# Lecture Notes in Computer Science 2624

Edited by G. Goos, J. Hartmanis, and J. van Leeuwen

T0240569

**Springer**
*Berlin*
*Heidelberg*
*New York*
*Barcelona*
*Hong Kong*
*London*
*Milan*
*Paris*
*Tokyo*

Henry G. Dietz (Ed.)

# Languages and Compilers for Parallel Computing

14th International Workshop, LCPC 2001
Cumberland Falls, KY, USA, August 1-3, 2001
Revised Papers

 Springer

Series Editors

Gerhard Goos, Karlsruhe University, Germany
Juris Hartmanis, Cornell University, NY, USA
Jan van Leeuwen, Utrecht University, The Netherlands

Volume Editor

Henry G. Dietz
University of Kentucky
Electrical and Computer Engineering Department
Lexington, KY 40506-0046, USA
E-mail: hankd@engr.uky.edu

Cataloging-in-Publication Data applied for

A catalog record for this book is available from the Library of Congress.

Bibliographic information published by Die Deutsche Bibliothek
Die Deutsche Bibliothek lists this publication in the Deutsche Nationalbibliografie;
detailed bibliographic data is available in the Internet at <http://dnb.ddb.de>.

CR Subject Classification (1998): D.3, D.1.3, F.1.2, B.2.1, C.2.4, C.2, E.1

ISSN 0302-9743
ISBN 3-540-04029-3 Springer-Verlag Berlin Heidelberg New York

Springer-Verlag Berlin Heidelberg New York
a member of BertelsmannSpringer Science+Business Media GmbH

http://www.springer.de

© Springer-Verlag Berlin Heidelberg 2003
Printed in Germany

Typesetting: Camera-ready by author, data conversion by Boller Mediendesign
Printed on acid-free paper      SPIN: 10873007      06/3142      5 4 3 2 1 0

# Preface

This volume contains (revised versions) of papers presented at the 14th Workshop on Languages and Compilers for Parallel Computing. Parallel computing used to be nearly synonymous with supercomputing research, but as parallel processing technologies have become common features of commodity processors and systems, the focus of this workshop also has shifted. For example, this workshop marks the first time that compiler technology for power management has been recognized as a key aspect of parallel computing. Another pattern visible in the research presented is the continuing shift in emphasis from simply finding potential parallelism to being able to use parallelism efficiently enough to achieve good speedup. The scope of languages and compilers for parallel computing has thus grown to encompass all relevant aspects of systems, ranging from abstract models to runtime support environments.

As in previous years, key researchers were invited to participate. Every paper submitted was reviewed in depth and quantitatively graded on originality, significance, correctness, presentation, relevance, need to revise the write-up, and overall how appropriate it would be to accept the paper. Any concerns raised were discussed by the program committee. In summary, the papers included here represent leading-edge work from North America, Europe, and Asia.

The workshop was hosted by the University of Kentucky. However, the workshop was not held at the host institution; instead, it was held in Kentucky's Cumberland Falls state park. It is a beautiful and quiet place for people to think together. The environment produced not only an increase in attendance over previous years, but also an increase in interactions between attendees, including a very lively panel discussion. Many of the papers in this volume benefited from revisions inspired by discussions at the workshop.

As General/Program Chair for LCPC 2001, I created a permanent website (www.lcpcworkshop.org) for the workshop series, recruited both the University of Kentucky and Advanced Micro Devices (AMD) as sponsors, and made all the arrangements for the workshop, its CD-ROM proceedings, and this publication. Throughout the process of creating and holding this workshop, the Founders' Committee (Utpal Banerjee, David Gelernter, Alex Nicolau, and especially David Padua) ensured that the best traditions of the workshop series continued. The Program Committee members (Larry Carter, Siddhartha Chatterjee, Jeanne Ferrante, Manish Gupta, Sam Midkiff, Jose Moreira, Jan Prins, Bill Pugh, and Chau-Wen Tseng) served in their primary function of ensuring that the papers were of high quality, also contributing many insights as to how to make the workshop really work.

November 2002                                                                 Henry Dietz

# **LCPC** Organization

The 14th workshop on Languages and Compilers for Parallel Computing, LCPC 2001, was organized and hosted by the Electrical and Computer Engineering Department of the University of Kentucky, Lexington, KY, USA.

## Program and General Chair

Henry Dietz                        University of Kentucky

## Founders' Committee

| | |
|---|---|
| Utpal Banerjee | Intel Corporation |
| David Gelernter | Yale University |
| Alex Nicolau | University of California at Irvine |
| David Padua | University of Illinois at Urbana-Champaign |

## Program Committee

| | |
|---|---|
| Larry Carter | University of California at San Diego |
| Siddhartha Chatterjee | University of North Carolina at Chapel Hill |
| Jeanne Ferrante | University of California at San Diego |
| Manish Gupta | IBM T.J. Watson Research Center |
| Sam Midkiff | IBM T.J. Watson Research Center |
| Jose Moreira | IBM T.J. Watson Research Center |
| Jan Prins | University of North Carolina at Chapel Hill |
| Bill Pugh | University of Maryland |
| Chau-Wen Tseng | University of Maryland |

## Sponsoring Institutions

Electrical and Computer Engineering Department, University of Kentucky, Lexington, KY, USA.
Advanced Micro Devices (AMD), Sunnyvale, California

## Workshop Attendees

# Table of Contents

# Optimizing Compiler Design for Modularity and Extensibility

Steven Carroll, Walden Ko, Mark Yankelevsky, and
Constantine Polychronopoulos

Center for Supercomputing Research and Development
University of Illinois at Urbana-Champaign
1308 W. Main St, Urbana IL 61801, USA
phone: +1.217.244.4654
{scarroll, w-ko, myankele, cdp}@csrd.uiuc.edu

**Abstract.** Implementing an optimizing compiler for a new target architecture has traditionally been a complex design/development effort requiring a large time scale. Existing machine descriptions and approaches based on pre-existing internal representations (IR) are not sufficient to build truly modular and extensible compilers. This paper describes the features of the Extensible Compiler Interface (ECI) implemented in the PROMIS compiler, which tackles several major problems concerning the reuse of compiler components, retargeting as well as extending existing compilers with new functionality. One of the main design issues is maintaining analysis information calculated by one module after another potentially unknown module modifies the IR. Another problem is expanding existing modules (or passes) to work with processor-specific instructions and data types added by the compiler developers. Our approach to compiler extensibility through the proposed ECI tackles and solves the above problems, and provides a simple yet powerful API for adding arbitrary functionality or entirely new optimizations to existing compilers. A case study is presented in which the components of a parallelizing compiler are reused to build a compiler for a vector architecture, thereby demonstrating the utility and convenience of ECI.

## 1 Introduction

As system architectures become more complex with deeper computational and memory hierarchies, the need for sophisticated compilation technology grows. As a result, compiler optimization issues are considered early in the design process and regarded as an integral part of the conception and design of new architectures. An example is Intel's IA-64 architecture for which an optimizing compiler is essential to achieving good performance. As processor and system architectures become more complex, the number of possible compiler optimizations also increases, and their interdependencies become even harder to optimally resolve.

Nevertheless, the design and implementation of optimizing compilers for new architectures is a development-intensive process, which often takes longer to

H. Dietz (Ed.): LCPC 2001, LNCS 2624, pp. 1–17, 2003.

complete, debug and fine-tune than the implementation of an new processor - from concept to working silicon. Compilers often outlive their original intended targets because of the high fixed cost of starting from ground zero. Therefore, compiler designers routinely reuse pieces of existing compilers to build new ones. For example, the part of the frontend that is responsible for lexical analysis and parsing the source files of common languages are rarely re-implemented. Several commercial-grade tools are available for performing these tasks, such as the frontends available from Edison Design Group [5].

The impact of the desire to minimize duplication of implementation effort is that often compilers are a collection of passes taken from older compilers and combined with newer modules created specifically for a new target system. After many generations of use and reuse, the result is a patchwork of optimizations and passes that, at best, is too complex for one individual to understand, extend and maintain and at worst, the cost of enhancing, maintaining and coping with undesirable side effects becomes prohibitively high.

Compiler generation tools were developed to speed compiler development by automatically generating common compiler components. These tools include lex [10] and yacc [8] for creating parsers and frontends, and code generator generators like BURG [4] for emitting native code. More recent research has focused on addressing some of these issues by means of Universal Internal Representations (UIRs); IRs that go beyond the ever popular abstract syntax tree (AST) in an attempt to serve as the common program representation for all (or nearly all) analysis and optimization phases of any compiler, facilitating (among other design goals) reuse of compiler modules.

Despite all these design approaches, a sufficiently extensible and modular compiler framework still does not exist. One of the prime goals of the PROMIS compiler project [11][12] is to create a fully extensible, retargetable and modular compiler framework. Its design is based on a universal unified internal representation capable of representing many different forms of parallelism at all levels of compilation. In this paper, we will examine the problem of compiler component reuse and propose a powerful and convenient solution to these problems. In this paper we briefly discuss our approach to ECI and present the External Data Structure (EDS) system. EDS, which we designed and implemented in the PROMIS compiler, allows analysis information to be maintained across arbitrary transformations. It also provides a mechanism for adding new machine instructions and new data types to the IR without creating inaccuracies in existing passes. In this paper, it is not our intention to present yet another UIR. Instead we present several mechanisms for making existing UIRs more extensible, modular and better-suited to cover a wider range of compiler applications than previous generations.

The following section describes the organization of the PROMIS compiler and shows how it lends itself to extensibility. The next section describes other related work on compiler extensibility. Subsequent sections discuss EDS in the PROMIS compiler and the resources available for extending its capabilities. These features are collectively known as the Extensible Compiler Interface (ECI). We conclude with a case study showing how the PROMIS compiler infrastructure can be used to build a vectorizing compiler quickly out of the components written for a parallelizing compiler, in order to demonstrate the effectiveness, generality and simplicity of our approach.

## 2   PROMIS Compiler Organization

The basic organization of the PROMIS compiler's extensibility architecture is shown in Figure 1. The Core IR is the basic set of all compiler data structures that are shared by all compilers constructed from the PROMIS framework. It consists of such data structures as Variables, Types, Expressions, Statement nodes, control and data flow arcs, and the Extensible Compiler Interface (ECI) for extending those structures. ECI allows external data structures (EDS) to be attached to any of the data structures of the core IR to capture and express any extra information about them. Section 5 describes this aspect of the design in more detail. The compiler developer can also add processor specific data types and instructions to the IR using intrinsic functions and custom types. These are described in Section 7.

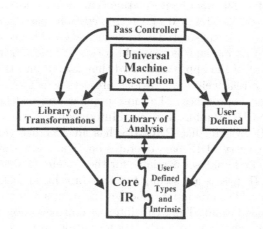

**Fig. 1.** Compiler organization

PROMIS is also distributed with a library of common analyses and transformation passes. These are the modular building blocks that a compiler designer can use to assemble a compiler. Analyses include control dependence, data dependence, data flow, privatization, reduction idiom recognition and others. Transformations include loop unrolling, function inlining, symbolic interpretation, loop distribution, loop fusion, strip mining and many others. The node labeled "User Defined" in the figure, represents the processor- or compiler-specific analyses added to the PROMIS framework by the compiler developer. All of these passes operate on the core IR augmented by the user-defined EDSs, data types and instructions.

The Machine Description is the storehouse for all information about the target system, such as: instruction pipeline, register characteristics, special purpose hardware, instruction mappings, and semantic information about processor specific instructions. It works in a query-response fashion. The analysis and transformation passes query the machine description about the target architecture to drive optimization. Most importantly, the machine description can help analysis passes and transformation passes handle user-defined instructions and data types as is described in Section 7.1.

## 3  Related Work

A common approach to extensible compiler design is to use IR syntax and associated tools that dump the IR into a file using "standard" formats and regenerate the IR from such files. The format is almost always a variant of the abstract syntax tree (AST). The simplicity and wide use of the AST makes this approach desirable in terms of generality. However, it is also extremely limiting in terms of the type of non-syntactic information (parallelism, flow and dependence analyses, etc) that can be dumped and recreated from pass to pass. The only information that can be encapsulated in these formats and hence passed down to successive optimization modules is that which can be reflected in the structure of the IR itself. Most of the approaches used thus far fall into this category.

There have been relatively few previous projects dedicated to compiler extensibility tools and approaches. The most popular and widely used of these frameworks is the SUIF (Stanford Universal Intermediate Format) compiler system [17]. The SUIF system, like PROMIS, has an AST-like common internal representation that every SUIF pass operates on. There are a number of standard optimizations and analyses available for the system. However, the similarities end there. SUIF passes are strung together in a linear fashion. Each pass takes a SUIF format file as its input, modifies the program and produces a new SUIF file of the same format. The SUIF internal representation is similar to an abstract syntax tree and has no analysis information stored in it, by default. Therefore, the only universal information exchanged between passes is the program structure itself. SUIF does allow the user to create annotations to the internal representation, but the library of passes that are distributed with the SUIF system will not be able to use information in the user-defined libraries. In other words, annotations allow analysis information to be exchanged only between passes that are constructed to understand those annotations. One of the primary goals of the PROMIS compiler infrastructure was to allow the compiler writer to use the provided library of standard optimizations and still maintain the user defined analysis information.

The Machine SUIF library [13] adds extensions for machine-dependent optimizations to the base SUIF package. The Optimization Programming Interface (OPI)[7] is an interface used by optimizations to hide target-specific details about the optimization. The target-dependent details then are implemented in libraries. A library must be implemented for each desired target machine.

Machine libraries in SUIF are primarily used for backend, low-level optimizations. System information is not used for high-level parallelization. PROMIS uses machine information for both high and low-level optimizations. Also, machine descriptors in PROMIS are bound dynamically. Optimizations obtain machine information through the machine description interface. The specific values of machine parameters are not obtained until compile time when the machine description is processed. Retargeting is accomplished by changing the contents of the machine description file. No libraries or source code modifications are needed to change the target machine.

The Zephyr [1]infrastructure provides a framework for building a compiler from individual components. A set of description languages provides the means to describe the intermediate representations used by different compiler modules. Additional tools are provided to store, manipulate, and exchange information between modules. As in SUIF, Zephyr IRs are based on abstract syntax trees. However, the IR's used by each module may be different. The Zephyr IR tools allow information to be exchanged between different IR's. In fact, these tools are used to provide a SUIF front end for Zephyr.

The difference in design philosophies between Zephyr and PROMIS begins with the IR. Whereas Zephyr allows each pass to use its own IR, PROMIS is based on a single IR that is used by all optimizations. Because each Zephyr module operates independently, its IR tools are the means of integrating the different modules. Although new optimizations may be added to the infrastructure, translations must occur from their IR to existing Zephyr passes. This IR translation cannot preserve all analysis information produced by each pass. This is in contrast to PROMIS, which is designed to retain all analysis information from the high to low level.

Gcc is one of the most widely used compilers and has code generators for many platforms. Its internal representation is based on register transfer lists (RTL). Although new passes can be added to gcc, its internal representation has limited expansion capabilities. The types and expressions in RTL are fixed. Also, instruction selection is based on pattern matching RTL sequences. While it is certainly possible to add types and operations to gcc by modifying the compiler source code, existing passes must be modified to support these additions. A clear interface for this process is not provided. Unlike PROMIS, gcc is not intended to be a high-level optimizer. As a result, there is very little high-level analysis information to preserve for the backend.

The PIGG system[2] shares some of the goals of PROMIS as well. It also attempts to preserve information in a single monolithic IR and attempts to build the compiler from a machine description. The project suffers from a similar problem as SUIF, namely that it maintains a certain preset set of information but has no mechanism for adding new maintainable structures to it.The MCAT compiler[6] has a tightly coupled frontend and backend that assures no loss of information, but to the best of our knowledge there is no mechanism for adding new analyses that will be pervasively maintained.

## 4   Adding Optimization Passes to a Compiler

The first aspect of extensibility that we will examine is adding new compiler passes to an existing compiler. The compiler pass is the basic module in a compiler system: typically, a pass is a module that implements a specific analysis, transformation or optimization algorithm, and often involves a complete sweep (or pass) through the IR - hence the term "pass". Ordering compiler passes in an optimal fashion, for a given input program, is a problem known to be NP-complete [16]. PROMIS provides facilities for both static and dynamic pass lists. A static pass list is used by PROMIS at compile time to direct the selection and the order of specific analyses and optimization algorithms to be applied for each compilation session.

Alternately, passes can be run dynamically based on the characteristics of the code being compiled. For instance, after a common subexpression pass is executed it may be possible to remove some assignments with dead code elimination. PROMIS provides a facility for passes to dynamically trigger other passes through a central pass controller interface. Each pass has a list of dependencies (prerequisite passes) associated with it, which are passes that must be run before this pass can safely be executed. For instance, if a certain pass requires data dependence information to be available, it lists the data dependence module as its prerequisite. When a pass is invoked by the compiler before its prerequisite passes have completed, PROMIS provides for the suspension of that pass and the automatic invocation of the required modules; following execution of those modules the suspended pass resumes execution.

## 5   Adding Analyses Modules to a Compiler

Analysis is the lifeblood of any optimizing compiler. The more information the compiler has about the program, the more likely it is that it will be able to intelligently decide how to generate efficient code. The PROMIS compiler provides data dependence, control flow, and call graphs as part of the core IR. All passes have access to this information and are required to maintain its consistency. In addition, the PROMIS compiler provides a number of optional analyses which can be calculated on demand, such as:

- Privatization and Reduction analysis
- Control Dependence analysis
- Data Flow Information
- Iteration Variable Analysis
- Subscript Analysis

Provisioning for new analysis information in the PROMIS compiler is done by adding an External Data Structure (EDS) to the components of the IR. EDSs are user defined data structures that supply extra information about whatever structure they are attached to. For example, a Privatization EDS is attached to loop nodes to identify which of the variables used in that loop are privatizable. EDSs can be attached to types, statements, arcs, expressions, and functions. For example, when data flow information was incorporated in the PROMIS IR, a data flow EDS was created and an instance of that EDS was added to each of the statements in the IR in order to hold the IN and OUT sets for corresponding statements. The control dependence graph (CDG) is also implemented as an EDS in PROMIS. An adjacency list is associated with each statement - collectively, they describe the graph structure. Implementing new analyses using the EDS system as presented here is similar, in principle, to the idea of annotations in SUIF, but the uniqueness of the PROMIS system is how these structures can be maintained across code transformations allowing for more flexible pass ordering and modularity.

## 6   Maintaining Consistency of Analysis Information

One of the distinct challenges that must be addressed in a compiler that is built out of pre-existing modules is correctly maintaining analysis information across transformations that have no knowledge about that information. For example, consider constructing a compiler that has one analysis pass and one transformation pass: privatization and dead code elimination, respectively. Assume also that the two passes are from the provided library of passes and have no knowledge of each other's existence. Moreover, assume that the privatization information must be valid throughout the compilation process. At the beginning of compilation, the privatization variables for all the loops in the code are computed, and a series of code improving optimizations are performed, including dead code elimination. The input code is shown in Figure 2.

```
DO I=1, 100
   T = A[0];
   IF FALSE_COMPILE_TIME_CONSTANT
      THEN B[0] = T;
   ...
ENDDO
```

**Fig. 2.** Example Code

$T$ is found to be privatizable because it is always assigned before it is used in the loop. Therefore, $T$ can be added to the list of privatizable variables for that loop. However, dead code elimination determines that the condition $FALSE\_COMPILE\_TIME\_CONSTANT$ is always false and so the only use of $T$ in the loop can be removed; by the same token, the assignment to $T$ can also be removed. This optimization has now invalidated the list of privatizable variables but there is no defined communication channel for the dead code elimination pass to communicate that information to the privatization information (since they were written without knowledge of each other). In a traditional compiler, the dead code elimination pass would be modified to explicitly maintain the privatization information, which would be a non-modular design choice, or the information would have to be fully re-computed after every transformation.

The ECI system provides a set of callback functions that are invoked when specific operations are performed on the IR. For instance, callbacks are invoked each time a statement is added or deleted from the internal representation, each time a new dependence arc is added or deleted, and each time a statement is modified. An analysis pass can simply register a function to be invoked for each of the operations that can potentially invalidate the information it has computed. In the example above, the privatization pass can simply register a callback function that is invoked each time a statement is about to be deleted. When a statement is deleted, the function is invoked with the deleted node as an argument. The function then removes the variable $T$ from its list of privatizable variables.

Part of our design and implementation of ECI specifies the AutoEDS system, which is provided for analysis information that does not need to be explicitly maintained. Instead, the developer simply chooses the types of modifications that will invalidate the analysis information. When any of those modifications are made, a dirty bit is automatically set. For instance, the CDG is constructed as an AutoEDS that automatically tracks changes to the control flow graph (CFG). If the CDG is dirty and a pass tries to access the information, the CDG is cleared and rebuilt.

## 7   Extending the Internal Representation

Compiler passes perform analysis and transformation on a well-defined Internal Representation (IR). If the IR definition is modified, existing passes must be rewritten to work properly. For this reason, it is difficult to add machine-specific instructions and data types to the IR of many compilers. An extensible IR would provide the ability to add new operations and data types while maintaining backward compatibility with existing passes. This section describes these capabilities in PROMIS. First, an overview of the processor description capabilities is provided. Then, the mechanism for inserting processor instructions into the IR is described. Finally, we discuss the support for new data types.

### 7.1   Target Architecture Encapsulation Through Machine Descriptors

The Universal Machine Descriptor (UMD) [9] maintains information about the target system. Unlike compilers that only use machine descriptions in the backend, UMD information is also used by PROMIS in the frontend. The communication between the UMD and the passes is shown conceptually in Figure 1. UMD descriptions provide many system characteristics. At the instruction level, there are data types, instructions, and intrinsic function semantics. Descriptions of hardware resources include the number and types of functional units, the depth of pipelines, and number of processing elements. The structure of caches and thread management features are also described in the UMD.

The UMD description is a text file that is processed and stored at compile-time, ready to be accessed by transformations. The file format and contents is described fully in the PROMIS manual [3]. The exact syntax of the machine descriptor file and the UMD API are out of the scope of this paper, and only references are made to attributes relevant to our discussion.

Once the machine description has been processed, individual transformations query the UMD whenever system information is needed. These queries return many different kinds of information. An example of a simple query is one to obtain the total number of processor registers, which simply returns an integer. A more complicated example is one for the result register of an operation. Given the type of IR operation and the type of the value, this method returns an IR variable representing the name of the physical register. This variable then can be used in the IR to represent a write operation to the physical register.

## 7.2   Support for Machine-Specific Instructions

Traditionally, compiler IRs are divided into two levels: a high level where semantic information from program structures like loops is retained, and a low-level which resembles assembly or machine code. At the low-level, much of the high-level information is lost. One of the main objectives of the PROMIS compiler as described in [15] is the maintenance of high-level information throughout compilation. This is accomplished with a unified IR in which IR data structures are the same in the frontend (high-level) and the backend (low-level). These data structures make it easier to maintain high-level analysis information that would otherwise be lost when lowering the IR from the high level to the low level.

Instruction assignment, also called opcode tagging, usually occurs during the final stages of compilation. This is the process by which IR operations are converted to machine instructions. Because the exact syntax of instructions and operands are machine-specific, the IR must support a general set of operations while the code generator must be capable of mapping these operations to all supported target machines. The disadvantage of this approach is the lack of support for machine instructions that do not correspond to a single IR operation. These instructions often perform the work of several IR operations combined. Pattern matching is one method of exploiting these instructions. For machines that provide a combined multiply-add operation, correlated multiplication and addition operations in the IR can be located, grouped together, and combined into a single multiply-add. However, this approach fails for more advanced instructions like those that use SIMD parallelism. Code generation for packed operations and multithreading require high-level analysis. The ability to insert these unique instructions in the IR while providing semantic information would allow for more powerful analyses.

The disconnect between frontend and backend analysis is bridged in PROMIS with the use of intrinsic functions as place-holders for machine specific instructions. The idea for PROMIS intrinsic functions comes from FORTRAN, where functions like MIN and MAX are a part of the language. Even though no function body is provided in the source, the compiler knows how to generate code for it. In PROMIS, an intrinsic function is a type of function that the compiler recognizes and handles in a special manner. The developer can add code generation rules and semantic information for the intrinsic function to the machine descriptor. Therefore, intrinsic functions provide a means to insert new operations into the IR transparently.

To the best of our knowledge, this approach (and its application to compiler extensibility) is unique. Other compilers either limit the use of machine idioms to backend optimizations, where custom optimization and code generation passes can be written, or require that transformations be rewritten to translate high level directives to low-level instructions. In SUIF, for example, a custom lowering pass must be written to identify a prefetch operation and lower it to *suifvm*, its low-level machine language [14]. The combination of intrinsic functions and machine descriptors in PROMIS allow for transparent lowering of these operations. No compiler passes need to be rewritten to support a new instruction.

```
// data flow gen function
switch (statement type) {
  case Assignment:
    gen_set = AssignmentGen();
  case Intrinsic Function:
    UMD->RunExtensionFunc("DataFlowGen", intrinsic_name,gen_set, params);
}
```

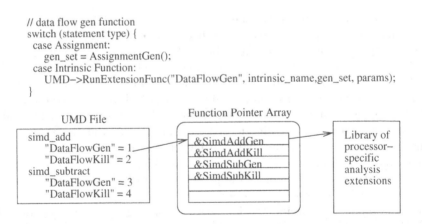

**Fig. 3.** Data Flow Analysis pass accesses UMD for Gen set of Intrinsic Function

In order to obtain more accurate analysis information in the presence of new instructions, the machine descriptor contains a list of functions that extend existing analysis passes for those instructions. For instance, in the *available expression* part of the dataflow analysis pass, each type of program statement in the core IR has an associated *Gen* and *Kill* function. A pseudo-code fragment of this analysis is shown in Figure 3. If the statement node is an intrinsic function representing a new instruction, the pass queries the UMD for a Gen function corresponding to the new instruction. The UMD searches for a matching string in the list of extension functions for this instruction. If it is found, the matching index in an array of function pointers is used to access the user-defined analysis extension function. These functions are a part of the user-defined block in Figure 1. If the compiler developer does not provide an analysis extension function for this new instruction, it is treated as a black box. In summary, the compiler developer can extend the analysis passes to work with new instructions without *any* code changes in the analysis module. This design feature is also novel in the context of compiler extensibility.

## 7.3   Data Type Extensions

Modern architectures often employ processor-specific data types, such as packed data types for vector operations, double-extended data types, and others. These new types must also be expressed in the compiler's IR because they are frequently the data type of the operands of new instructions. For example, the operands to a vector add instruction that was added using the mechanisms described in the previous section takes packed data as operands.

A composite "intrinsic" type represents new types. Intrinsic types also contain a string that identifies the corresponding type in the machine descriptor file. Much like intrinsic functions, they are treated as exceptional cases in existing passes. Register allocation, and code generation both use information in the machine description to work with new processor-specific types.

When the register allocator needs to determine the set of valid registers for an operand, it examines the type. For intrinsic types, the allocator queries the machine descriptor for the registers used for this particular type using the intrinsic type's name field. After register allocation, the next stage is instruction selection. Instructions are selected using the types of their operands. For example, if *temp1* and *temp2* have a double-extended intrinsic data type, the statement

```
temp1 = *addr
```

will be treated as [double-extended] <= READ[memory]. This pattern matches the corresponding instruction for a double-extended *load* specified in the machine descriptor file. Similarly, the

```
*addr2 = temp1
```

statement maps to a *store* instruction for double-extended types. The key benefit of our approach is that none of the existing code for lowering and code generation needs to be modified. The changes are localized to the user defined code and the machine description file.

## 8  Vectorizing Compiler: A Case Study

It is rather difficult to quantitatively evaluate compiler design architectures or otherwise establish the resulting advantages and flexibility. Therefore, in order to demonstrate the advantages of our design approach within the space limitations of a research paper, we use the example of extending compiler transformations aimed at multiprocessing for vector architectures. Specifically, we describe how the analyses and transformations developed for loop parallelization in PROMIS can be reconfigured with minimal effort to build a vectorizing compiler. We will then compare the implementation effort in the proposed framework to the effort that would be necessary in a more traditional compiler and the SUIF compiler. An organizational view of the compiler constructed is shown in Figure 4. The existing components that were reused in the vectorizing compiler were the following:

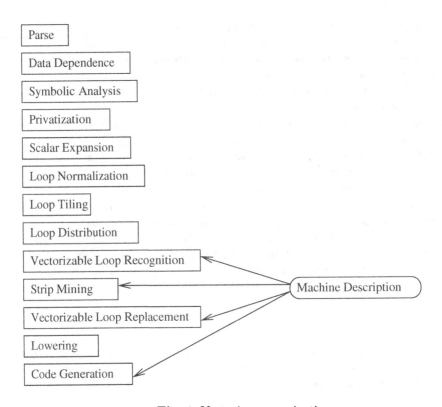

**Fig. 4.** Vectorizer organization

- Parsing (FORTRAN and C) - reads in the code and constructs the IR
- Data Dependence - collect data dependence information about each function, builds the data dependence graph and calculates distance vectors.

- Symbolic Analysis - a complex module that uses symbolic interpretation to perform SSA conversion, iteration variable analysis, loop invariant code motion, and determines which loops are fixed-iteration loops.
- Loop Normalization - normalizes all loops to start at iteration 1 (or 0) with iteration increment of 1.
- Scalar Privatization - determines which scalars are always assigned before they are used in each iteration. In loop parallelization, cross-iteration dependences on these scalars can be broken safely by allocating a copy of the scalar for each iteration.
- Loop Distribution - computes the strongly connected components (SCC) for the data dependences on each loop and splits each SCC into its own loop.
- Loop Strip Mining - converts a one-dimensional loop into a doubly-nested loop where the inner loop has a fixed iteration count, according to some optimization objective.
- Loop-carried Dependence Analysis - determines which data dependences are loop-carried and whether those dependences can be ignored or enforced.
- Lowering - takes the high-level representation of the IR and breaks complex expressions to create the low-level representation.
- Code Generator - uses the machine description to generate assembly code.

Next, we describe the vector related passes that were added. First, a scalar expansion pass was constructed that reads the Privatization EDS variables and expands the privatizable scalars into arrays to increase the opportunities for vectorization. Because the privatization information is maintained using the EDS system, the scalar expansion pass can be called multiple times as other transformations create new privatizable scalars without complete recalculation of the privatization information. In a traditional compiler, the privatization information would have to be explicitly maintained by all transformations.

Next, a vectorizable-loop recognition pass was constructed. The loop distribution module previously distributed all loops, so this pass searches for innermost loops with a single instruction in the loop body and without loop carried dependences. The loop carried dependence analysis indentifier was constructed for parallel loop detection, but can be reused in this case without changes. Loops that match these conditions are vectorizable, so an EDS structure that marks the loop as vectorizable is created and attached to the loop node in the IR. Reduction analysis information is also available to vectorize simple recurrence loops.

We can now query the machine descriptor to determine the vector size for the target architecture. The PROMIS strip-mining pass is subsequently called on each of the vectorizable loops, which are recognizable via the EDS that was attached in the previous step. Strip mining takes a vectorizable loop and splits it into a doubly nested loop. The inner loop has a number of iterations equal to the vector size as is seen in Figure 5. The corresponding EDS can now be moved to the inner loop, and vector instructions can be emitted.

The vectorizable-loop replacement routine replaces all vector loops (identified by the corresponding EDS) with the appropriate intrinsic function. All of the parameters to this function have an intrinsic type representing packed data assigned to them.

```
// BEFORE STRIP MINING
DO I=1, 1024  //VECTORIZABLE
   A[I] = B[I] + C[I];
ENDDO

// AFTER STRIP MINING
DO I=1, 256
   DO J=1, 4 //VECTORIZABLE
      A[4*I + J] = B[4*I + J] + C[4*I + J];
   ENDDO
ENDDO

// AFTER REPLACEMENT
DO I=1, 256
   // A[4*I], B[4*I] and C[4*I] are tagged as SIMD packed data
   A[4*I] = SIMD_ADD(B[4*I],C[4*I])
ENDDO
```

**Fig. 5.** Strip Mining Example

The lowering pass can then convert the IR into three-address code. The conversion propagates the SIMD tagging automatically as described above. Next, register allocation replaces the scalar variables with registers. SIMD registers are introduced in place of the variables tagged as having the SIMD type intrinsic by consulting the MD.

Code generation, the final pass, assigns the specific (vector) instruction to each of the statements and emits the code. Instructions for the intrinsic functions are extracted from the MD file. Note that instructions are matched to program statements based on the register and constant types. Therefore, if a register is marked as SIMD, and it is on the receiving end of a load, the appropriate SIMD load instruction will be located in the MD file.

```
(arg_simd_add dest1(SIMD_REG) src1(SIMD_REG) src2(SIMD_REG)
    format("%s, %s, %s",dest1, src1, src2))
(op_simd_add args(arg_simd_add) format("padd %s",args))
```

**Fig. 6.** Format description of the simd_add instruction in the md

Figure 6 demonstrate the md file component that is added to support SIMD ADD instruction. The format in figure 6 describes simd add instruction. The

```
// AFTER LOWERING
I=1
START:
    if I > 256 GOTO EXIT
    T0 = 4*I
    ADDR1 = A+T0
    ADDR2 = B+T0
    ADDR3 = C+T0
    T2 = *ADDR2
    T3 = *ADDR3
    // ADDR1, ADDR2, ADDR3, T2, T3 are tagged as an SIMD expressions
    [ADDR1] = SIMD_ADD(T2,T3)
    I = I + 1;
    GOTO START
EXIT:

// AFTER REGISTER ALLOCATION
R10=1
START:
    IF R10 > 256 GOTO EXIT
    R0 = 4*R10
    R1 = A+R0
    R5 = B+R0
    R6 = C+R0
    // ADDRx are replaced by non-simd registers,
    // since they contain addresses
    SIMD_R2 = *R5
    SIMD_R3 = *R6
    // SIMD_R1 is a register replacement for [ADDR1]
    SIMD_R1 = SIMD_ADD(SIMD_R2,SIMD_R3)
    [R1] = SIMD_R1
    R10 = R10 + 1
    GOTO START
EXIT:

// AFTER ASSEMBLY GENERATION
    R10 = 1
START:
    BGT R10, 256, EXIT
    MUL R0, R10, 4
    ADD R1, R0, A
    ADD R5, R0, B
    ADD R6, R0, C
    LOAD_SIMD SIMD_R2, 0x0[R5]
    LOAD_SIMD SIMD_R3, 0x0[R6]
    SIMD_ADD SIMD_R1, SIMD_R2, SIMD_R3
    STORE_SIMD SIMD_R1, 0x0[R1]
    ADD  R10, R10, 1
    J START
EXIT:
```

**Fig. 7.** Example Of Back End Passes (cont. from Strip Mining Example)

tag in this case is `simd_add` . And PROMIS will output this instruction as `padd mm1, mm3, mm4`.

The previous example illustrates a number of direct and second-order advantages of the ECI and EDS architecture used in PROMIS. First, the variety of passes and their inter-operability allows the user to quickly assemble and reconstruct most of the important components of a vectorizer without writing any code. It is worth noting that neither the lowering pass nor the register allocator needs to be rewritten. In addition, the backend optimizations that use data flow information were made to work with the new instructions using the MD indirection described above. There was no need to modify the optimization code, thus maintaining modularity.

## 9    Conclusion

The ability to rapidly and efficiently retarget existing compilers to new architectures or extensions of existing architectures without compromising performance has profound impact on cost and development time (of both compiler and architecture design). The approaches used thus far rely primarily on IR format specifications and tools that facilitate the re-use of existing compiler modules. New modules were made to adhere to those formats, in order to cope with the inherent complexity and reduce deployment time. The main disadvantage of these approaches is that valuable information is lost as compilation proceeds between passes, impacting the quality of the generated code.

In this paper we presented an elegant but powerful approach to compiler extensibility based on a simple API, the Extensible Compiler Interface. ECI provides simple mechanisms for extending the IR with new instructions, new types or other information in a fashion that requires no modifications to existing optimizations whatsoever. At the same time, new modules written to take advantage of IR extensions still operate on the same IR. The result is a seamless maintenance of all analyses information between compiler passes, which greatly facilitates optimization and efficient code generation.

Furthermore, the extensible addition of new optimizations and processor specific features to the compiler with maximum reuse of existing structure, minimum changes in the core IR and clear separation of the newly plugged-in components greatly reduces design and development time. The simple case study demonstrated the step-by-step methods used in augmenting a parallelizing compiler with a vectorizer using our PROMIS research compiler.

## Acknowlegments

This work was supported in part by NSF grant EIA 99-75019 with research support from NSA, and a grant from Intel Corp. The views of this paper do not necessarily reflect the views of the funding agencies.

# References

[1]  A. Appel, J. Davidson, and N. Ramsey. The Zephyr compiler infrastructure, 1998.

[2]  W.E. Cohen. *Automatic Construction of Optimizing, Parallelizing Compilers from Specifications.* PhD thesis, Purdue University, December 1994.

[3]  CSRD. *PROMIS Manual (http://promis.csrd.uiuc.edu/).* Urbana, Illinois.

[4]  C. Fraser, R. Henry, and T. Proebsting. BURG – Fast Optimal Instruction Selection And Tree Parsing, April 1992.

[5]  Edison Design Group. http://www.edg.com/.

[6]  L.J. Hendren, C. Donawa, M. Emami, G. R. Gao, Justiani, and B. Sridharan. Designing the McCAT Compiler Based on a Family of Structured Intermediate Representations. In *Proceedings of the 5th International Workshop on Languages and Compilers for Parallel Computing*, pages 406–420. Springer-Verlag, LNCS 757, 1993.

[7]  G. Holloway and M.D. Smith. An Extender's Guide to the Optimization Programming Interface and Target Descriptions. Harvard University, 2000.

[8]  S. C. Johnson. Yacc: Yet another compiler compiler. In *UNIX Programmer's Manual*, volume 2, pages 353–387. Holt, Rinehart, and Winston, New York, NY, USA, 1979.

[9]  W. Ko. The Promis Universal Machine Descriptor: Concepts, Design, and Implementation. Master's thesis, University of Illinois, Urbana, Illinois, 2001.

[10]  M. E. Lesk. Lex — A lexical analyzer generator. Technical Report No. 39, AT&T Bell Laboratories, Murray Hill, N.J., 1975.

[11]  H. Saito, N. Stavrakos, Steve Carroll, Constantine Polychronopoulos, and Alex Nicolau. The design of the PROMIS compiler. In *Proceedings of the International Conference on Compiler Construction (CC)*, March 1999. Also available in Lecture Notes in Computer Science No. 1575 (Springer-Verlag) and as CSRD Technical Report No.1539 (rev.1).

[12]  H. Saito, N. Stavrakos, C. Polychronopoulos, and A. Nicolau. The Design of the PROMIS Compiler — Towards Multi-Level Parallelization. *International Journal of Parallel Programming*, 28(2), 2000.

[13]  M. Smith. Extending SUIF for Machine-dependent Optimizations. In *Proc. First SUIF Compiler Workshop*, January 1996.

[14]  M.D. Smith and G. Holloway. An Introduction to Machine SUIF and Its Portable Libraries for Analysis and Optimization. Harvard University, 2000.

[15]  N. Stavrakos, S. Carroll, H. Saito, C. Polychronopoulos, and A. Nicolau. Symbolic analysis in the PROMIS compiler. In *Proceedings of the International Workshop on Languages and Compilers for Parallel Computing (LCPC)*, August 1999. Also available in Lecture Notes in Computer Science (Springer-Verlag). Extended version available as CSRD Technical Report No.1564.

[16]  D. Whitfield and M.L. Soffa. An approach to ordering optimizing transformations. In *Proceedings of ACM SIGPLAN Symposium on Principles and Practices of Parallel Programming (PPoPP)*, March 1990.

[17]  R. Wilson, R. French, C. Wilson, S. Amarasinghe, J. Anderson, S. Tjiang, S. Liao, C. Tseng, M. Hall, M. Lam, and J. Hennessy. The SUIF compiler system: a parallelizing and optimizing research compiler. Technical Report CSL-TR-94-620, Stanford University, May 1994.

# Translation Schemes for the *HPJava* Parallel Programming Language

Bryan Carpenter, Geoffrey Fox, Han-Ku Lee, and Sang Boem Lim

School of Computational Science and Information Technology,
400 Dirac Science Library,
Florida State University,
Tallahassee, Florida 32306-4120
{dbc,fox,hkl,slim}@csit.fsu.edu

**Abstract.** The article describes the current status of the authors' HP-Java programming environment. HPJava is a parallel dialect of Java that imports Fortran-like arrays—in particular the distributed arrays of High Performance Fortran—as new data structures. The article discusses the translation scheme adopted in a recently developed translator for the HPJava language. It also gives an overview of the language.

## 1 Introduction

HPJava [3] is a language for parallel programming, especially suitable for programming massively parallel, distributed memory computers.

Several of the ideas in HPJava are lifted from the High Performance Fortran (HPF) programming language. However the programming model of HPJava is "lower level" than the programming model of HPF. HPJava sits somewhere between the explicit SPMD (Single Program Multiple Data) programming style—often implemented using communication libraries like MPI—and the higher level, data-parallel model of HPF. An HPF compiler generally guarantees an equivalence between the parallel code it generates and a sequential Fortran program obtained by deleting all distribution directives. An HPJava program, on the other hand, is defined from the start to be a distributed MIMD program, with multiple threads of control operating in different address spaces. In this sense the HPJava programming model is "closer to the metal" than the HPF programming model. HPJava *does* provide special syntax for HPF-like distributed arrays, but the programming model may best be viewed as an incremental improvement on the programming style used in many hand-coded applications: explicitly parallel programs exploiting collective communication libraries or collective arithmetic libraries.

We call this general programming model—essentially direct SPMD programming supported by additional syntax for HPF-like distributed arrays—the *HP-spmd model*. In general SPMD programming has been very successful. Many high-level parallel programming environments and libraries assume the SPMD style as their basic model. Examples include ScaLAPACK [1], DAGH [14], Kelp

H. Dietz (Ed.): LCPC 2001, LNCS 2624, pp. 18–32, 2003.
© Springer-Verlag Berlin Heidelberg 2003

[6] and the Global Array Toolkit [13]. While there remains a prejudice that HPF is best suited for problems with rather regular data structures and regular data access patterns, SPMD frameworks like DAGH and Kelp have been designed to deal directly with irregularly distributed data, and other libraries like CHAOS/PARTI [5] and Global Arrays support unstructured access to distributed arrays. Presently, however, the library-based SPMD approach to data-parallel programming lacks the uniformity and elegance that was promised by HPF. The various environments referred to above all have some idea of a distributed array, but they all describe those arrays differently. Because the arrays are managed entirely in libraries, the compiler offers little support and no safety net of compile-time or compiler-generated run-time checking. The HP-spmd model is one attempt to address such shortcomings.

HPJava is a particular instantiation of this HPspmd idea. As the name suggests, the *base language* in this case is the Java$^{TM}$ programming language. To some extent the choice of base language is incidental, and clearly we could have added equivalent extensions to another language, such as Fortran itself. But Java does seem to be a better language in various respects, and it seems plausible that in the future more software will be available for modern object-oriented languages like Java than for Fortran.

HPJava is a strict extension of Java. It incorporates all of Java as a subset. Any existing Java class library can be invoked from an HPJava program without recompilation. As explained above, HPJava adds to Java a concept of multidimensional, distributed arrays, closely modelled on the arrays of HPF[1]. Regular sections of distributed arrays are fully supported. The multidimensional arrays can have any rank, and the elements of distributed arrays can have any standard Java type, including Java class types and ordinary Java array types.

A translated and compiled HPJava program is a standard Java class file, which will be executed by a distributed collection of Java Virtual Machines. All externally visible attributes of an HPJava class—e.g. existence of distributed-array-valued fields or method arguments—can be automatically reconstructed from Java signatures stored in the class file. This makes it possible to build libraries operating on distributed arrays, while maintaining the usual portability and compatibility features of Java. The libraries themselves can be implemented in HPJava, or in standard Java, or through Java Native Interface (JNI) wrappers to code implemented in other languages. The HPJava language specification carefully documents the mapping between distributed arrays and the standard-Java components they translate to.

While HPJava does not incorporate HPF-like "sequential" semantics for manipulating its distributed arrays, it does add a small number of high-level features designed to support direct programming with distributed arrays, including a distributed looping construct called **overall**. To directly support lower-level SPMD programming, it also provides a complete set of inquiry functions that

---

[1] "Sequential" multi-dimensional arrays—essentially equivalent to Fortran 95 arrays—are available as a subset of the HPJava distributed arrays.

allow the local array segments in distributed arrays to be manipulated directly, where necessary.

In the current system, syntax extensions are handled by a preprocessor that emits an ordinary SPMD program in the base language. The HPspmd syntax provides a relatively thin veneer on low-level SPMD programming, and the transformations applied by the translator are correspondingly direct—little non-trivial analysis should be needed to obtain good parallel performance. What the language does provide is a uniform model of a distributed array. This model can be targetted by reusable libraries for parallel communication and arithmetic. The specific model adopted very closely follows the distributed array model defined in the High Performance Fortran standard.

This article describes ongoing work on refinement of the HPJava language definition, and the development of a translator for this language.

## 2   HPJava — An HPspmd Language

HPJava extends its base language, Java, by adding some predefined classes and some additional syntax for dealing with distributed arrays. We aim to provide a flexible hybrid of the data parallel and low-level SPMD paradigms. To this end HPF-like distributed arrays appear as language primitives. The distribution strategies allowed for these arrays closely follow the strategies supported in HPF—any dimension of an array can independently be given blockwise, cyclic, or other distribution format[2], array dimensions can have strided alignments to dimensions other arrays, arrays as a whole can be replicated over axes of processor arrangements, and so on.

A design decision is made that all access to *non-local* array elements should go through explicit calls to library functions. These library calls must be placed in the source HPJava program by the programmer. This requirement may be surprising to people expecting to program in high-level parallel languages like HPF, but it should not seem particularly unnatural to programmers presently accustomed to writing parallel programs using MPI or other SPMD libraries. The exact nature of the communication library used is not part of the HPJava language design, per se. An appropriate communication library might perform collective operations on whole distributed arrays (as illustrated in the following examples), or it might provide some kind of get and put functions for access to remote blocks of a distributed array, similar to the functions provided in the Global Array Toolkit [13], for example.

A subscripting syntax can be used to directly access *local* elements of distributed arrays. A well-defined set of rules—automatically checked by the translator—ensures that references to these elements can only be made on processors that hold copies of the elements concerned. Alternatively one can access local

---

[2] The current HPJava translator does not implement block-cyclic distribution format, and in general the HPJava language design can't very easily accomodate the INDIRECT mappings present in the extended version of HPF. To our knowledge these are the only major omission from the HPF standards.

```
Procs2 p = new Procs2(P, P) ;
on(p) {
  Range x = new BlockRange(M, p.dim(0)) ;
  Range y = new BlockRange(N, p.dim(1)) ;

  float [[-,-]] a = new float [[x, y]], b = new float [[x, y]],
                c = new float [[x, y]] ;

  ... initialize values in 'a', 'b'

  overall(i = x for :)
    overall(j = y for :)
      c [i, j] = a [i, j] + b [i, j] ;
}
```

**Fig. 1.** A parallel matrix addition.

elements of a distributed array indirectly, by first extracting the locally held
block of elements, then subscripting this block as a local sequential array.

To facilitate the general scheme, the language adds three *distributed control*
constructs to the base language. These play a role something like the ON HOME
directives of HPF 2.0 and earlier data parallel languages [8]. One of the special
control constructs—a distributed parallel loop—facilitates traversal of locally
held elements of distributed arrays.

Mapping of distributed arrays in HPJava is described in terms of a two special
classes: **Group** and **Range**. *Process group* objects generalize the processor arrangements of HPF, and *distributed range* objects are used in place HPF templates. A
distributed range is comparable with a single dimension of an HPF template. The
changes relative to HPF (with its processor arrangements and multi-dimensional
templates) are best be regarded as a modest change of *parametrization* only: the
set of mappings that can be represented is unchanged.

Figure 1 is a simple example of an HPJava program. It illustrates creation
of distributed arrays, and access to their elements. The class **Procs2** is a standard library class derived from the special base class **Group**, and representing
a two-dimensional grid of processes. The distributed range class **BlockRange**
is a library class derived from the special class **Range**; it denotes a range of
subscripts distributed with BLOCK distribution format. Process dimensions associated with a grid are returned by the **dim()** inquiry. The **on(p)** construct is
a new control construct specifying that the enclosed actions are performed only
by processes in group **p**.

The variables **a**, **b** and **c** are all distributed array objects. The type signature
of an $r$-dimensional distributed array involves double brackets surrounding $r$
comma-separated slots. The constructors specify that these all have ranges **x**
and **y**—they are all M by N arrays, block-distributed over **p**.

A second new control construct, **overall**, implements a distributed parallel
loop. The symbols **i** and **j** scoped by these constructs are called *distributed*

```
Procs2 p = new Procs2(P, P) ;
on(p) {
  Range x = new ExtBlockRange(N, p.dim(0), 1, 1) ;
  Range y = new ExtBlockRange(N, p.dim(1), 1, 1) ;

  float [[-,-]] u = new float [[x, y]] ;

  ... some code to initialise 'u'

  for(int iter = 0 ; iter < NITER ; iter++) {

    Adlib.writeHalo(u) ;

    overall(i = x for 1 : N - 2)
      overall(j = y for 1 + (i' + iter) % 2 : N - 2 : 2)
        u [i, j] = 0.25 * (u [i - 1, j] + u [i + 1, j] +
                           u [i, j - 1] + u [i, j + 1]) ;
  }
}
```

**Fig. 2.** Red-black iteration.

*indexes.* The indexes iterate over all locations (selected here by the degenerate interval ":") of ranges x and y.

In HPJava, with a couple of exceptions noted below, the subscripts in element references must be distributed indexes. The locations associated with these indexes must be in the range associated with the array dimension. This restriction is a principal means of ensuring that referenced array elements are held locally.

This general policy is relaxed slightly to simplify coding of stencil updates. A subscript can be a *shifted index*. Usually this is only legal if the subscripted array is declared with suitable *ghost regions* [7]. Figure 2 illustrates the use of the standard library class ExtBlockRange to create arrays with ghost extensions (in this case, extensions of width 1 on either side of the locally held "physical" segment). A function, writeHalo, from the communication library Adlib updates the ghost region. If i is a distribute index, the expression i' (read "i-primed") yields the integer global loop index.

Distributed arrays can be defined with some sequential dimensions. The sequential attribute of an array dimension is flagged by an asterisk in the type signature. As illustrated in Figure 3, element reference subscripts in sequential dimensions can be ordinary integer expressions.

The last major component of the basic HPJava syntax is support for Fortran-like array sections. An *array section expression* has a similar syntax to a distributed array element reference, but uses double brackets. It yields a new array contains a subset of the elements of the parent array. Those elements can

```
Procs1 p = new Procs1(P) ;
on(p) {
  Range x = new BlockRange(N, p.dim(0)) ;

  float [[-,*]] a = new float [[x, N]], c = new float [[x, N]] ;
  float [[*,-]] b = new float [[N, x]], tmp = new float [[N, x]] ;

  ... initialize 'a', 'b'

  for(int s = 0 ; s < N ; s++) {

    overall(i = x for :) {

      float sum = 0 ;
      for(int j = 0 ; j < N ; j++)
        sum += a [i, j] * b [j, i] ;

      c [i, (i' + s) % N] = sum ;
    }

    // cyclically shift 'b' (by amount 1 in x dim)...

    Adlib.cshift(tmp, b, 1, 1) ;
    Adlib.copy(b, tmp) ;
  }
}
```

**Fig. 3.** A pipelined matrix multiplication program.

subsequently be accessed either through the parent array or through the array section—HPJava sections behave something like array pointers in Fortran, which can reference an arbitrary regular sections of a target array. As in Fortran, subscripts in section expressions can be index triplets. The language also has built-in ideas of *subranges* and *restricted groups*. These can be used in array constructors on the same footing as the ranges and grids introduced earlier, and they enable HPJava arrays to reproduce any mapping allowed by the ALIGN directive of HPF.

The examples here have covered the basic syntax of HPJava. The language itself is relatively simple. Complexities associated with varied and irregular patterns of communication would be dealt with in libraries, which can implement many richer operations than the writeHalo and cshift functions of the examples.

The examples given so far look very much like HPF data-parallel examples, written in a different syntax. We will give one final example to emphasize the point that the HPspmd model is *not* the HPF model. If we execute the following

HPJava program

```
Procs2 p = new Procs2(2, 3) ;
on(p) {
  Dimension d = p.dim(0), e = p.dim(1) ;

  System.out.println("My coordinates are (" + d.crd() +
                                   ", " + e.crd() + ")") ;
}
```

we could see output like:

```
My coordinates are (0, 2)
My coordinates are (1, 2)
My coordinates are (0, 0)
My coordinates are (1, 0)
My coordinates are (1, 1)
My coordinates are (0, 1)
```

There are 6 messages. Because the 6 processes are running concurrently in 6 JVMs, the order in which the messages appear is unpredictable. An HPJava program is a MIMD program, and any appearance of collective behavior in previous examples was the result of a particular programming style and a good library of collective communication primitives. In general an HPJava program can freely exploit the weakly coupled nature of the process cluster, often allowing more efficient algorithms to be coded.

## 3   Miscellaneous Language Issues

Early versions of HPJava (see for example, [17]) adopted the position that a distributed array should be a kind of Java object. After working with this approach for some time, our position changed. In our current language definition a distributed array type is not an ordinary Java reference type. It is a new kind of reference type that does not extend Object. In practise a single distributed array is translated to several Java objects in the emitted code.

An early motivation for this change was to avoid introducing infinitely many different Java classes for the different distributed array types. However the change has other advantages. Now that a distributed array type no longer extends Object we are liberated from having to support various object-like behaviors, that would make efficient translation of operations on distributed arrays harder than it needs to be.

The HPJava translator only applies its transformations code in *HPspmd classes*. These are classes that implement a marker interface called HPspmd. Classes that do not implement this interface are not transformed and cannot use the special syntax extensions of HPJava.

Many of the special operations in HPJava rely on the knowledge of the currently active process group—the *APG*. This is a context value that will change during the course of the program as distributed control constructs limit control to different subsets of processors. In the current HPJava translator the value of the APG is passed as a hidden argument to methods and constructors of HPspmd classes (so it is handled something like the `this` reference in typical object-oriented languages).

The HPJava language has a set of rules that the translator enforces to help ensure a rational parallel program. These govern where in a program certain constructs can legally appear, and the allowed subscripts in distributed arrays.

The value of the current active process group is used to determine whether particular distributed control contructs and certain collective array operations are legal at particular points in a program. So long as these basic rules are respected, distributed control constructs can be nested freely, and generally speaking collective operations will operate properly within the restricted APGs in effect inside the constructs.

So far as subscripting is concerned, a characteristic rule is that distributed array element reference in:

```
overall(i = x for l : u : s) {
    ... a[e_0,...,e_{r-1},i,e_{r+1},...]  ...
}
```

is allowed if and only if

1. The expression $a$ is invariant in the `overall` construct.
2. All locations in $x[l:u:s]$ are of elements $a.\texttt{rng}(r)$.

The syntax $x[l:u:s]$ represents a subrange, and the inquiry $a.\texttt{rng}(r)$ returns the $r$th range of $a$. This rule is a statement about the `overall` construct as a whole, not about the array accesses in isolation. The rule applies to any access that appears textually inside the constructs, even if some conditional test in the body of the construct might prevent those accesses from actually being executed. This is important because it allows any associated run-time checking code to be lifted outside the local loops implied by an `overall`.

## 4    Basic Translation Scheme

In some ways the philosophy behind our HPspmd translator is orthogonal to the approach in writing a true compiler. There is a deliberate effort to keep the translation scheme simple and apparent to the programmer. Aggressive optimizations of the local code are left to the compiler (or JVM) used as a backend. The full translation scheme is documented in the HPJava report at [4]. This is a work in progress, and the document evolves as the translator matures.

### 4.1    Translation of Distributed Arrays

Figure 4 gives a schema for translating a distributed array declaration in the source HPJava program. Here $T$ is some Java type, $a'_{\text{dat}}$, $a'_{\text{bas}}$ and $a'_0 \ldots a'_{R-1}$ are

**SOURCE:**
$$T \ [[attr_0, \ \ldots, \ attr_{R-1}]] \ a \ ;$$

**TRANSLATION:**

$$T \ [] \ a'_{\text{dat}} \ ;$$

$$\texttt{ArrayBase} \ a'_{\text{bas}} \ ;$$

$$DIMENSION\_TYPE(attr_0) \ a'_0 \ ;$$
$$\ldots$$
$$DIMENSION\_TYPE(attr_{R-1}) \ a'_{R-1} \ ;$$

**Fig. 4.** Translation of a distributed-array-valued variable declaration.

new identifiers, typically derived from $a$ by adding some suffixes, the strings $attr_r$ are each either a hyphen, -, or an asterisk, *, and the "macro" $DIMENSION\_TYPE$ is defined as

$$DIMENSION\_TYPE(attr_r) \equiv \texttt{ArrayDim}$$

if the term $attr_r$ is a hyphen, or

$$DIMENSION\_TYPE(attr_r) \equiv \texttt{SeqArrayDim}$$

if the term $attr_r$ is an asterisk.

If, for example, a class in the source program has a field:

```
float [[-,-,*]] bar ;
```

the translated class may be assumed to have the five fields:

```
float [] bar__$DDS ;

ArrayBase bar__$bas ;

ArrayDim bar__$0 ;
ArrayDim bar__$1 ;
SeqArrayDim bar__$2 ;
```

In general a rank-$r$ distributed array in the source program is converted to $2 + r$ variables in the translated program. The first variable is an ordinary, one-dimensional, Java array holding local elements. A simple "struct"-like object of type `ArrayBase` contains a base offset in this array and an HPJava `Group` object (the distribution group of the array). $r$ further simple objects of type `ArrayDim` each contain an integer stride in the local array and an HPJava `Range`

---

**SOURCE:**

overall ($i$ = $x$ for $e_{\mathrm{lo}}$ : $e_{\mathrm{hi}}$ : $e_{\mathrm{stp}}$) $S$

**TRANSLATION:**

Block $b$ = $x$.localBlock($\mathbf{T}\left[e_{\mathrm{lo}}\right]$, $\mathbf{T}\left[e_{\mathrm{hi}}\right]$, $\mathbf{T}\left[e_{\mathrm{stp}}\right]$) ;

Group $p$ = ((Group) $apg$.clone()).restrict($x$.dim()) ;

for (int $l$ = 0 ; $l$ < $b$.count ; $l$++) {
    int $sub$ = $b$.sub_bas + $b$.sub_stp * $l$ ;
    int $glb$ = $b$.glb_bas + $b$.glb_stp * $l$ ;

    $\mathbf{T}\left[S\,|p\right]$
}

where:

$i$ is an index name in the source program,
$x$ is a simple expression in the source program,
$e_{\mathrm{lo}}$, $e_{\mathrm{hi}}$, and $e_{\mathrm{stp}}$ are expressions in the source,
$S$ is a statement in the source program, and
$b$, $p$, $l$, $sub$ and $glb$ are names of new variables.

---

**Fig. 5.** Translation of overall construct.

object describing the dimensions of the distributed array. The class `SeqArrayDim` is a subclass of `ArrayDim`, specialized to parameterize sequential dimensions conveniently.

One thing to note is that a class file generated by compiling the translated code will contain the generated field names. These follow a fixed prescription, so that when a pre-compiled class file (from some library package, say) is read by the HPJava translator, it can reconstruct the original distributed array signature of the field from the $2+r$ fields in the class file. It can then correctly check usage of the external class. By design, the translator can always reconstruct the HPspmd class signatures from the standard Java class file of the translated code.

## 4.2 Translation of the Overall Construct

The schema in Figure 5 describes basic translation of the overall construct. The `localBlock()` method on the `Range` class returns parameters of the locally held block of index values associated with a range. These parameters are returned in another simple "struct"-like object of class `Block`. Terms like $\mathbf{T}\left[e\right]$ represent the translated form of expression $e$.

The *local subscript* for the index $i$ is the value of $sub$. This value is used in subscripting distributed arrays. The *global index* for the index $i$ is the value of $glb$. This value is used in evaluating the global index expression $i$'.

---

**SOURCE:**

$$e \equiv a \; [e_0, \; \ldots, \; e_{R-1}]$$

**TRANSLATION:**

$$\mathbf{T}\,[e] \equiv \mathbf{T}_{\mathrm{dat}}\,[a] \; [OFFSET(a, e_0, \ldots, e_{R-1})]$$

where:

    The expression $a$ is the subscripted array,
    each term $e_r$ is either an integer, a distributed index name,
        or a shifted index expression, and
    the macro $OFFSET$ is defined in the text.

---

**Fig. 6.** Translation of distributed array element access.

Because we use the run-time inquiry function `localBlock()` to compute parameters of the local loop, this translation is identical for every distribution format supported by the language (block-distribution, simple-cyclic distribution, aligned subranges, and several others). Of course there is an overhead associated with abstracting this computation into a method call; but the method call is made at most once at the start of each loop, and we expect that in many cases optimizing translators will recognize repeat calls to these methods, or recognize the distribution format and inline the computations, reducing the overhead further.

$\mathbf{T}\,[S\,|p]$ means the translation of $S$ in the context of $p$ as active process group.

## 4.3   Translating Element Access in Distributed Arrays

We only need to consider the case where the array reference is a distributed array: the general scheme is illustrated in Figure 6. The macro $OFFSET$ is defined as

$$OFFSET(a, e_0, \ldots, e_{R-1}) \equiv$$

$$\mathbf{T}_{\mathrm{bas}}\,[a].\texttt{base} \;+\; OFFSET\_DIM(\mathbf{T}_0\,[a], e_0)$$

$$\ldots$$

$$+\; OFFSET\_DIM(\mathbf{T}_{R-1}\,[a], e_{R-1})$$

There are three cases for the macro $OFFSET\_DIM$ depending on whether the subscript argument is a distributed index, a shifted index, or an integer subscripts (in a sequential dimension). We will only illustrate the case where $e_r$ is a distributed index $i$. Then

$$OFFSET\_DIM(a_r', e_r) \equiv \quad a_r'.\texttt{stride} \; * \; sub$$

where $sub$ is the local subscript variable for this index (see the last section).

Ultimately—as we should expect for regular access patterns—the local subscript computations reduce to expressions linear in the indices of local loops. Such subscripting patterns are readily amenable to optimization by the compiler back-end, or, more likely, they can be further simplified by the HPspmd translator itself.

We have only sketched three of the more important schema, leaving out details. The full translation scheme for HPJava, recorded in [4], involves perhaps a couple of dozen such schema of varying complexity. In practice the translation phase described here is preceded by a "pre-translation" phase that simplifies some complex expressions by introducing temporaries, and adds run-time checking code for some of the rules described in section 3.

# 5   Status and Prospects

The first fully functional version of the HPJava translator is now operational. Over the last few weeks the system as been tested and debugged against a small test suite of available HPJava programs. Currently most of the examples are short, although the suite does include an 800-line Multigrid code, transcribed from an existing Fortran 90 program. One pressing concern over the next few months is to develop a much more substantial body of test code and applications.

As we have emphasized, HPJava includes all of standard Java as a subset. "Translation" of the conventional Java part of the language is very easy. It is a design feature of HPJava that the translation system handles code that *looks like* base language code in *exactly* the same way as it would be handled by a compiler for the base language. In our source-to-source translation strategy, this means that standard Java statements and expressions are copied through essentially unchanged. On the other hand the inclusion of Java means that we do need a front-end that covers the whole of Java. The translation scheme for HPJava depends in an important way on type information. It follows that we need type analysis for the whole language, including the Java part. Writing a full type-checker for Java is not trivial (especially since the introduction of nested types). In practice development of the front-end, and particularly the type-checker, has been the most time-consuming step in developing the whole system. The HPJava translator is written in Java. The parser was developed using the JavaCC and JTB tools.

It is too early to give detailed benchmarks. However we will give some general arguments that lead us to believe that in the near future we can hope to obtain effective performance using our system. For the sake of definiteness, consider the Multigrid example referred to above. This is a good example for HPJava, because it is an example of an algorithm that is quite complex to code "by hand" as a parallel program, and relatively easy to code using HPJava together with the communication library Adlib. The detailed logic of the Multigrid algorithm has an interesting recursive structure, but the core of the computational work boils down to red-black relaxation (Figure 2). If we can code this simple algorithm well, we expect the whole of the solver should work reasonably well.

The general feasibility of programming this kind of algorithm on a massively parallel, distributed memory computer is presumably not at issue. As discussed in the previous section, the translation scheme for HPJava ultimately reduces the **overall** constructs of the source program to simple **for** loops—much the same as the kind of **for** loops one would write in a hand-coded MPI program[3]. Earlier experiences, using the high-level Adlib communication library as run-time support for research implementations of HPF, lead us to believe that this library should not introduce unacceptable overheads. (Adlib is a C++ library built on top of MPI. The Java binding is through JNI.) So this leaves us with the question of whether Java will be the weak link, in terms of performance. The answer seems to be "perhaps not". Recent benchmarking efforts [2] indicate that—at least on major commodity platforms—Java JIT performance is approaching parity with C and even Fortran compilers. We believe that these results will carry over to our applications.

## 6  Conclusion

HPJava is conceived as a parallel programming language extended from, and fully compatible, with, Java—perhaps the most modern programming language in widescale use at the time of writing. It imports language constructs from Fortran 90 and High Performance Fortran that are believed to be important to support effective scientific programming of massively parallel computers.

HPJava is an instance of what we call the *HPspmd model*: it is not exactly a high-level parallel programming language in the ordinary sense, but rather a tool to assist parallel programmers in writing SPMD code. In this respect the closest recent language we are familiar with is probably F-- [15], but HPJava and F-- have many obvious differences.

Parallel programming aside, HPJava is also one of several recent efforts to put "scientific", Fortran-like arrays into Java. At meetings of the Java Grande Forum, for example, this has been identified as an important requirement for wider deployment of scientific software in Java. Work at IBM over the last few years [10, 9, 12, 16] has been particularly influential in this area, leading to a JSR (Java Specification Request) for standardized scientific array classes. The approach taken in HPJava—using a preprocessor to break arrays into components rather than introducing multidimensional array classes as such—is somewhat different. For us the preprocessor approach was essentially mandated by the proliferation of distinct distributed array types in our model. Generating the large number of array classes that would be needed seems to be impractical. In recent talks the IBM group have also discussed comparable approaches for sequential multiarrays without introducing specific array classes [11].

---

[3] More precisely, they will be much the same once the raw code, generated by the basic translation scheme, has been cleaned up by some straightforward optimizations. This is the step that is missing at the time of writing.

# 7    Acknowledgements

This work was supported in part by the National Science Foundation Division of Advanced Computational Infrastructure and Research, contract number 9872125.

# References

[1] L. S. Blackford, J. Choi, A. Cleary, E. D'Azevedo, J. Demmel, I. Dhillon, J. Dongarra, S. Hammarling, G. Henry, A. Petitet, K. Stanley, D. Walker, and R. C. Whaley. *ScaLAPACK User's Guide.* SIAM, 1997.

[2] M. Bull, L. Smith, L. Pottage, and R. Freeman. Benchmarking Java against C and Fortran for scientific applications. In *ACM 2001 Java Grande/ISCOPE Conference.* ACM Press, June 2001.

[3] Bryan Carpenter, Guansong Zhang, Geoffrey Fox, Xiaoming Li, Xinying Li, and Yuhong Wen. Towards a Java environment for SPMD programming. In David Pritchard and Jeff Reeve, editors, *4th International Europar Conference*, volume 1470 of *Lecture Notes in Computer Science.* Springer, 1998. http://aspen.csit.fsu.edu/pss/HPJava.

[4] Bryan Carpenter, Guansong Zhang, and Han-Ku Lee. Parallel programming in HPJava. http://aspen.csit.fsu.edu/pss/HPJava.

[5] R. Das, M. Uysal, J.H. Salz, and Y.-S. Hwang. Communication optimizations for irregular scientific computations on distributed memory architectures. *Journal of Parallel and Distributed Computing*, 22(3):462–479, September 1994.

[6] Stephen J. Fink and Scott B. Baden. Run-time data distribution for block-structured applications on distributed memory computers. In *Proceedings of the 7th SIAM Conference on Parallel Processing for Scientific Computing*, February 1995.

[7] Michael Gerndt. Updating distributed variables in local computations. *Concurrency: Practice and Experience*, 2(3):171–193, 1990.

[8] C. Koelbel and P. Mehrotra. Compiling global name-space parallel loops for distributed execution. *IEEE Transactions on Parallel and Distributed Systems*, 2(4):440–451, 1991.

[9] J.E. Moreira. Closing the performance gap between Java and Fortran in technical computing. In *First UK Workshop on Java for High Performance Network Computing, Europar '98*, September 1998. http://www.cs.cf.ac.uk/hpjworkshop/.

[10] J.E. Moreira, S.P. Midkiff, and M. Gupta. From flop to MegaFlops: Java for technical computing. In *Languages and Compilers for Parallel Computing*, volume 1656 of *Lecture Notes in Computer Science.* Springer, 1998.

[11] J.E. Moreira, S.P. Midkiff, and M. Gupta. A comparision of three approaches to language, compiler and library support for multidimensional arrays in Java. In *ACM 2001 Java Grande/ISCOPE Conference.* ACM Press, June 2001.

[12] J.E. Moreira, S.P. Midkiff, M. Gupta, and R. Lawrence. High performance computing with the Array package for Java: A case study using data mining. In *Supercomputing '99.* IEEE Computer Society Press, 1999.

[13] J. Nieplocha, R.J. Harrison, and R.J. Littlefield. The Global Array: Non-uniform-memory-access programming model for high-performance computers. *The Journal of Supercomputing*, 10:197–220, 1996.

[14] Manish Parashar and J.C. Browne. Systems engineering for high performance computing software: The HDDA/DAGH infrastructure for implementation of parallel structured adaptive mesh. In *Structured Adaptive Mesh Refinement Grid Methods*, IMA Volumes in Mathematics and its Applications. Springer-Verlag.

[15] R.W.Numrich and J.L.Steidel. F - -: a simple parallel extension to Fortran 90. *SIAM News*, page 30, 1997.

[16] Peng Wu, Sam Midkiff, Jose Moreira, and Manish Gupta. Efficient support for complex numbers in Java. In *ACM 1999 Java Grande Conference*. ACM Press, June 1999.

[17] Guansong Zhang, Bryan Carpenter, Geoffrey Fox, Xinying Li, and Yuhong Wen. Considerations in HPJava language design and implementation. In *11th International Workshop on Languages and Compilers for Parallel Computing*, 1998.

# Compiler and Middleware Support for Scalable Data Mining*

Gagan Agrawal, Ruoming Jin, and Xiaogang Li

Department of Computer and Information Sciences
University of Delaware, Newark DE 19716
{agrawal,jrm,xili}@cis.udel.edu

**Abstract.** The parallelizing compiler community has traditionally focused its efforts on scientific applications. This paper gives an overview of a compiler/runtime project targeting parallel and scalable execution of data mining algorithms. To the best of our knowledge, this is the first project with such a focus.

Data mining is the process of analyzing large datasets for extracting novel and useful patterns or models. Though a lot of effort has been put into developing parallel algorithms for data mining tasks, the expertise and effort currently required in implementing, maintaining, and performance tuning a parallel data mining application is an impediment in the wide use of parallel computers for data mining.

We have developed a data parallel dialect of Java that can be used for expressing common data mining algorithms at a high level. Our compiler generates a middleware specification from this dialect of Java. The middleware supports both distributed memory and shared memory parallelization, and performs a number of I/O optimizations to support efficient processing of disk resident datasets. Our final goal is to start from declarative mining operators, and translate them to data parallel Java.

In this paper, we describe the commonality among different data mining algorithms, the middleware and its interface, the data parallel dialect of Java, and the compilation techniques required for generating the middleware specification. Experimental evaluations of the middleware and the compiler are also presented.

## 1 Introduction

The parallelizing compiler community has traditionally focused its efforts on scientific applications. Over the last two decades, various data-parallel and task-parallel compilers have been developed for a number of classes of scientific applications. Examples of classes of applications targeted include regular, irregular, multi-grid, out-of-core, and pointer-based applications. Many of the parallelizing compilers have heavily used application-class specific runtime systems, like

---

* This work was supported by NSF grant ACR-9982087, NSF CAREER award ACI-9733520, and NSF grant CCR-9808522.

H. Dietz (Ed.): LCPC 2001, LNCS 2624, pp. 33–51, 2003.

PARTI/CHAOS for sparse applications [40], and PASSION for out-of-core applications [8].

This paper gives an overview of a compiler/runtime project targeting parallel and scalable execution of data mining algorithms. To the best of our knowledge, this is the first project with such a focus.

Data mining is the process of analyzing large datasets for extracting novel and useful patterns or models. In recent years, very large datasets have become available for analysis in a number of scientific fields, like genomics, geology and earth sciences, and computational simulations; and in commercial settings like large retail chains, financial institutions, insurance companies, etc. Data mining and knowledge discovery from these large data sets can lead to significant advances in scientific domains, as well as improvements in business practices.

As the amount of data available for analysis has exploded, scalability of data mining implementations has become a critical factor. To this end, parallel algorithms for most of the well-known data mining techniques have been developed in recent years [2, 18, 27, 34, 42, 43]. However, the expertise and effort currently required in implementing, maintaining, and performance tuning a parallel data mining application is a severe impediment in the wide use of parallel computers for scalable data mining. There is a clear need for high-level support for developing parallel data mining implementations.

## 1.1   Overview of the Project

We are developing a series of successively higher level interfaces to enable rapid specification or development of scalable data mining applications. The components of our research project are outlined in Figure 1.

Our target environment are clusters of SMPs, which are emerging as a cost-effective, flexible, and popular parallel processing configuration. Clusters of SMP workstations, where each workstation has an attached disk farm, offer both shared-nothing parallelism (across nodes of the cluster) and shared-memory parallelism (within a node). Thus, the tools and techniques we develop can also be used on purely shared memory configurations (like a large SMP machine) or purely distributed memory configurations (like a cluster of uniprocessor workstations).

Our work is based on the observation that parallel versions of several well-known data mining techniques share a relatively similar structure. We have carefully studied parallel versions of apriori association mining [2], k-means clustering [21], k-nearest neighbor classifier [19], and decision tree classifier [30]. In each of these methods, parallelization can be done by dividing the data instances (or records or transactions) among the nodes. The computation on each node involves reading the data instances in an arbitrary order, processing each data instance, and performing a *local reduction*. The reduction involves only commutative and associative operations, which means the result is independent of the order in which the data instances are processed. After the local reduction on each node, a *global reduction* is performed.

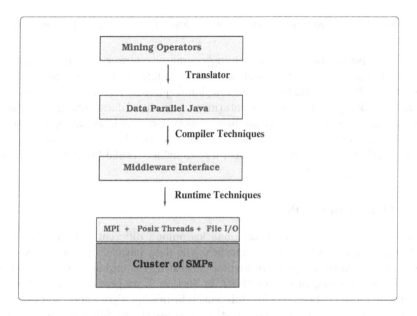

**Fig. 1.** Overview of the Research Project

Currently, developing a parallel data mining implementation on a clusters of SMPs involves programming using the Message Passing Interface (MPI), Posix threads, and file I/O, thereby requiring both high effort and expertise. We are developing the following series of successively higher-level interfaces for enabling much simpler development or specification of scalable data mining applications.

**Middleware Interface:** Our middleware interface exploits the similarity between a number of common data mining algorithms and allows a high-level specification of a parallel data mining algorithm. Runtime techniques achieve shared-nothing and shared-memory parallelization starting from such high-level specification. It enables high I/O performance by minimizing disk seek time and using asynchronous I/O operations, thereby achieving efficient execution on disk resident datasets. I/O, communication, and synchronization optimizations can be implemented in such a middleware, enabling different parallel data mining applications to benefit. If the middleware is successfully ported to a new parallel configuration, all applications developed on top of it can be executed on the new configuration without requiring any extra effort.

**Data Parallel Java Interface:** We are using a dialect of Java for expressing data mining algorithms at a higher level than our middleware interface. Our dialect of Java includes extensions for declaring multi-dimensional collections of objects, parallel loops over such collections, and a reduction interface. Starting from a sequential implementation that only processes main memory datasets, a data parallel version can be conveniently developed by inserting a few simple directives.

**Mining Operators:** The data mining community is working on developing a set of mining operators that will allow data mining tasks to be specified in a declarative fashion, similar to the relational queries [19]. We believe that by having a library of Java implementations of common data mining algorithms, we can easily create data parallel Java versions from such mining operators. By utilizing the compiler and runtime technology, supporting the data parallel Java dialect and the middleware interface, we can achieve scalable execution starting from mining operators.

## 1.2    Outline of the Paper

This paper focuses on the commonalities among different data mining algorithms, the middleware and its interface, the data parallel dialect of Java, and the compilation techniques required for generating the middleware specification.

The paper is organized as follows. In Section 2, we give an overview of parallelization approaches used for different data mining algorithms, and establish the commonality between those. Section 3 covers the middleware, including an overview, its interface, an example, and a brief experimental evaluation. Section 4 describes the language framework and compilation techniques. We compare our work with related research efforts in Section 5, and conclude in Section 6.

# 2    Parallel Data Mining Algorithms

In this section, we describe how parallel versions of several commonly used data mining techniques share a relatively similar structure. We focus on four important techniques: apriori associating mining [2], k-means clustering [21], k-nearest neighbors [19], and decision tree classifiers [30]. For each of these techniques, we describe the basic problem and then the parallelization strategy.

## 2.1    Apriori Association Mining

Association rule mining is the process of analyzing a set of transactions to extract *association rules* and is a very commonly used and well-studied data mining problem. Given a set of transactions[1] (each of them being a set of items), an association rule is an expression $X \rightarrow Y$, where $X$ and $Y$ are the sets of items. Such a rule implies that transactions in databases that contain the items in $X$ also tend to contain the items in $Y$.

Formally, the goal is to compute the sets $L_k$. For a given value of $k$, the set $L_k$ comprises the frequent itemsets of length $k$. A well accepted algorithm for association mining is the *apriori* mining algorithm [3]. The main observation in the apriori technique is that if an itemset occurs with frequency $f$, all the

---

[1] We use the terms *transactions, data items,* and *data instances* interchangeably.

subsets of this itemset also occur with at least frequency $f$. In the first iteration of this algorithm, transactions are analyzed to determine the frequent 1-itemsets. During any subsequent iteration $k$, the frequent itemsets $L_{k-1}$ found in the $(k-1)^{th}$ iteration are used to generate the candidate itemsets $C_k$. Then, each transaction in the dataset is processed to compute the frequency of each member of the set $C_k$. k-itemsets from $C_k$ that have a certain pre-specified minimal frequency (called the *support level*) are added to the set $L_k$.

A straight forward method for parallelizing the apriori association mining algorithm is *count distribution* [2]. Though a number of other parallelization techniques have been proposed [17, 43], the count distribution method is easy to implement and very efficient as long as the number of candidates does not become very large and/or sufficient memory is available on each node. The outline of the count distribution parallelization strategy is as follows. The transactions are partitioned among the nodes. Each nodes generates the complete $C_k$ using the frequent itemset $L_{k-1}$ created at the end of the iteration $k-1$. Next, each node scans the transactions it owns to compute the count of local occurrences for each candidate k-itemset in the set $C_k$. After this *local* phase, all nodes perform a *global reduction* to compute the global count of occurrences for each candidate in the set $C_k$.

## 2.2   k-means Clustering

The second data mining algorithm we describe is the k-means clustering technique, which is also very commonly used. This method considers transactions or data instances as representing points in a high-dimensional space. Proximity within this space is used as the criterion for classifying the points into clusters.

Three steps in the sequential version of this algorithm are as follows: 1) start with $k$ given centers for clusters; 2) scan the data instances, for each data instance (point), find the center closest to it, assign this point to the corresponding cluster, and then move the center of the cluster closer to this point; and 3) repeat this process until the assignment of points to cluster does not change.

This method can also be parallelized in a fashion very similar to the count distribution method for apriori association mining [4, 15, 36]. The data instances are partitioned among the nodes. Each node processes the data instances it owns. Instead of moving the center of the cluster immediately after the data instance is assigned to the cluster, the *local sum* of movements of each center due to all points owned on that node is computed. A *global reduction* is performed on these local sums to determine the centers of clusters for the next iteration.

## 2.3   k-nearest Neighbors

k-nearest neighbor classifier is based on learning by analogy [19]. The training samples are described by an n-dimensional numeric space. Given an unknown sample, the k-nearest neighbor classifier searches the pattern space for k training samples that are closest, using the euclidean distance, to the unknown sample.

Again, this technique can be parallelized as follows. The training samples are distributed among the nodes. Given an unknown sample, each node processes the training samples it owns to calculate the k-nearest neighbors *locally*. After this local phase, a *global reduction* computes the overall k-nearest neighbors from the k-nearest neighbors on each node.

### 2.4   Decision Tree Classifiers

The final set of data mining techniques we examine is decision tree classifiers [30]. In a decision tree, each leaf node is associated with a class label, and each internal node is associated with a split condition on an attribute. A decision tree is primarily built by recursively splitting the training dataset into partitions, until all or most of the records in the partitions have the same class label. Two most time consuming phases in a decision tree construction algorithm are: 1) finding the best split point for each internal node, and 2) performing the split, which means that the data items associated with the node split are divided into two partitions.

The parallelization strategy typically used for a decision tree classifier is also quite similar to the approach used for the previous three techniques. The training dataset is partitioned between the nodes. Each node processes the data items it owns, to compute the *local* counts used for selecting between candidate splitting conditions. After local counts have been computed on each node, a *global reduction* needs to performed.

There are two major additional issues in implementing an efficient parallel version of a decision tree classifier. First, in distributing the data items among different nodes, numerical attributes are sorted. Second, the split operation can be I/O intensive, though it does not require communication between the nodes.

## 3   Middleware for Parallel Data Mining Implementations

Our middleware interface is the first high-level interface we offer for expressing parallel data mining tasks. In this section, we describe the middleware interface, the runtime support techniques used, an example of the use of the middleware, and a brief experimental evaluation.

### 3.1   Middleware Interface

The following functions need to be written by the application developer using our middleware. Most of these functions can be easily extracted from a sequential version that processes main memory resident datasets.

**Initial Processing:** Many data mining applications involve an initial processing of the data instances to modify the format of certain fields, or pre-process for some exceptional cases, etc. This processing is performed independently on each data instance, and therefore, can be performed in parallel and in an arbitrary order on each processor.

**Specifying the Subset of Data to be Processed:** In many case, only a subset of the available data needs to be analyzed for a given data mining task. For example, while creating associations rules from customer purchase record at a grocery store, we may be interested in processing records obtained in certain months, or for customers in a certain age groups, etc.

**Local Reductions:** The data instances owned by a processor and belonging to the subset specified are read. A local reduction function specifies how, after processing one data instance, a *reduction object* (declared by the programmer), is updated. The result of this processing must be independent of the order in which data instances are processed on each processor. The order in which data instances are read from the disks is determined by the runtime system. The reduction object is maintained in the main memory.

**Global Reductions:** The reduction objects on all processors are combined using a global reduction function.

**Iterator:** A parallel data mining application comprises of one or more distinct pairs of local and global reduction functions, which may be invoked in an iterative fashion. An iterator function specifies a loop which is initiated after the initial processing and invokes local and global reduction functions.

## 3.2   Runtime Techniques

In this subsection, we discuss the runtime techniques implemented in the middleware for I/O performance enhancement, shared-nothing parallelization, and shared-memory parallelization.

**Shared-Nothing Parallelization** As we described in Section 2, the structure of parallel algorithms for common data mining techniques makes shared-nothing parallelization relatively simple. After data has been distributed (declustered) between different nodes, each node can execute initial processing and local reduction functions on data items it owns. After each invocation of local reduction function, local copies of reduction objects on each node are broadcasted to all other nodes, and local copies of reduction objects from all other nodes are received on each node. This communication is facilitated by the middleware. After the communication phase, global reduction function is invoked on each node.

**I/O Performance Enhancement** Efficient I/O is critical for mining over disk resident datasets. For this purpose, a preprocessing phase, known as *task planning*, is used to create a schedule for each invocation of local reduction. Task planning is somewhat similar in nature to the *inspector* used as part of the inspector/executor paradigm for improving communication performance on distributed memory machines [32] or performing runtime parallelization [33]. A schedule or task plan specifies the order in which data items locally owned are accessed and processed. The task plan is created to minimize disk seek time on each disk, while maximizing parallelism in accessing each disk. Within each disk, the data items that are within the subset of data to be processed are accessed in the order in which they are stored. For achieving high bandwidth retrieval, the dataset owned by each node is partitioned into a set of *chunks*. A chunk is typically of the size of a small number of disk blocks and is the unit of I/O. During task processing, I/O and processing is overlapped as much as possible. It does this by maintaining explicit queues for both kind of operations (data retrieval and data processing) and switching between them as required.

One of the features of the our task processing is the integration of data retrieval and processing. This is achieved by pushing processing operations into the storage manager and allowing processing operations to access the buffer used to hold data arriving from disk. As a result, the system avoids one or more levels of copying that would be needed in a layered architecture where the storage manager and the processing are not coupled together.

The I/O and shared-nothing parallelization support in our middleware has been developed on top of the Active Data Repository (ADR) developed at University of Maryland [10, 11, 12], which targets data intensive computations from domains like satellite data processing and medical informatics. Unlike our middleware, ADR targets strictly distributed memory parallel machines and is not specifically targeted towards data mining applications.

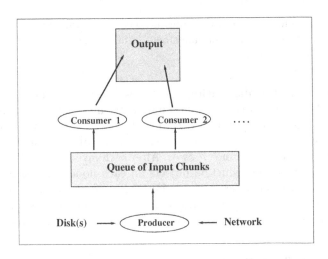

**Fig. 2.** Producer / Consumer Framework for Runtime Parallelization

**Runtime Shared-Memory Parallelization** We now describe the framework we have implemented for efficiently using multiple processors available on each node of a SMP workstation for data mining applications.

The processors available on each node need to perform the following tasks: 1) perform task scheduling, 2) manage disk operations and file I/O, 3) manage communication with other nodes, 4) execute the *Iterator* loop described earlier,

5) assign local reductions on data items being processed by the node to different processors, and 6) perform local reductions.

To perform the above tasks, we use one *producer* thread and one or more *consumer* threads. The producer thread is responsible for the tasks 1, 2, 3, 4, and 5 in the list above. Typically, one consumer thread is scheduled on a single processor, and perform local reductions (task 6) on the data items assigned to it.

The producer/consumer framework is shown in Figure 2. As we mentioned earlier in this section, the unit for I/O in our middleware is a *chunk*, which is typically one disk block or a small number of disk blocks. We use the same unit for dividing the local reductions among processors on a node. The idea is that chunk size can be chosen to be of sufficiently low granularity to allow effective load balancing at runtime, and of sufficiently high granularity to keep the overhead of runtime scheduling acceptable.

As we discussed earlier, in most of the parallel data mining algorithms, local reductions on data items are independent operations, except for race conditions in updating the same reduction object. In avoiding these race conditions, the main complication is that the particular element(s) in the reduction object that need to be modified after processing a data item is not known until after performing the computation associated with the data item. With this constraint, we have developed four different approaches for avoiding race conditions as different consumer threads may want to update the same elements in the reduction object. These techniques are: *full locking*, *fixed locking*, *full replication*, and *partial replication*.

*Full Locking:* One obvious solution to avoiding race conditions is to associate one lock with every element in the reduction object. After processing a data item, the consumer thread needs to acquire the locks associated with all elements in the reduction object it needs to update.

*Fixed Locking:* To alleviate the overheads associated with the large number of locks required in the full locking scheme, we have designed the fixed locking scheme. As the name suggests, a fixed number of locks are used. The number of locks chosen is a parameter to this scheme. If the number of locks is $l$, then the element $i$ in the reduction object is assigned to the lock $i \bmod l$.

*Full Replication:* One simple way of avoiding race conditions is to replicate the reduction object and create one copy for every consumer thread. The copy for each consumer thread needs to be initialized in the beginning. After the local reduction has been performed using all the data items on a particular node, the increments made in all the copies are *merged*.

*Partial Replication:* Instead of creating copies of the reduction object for each consumer thread (as in the full replication scheme), we create a buffer for every consumer thread. The consumer thread stores the updates to elements of the reduction object in this buffer. A separate thread works on updating the reduction object using the values from these buffers.

## 3.3   Case Study: Association Mining

We have so far used our middleware for implementing parallel versions of apriori association mining, k-means clustering, and k-nearest neighbors. In this subsection, we describe our implementation experience with apriori association mining, and illustrate several important aspects of the middleware interface.

We started from a sequential apriori code that processes datasets that fit in main memory. This sequential code was developed by Borgelt [9] and uses a prefix tree to represent candidate itemsets. The dataset is partitioned between different nodes in the cluster. On each node, the set of transactions is further divided into chunks, which is the unit for processing in our middleware.

The parallelization strategy we use across nodes is the same as the well known count distribution scheme [2], except that we use middleware for handling message passing.

The middleware's producer/consumer framework is used for parallelization within the node. The use of four mechanisms implemented in the middleware for avoiding race conditions while updating candidate counts leads to a family of new parallel apriori algorithms for hierarchical ((i.e. combining both shared-nothing and shared-memory parallelization) systems. Our shared-memory parallelization has some similarities with the Common Candidate Partitioned Database (CCPD) scheme developed by Zaki et al. [42], in the sense that there is only one itemset tree stored in the main memory. However, there are two main differences in our approach. First, the use of middleware and a producer thread allows asynchronous and efficient I/O, and therefore, good performance on disk resident datasets. Second, depending upon the scheme used for avoiding race conditions, the candidate counts may be fully or partially replicated across processors, enabling higher parallelism.

```
LocalReduc(Chunk p, int k)
{
    for (each transaction t in p)
    {
        prefixtree.count(c,t,k);
    }
}

GlobalReduc(CountVector c, MessageReceiveBuffer buffer)
{
    combine(c,buffer);
}
```

```
Iterator()
{
    for (k = 1 ; not end_condition() ; k++)
    {
        for (each chunk p)
            LocalReduction(p,k);
        GlobalCombination(c,buffer);
        prefixtree.expand(k);
    }
}
Bool end_condition(k)
{
    return prefixtree.newcandidate == 0;
}
```

**Fig. 3.** Main functions used in Middleware Specification

The major functions used in middleware specification are shown in Figure 3. The function `LocalReduc` just invokes the function `prefixtree.count` from the sequential implementation. After the local reduction, the reduction object on each processor (counts of all candidates) are broadcasted to all other processors. The processing in the `GlobalReduc` function is very simple. In the function shown in the figure, counts of all candidates received from another processor are combined with the local counts. This is repeated for the buffer received from each processor. The `Iterator` function invokes local and global reductions and adds candidates to the prefix tree.

We believe that our implementation is the first hierarchical parallel implementation of apriori on disk resident datasets.

### 3.4   Preliminary Experimental Data

In this section, we give preliminary evaluation of our middleware using implementations of association mining and k-nearest neighbor classifier.

The experiments were conducted on a cluster of SMP workstations. We used 8 Sun Microsystem Ultra Enterprise 450's, each of which has 4 250MHz Ultra-II processors. Each node has 1 GB of main memory which is 4-way interleaved. Each of the node have a 4 GB system disk and a 18 GB data disk.

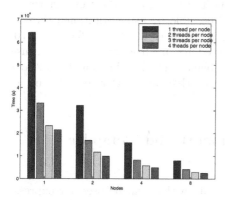

**Fig. 4.** Performance of Apriori Association Mining

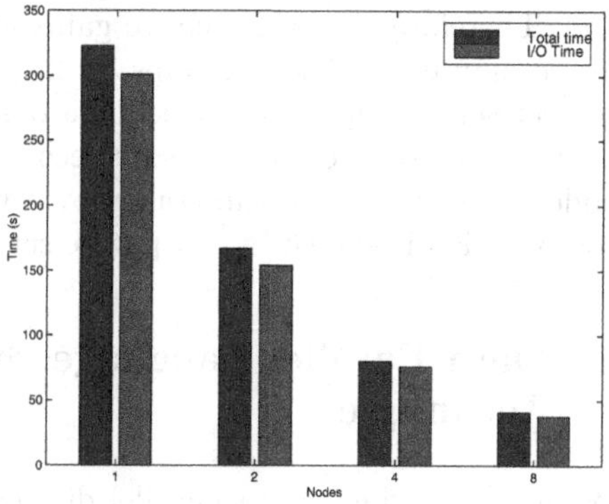

**Fig. 5.** Performance of k-nearest Neighbor

The dataset we used for evaluating our implementation of association mining has 64 million transactions, with an average of 30 items per transaction. The total number of distinct items is 1000. The total size of the dataset is 8 GB, and exceeds the total main memory on 8 nodes. The support and confidence levels used in our experiments are 1% and 90%, respectively. Since we wanted to see the best performance than can achieved using our system, we have used the full replication scheme.

The performance on the 8GB dataset is presented in Figure 4. This dataset resulted in 9 iterations of the outer-loop of the apriori association mining algorithm. The number of candidate whose support is counted during these iterations is 1,000, 344,912, 858,982, 25,801, 22,357, 14,354, 6,257, 55, and 1, for the first through ninth iterations, respectively. Each node has to broadcast and receive 5.1 MB of data (broken over 9 messages) during the course of the execution.

Our implementation achieves high shared-nothing parallel efficiency. With the use of 1 thread per node, the speedups on 2,4, and 8 nodes are 1.99, 4.05, and 8.07, respectively. As the data is distributed over multiple nodes, the amount of I/O needed on each node reduces, and helps achieve somewhat higher than linear speedups.

Use of up to 3 consumer threads per node results in almost linear performance improvements. With 3 consumer threads per node, the speedups on 1, 2, 4, and 8 nodes are 2.77, 5.50, 11.08, and 21.98, respectively. The parallel efficiency on 8 nodes with 3 consumer thread per node is 91.6%. With 4 consumer threads per node, the speedups on 1, 2, 4, and 8 nodes are 3.0, 6.5, 13.03, and 25.50, respectively, showing only marginal improvements from the results with 3 consumer threads. This is because each node has 1 producer thread, so the use of 4 consumer threads results in a total of 5 threads on 4 processors.

For evaluating k-nearest neighbor, we used a 2.7 GB dataset with points in a 3-dimensional space and 10 as the value of $k$. The performance on 1, 2, 4, and 8 nodes, with 1 thread per node, is shown in Figure 5. This code is I/O bound, i.e., there is very little computation and most of the time is spent in performing I/O. Therefore, no performance gains are possible by using additional threads for computation. The speedups on 2, 4, and 8 nodes are 1.93, 4.04, and 7.70, respectively. A superlinear speedup is observed in going from 2 to 4 nodes because he data owned by each processor becomes memory resident in going from 2 to 4 nodes. The amount of time taken by a version that only performed I/O and no computation is shown by a separate set of bars in Figure 5.

# 4   Data Parallel Language Support and Compiler Techniques

We now describe a data parallel dialect of Java that can be used for expressing parallel algorithms for common data mining techniques, including all the techniques we described in Section 2. This data parallel Java dialect offers a significantly higher level interface than the middleware interface described in the previous section. We also describe the compiler techniques for translate from this Java dialect to the middleware interface.

## 4.1   Java Extensions for Expressing Data Mining Algorithms

We use three main directives in our data parallel dialect. These are for specifying a multi-dimensional collections of objects, a parallel for loop, and a reduction interface. The first two have been commonly used in other object-oriented parallel systems like Titanium [41], HPC++ [7], and Concurrent Aggregates [13]. The concept of reduction interface is, to the best of our knowledge, novel to our approach.

```
Interface Reducinterface {
    { * Any object of any class implementing *}
    { * this interface is a reduction variable *}
}
public class Transaction {
    { * Implements a set of items *}
}
public class PrefixTree
            implements Reducinterface; {
    { * Implements a prefix tree of *}
    { * candidates with counts *}
}

static RectDomain[1] trans = [0:numTrans - 1];
static Transaction[2d] dataset = new Transaction[trans];
static PrefixTree prefixtree ;
public static void main(String[] args) {
    for (k = 1 ; !prefixtree.end_condition() ; k++) {
        foreach(t in trans) {
            prefixtree.count(dataset[t],k);
        }
        prefixtree.expand(k);
    }
}
```

**Fig. 6.** Parallel Apriori Association Mining in Data Parallel Java

**Rectdomain:** A rectdomain is a collection of objects of the same type such that each object in the collection has a *coordinate* associated with it, and this coordinate belongs to a pre-specified rectilinear section.

**Foreach loop:** A foreach loop iterates over objects in a rectdomain, and has the property that the order of iterations does not influence the result of the associated computations.

**Reduction Interface:** Any object of any class implementing the reduction interface acts as a *reduction variable* [20]. The semantics of a reduction variable are analogous to those used in version 2.0 of High Performance Fortran (HPF-2) [20]. A reduction variable has the property that it can only be updated inside a *foreach* loop by a series of operations that are associative and commutative. Furthermore, the intermediate value of the reduction variable may not be used within the loop, except for self-updates.

The goals of these extensions is to give the compiler information about independent collections of objects (with no aliasing between the elements), parallel loops, and reduction operations. We also require that no Java threads be spawned within such loop nests, and no memory locations read or written to inside the loop nests may be touched by another concurrent thread. Our compiler will also assume that no Java exceptions are raised in the loop nest.

The outline of the data parallel Java code for apriori association mining is shown in Figure 6. The outline of the middleware specification for the same data mining task was previously shown in Figure 3. We believe that programming in this data parallel dialect is much simpler than directly programming at the middleware interface. This is mainly because a programmer just needs to insert directives for parallel collections and loops in a sequential program, rather than having to generate separate functions for the middleware interface. The data parallel Java program written by a programmer assumes a single processor and a flat memory. It also assumes that the data is available as collections of objects, and is not in persistent storage.

```
foreach(r ∈ R) {
    O = F(O, I[r])
}
```

**Fig. 7.** Canonical Loop for Parallel Data Mining Codes

## 4.2   Compilation Problem

In generating the code for the middleware interface (described in Section 3.1), the compiler needs to generate:

- An *Iterator* function that invokes local and global reduction functions.
- For each data parallel loop that updates a reduction object, we need to generate 1) a specification of the subset of the data processed in that loop, 2) a local reduction function, and 3) a global reduction function.

Extracting the iterator function is relatively simple, as each data parallel loop can be replaced by invocations to local and global reduction functions, and the resulting code is simply the iterator function.

Before describing how the processing range, the local reduction function, and the global reduction functions are extracted from each data parallel loop, we state the canonical form of loop. This form is shown in Figure 7, and is sufficient for expressing any of the parallel data mining algorithms described in Section 2. $I$ is the collection of transactions or data items processed in the loop. $O$ is the reduction object whose values is updated during the iterations of the loop. The range over this the loop iterates is denoted by $R$.

**Extracting the Processing Range:** For extracting the description of the range over which the loop operates, we use the general technique of interprocedural static program slicing [39]. A number of techniques have been developed for slicing in the presence of object-oriented features like object references and polymorphism. Harrold *et al.* and Tonnela *et al.* have particularly focused on slicing in the presence of polymorphism, object references, and across procedure boundaries. Slicing in the presence of aliases and reference types has also been addressed [1]. Thus, the use of slicing for extracting range enables our compiler to work accurately in the presence of object-oriented features and frequent procedure boundaries.

**Extracting the Local Reduction Function:** Extracting the local reduction function is straight-forward. The computations performed in the loop are put in a separate function, which simply becomes the local reduction function.

**Extracting the Global Reduction Function:** Extracting the global reduction function from the computations in the loop is a more challenging problem. Formally, we want to synthesize a function $op$, such that the computation in Figure 7 can be stated as $O = O \, op \, F'(I[r])$.

This function $op$ can be used as $O = O \, op \, O1$ to perform the global reduction, using the objects $O$ and $O1$ computed on individual processors after the local reduction phase. This problem is significantly different from the previous work on analysis of reduction statements [6, 16, 26], because we are considering an object-oriented language where several members of an output object may be updated within the same function.

Consider any statement in the local reduction function that updates a data member of the reduction object $O$. If this statement includes any temporary variables that are defined in the local reduction itself, we perform forward substitution and replace these temporary variables. After such forward substitution, the update to the data member can be classified as being one of the following: 1) assignment to a *loop constant* expression, i.e., an expression whose value is constant within each invocation of the data intensive loop from which the local reduction function is extracted. 2) assignment to the value of another data member of the LHS object, or an expression involving one or more other data members, and loop constants, and 3) update using a commutative and associative function $op_i$, such that the data member $O.x$ is updated as $O.x = O.x\ op_i\ g(\ldots)$, where the function $g$ does not involve any members of the reduction object $O$.

The set of statements in the local reduction function that update the data members of the LHS object is denoted by $S$. In synthesizing the function $op$, we start with the statements in the set $S$. The statements that fall in groups 1 or 2 above are left unchanged. The statements that fall in the group 3 are replaced by the statement of the form $O.x = O.x\ op_i\ O1.x$. Within the original local reduction function, we use the statements in the set $S$ as the slicing criteria [39], and use program slicing to construct an executable function that will produce the same results (except as modified for the statements in the group 3) for these statements.

### 4.3   Preliminary Experimental Results from Our Current Implementation

We have recently finished a prototype implementation incorporating the techniques described above. Our current compiler can be used for distributed memory parallelization, and for handling disk-resident datasets, but not for shared memory parallelization. We present experimental results from k-means and k-nearest neighbors. The results are obtained on the same cluster we used for evaluating the middleware (Section 3.4).

A 1.5 GB dataset was used for both k-means and k-nearest neighbors. The value of $k$ used for k-means was 20 and the value of $k$ used for k-nearest neighbors was 3.

The results are shown in Figure 8 and 9. Execution times and speedups compared to the one processor version are shown here. The speedups for k-means are nearly linear. Superlinear speedup is seen in going from 2 to 4 processors for k-means and from 1 to 2 processors for k-nearest neighbors. This is because the size of dataset processed on each processor reduces in going to a larger number of processors. Speedups for k-nearest neighbors on 8 processors is relatively low, especially compared to the speedups achieved by hand programming the middleware (Figure 5). Examining the reasons for this performance difference is a topic for our future work.

| No. of Proc. | Execution Time (sec.) | Speedup |
|---|---|---|
| 1 | 2327 | 1 |
| 2 | 1245 | 1.87 |
| 4 | 597 | 3.90 |
| 8 | 304 | 7.65 |

| No. of Proc. | Execution Time (sec.) | Speedup |
|---|---|---|
| 1 | 161.5 | 1 |
| 2 | 79.4 | 2.03 |
| 4 | 42.8 | 3.77 |
| 8 | 26.53 | 6.21 |

**Fig. 8.** Performance of k-means

**Fig. 9.** Performance of k-nearest neighbor

## 5 Related Work

One effort somewhat similar to our middleware effort is from Becuzzi *et al.* [5]. They use a structured parallel programming environment PQE2000/SkIE for developing parallel implementation of data mining algorithms. Darlington *et al.* [14] have also used structured parallel programming for developing data mining algorithms. Our work is distinct at least two important ways. First, they only target distributed memory parallelism (while they report results on an SMP machine, it is using MPI). Second, I/O is handled explicitly by the programmers in their approach.

The similarity among parallel versions of different data mining techniques that we described in Section 2 has also been observed by Skillicorn [35, 34]. Darlington *et al.* have also used cost models for choosing between different parallelization strategies, but only for a classification technique [14].

Our work at the data parallel Java level can be considered as developing an out-of-core Java compiler. Compiler optimizations for out-of-core data-structures have been considered by several projects. The PASSION project at Northwestern University has considered several different optimizations for improving locality in out-of-core applications [8, 25, 23, 22, 24, 37, 38]. Some of these optimizations have also been implemented as part of the Fortran D compilation system's support for out-of-core applications [31]. Mowry *et al.* have shown how a compiler can generate prefetching hints for improving the performance of a virtual memory system [29]. These projects have concentrated on on stencil computations written in Fortran. Our work is different in considering a different applications class, which has very different communication and data access patterns, a different language, and targeting an application-class specific middleware as the compiler output. Moreira *et al.* have developed a particular data mining algorithm using Java [28]. They show how a technique they developed for removing array bound checks is crucial for obtaining high sequential performance and efficient shared memory parallelization. Our work is different because we focus on several important data mining algorithms, and include distributed memory parallelization and I/O optimizations.

# 6   Summary

Our goal is to allow rapid development of parallel data mining implementations. For this purpose, we are developing a series of successively higher level interfaces. We have already developed a middleware that allows a high-level specification of a parallel data mining algorithm. The preliminary experimental results have demonstrated the middleware's ability to achieve efficient distributed memory and shared memory parallelization. We have proposed a data parallel dialect of Java that enables an even higher level specification of a data mining task. An initial prototype compiler translating this dialect to a middleware specification has been implemented.

# References

[1] H. Agrawal, R. A. DeMillo, and E. H. Spafford. Dynamic slicing in the presence of unconstrained pointers. In *Proceedings of the ACM Fourth Symposium on Testing, Analysis and Verification (TAV4)*, pages 60–73, 1991.

[2] R. Agrawal and J. Shafer. Parallel mining of association rules. *IEEE Transactions on Knowledge and Data Engineering*, 8(6):962 – 969, June 1996.

[3] R. Agrawal and R. Srikant. Fast algorithms for mining association rules. In *Proc. 1994 Int. conf. Very Large DataBases (VLDB'94)*, pages 487–499, Santiago,Chile, September 1994.

[4] R. Baraglia, D. Laforenza, S. Orlando, P. Palmerini, and R. Perego. Implementation issues in the design of i/o intensive data mining applications on clusters of workstations. In *Proceedings of Workshop on High Performance Data Mining IPDPS 2000, LNCS Volume 1800*, pages 350 – 357. Springer Verlag, 2000.

[5] P. Becuzzi, M. Coppola, and M. Vanneschi. Mining of association rules in very large databases: A structured parallel approach. In *Proceedings of Europar-99, Lecture Notes in Computer Science (LNCS) Volume 1685*, pages 1441 – 1450. Springer Verlag, August 1999.

[6] W. Blume, R. Doallo, R. Eigenman, J. Grout, J. Hoelflinger, T. Lawrence, J. Lee, D. Padua, Y. Paek, B. Pottenger, L. Rauchwerger, and P. Tu. Parallel programming with Polaris. *IEEE Computer*, (12):78–82, December 1996.

[7] Francois Bodin, Peter Beckman, Dennis Gannon, Srinivas Narayana, and Shelby X. Yang. Distributed pC++: Basic ideas for an object parallel language. *Scientific Programming*, 2(3), Fall 1993.

[8] R. Bordawekar, A. Choudhary, K. Kennedy, C. Koelbel, and M. Paleczny. A model and compilation strategy for out-of-core data parallel programs. In *Proceedings of the Fifth ACM SIGPLAN Symposium on Principles & Practice of Parallel Programming (PPOPP)*, pages 1–10. ACM Press, July 1995. ACM SIGPLAN Notices, Vol. 30, No. 8.

[9] Christan Borgelt. Apriori. http://fuzzy.cs.Uni-Magdeburg.de/ borgelt/Software. Version 1.8.

[10] C. Chang, A. Acharya, A. Sussman, and J. Saltz. T2: A customizable parallel database for multi-dimensional data. *ACM SIGMOD Record*, 27(1):58–66, March 1998.

[11] Chialin Chang, Renato Ferreira, Alan Sussman, and Joel Saltz. Infrastructure for building parallel database systems for multi-dimensional data. In *Proceedings of*

the Second Merged IPPS/SPDP (13th International Parallel Processing Symposium & 10th Symposium on Parallel and Distributed Processing). IEEE Computer Society Press, April 1999.

[12] Chialin Chang, Tahsin Kurc, Alan Sussman, and Joel Saltz. Query planning for range queries with user-defined aggregation on multi-dimensional scientific datasets. Technical Report CS-TR-3996 and UMIACS-TR-99-15, University of Maryland, Department of Computer Science and UMIACS, February 1999.

[13] A.A. Chien and W.J. Dally. Concurrent aggregates (CA). In Proceedings of the Second ACM SIGPLAN Symposium on Principles & Practice of Parallel Programming (PPOPP), pages 187–196. ACM Press, March 1990.

[14] John Darlington, Moustafa M. Ghanem, Yike Guo, and H. W. To. Performance models for co-ordinating parallel data classification. In Proceedings of the Seventh International Parallel Computing Workshop (PCW-97), Canberra, Australia, September 1997.

[15] Inderjit S. Dhillon and Dharmendra S. Modha. A data-clustering algorithm on distributed memory multiprocessors. In In Proceedings of Workshop on Large-Scale Parallel KDD Systems, in conjunction with the 5th ACM SIGKDD International Conference on Knowledge Discovery and Data Mining (KDD 99), pages 47 – 56, August 1999.

[16] M. W. Hall, S. Amarsinghe, B. R. Murphy, S. Liao, and Monica Lam. Detecting Course-Grain Parallelism using an Interprocedural Parallelizing Compiler. In Proceedings Supercomputing '95, December 1995.

[17] E-H. Han, G. Karypis, and V. Kumar. Scalable parallel datamining for association rules. In Proceedings of ACM SIGMOD 1997, May 1997.

[18] E-H. Han, G. Karypis, and V. Kumar. Scalable parallel datamining for association rules. IEEE Transactions on Data and Knowledge Engineering, 12(3), May / June 2000.

[19] Jiawei Han and Micheline Kamber. Data Mining: Concepts and Techniques. Morgan Kaufmann Publishers, 2000.

[20] High Performance Fortran Forum. Hpf language specification, version 2.0. Available from http://www.crpc.rice.edu/HPFF/versions/hpf2/files/hpf-v20.ps.gz, January 1997.

[21] A. K. Jain and R. C. Dubes. Algorithms for Clustering Data. Prentice Hall, 1988.

[22] M. Kandemir, A. Choudhary, and A. Choudhary. Compiler optimizations for i/o intensive computations. In Proceedings of International Conference on Parallel Processing, September 1999.

[23] M. Kandemir, A. Choudhary, J. Ramanujam, and R. Bordawekar. Compilation techniques for out-of-core parallel computations. Parallel Computing, (3-4):597–628, June 1998.

[24] M. Kandemir, A. Choudhary, J. Ramanujam, and M. A.. Kandaswamy. A unified framework for optimizing locality, parallelism, and comunication in out-of-core computations. IEEE Transactions on Parallel and Distributed Systems, 11(9):648–662, 2000.

[25] M. Kandemir, J. Ramanujam, and A. Choudhary. Improving the performance of out-of-core computations. In Proceedings of International Conference on Parallel Processing, August 1997.

[26] Bo Lu and John Mellor-Crummey. Compiler optimization of implicit reductions for distributed memory multiprocessors. In Proceedings of the 12th International Parallel Processing Symposium (IPPS), April 1998.

[27] William A. Maniatty and Mohammed J. Zaki. A requirements analysis for parallel kdd systems. In *Proceedings of Workshop on High Performance Data Mining, IPDPS 2000, LNCS Volume 1800*, pages 358 – 365. IEEE Computer Society Press, May 2000.

[28] Jose E. Moreira, Samuel P. Midkiff, Manish Gupta, and Richard D. Lawrence. Parallel data mining in Java. Technical Report RC 21326, IBM T. J. Watson Research Center, November 1998.

[29] Todd C. Mowry, Angela K. Demke, and Orran Krieger. Automatic compiler-inserted i/o prefetching for out-of-core applications. In *Proceedings of the Second Symposium on Operating Systems Design and plementation (OSDI '96)*, Nov 1996.

[30] S. K. Murthy. Automatic construction of decision trees from data: A multidisciplinary survey. *Data Mining and Knowledge Discovery*, 2(4):345–389, 1998.

[31] M. Paleczny, K. Kennedy, and C. Koelbel. Compiler support for out-of-core arrays on parallel machines. In *Proceedings of the Fifth Symposium on the Frontiers of Massively Parallel Computation*, pages 110–118. IEEE Computer Society Press, February 1995.

[32] Joel Saltz, Kathleen Crowley, Ravi Mirchandaney, and Harry Berryman. Runtime scheduling and execution of loops on message passing machines. *Journal of Parallel and Distributed Computing*, 8(4):303–312, April 1990.

[33] Joel H. Saltz, Ravi Mirchandaney, and Kay Crowley. Run-time parallelization and scheduling of loops. *IEEE Transactions on Computers*, 40(5):603–612, May 1991.

[34] David B. Skillicorn. Strategies for parallel data mining. *IEEE Concurrency*, Oct-Dec 1999.

[35] D.B. Skillicorn. Strategies for parallelizing data mining. In *Proceedings of the Workshop on High-Performance Data Mining, in association with IPPS/SPDP 1998*, April 1998.

[36] Kilian Stoffel and Abdelkader Belkoniene. Parallel k/h-means clustering for large datasets. In *Proceedings of Europar-99, Lecture Notes in Computer Science (LNCS) Volume 1685*, pages 1451 – 1454. Spring Verlag, August 1999.

[37] R. Thakur, A. Choudhary, R. Bordawekar, S. More, and S. Kutipudi. Passion: Optimized I/O for parallel applications. *IEEE Computer*, 29(6):70–78, June 1996.

[38] Rajeev Thakur, Rajesh Bordawekar, and Alok Choudhary. Compilation of out-of-core data parallel programs for distributed memory machines. In *Proceedings of the IPPS'94 Second Annual Workshop on Input/Output in Parallel Computer Systems*, pages 54–72, April 1994. Also appears in ACM Computer Architecture News, Vol. 22, No. 4, September 1994.

[39] F. Tip. A survey of program slicing techniques. *Journal of Programming Languages*, 3(3):121–189, September 1995.

[40] Janet Wu, Raja Das, Joel Saltz, Harry Berryman, and Seema Hiranandani. Distributed memory compiler design for sparse problems. *IEEE Transactions on Computers*, 44(6):737–753, June 1995.

[41] K. Yelick, L. Semenzato, G. Pike, C. Miyamoto, B. Libit, A. Krishnamurthy, P. Hilfinger, S. Graham, D. Gay, P. Colella, and A. Aiken. Titanium: A high-performance Java dialect. *Concurrency Practice and Experience*, 9(11), November 1998.

[42] M. J. Zaki, M. Ogihara, S. Parthasarathy, and W. Li. Parallel data mining for association rules on shared memory multiprocessors. In *Proceedings of Supercomputing'96*, November 1996.

[43] Mohammed J. Zaki. Parallel and distributed association mining: A survey. *IEEE Concurrency*, 7(4):14 – 25, 1999.

# Bridging the Gap between Compilation and Synthesis in the DEFACTO System*

Pedro Diniz, Mary Hall, Joonseok Park, Byoungro So, and Heidi Ziegler**

University of Southern California / Information Sciences Institute
4676 Admiralty Way, Suite 1001
Marina del Rey, California, 90292
{pedro, mhall, joonseok, bso, ziegler}@isi.edu

**Abstract.** The DEFACTO project - a Design Environment For Adaptive Computing TechnOlogy - is a system that maps computations, expressed in high-level languages such as C, directly onto FPGA-based computing platforms. Major challenges are the inherent flexibility of FPGA hardware, capacity and timing constraints of the target FPGA devices, and accompanying speed-area trade-offs. To address these, DEFACTO combines parallelizing compiler technology with behavioral VHDL synthesis tools, obtaining the complementary advantages of the compiler's high-level analyses and transformations and synthesis' binding, allocation and scheduling of low-level hardware resources. To guide the compiler in the search of a good solution, we introduce the notion of *balance* between the rates at which data is fetched from memory and accessed by the computation, combined with *estimation* from behavioral synthesis. Since FPGA-based designs offer the potential for optimizing memory-related operations, we have also incorporated the ability to exploit *parallel memory accesses* and customize *memory access protocols* into the compiler analysis.

## 1 Introduction

The extreme flexibility of field programmable gate arrays (FPGAs), coupled with the widespread acceptance of hardware description languages (HDL) such as VHDL or Verilog, have made FPGAs the medium of choice for fast hardware prototyping and a popular vehicle for the realization of custom computing machines. Programming these reconfigurable systems, however, is an elaborate and lengthy process. The programmer must master all of the details of the hardware architecture, partitioning both the computation to each of the computing FPGAs and the data to the appropriate memories.

The standard approach to this problem requires that the programmer manually translate the program into an HDL representation, applying his or her

---

* The DEFACTO project is funded by the Defense Advanced Research Project Agency (DARPA) under contract #F30602-98-2-0113.
** H. Ziegler is funded through a Boeing Satellite Systems Doctoral Scholars Fellowship.

H. Dietz (Ed.): LCPC 2001, LNCS 2624, pp. 52–70, 2003.

knowledge of the FPGA specifics, identifying available parallelism and performing the necessary code transformations at that time. Using commercially available synthesis tools, typically the programmer can specify the maximum number of components of a given kind and/or the maximum area or clock period of the resulting design. The tool then determines the feasibility of the design by negotiating area and speed trade-offs, and generates a realizable design. Throughout the process, the burden is on the programmer to ensure that the intermediate representation of the program is kept consistent with the original version.

We believe the way to make programming of FPGA-based systems more accessible is to offer a high-level imperative programming paradigm, such as C, coupled with new compiler technology oriented towards FPGA designs. Programmers retain the advantages of a simple computational model via a high-level language but rely on powerful compiler analyses to identify parallelism, provide high-level loop transformations, and automate most of the tedious and error-prone mapping tasks. This paper describes preliminary experiences with DEFACTO - a Design Environment For Adaptive Computing TechnOlogy. The DEFACTO system integrates compilation and behavioral synthesis to automatically map computations expressed in C to FPGA-based computing engines.

In DEFACTO, we explore the interaction between compiler transformations, most notably loop transformations, and their hardware realizations on FPGAs using commercially available synthesis tools. Since the hardware implementation is bound in terms of capacity, the compiler transformations must be driven by the space constraints and timing requirements for the design. Also, high latency and low bandwidth to external memory, relative to the computation rate, are often performance bottlenecks in FPGA- based systems, just as in conventional architectures. A compiler using high-level analysis information such as data dependence analysis, is in a privileged position to make decisions about which code transformations will lead to good hardware designs. To this end, we introduce the notion of *balance* to select the appropriate set of transformations.

A balanced solution is one where data is fetched from memory at approximately the same rate as it is consumed by the computation. To determine balance, we must examine the output of synthesis for a candidate design. Due to the complexity of resource binding and other by-products of synthesis, the compiler cannot accurately predict a priori the performance and space characteristics of the resulting design. Completely synthesizing a design is prohibitively slow (hours to days) and further, the compiler must try several designs to arrive at a good solution. For these reasons, we exploit *estimation* from behavioral synthesis tools such as Mentor Graphics' Monet™[12] to determine specific hardware parameters (*e.g.*, size and speed) with which the compiler can quantitatively evaluate the application of a high-level transformation to derive a balanced and feasible implementation of the loop nest computation. The compilation system uses data dependence and related analyses in combination with estimation information from a commercially available behavioral synthesis tool for the rapid evaluation of implementation options to steer a successful implementation of a selected portion of the computation to hardware. DEFACTO performs several code transformations that are useful for tailoring code to space constraints, such as *loop tiling*, and *loop unrolling*.

An additional focus of optimization in the DEFACTO system is to decrease latency and increase the effective bandwidth to external memory. While many locality optimizations used in conventional systems can be applied (*e.g.*, loop permutation, tiling, unrolling, scalar replacement), new optimizations are possible such as *parallelization of memory accesses* and *customization of memory access protocols*. Further, the configurability of FPGA hardware leads to new decision procedures for applying existing transformations. In this paper we describe how these techniques borrowed and adapted from compiler technology have been combined with a commercial behavioral synthesis tool, to automatically derive balanced and optimized designs on FPGA-based architectures.

The rest of this paper is organized as follows. In the next section we compare parallelizing compiler technology with behavioral synthesis technology used in commercially available tools. Section 3 presents an overview of the DEFACTO system. Section 4 describes analyses to uncover data reuse and exploit this knowledge in the context of FPGA-based data storage structures. Section 5 describes a transformation strategy for automating design space exploration in the presence of multiple loop transformations. This strategy uses a specific performance metric that takes data reuse and the space and time estimates derived by behavioral synthesis estimation. Section 6 describes the application of data partitioning and customization of memory controllers to substantially reduce the costs of accessing external memory from the FPGA. We survey related work in section 7. In section 8 we describe the current status of the DEFACTO system implementation and present some preliminary conclusions of its applicability to simple kernel applications.

## 2    Comparing Parallelizing Compiler Technology and Behavioral Synthesis

Behavioral synthesis tools map computations expressed in hardware-oriented programming languages, such as VHDL or Verilog, to FPGA and ASIC hardware designs. Behavioral specifications, as opposed to lower level logic or structural specifications, specify their computations without committing to a particular hardware implementation. In the same way that behavioral synthesis has raised the level of abstraction from logic synthesis, permitting designers to develop much more complex designs than previously possible, the goal of the DEFACTO system is to raise the level of abstraction even higher, to the C application level. While at first glance it may seem obvious that a compiler can generate correct VHDL code from a C input (in fact, some commercial systems already do this for restricted C dialects), what is less obvious is that existing compiler technology, developed for parallelization and optimizing memory hierarchies, can automate important optimizations that are difficult for a human designer to perform and exceed the capabilities of today's synthesis tools.

| Behavioral Synthesis | Parallelizing Compiler |
|---|---|
| . Optimization on Scalar Variables | . Optimization on Scalars and Arrays |
| . Optimizations only inside loop body | . Optimization inside loop body and across loop iterations |
| . Supports user-controlled loop unrolling | . Analysis guides automatic loop transformations |
| . Manages registers and inter-operator communication | . Optimizes memory accesses; evaluates trade-offs of different storage on- and off-chip |
| . Considers only a single FPGA | . System-level view; multiple FPGAs, memories |
| . Performs allocation, binding and scheduling of hardware resources | . No knowledge of hardware implementation of computation |

**Table 1.** Comparison of Capabilities.

While there are some similarities between the optimizations performed in these two technologies, in many ways they offer complementary capabilities, as shown in Table 1. Behavioral synthesis performs three core functions: (1) binding operators and registers in the specification to hardware implementations (*e.g.*, selecting a ripple-carry adder to implement an addition); (2) resource allocation (*e.g.*, deciding how many ripple-carry adders are needed); and, (3) scheduling operations in particular clock cycles. In addition, behavioral synthesis supports some optimizations, but relies heavily on programmer pragmas to direct some of the mapping steps. For example, after loop unrolling, the tool will perform extensive optimizations on the resulting inner loop body, such as parallelizing and pipelining operations and minimizing registers and operators to save space. However, deciding the unroll amount is left up to the programmer.

The key advantage of parallelizing compiler technology over behavioral synthesis is the ability to perform data dependence analysis on array variables, used as a basis for parallelization, loop transformations and optimizing memory accesses. This technology permits optimization of designs with array variables, where some data resides in off-chip memories. Further, it enables reasoning about the benefits of code transformations (such as loop unrolling) without explicitly applying them.

In DEFACTO, we combine these technologies, as will be described in the next section. Behavioral VHDL specifications permit use of variables and high-level control constructs such as loops and conditions, reducing the gap between parallelizing compiler technology and logic synthesis tools.

## 3   Overview of DEFACTO Compilation and Synthesis System

### 3.1   Design Flow

Figure 1 shows the steps of automatic application mapping in the DEFACTO compiler. In the first step, the DEFACTO compiler takes an algorithm description written in C or FORTRAN, and performs pre-processing and several common optimizations. In the second step, the code is partitioned into what will execute in software on the host and what will execute in on the FPGAs.

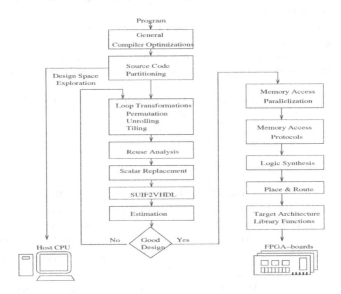

**Fig. 1.** DEFACTO Design Flow.

The following steps are loop transformations and analyses to optimize the parallelism and data locality. Loop permutation [13] changes the nesting order of loops; we use it in DEFACTO to move loops that carry the most data reuse to the innermost loops where it can be better exploited. Loop unrolling [13] duplicates the loop body. Tiling [17] divides computation and data that are allocated to an FPGA into blocks. The next step is data reuse analysis, which identifies multiple accesses to the same memory location. Scalar replacement [5] makes the data reuse explicit by using the same register for read/write references that access the same memory location. SUIF2VHDL translates from SUIF to VHDL, which is the input to the synthesis process.

When the final computation part of the behavioral VHDL design has been derived, we optimize memory accesses by reorganizing data, and customizing memory access protocols. The resulting design is sent on to logic synthesis and place-and-route. Invocations to library functions are added to the portion of the code that will execute in software to load FPGA configurations and memories, synchronize and retrieve results.

A major issue in the automation process in DEFACTO is to understand how much and which set of loop transformations to apply and what are the good metrics by which to evaluate the resulting design. Our approach uses the estimation features of commercially available synthesis tools, which deliver fast (and presumably reasonably accurate) estimates for a given design. The synthesis

tool provides area estimates and the number of clock cycles required for its
scheduling. Using this information, DEFACTO refines the set of constraints for
the design and evaluates what the resulting implementation estimate is. This
estimation helps the DEFACTO system to quickly explore area and speed tradeoffs in the design space.

## 3.2   Target Architectures

The compilation techniques designed for DEFACTO focus on targeting board-
level systems similar to the WildStar/PCI board from Annapolis Micro Systems [2], depicted in figure 2. Such systems consist of multiple interconnected
FPGAs; each can access its own local memories. A larger shared system memory and general-purpose processor (GPP) are directly connected to the FPGA
(this connection varies significantly across boards). The GPP is responsible for
orchestrating the execution of the FPGAs by managing the flow of control and
data from local memory to shared system memory in the application.

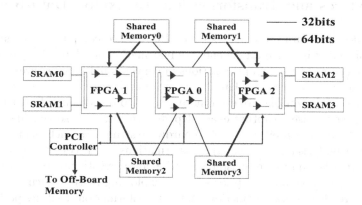

**Fig. 2.** Target Architecture: The Annapolis WildStar/PCI Board

We chose a board-level architecture as a target for DEFACTO because it
can be assembled with commodity parts, and commercial systems composed
of such components are available. We expect the compilation approaches to
form a solid foundation for a multi-board system, and also be applicable to
system-on-a-chip devices that have multiple independent memory banks, each
with configurable logic. The WildStar/PCI board in figure 2 consists of three
Xilinx Virtex FPGAs parts with up to a million gates each. One FPGA serves as
a controller; the other two FPGAs are connected by a 64-bit channel, and each
has two local SRAMs with 32-bit dedicated channels. The three FPGAs share
additional system memory. When logic is effectively mapped to the FPGAs, the
rate data is consumed by the computation is significantly higher than the rate
the local memories can provide making it desirable to exploit temporal reuse
within the FPGA.

### 3.3   Target Applications and Examples

Image processing applications are one of the primary domains for the DEFACTO system. These applications typically manipulate large volumes of fine-grain data that, despite recent increases in FPGA capacity, must be mapped to external memories and then streamed through the FPGAs for processing. These applications typically combine the manipulation data organized as images in a regular fashion. They also tend to combine bit-level operations with sliding-window techniques making them amenable for data dependence and data reuse analysis which are a significant part of the focus of the DEFACTO compilation flow. In the next section we introduce these analyses and present a running example - a binary image correlation kernel application - that fits this class of applications. In addition, the example offers opportunities for the application of loop level transformations, such as loop unrolling and tiling, and because of its complexity, requires that the compiler negotiate the space-time trade-off.

## 4   Analyses and Transformations to Exploit Data Reuse

We next describe data reuse analysis for FPGA-based computing engines. The core of this analysis uses data dependence information developed for parallelization and memory hierarchy optimizations in conventional architectures. FPGAs have no cache to reduce the latency of memory accesses. As a result, reuse analysis and optimizations are even more critical to our domain. Further, reuse analysis must precisely capture exact dependence distances so that data reuse can be exploited in compiler-controlled hardware structures, such as in registers. Thus, reuse analysis and associated transformations in our context more closely resemble what is required in register allocation for conventional architectures [5], rather than the large body of prior work on exploiting reuse in cache.

There are also several distinctions in the transformations that are performed in FPGA-based systems. The number of registers is not fixed as in a conventional architecture, so it is possible to tailor the number of registers to the requirements of the design. Second, customized hardware structures, not just registers, can be used to exploit the reuse in a way that maps to a time- and space-efficient design. The remainder of this section describes these differences.

### 4.1   Data Reuse Analysis

Data reuse analysis, as implemented in our compiler, identifies reuse opportunities, and builds a reuse graph for a given loop nest. A reuse graph G=(V,E) includes all array references (V) and the reuse edges (E) between them. Reuse edges are represented by the reuse distance between two array references. The reuse distance is defined by the difference in iteration counts between the dependent references. The reuse distance is different from the dependence distance in two ways. First, only input and true dependences are candidates for data reuse. Our analysis also considers output dependences as candidates for redundant write access elimination, which also reduces memory accesses. Anti-dependences are not considered, as they do not represent data reuse. Secondly, as reuse analysis must precisely capture the distance between dependences, we do not include dependences with an inconsistent distance, where the iteration counts between the dependent references are not always a fixed constant. These references require a non-constant number of registers to exploit reuse. Further, the candidate array references for data reuse must be in the affine domain. In other words, the array access expression is composed of linear functions of loop indices and constants.

The reuse distance is represented in the same form as dependence vectors, *i.e.*, a vector with the same number of elements as the number of loops in the loop nest. For example, a reuse distance of <1,2> means that there are two loops in the nest and the reuse occurs in one iteration of the outer loop and two iterations of the inner loop. A loop-independent data reuse represented by a vector of all zeros, occurs when the same array element is referenced multiple times in the same iteration of the loop nest. A reuse chain includes all the array references that access the same memory location. A reuse instance includes two array references, one source and one sink, and the reuse distance vector (reuse edge) between the two array references. References with no incoming reuse edges are called generators; each reuse chain has one generator. A generator provides the data that is used by all the references in the reuse chain.

Figure 3(a) shows an example, organized as a four-deep loop nest with a conditional accumulation. At each iteration, the code determines whether or not a pixel of the input image should be accumulated with a running sum depending on the value of a mask array. An array reference mask[i][j] is read in every iteration of loops m and n. The reuse distance <+,*,0,0> from mask[i][j] to itself means the same array element is referenced repeatedly in every iteration of loop m and n. The array image also carries reuse, but the reuse distance is not consistent to avoid the accesses to the same memory location using a fixed number of registers. Therefore, we give up the reuse opportunities and the array image is read from memory.

## 4.2   Scalar Replacement

When the code shown in Figure 3(a) is mapped to an FPGA-based system, it will result in repeated accesses to the same external memory location. The compiler must transform the code to guide behavioral synthesis to exploit the reuse that the previously described analysis has identified.

Scalar replacement replaces certain array references with temporary scalar variables that will be mapped to on-chip registers by behavioral synthesis. Scalar replacement makes the data reuse explicit, resulting in a reduction in the memory accesses. It also avoids multiple write references by writing the redundant memory writes to a register and only writing the data to memory for the last write.

```
intth[60] [60];

int  th[60] [60];              for(m = 0; m < 60; m++){
char mask[4][4];                  for(n = 0; n < 60; n++){
char image[63][63];                  sum = 0;
for(m=0; m<60; m++){                  for(i = 0; i < 4; i++){
   for(n=0; n<60; n++){                  for(j = 0; j < 4; j++){
      sum = 0;                              if (m == 0 && n == 0)
      for(i=0; i<4; i++){                      mask_0 = mask[i][j];
         for(j=0; j<4; j++){                 if (mask_0 != 0)
            if(mask[i][j] != 0)                 sum += image[m+i][n+j];
               sum += image[m+i][n+j];       rotate_register(mask_0,
         }                                     mask_1,mask_2,mask_3,
      }                                        mask_4,mask_5,mask_6,
      th[m][n] = sum;                          mask_7,mask_8,mask_9,
   }                                           mask_10,mask_11,mask_12,
}                                              mask_13,mask_14,mask_15);
```

(+,*,0,0)  ( mask[i][j]                         }
                                             th[m][n] = sum;
                                          }
**(a) Source Code & Reuse Graph**        **(b) Scalar Replacement**

```
for(m=0; m<60; m++)       {
   for(n=0; n<60; n++)       {
      sum = 0;
      for(i=0; i<4; i++)       {
         for(j=0; j<4; j += 2)       {
            if(mask[i][j]  != 0) sum += image[m+i][n+j];
            if (mask[i][j+1] != 0) sum += image[m+i][n+j+1];
         }
      }
      th[m][n] = sum;
   }
}
```
**(c) Loop Unrolling**

```
for (m = 0; m < 60; m++)       {
   for (n = 0; n < 60; n++)       {
      sum = 0;
      for (i = 0; i_tile < 2; i++)       {
         if (m == 0 && n == 0)       {
            mask_0_0 = mask[2*i][0]; mask_1_0 = mask[2*i][1];
            mask_2_0 = mask[2*i][2]; mask_3_0 = mask[2*i][3];
            mask_4_0 = mask[2*i+1][0]; mask_5_0 = mask[2*i+1][1];
            mask_6_0 = mask[2*i+1][2]; mask_7_0 = mask[2*i+1][3];
         }
         if (mask_0_0 != 0) sum += image[m+2*i][n];
         if (mask_1_0 != 0) sum += image[m+2*i][n+1];
         if (mask_2_0 != 0) sum += image[m+2*i][n+2];
         if (mask_3_0 != 0) sum += image[m+2*i][n+3];
         if (mask_4_0 != 0) sum += image[m+2*i+1][n];
         if (mask_5_0 != 0) sum += image[m+2*i+1][n+1];
         if (mask_6_0 != 0) sum += image[m+2*i+1][n+2];
         if (mask_7_0 != 0) sum += image[m+2*i+1][n+3];
         swap_reg(mask_0_0, mask_0_1); swap_reg(mask_1_0, mask_1_1);
         swap_reg(mask_2_0, mask_2_1); swap_reg(mask_3_0, mask_3_1);
         swap_reg(mask_4_0, mask_4_1); swap_reg(mask_5_0, mask_5_1);
         swap_reg(mask_6_0, mask_6_1); swap_reg(mask_7_0, mask_7_1);
      }
      th[m][n] = sum;       (d)Unroll-and-Jam
   }
}
```

**Fig. 3.** ATR Kernel.

Our scalar replacement has more freedom than previously proposed work [5] in that it can utilize the flexibility of FPGAs, *i.e.*, the number of registers to keep the frequently used data does not have a rigid limit, and is only constrained by the space limitation of the FPGA device and the complexity of designs involving very large numbers of registers.

The reuse distance between the generator and the tail reference in a reuse chain decides the required number of registers to exploit a possible data reuse. Intuitively, all the array references in the reuse chain can be replaced by accesses to registers and the generators are assigned data from memory.

Figure 3(b) shows the output of our scalar replacement. From the reuse information given by the reuse analysis, the reuse carrying array reference mask[i][j] is replaced with a scalar variable mask_0. Each array element mask[i][j] is kept in 16 different registers, mask_0 through mask_15. Data in these registers are loaded when m and n are 0 and rotated in each iteration of the j loop so that `mask_0` always contains the correct data, avoiding checking loop variable `i` and `j` repeatedly. The rotate operation can be done in parallel in hardware. Our compiler also performs loop peeling to isolate the condition (`m==0 && n==0`) to eliminate the conditional read to memory. For clarity of presentation, the results of this transformation are not shown here.

### 4.3    Tapped Delay Lines

An alternative to scalar replacement can be used if reuse is further restricted to input dependences with a consistent dependence carried by the innermost loop in a nest (or other loops in the nest if inner loops are fully unrolled). For example, if a computation accesses consecutive and overlapping elements of a given array (such as scanning an array corresponding to rows or columns of an image) over consecutive iterations of a loop, it is possible to store the values across iterations in a linearly-connected set of registers - known as tapped delay lines. The data accessed in one iteration differs from the data in the previous iteration by an ajacent memory location. All but one element of the delay line can be reused, substantially reducing the number of memory accesses. This important improvement opportunity has long been recognized by experienced designers who map computations by hand to hardware, by mapping elements in memory to tapped delay lines. As part of our previous work, we developed several compiler analyses that recognize and exploit opportunities in the source program for data reuse and can be subsequently mapped to tapped delay lines [6,13].

The application reuses the data in different registers by moving in tandem, across loop iterations, the data stored in all of the registers in the tapped delay line. By doing this shifting operation, the computation effectively reuses the data in all but one of the registers in the tapped delay line, therefore reducing the number of memory accesses. Although the same sort of reuse could be exploited by scalar replacement, the tapped delay line structure results in a more efficient hardware mapping, as we can incorporate a library with hand-placed components.

Our approach for identifying this reuse and exploiting tapped delay lines in FPGA designs is described elsewhere [7]. While the current analysis for tapped delay lines is limited to input data dependences on innermost loops, we feel this covers a substantial set of image processing applications that scan subsections of images stored in arrays.

## 5    Transformation Strategy for Automating Design Space Exploration

Current practice when developing designs for FPGA-based systems is for the application programmer to develop a series of designs and go through numerous iterations of synthesizing the design, examining the results, and modifying the design to trade off performance and space. To automate this process, called design space exploration, we must define a set of transformations to be applied and metrics to evaluate specific optimized designs among candidates in the design space. Simply stated, the optimization criteria for mapping a single loop nest to FPGA-based systems are as follows: (1) the design must not exceed the capacity constraints of the system; (2) the execution time should be minimized; and, (3) for a given performance, FPGA space usage should be minimized. The motivation for the first two criteria is obvious, but the third criterion is also needed for several reasons. First, if two designs have equivalent performance, the smaller design is more desirable, in that it frees up space for other uses of the FPGA logic, such as to map other loop nests. In addition, a smaller design usually has less routing complexity, and may achieve a faster target clock rate. Moreover, the third criterion suggests a strategy for selecting among a set of candidate designs that meet the first two criteria.

The DEFACTO compiler uses two metrics to guide the selection of a design. First, results of estimation provide space usage of the design, related to criterion 1 above. Another important metric used to guide the selection of a design, related to criteria 2 and 3, is balance, defined by the following equation.

$$Balance = \frac{F}{C} \qquad (1)$$

where F refers to the data fetch rate, the total data bits that memory can provide per cycle, and C refers to the data consumption rate, total data bits that computation can consume during the computational delay. If balance is close to one, both memories and FPGAs are busy. If balance is less than one, the design is memory bound; if greater than one, it is compute bound. When a design is not balanced, this metric suggests whether more resources should be devoted to improving computation time or memory time.

The DEFACTO compiler adjusts balance by trading off operator and memory parallelism and on-chip storage. For example, consider loop unrolling [13]. Figure 3(c) shows the result of unrolling the inner loop j once on the original code in Figure 3(a). The number of memory accesses in one iteration in the unrolled code is doubled, and, since behavioral synthesis will only schedule independent memory accesses in parallel if they appear in the same inner loop body, the unrolled code fetches data at twice the rate of the original loop body. In addition, if the clock period is sufficiently long, even the dependent computations, two accumulations, can be scheduled in the same cycle. Therefore, unrolling can increase both the consumption rate and the fetch rate.

We can model the relationship between the unroll factor and the fetch and consumption rates under the following assumptions: (1) computation and memory accesses are completely overlapped, requiring that addresses for memory accesses can be calculated at the rate at which the memory can provide data; (2) the target architecture, target clock rate, and memory latency are fixed; (3) data is laid out in independent memories to maximize memory parallelism, as described in the next section; and, (4) estimates derived from a combination of behavioral synthesis and compiler analysis are accurate. Then, the fetch rate increases linearly in the unroll amount until it saturates at an upper limit based on memory parallelism in the application and the bandwidth of the architecture,

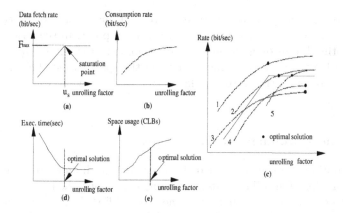

**Fig. 4.** Data Fetch and Consumption Rates.

as shown in Figure 4(a). The consumption rate, which combines the estimate of computation delay (ignoring memory latency) taken directly from behavioral synthesis with the compiler's model of the data fetch rate, increases with the unroll amount, but not linearly, and does not saturate, as shown in Figure 4(b). The relationship is sublinear because executing operations in parallel depends on the availability of operands (the data fetch rate) and data dependences across operations in the unrolled loop body.

## 5.1 Optimal Unrolling Factor Search

Given the above model, the compiler uses balance to guide determining the optimal unroll amount. Given the properties of the data consumption rate and the data fetch rate described in the previous section, there could be five possible scenarios that can happen between the data fetch rate and the consumption rate, as shown in Figure 4(c). In any scenario, the slower rate dominates the overall execution time, and the faster rate cannot get its full performance. In scenario one and four, the data fetch rate and the consumption rate do not cross each other. In scenario three and five, there is one crossing point, where the balance is one. In scenario two, there are two crossing points. The solution with higher rates between the two crossing points, of course, results in better performance, provided the solution meets the space constraint.

In all cases, the optimal solution can be found beyond the saturation point, if the solution meets the space constraint. In scenario two and three, for example, even though there is a balanced solution before the saturation point, a greater unrolling factor performs better than the balanced solution because its dominant rate is greater. If a balanced solution exists beyond the knee (saturation point) of the fetch rate, increasing the unrolling factor further will not improve the overall performance, since the slower memory operations dominate the overall performance. Figure 4(d) illustrates the relationship between the unrolling factor and overall performance. The knee of the graph is the optimal solution. It is a balanced solution in scenarios two and five if it meets the space constraint. In scenario one, it is the solution at the saturation point. In scenario three and four, the optimal solution is the maximum unrolling factor. Figure 4(e) shows the relationship between the unrolling factor and the space usage. The space usage of a design grows as the unrolling factor increases, even beyond the optimal solution.

## 5.2   Beyond Unrolling: Unroll-and-Jam

A similar optimization strategy can be used for unroll-and-jam, which is the multi-loop analog of unrolling. After unrolling outer loops, the resulting duplicate inner loop bodies are fused back together. In DEFACTO, we use unroll-and-jam to increase the instruction-level parallelism and manage the space for on-chip data storage. By changing the unrolling factor, we control the parallelism, locality, and space usage for on-chip storage. Figure 3(d) shows an example of unroll-and-jam. Two inner loops of the original program in Figure 3(a) are unroll by a factor of 2 and loop j is completely unrolled.

# 6   Parallelization and Customization of Memory Accesses

In DEFACTO we explore several techniques to increase aggregate external memory bandwidth and to decrease the amount of latency per memory access. These include 1) introducing a new architecture to create an optimized external-memory-to-FPGA interface and designing optimized circuitry to implement the architecture; 2) customizing data partitioning across a set of memories to gain parallel accesses; and 3) performing data reorganization and packing to create a tailored data layout.

## 6.1   Memory Interface Architecture

FPGAs offer a unique opportunity to exploit application specific characteristics in terms of the design and implementation of the datapath-to-external-memory interface. In order to build a modular, yet efficient interface to external memory, we defined two interfaces and a set of parameterizable abstractions that can be integrated with existing synthesis tools. These interfaces decouple target-architecture dependent characteristics between the datapath and external memories. One interface generates all the external memory control signals matching the vendor-specific interface signals - physical address, enable, write_enable, data_in/out, etc. In addition, this interface allows the designer to exploit application-specific data access patterns by providing support for pipelined memory accesses. The second interface defines the scheduling of the various memory operations allowing the designer to define application specific scheduling strategies. We have implemented these two interfaces over a simple, yet modular, architecture a described in detail in [14]. This architecture consists of conversion FIFO queues, and channels, an address generation unit (AGU), and a memory controller for each of the external memories in the design.

In this context, we introduce two abstractions, data ports and data channels. A data port defines several hardware attributes for the physical connection of wires from the memory controller (the entity responsible for moving data bits to and from the external memory) to the datapath ports. A data channel characterizes (for a given loop execution) the way the data is to be accessed from/to memory to/from a datapath port. Examples include sequential or strided accesses. A channel also includes a conversion FIFO. The FIFO queue allows for the prefetching of data from a memory, and also allows for deferred writebacks to memory such that incoming data transfers, necessary to keep the computation executing, take priority. The conversion FIFO queue also allows for the implementation of data packing and unpacking operations implicitly, if any, so that no modifications to the datapath either producing or consuming the data are necessary. Over the lifetime of the execution of a given computation it is possible to map multiple data channels to the same datapath port by redefining the parameters of the data stream associated with it.

## 6.2   Memory Interface Controller and Scheduling Optimizations

Part of the target hardware design consists of auxiliary circuitry to deal with the external memories. These less glamorous and often neglected entities provide the means to generate addresses, carry out memory signaling and temporarily store data to and from external memories dealing with the pins and timing vagaries of the vendor-specific memory and FPGA interfaces. Because of its key role in exploiting application-specific features to reduce memory latency, we focus our attention on the memory channel controller.

The role of a memory channel controller is to serialize multiple memory requests for a set of data channels associated with a single memory. A naive implementation of the memory controller would call for the controller to determine for each data channel whether or not a memory access is required. If required the controller must issue an address and engage in the memory signaling protocol. All these phases are implemented via finite state machines that the compiler synthesizes from parameterized VHDL code generation templates and which correspond to a substantial amount of complexity of the final design.

The current implementation allows for application-specific scheduling by defining a distinct ordering of the memory accesses for the different channels. While predicting exact memory access order is impossible, our compiler can reduce the number of clock cycles required to access the data corresponding to many memory channels by bypassing memory controller states. These "test" states can be eliminated when the controller is assured that if a datum is required by a given channels, it is also true that it is required by a set of other channels. In this situation the controller need not explicitly check whether or not a memory access is required. The benefits of this optimization when compounded with pipelined memory access mode can lead to a substantial performance improvement of up to 50% for a small set of image processing kernels [14]

## 6.3  Data Partitioning

To take advantage of the multiple external memories associated with an FPGA, in such a way as to obtain the maximum number of parallel reads and writes, we want to divide program data among them in a useful way. For very simple programs, it may be easy for the programmer to simply divide each array into equal parts, assigning each to an associated memory to gain some parallel memory accesses. Determining exactly how to divide the data and place it in a memory to gain the maximum amount of parallelism requires further analysis. Therefore, in contrast to having the programmer specify a data partition by hand, we automatically partition an array across available external memories by identifying data access patterns from array subscript expressions. Host code, initially transferring data to the FPGA memories before program execution and also returning data to the host memory upon program completion, implements the partitioning scheme.

## 6.4  Data Reorganization and Packing

Similar in concept to increasing spatial locality in a cache line described by Anderson et. al.[1], we use data reorganization and packing techniques to increase spatial locality and decrease access latency inherent in the system. By reorganizing data assigned to a particular memory, we can create a tailored layout that will allow the channel access pattern to be sequential or strided, thus taking advantage of the optimized circuitry. By identifying and packing array elements whose sizes are less than the width of one data transfer, we are able to match the computation rate. We may even be able to uncover further information that could be used to direct additional loop transformations to optimize the system. An example would be that by packing data, we gain increased bandwidth and realize that we could further unroll the loop.

## 6.5  Example

We now illustrate the application of the two compiler techniques described in the previous sections to the running example described earlier in this paper. First we partition the arrays mask and image across the two external memories. From the program, we build a set of constraints and solve for the partitions. Both the mask and image arrays have similar access patterns; therefore, the resulting partitions are similar. Within the loop body, the 16 elements of the mask array are accessed in a row wise manner. The even rows of the mask array are partitioned to one memory and the odd to the other. The array image is also accessed in a row wise manner, in blocks of four by four elements, within the loop body. Since square blocks are accessed on each loop iteration, we can partition either row or column wise. Since no code transformations are necessary for a row wise partition, we choose that scheme. The even rows of array image are assigned to one memory and the odds to the other. Similarly shaded data in each memory are accessed by the FPGA in parallel.

We reorganize the partitioned data so that the even rows of the array mask are contiguous in the assigned external memory. We reorganize the odd rows in a similar manner for both arrays. Image processing applications, such as the example, that operate on pixel-based images using eight bit values can have a substantial reduction in the number of memory accesses as a single 32-bit memory transfer can retrieve/store four consecutive pixel values. We pack data elements in memory to take advantage of the full channel width.

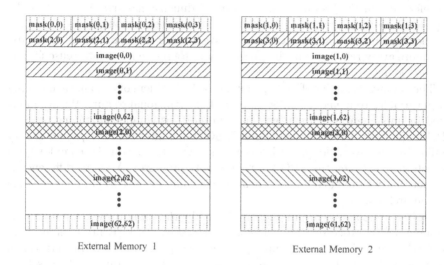

**Fig. 5.** Example Data Layout.

# 7  Related Work

## 7.1  Configurable Architectures

Several research efforts have concentrated on the development of new reconfigurable architectures (*e.g.*, [6,10,11]). These efforts differ from our research in two main aspects. First, as new architectures, they chose which components of the systems are reconfigurable and what are the macro instructions the non-reconfigurable portion can execute. As such they have develop target architecture-specific compiler and synthesis tools and have not taken advantage of the wealth of techniques available in behavioral synthesis tools.

In DEFACTO we use commercially available FPGAs and corresponding tools and synthesize from the ground up all of the control structures in the FPGA to allow them to operate autonomously. Because other approaches do not use commercial synthesis tools they avoid the performance and interface issues with place-and-route.

## 7.2   Compilation Systems for Configurable Architectures

Like our effort other researchers have focused on using automatic data dependence and compiler analysis to aid the mapping of computations to FPGA-
based machines. Weinhardt [16] describes a set of program transformations for
the pipelined execution of loops with loop-carried dependences onto custom machines using a pipeline control unit and an approach similar to ours. He also
recognizes the benefit of data reuse but does not present a compiler algorithm.
No references in the literature mention multi-dimensional arrays as well as the
implementation of a decision procedure to analyze the various trade-off choices
for the implementation of data queues. We further use loop unrolling to ex-
pose more array references in the program and therefore infer data reuse for the
unrolled loops.

The Napa-C compiler effort [8,9] explores the problem of automatic mapping
array variables to memory banks. This work is orthogonal to ours. We are interested in implementing an efficient and autonomous computing engine on each
FPGA of a multi-FPGA board. Their RISC-based interface as expected is very
similar to our target design architecture as a way to control the complexity of
the interface between the FPGAs and the host processor. A major difference is
the fact that we target commercially available components and not an embedded
custom architecture.

Multiprocessor systems are highly effected by the computation and data partitioning across processors and memory. Anderson's work [1] presents an algorithm that automates this mapping to free the programmer from performing
the process by hand. The process uses a linear algebra framework to set up
constraints contained in the user program and then solves for a data and computation distribution. Data reorganization [1] may need to be calculated as the
algorithm looks within procedures as well as across procedure boundaries. This
work takes into account effects from the cache(s) and sequential code execution
on a processor. We replace these processor specifics with hardware-synthesis-
specific information.

In the context of the MIT Raw project - a tiled and configurable architecture [3] the compiler partitions the computation and data among the cores and
programs the communication channels to best suite the communication pattern
for each application. Barua *et. al.* [4] present a code transformation technique
using compile-time information to manage a distributed address space memory, with exposed memory banks. A memory reference instruction is said to
be bank-disambiguated when the compiler guarantees that every dynamic instance of that instruction references the same compile-time-known bank. Using
the bank information, array accesses are uniformly laid out across tiles, via a low
order interleaving scheme. The low order bits of the address specify the tile. To
achieve program correctness, the loop body must be unrolled. While arrays are
partitioned across memories similar to our work, the only scheme is low order
interleaving and we propose several others.

## 7.3   Data Reuse Analysis

The data reuse analysis developed for the DEFACTO system differs from the data reuse analysis described by Carr and Kennedy [5] in several points. First, our analysis includes output dependence in addition to the true and input dependences in [5] to decrease unnecessary store operations. Secondly, we exploit reuse along all loops of a loop nest and unlike [5] we are not restricted to the innermost loop only. Since loop permutation moves the loop that exploits the most reuse innermost and it takes more register to exploit reuse in outer loops, this approach is sufficient to get the most benefit if the number of registers are limited or if cache is the target memory hierarchy, where it is hard to exploit outer loop's locality due to cache size limitation. In addition, considering localized iteration space where register contents are reused throughout all the iterations without shifting between registers, the number of registers can be significantly reduced. Thirdly, Carr/Kennedy's analysis use Callahan's balance model to evaluate how the loop matches the capabilities of a specific architecture. Our notion of balance can explain whether either memory side or computation side is the bottleneck. It also can guide whether the limited space on an FPGA must be devoted more to memory operations or computations. Fourth, their complexity of optimization problem is greater than ours. Our analysis employs a commercial synthesis tool to get a feedback on the space use and execution rate. By doing so, our reuse analysis reduces the size of the candidate tile size search space and tunes the unrolling factors.

## 8   Project Status and Conclusion

We have implemented the bulk of what has been presented in this paper in the DEFACTO system. We have demonstrated a fully automatic design flow for DEFACTO that consists of a subset of the passes described in Section 3 on three image processing kernels, mapping from a C specification to working designs on the Annapolis WildStar™ computing board described in Section 3.2.

A major focus of our current work is integrating the compiler and synthesis tool via estimation for design space exploration. We have developed an interface to estimation from the Synopsys Behavioral Compiler as well as Monet™ [12], and are using it to automatically calculate balance for a particular optimized loop nest design.

With the growing size of FPGA devices and the increased complexity of the place-and-route and mapping related passes in commercially available synthesis tools, we envision estimation as a fundamental technique for quickly exploring a wide range of implementation options while keeping the compilation/synthesis time at a reasonable cost. The DEFACTO system shows that it is possible to successfully map applications written in imperative programming languages directly to FPGA-based computing boards combining the application of traditional data dependence analysis techniques with commercially available behavioral synthesis tools.

# References

1. J. Anderson, S. Amarasinghe, and M. Lam, "Data and Computation Transformations for Multiprocessors," in *In Proc. of the ACM Symp. on Principles and Practice of Parallel Programming (PPoPP'95)*, Jul. 1995, pp. 19–21, ACM Press.
2. Annapolis Micro Systems Inc., " WildStar™ Reconfigurable Computing Engines". newblock User's Manual R3.3, 1999.
3. J. Babb, M. Rinard, A. Moritz, W. Lee, M. Frank, R. Barua and S. Amarasinghe, "Parallelizing Applications into Silicon", in *Proc. of the IEEE Symposium on FPGAs for Custom Computing Machines (FCCM'99)*, IEEE Computer Society Press, Los Alamitos, 1999, pp. 70-81.
4. R. Barua, W. Lee, S. Amarasinghe, and A. Agarwal, "Memory bank disambiguation using modulo unrolling for Raw machines," in *In Proc. of the ACM/IEEE Fifth Int'l Conference on High Performance Computing(HIPC)*, Dec. 1998.
5. S. Carr and K. Kennedy, "Improving the ratio of memory operations to floating-point operations in loops," *ACM Transactions on Programming Languages and Systems*, vol. 15, no. 3, pp. 400–462, July 1994.
6. D. Cronquist, P. Franklin, S. Berg, and C. Ebeling, "Specifying and compiling applications for RaPiD," in *In Proc. IEEE Symp. on FPGAs for Custom Computing Machines (FCCM'98)*. 1998, pp. 116–125, IEEE Press.
7. P. Diniz and J. Park, "Automatic synthesis of data storage and contol structures for FPGA-based computing machines," in *In Proc. IEEE Symp. on FPGAs for Custom Computing Machines (FCCM'00)*. Apr. 2000, pp. 91 – 100, IEEE Press.
8. M. Gokhale and J. Stone, "Automatic Allocation of Arrays to Memories in FPGA Processors with Multiple Memory Banks". in *Proc. of the IEEE Symp. on FPGAs for Custom Computing Machines (FCCM'99)*, IEEE Computer Society Press, Los Alamitos, 1999, pp. 63-69.
9. M. Gokhale and J. Stone, "Napa-C: Compiling for a hybrid RISC/FPGA architecture," in *Proc. of the IEEE Symp. on FPGAs for Custom Computing Machines (FCCM'98)*. 1998, pp. 126–135, IEEE Computer Society Press.
10. S. Goldstein, H. Schmit, M. Moe, M. Budiu, S. Cadambi, R. Taylor, and R. Laufer, "PipeRench: A coprocessor for streaming multimedia acceleration," in *Proc. of 26th Intl. Symp. on Computer Architecture (ISCA'99)*. 1999, pp. 28–39, ACM Press.
11. J. Hauser and J. Wawrzynek, "Garp: A MIPS processor with a reconfigurable coprocessor," in *Proc. of the IEEE Symp. on FPGAs for Custom Computing Machines*. 1997, pp. 12–21, IEEE Computer Society Press.
12. "Mentor Graphics Inc.", "Monet™" User's Manual R43.
13. S. Muchnick, *Advanced Compiler Design and Implementation*, Morgan Kaufmann, San Fransisco, Calif., 1997.
14. J. Park and P. Diniz, "Synthesis of memory access controller for streamed data applications for FPGA-based computing engines," in *Proc. of the 14th Intl. Symp. on System Synthesis (ISSS'2001)*. Oct. 2001, IEEE Computer Society Press.
15. "The Stanford SUIF Compilation System," Public Domain Software and Documentation.
16. M. Weinhardt and W. Luk, "Pipelined vectorization for reconfigurable systems," in *Proc. of the IEEE Symp. on FPGAs for Custom Computing Machines (FCCM'99)*. 1999, pp. 52–62, IEEE Computer Society Press.
17. M. Wolf and M. Lam, "A Loop Transformation Theory and an Algorithm for Maximizing Parallelism", In IEEE Trans. on Parallel and Distributed Systems, Oct. 1991.

# Instruction Balance and Its Relation to Program Energy Consumption

Tao Li and Chen Ding

Computer Science Department
University of Rochester
Rochester, New York
{taoli,cding}@cs.rochester.edu

**Abstract.** A computer consists of multiple components such as functional units, cache and main memory. At each moment of execution, a program may have a varied amount of work for each component. Recent development has exploited this imbalance to save energy by slowing the components that have a lower load. Example techniques include dynamic scaling and clock gating used in processors from Transmeta and Intel. Symmetrical to reconfiguring hardware is reorganizing software. We can alter program demand for different components by reordering program instructions. This paper explores the theoretical lower bound of energy consumption assuming that both a program and a machine are fully adjustable. It shows that a program with a balanced load always consumes less energy than the same program with uneven loads under the same execution speed. In addition, the paper examines the relation between energy consumption and program performance. It shows that reducing power is a different problem than that of improving performance. Finally, the paper presents empirical evidence showing that a program may be transformed to have a balanced demand in most parts of its execution.

## 1 Introduction

Many devices for personal and network computing are portable devices powered by batteries. Higher energy efficiency would allow for smaller batteries, lower device weight, and longer uninterrupted operation. As a result, managing the energy consumption of portable processors has become important because it directly leads to lower cost and better service. In addition, power reduction also helps traditional computing platforms such as desktop PCs and even supercomputers by reducing their packaging complexity and cost. As computing devices permeate our daily life, saving energy has broad benefits to the society and environment.

Energy is consumed by all parts of a computer system, including functional units, cache and main memory. For each component, the power usage is largely determined by its operating speed. On most machines, the hardware configuration is fixed. When a program does not utilize all available capacity, some components are underutilized and waste energy. The recent interest in energy

H. Dietz (Ed.): LCPC 2001, LNCS 2624, pp. 71–85, 2003.

efficiency has prompted rapid development of reconfigurable processors, which adjust hardware speed to match the dynamic demand of applications. For example, when CPU is under-utilized due to slow memory, its frequency and voltage are switched down to save energy. This technique is called *dynamic scaling*. It has already found its way into commercial processors such as Transmeta Crusoe and Intel XScale. For example, during execution, Crusoe TM5800 can switch its voltage between 0.9 volt to 1.3 volt and adjust its frequency between 367MHz and 800MHz. Given the improvement in hardware, a natural subsequent question is whether software can be adapted to fully utilize the emerging reconfigurable processors.

For many years, programs have been analyzed and optimized for performance. One effective optimization is demand reduction, which eliminates redundant program instructions and memory access. While the fastest instructions are those that do not exist, those are also the most energy efficient. Although demand reduction saves power, it does not specifically utilize the adaptiveness of hardware. The question remains open on whether we can save additional energy after demand reduction has been applied. The following example will demonstrate that such opportunity exists. In particular, it will show that *demand reordering* can save energy on reconfigurable processors such as Transmeta Crusoe and Intel XScale.

## A Motivating Example

For this example, we assume a simple machine with two components: CPU and main memory. We model each program as a sequence of instruction blocks, where blocks must be executed sequentially but operations within each block are fully parallel. We call the ratio of CPU operations (*cpu op*) to memory operations (*mem op*) the *instruction balance*. Part (a) of Figure 1 shows a program with two blocks with instruction balances 4 and $\frac{1}{4}$. Part (b) shows a reordered program that has an identical instruction balance of 1.

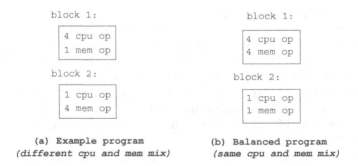

block 1:

| 4 cpu op |
| 1 mem op |

block 2:

| 1 cpu op |
| 4 mem op |

block 1:

| 4 cpu op |
| 4 mem op |

block 2:

| 1 cpu op |
| 1 mem op |

(a) Example program
(different cpu and mem mix)

(b) Balanced program
(same cpu and mem mix)

**Fig. 1.** Example of program reordering

| Program | Block | Frequency | Exe. time (t) | Energy $E \approx tf^3c$ |
|---|---|---|---|---|
| Example program with no dynamic scaling | block 1 | $f_{cpu} = f_{mem} = f_{max}$ | $\frac{4}{f_{max}}$ | $8f_{max}^2 c$ |
| | block 2 | $f_{cpu} = f_{mem} = f_{max}$ | $\frac{4}{f_{max}}$ | $8f_{max}^2 c$ |
| | total | | $\frac{8}{f_{max}}$ | $16f_{max}^2 c$ |
| Example program with dynamic scaling | block 1 | $f_{cpu} = f_{max}, f_{mem} = \frac{1}{4}f_{max}$ | $\frac{4}{f_{max}}$ | $4\frac{1}{16}f_{max}^2 c$ |
| | block 2 | $f_{cpu} = \frac{1}{4}f_{max}, f_{mem} = f_{max}$ | $\frac{4}{f_{max}}$ | $4\frac{1}{16}f_{max}^2 c$ |
| | total | | $\frac{8}{f_{max}}$ | $8.13f_{max}^2 c$ |
| Balanced program with dynamic scaling | block 1 | $f_{cpu} = \frac{5}{8}f_{max}, f_{mem} = \frac{5}{8}f_{max}$ | $\frac{32}{5f_{max}}$ | $3\frac{3}{8}f_{max}^2 c$ |
| | block 2 | $f_{cpu} = \frac{5}{8}f_{max}, f_{mem} = \frac{5}{8}f_{max}$ | $\frac{32}{5f_{max}}$ | $\frac{25}{32}f_{max}^2 c$ |
| | total | | $\frac{8}{f_{max}}$ | $3.91f_{max}^2 c$ |

**Table 1.** Power consumption of example programs

Table 1 shows energy consumption for three configurations. The first is original program without dynamic scaling, where both hardware and software are fixed. The second is original program with dynamic scaling, where software is fixed but hardware is adaptive. The last is the balanced program with dynamic scaling, where software is reorganized and hardware is adaptive. Each configuration includes three rows: two for instruction blocks and one for their total. The data for each configuration are listed in columns. The third column lists the frequency used by CPU and memory unit, $f_{cpu}$ and $f_{mem}$. The fourth column shows the execution time, $t$, which is the number of operations divided by the operating frequency. The total energy, $E$, shown in the last column, is summed for two units. Each unit consumes energy $tf^3c$, where $t$ is the time, $f$ is the frequency, and $c$ is a architectural dependent constant. We assume the same constant for CPU and memory.

In the first configuration, all units run at the peak speed, $f_{max}$. In the second configuration, only one unit runs at the peak speed, the other unit runs at a lower frequency, $\frac{1}{4}f_{max}$. In the third configuration, both units run at a lower speed, $\frac{5}{8}f_{max}$. The three rows labeled with "total" give the overall speed and energy consumption. All three configurations have the same execution time, $\frac{8}{f_{max}}$. The energy consumption, however, is very different. Dynamic scaling saves about half of the energy (49%) compared to no scaling. Program reordering further reduces the energy consumption by over a half (another 52%). In other words, program reordering is able to double the energy saving without removing any instruction from the program.

The rest of this paper presents a theoretical basis for program reordering for the purpose of energy reduction. Section 2 defines the program and machine model. Section 3 and 4 prove the basic and extended theorems. Section 5 addresses the relation with performance optimization. Section 6 evaluates a benchmark program. Finally, Section 7 discusses related work, and Section 8 concludes.

## 2   Program and Machine Model

This section describes our system model. Since we intend to find the highest energy efficiency possible, we impose the least restrictions on our model. To simplify the presentation, we assume a machine with only two identical components running at any non-negative frequency. The extended theorems that include $N$ asymmetrical components and discrete frequencies are given in Section 4.

*Program Model* We view a program, $P$, by its execution trace, which we model as a sequence of instruction blocks, $B_1, B_2, ..., B_n$. Each block, $B_i$, is a pair $(a_i, b_i)$, where $a_i$ is the number of CPU operations, and $b_i$ is the number of memory operations. We assume a sequential execution of blocks but no dependence among different types of operations inside a block. For example, we assume that CPU and memory operations can be executed independent of each other. This program model is not as unreasonable as it seems. For example, we can view the set of instructions executed at each machine cycle as a block.

The *instruction balance* for a block $B_i$ is the ratio $\dfrac{a_i}{b_i}$. If the balance of all blocks is the same, that is, for any $i$ and $j$, $\frac{a_i}{b_i} = \frac{a_j}{b_j}$, we say the program has a constant instruction balance. We call the program a *balanced program*. The condition can be rewritten as $\frac{a_i}{a_j} = \frac{b_i}{b_j}$. The second format is more convenient when we extend the formulation to instructions of more than two types in Section 4. We note that a constant balance is not necessarily a unit balance. The number of CPU and memory operations does not need to be the same. In fact, a balanced program can have any number of instructions in each type. Finally, to find the theoretical maximum, we assume that a compiler can freely move instructions from one block to another but cannot eliminate any instruction in any block.

*Machine Model* A machine consists multiple functional units whose frequency can be independently adjusted by hardware to match software demand (i.e. dynamic scaling). The total energy cost is the power consumption of each unit multiplied by the execution time. Burd and Brodersen divided CMOS power into static and dynamic dissipation [2]. Static power due to bias and leakage currents can be made insignificant by improved circuit design. Dynamic power, which dominates overall power, is proportional to $V^2 \cdot f \cdot C$ where $V$ is the supply voltage, $f$ is the clock speed and $C$ is the effective switching capacitance [2]. Here we assume that the voltage can be scaled linearly with frequency. Therefore, power consumption is a cubic function of frequency, that is, for unit $i$, $P_i \approx f_i^3 c_i$, where $c_i$ is an architectural dependent constant. We assume that all $c_i$s are identical in proving the basic theorem. The extend theorems will remove this assumption in Section 4.2. We do not explicitly consider any overhead incurred by dynamic scaling. However, switching overhead does not change our theorem because in the optimal case, program demand is constant and incurs no switching cost.

The above machine and program model is too simple to model a real system. Program instructions cannot be arbitrarily reordered. The scaling between voltage and frequency is not linear [10]. However, the simplified model is useful in our theoretical study because it allows for the most freedom in software reorganization and gives a closed formula for energy consumption.

## 3   Instruction Balance and Energy Consumption

We now present the basic theorem: a program organization is optimal for energy if and only if all instruction blocks have the same instruction balance. To prove, we show that for any program with uneven instruction balances, its balanced counterpart can finish execution in the same amount of time but consume less energy. We next formulate the energy consumption of a program and its balanced counterpart.

### 3.1   Problem Formulation

Assume a program of $n$ instruction blocks, $P = (B_1, ..., B_i, ..., B_n)$, $B_i = (a_i, b_i)$, $i = 1, ..., n$. Let $f$ be the maximum processor frequency. The original energy consumption $E_{original}$ is computed in the following three steps.

- The execution time of each block is $t_i = \dfrac{M_i}{f}$, where $M_i = max(a_i, b_i)$, and $f$ is the maximal frequency of functional units.
- The power consumption of each block is $P_i = f^3 + (\dfrac{m_i}{M_i} f)^3$, where $m_i = min(a_i, b_i)$ and $M_i = max(a_i, b_i)$. The second term includes the effect of dynamic scaling.
- The energy consumption of the program is

$$E_{original} = \sum_{i=1}^{n} t_i P_i = \sum_{i=1}^{n} \frac{M_i}{f}(f^3 + (\frac{m_i}{M_i} f)^3) = \sum_{i=1}^{n} \frac{M_i^3 + m_i^3}{M_i^2} f^2 = \sum_{i=1}^{n} \frac{a_i^3 + b_i^3}{M_i^2} f^2$$

The overall balance of the program is $\frac{A}{B}$, where $A = \sum_{i=1}^{n} a_i$, and $B = \sum_{i=1}^{n} b_i$. If we re-balance the program, i.e. transforming the program into $P' = (B'_1, ..., B'_i, ..., B'_n)$, $B'_i = (a'_i, b'_i)$, then all balances are the same, i.e. $\frac{a'_i}{b'_i} = \frac{A}{B}$. Let $P'$ runs in the same time as $P$, which is $t_{total} = \sum_{i=1}^{n} t_i = \sum_{i=1}^{n} \frac{M_i}{f}$. The following three steps compute the energy consumption, $E_{balanced}$, for the transformed program $P'$.

- The frequency of CPU is $f_{cpu} = \frac{A}{t_{total}}$
- The frequency of the memory unit is $f_{mem} = \frac{B}{t_{total}}$
- The energy consumption is

$$E_{balanced} = t_{total}(f_{cpu}^3 + f_{mem}^3) = \frac{A^3 + B^3}{(\sum_{i=1}^{n} M_i)^2} f^2 = \frac{(\sum_{i=1}^{n} a_i)^3 + (\sum_{i=1}^{n} b_i)^3}{(\sum_{i=1}^{n} M_i)^2} f^2$$

We now remove the common positive term $f^2$ from $E_{original}$ and $E_{balanced}$. The following theorem states their inequality and the condition for equality.

## 3.2   The Basic Theorem

The following theorem says that the energy consumption of any program, represented by the left-hand side formula, is always greater than or equal to the energy consumption of its balanced self, represented by the right-hand side formula, assuming the same execution time. Therefore, program re-balancing saves energy. The theorem is stronger than required by the formulation. It allows for $M_i \geq max(a_i, b_i)$, while the formulation needs only $M_i = max(a_i, b_i)$. The generalization turns out to be the key to our proof. It makes the induction possible.

**Theorem 1** *The following inequality holds.*

$$\sum_{i=1}^{n} \frac{a_i^3 + b_i^3}{M_i^2} \geq \frac{(\sum_{i=1}^{n} a_i)^3 + (\sum_{i=1}^{n} b_i)^3}{(\sum_{i=1}^{n} M_i)^2}$$

*where $a_i, b_i \geq 0$, $\sum_{i=1}^{n} a_i > 0$, $\sum_{i=1}^{n} b_i > 0$, and $M_i \geq max(a_i, b_i) > 0$. The equality holds when and only when $\frac{a_i}{b_i} = \frac{a_j}{b_j}$ for all $i$ and $j$.*

**Proof:** We first use induction and then reduce the case of $n + 1$ to the case of $n = 2$, which we prove with a calculus method.

If $n = 1$, the inequality holds trivially. Now suppose it holds for $n$.

$$\sum_{i=1}^{n} \frac{a_i^3 + b_i^3}{M_i^2} \geq \frac{(\sum_{i=1}^{n} a_i)^3 + (\sum_{i=1}^{n} b_i)^3}{(\sum_{i=1}^{n} M_i)^2}$$

We need to prove

$$\sum_{i=1}^{n+1} \frac{a_i^3 + b_i^3}{M_i^2} \geq \frac{(\sum_{i=1}^{n+1} a_i)^3 + (\sum_{i=1}^{n+1} b_i)^3}{(\sum_{i=1}^{n+1} M_i)^2}$$

After separating the terms involved in the case of $n$ and applying the induction hypothesis, the inequality becomes

$$\frac{(\sum_{i=1}^{n} a_i)^3 + (\sum_{i=1}^{n} b_i)^3}{(\sum_{i=1}^{n} M_i)^2} + \frac{a_{n+1}^3 + b_{n+1}^3}{M_{n+1}^2} \geq \frac{(\sum_{i=1}^{n} a_i + a_{n+1})^3 + (\sum_{i=1}^{n} b_i + b_{n+1})^3}{(\sum_{i=1}^{n} M_i + M_{n+1})^2}$$

Now let $a' = \sum_{i=1}^{n} a_i$, $b' = \sum_{i=1}^{n} b_i$, $M' = \sum_{i=1}^{n} M_i$. We have $M' \geq max(a', b')$ because $M_i \geq max(a_i, b_i), i = 1, ..., n$. So we arrive at the same inequality as the case $n = 2$, which is

$$\frac{a_1^3 + b_1^3}{M_1^2} + \frac{a_2^3 + b_2^3}{M_2^2} \geq \frac{(a_1 + a_2)^3 + (b_1 + b_2)^3}{(M_1 + M_2)^2}$$

where $M_1 \geq max(a_1, b_1)$, $M_2 \geq max(a_2, b_2)$. Next, we split the inequality into two parts: $\frac{a_1^3}{M_1^2} + \frac{a_2^3}{M_2^2} \geq \frac{(a_1 + a_2)^3}{(M_1 + M_2)^2}$ and $\frac{b_1^3}{M_1^2} + \frac{b_2^3}{M_2^2} \geq \frac{(b_1 + b_2)^3}{(M_1 + M_2)^2}$

Since the above two inequalities are equivalent, we prove the first one in the following lemma. Note that the lemma is stronger than required: $M_1$ and $M_2$ can be any positive number and do not have to be greater than $a_1$ and $a_2$.

**Lemma 1.** $\dfrac{a_1^3}{M_1^2} + \dfrac{a_2^3}{M_2^2} \ge \dfrac{(a_1 + a_2)^3}{(M_1 + M_2)^2}$, *where* $a_1, a_2, \ge 0$ *and* $M_1, M_2 > 0$.

**Proof:** We first convert $M_2$ to 1 by dividing both sides with $M_2^2$. Then we multiply both sides with the product of their denominators. The inequality is converted to

$$(2M^{-1} + M^{-2})a_1^3 + (2M + M^2)a_2^3 \ge 3a_1 a_2 (a_1 + a_2)$$

where $a_1, a_2, b_1, b_2 \ge 0$, and $M > 0$. If $a_1 = 0$ or $a_2 = 0$, the inequality holds trivially. Now we assume that $a_1, a_2 > 0$. Define

$$f(M) = (2M^{-1} + M^{-2})a_1^3 + (2M + M^2)a_2^3$$

where $M, a_1, a_2 > 0$. We will show that $f(M)$ researches its minimum value at $\dfrac{a_1}{a_2}$, which is $f(\dfrac{a_1}{a_2}) = 3a_1 a_2 (a_1 + a_2)$. The first and second derivatives are
$f'(M) = (-2M^{-2} - 2M^{-3})a_1^3 + (2 + 2M)a_2^3$, and
$f''(M) = (4M^{-3} + 6M^{-4})a_1^3 + 2a_2^3 > 0$
Since $f''(M) > 0$, so $f(M) \ge f(\dfrac{a_1}{a_2}), \forall M > 0$. The lemma holds and the theorem follows.

# 4    Extended Theorems

The basic theorem assumes a machine that has two components and operates on any non-negative frequency. This section extends the theorem to a machine that has more than two components and operates on a set of fixed frequencies. The set of frequencies needs not to be the same for each component, nor does the constant factor in the energy equation. In the case of clock gating, a component has two frequencies: one is the operating frequency and the other is zero.

## 4.1    Multiple Functional Units

We generalize first the definition of instruction balance and then the theorem.

**Definition 1.** *Assume a program* $P$, $P = (B_1, ..., B_i, ..., B_n), B_i = (a_{i1}, ..., a_{im})$, $i = 1, ..., n$. *The instruction balance for each block* $B_i$ *is an* $m$-*tuple* $(a_{i1}, ..., a_{im})$. *A program is said to have a constant instruction balance if* $\dfrac{a_{i1}}{a_{j1}} = \cdots = \dfrac{a_{im}}{a_{jm}}$, *for any* $B_i, B_j$.

**Theorem 2** *(Generalization of Theorem 1 for N functional units)*:

$$\sum_{i=1}^{n} \frac{a_{i1}^3 + \cdots a_{im}^3}{M_i^2} \ge \frac{(\sum_{i=1}^{n} a_{i1})^3 + \cdots (\sum_{i=1}^{n} a_{im})^3}{(\sum_{i=1}^{n} M_i)^2}$$

*where* $a_{i1}, ..., a_{im} \ge 0$ *and* $M_i \ge max(a_{i1}, ..., a_{im}) > 0$.

**Proof**: We prove the generalized theorem by induction on m. The inductive case is established by applying theorem 1.

Since $M_i \geq max\{a_{i1}, ..., a_{im}, a_{im+1}\} \geq max\{a_{i1}, ..., a_{im}\}$, by induction hypothesis we have

$$\sum_{i=1}^{n} \frac{a_{i1}^3 + a_{i2}^3 + \cdots + a_{im}^3 + a_{im+1}^3}{M_i^2} = \sum_{i=1}^{n} \frac{a_{i1}^3 + a_{i2}^3 + \cdots + a_{im}^3}{M_i^2} + \sum_{i=1}^{n} \frac{a_{im+1}^3}{M_i^2}$$

$$\geq \frac{(\sum_{i=1}^{n} a_{i1})^3 + (\sum_{i=1}^{n} a_{i2})^3 + \cdots + (\sum_{i=1}^{n} a_{im})^3}{(\sum_{i=1}^{n} M_i)^2} + \sum_{i=1}^{n} \frac{a_{im+1}^3}{M_i^2}.$$

Note that $\sum_{i=1}^{n} \frac{a_{im+1}^3}{M_i^2} = \sum_{i=1}^{n} \frac{a_{im+1}^3 + b_{im+1}^3}{M_i^2}$, where $b_{im+1} = 0, \forall i = 1, ..., n$,

and $M_i \geq max\{a_{i1}, ..., a_{im}, a_{im+1}\} \geq max\{a_{im+1}\} \geq max\{a_{im+1}, b_{im+1}\}$. Now we apply Theorem 1 and get

$$\sum_{i=1}^{n} \frac{a_{im+1}^3 + b_{im+1}^3}{M_i^2} \geq \frac{(\sum_{i=1}^{n} a_{im+1})^3 + (\sum_{i=1}^{n} b_{im+1})^3}{(\sum_{i=1}^{n} M_i)^2} = \frac{(\sum_{i=1}^{n} a_{im+1})^3}{(\sum_{i=1}^{n} M_i)^2}.$$

Hence we have

$$\sum_{i=1}^{n} \frac{a_{i1}^3 + a_{i2}^3 + \cdots + a_{im}^3 + a_{im+1}^3}{M_i^2}$$

$$\geq \frac{(\sum_{i=1}^{n} a_{i1})^3 + (\sum_{i=1}^{n} a_{i2})^3 + \cdots + (\sum_{i=1}^{n} a_{im})^3}{(\sum_{i=1}^{n} M_i)^2} + \sum_{i=1}^{n} \frac{a_{im+1}^3}{M_i^2}$$

$$\geq \frac{(\sum_{i=1}^{n} a_{i1})^3 + (\sum_{i=1}^{n} a_{i2})^3 + \cdots + (\sum_{i=1}^{n} a_{im})^3}{(\sum_{i=1}^{n} M_i)^2} + \frac{(\sum_{i=1}^{n} a_{im+1})^3}{(\sum_{i=1}^{n} M_i)^2}$$

$$= \frac{(\sum_{i=1}^{n} a_{i1})^3 + (\sum_{i=1}^{n} a_{i2})^3 + \cdots + (\sum_{i=1}^{n} a_{im+1})^3}{(\sum_{i=1}^{n} M_i)^2}.$$

So the generalized theorem holds.

The generalized theorem says that on machines with any number of components, a balance program consumes less energy than its unbalanced counterpart, given the same execution time.

## 4.2  Discrete Operating Frequencies

So far we have assumed that a frequency can be any non-negative rational number. On real machines, a frequency must be an integer and *valid frequencies* are pre-determined. For example, Transmeta Crusoe has 32 steps in its range of operating frequency and voltage. A less obvious case is clock gating, where a component either runs in full speed or is shut down completely. This case is equivalent to having two valid frequencies. The optimal frequency, as determined by the instruction balance and execution time, may lie between two valid frequencies. The solution in this case is to alternate between two closest valid frequencies. We now show the optimality of the alternation scheme by proving it for each component.

Assuming that the optimal frequency, $f_{opt}$, lies between two (closest) valid frequencies $g_1$ and $g_2$, we will show that alternating between these two frequencies consumes less energy than any other scheme that uses frequencies outside the range of $g_1$ and $g_2$. In other words, running the program at any other frequency at any time would consume more energy. In our proof, we compare the optimal scheme with schemes that can use all frequencies outside $g_1$ and $g_2$, not just those of a fixed set of valid frequencies. In addition, our program and machine model (Section 2) does not permit a frequency that is higher than the maximal machine frequency. So the following proof covers all cases of discrete frequencies and does not lose any generality.

We now formulate the problem. Assume a component that can operate on any frequency except between a lower point $g_1$ and a higher point $g_2$ (although $g_1$ and $g_2$ are valid). Assume a program with $N$ blocks, each has $a_i$ operations and takes $t_i$ to execute. The operating frequency for each block is $f_i = \frac{a_i}{t_i}$, which must lie outside $g_1$ and $g_2$. From Theorem 2, the optimal frequency, $f$, is $\frac{\sum_{i=1}^{i=n} a_i}{\sum_{i=1}^{i=n} t_i}$. Assume that the optimal frequency is not a valid frequency, i.e., $f > g_1$ and $f < g_2$. The alternation scheme runs the component by frequency $g_1$ in time $T_1$ and by $g_2$ in $T_2$, where $T_1 + T_2 = \sum_{i=1}^{i=n} t_i$ and $g_1 T_1 + g_2 T_2 = \sum_{i=1}^{i=n} a_i$. The energy consumption of the original scheme, $E_{original}$, is $\sum_{i=1}^{i=n} f_i^3 t_i$. The energy consumption of the alternation scheme, $E_{opt}$, is $g_1^3 T_1 + g_2^3 T_2$. The following theorem states that the alternation scheme consumes the least amount of energy.

**Theorem 3** (*Theorem for discrete frequencies*): $\sum_{i=1}^{i=n} f_i^3 t_i \geq g_1^3 T_1 + g_2^3 T_2$, where $f_i, g_1, g_2 \geq 0$, $t_i > 0$, $T_1 + T_2 = \sum_{i=1}^{i=n} t_i$, $\sum_{i=1}^{i=n} f_i t_i = g_1 T_1 + g_2 T_2$, and either $f_i \geq g_2$ or $f_i \leq g_1$.

As in the proof of Theorem 1, we use induction on $n$ and reduce the case of $n = n + 1$ to the case of $n = 2$, which is equivalent to the following lemma.

**Lemma 2.** $f_1^3 t_1 + f_2^3(T - t_1) \geq g_1^3 t_2 + g_2^3(T - t_2)$, where $0 \leq f_1 \leq g_1 < g_2 \leq f_2$, $t_1, t_2 > 0$, and $f_1 t_1 + f_2(T - t_1) = g_1 t_2 + g_2(T - t_2)$.

**Proof:** Let $W = f_1 t_1 + f_2(T - t_1)$. We can represent $t_1$ and $t_2$ with $W$, that is, $t_1 = \frac{W - f_2 T}{f_1 - f_2}$ and $t_2 = \frac{W - g_2 T}{g_1 - g_2}$. In addition, let $fT = W$. Substitute $t_1$ and $t_2$ with $f$ in the inequality and simplify the equation to the following inequality, which is surprisingly well behaved considering that it has five variables that are only loosely constrained.

$$f f_1^2 + f_2(f - f_1)(f_1 + f_2) \geq f g_1^2 + g_2(f - g_1)(g_1 + g_2)$$

where $f_1 \leq g_1 \leq f \leq g_2 \leq f_2$.

Since $f_1 \geq g_1$ and $f_2 \geq g_2$, it is sufficient to show $(f - f_1)(f_1 + g_2) \geq (f - g_1)(g_1 + g_2)$. Define a function $F(x) = (f - x)(x + g_2) = -x^2 + (f - g_2)x + f g_2$. $F(x)$ hits its maximal point at $x = -\frac{f - g_2}{2}$. Since $f \leq g_2$, $F(x)$ is decreasing when $x \geq 0$. Hence, $F(f_1) \geq F(g_1)$ when $f_1 \leq g_1$. Thus, the inequality holds, so is the lemma and Theorem 3.

We make three additional comments on the proof. First, the solution for discrete frequencies can be generalized to multiple components by applying the alternation scheme on each unit. Components can be asymmetrical. The minimal energy consumption of the whole system is minimal if and only if the energy consumption of each component is minimal. Second, this alternation scheme is best among all execution schemes that require the same or less execution time. Finally, the optimality holds when considering the overhead of switching between valid frequencies. The optimal alternation scheme switches only once, which is optimal.

In essence, Lemma 2 is a constrained version of Lemma 1. These two lemmas form the basis for the entire proof of the paper. Intuitively, they establish the optimality condition for a single component in two execution cycles. The rest of the proof extends them to multiple components and time cycles.

## 5    Energy Consumption and Program Performance

Program reordering has been studied for improving program performance. However, the problem is a new one in the case of energy reduction because the optimal order for energy is different from that for performance. We show this difference with an example.

We assume a machine with one integer unit and one floating-point unit, with the same maximal frequency $f$. Figure 2 shows three versions of the same program: unoptimized, optimized for performance, optimized for energy and performance. The execution time of the unoptimized program is $\frac{9}{f}$. The second version runs faster—in time $\frac{8}{f}$, which is optimal because FPU must execute all 8 floating-point operations. However, the second version is not most energy efficient because it has uneven instruction balances. The third program has constant instruction balances and, according to our theorem, consumes minimal energy. The third program also yields optimal performance, $\frac{8}{f}$.

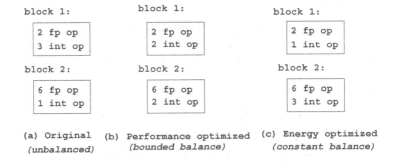

**Fig. 2.** Difference between performance and energy optimization

The simplified machine and program model does not consider the dependence and latency among program instructions. So the primary factor affecting performance is the utilization of critical resource. If the critical resource is fully utilized, the performance is optimal (assuming we cannot remove any instruction). In the previous example, the program has more floating-point operations than integer operations, so FPU is the critical resource. To keep the resource fully utilized, the ratio of floating-point operations to integer operations must be no less than one. The first program is not performance optimal because the first block has more integer operations than floating-point operations and therefore cannot fully utilize the critical resource. Both the second and third programs correct this problem and obtain the fastest speed. In fact, any reordering scheme is performance optimal if it bounds the balance to be no less than one.

The difference can now be described in terms of instruction balance. For best performance, we want full utilization of the critical resource and therefore a bounded balance. For minimal energy, we need a stronger condition that all blocks must have the same instruction balance. The requirement for a constant balance is even more important considering the switching cost of hardware. Constant balances do not require dynamic reconfiguration during execution. Table 2 summarizes the differences between issues of performance and those of energy.

|  | Improving Performance | Saving Energy |
|---|---|---|
| Goal | full utilization of critical resource | balanced use of all resources |
| Reordering | bounded instruction balances | constant instruction balances |

**Table 2.** Comparison of Program Reordering for Performance and for Energy

## 6   Evaluation

This section studies the effect of program reordering in a benchmark program, *Swim* from Spec95 suite. The program solves shallow water equations, a computation that is common in applications such as weather prediction. The main body of *Swim* consists of three loop nests enclosed in a time-step loop. Since different loops tend to have different instruction balances, we tried to combine them through loop fusion. We used a research compiler [7] that implements more aggressive loop fusion than current commercial compilers from Compaq, Sun, and SGI. It fused all three loop nests in *Swim*. Next we examine the effect of loop fusion on instruction balance.

We collected the execution trace and divided it into blocks of 500 instructions. For each block, we counted the number of different types of instructions and computed the balance. The trace collection and instruction enumeration were done on a Compaq Alpha 4000 Server using the ATOM tool [14]. To simplify the presentation, we will limit the discussion to only the ratio of floating-point to integer operations.

For this experiment, we ran the program in one iteration with an input size of 512x512. The original version has a total of 339 million instructions, out of which 166 million are floating-point and 43 million are integer operations. The upper two graphs of Figure 3 show the temporal graph and histogram of instruction balances. The temporal graph shows three segments, likely corresponding to the three loop nests. The ranges of instruction balances differ significantly in three segments: they are between 7 and 12, between 4 and 7, and between 2 and 3. The histogram shows the variation cumulatively. Instruction balances range from nearly 0 to 12 with high concentration points at 2.6 and 8.0 as well as a spread between 4.6 and 6.8. The largest single-point concentration covers no more than 15% of the program.

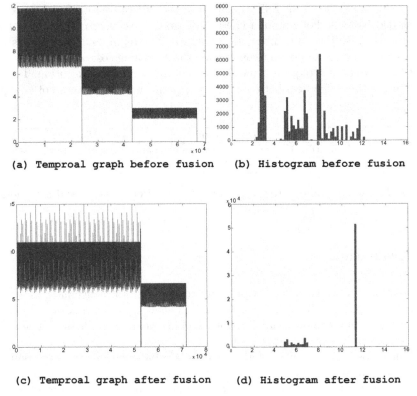

(a) **Temproal graph before fusion**     (b) **Histogram before fusion**

(c) **Temproal graph after fusion**     (d) **Histogram after fusion**

**Fig. 3.** Program balances of SPEC/Swim before and after loop fusion

Loop fusion altered the distribution of instruction balances, as shown by the lower two graphs in Figure 3. In the temporal graph, the number of segments has been reduced to two, one ranges between 6 and 12 and the other between 4 and 6. The histogram shows a dramatic change: over 70% of the program has an identical balance of 11.2, and all the rest are between 4.8 and 6.8. The histogram also shows that the seeming variation in the first segment in the temporal graph does not materialize in the histogram. Effectively, the fused version has a constant program demand in the first part of the computation. The number of instruction balances that are not 11.2 is too small to be seen on the histogram. Not shown in the figure, we also observed that loop fusion removed about 40% of integer operations because of the reduction in loop and data access overhead. The number of floating-point operations remained unchanged. Further study is needed to examine the full effect of program transformation, which is beyond the scope of this paper.

In summary, the study of *Spec/Swim* program has shown that program reordering can significantly alter program demand and re-balance the mix of instructions. For the ratio of floating-point to integer operations, program portion that has a constant balance is increased from under 15% to over 70%. The result of this experiment provides preliminary evidence that changing instruction balances is not only desirable but also feasible in a real application.

# 7   Related Work

A significant effort has been devoted to circuit or architectural improvement for power efficiency. Circuit-level features cannot be directly controlled by software, but architectural ones sometimes can. Our strategy depends on dynamic voltage and frequency scaling [2], which is being used by commercial processors such as Transmeta Crusoe and Intel XScale. Other architectural techniques such as clock gating [9] are also included in our model. Recently, Semeraro et al. studied fine-grained dynamic scaling, where funtional units within a processor may be scaled independently with each other [13]. The goal of our work is complementary and is to examine how can software better utilize these hardware features so that the whole system is optimized.

Software techniques have been studied for reducing energy usage [16, 15, 17]. Tiwari et al. reported that the most energy saving was obtained by reducing memory misses (up to 40% saving) and the least effective was energy-based code generation and instruction scheduling [17]. Better caching leads to power saving in the memory system. Vijaykrishnan et al. evaluated a set of cache optimizations by a compiler [18]. Most techniques save energy by reducing program demand. In contrast, we show the potential of demand reordering, which is targeted specifically at reconfigurable hardware. Demand reordering at the instruction level is the subject of two recent work. Both tried to spread out non-critical instructions and make program demand less concentrated. Greg et al. studied the potential benefit by rescheduling the execution trace [13]. Yang et al. modified software pipelining and measured its effect on the SPEC Integer benchmark suite [19]. Both reported double-digit percentage energy saving with no or little performance degradation.

In the past, power models at the CMOS level were studied for the processor core [2] and for memory hierarchy [5]. Instruction-level power consumption for fixed-configuration processors was measured for real machines [16, 12].

Architectural-level simulators have been developed [1, 18, 13]. Furthermore, researchers also studied better software feedback for reconfigurable hardware [10] and OS support for paging [11] and disk scheduling [8]. These techniques do not change the demand of software but improve the effectiveness of hardware adaptation. Techniques of program reordering like ours will benefit from power models and advanced system support.

Program optimization has been studied for many years for improving program performance. Here we review the ones that are related to instruction balance. Balance was introduced to model FPU throughput and load/store bandwidth [3]. Transformations such as unroll-and-jam are used to improve program balance [4]. To consider all levels of memory hierarchy, our earlier work extended the definition of balance from a ratio to a tuple [6]. In this paper, we further extend the definition to include all components of a computer including functional units within the CPU.

## 8   Conclusion and Future Work

This paper has presented a theoretical result to an important optimization problem regarding the best program organization on a machine of different components operating on a different set of frequencies. It has proved that a program with constant instruction balances consumes the least amount of energy, that balancing program instructions guarantees power saving without performance degradation, and that energy-based reordering is a different problem than performance-based reordering.

We are currently measuring instruction balance in programs and its exact role in energy consumption. We are also designing a *Smooth* compiler for improving instruction balances by building upon the global program and data transformations that we have developed previously [7].

## Acknowledgment

The idea of this work was originated from a discussion with the PIs of the CAP project, Micheal Scott, Dave Albonesi, and Sandhya Dwarkadas. Bin Han provided an important hint that led to the proof of Lemma 1. We are also grateful to Xianghui Liu and members of the system group at the Computer Science Department of University of Rochester for their helpful discussions.

## References

[1] D. Brooks, V. Tiwari, and M. Martonosi. Wattch: A framework for architectural-level analysis and optimization. In *Proceedings of the 27th International Symposium on Computer Architecture*, Vancouver, BC, 2000.

[2] T. Burd and R. Brodersen. Processor design for portable systems. *Journal of LSI Signal Processing*, 13(2-3):203–222, 1996.

[3]  D. Callahan, J. Cocke, and K. Kennedy. Estimating interlock and improving balance for pipelined machines. *Journal of Parallel and Distributed Computing*, 5(4):334–358, August 1988.

[4]  S. Carr and K. Kennedy. Improving the ratio of memory operations to floating-point operations in loops. *ACM Transactions on Programming Languages and Systems*, 16(6):1768–1810, 1994.

[5]  A. M. Despain and C. Su. Cache designs for energy efficiency. In *Proceedings of 28th Hawaii International Conference on System Science*, 1995.

[6]  C. Ding and K. Kennedy. Memory bandwidth bottleneck and its amelioration by a compiler. In *Proceedings of 2000 International Parallel and Distribute Processing Symposium (IPDPS)*, Cancun, Mexico, May 2000.

[7]  C. Ding and K. Kennedy. Improving effective bandwidth through compiler enhancement of global cache reuse. In *Proceedings of International Parallel and Distributed Processing Symposium*, San Francisco, CA, 2001. http://www.ipdps.org.

[8]  F. Douglis, R. Caceres, B. Marsh, F. Kaashoek, K. Li, and J. Tauber. Storage alternatives for mobile computers. In *Proceedings of the first symposium on operating system design and implementation*, Monterey, CA, 1994.

[9]  S. Gary et al. PowerPC 603, a microprocessor for portable computers. In *IEEE Design and Test of Computers*, pages 14–23, 1994.

[10]  C.-H. Hsu, U. Kremer, and M. Hsiao. Compiler-directed dynamic frequency and voltage scaling. In *Workshop on Power-Aware Computer Systems*, Cambridge, MA, 2000.

[11]  A. R. Lebeck, X. Fan, H. Zeng, and C. Ellis. Power aware page allocation. In *Proceedings of the 9th international conference on architectural support for programming languages and operating systems*, Cambridge, MA, 2000.

[12]  J. T. Russell and M. F. Jacome. Software power estimation and optimization for high performance, 32-bit embedded processors. In *Proceedings of International Conference on Computer Design*, Austin, Texas, 1998.

[13]  G. Semeraro, M. Grigorios, R. Balasubramanian, D. H. Albonesi, S. Dwarkadas, and M. L. Scott. Energy-efficient processor design using multiple clock domains with dynamic voltage and frequency scaling. Submitted for publication, 2001.

[14]  A. Srivastava and A. Eustace. ATOM: A system for building customized program analysis tools. In *Proceedings of ACM SIGPLAN Conference on Programming Language Design and Implementation*, Orlando Florida, June 1994.

[15]  C. Su, C. Tsui, and A. M. Despain. Low power architecture design and compilation techniques for high-performance processors. In *Proceedings of the IEEE COMPCON*, pages 489–498, 1994.

[16]  V. Tiwari, S. Maik, and A. Wolfe. Power analysis of embedded software: a first step towards software power minimization. *IEEE Transaction on VLSI Systems*, 1994.

[17]  V. Tiwari, S. Maik, A. Wolfe, and M. Lee. Instruction level power analysis and optimization of software. *Journal of VLSI Signal Processing*, 13(2):1–18, 1996.

[18]  N. Vijaykrishnan, M. Kandemir, M. J. Irwin, H. S. Kim, and W. Ye. Energy-driven integrated hardware-software optimizations using SimplePower. In *Proceedings of the 27th International Symposium on Computer Architecture*, Vancouver, BC, 2000.

[19]  H. Yang, G. R. Gao, and G. Cai. Maximizing pipelined functional unit usage for minimum power software pipelining. Technical Report CAPSL Technical Memo 41, University of Delaware, Newark, Delaware, September 2001.

# Dynamic Voltage and Frequency Scaling for Scientific Applications*

Chung-Hsing Hsu and Ulrich Kremer

Department of Computer Science
Rutgers University
Piscataway, New Jersey, USA
{chunghsu, uli}@cs.rutgers.edu

**Abstract.** Dynamic voltage and frequency scaling (DVFS) of the CPU has been shown to be one of the most effective ways to reduce energy consumption of a program. This paper discusses the benefit of dynamic voltage and frequency scaling for scientific applications under different optimization levels. The reported experiments show that there are still many opportunities to apply DVFS to the highly optimized codes, and the profitability is significant across the benchmarks. It is also observed that there are performance and energy consumption tradeoffs for different optimization levels in the presence of DVFS. While in general compiling for performance will improve energy usage as well, in some cases the less successful optimization lead to higher energy savings. Finally, a comparison of the benefits of operating system support versus compiler support for DVFS is discussed.

## 1 Introduction

Modern architectures have a large gap between the speeds of the memory and the processor. Techniques exist to bridge this gap, including memory pipelines, cache hierarchies, and large register sets. Most of these architectural features exploit the fact that computations have temporal and/or spatial locality. However, many computations have limited locality, or even no locality at all. In addition, the degree of locality may be different for different program regions. Such computations may lead to a significant mismatch between the actual machine balance and computation balance, resulting in frequent stalls of the processor waiting for the memory subsystem to provide the data.

Minimizing the power/energy consumption of scientific computations leads to a reduction in heat dissipation and cooling requirements, which in turn reduces design and packaging costs of advanced architectures, and operating costs of such machines in computing and data centers. In particular, electric bills due to air conditioning of machine rooms have become an important concern. It is reasonable to assume that the amount of energy needed to drive a computer system is comparable to the amount of energy needed to remove the resulting dissipated heat from the physical environment.

---

* This research was partially supported by NSF CAREER award No. CCR-9985050.

H. Dietz (Ed.): LCPC 2001, LNCS 2624, pp. 86–99, 2003.

Dynamic voltage and frequency scaling (DVFS) has been recognized as an effective technique to reduce power dissipation. Commercial processors that support DVFS have recently become available, including Transmeta's Crusoe, Intel's XScale, and AMD's K6-IIIE+. To use the DVFS capability of such microprocessor, values in appropriate system registers or data structures have to be set that reflect the desired clock frequencies and voltage levels. These values may be changed during the course of program execution.

Current research on DVFS is mostly done in the context of real-time operating systems where the operating system determines the voltage and frequency levels with the lowest power/energy consumption, given the constant of a hard or soft program deadline. Almost all the proposed scheduling algorithms use the idea of eliminating CPU slacks to determine the desired frequencies. Given the frequencies, the lowest voltage is selected that is needed to support this frequency.

CPU slacks come from many sources. In this paper, we study those from the *imbalance* between CPU and memory activities. A recent study [14] has shown that even with an aggressive, next-generation memory system, a processor still spends over half of its time stalling for L2 cache misses. It is these stalls that we can exploit to save processor power.

Most advanced locality optimizations try to reduce the memory stalls to improve performance. This is typically done by reducing the number of memory references, or overlapping memory references with computation. In this paper, we investigate the impact of these transformations to the reduction of memory stalls, which are an indication of DVFS applicability and profitability. We analyzed five scientific codes that were compiled with Compaq's (formerly DEC's) V5.3-1155 Fortran compiler, arguably one of the best optimizing compilers available today. Energy and performance simulation results showed that

- There are still many opportunities to apply DVFS to the highly optimized codes, and the profitability is significant across the benchmarks;
- There are performance and energy consumption tradeoffs for different optimization levels in the presence of DVFS; given a fixed execution time deadline, choosing the highest optimization level, followed by DVFS, may not be the best strategy for maximal energy savings.

Whether to exploit this significant opportunity for DVFS through hardware, operating systems, or compilation techniques is an open problem. The best strategy will depend on the overhead of frequency and voltage adjustment operations, and the number of times the frequency and voltage needs to be changed during program execution. This paper tries to give a first assessment with respect to this issue.

The paper is organized as follows. We first present the methodology used to conduct the experiments in Section 2. Power, energy, and performance tradeoffs are discussed in Section 3, followed by a discussion of DVFS applicability and its profitability in terms of energy savings in Section 4. A comparison of the benefits of operating system support vs. compiler support for DVFS is presented in

Section 5. Finally, Section 6 gives a brief summary of related work, and Section 7 concludes the paper.

## 2   Our Platform and Methodology

The *Wattch* CPU energy and performance simulator [1] was used for our experiments to determine execution times, power dissipation, and energy consumption. We configured the simulator to reflect most of the characteristics of DEC's Alpha 21264, a quad-issue dynamically-scheduled general-purpose processor. As suggested in [4], the combined LSQ (Load Store Queue) is set to 64 entries, and the RUU (Register Update Unit) uses 64 entries. The memory system in our study contains a 64KB, 2-way set associative instruction and data cache, and a 2MB direct-mapped L2 cache. All caches are write-back and have the block size of 64 bytes. The main memory runs at 1/4 of the processor speed and is connected to the CPU via a 8-byte memory bus. Disks are not modeled.

The default setting assumes a fully pipelined main memory, i.e., memory can service arbitrarily many access requests at any cycle. However, we found that the simulation results are inconsistent with the real measurements of programs optimized at different levels. We believe that the assumption that memory is fully pipelined was too optimistic, and therefore chose to use *non-pipelined* memory in our simulation. That is, memory can service at most one request at any given time. All the other requests are buffered until the memory is available. The memory latency was set to be 40 cycles for all experiments.

We selected five programs from the SPECfp95 benchmarks, and compiled each program with Compaq's (formerly DEC's) Fortran V5.3-1155 f90 compiler. All benchmarks were compiled with -arch ev6 -non_shared flags and different optimization levels. The default optimization level is -O4. Optimization level -O5 performs all the optimizations in -O4, plus software pipelining and various loop transformations. It is the highest available optimization level in -O[n]. The resulting Alpha EV6 binaries were "executed" by our simulator to obtain performance, power, and energy results.

The SPECfp95 benchmark programs have a common structure, consisting of an initialization phase followed by an execution phase which can be iterated multiple times. The number of iterations of the execution phase is part of an input file and can be adjust in order to reduce simulation time. For our experiments, all benchmarks took the provided reference data sets as input, with the number of iterations for the execution phase reduced to 10 iterations.

We used *Wattch*'s default manufacturing process parameter of .35μm at 600MHz. The simulator reported 98.86W peak power for our Alpha21264-style processor. Power is assumed to scale linearly with port or unit usage, and that unused units dissipate 10% of their maximum power. Besides the total energy and total execution time reported for the entire program, we extended *Wattch* to record all these values for intervals of 1,000,000 cycles. This was done to capture the time varying behavior of the programs, as described in [20].

**Table 1.** The effects of standard optimizations on power/energy/performance. All the reported energy values are in Joules, execution times in cycles, and average powers in watts (Joules/sec). **Insts** is the total number of instructions executed. **Misses** is the total number of L2 cache misses (memory accesses).

| Benchmark | Opt Level | Energy Joules | Exec Time $10^6$ cycles | Avg Power Watts | Insts $10^6$ | Misses $10^6$ |
|---|---|---|---|---|---|---|
| swim | -O4 | 17.09 | 404.63 | 25.34 | 433.92 | 4.87 |
|  | -O5 | 16.23 | 387.74 | 25.12 | 429.09 | 4.43 |
| tomcatv | -O4 | 69.86 | 1323.13 | 31.57 | 2159.69 | 9.39 |
|  | -O5 | 67.00 | 1226.37 | 32.78 | 2153.52 | 7.99 |
| applu | -O4 | 62.79 | 1555.48 | 24.27 | 1606.90 | 16.61 |
|  | -O5 | 50.64 | 1420.04 | 21.40 | 1081.22 | 17.91 |
| hydro2d | -O4 | 99.79 | 2710.61 | 22.09 | 2268.55 | 33.11 |
|  | -O5 | 101.75 | 2747.82 | 22.22 | 2365.39 | 33.31 |
| turb3d | -O4 | 273.42 | 4402.67 | 37.26 | 9179.82 | 18.53 |
|  | -O5 | 273.41 | 4402.56 | 37.26 | 9179.63 | 18.53 |

# 3   Power/Energy/Performance Tradeoffs

In general, compiling for performance will also result in more power and energy efficient programs, at least for optimizations that reduce CPU workloads. For advanced locality optimizations, compiling for performance tends to introduce considerable CPU workload with possibly marginal performance improvement. As a result, CPU power dissipation may increase. Kandemir et al. have shown that loop transformations such as loop tiling can reduce memory energy costs, but at the same time can increase CPU energy consumption, which may result in an overall energy increase [13].

Table 1 shows the simulation results obtained when five SPECfp95 benchmarks are compiled with different optimization levels. The results show that, for each benchmark, the version that has the better performance always has the lower energy consumption. For most cases, this version has less CPU workload (approximated by **Insts**) and less memory workload (approximated by **Misses**). In the case of the applu benchmark, -O5 version slightly increases memory workload. But it significantly reduces CPU workload and results in better performance and lower energy cost than -O4 version.

To further illustrate the tradeoffs between power, energy, and performance, we performed simulation on several highly optimized versions of the swim benchmark. Swim is an iterative stencil computation. It has been a popular benchmark used by researchers in the optimizing compiler community. The first version was provided by Chen Ding from the University of Rochester, and uses *loop fusion* and *array regrouping* [5]. All the other versions were provided by Marta Jimenez from the Universitat Politecnica de Catalunya, Barcelona, Spain. Her optimizations include *loop tiling* at the cache level [22] and/or register level [11]. All these transformations tend to reduce the memory workload, and have been shown to be effective for `swim`. Table 2 presents the simulation results for the different versions of `swim`.

**Table 2.** The effects of various additional optimizations on power/energy/performance of the `swim` benchmark. All programs were optimized with `-O5`, with the exception of tiled versions where loop transformations and loop unrolling was disabled [10]. All the reported energy values are in Joules, execution times in cycles, and average power dissipation in watts (Joules/sec). **Insts** is the total number of instructions executed. **Misses** is the total number of L2 cache misses (memory accesses).

| Opt Level | Energy | Exec Time | Avg Power | Insts | Misses |
|---|---|---|---|---|---|
| | Joules | $10^6$ cycles | Watts | $10^6$ | $10^6$ |
| O5 | 16.23 | 387.74 | 25.12 | 429.09 | 4.43 |
| O5+AR+LF | 14.98 | 358.89 | 25.04 | 348.30 | 4.35 |
| O5+AR+2dLT | 18.58 | 338.47 | 32.94 | 597.46 | 2.16 |
| O5+AR+1dLT | 17.65 | 288.96 | 36.66 | 550.97 | 1.86 |
| O5+AR+RT+2dLT | 14.42 | 273.54 | 31.64 | 404.43 | 2.25 |
| O5+AR+RT+1dLT | 14.25 | 259.08 | 33.01 | 403.00 | 1.95 |

LF - loop fusion
AR - array regrouping
LT - 1-dim/2-dim loop tiling
RT - register tiling

Loop tiling appears to improve performance better than simply fusing loops together. Tiling at the cache level significantly cuts down the number of memory accesses at the expense of increasing the CPU workload. Unlike the previous results in Table 1, performance is improved but the energy consumption goes up. It is one more evidence that compiling for performance and compiling for low power/energy may sometimes not be the same. With the help of register tiling, the CPU workload can be effectively reduced while similar memory workload as tiling at the cache level is preserved. Not only the program performance is further improved, the corresponding energy cost is reduced as well. As a matter of fact, the version `O5+AR+RT+2dLT` runs the fastest and consumes the least energy. But we want to point out that it has the second highest average power.

## 4   DVFS for Highly Optimized Codes

Extensive research on optimizing compilers has been carried out in the last decades, especially the loop and data layout transformations for scientific applications. All these high-level transformations try to improve the cache locality, and have been proved to be quite effective in reducing memory stalls. However,

DVFS relies on exploiting memory stalls to save power and energy. In this section we will discuss the impact of loop transformations on the applicability and profitability of DVFS.

## 4.1   Quantify DVFS Applicability

It is not yet clear how to capture the DVFS applicability. In earlier work, we introduced a metric, called slow-down factor $\delta$ [8], to capture DVFS opportunities. The slow-down factor is defined by how much the CPU can be slowed down without exceeding a prescribed performance penalty (soft deadline). The slow-down factor is never less than one, and larger factors represent slower clock frequencies.

The slow-down factor is defined as follows:

$$\delta \overset{\text{def}}{=} 1 + \min(\frac{r}{R_c}, \frac{R_m}{R_b})$$

where $R_b$ represent the fraction of an interval in which CPU activity (including L1 and L2 activity) is overlapped with memory access, $R_c$ is the fraction in which only CPU has activity, and $R_m$ is the fraction in which CPU is stalled due to memory bandwidth and latency. The ratio $r$ indicates the prescribed relative performance penalty. In this paper we set it to be 10%.

Figure 1 gives the DVFS applicability of the five benchmarks optimized with -O5 over intervals of 1,000,000 cycles. All graphs show an initialization phase, followed by an execution phase consisting of repeated patterns. The regular patterns suggest that the compiler may be able to recognize them. If we consider the entire execution phase except the last few intervals, benchmarks such as swim and tomcatv have a minimum slow-down factor across all intervals that is significantly greater than one. This indicates that the default CPU speed is too high for the benchmark. As a result, choosing a single, fixed slow-down factor for the entire execution phase, namely the minimum value, will reduce energy consumption without incurring any switching overhead.

Inside each repeated pattern, there are regions that have slow-down factors much higher than the minimum value. These regions spend a considerable amount of time in each pattern. These are the places that the *dynamic* voltage and frequency scaling can be applied to further reduce the energy costs. In summary, there are still significant opportunities to apply DVFS to highly optimized scientific applications, a somewhat surprising result.

## 4.2   DVFS Profitability

To quantify the benefit of applying DVFS to highly optimized codes, we introduced a simple analytical energy model. The model is based on associating with each CPU cycle an energy cost, and separating active cycles from idle cycles. The energy model is defined as follows.

$$E = \rho \cdot 10^6 \cdot [R_c + R_b + \frac{1}{10} \cdot R_m] \tag{1}$$

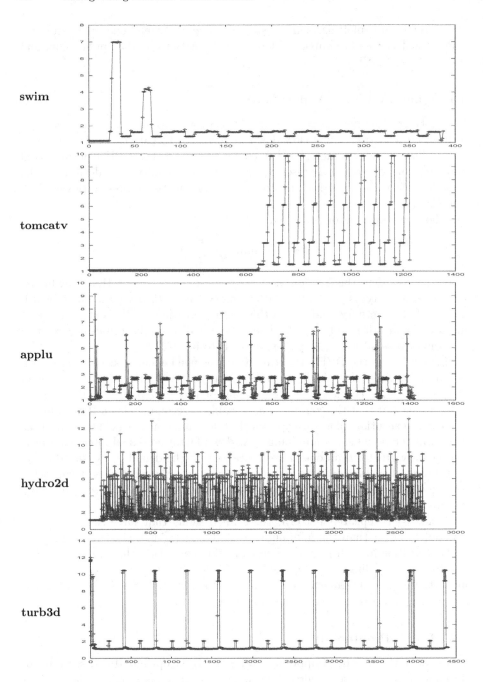

**Fig. 1.** DVFS applicability of the five SPECfp95 benchmarks optimized with -O5. The x-axis represents intervals of 1,000,000 cycles and the y-axis represents the DVFS applicability in terms of the slow-down factor $\delta$.

**Table 3.** DVFS profitability for benchmarks optimized with -O5. Energy savings and performance penalty are relative to the codes executed without DVFS. They are all represented as percentages.

| Benchmark | Energy Saving (%) | Performance Penalty (%) |
|---|---|---|
| swim | 58.54 | 9.50 |
| tomcatv | 39.09 | 8.42 |
| applu | 70.61 | 7.27 |
| hydro2d | 64.88 | 7.32 |
| turb3d | 26.36 | 9.27 |

$$E' = \frac{\rho}{\delta^2} \cdot 10^6 \cdot [R_c + R_b + \frac{1}{10} \cdot \frac{1}{\delta} \cdot (\max\left(\frac{\delta R_b}{R_b + R_m}\right) - \delta R_b)] \qquad (2)$$

Energy measure $E$ is for the interval without DVFS, which we had profiled in the simulation. An active CPU cycle consumes $\rho$ Joules, while an idle one consumes only 10% of this figure. Energy measure $E'$ is for the interval after applying DVFS using slow-down factor $\delta$. The energy cost of an active CPU cycle is scaled down by a factor of $\delta^2$. The CPU workload is kept the same after applying DVFS [1], as reflected by $10^6 \cdot (R_c + R_b)$. However, the total execution time in *seconds* increases due to slower CPU speed. As a consequence, the number of idle CPU cycles for a DVFS'ed program is reduced. This can be reflected by the inequality $\frac{1}{\delta} \cdot (\max\left(\frac{\delta R_b}{R_b + R_m}\right) - \delta R_b) \leq R_m$. Finally, the DVFS profitability can be estimated through the relative energy reduction $1 - E'/E$ using Equations (1) and (2).

Table 3 shows the possible energy savings and performance degradation if at every interval we slowed down the CPU according to the slow-down values shown in Figure 1. Energy may be saved up to 71% if the switching cost between different voltages and frequencies is negligible. Again, this is an optimistic approximation, but it clearly indicates the possibility of applying DVFS without significant performance penalties even for highly optimized codes.

## 5   Discussion

Compiling for low power and energy, and compiling for performance may require different optimization strategies. In the previous section we have shown that DVFS can be applied to codes which are already highly optimized for performance. In this section we would like to address a few other issues of using DVFS from the compiler's point of view.

---

[1] It is an ideal assumption and may not be the case in practice, for instance due to out-of-order instruction execution.

**Table 4.** DVFS profitability on various version of the `swim` benchmark. All the reported energy values are in Joules and execution times in $10^6$ cycles.

| Opt Level | w/o DVFS | | w/ DVFS | | Profitability | |
|---|---|---|---|---|---|---|
| | Energy | Exec Time | Energy | Exec Time | Energy Saving (%) | Performance Penalty (%) |
| O5 | 16.23 | 387.74 | 6.73 | 424.57 | 58.54 | 9.50 |
| O5+AR+LF | 14.98 | 358.89 | 5.15 | 392.78 | 65.63 | 9.44 |
| O5+AR+2dLT | 18.58 | 338.47 | 12.17 | 370.88 | 34.49 | 9.58 |
| O5+AR+1dLT | 17.65 | 288.96 | 11.60 | 316.34 | 34.29 | 9.48 |
| O5+AR+RT+2dLT | 14.42 | 273.54 | 8.37 | 299.36 | 41.96 | 9.44 |
| O5+AR+RT+1dLT | 14.25 | 259.08 | 8.69 | 283.55 | 39.07 | 9.44 |

LF - loop fusion
AR - array regrouping
LT - 1-dim/2-dim loop tiling
RT - register tiling

As discussed in Section 3, sometimes the compiler optimizations introduce a considerable amount of processor workload, often only for marginal performance gains. In such situations, the CPU power dissipation goes up, and possibly the total energy consumption increases as well. Aggressive optimizations, if not applied carefully, may prohibit DVFS, and therefore will not benefit from this effective power/energy reducing technique.

Consider the various versions of the `swim` program with and without DVFS. First of all, as in the case of our five benchmark programs, there is significant opportunity and benefit for DVFS across the highly optimized versions of the benchmark. Table 4 gives the estimates of DVFS profitability. Notice that even though version `O5+AR+RT+1dLT` consumes the least energy without DVFS, it does not allow large energy reduction due to DVFS. On the other hand, version `O5+AR+LF` consumes slightly more energy but preserves the DVFS applicability, and in the final consumes the least amount of energy when DVFS is applied. The result shows that, while compiling for performance is in general good for compiling for low power, the DVFS applicability needs to be taken into account as well.

In a computation environment with limited energy resources, a compiler may trade-off execution speed for power and energy savings. In one possible optimization scenario, the compiler is presented with a fixed program execution deadline. The optimization goal is to minimize energy consumption while honoring this deadline. One possible compilation approach consists of applying advanced data locality optimizations, and using the resulting performance gain as the performance penalty $r$ (see Section 4.1) that can be tolerated for choosing a slow-down factor $\delta$. Table 5 shows the result of this approach for the `swim` benchmark with an execution deadline equal to the execution time of the O5 optimization level version. Although the fastest optimization turned out to be the most energy

**Table 5.** The profitability of DVFS on various version of the `swim` benchmark with respect to a global deadline: the execution time of version O5. All the reported energy values are in Joules and execution times in $10^6$ cycles. $r$ is the relative performance penalty used to determine slow-down factor $\delta$ as discussed in Section 4.1.

| Opt Level | w/o DVFS | | | w/ DVFS | | Profitability | |
|---|---|---|---|---|---|---|---|
| | Energy | Exec Time | $r$ | Energy | Exec Time | Energy Saving (%) | Performance Penalty (%) |
| O5 | 16.23 | 387.74 | 0.00 | | | | |
| O5+AR+LF | 14.98 | 358.89 | 0.08 | 5.97 | 386.39 | 63.23 | -0.35 |
| O5+AR+2dLT | 18.58 | 338.47 | 0.15 | 10.62 | 385.95 | 34.56 | -0.46 |
| O5+AR+1dLT | 17.65 | 288.96 | 0.34 | 7.30 | 368.46 | 55.03 | -4.97 |
| O5+AR+RT+2dLT | 14.42 | 273.54 | 0.42 | 4.64 | 357.04 | 71.44 | -7.92 |
| O5+AR+RT+1dLT | 14.25 | 259.08 | 0.50 | 4.52 | 349.39 | 72.14 | -9.89 |

LF - loop fusion
AR - array regrouping
LT - 1-dim/2-dim loop tiling
RT - register tiling

efficient one in this case (`O5+AR+RT+1dLR`), the ranking of the other versions switched, i.e., the less successful optimization lead to higher energy savings for the given deadline.

The previous experimental results assume that the cost of scaling to the desired voltage and frequency is negligible. In current technology, it is not the case. Right now the switching latency is as long as 75-520$\mu$s. If the switching overhead is significant, DVFS cannot be applied too frequently during the entire program execution. Fortunately, Figure 1 shows that four of the five benchmarks have stable regions that we can simply change the voltage and frequency at the beginning and end of these regions. We believe that DVFS at the compiler level, OS level, or microarchitecture level will perform equally well for these four programs.

Difficulties for effective DVFS at OS and microarchitecture levels arise in programs like `hydro2d`. There are too many peaks that prohibit effective application of OS or hardware guided DVFS approaches which rely on limited windows of observed past program behavior. In contrast, the compiler has a *more global* view of the program regions and their execution characteristics, and therefore can better tolerate frequent changes in CPU slack. For example, if we apply the technique in [9], the compiler is able to find a program region in the execution phase to slow down, as shown in Figure 2. The total execution time increases by 12.25%, but the energy is reduced by 64.62%. More importantly, there are only 20 voltage/frequency switches, compared to 2748 switches in the ideal case.

There is an additional reason why compiler-directed DVFS is *complementary* to the OS-directed DVFS. In general, the operating system receives a given

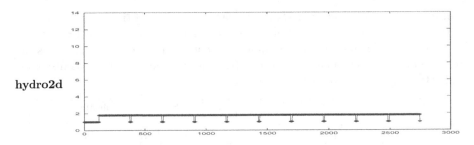

**Fig. 2.** The compiler-directed DVFS application of the `hydro2d` benchmarks optimized with `-O5`. The x-axis represents intervals of 1,000,000 cycles and the y-axis represents the DVFS applicability in terms of the slow-down factor $\delta$.

binary to execute, while the compiler has a version of the source code which may be translated to many different semantically equivalent binaries. If, for example, the compiler generates the tiled version of `swim`, OS-directed DVFS will not be able to reduce energy too much since the binary does not provide the opportunity. In contrast, the compiler has the choice of considering different DVFS opportunities with different power/energy/performance tradeoffs.

## 6   Related Work

There exist processors that support dynamic voltage and frequency scaling, such as Transmeta's Crusoe, Intel's Xscale, AMD's K6-IIIE+, and the prototypes from U.C., Berkeley [2] and from Delft University of Technology [19]. Current implementations involve draining instruction pipeline and waiting until the desired voltage is supplied through an external DC-DC regulator when DVFS is applied. It usually takes a long time to switch (75-520 $\mu$s). With such high latency the frequency of dynamically changing voltage may need to be taken extreme care.

Extensive research on optimizing compilers has been carried out in the last decade [18], mostly stressing on high performance. Until recently, power becomes an increasingly important issue and there is a growing interest in optimizing software for low power. While most of the researches focus on the back-end optimizations such as reducing bit switching activity in buses, we address in this paper the high-level optimizations, especially loop transformations for scientific applications.

Kandemir et. al. evaluated the influence of high-level compiler optimizations on the power/energy behavior of a program. They showed in [13] that optimizations such as loop tiling and data transformations may increase the CPU energy usage while reducing memory system energy. Valluri and John in [23] presented a quantitative study of the standard optimizations levels on power and energy of the processor. They concluded that optimizations that improve performance by reducing the workload (such as common subexpression elimination and copy propagation) are optimized for energy, and optimizations that improve performance by increasing the workload overlap (such as aggressive instruction scheduling) increase the average power dissipated in the processor.

It is interesting to note that several researchers have found that compiling for low power is quite different from compiling for performance. For example, in [12], Kandemir et al. found that the best tile size for the least energy consumed is different from that for the best performance. And in [16], Marculescu found that an optimal level of parallelism for energy consumption in modern processors is not necessarily the same as the one for performance.

To capture DVFS opportunity, most of the work has been done at the operating system level. Previous studies that adapted frequency to CPU activity based on intervals used ad hoc heuristics and "hand tuned" these heuristics. In each case, the goal was to reduce energy without compromising performance. A recent study, based on actual execution not on simulation, showed that this goal is not quite achieved [7].

Applying DVFS at the microarchitecture level is also advocated in recent years. For example, Ghiasi et al. in [6] and Childers et al. in [3] suggested using IPC (or IPS) to adapt the frequency to the current workload to save energy. Marculescu in [15] proposed to use cache misses as the scaling points.

To the best of our knowledge, compiler-directed DVFS has yet to be explored. In an early paper [8] we proposed a simple model to compute the CPU slow-down factor, and showed in a later paper [9] that it can save energy of 3.97%-23.75% for the SPECfp95 benchmark suite with performance penalty of at most 2.53%. Other approaches include the ones proposed by [17,21] to instrument program regions so as to exploit the CPU slacks missing when using the worst-case execution time assumption to determine the voltage schedule in the operating systems.

## 7  Conclusions

Dynamic voltage and frequency scaling (DVFS) has been recognized as an effective technique to reduce power dissipation. Since it relies on exploiting memory stalls and most advanced locality optimizations try to reduce the stalls, we investigate in this paper the impact of these transformations to the applicability and profitability of DVFS.

Five scientific codes were compiled with Compaq's Fortran compiler, arguably one of the best optimizing compilers available today. Energy and performance simulation results showed that there are still many opportunities to apply DVFS to the highly optimized codes, and the profitability is significant across the benchmarks. It is also observed that there are performance and energy consumption tradeoffs for different optimization levels in the presence of DVFS. A comparison of the benefits of operating system support vs. compiler support for DVFS is discussed as well.

# Acknowledgements

The authors wish to thank Chen Ding from University of Rochester for a version of the `swim` code and the support of using their Alpha compiler. In addition, they want to thank Marta Jimenez from Universitat Politecnica de Catalunya (UPC) for tiled versions of the `swim` code.

# References

1. D. Brooks, V. Tiwari, and M. Martonosi. Wattch: A framework for architectural-level power analysis and optimizations. In *27th International Symposium on Computer Architecture (ISCA)*, June 2000.
2. T. Burd and R. Brodersen. Design issues for dynamic voltage scaling. In *Proceedings of 2000 International Symposium on Low Power Electronics and Design (ISLPED'00)*, July 2000.
3. B. Childers, H. Tang, and R. Melhem. Adapting processor supply voltage to instruction-level parallelism. In *Kool Chips 2000 Workshop*, December 2000.
4. R. Desikan, D. Burger, and S. Keckler. Measuring experimental error in microprocessor simulation. In *the 28th Annual International Symposium on Computer Architecture (ISCA'01)*, July 2001.
5. C. Ding and K. Kennedy. Improving effective bandwidth through compiler enhancement of global cache reuse. In *Proceedings of International Parallel and Distributed Processing Symposium*, April 2001.
6. S. Ghiasi, J. Casmira, and D. Grunwald. Using IPC variation in workloads with externally specified rates to reduce power consumption. In *Workshop on Complexity Effective Design*, June 2000.
7. D. Grunwald, P. Levis, K. Farkas, C. Morrey III, and M. Neufeld. Policies for dynamic clock scheduling. In *Proceedings of the 4th Symposium on Operating System Design and Implementation (OSDI-2000)*, October 2000.
8. C.-H. Hsu, U. Kremer, and M. Hsiao. Compiler-directed dynamic frequency and voltage scheduling. In *Workshop on Power-Aware Computer Systems (PACS)*, November 2000.
9. C.-H. Hsu, U. Kremer, and M. Hsiao. Compiler-directed dynamic voltage/frequency scheduling for energy reduction in microprocessors. In *Proceedings of the International Symposium on Low-Power Electronics and Design (ISLPED'01)*, August 2001.
10. M. Jimenez. Private communication.
11. M. Jimenez, J.M. Llaberia, A. Fernandez, and E. Morancho. A general algorithm for tiling the register level. In *Proceedings of the 12th ACM International Conference on Supercomputing*, July 1998.
12. M. Kandemir, N. Vijaykrishnan, M.J. Irwin, and H.S. Kim. Experimental evaluation of energy behavior of iteration space tiling. In *International Workshop on Languages and Compilers for Parallel Computing (LCPC)*, August 2000.
13. M. Kandemir, N. Vijaykrishnan, M.J. Irwin, and W. Ye. Influence of compiler optimizations on system power. In *Design Automation Conference (DAC)*, June 2000.
14. W.-F. Lin, S. K. Reinhardt, and D. Burger. Reducing DRAM latencies with an integrated memory hierarchy design. In *Proc. 7th Int'l Symp. on High-Performance Computer Architecture (HPCA)*, January 2001.

15. D. Marculescu. On the use of microarchitecture-driven dynamic voltage scaling. In *Workshop on Complexity-Effective Design*, June 2000.

16. D. Marculescu. Profile-driven code execution for low power dissipation. In *Proceedings of International Symposium on Low Power Electronics and Design (ISLPED)*, July 2000.

17. D. Mossé, H. Aydin, B. Childers, and R. Melhem. Compiler-assisted dynamic power-aware scheduling for real-time applications. In *Workshop on Compiler and Operating Systems for Low Power (COLP'00)*, October 2000.

18. S. Muchnick. *Advanced Compiler Design and Implementation*. Morgan Kaufmann Publishers, Inc., 1997.

19. J. Pouwelse, K. Langendoen, and H. Sips. Dynamic voltage scaling on a low-power microprocessor. In *Proceedings of the 7th Annual International Conference on Mobile Computing and Networking*, July 2001.

20. T. Sherwood and B. Calder. Time varying behavior of programs. Technical Report UCSD-CS99-630, Department of Computer Science and Engineering, University of California, San Diego, August 1999.

21. D. Shin, J. Kim, and S. Lee. Intra-task voltage scheduling for low-energy hard real-time applications. In *To appear in IEEE Design and Test of Computers*, March 2001.

22. Y. Song and Z. Li. New tiling techniques to improve cache temporal locality. In *Proceedings of the ACM SIGPLAN'99 Conference on Programming Language Design and Implementation (PLDI'99)*, pages 215–228, May 1999.

23. M. Valluri and L. John. Is compiling for performance == compiling for power? In *The 5th Annual Workshop on Interaction between Compilers and Computer Architectures (INTERACT-5)*, January 2001.

# Improving Off-Chip Memory Energy Behavior in a Multi-processor, Multi-bank Environment

Victor De La Luz[1], Mahmut Kandemir[1], and Ugur Sezer[2]

[1] Department of Computer Science and Engineering,
Pennsylvania State University, University Park, PA 16802-6106.
delaluzp@cse.psu.edu, kandemir@cse.psu.edu
[2] Department of Electrical and Computer Engineering,
University of Wisconsin-Madison, Madison, WI 53706-1691.
sezer@ece.wisc.edu

**Abstract.** Many embedded/portable applications from image and video processing domains are characterized by spending a large fraction of their energy in executing load/store instructions that access off-chip memory. Although most performance-oriented locality optimization techniques reduce the number of memory instructions and, consequently, improve memory energy consumption, we also need to consider energy-oriented approaches if we are to improve energy behavior further.
Our focus in this paper is on a system with multiple homogeneous processors and a multi-bank memory architecture that process large arrays of signals. To reduce energy consumption in such a system, we use a compiler-based approach which exploits low-power operating modes. In such an architecture, one of the major problems is to address the conflicting requirements of maximizing parallelism and reducing energy consumption. This conflict arises because maximizing parallelism requires independent concurrent accesses to different memory banks, whereas reducing energy consumption implies limiting the accesses at a given period of time to a small set of memory banks (so that the remaining banks can be placed into a low-power operating mode). Our approach consists of three complementary steps, namely, parallel access pattern detection, array allocation across memory banks, and data layout transformations. Our preliminary results indicate that our approach leads to significant off-chip memory energy savings without sacrificing the available parallelism.

## 1   Introduction

Embedded/portable devices are becoming increasingly popular. These devices are used in a wide spectrum of environments, from PDAs and mobile phones to digital cameras to car navigation systems. We observe three trends in embedded computing world. The first is the clustering of hardware components into smaller and less energy consuming components. An example is the multi-clustered architecture where the register file, issue window, and functional units are distributed across multiple clusters on a chip. Zyuben and Kogge [10] show

H. Dietz (Ed.): LCPC 2001, LNCS 2624, pp. 100–114, 2003.

that such a multi-clustered architecture can be up to twice as energy efficient as wide-issue superscalar processors. The second trend is the support for different low-power operating modes, each consuming a different amount of energy. This provision is available in processors (e.g., the mobile Pentium III has five power management modes [6]), memory (e.g., the RDRAM technology [8] provides up to six power modes), disks [4], and other peripherals. While these energy-saving modes might be very useful during idle periods, one has to pay a cost of exit latency (re-synchronization time) to transition them back to the operational (active) state once the idle period is over. The third trend is the employment of multiple processor cores in a single chip. In particular, many current DSP multi-processors allow multi-processing based on a shared memory architecture. A typical example is the Analog Devices Quad-SHARC, which contains four 32-bit ADSP-21060 DSPs linked via an interconnection network. Considering these three trends, we can conclude that, in the future, optimizing the performance and energy characteristics of multi-processor embedded devices with multiple memory banks using low-power operating modes will be important.

Unfortunately, previous work in the literature does not target the problem of reducing off-chip energy consumption directly or completely. Except for a few studies (e.g., [5,3]), many approaches rely on the observation that performance-oriented program optimizations are also beneficial from an energy perspective. While this holds true in many cases, it is also important to investigate energy-oriented optimizations that further increase energy savings without causing a negative impact on execution time.

This paper is a step in this direction. Our focus is on a system with multiple homogeneous processors and a multi-bank memory architecture that processes large arrays of signals. To reduce energy consumption in such a system, we use a *compiler-based approach* which exploits the low-power operating modes available. In such an architecture, one of the major problems is to address the conflicting requirements of maximizing parallelism and reducing energy consumption. This conflict arises because maximizing parallelism requires independent concurrent accesses to different memory banks, whereas reducing energy consumption implies limiting the accesses at a given period of time to a small set of memory banks (so that the remaining banks can be placed into a low-power operating mode).

The rest of this paper is organized as follows. Section 2 revises the concepts of multi-bank memory system and low-power operating modes. Section 3 discusses the conflicting goals of obtaining maximum parallelism and reducing energy consumption in a multi-bank off-chip memory system. Section 4 presents our approach which consists of parallel access pattern detection, array allocation across memory banks, and data layout transformations. Section 5 introduces the benchmarks used in this study, gives our experimental methodology, and presents experimental data showing the usefulness of our approach. Finally, Section 6 summarizes our major conclusions.

## 2    Multi-bank Memory System

The target memory system for this work is a memory architecture that consists of a number of memory modules organized into banks (rows) and columns as shown in Figure 1. Accessing a data in such an architecture would require activating the corresponding modules. There are several ways of saving power in such a memory organization. The approach adopted in this paper is to put the unused memory banks into low-power operating modes.

In all our experiments, we use one module in a bank; consequently, the terms 'bank' and 'module' are used interchangeably. Each bank operates independently, and when not in active use, it can be placed into a *low-power operating mode* to conserve energy. Each low-power operating mode works by activating only specific parts of the memory circuitry such as column decoders, row decoders, clock synchronization circuitry and refresh circuitry (instead of all parts of the circuit) [7], and can be characterized using two metrics: *per access energy consumption* and *re-synchronization time (re-activation cost)*. The re-synchronization time is the time (in cycles) it takes to bring back a bank from a low-power mode to the active (i.e., fully-operational) mode. Typically, lesser the per access energy consumption, higher the re-synchronization time. Consequently, the selection of low-power operating mode has both energy and performance impacts, and usually involves a trade-off between them [3,5].

For the purposes of this paper, we assume five operating modes: an *active* mode (the only mode during which the memory read or write activity can occur) and three low-power modes, namely, *standby, nap,* and *power-down.* Current DRAMs [8] support up to six energy modes of operation with a few of them supporting only two modes. We collapse the read, write, and active without read or write modes into a single mode (called active mode) in our experimentation. However, one may choose to vary the number of modes based on the target DRAM. The energy consumptions and re-synchronization times for these operating modes are given in Figure 2. The energy values shown in this figure have been obtained from the measured current values associated with memory modules documented in memory data sheets (for a 3.3 V, 2.5 nanoseconds cycle time, 8 MB memory) [7]. The re-synchronization times are also obtained from data sheets. These are the values used in our experiments. Based on trends gleaned from data sheets, the energy values are increased by 30% when module size is doubled, and by 50% when the number of ports is doubled.

A bank can be placed into a low-power mode using a hardware-based, software-based, or a hybrid approach [3,5]. In this work, we adopt a hardware-based scheme. Typically, several of the DRAM modules are controlled by a memory controller which interfaces with the memory bus. The interface is used not only for latching the data and addresses, but is also used to control the configuration and operation of the individual modules as well as their operating modes. The controller also contains some *prediction hardware* to estimate the time until the next access to a memory module (called bank inter-access time) and circuitry to ask the memory controller to initiate mode transitions. A limited amount of such self-monitored power-down is already present in current memory con-

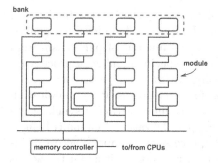

**Fig. 1.** Multi-bank memory architecture.

| | Energy Consumption (nJ) | Re-synchro-nization Time (cycles) |
|---|---|---|
| Active | 3.570 | 0 |
| Standby | 0.830 | 2 |
| Nap | 0.320 | 30 |
| Power-Down | 0.005 | 9,000 |

**Fig. 2.** Energy consumption and re-synchronization times for different operating modes.

trollers (e.g., Intel 82443BX and Intel 820 Chip Set). In this paper, we employ a predictor, called *constant threshold predictor* (or CTP), details of which can be found elsewhere [3]. This mechanism is similar to the mechanisms used in current memory controllers. After 10 cycles of idleness, the corresponding module is put in standby mode. Subsequently, if the module is not referenced for another 100 cycles, it is transitioned into the napping mode. Finally, if the module is not referenced for a further 1,000,000 cycles, it is put into power-down mode. We do not utilize the disabled state that shuts off the refresh circuitry to avoid loss of data in the memory modules. Whenever the module is referenced, it is brought back into the active mode incurring the corresponding re-synchronization costs (based on what mode it was in).

Each memory bank is assumed to have a specific number of read/write ports. If the number of processors that want to simultaneously access a given memory bank is larger than the number of ports available, one or more processors are delayed (that is, the accesses are sequentialized). This delay along with the re-synchronization costs should be taken into account in evaluating an array allocation strategy across memory banks.

## 3   Conflicting Goals

In this article, we focus on compiler-directed allocation of array data across a multi-bank memory system which is shared by a number of parallel processors. In this respect, this work is complementary to studies in [5,3] that focus on a single processor system. We have developed a compiler algorithm that takes a parallelized code as input and generates as output a mapping of array elements into memory banks. The input code might be a code explicitly parallelized by programmer (e.g., by using directives/annotations), or it might be an intermediate code obtained through a previous automatic parallelization step.

The objective of our array allocation mechanism is two-fold: *reducing memory energy consumption* and *not restricting available parallelism*. Reducing memory energy can be achieved by restricting the accesses to a small number of banks in a given time frame. The remaining banks (that is, the unused banks) can then be placed into a low-power operating mode. Existing loop-level parallelization strategies in general try to extract maximum amount of parallelism from a given nested loop. A parallelized code (using a specific number of processors) has an inherent degree of parallelism; ideally, we want all processors to execute in parallel without frequently waiting for inter-processor communication or synchronization. These issues, inter-processor communication or synchronization, are, in general, taken into account during parallelization. In a multi-banked shared memory system, however, if multiple processors attempt to access a single bank, this can result in one (or more) of the processors waiting for the access to be granted depending on the number of ports available for servicing memory requests. Therefore, maximizing parallelism demands spreading data accesses originating from different processors across the address space. Obviously, this implies an increase in the number of active banks for a given time.

The preceding discussion indicates that these two objectives, namely, reducing memory energy consumption and not restricting parallelism do conflict; the degree of this conflict depends on a number of factors such as the array allocation strategy, the number and types of available low-power operating modes, and the sizes and number of ports of the banks. Consider a scenario where four processors access an array stored in a four-bank shared memory. Each bank is assumed to have two ports (that is, it can service two memory requests, each from a different processor, concurrently). If the array in question is stored across four banks, the corresponding bank access pattern exhibits maximum parallelism as shown in Figure 3(a). However, this access pattern may not be very desirable from an energy perspective as all banks are active all the time. Figure 3(b) shows the other extreme where the entire array is stored in a single bank (provided that the bank is large enough) and all processors access the same bank. Since the bank has only two ports, this access pattern, although might be beneficial from energy perspective, will force two of the processors experience delays in accessing data. Figure 3(c) represents an ideal access pattern for this example. The array is stored in two banks, and each bank is shared by two processors. Therefore, each processor can access its data without any delay (maximum parallelism); in addition, two of the banks (bank 1 and bank 3) can be put in a low-power operating mode to save energy. It should be noted that this is not the only possible ideal bank access pattern in this example. An alternative bank access pattern is depicted in Figure 3(d). This example clearly illustrates that array placement has both energy and performance (parallelism) consequences; therefore, a placement strategy needs to consider both the factors.

## 4    Our Approach

Our data allocation strategy tries to achieve its objectives using a three-step approach:

- *Detecting Parallel Access Pattern:* This step detects a dominant parallel access pattern for each array manipulated by the application. This access

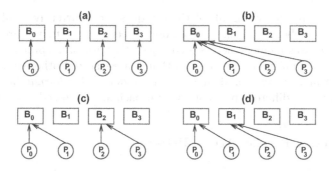

**Fig. 3.** Different bank access patterns for a four-processor ($P_0$, $P_1$, $P_2$, and $P_3$), four-bank ($B_0$, $B_1$, $B_2$, and $B_3$) case.

pattern is independent from the bank architecture available in the system, and is derived from the parallelization information available to our strategy.

– *Determining Array Allocation:* This step decides what portions of the arrays manipulated by the code should go to which memory banks. The parallel access pattern found in the previous step and the sizes and the number of memory banks as well as the number of ports per bank are taken into account in this step. It should be noted that the sections of different arrays can have an entirely different distribution styles (i.e., mappings). For instance, a given array might be distributed across memory banks in a row-major fashion (row-wise) whereas some other array might be distributed column-wise.

– *Transforming Data Layouts:* A given array allocation can result in complexities in addressing. For example, if different portions of a given array are mapped to different banks and each of these sections interleaves with sections of other arrays (on the same bank), this might present difficulties in addressing array elements (during code generation) that are not consecutive in physical address space. To address this issue, our approach uses a data space transformation technique, whose purpose is to make (for each array variable) the elements that are accessed by a processor consecutive in memory. The practical effect of this transformation is that the array elements are re-numbered such that the elements in a given section (mapped to a bank) have consecutive addresses.

Before going into details of these steps, let us discuss the assumptions we make. First, we assume that there is no virtual memory (VM) support; that is, the compiler is in full control of the physical address space. Note that there exist many embedded systems without any VM support. Second, we consider port restrictions by only taking into account the parallel accesses originating from *multiple (different) processors*. Depending on the code being optimized, each processor might need to access multiple array elements simultaneously. If this is the case and there is not sufficient bandwidth, we assume that these accesses (coming from a single processor) are sequentialized. Since a processor might need to access a large number of array elements (e.g., to execute an iteration of an inner loop), satisfying all of these requests concurrently would demand an excessive number of ports. Instead, our objective is to make sure that each processor executes memory accesses concurrently with other processors. Third, for the sake of uniformity, we assume that, unless stated otherwise, all multi-dimensional arrays are stored in memory in *row-major format* (as in C and C++). Below the different parts of our approach are discussed in detail.

## 4.1   Detecting Parallel Access Pattern

A parallel access pattern corresponds to the fashion that a given data set (e.g., a multi-dimensional array) is accessed by multiple processors. It should be noted that this access might be either for read or write. To represent a given access pattern in a concise manner, we simply indicate how each dimension of the array is decomposed (divided, distributed) between processors. For instance, if we have four processors, there are a number of ways these processors might access the elements of a given, say, two-dimensional array. One approach might be such that each processor accesses a group of consecutive columns from the array. We refer to this access pattern as *column-wise* (or *column-major*) access pattern, indicating that the second dimension (the column dimension) is decomposed across (four) processors, whereas the first dimension (the row dimension) is not decomposed. If, instead, each processor accesses a group of consecutive rows, we call the resulting access pattern *row-wise* (or *row-major*). Alternatively, the processors might be organized by a two-by-two array, with each processor accessing a sub-array of the said array; this access pattern can be termed as *blocked* access pattern.

A parallel access pattern is a direct result of the loop parallelization strategy adopted (e.g., [2]). Specifically, each array reference in the program code generates an access pattern that can be determined by considering the number of processors and the parallelization strategy. For example, an array reference such as a[i][j] to an array a in a two-level nested loop consisting of loops i (outer) and j (inner) causes row-wise access pattern if only the loop i is parallelized. Similarly, the same reference corresponds to column-wise and blocked access patterns if only the loop j is parallelized and if both the loops are parallelized, respectively. A problem occurs when different references exhibit different access patterns for the *same* array. In this case, since it is not practical to have multiple distributions of a given array across banks, the compiler needs to determine a *dominant parallel access pattern* — the access pattern that occurs most frequently. Our current approach to this problem is based on profile information. In this work, we assume that the compiler will determine a single dominant access pattern for each array in a given application. Note that when the array is stored in the banked memory system using the dominant parallel access pattern (as explained below), other references (non-dominant ones) might exhibit suboptimal bank access patterns. That is, a large number of banks may need to be activated when those references are touched by multiple processors. However, if the dominant reference (hence the dominant access pattern) is determined carefully, the impact of these sub-optimal accesses on the overall energy behavior of the memory system will be minimal.

## 4.2   Determining Array Allocation

Once parallel access patterns have been determined, the next step is the allocation of arrays into memory banks. Let us first focus on a single array case where multiple processors operate on a single shared array in parallel. In performing array allocation, we observe the following rule:

> *"Array portions that belong to different processors are stored in the same bank if doing so does not restrict available parallelism and does not exceed the bank capacity."*

According to this rule, there may be two reasons to prevent a given portion of an array from being stored in a given bank: either the bank capacity is exceeded, or the bank does not have sufficient number of ports to satisfy concurrent requests from different processors (this, in turn, restricts parallel accesses). Let us consider the following nested loop:

```
pfor(i=0;i<N;i++)
  for(j=0;j<N;j++)
    ... a[i][j] ...
```

In this fragment, `pfor` represents a parallel `for` loop. Therefore, in this example, the outer loop is parallelized whereas the inner loop is run sequentially by each processor. Assuming four processors, Figure 4 shows different allocations of array portions ($a_0$, $a_1$, $a_2$, and $a_3$, each for a given processor) across banks of four-bank and two-bank memory systems. An array portion accessed by a processor is called a *slab* in the rest of this paper. Let us first focus on the 4-bank case. If each bank has only a single port, then co-locating any two slabs in a single bank will sequentialize accesses. Therefore, each slab should be stored in its own bank. If each bank has two ports, however, two slabs can share a bank *without* restricting available parallelism. The remaining two banks can then be placed into a low-power operating mode. Note that, in this case, using more than two banks increases energy consumption without any performance benefits. Similarly, if we have four ports per bank, all slabs can be co-located in a single bank. All these allocations assume that the banks in each case have sufficient capacities. In Figure 4, the sixth column (marked 'Delay') gives the *delay factor* of the array allocation. We define delay factor as the maximum number of steps a processor needs to wait (due to port conflict) before accessing the memory bank. For instance, if we have two ports (per bank) and allocate all four slabs in the same bank, a processor may have to wait for one step (for the first two processors to complete their accesses) to start accessing the bank (assuming a four-processor setting). The last column (marked '# of Lows') in the figure, on the other hand, gives the number of idle banks that can be placed into low-power modes. Ideally, for a given port size, the compiler should select an allocation with a zero delay factor (not to sacrifice any parallelism) and maximum number of idle banks (to optimize energy consumption). If a zero delay factor is not possible, our compiler considers the allocation with the minimum delay factor, and among them, selects the one with the maximum number of idle banks. In Figure 4, for each port size, the preferable array allocation is marked using the symbol '*' next to the number of ports in the first column.

Now let us concentrate on the case with two banks. The lower portion of Figure 4 shows the array allocation alternatives when we have a two-bank system. If we have one port per bank, any allocation of slabs will lead to a conflict; so, in this case, we cannot obtain a delay factor of zero. If each bank has two ports, on the other hand, we can avoid any delay by fully utilizing both the banks. Finally, in case of four-port banks, we can cluster all slabs in a single bank; that other bank can be put in a low-power mode.

| 4-Bank Memory System | | | | | | |
|---|---|---|---|---|---|---|
| # of Ports | Bank 0 | Bank1 | Bank 2 | bank3 | Delay | # of Lows |
| 1* | $a_0$ | $a_1$ | $a_2$ | $a_3$ | 0 | 0 |
| 1 | $a_0\ a_1$ | $a_2\ a_3$ | - | - | 1 | 2 |
| 1 | $a_0\ a_1\ a_2\ a_3$ | - | - | - | 3 | 3 |
| 2 | $a_0$ | $a_1$ | $a_2$ | $a_3$ | 0 | 0 |
| 2* | $a_0\ a_1$ | $a_2\ a_3$ | - | - | 0 | 2 |
| 2 | $a_0\ a_1\ a_2\ a_3$ | - | - | - | 1 | 3 |
| 4 | $a_0$ | $a_1$ | $a_2$ | $a_3$ | 0 | 0 |
| 4 | $a_0\ a_1$ | $a_2\ a_3$ | - | - | 0 | 2 |
| 4* | $a_0\ a_1\ a_2\ a_3$ | - | - | - | 0 | 3 |

| 2-Bank Memory System | | | |
|---|---|---|---|
| # of Ports | Bank 0 | Bank1 | Delay | # of Lows |
| 1* | $a_0\ a_1$ | $a_2\ a_3$ | 1 | 0 |
| 1 | $a_0\ a_1\ a_2\ a_3$ | - | 3 | 1 |
| 2* | $a_0\ a_1$ | $a_2\ a_3$ | 0 | 0 |
| 2 | $a_0\ a_1\ a_2\ a_3$ | - | 1 | 1 |
| 4 | $a_0\ a_1$ | $a_2\ a_3$ | 0 | 0 |
| 4* | $a_0\ a_1\ a_2\ a_3$ | - | 0 | 1 |

**Fig. 4.** Different array allocations with four and two memory banks.

We now focus on the case where multiple arrays might be accessed in parallel. While there might be different strategies to adopt for handling this case, our current approach considers the slabs (of different arrays) that are required by the same processor, and tries to cluster them in the minimum number of banks. Specifically, we adhere to the following rule:

*"Slabs (of different arrays) that are used by the same processor in a given nested loop are stored in the same bank subject to the bank capacity constraint."*

An alternate strategy would be to store these slabs in different banks. However, since they are required by the same processor during the same computation, this would most probably lead to the activation of multiple banks, thereby increasing the energy consumption in memory. By storing the related slabs in the same bank, we (i) localize the accesses from a given processor, and (ii) enable the processor to bring elements of multiple slabs at the same time (from the same bank) if there exists enough bandwidth. Figure 5 illustrates a scenario in which four processors manipulate three two-dimensional arrays using different parallel access patterns. We assume that $a_i$, $b_i$, and $c_i$ denote the slabs that belong to the $i$th processor. Note that this strategy (as the one in the single array case) tries to eliminate the inter-processor conflicts in accessing memory banks as much as possible. Note also that in this scenario, if there are more than four banks in the system, all but these four can be placed in a low-power operating mode, thereby saving energy.

### 4.3   Transforming Data Layouts

While determining the most suitable array allocation is crucial, it is of little value without accompanying data transformations. This is because, depending on the type of the array distribution, the elements that map to a slab might not be consecutive in memory. A consequence of this is that addressing these elements (in the slab) may not be trivial. To illustrate the problem, we consider a given (row-major) array distributed column-wise across four memory banks. For each slab, the elements in each sub-row are consecutive in memory whereas there is a large gap between the last element of a given sub-row and the first element of the following sub-row.

In this case, we have two options. First, we can store each slab (as it is) in the corresponding bank As mentioned above, the problem with this approach is that due to non-consecutiveness of majority of the elements in the slab, addressing these elements will be a problem. Second, instead of adopting a slab-based allocation (which is a direct result of the parallelization strategy), we simply perform a default (row-wise) allocation (independent of the parallelization strategy), and let each processor to access its slab. This strategy would, unfortunately, lead to activation of multiple banks as the elements in a given slab could span (in general) a number of banks.

To address this problem, we propose to employ data (layout) transformations. Informally, a data layout transformation takes an array layout and converts it to another form. Each processor can then access the elements belonging to its slab from a single bank. In addition, the elements in a given slab are consecutive; that is, they can be addressed easily. Our current data transformation model is similar to that proposed by [2], but also handles non-rectilinear data decompositions. The basic idea is to restructure the array so that all the data accessed by the same processor are contiguous in the address space. The data transformations that we use are analogous to the well-known loop transformations. The details are omitted due to lack of space.

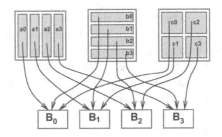

**Fig. 5.** Bank allocation of multiple arrays.

## 5   Experiments

This section investigates the impact of our approach on both energy and performance using several benchmarks and bank configurations.

### 5.1   Benchmarks and Default Configuration

The programs used in this study include a two-dimensional FFT routine (`fft`), an array-based code from the Specfp benchmarks (`tomcatv`), a digital filtering routine (`flt`), an ADI computation routine that uses only two-dimensional arrays (`adi`), and an array-dominated code from the Perfect Club benchmarks (`eflux`). These benchmark codes were parallelized using the SGI MIPSpro compiler's automatic parallelization option. The input sizes used are 26.3MB, 28.8MB, 29.0MB, 27.1MB, and 25.2MB for `fft`, `tomcatv`, `flt`, `adi`, and `eflux`, respectively. These input sizes are selected to make sure that the aggregate array size for each code is close to 32MB, which is the total (aggregate) capacity of our banked memory system. The default system consists of 8 banks, each is 4MB and has two ports, and 8 processors. Since our main objective is to evaluate our array allocation strategy under a given parallelization, we consider a cacheless system to isolate the impact of parallelization and array allocation.

### 5.2   Code Versions

For each benchmark code, we performed experiments with three different versions (under the same parallelization strategy):

- p-P   This is a pure parallelism-oriented version which does not take into account energy consumption. It tries to prevent port conflicts as much as possible by spreading the slabs across available banks.
- p-E   This is a pure energy-oriented version. It clusters the arrays with temporal affinity to the highest extent possible. Obviously, in general, this strategy might result in excessive port conflicts.
- EP   This is the strategy discussed in this paper. As explained earlier, it tries to eliminate all port conflicts; but, at the same time, it tries to limit the number of active banks.

All these three versions has been implemented within the SUIF compilation framework [1]. Our current implementation takes as input a parallelized code from the SGI's MIPSpro compiler. For the p-P version, it distributes the slabs in such a way that no port conflict occurs. For the p-E version, on the other hand, it clusters the array elements in minimum set of banks as discussed in [3]. The EP version leads to an increase in compilation time by 2.3%, 4.7%, 2.8%, 3.0%, and 4.1% for fft, tomcatv, flt, adi, and eflux, respectively, as compared to an unoptimized code. What this means is that the increase in compilation time is less than 5 percent. After obtaining different versions for each code, they are input to a custom simulator [3] which simulates a banked memory architecture.

Unless otherwise stated, the figures reported in this paper are energy and time (spent in memory accesses) results *normalized* with respect to a *sequential array allocation scheme* (under the same parallelization strategy). The sequential scheme stores arrays (in their declaration order in the code) one after another starting from the first available location of the first bank. Arrays are normally stored without leaving a gap between them unless only a few elements of a given array are left in the previous bank (in our experiments this number is 10). In other words, to minimize false sharing of banks, the arrays are aligned along the memory bank boundaries whenever necessary. For all benchmark codes and all versions, the same set of operating modes (explained in Section 2) are used. Therefore, the difference between energy consumptions and that between memory times of different versions are due to array allocation.

### 5.3 Impact on Energy Consumption and Time

We first present in Figure 6 the (normalized) energy consumptions for all three versions. We observe that in three out of five codes, p-P increases energy consumption. In other two codes, it slightly reduces the energy consumption (as the modifications in access pattern enabled the selection of more aggressive power modes). We also see that the p-E version saves 11.58% more energy than EP. The average energy savings for p-E and EP are 79.06% and 67.48%, respectively. The memory time trends depicted in Figure 7! are, however, entirely different. The p-E version increases the time spent in memory for all benchmarks tested. As the EP version never sacrifices parallelism, its memory access time is the same as the p-P version. The average difference between EP and p-E is 44.22%. When we consider Figures 6 and 7 together, we see that EP strikes a balance between energy and performance. Note that all memory access times reported in this section also include overheads due to our prediction hardware.

### 5.4 Sensitivity to the Number of Ports

The next set of experiments study the impact of the port size on energy consumption and time. We focus on two benchmark codes, fft and tomcatv, as other codes exhibit similar behavior. We performed experiments with (*per bank*) port sizes of 1, 2, 3, 4, and 5. We observe from the results given in Figure 8 that increasing the number of ports, in general, reduces the energy consumption

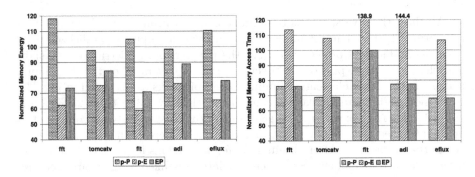

**Fig. 6.** Normalized memory energy consumptions.

**Fig. 7.** Normalized memory access times.

up to a port size beyond which the energy consumption starts to increase as the irregularity (due to excessive number of requests) in bank access pattern prevents suitable power mode selection. Figure 9 illustrates the memory time variations due to port size. We observe that (for a given version), beyond a port size, increasing the port size does not bring any performance benefit. This is because there is an inherent degree of parallelism for any given benchmark; once this degree has been reached, further increasing resources does not help much.

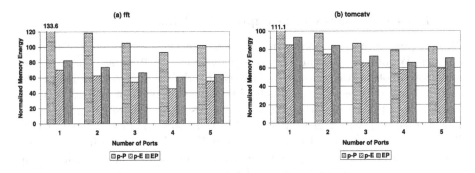

**Fig. 8.** Impact of the number of ports on energy consumption.

## 5.5    Sensitivity to the Number of Processors

Figures 10 and 11 give, respectively, energy consumptions and memory access times for the fft and tomcatv benchmarks when the number of processors is varied. In all these experiments, the port size per bank is fixed at two. It can be observed from Figure 10 that increasing the number of processors leads to an increase in the energy consumption of p-P as more processors demand a larger number of active banks as a given time. The EP and p-E versions, on the other

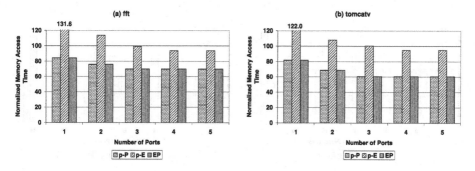

**Fig. 9.** Impact of the number of ports on performance.

hand, exhibit a consistent energy behavior when the number of processors are varied. The trends observed in Figure 11 indicate that, for the p-E version, the time in spent in memory increases with the increased number of processors. For example, when the number of processors is increased from two to thirty two, there is nearly a 23% increase in memory access time.

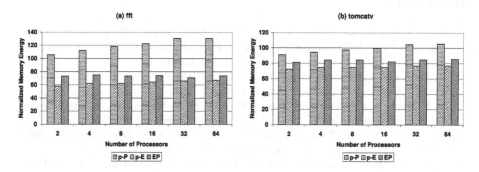

**Fig. 10.** Impact of the number of processors on energy consumption.

## 6   Conclusions

The increasing prevalence of portable computing has promoted energy efficiency to a first-class parameter in system design. While architectural techniques such as partitioned memories and low-power operating modes can help reduce energy consumption, compiler-based optimizations might lead to further energy savings. This paper has proposed a compiler-based approach for optimizing memory energy consumption in a multi-processor system with a multi-bank memory architecture using low-power operation modes. Our approach first detects the prevalent parallel access pattern for each array, and then allocates arrays in memory banks taking into account the access pattern and port restrictions. It

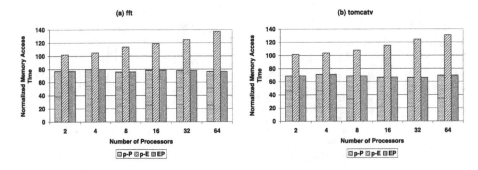

**Fig. 11.** Impact of the number of processors on performance.

then uses a data layout transformation technique to make sure that the array elements accessed by each processor are consecutive in the shared address space. Our preliminary results show that our approach is able to reduce memory energy and, at the same time, maintain a decent degree of parallelism.

# References

1. S. P. Amarasinghe, J. M. Anderson, M. S. Lam, and C. W. Tseng The SUIF compiler for scalable parallel machines. In Proc.*the Seventh SIAM Conference on Parallel Processing for Scientific Computing,* February, 1995.
2. J. Anderson. *Automatic Computation and Data Decomposition for Multiprocessors.* Ph.D. dissertation, Stanford University, March 1997.
3. V. Delaluz, M. Kandemir, N. Vijaykrishnan, A. Sivasubramaniam, and M. J. Irwin. DRAM energy management using software and hardware directed power mode control. In Proc. *the 7th International Conference on High Performance Computer Architecture,* Monterrey, Mexico, January 2001.
4. F. Douglas, P. Krishnan, and B. Marsh. Thwarting the power-hungry disk. In Proc. *Winter Usenix,* 1994.
5. A. R. Lebeck, X. Fan, H. Zeng, and C. S. Ellis. Power aware page allocation. In *Proc. Ninth International Conference on Architectural Support for Programming Languages and Operating Systems,* November 2000.
6. Pentium III Processor Mobile Module MMC-2, Data-sheet 243356–001, Intel Corporation.
7. Rambus Inc. http://www.rambus.com/.
8. 128/144-MBit Direct RDRAM Data Sheet, Rambus Inc., May 1999.
9. N. Vijaykrishnan, M. Kandemir, M. J. Irwin, H. Y. Kim, and W. Ye. Energy-driven integrated hardware-software optimizations using SimplePower. In Proc. *the International Symposium on Computer Architecture,* June 2000.
10. V. Zyuban and P. Kogge. Split register file architectures for inherently lower power microprocessors. In Proc. *Power-Driven Micro-architecture Workshop,* in conjunction with *ISCA'98,* pages 32–37, 1998.

# A Compilation Framework for Power and Energy Management on Mobile Computers*

Ulrich Kremer[1], Jamey Hicks[2], and James Rehg[2]

[1] Department of Computer Science
Rutgers University
Piscataway, New Jersey, USA
{uli}@cs.rutgers.edu
[2] Compaq Computer Corporation
Cambridge Research Lab
Cambridge, Massachusetts, USA
{hicks,rehg}@crl.dec.com

**Abstract.** Power and energy management is crucial for mobile devices that rely on battery power. In addition to voice recognition, image understanding is an important class of applications for mobile environments. We propose a new compilation strategy for remote task mapping, and report experimental results for a face detection and recognition system.

Our compilation strategy generates two versions of the input program, one to be executed on the mobile device (client), and the other on a machine connected to the mobile device via a wireless network (server). Compiler supported checkpointing is used to allow the client to monitor program progress on the server, and to request checkpoint data in case of anticipated server and/or network failure. The reported results have been obtained by actual power measurements, not simulation. Experiments show energy savings of up to one order of magnitude on the mobile machine. A prototype implementation of the discussed compilation framework is underway, and preliminary results are reported.

## 1 Introduction

Power dissipation has become one of the crucial design challenges of current and future computer systems. In a mobile environment, power savings are important to prolong battery life. For a desk-top "wall-powered" system, heat emission has become a severe design limitation with respect to transistor densities and clock frequencies. Power and energy management addresses both of these issues. However, in the context of this paper, prolonging battery life is the main objective[1].

Mobile devices come in many flavors, including laptop computers, webphones, pocket computers, Personal Digital Assistance (PDAs), and intelligent sensors. Many

---

* This research was partially conducted while the first author was a visiting researcher at Compaq's Cambridge Research Lab (CRL). Additional funding has been provided by NSF CAREER award No. 9985050.

[1] In this paper, we consider a reduction in power and energy as the same optimization goal. This is a simplifying assumption, and not true in general.

H. Dietz (Ed.): LCPC 2001, LNCS 2624, pp. 115–131, 2003.

such devices already have wireless communication capabilities, and we expect most future systems to have such capabilities. There are two main differences between mobile and desk-top computing systems, namely the source of the power supply and the amount of available resources. Mobile systems operate entirely on battery power most or all the time. The resources available on a mobile system can be expected to be at least one order of magnitude less than those of a "wall-powered" desk-top system with similar technology. This fact is mostly due to space, weight, and power limitations placed on mobile platforms. Such resources include the amount and speed of the processor, memory, secondary storage, and I/O. With the development of new and even more power-hungry technology, we expect this gap to widen even more.

Image processing and image understanding will be one of the key applications for low-power mobile devices, in addition to speech recognition. Image processing can be used in autonomous robot navigation, target acquisition/classification, keyboard-less input, and aerial surveillance (Micro Air Vehicles), just to mention a few. Low power single-chip imagers, such as the Photobit PB-0100, are becoming available that will allow mobile devices to capture high-quality images. Image processing can be used in the context of robot control and navigation, wide-scale video surveillance, guidance systems for blind people to identify and classify objects, keyboard-less human-computer interfaces, and Micro Air Vehicles (MAVs) to support aerial surveillance, target acquisition and target classification. Face detection and recognition in video images is a key technology for several of these applications.

The compilation approach for power and energy management discussed in this paper is complementary to operating systems and hardware techniques. The latter techniques rely on observed past program behavior and resource requirements to predict future program characteristics. A compile-time whole program analysis is often able to determine future behavior and requirements since the entire program is available to the compiler and not just a limited window of recent events. In addition, a compiler may perform high-level transformations and thereby "reshape", i.e., change program behavior and resource requirements, allowing further program optimizations. In cases where compile-time information is not available to perform a particular optimization task, the compiler may generate code that will make optimization decisions at run time based on run-time values of compile-time determined variables and conditions.

In this paper, we give a first assessment of the potential benefits of compiler-directed remote task mapping as an optimization to save energy on mobile devices. We use the tasks of face detection and recognition, in the context of a TourGuide system for visitors to Compaq's CRL lab, as an experimental vehicle for our investigation. The main challenges in remote task mapping is the identification of suitable remote tasks where the communication overhead is more than compensated for by the expected power savings. We discuss a compilation framework for remote task execution, and give experimental results for a hand-simulated compilation of our face detection and recognition program. The framework addresses the problem of network disconnection. Power measurements are reported for three platforms: a low-power single-board system called Skiff [8], which was developed at CRL, a recently introduced new handheld PC by Compaq (iPAQ H3650), and a PentiumII based laptop computer. Initial results with a

Ulrich Kremer: match distance 192

**Fig. 1.** Example Image and TourGuide 's output.

prototype implementation of the compilation framework indicate the feasibility of our approach.

## 2   Remote Task Mapping

The input to the envisioned compilation system is a program written in C or Java that does not contain any user annotations, for instance, to specify tasks for remote execution. Compiler-directed remote task mapping for power and energy management identifies program tasks that (1) can be safely executed on a remote server, and that (2) will lead to power savings on the mobile client system. The profitability of remote task execution will depend on the amount of communication needed between the mobile client and remote server, the time it takes to complete the remote task, and the communication time itself. The latter two points are of particular importance in mobile systems that have a significant power consumption during the time the system is waiting for the response of the server.

Our proposed power management strategy considers disconnectedness. The system will be able to continue program execution while being disconnected from the server, possibly with a degradation of program performance such as an increase in execution time. This is an important feature for any mission critical program with real-time response requirements. Simply putting the mobile system into a hibernation state until the connection to the server has been reestablished is not acceptable. The goal of power management is to save as much energy as possible while running the program to completion within a set of real-time constraints required by the given application. For example, leaving a robot or a MAV without image processing capabilities for extended periods of time may lead to total system loss.

## 3   TourGuide : A Face Detection and Recognition System

We have developed a prototype application based on face detection and recognition, called TourGuide , which identifies researchers and staff members at Compaq's Cambridge Research Laboratory (CRL). The TourGuide system will consist of a mobile client and a network of embedded servers. The client can be given to visitors to the lab. It allows them to more easily identify and keep track of the members of the laboratory that they encounter during their visit. The system is designed to run on a portable low-power device with wireless communication capabilities that is equipped with a digital camera.

The face detection component of the TourGuide architecture utilizes a neural network-based detector for frontal, upright faces developed at Carnegie Mellon Univ. by Rowley et. al. [17]. The detector uses two networks which were trained to detect faces in windows of $20 \times 20$ and $30 \times 30$ pixels. These networks are scanned across an image pyramid in a coarse-to-fine fashion. The resulting system can detect any number of frontal, upright faces in a single image, regardless of their size or position. Faces which are tilted in the plane of the image or away from the camera will not be detected. However, if the detector is applied to a sequence of video frames taken from an interaction with a person, it is quite likely that there will be several correct detections.

The face recognition module in TourGuide is applied whenever a face is successfully detected. It is based on the ARENA [23, 22] system developed by Sim et. al. from CMU and JustResearch. ARENA uses a nearest neighbor classifier to identify faces by comparing their distance using an L1 norm to labeled example faces (prototypes) taken from a training set. Input faces are correctly identified when they fall within some predefined distance threshold of the correct prototype face. On relatively small populations the ARENA system has generated impressive results using fairly unconstrained input imagery.

An example input image and the resulting output is shown in Figure 1. A $320 \times 320$ central section of the $640 \times 480$ input image is passed through the face detector. If successful, the detected face is first enlarged by 20%, summarized, and then processed by the face recognizer. In the shown example, the recognizer reports a successful match and a confidence level for that match.

The overall code structure of the face detection and recognition system is shown in the appendix. In the envisioned application environment, the system may process several input images before successfully recognizing a person. The entire system has been implemented in C and runs under the Linux operating system. The source code is approx. 6000 lines, including comments. Since the current family of StrongARM processors does not have a floating-point unit, we have developed a fixed-point package for efficient floating-point emulation.

The TourGuide system is an interesting application for our benefit analysis of remote task execution for power management purposes since it exhibits important aspects of mobile applications, including

- *necessary mobility*: The system will be carried by the laboratory visitor who is meeting with researchers inside and outside the laboratory space.
- *potential disconnection*: Some part of the laboratory may not be covered by the wireless communication network. In addition, the communication is interrupted while the visitor is leaving the laboratory space.
- *continuous operation*: Even if the visitor is not within the range of a base station, the system should continue to work, although not at the same performance level as within the range of the network.

Dealing with all or just a subset of these aspects is a challenge, and we believe that compiler support will play a crucial role for effective power management of such applications.

## 4   Compilation Strategy

The basic idea of our compilation strategy is to identify program tasks that are safe to be executed remotely, and that will lead to power savings on the mobile architecture due to remote execution. During remote execution, the mobile machine will enter a hibernation state in order to save as much energy as possible. It is the compiler's responsibility to insert code that will initiate power state transitions on the mobile machine. While waiting for the completion of a remote task, the mobile client and server may get disconnected. If after a predetermined waiting time the remote server has not finished executing the assigned task, the local client will reexecute the task locally.

The proposed compilation strategy is based on a client/server model and consists of several steps. In the first step, program tasks have to be identified that can safely be executed remotely, i.e., on the server. In the second step, the profitability of remote task execution is examined for remote task candidates. In the final step, two versions of application are generated, one that will be executed on the mobile machine, and one on the remote server accessible from the mobile machine via a wireless connection.

Disconnection events are dealt with through a checkpointing mechanism that provides on-demand data exchange at compile-time determined program points. This checkpointing mechanism serves two purposes, namely (1) informing the client about the progress of the remote task on the server, and (2) allowing the client to receive partial results in order to avoid entire task reexecution in the event of a server or network failure. The version of the application running on the remote server can be considered a specialized server for that application.

The compilation strategy assumes that the entire source program is available during compilation. The compiler will classify I/O operations as performed on *replicated* data or *client* data.

Copies of replicated data are stored on the client and the server machines at the time the client and server programs are compiled on the two platforms, i.e., are made available to the client and server as part of the program installation process. Neither replicated data nor program code will need to be communicated during program execution. Client data is acquired by the client, and may lead to communication to the remote server. We will refer to I/O operations such as image acquisition as client I/O. Figure 2(A) shows the task graph of our TourGuide  system, together with its object life ranges. The task graph nodes represent system initialization (SI:1), image acquisition (I/O:2), face detection preprocessing (PFD:3), face detection (FD:4), face recognition preprocessing (PFR:5), face recognition (FR:6), and final answer (I/O:7). Table 1 summarizes the data objects and their life ranges relative to the subtask nodes in the task graph.

A strategy for remote task execution may evaluate the profitability of remote execution for each individual task between a pair of client I/O operations. Our basic strategy is not as general, and is based on the assumption that the network and server is available

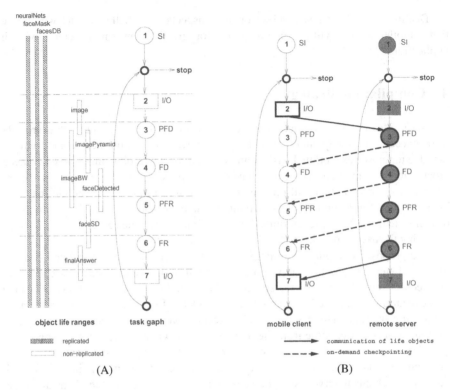

**Fig. 2.** (A): Task graph with object life ranges for the TourGuide system. (B): Client and server task graphs for remote thread **PFD+FD+PFR+FR**. The remote thread has three possible checkpoints.

most of the time. In such a scenario, the client may want to initiate remote execution as early as possible, and once initiated, may want to execute as many tasks as possible remotely, i.e., execute all subsequent tasks remotely until the next client I/O operation is reached. During remote execution, the client may enter a hibernation state. The client may wake up periodically to check the progress on the server, and may request checkpoint data from the server before entering the next hibernation interval. Suitable policies for wake-up and on-demand checkpointing are currently under investigation. For example, a client may request the execution of a checkpoint if the wireless signal strength is below a predefined threshold, indicating a potential disconnection event in the near future. The wake-up and checkpointing policies will be implemented through a runtime library and code generated by the compiler as part of the client and server programs. No communication is necessary between the client and the server once the remote execution has been initiated, except for checkpointing purposes and the final answer computed by the server. The resulting execution model has strong similarities with the concept of program continuations in the sense that once a remote task execution is initiated, it will be able to execute the task to completion without any further commu-

| objects | life range[1] | size in bytes | comments |
|---------|------|---------|----------|
| replicated | | | |
| neuralNets | 2 - 7 | 300K | neural networks |
| faceMask | 2 - 7 | 412 | 20 × 20 pnm image |
| facesDB | 2 - 7 | 2.8M | faces data base of CRL staff members |
| non-replicated | | | |
| image | 3 | 60K | 640 × 480 jpeg image |
| imageBW | 4 - 5 | 310K | 640 × 480 pnm image |
| imagePyramid | 4 | 153K | 10 levels, based on cropped 320 × 320 "imageBW" |
| faceDetected | 5 | 12 | location & size of det. face |
| faceSD | 6 | 269 | 16 × 16 scaled-down image |
| finalAnswer | 7 | 200 | output of recognizer |

[1] life on entry to node(s).

**Table 1.** Data objects and their life ranges for the main routine of the TourGuide system program.

nication. Due to space limitations, a discussion of our checkpointing mechanisms is beyond the scope of this paper.

A *candidate thread* starts with the initial client I/O operation and ends with the final client I/O operation. Once a remote execution has been initiated, the thread will execute all remaining tasks remotely, returning the final answer to the client just before the final I/O operation. The first task executed remotely is called the *remote entry point*. It is important to note that this remote task execution strategy serves as a base-line strategy, and may need to be refined further.

The communication necessary before the initiation of each remote execution corresponds to the set of non-replicated data objects that are life at the remote entry point. A candidate thread is safe if all data object instances that need to be communicated to the remote server are known. For example, an object instance that cannot be uniquely identified at compile time must not be life at a remote entry point. Such a life range will force the compiler to eliminate this particular candidate thread. Compile-time techniques such as *points-to* analysis (e.g.: [3]), *escape analysis* (e.g.: [16], and type analysis will be used to determine *what* objects and *how* objects need to be transmitted between client and server.

For example, Figure 2(B) shows the candidate thread PFD+FD+PFR+FR (entry point 3) of our TourGuide application with its three compile-time determined on-demand checkpoints. The compiler determines the data objects that need to be communicated at a checkpoint in order to resume program execution on the mobile client. The decision whether or not to execute a checkpoint will depend on the selected checkpointing policy and will be evaluated at runtime. The only life object at entry point 3 is image. The object is communicated to the server as part of initiating remote execution.

| mobile client | remote server |
|---|---|
| SA110 (SKIFF) 233 MHz | PentiumII 300 MHz |
| SA110 (SKIFF) 233 MHz | Dual Proc. PentiumIII 450 MHz |
| SA1100 (iPAQ) 206 MHz | Dual Proc. PentiumIII 450 MHz |
| PentiumII 300 MHz | Dual Proc. PentiumIII 450 MHz |

**Table 2.** The target systems for the case study.

The remote server will send object `finalAnswer` to the mobile client once the task `FR` has been successfully executed on the server.

## 5   Benefit Experiments

The TourGuide face detection and recognition system serves as a test case for the discussed compilation strategy. The four target configurations for this study are shown in Table 5. All machines run the Linux operating system and used wireless 802.11b PC cards as their wireless network connection. The experiments focus on the execution time reductions obtained through remote task execution for the different configurations.

In general, most performance oriented transformations will also improve the overall energy consumption of an application [25, 26]. However, Kandemir et al. showed that for loop tiling, the best tile sizes for performance and energy consumption are different, i.e., energy consumption and execution time improvements are different optimization goals [11].

In this paper, we focus on execution time reduction as the main tool to decrease energy consumption on a mobile computer, taking advantage of the significant resource gap between mobile computers and high-performance servers and workstation. In the presence of resource hibernation [24], remote execution is an *enabling* transformation, allowing significant energy savings even in cases where the overall program execution time is increased.

### 5.1   Skiff

Skiff has been designed as a low-power computing appliance and is based on a 233MHz StrongARM processor (SA-110). It has 32MB of SDRAM, 16KB I-cache, 16KB D-cache, 8MB flash memory, one 10Mbps Ethernet port, and two PCMCIA card slots, but no floating point unit. A full system specification is given elsewhere [8]. The system has separate power planes (2V, 3.3V, and 5V) and allows power measurements for individual system components such as the processor, memory subsystem, and controllers. The power measurements were taken using a Tektronix oscilloscope at each of these power

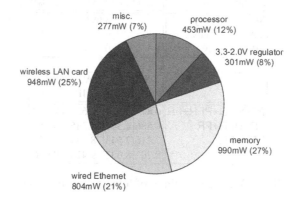

**Fig. 3.** Average power measurements for TourGuide on Skiff.

measurement points. In addition, the power supply reported the overall power consumption of the entire system, allowing power measurements for system components such as the power regulators.

Although Skiff has been designed to serve as a low-power computing appliance and not a mobile device, its system characteristics are similar to other handheld computers such as Compaq's Itsy [5] and Compaq's iPAQ H3600, which are also based on a StrongARM processor (SA-1100). Figure 3 shows the average power dissipation and distribution of Skiff for the four main tasks of TourGuide in a stand-alone mode. The TourGuide system program was compiled using gcc -O3 and then executed and measured for several input images. For the Skiff experiments, we used Compaq's WL100 11 Mbps wireless PC card. Overall, Skiff dissipates 3.77W with the wireless PC card, and 2.82W without such a card. Note that even though the wired Ethernet connection is not "in use", the Ethernet controller consumes significant power. The same holds for the wireless LAN card.

## 5.2 iPAQ Handheld and PentiumII Laptop

We were only able to take overall power measurements for these two systems. Compaq's iPAQ H3600 has a 206MHz Intel StrongARM SA-1100 processor. Since the basic unit does not have a PCMCIA slot, we used a PCMCIA expansion pack for the wireless PC card. For the image processing application, the iPAQ dissipates on average 2.20W with a wireless Orinoco (Lucent WaveLan) 11 Mbps card, and 1.25W without the card. Throughout the experiments, the back light of the color display was disabled.

The 300MHz PentiumII based laptop dissipates 19W on average without the display. Here, we used Compaq's WL100 11 Mbps PC card as the wireless network connection.

| candidate thread | execution time (in seconds) |
|---|---|
| Skiff local only | 8.691 |
| iPAQ local only | 9.510 |
| PII local only | 0.708 |

| | Skiff & | | iPAQ & | PII & |
|---|---|---|---|---|
| | PII | PIII | PIII | PIII |
| PFD+FD+PFR+FR | 0.877 | 0.624 | 0.620 | 0.469 |
| FD+PFR+FR | 4.586 | 4.347 | 4.345 | 0.655 |
| PFR+FR | 7.716 | 7.543 | 8.089 | 0.655 |
| FR | 8.702 | 8.632 | 9.425 | 0.626 |

**Table 3.** Execution times of four candidate threads.

### 5.3    Initial Benefit Analysis

In the initial experiment, we measured the execution times of the basic tasks in the task graph and the cost of communicating non-replicated life objects at each of the four remote entry points. The communication was performed by reading (receiving) and writing (sending) the life data objects to and from files residing on the remote host. In other words, communication was done through the network file system (NFS). The reported results are based on four input pictures. Three measurements were performed for each picture, and the reported numbers are the medians over all runs and images. Timings are wall clock times in seconds.

Mainly due to the fact that the StrongARM (Skiff and iPAQ) does not have a floating point unit, floating point intensive computations such as in PFD and FD are executed on the order of $35\times$ faster on the dual processor PentiumIII system than on Skiff. For this case study, all four possible candidate threads, namely PFD+FD+PFR+FR (entry point 3) , FD+PFR+FR (entry point 4), PFR+FR (entry point 5), and FR (entry point 6) are safe. Table 3 shows the expected overall execution times for the different candidate threads and target systems. The figures were computed as the sum of execution times for tasks and communications performed on the client and host. Communicating a data object involves writing the object into a file on the sender side, and reading it out of the file on the receiver side. The reported figures exclude system initialization times (SI), and the time needed to acquire the input jpeg image.

Execution time reductions correspond to the expected energy savings if the mobile client does not support hibernation states for its components. The wireless PC cards lead to additional power dissipation of approximately 950mW as shown in Figure 3. A Skiff board without the wireless LAN card dissipates 2.82W. Figure 4 shows the expected energy consumption for Skiff given the additional power costs of the wireless connection. The stand-alone version does not initiate any remote execution and does not use the wireless PC card, i.e., the PC card is not inserted into one of Skiff's PCMCIA slots and therefore does not consume any power.

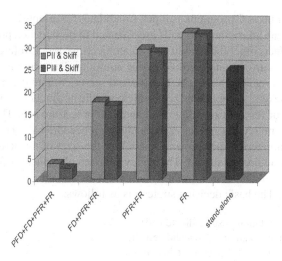

**Fig. 4.** Expected energy consumption on Skiff in Joules for the four remote candidate threads of the TourGuide system and two server target architectures. Reported figures are based on candidate threads execution times and Skiff's average power dissipation (3.77W with wireless LAN card, 2.82W without).

For the iPAQ, the power dissipation difference is even more significant, namely 2.20W with, and 1.25W without the card, i.e., over 40% of the overall power budget are due to the wireless connection.

For the PentiumII laptop, the additional power consumption of the wireless card is not significant (5% increase). For all target systems, we did not observe a significant difference in power consumption due to program initiated communication over the wireless Ethernet connection, i.e., the costs for sending and receiving were comparable.

The results show speedups of up to 13.9x with resulting energy savings of up to 10x on Skiff, and speedups of up to 15.3x with resulting energy savings of up to 8.6x on the iPAQ. However, the energy consumption can be significantly larger for some candidate threads as compared to the version of the code that is executed only on the mobile client due to the additional energy consumed by the plugged-in wireless LAN card. On the laptop, energy savings on the order of 30% are possible. In contrast to Skiff and iPAQ, all candidate threads lead to energy savings. The reported figures do not consider power savings due to transitions into low-power hibernation states on the mobile client.

## 6   Prototype Compiler

The implementation of a prototype system is currently underway and is based on the SUIF2 compilation infrastructure. The current prototype compiler is limited, and the final paper will contain updated results with respect to this compilation system.

The compiler takes C programs as input. Candidates for remote execution are procedure calls in the `main` routine. All calls are assumed to be safe, i.e., procedure calls do not have side effects other than modifying data objects passed as reference parameters. This condition is currently not verified by the compiler. The compiler generates separate client and server programs, where client and server communicate with each other through Unix sockets. A parameterized, static performance model is used to determine the profitability of remote execution of a candidate procedure call. The compiler generates a call to a policy routine for each candidate procedure call. The policy routines evaluate the parameterized performance model for the sizes of the actual parameters at each particular candidate call site. The policy routines also check whether a communication link is available or not. In the latter case, the candidate procedure call will be executed locally. The basic decision strategy is as follows:

```
if  local_computation_cost(candidate_call) >
    (remote_computation_cost(candidate_call) +
    communication_cost(parameter_list_with_sizes)
then
    remote_call(candidate_call)
else
    local_call(candidate_call)
```

The used cost functions have been derived by a micro-benchmarking approach [2, 20], and reflect only expected execution times as an approximation to energy consumption. Executing a remote call requires the marshaling and unmarshaling of the actual parameters and final function value at the client and server sides. The compiler inserts the appropriate code based on the types of the formal parameters. Once a remote call is initiated, the client blocks until the remote call terminates. The preliminary prototype does not support on-demand checkpointing, and the client program will block in case of a disconnection event.

Preliminary experiments were performed for two simple programs, a selection sort and accumulation code, and a program that performs private RSA encryption [4]. The first code takes as input an integer array of size $n$ and returns its sum, while the encryption code takes as input a message of size $n$, and returns the encrypted message. The experiments used a 233MHz Skiff board as its client machine, and a 440MHz SUN UltraSparc-10 workstation as the server. Figure 5 shows the execution times of the local and remote versions of the two example programs. A simple performance model is able to detect the cross-over points, allowing the correct selection between local and remote procedure execution. For large problem sizes, the remote version is up to 2.3x and 2.7x faster for the sort/accumulation and encryption programs, respectively, resulting in corresponding energy savings of up to 41% and 50%.

# 7   Related Work

Code generation for reducing energy consumption of an application has been discussed by researchers at Princeton and Fujitsu [25]. Their work showed that most classical optimizing for execution speed alone will also improve the overall power efficiency of

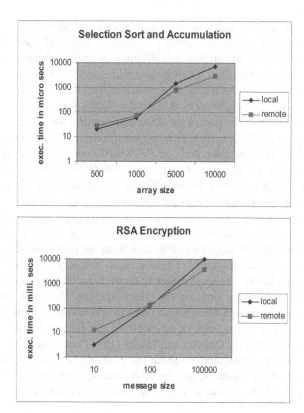

**Fig. 5.** Measured execution times of local and remote versions of two sample programs.

an application. For instance, improving the locality of a computation will avoid cache misses which may require off-chip data to be fetched, an operation that consumes several orders of magnitude more energy than an access to an on-chip cache or register. In the context of wireless communications, most work has concentrated on low-power communication protocols [12] or using the wireless network as a secondary storage device [13]. The latter work mainly deals with problems arising from limited network bandwidth.

The Odyssey from CMU was designed by Satyanarayanan et al. to support a variety of mobile information access applications [14]. The applications run on the mobile client and access data objects on the remote server. The client tries to adapt to changes in the network bandwidth or other resources such as remaining battery life [7] by requesting data at different levels of fidelity or quality. For example, fewer image frames may be requested in response to a reduction in communication bandwidth. The discussed approach relies on the semantic properties of the data processing done by the client. Data loss or skipping data, for instance by dropping a frame in the context of an image processing application, is not acceptable for all classes of applications. This application dependent aspect is important and effective, but orthogonal to the compiler approach discussed in this paper. In addition, their work does not deal with disconnection, i.e., total loss of network connectivity. However, Satyanarayanan et al. have developed operating system techniques that can deal with disconnectedness in the context of CODA, a distributed file system [21]. The CODA project addressed the important problem of establishing a consistent state of the file system across the client and server after network reconnection. More recently, Flinn et al. have developed Spectra, an environment that supports remote execution as part of the Aura architecture, which includes the CODA and Odyseey systems [6]. Spectra uses monitoring technology to balance different optimization goals of an application that contains Spectra operations and system calls.

Executing task on a remote server for the purpose of power savings is not a new idea. Researchers at UCLA and the University College London have investigated the profitability of remote task execution for operating system level tasks [19, 15]. In contrast, our compilation framework identifies within a single program candidate computations that are profitable to be executed remotely. Rudenko et al. have developed a remote processing framework that supports remote task mapping [19] at the OS level. Files are the objects that are communicated between a client and server. For a set of compilation tasks, the framework achieved power reductions on the order of 3 to 6 times as compared to the compilation done on the client machine. On a task set that includes text processing and Gaussian Elimination tasks in addition to compilation tasks, they report power consumption savings of up to 50% [18]. Battery lifetime extensions of up to 21% were reported by Othman and Hailes [15]. These results were obtained by simulation, and different assumptions about the available network bandwidth and CPU processing power of the client vs. the server machines. To the best of our knowledge, no compiler work has been done to support remote task execution for the purposes of energy savings.

Our proposed compile-time techniques identify remote subtask within a single program and determine when their execution may be profitable in terms of overall energy savings. For many applications, compilers are able to analyze entire programs and predict their future behavior and resource requirements. Operating systems and hardware approaches rely on the past observed program behavior to predict future program characteristics. Preliminary results of compiler support for dynamic voltage and frequency scaling for power and energy management purposes has been very encouraging [9, 10]. In addition, our work addresses the important issue of network disconnection and failure recovery. Finally, our power measurements are more precise than previously reported figures since we are able to measure instantaneous power directly at the hardware level, in particular for the Skiff system.

# 8  Conclusions and Future Work

This paper presents a compilation framework that identifies program regions that may be candidates for remote execution. To the best of our knowledge, we are the first to discuss image processing application in the context of mobile environments, and report actual power measurements for such an application on existing low-power platforms, instead of reporting power predictions based on simulation.

Remote task execution can be an effective compiler optimization for image processing applications. Preliminary experiments on StrongARM based systems show potential energy savings of one order of magnitude, mainly due to the reduction in overall execution times. On a PentiumII based laptop computer, up to 30% of the energy was saved. However, the experiments also show that remote tasks have to be selected carefully since a poor choice can lead to a significant increase in overall energy consumption. An initial prototype system has been implemented based on the SUIF2 compiler infrastructure [1]. Experimental results show the effectiveness of our compilation framework for two sample programs. The compiler was able to correctly choose between local and remote execution of procedure calls, resulting in up to 41% overall energy savings for the first, and 50% overall energy savings for the second sample code.

The initial compiler prototype is currently extended to perform interprocedural safety and more advanced profitability analyses for remote execution. In addition, compiler techniques are investigated that will initiate transitions between hibernation states of system components, allowing additional energy savings.

## Acknowledgement

We would like to thank Christoph Peery, Steve Sanbeg and Kiran Nagaraja for their work on the preliminary prototype implementation of the compilation framework.

## References

[1] National Compiler Infrastructure (NCI) project. Overview available online at http://www-suif.stanford.edu/suif/nci/index.html., Co-funded by NSF/DARPA, 1998.
[2] V. Balasundaram, G. Fox, K. Kennedy, and U. Kremer. A static performance estimator to guide data partitioning decisions. In *ACM SIGPLAN Symposium on Principles and Practice of Parallel Programming*, pages 213–223, Williamsburg, VA, April 1991.
[3] R. Chatterjee, B. Ryder, and W. Landi. Relevant context inference. In *ACM SIGPLAN Symposium on the Principles of Programming Languages (POPL)*, pages 133–146, January 1999.
[4] T. H. Cormen, C. E. Leiserson, and R. L. Rivest. *Introduction to Algorithms*. The MIT Press, Cambridge, MA, 1990.
[5] K. Farkas, J. Flinn, G. Back, D. Grunwald, and J. Anderson. Quantifying the energy consumption of a pocket computer and a Java virtual machine. In *ACM International Conference on Measurement and Modeling of Computer Systems (SIGMETRICS)*, Santa Clara, CA, June 2000.
[6] J. Flinn, D. Narayanan, and M. Satyanarayanan. Self-tuned remote execution for pervasive computing. In *Hot Topics on Operating Systems (HotOS-VIII)*, Schloss Elmau, Germany, May 2001.
[7] J. Flinn and M. Satyanarayanan. Energy-aware adaptation for mobile applications. In *ACM Symposium on Operating Systems Principles (SOSP)*, December 1999.
[8] J. Hicks and U. Kremer. Skiff - a platform for pervasive computing. Technical Report 2000-3, Compaq Cambridge Research Laboratory (CRL), 2000.
[9] C-H. Hsu, U. Kremer, and M. Hsiao. Compiler-directed dynamic frequency and voltage scheduling. In *Workshop on Power-Aware Computer Systems (PACS'00)*, Cambridge, MA, November 2000.

[10] C.-H. Hsu, U. Kremer, and M. Hsiao. Compiler-directed dynamic voltage/frequency scheduling for energy reduction in microprocessors. In *Proceedings of the International Symposium on Low-Power Electronics and Design (ISLPED'01)*, August 2001.

[11] M. Kandemir, N. Vijaykrishnan, M.J. Irwin, and H.S. Kim. Experimental evaluation of energy behavior of iteration space tiling. In *International Workshop on Languages and Compilers for Parallel Computing (LCPC)*, August 2000.

[12] R. Kravets and P. Krishnan. Power management techniques for mobile communication. In *Proceedings of the Annual International Conference on Mobile Computing and Networking (MOBICOM)*, Dallas, TX, 1999.

[13] J. Lorch and A. Smith. Software strategies for portable computer energy management. *IEEE Personal Communications Magazine*, 5(3), June 1998.

[14] B. Noble. System support for mobile, adaptive applications. *IEEE Personal Communications*, 7(1):44–49, February 2000.

[15] M. Othman and S. Hailes. Power conservation strategy for mobile computers using load sharing. *Mobile Computing and Communications Review*, 2(1):44–50, 1998.

[16] Y. Park and B. Goldberg. Escape analysis on lists. In *ACM SIGPLAN Conference on Programming Language Design and Implementation (PLDI'92)*, pages 116–127, June 1992.

[17] H.A. Rowley, S. Baluja, and T. Kanade. Neural network-based face detection. *IEEE Transactions on Pattern Analysis and Machine Intelligence*, 20(1):23–38, 1998.

[18] A. Rudenko, P. Reiher, G. Popek, and G. Kuenning. Saving portable computer battery power through remote process execution. *Mobile Computing and Communications Review*, 2(1):19–26, 1998.

[19] A. Rudenko, P. Reiher, G. Popek, and G. Kuenning. The remote processing framework for portable computer power saving. In *Proceedings of the ACM Symposium on Applied Computing (SAC99)*, San Antonio,TX, February 1999.

[20] R. Saavedra-Barrera. *CPU Performance Evaluation and Execution Time Prediction Using Narrow Spectrum Benchmarking*. PhD thesis, U.C. Berkeley, February 1992. UCB/CSD-92-684.

[21] M. Satyanarayanan. Mobile information access. *IEEE Personal Communications*, 3(1):26–33, February 1996.

[22] T. Sim, R. Sukthankar, M. Mullin, and S. Baluja. High-performance memory-based face recognition for visitor identification. Technical report, Just Research, 1999.

[23] T. Sim, R. Sukthankar, M. Mullin, and S. Baluja. Memory-based face recognition for visitor identification. In *Proc. 4th Intl. Conf. on Face and Gesture Recognition*, pages 214–220, Grenoble, France, March 2000.

[24] T. Simunic, L. Benini, P. Glynn, and G. De Micheli. Dynamic power management for portable systems. In *Proceedings of the Sixth Annual International Conference on Mobile Computing and Networking (MobiCom)*, Boston, MA, August 2000.

[25] V. Tiwari, S. Malik, A. Wolfe, and M. Lee. Instruction level power analysis and optimization of software. *Journal of VLSI Signal Processing*, 13(2/3):1–18, 1996.

[26] M. Valluri and L. John. Is compiling for performance == compiling for power? In *The 5th Annual Workshop on Interaction between Compilers and Computer Architectures (INTERACT-5)*, January 2001.

# A    Basic Structure of TourGuide

### System Initialization (SI)
create in-memory representation of neural networks (for face detection)
read-in face mask
create in-memory representation of faces data base (for face recognition)

**while** active **do**

### Image Acquisition (IA)
obtain $640 \times 480$ pixel jpeg image

### Preprocessing for Face Detection (PFD)
decompress jpeg image into black&white pnm image
crop image to $320 \times 320$ pixels (center section)
normalize image for contrast
build image pyramid with scale factor 1.1, where last five
levels are pruned, resulting in 10 remaining levels

### Face Detection (FD)
**for** i = highest_pyramid_level **downto** lowest_pyramid_level **do**
compute set of $30 \times 30$ pixels target regions that may contain a face (pre-filter)
**foreach** target region **do**
detect $20 \times 20$ pixels face in target region
**if** detection successful **then** exit both surrounding loops
**endforeach**
**endfor**

### Preprocessing for Face Recognition (PFR)
Increase size of region with detected face by 20%
Normalize detected face for contrast
Scale-down detected face to $16 \times 16$ pixels

### Face Recognition (FR)
determine best matching score with $16 \times 16$ pixels faces in data base
**if** best match is above predefined quality threshold **then**
report successful recognition and return persons identity
**else**
report unsuccessful recognition
**endif**
**enddo**

# Locality Enhancement by Array Contraction[*]

Yonghong Song[1], Cheng Wang[2], and Zhiyuan Li[2]

[1] Sun Microsystems, Inc, 901 San Antonio Rd,
Palo Alto, CA 94303, USA,
yonghong.song@sun.com
[2] Department of Computer Sciences, Purdue University,
West Lafayette, IN 47907, USA,
{wangc,li}@cs.purdue.edu

**Abstract.** In this paper, we study how array contraction can enhance locality and improve performance. In our previous work, we have developed a memory minimization scheme, SFC, which is a combination of loop shifting, loop fusion and array contraction. SFC focuses on reducing the memory requirement, and as a by-product, it may enhance cache locality. In this paper, we study how array contraction can contribute to cache locality and performance enhancement. We develop a memory cost model for SFC. We also present a fusion algorithm so that the predicted locality enhancement can be realized. Experimental results on both a real machine and a simulator demonstrate the effectiveness of array contraction on cache locality enhancement and performance improvement.

## 1 Introduction

Due to the increasing gap between processor and memory speed, the importance of exploiting cache locality has been well recognized. Array contraction is a technique to contract a high-dimensional array to a lower one. Array contraction has long been recognized for locality enhancement and register utilization [1, 4].

In our recent work, we have presented a work which combines loop shifting, loop fusion and array contraction for memory requirement minimization [14]. In this paper, we call such an approach SFC. Loop shifting is an enabling technique which shifts the loop iteration space by a certain amount [8]. Without loop shifting, some loop nests cannot be fused because of otherwise introduced backward dependences after fusion [14]. Given a fused loop, live analysis and region analysis [5] can be used to determine *contractable* arrays. Array contraction can then be applied to these contractable arrays using the algorithm in [14].

This paper tries to explain why and how array contraction can enhance locality and improve performance. Unlike the previous work in [1, 4], our array contraction allows an array to be contracted from a higher dimension to a lower

---

[*] This work is sponsored in part by National Science Foundation through grants CCR-9975309, ACI/ITR-0082834 and MIP-9610379, by Indiana 21st Century Fund, by Purdue Research Foundation, and by a donation from Sun Microsystems, Inc.

H. Dietz (Ed.): LCPC 2001, LNCS 2624, pp. 132–146, 2003.

```
DO T = 1, ITMAX
L₁: DO J₁ = 2, N − 1
    DO I₁ = 2, N − 1
        L(I₁, J₁) = (A(I₁ + 1, J₁)
            +A(I₁ − 1, J₁) + A(I₁, J₁ + 1)
            +A(I₁, J₁ − 1))/4
    END DO
END DO
L₂: DO J₂ = 2, N − 1
    DO I₂ = 2, N − 1
        A(I₂, J₂) = L(I₂, J₂)
    END DO
END DO
END DO
```

(a)

```
DO T = 1, ITMAX
DO J₁ = 2, N − 1
    DO I₁ = 2, N − 1
        L(I₁, J₁) = (A(I₁ + 1, J₁)
            +A(I₁ − 1, J₁) + A(I₁, J₁ + 1)
            +A(I₁, J₁ − 1))/4
    END DO
END DO
DO J₂ = 3, N
    DO I₂ = 2, N − 1
        A(I₂, J₂ − 1) = L(I₂, J₂ − 1)
    END DO
END DO
END DO
```

(b)

```
DO T = 1, ITMAX
DO J₁ = 2, N
    DO I₁ = 2, N − 1
        IF (J₁.EQ.2) THEN
            L(I₁, J₁) = (A(I₁ + 1, J₁)
                +A(I₁ − 1, J₁) + A(I₁, J₁ + 1)
                +A(I₁, J₁ − 1))/4
        ELSE IF (J₁.EQ.N) THEN
            A(I₁, J₁ − 1) = L(I₁, J₁ − 1)
        ELSE
            L(I₁, J₁) = (A(I₁ + 1, J₁)
                +A(I₁ − 1, J₁) + A(I₁, J₁ + 1)
                +A(I₁, J₁ − 1))/4
            A(I₁, J₁ − 1) = L(I₁, J₁ − 1)
        END IF
    END DO
END DO
END DO
```

(c)

```
DO T = 1, ITMAX
DO J₁ = 2, N
    DO I₁ = 2, N − 1
        IF (J₁.EQ.2) THEN
            LL(I₁) = (A(I₁ + 1, J₁)
                +A(I₁ − 1, J₁) + A(I₁, J₁ + 1)
                +A(I₁, J₁ − 1))/4
        ELSE IF (J₁.EQ.N) THEN
            A(I₁, J₁ − 1) = LL(I₁)
        ELSE
            temp = (A(I₁ + 1, J₁)
                +A(I₁ − 1, J₁) + A(I₁, J₁ + 1)
                +A(I₁, J₁ − 1))/4
            A(I₁, J₁ − 1) = LL(I₁)
            LL(L₁) = temp
        END IF
    END DO
END DO
END DO
```

(d)

**Fig. 1.** The Jacobi example

dimension, not just scalars. Also, by incorporating loop shifting into the framework, SFC has more opportunities for array contraction than [1, 4]. We develop a memory cost model to analytically estimate the number of cache misses during different stages of SFC (before fusion, after fusion but before array contraction, and after array contraction). (Loop shifting does not change the number of cache misses when compared with the unfused codes.) We develop an algorithm to partition the loop nests into different partitions such that all loop nests within the same partition will be fused. Array contraction will then be applied to each partition. We present experimental results on both a real machine and a simulator to show how array contraction is able to enhance locality.

In the rest of this paper, we first present a motivating example through Jacobi in Section 2. We present our program model and develop our memory cost model in Section 3. In Section 4, we present a fusion algorithm which takes into account loop shifting and array contraction. We present our experimental results in Section 5. We discuss related work in Section 6 and conclude in Section 7.

## 2   An Example

In this section, we estimate the number of cache misses of the Jacobi code to show how array contraction can enhance locality and improve performance.

Figure 1(a) shows the original Jacobi code, for which the convergence test is omitted. Loops $L_1$ and $L_2$ cannot be fused because of an anti-dependence from $L_1$ to $L_2$ with the distance vector $(-1, 0)$. Figure 1(b) shows the code after loop shifting. Figure 1(c) shows the fused code. After loop fusion, array $L$ can be contracted from a 2-D array to an 1-D array. Figure 1(d) shows the code after array contraction, where array $LL$ represents the contracted array for array $L$. In this paper, we assume Fortran column major.

We follow the classification in [6], partitioning all cache misses into three classes: compulsory misses, capacity misses and conflict misses. Compulsory misses cannot be avoided and thus be omitted in this paper. Conflict misses can be attributed to self-conflict or cross-conflict misses, depending on whether the two involved references are from the same array or not.

In this paper, we only count the number of capacity misses. The cache conflict misses are ignored. In Section 5.3, we show that for fused codes, conflict misses change little before and after array contraction and the capacity misses dominate the difference.

The following assumptions are made in order to estimate the number of cache misses for different versions of Jacobi codes:

- Both the cache line size and the data element size are equal to 1. This assumption is used only for this section to simplify presentation.
- The original array size $N^2$ is greater than the cache size but $3N$ is smaller than the cache size. With this range of $N$, the group reuses can be translated to cache hits in a fully-associative cache for all versions of codes in Figure 1 (see Section 4 for details). (Other $N$ value is possible but is omitted here. We only count for this particular range and other ranges can be estimated based on the formulas in Section 3.2.)
  With the above chosen N and omission of conflict misses, group reuses for array A can be realized to cache hits in all versions of codes.

For the original code (in Figure 1(a)), the number of cache misses can be estimated as $(4 * N^2 * ITMAX)$. The shifting code (in Figure 1(b)) has the same number of cache misses as the original code. After fusion (in Figure 1(c)), the number of cache misses can be estimated as $(2 * N^2 * ITMAX)$. After array contraction (in Figure 1(d)), the number of cache misses is $(N^2 * ITMAX + N)$, since array $LL$ can be reused even across different $T$ iterations.

We run the above example on one R10K processor of an SGI Origin 2000 multiprocessor with an arbitrary $N = 1100$. (Some additional codes are added to initialize array $A$.) The L1 cache size for the R10K is 4K in terms of the number of data elements. The outside time-step loop trip counts are 1 ($ITMAX = 1$) and 1000 ($ITMAX = 1000$) respectively. Figure 3 shows the result, where "Original" represents the normalized execution time for the original program (in Figure 1(a)), "Fusion" for the program after fusion but before array contraction

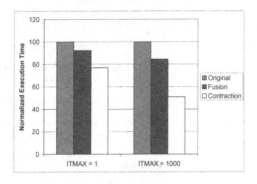

**Fig. 2.** Execution time for Jacobi on the R10K

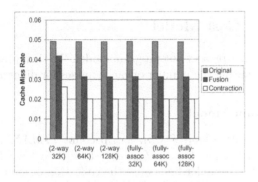

**Fig. 3.** Cache miss rate for Jacobi with simulation with $ITMAX = 1$

(in Figure 1(c)) and "Contraction" for the program after array contraction (in Figure 1(d)). For both trip counts 1 and 1000, the fusion version performs better than the original code and the array contraction version performs better than the fusion version. After array contraction, compared with "$ITMAX = 1$" version, the "$ITMAX = 1000$" version achieves greater speedup because array $LL$ is able to be reused even across the $T$ loop.

We also run simulation using SimpleScalar [2] on the Jacobi example. Figure 3 shows the result with $ITMAX = 1$, where "2-way 32K" represents a two-way set-associative cache with a size of 32 kilobytes . The other legends in Figure 3 have similar meaning. All the cache lines for the runs in Figure 3 are 16 bytes. The set associativity is at least two to minimize the effect of conflict misses. Simulation results confirm our analysis such that the fusion version has a smaller cache miss rate than the original version, and that the array contraction version has a smaller cache miss rate than the fusion version. (We did not run simulation with $ITMAX = 1000$ because of its long simulation time.)

```
DO T = 1, ITMAX                          DO T = 1, ITMAX
L₁ : DO L_{1,1} = l_{1,1}, u_{1,1}       L₁ : DO L_{1,1} = l_{1,1} + p¹(L₁), u_{1,1} + p¹(L₁)
       DO L_{1,2} = l_{1,2}, u_{1,2}            DO L_{1,2} = l_{1,2} + p²(L₁), u_{1,2} + p²(L₁)
         ...                                      ...
           DO L_{1,n} = l_{1,n}, u_{1,n}            DO L_{1,n} = l_{1,n} + pⁿ(L₁), u_{1,n} + pⁿ(L₁)
  ...                                       ...
Lᵢ : DO L_{i,1} = l_{i,1}, u_{i,1}       Lᵢ : DO L_{i,1} = l_{i,1} + p¹(Lᵢ), u_{i,1} + p¹(Lᵢ)
       DO L_{i,2} = l_{i,2}, u_{i,2}            DO L_{i,2} = l_{i,2} + p²(Lᵢ), u_{i,2} + p²(Lᵢ)
         ...                                      ...
           DO L_{i,n} = l_{i,n}, u_{i,n}            DO L_{i,n} = l_{i,n} + pⁿ(Lᵢ), u_{i,n} + pⁿ(Lᵢ)
  ...                                       ...
Lₘ : DO L_{m,1} = l_{m,1}, u_{m,1}       Lₘ : DO L_{m,1} = l_{m,1} + p¹(Lₘ), u_{m,1} + p¹(Lₘ)
       DO L_{m,2} = l_{m,2}, u_{m,2}            DO L_{m,2} = l_{m,2} + p²(Lₘ), u_{m,2} + p²(Lₘ)
         ...                                      ...
           DO L_{m,n} = l_{m,n}, u_{m,n}            DO L_{m,n} = l_{m,n} + pⁿ(Lₘ), u_{m,n} + pⁿ(Lₘ)
END DO                                   END DO

            (a)                                      (b)
```

**Fig. 4.** The original and transformed loop nests

## 3  A Memory Cost Model

In this section, we first present out program model. We then present our memory cost model by estimating the number of cache misses for different stages of SFC.

### 3.1  The Program Model

We consider an iterative loop $T$ with a trip count $ITMAX$, which contains a collection of loop nests, $L_1$, $L_2$, ..., $L_m$, $m \geq 1$, in their lexical order, as shown in Figure 4(a). If the compiler finds only the collection of loop nests, it can add an artificial $T$ loop with $ITMAX = 1$ in the outer position. The label $L_i$ denotes a perfect nest of loops with indices $L_{i,1}$, $L_{i,2}$, ..., $L_{i,n}$, $n \geq 1$, starting from the outmost loop. Loop $L_{i,j}$ has the lower bound $l_{i,j}$ and the upper bound $u_{i,j}$ respectively, where $l_{i,j}$ and $u_{i,j}$ are loop invariants. For simplicity of presentation, all the loop nests $L_i$, $1 \leq i \leq m$, are assumed to have the same nesting level $n$. If they do not have the same nesting level, we can apply our technique to different loop levels incrementally [14].

Figure 4(b) shows the loop nests after loop shifting. Each loop $L_{i,j}$ is associated with a shifting factor $p^j(L_i)$. For the perfect nest $L_i$, we denote its associated shifting factor as $\boldsymbol{p}(L_i) = (p^1(L_i), \ldots, p^n(L_i))$.

After loop shifting, the loop nests shown in Figure 4(b) are partitioned into different *partitions*. All loop nests within the same partition are fused together. Array contraction is then applied to the fused loops.

### 3.2  The Memory Cost Model

As stated in Section 2, we only count the number of capacity misses. We assume an LRU cache replacement policy. For all versions of codes (the original unfused code, the fused code and the code after array contraction), we make the following assumptions in order to estimate the number of cache misses.

- **Assumption 1**: Spatial locality is fully exploited in the innermost loop.
- **Assumption 2**: All group reuses [15] can be realized and translated into cache hits.

Assumption 1 can be satisfied by interchanging the loop, which accesses the first array dimension, into the innermost position. In extreme case, where the array elements from different array columns map to the same cache location, intra-array padding can be applied [11].

Assumption 2 is satisfied by our heuristic in Section 4, which requires the cache size must be greater than the total memory requirement necessary to realize all group reuses.

Before estimating the number of cache misses, we first define the following terms:

- $W_i$ is the total array footprint size of loop nest $L_i$ in Figure 4(a).
- $W_f$ is the total array footprint size for the fused loop, assuming all $m$ loops in Figure 4(a) are fused together. The inequality $W_f \leq \Sigma_{i=1}^{m} W_i$ is true.
- $W_n$ is the total array footprint size which cannot be contracted after array contraction. Hence, $(W_f - W_n)$ represents the total array footprint size which can be contracted after fusion but before array contraction.
- $W_c$ is the size of contracted arrays after array contraction. The inequality $W_c < (W_f - W_n)$ is true.
- $C_b$ and $C_s$ represent the cache line size and the cache size respectively.

We assume all $W_i$ and $W_f$ are greater than the cache size. This is often true for practical applications. We can estimate the number of cache misses for the original loop nest as follows:

$$\frac{\Sigma_{i=1}^{m} W_i}{C_b} * ITMAX. \tag{1}$$

The number of cache misses after loop fusion before array contraction can be estimated as

$$\frac{W_f}{C_b} * ITMAX. \tag{2}$$

Suppose $W_c$ is greater than the cache size $C_s$, the contracted arrays are not able to be reused across different dynamic references to themselves. For example in Figure 1(d), the repeated accesses to array $LL$ will still cause cache misses. Therefore, the number of cache misses after array contraction is the same as the version after fusion but before array contraction, which is

$$\frac{W_f}{C_b} * ITMAX \text{ if } W_c > C_s. \tag{3}$$

Suppose $W_c$ is smaller than or equal to $C_s$ and the total array footprint size after array contraction is greater than the cache size. The contracted arrays can be reused across different dynamic references to themselves. Therefore, the number of cache misses after array contraction in this case can be estimated as

$$\frac{W_n}{C_b} * ITMAX + \frac{W_c}{C_b} \text{ if } W_c \leq C_s \wedge (W_n + W_c) > C_s. \tag{4}$$

**Procedure** Partition
**Input:** (1) a collection of $m$ loop nests, (2) the simplified loop dependence graph [14], (3) the cache size $C_s$ and the number of available registers $R$ for the given architecture.
**Output:** A set of partitions, $P$.
**Procedure:**
    Compute the shifting factors [14].
    Sort the contractable arrays starting with the one which reduces the memory most.
    Initialize the partition set $P$ to $\phi$.
    **for** (each contractable array $a$ in order)
       Let $S$ be the set of loop nests in which $a$ is accessed.
       Let $P_{k_i} (1 \le i \le s)$ be partitions such that $P_{k_i} \cap S \ne \phi$.
       Let $M = \cup_{i=1}^{s} P_{k_i} \cup S$.
       **if** ($num\_ref\_size(M) < C_s$ and $num\_reg(M) < R$)
          **for** $i \leftarrow 1$ to $s$ **do**
             $P = P - P_{k_i}$
          **end for**
          $P = P \cup \{M\}$
       **end if**
    **end for**

**Fig. 5.** Procedure *Partition*

Otherwise, if the total array footprint size after array contraction is equal to or smaller than the cache size, the number of cache misses can be estimated as

$$\frac{W_n + W_c}{C_b} \text{ if } (W_c + W_n) \le C_s. \tag{5}$$

From formulas (1) to (5), in general case, the fusion version can generate less number of cache misses than the non-fusion version. The array contraction can further reduce the number of cache misses if the contracted array size $W_c$ can fit in the cache, according to formulas (4) and (5). If the total array footprint size after array contraction can fit in the cache and the number of $T$ iterations ($ITMAX$) is much greater than 1, the number of cache misses can be reduced dramatically, according to formula (5). Our Jacobi example in Section 2 fits the formula (4).

## 4    A Fusion Scheme

Given a collection of loop nests, different schemes exist to partition them into different partitions such that the loop nests within the same partition will be fused together. In [7], Kennedy and McKinley proves that fusion for locality is NP-hard [7]. Their work does not consider either loop shifting or array contraction. On the other hand, adding loop shifting and array contraction can only make the fusion-for-locality problem harder. (We can have a case where all arrays are non-contractable and no loop shifting is necessary.) In this section, we present a greedy fusion heuristic considering loop shifting and array contraction. Our algorithm favors array contraction since this paper is to study how array contraction can enhance locality.

In [14], the concept of *reference window* is used to characterize the minimum memory requirement such that all the reusable data can be placed in the cache while all the dependences are satisfied. Our fusion scheme requires that the total reference window size should be equal to or smaller than the cache size so that Assumption 2 in Section 3.2 can be satisfied in a fully-associative cache. Such a requirement is called the *reference window constraint*. Since dependences imply reuses, all the dependences, including flow, anti, output and input dependences, are considered to enforce reference window constraint. Refer to [14] for the details of how to compute the reference window size given a set of data dependences. For Jacobi example after loop fusion in Figure 1(c), the reference window size for the flow dependences due to array $L$ is $N$ and it is $2N$ for the dependences due to array $A$. Therefore, the total reference window size is $3N$.

Register spills generate more accesses to the cache, which make our estimation imprecise. They also generate more loads and stores in the innermost loop body and may hurt the performance. We require that the total required number of registers should be less than the number of available registers, to avoid register spills. Such a requirement is called *register pressure constraint*.

Figure 5 shows our fusion algorithm, *Partition*. Our algorithm first computes the optimal shifting factors for memory minimization [14]. It then fuses the loops based on their contribution to memory reduction. The loops which can save more memory after being fused have the priority to be fused first. Given a contractable array $a$, the set of loop nests in which $a$ is accessed, $S$, is computed first. If these loop nests in $S$ are also included in some other partitions, try to fuse all these partitions and $S$ together to form a new partition. If fusion is successful, the new partition is put into the partition set $P$ and all the old partitions in which $a$ is accessed are removed from $P$. If fusion is unsuccessful because of the reference window constraint or the register pressure constraint, the algorithm continues to the next contractable array. Function $num\_ref\_size(S)$ returns the reference window size assuming all the loops in $S$ are fused together. We use the method in [14] to compute the reference window size. Function $num\_reg(S)$ returns the number of required registers to execute one iteration of the innermost loop, assuming all the loops in $S$ are fused together. Similar to [12], we estimate the number of required registers as the number of distinct array references.

In order to compute the shifting factor, data dependence analysis is necessary, which is exponential in the worst case. Data dependence analysis will build a loop dependence graph (LDG), which is an extension to the traditional data dependence graph with each node representing one loop nest [14]. The loop dependence graph can also be simplified before computing the optimal shifting factors [14]. The simplification takes time in the order of the number of original data dependence edges. Our algorithm takes the simplified loop dependence graph as one of its inputs. Let $n_a$ be the number of contractable arrays. The total complexity of our heuristic is $O((m * n_a)^3)$.

Our heuristic favors to fuse loops which can save memory since we are interested in studying the effect of array contraction on locality enhancement. Such a heuristic, however, may not generate the optimal solution for locality enhancement.

**Table 1.** Test programs

| Benchmark | Description | Input Parameters | m/n |
|-----------|-------------|------------------|-----|
| LL14 | Livermore Loop No. 14 | $N = 1001$, $ITMAX = 50000$ | 3/1 |
| LL18 | Livermore Loop No. 18 | $N = 400$, $ITMAX = 100$ | 3/2 |
| Jacobi | Jacobi Kernel w/o convergence test | $N = 1100$, ITMAX $= 1050$ | 2/2 |
| tomcatv | A mesh generation program from SPEC95fp | reference input | 5/1 |
| swim95 | A weather prediction program from SPEC95fp | reference input | 2/2 |
| swim00 | A weather prediction program from SPEC2000fp | reference input | 2/2 |
| hydro2d | An astrophysical program from SPEC95fp | reference input | 10/2 |
| lucas | A promality test from SPEC2000fp | reference input | 3/1 |
| mg | A multigrid solver from NPB2.3-serial benchmark | Class 'W' | 2/1 |
| combustion | A thermochemical program from UMD Chaos group | $N1 = 10$, $N2 = 10$ | 1/2 |
| purdue-02 | Purdue set problem02 | reference input | 2/1 |
| purdue-03 | Purdue set problem03 | reference input | 3/2 |
| purdue-04 | Purdue set problem04 | reference input | 3/2 |
| purdue-07 | Purdue set problem07 | reference input | 1/2 |
| purdue-08 | Purdue set problem08 | reference input | 1/2 |
| purdue-12 | Purdue set problem12 | reference input | 4/2 |
| purdue-13 | Purdue set problem13 | reference input | 2/1 |
| climate | A two-layer shallow water climate model from Rice | reference input | 2/4 |
| laplace-jb | Jacobi method of Laplace from Rice | $ICYCLE = 500$ | 4/2 |
| laplace-gs | Gauss-Seidel method of Laplace from Rice | $ICYCLE = 500$ | 3/2 |

In [14], we also have developed a controlled fusion heuristic, called *Pick_and_Reject*. The *Pick_and_Reject*, however, does not enforce the reference window constraint. Therefore, it may not reduce the number of cache misses if too many loops are fused together. For all our particular set of benchmarks in Section 5, however, both heuristics produce the same shifting factor and fusion partitioning scheme.

## 5   Experimental Evaluation

In this section, we first present our experimental methodology. We then present the results on one real machine. Lastly, we present simulation results.

### 5.1   Methodology

We have implemented our previous memory reduction technique in a research compiler, Panorama [5, 14]. We also implemented our heuristic in Figure 5 and applied it in our experiments. To evaluate the effectiveness of array contraction, we measure the performance on one processor of an SGI Origin 2000 multiprocessor. The MIPS R10K has a 32KB 2-way set-associative L1 data cache with a 32-byte cache line, and it has a 4MB 2-way set-associative unified L2 cache with an 128-byte cache line. It has totally 16GB main memory in which 1GB is local to the processor. It has 32 integer registers and 32 floating-point registers. The cache miss penalty is 9 CPU cycles for the L1 data cache and 68 CPU cycles for the L2 cache.

Table 1 lists the benchmarks used in our experiments, their descriptions and their input parameters. (We use the same set of benchmarks as in [14]). These benchmarks are chosen because they either readily fit our program model or they can be transformed by our enabling algorithms [14] to fit. In this table, "m/n" represents the number of loops in the loop sequence (m) and the maximum loop nesting level (n). Note that the array size and the iteration counts are chosen arbitrarily for LL14, LL18 and Jacobi. To differentiate benchmark swim from SPEC95 and SPEC2000, we denote the SPEC95 version as swim95 and the SPEC2000 version as swim00. Program swim00 is almost identical to swim95 except for its larger data size. For combustion, we change the array size (N1 and N2) from 1 to 10, so the execution time will last for several seconds. Programs climate, laplace-jb, laplace-gs and all the Purdue set problems are from an HPF benchmark suite at Rice University [9, 10]. Except for lucas, all the other benchmarks are written in F77. We manually apply our technique to lucas, which is written in F90. Among 20 benchmark programs, our algorithm finds that the purdue-set programs, lucas, LL14 and combustion do not need to perform loop shifting. For each of the benchmarks in Table 1, all $m$ loops are fused together. For swim95, swim00 and hydro2d, where $n = 2$, only the outer loops are fused. For all other benchmarks, all $n$ loop levels are fused. Except tomcatv, swim95 and swim00, all other benchmarks target the L1 cache, trying to improve the L1 cache locality. These three programs target the L2 cache because of their large array column size and large number of arrays, which make difficult to satisfy Assumption 2 in Section 3.2.

For each of the benchmarks, we examine three versions of the code, i.e. the original one, the one after loop fusion but before array contraction, and the one after array contraction.

For all versions of the benchmarks, we use the native Fortran compilers to produce the machine codes. We simply use the optimization flag "-O3" with the following adjustments. We switch off prefetching for laplace-jb, software pipelining for laplace-gs and loop unrolling for purdue-O3. For swim95 and swim00, the native compiler fails to insert prefetch instructions in the innermost loop body after memory reduction. We manually insert prefetch instructions into the three key innermost loop bodies, following exactly the same prefetching patterns used by the native compiler for the original codes.

We use the Cheetah cache simulator in Simplescalar 3.0 suite [2] to perform simulation in order to understand the underlying cache behavior. The program is compiled by gcc with the optimization level "-O3". By using a simulator, we are able to separate capacity misses from conflict misses.

## 5.2   Results on the Real Machine

In [14], we have presented performance results with the inputs in Table 1 for all our benchmarks. Here, only the summarized results are presented. Loop fusion, although being able to reduce capacity misses, may sometimes make performance even worse by increasing conflict misses. Array contraction, on the other hand, is able to further reduce capacity misses after loop fusion with comparable conflict misses, thus improving proerformance. Overall, the contraction version achieves

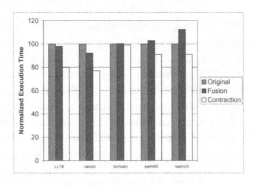

**Fig. 6.** Performance comparision with $ITMAX = 1$

an average speedup of 1.40 over the original programs, with a geometric mean. It has an average speedup of 1.25 over the fusion version.

Out of 20 benchmarks, 13 benchmarks conforms to our program model in Figure 4(a) with $ITMAX > 1$, except for simple scalar operations or convergence tests before $L_1$ or after $L_m$. (The benchmarks hydro2d, lucas, mg, combustion, purdue-07, purdue-12 and climate have an artificial outer loop with $ITMAX = 1$.) For these 13 benchmarks, we change their $ITMAX$ value to 1 and examining how the relative performance of different versions of codes will change when the $ITMAX$ value changes.

Figure 6 shows the results with $ITMAX = 1$. Because of available precision of the time utility, the smaller execution time is hard to exhibit the difference between different versions although they should have. In Figure 6, we only show the results of 5 programs whose execution time exceed 0.3 seconds. For different $ITMAX$ values, the same trend can be observed such that if the fusion version (or the version after array contraction) with a large $ITMAX$ citesong.ics01 performs better than the original version (or the fusion version), it is also true in Figure 6, and vice versa. Further, the speedup of the codes after array contraction over the fused codes for a large $ITMAX$ is greater than that in Figure 6. This is consistent with the formulas in Section 3.2 where the relative saving of cache misses will be larger if the $ITMAX$ value becomes larger.

### 5.3   Simulation Results

Unlike the execution on a real machine in Section 5.2, we use the reduced data set size and smaller iterative-loop trip counts for simulation, in order to reduce the long simulation time. In this subsection, we pick three benchmarks to study their cache behavior, with arbitrarily-chosen inputs. For the purpose to study the effect of array contraction, we assume both the size of the target cache and the number of available registers large enough so that we can always apply array contraction. We count the number of cache misses for the whole program which also contains some initialization and output codes.

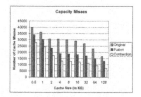
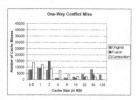
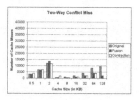

**Fig. 7.** Cache statistics for Jacobi ($N = 110$, $ITMAX = 1$)

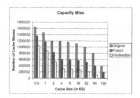
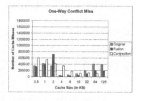
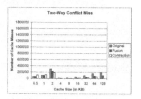

**Fig. 8.** Cache statistics for Jacobi ($N = 110$, $ITMAX = 50$)

**Jacobi** Figure 7 shows the results for Jacobi with the input ($N = 110, ITMAX = 1$). Each data element is assumed to take 8 bytes. The original codes include two loop nests each of which accesses two 2-D arrays, $A$ and $L$, as in Figure 1(a). After fusion, two 2-D arrays, $A$ and $L$, are accessed in the fused loop nest. After array contraction, one 2-D array $A$ and one 1-D array $LL$ are accessed in the loop nest. Based on the analysis in Section 3.2, the number of capacity misses should be reduced by half after fusion. The number of capacity misses should be reduced further by half after array contraction.

From Figure 7, the fused codes achieve smaller number of capacity misses than the original unfused codes. The codes after array contraction further reduces the number of capacity misses. Also the tend is very close to our analysis. For conflict misses, however, the trend is not clear. But in most cases, the fused codes and the codes after array contraction achieve comparable number of conflict misses either for a directly-mapped cache or for a two-way set-associative cache. Note that for small cache sizes (equal to or less than 2KB), Assumption 2 in Section 3.2 is not satisfied for both the fused codes and the codes after array contraction. Therefore, the number of conflict misses for such small cache sizes is significantly higher than that for the larger cache sizes.

Figure 8 shows the result with the input ($N = 110, ITMAX = 50$). When compared with Figure 7, the reduction of the number of capacity misses is larger for the codes after array contraction over the fused codes. This is consistent with our analysis in Section 3.2. For the cache size 128KB, the cache misses after array contraction are almost completely ignored because both arrays can fit in the cache now. (The data size is $(110 * 110 + 110) * 8 = 97680B$, which is smaller than the cache size 128KB.)

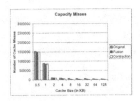
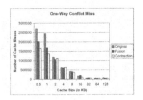
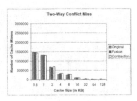

**Fig. 9.** Cache statistics for `tomcatv` ($N = 80$, $ITMAX = 1$)

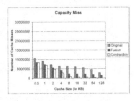
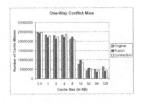
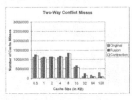

**Fig. 10.** Cache statistics for `tomcatv` ($N = 80$, $ITMAX = 100$)

`tomcatv` The original `tomcatv` has seven 2-D arrays accessed in 5 loop nests. After fusion, the same seven 2-D arrays are accessed in the fused loop. After array contraction, five 2-D arrays are contracted to 7 1-D arrays, where each of 2-D arrays $RX$ and $RY$ is contracted to two 1-D arrays. Based on our analysis in Section 3.2, the number of original capacity misses will be reduced by 67% after fusion. After array contraction, the number of capacity misses will be reduced by 70%, compared with the fusion version.

Figure 9 shows the results for `tomcatv` with the input ($N = 80$, $ITMAX = 1$). For capacity misses, the trend is very close to our analysis. However, for `tomcatv`, conflict misses are more important than capacity misses for 1-way and 2-way set-associative caches. Similar to Jacobi, the trend for conflict misses is not clear. However, both the fusion and array contraction versions achieve comparable results in most cases.

Figure 10 shows the results with the input ($N = 80$, $ITMAX = 100$). Similar to Jacobi, larger $ITMAX$ value can increase the relative reduction on the number of capacity misses after array contraction.

## 6 Related Work

This work directly follows our previous work in [14], where we develop SFC to minimize memory requirement. In this paper, we further studied why and how array contraction is able to enhance locality and improve performance.

Gao *et al.* combines loop fusion and array contraction to improve performance [4]. Their array contraction, however, only contracts arrays to scalars. They also do not consider loop shifting.

Loop shifting is not new. Darte claims that the problem of maximum fusion of parallel loops with constant dependence distances is NP-complete when combined with loop shifting [3]. His goal is to find the minimum number of partitions such that the loops within each partition can be fused, possibly enabled by loop shifting, and the fused loop remains parallel. His formulation is quite different from ours. Manjikian and Abdelrahman present *shift-and-peel* [8]. They shift the loops in order to enable fusion.

Loop fusion has been studied extensively. To name a few publications, Kennedy and McKinley prove maximizing data locality by loop fusion is NP-hard [7]. They provide two polynomial-time heuristics. Singhai and McKinley present *parameterized loop fusion* to improve parallelism and cache locality [13]. They do not perform loop shifting or array contraction.

# 7   Conclusion

In this paper, we have studied the role of array contraction on locality enhancement. We developed a memory cost model for our previous technique SFC, a combination of loop shifting, loop fusion and array contraction. Our cost model shows array contraction is able to reduce the number of capacity misses for the fused codes. We also developed a fusion heuristic in order to realize the predicted cache locality enhancement. Experiments are performed on both a real machine and a simulator. The results from the real machine show that array contraction can improve the performance with a speedup of 1.40 over the original codes and with a speedup of 1.25 over the fused codes. The simulation results show that array contraction indeed is able to reduce the number of capacity misses while having the comparable number of conflict misses to the fused codes, thus being able to improve the overall performance.

# References

[1] Bacon, D., Graham, S., Sharp, O.: Compiler transformations for high-performance computing. *ACM Computing Surveys*, 26(4):345–420, December 1994.

[2] Burger D., Austin, T.: The simplescalar tool set, version 2.0. Technical Report TR-1342, Department of Computer Sciences, Univ. of Wisconsin, Madison, June 1997.

[3] Darte, A.: On the complixity of loop fusion. In *Proceedings of International Conference on Parallel Architecture and Compilation Techniques*, pages 149–157, Newport Beach, California, October 1999.

[4] Gao, G., Olsen, R., Sarkar V., Thekkath, R.: Collective loop fusion for array contraction. In *Proceedings of the Fifth Workshop on Languages and Compilers for Parallel Computing*. Also in No. 757 in *Lecture Notes in Computer Science*, pages 281-295, Springer-Verlag, 1992.

[5] Gu, J., Li, Z., Lee, G.: Experience with efficient array data flow analysis for array privatization. In *Proceedings of the Sixth ACM SIGPLAN Symposium on Principles and Practice of Parallel Programming*, pages 157-167, Las Vegas, NV, June 1997.

[6] Hennessy, J., Patterson, D.: *Computer Architecture: A Quantitative Approach.* Morgan Kaufmann Publishers, 1996.

[7] Kennedy K., McKinley, K.: Maximizing loop parallelism and improving data locality via loop fusion and distribution. In *Springer-Verlag Lecture Notes in Computer Science, 768. Proceedings of the Sixth Workhsop on Languages and Compilers for Parallel Computing*, Portland, Oregon, August, 1993.

[8] Manjikian, N., Abdelrahman, T.: Fusion of loops for parallelism and locality. *IEEE Transactions on Parallel and Distributed Systems*, 8(2):193–209, February 1997.

[9] Mohamed, A., Fox, G., Laszewski, G., Parashar, M., Haupt, T., Mills, K., Lu, Y., Lin, N., Yeh, N.: Applications benchmark set for fortran-d and high performance fortran. Technical Report CRPS-TR92260, Center for Research on Parallel Computation, Rice University, June 1992.

[10] Rice, J., Jing, J.: Problems to test parallel and vector languages. Technical Report CSD-TR-1016, Department of Computer Science, Purdue University, 1990.

[11] Rivera, G., Tseng, C,: Eliminating conflict misses for high performance architectures. In *Proceedings of the 1998 ACM International Conference on Supercomputing*, pages 353–360, Melbourne, Australia, July 1998.

[12] Sarkar, V.: Optimized unrolling of nested loops. In *Proceedings of the ACM International Conference on Supercomputing*, pages 153–166, Santa Fe, NM, May 2000.

[13] Singhai, S., McKinley, K.: A parameterized loop fusion algorithm for improving parallelism and cache locality. *The Computer Journal*, 40(6), 1997.

[14] Song, Y., Xu, R., Wang, C., Li, Z.: Data locality enhancement by memory reduction. In *Proceedings of the 15th ACM International Conference on Supercomputing*, Naples, Italy, June 2001.

[15] Wolf, M., Lam, M.: A data locality optimizing algorithm. In *Proceedings of ACM SIGPLAN Conference on Programming Languages Design and Implementation*, pages 30–44, Toronto, Ontario, Canada, June 1991.

# Automatic Data Distribution Method
# Using First Touch Control
# for Distributed Shared Memory Multiprocessors

Takashi Hirooka[1,2], Hiroshi Ohta[3], and Takayoshi Iitsuka[1,2]

1 Advanced Parallelizing Compiler Project
2 Systems Development Laboratory, Hitachi, Ltd.
3 Information & Computer Systems, Hitachi, Ltd.

**Abstract.** We propose an interprocedural automatic data distribution method for a parallelizing compiler on distributed shared memory multiprocessors. In this paper we present the algorithm and its implementation and evaluation. This method combines "first touch control (FTC)" with data distribution directives. The characteristics of the FTC method are that our compiler controls first touch data distribution of the operating system and accurately determines a complex distribution of data. This method appropriately distributes data for those program patterns which conventional data distribution methods are unable to properly treat. In addition, we implemented an interprocedural analysis which improves data locality for the program as a whole. We evaluated the parallel performance, on SGI Origin2000, of applying this method to NPB2.3serial/FT, SP, and CG, and SPECfp95/tomcatv. On 16 processors, these benchmarks ran 2.1 times faster (on average) than they did without our method.

## 1. Introduction

Distributed shared memory multiprocessors (DSMs) have attracted the attention of users because such architectures provide both good performance scalability in terms of distributed memory multiprocessors and an easy parallel programming environment for shared memory multiprocessors. For users to efficiently use DSMs, parallel coverage, load balance, and data locality are all important. In this study, we focus on the optimization of data locality. An appropriate data distribution is indispensable for obtaining better performance from DSMs with their physically-distributed memory. We think that compilers have an important role to play in this optimization. In this paper we propose an algorithm for automatically determining an appropriate data distribution, describe its implementation, and present the results of its evaluation.

Data distribution directives by users [1] and the first touch data distribution of the operating system [1] have conventionally been studied for use in physically-distributed memory multiprocessors. However, these conventional data distribution methods are not able to easily determine an appropriate data distribution for such relatively common program patterns as indirect reference arrays and array section references. As a first step towards solving this problem, we propose our first touch control (FTC) method, in which the compiler controls the first touch data distribution of the operating system. Next, we present an implementation of the interprocedural automatic data distribution method to which our FTC method is

H. Dietz (Ed.): LCPC 2001, LNCS 2624, pp. 147-161, 2003.

applied and evaluate the respective performances of NPB2.3serial/FT, SP and CG [10], and SPEC95fp/tomcatv [11]. Our automatic data distribution method uses the FTC method and data distribution directives in an appropriate way to determine an appropriate data distribution for indirect reference array and array section references. With conventional methods, it is difficult to treat such references in an appropriate way, but our method is able to do so while obtaining good performance scalability across a broad range of programs.

The remainder of this paper is organized in the following way: Section 2 explains our method for the data distribution, the 'first touch control' (FTC) method for DSM. Section 3 describes the implementation of an automatic interprocedural data distribution method for DSMs. Section 4 describes our methods of evaluation and the results of evaluation are analyzed in section 5. Related work is introduced in section 6 and we present our conclusions in section 7.

## 2. The First Touch Control (FTC) Method

In this section we give a few examples in which conventional data distribution methods do not work appropriately and explain our new data distribution method.

### 2.1 Conventional Methods of Data Distribution

One of the ways of implementing DSM is to divide a virtual memory space into pages and to assign the pages to physical memory at nodes. SGI Origin2000 is a typical DSM and uses this method. We adopted Origin2000 as the platform for our experiment. The system applies two methods of assigning data to physical memory at each of its distributed nodes to improve data locality [1].

(1) Data distribution by directives

The user inserts data distribution directives into the program and the compiler assigns data to the nodes on the basis of the directives.

(2) First touch data distribution

The OS assigns each page to the node which is the first to access the page.

In some cases these conventional methods are unable to determine an appropriate data distribution. In the following paragraphs, we show examples of this and then propose the FTC method to solve this problem.

### 2.2 The First Touch Control (FTC) Method

#### 2.2.1 Basic Idea

We propose our first touch control (FTC) method of data distribution in which the compiler controls first touch data distribution of the operating system. To simplify the explanation in this paragraph, we don't consider data redistribution. In this case, an appropriate static data distribution is a distribution that places the data in a 'good' way in terms of those kernel loops which have high execution ratios in the program.

In the FTC method, the compiler generates a dummy loop which imitates the reference patterns of the kernel loop of the program and inserts it at the head of the program. Data is then distributed according to the first accesses to data in the dummy loop, that is, first touch data distribution of the operating system is applied. The resulting distribution then fits the patterns of reference in the kernel loop well. In the following, arrays which are the objects of data distribution in the FTC method are called "target arrays".

Example program 1 is given in Fig. 1 (a). The initialization loop of this program refers to all of the elements of array A(1:100), but only the array section A(41:100) is referred to in the kernel loop. Such a reference pattern appears comparatively often in actual programs, e.g., when an array section is passed in a procedure call. This pattern is semantically the same as the situation in example program 1. We use an intraprocedural example for the simple explanation in Fig.1.

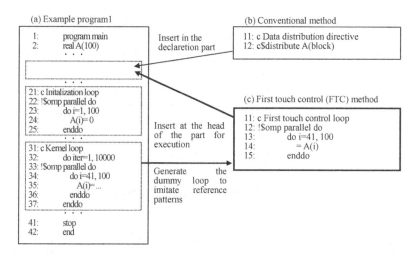

**Fig. 1**   First touch control method.

In the conventional method, a data distribution directive is inserted in the declaration part of the program (Fig. 1(b)) [5]. In this case, data is equally distributed to each processor as shown in Fig. 2(a). However, if the distribution of the loop iteration space is assumed to be a block distribution, the appropriate distribution for the kernel loop's reference pattern is to have array section A(41:100) uniformly distributed among the processors as shown in Fig. 2(b). Therefore the difference between Fig. 2(a) and Fig. 2(b) becomes remote references (Fig.2(c)). Up to 67% of the references in the kernel loop are remote references, and we cannot get enough of a performance benefit from parallel execution because of the low level of data locality. In another conventional method, the program is not modified and the data distribution is by the first touch data distribution of the operating system. Since the initialization loop refers to all elements of the array A(1:100), the resulting distribution of data is the same as is shown in Fig. 2(a). So this method doesn't improve data locality, either.

Our FTC method generates a dummy loop which imitates the pattern of references to target array A in the kernel loop (Fig. 1(c)). We call this dummy loop the "first touch control (FTC) loop". This FTC loop is inserted at the head of the execution part of the program. The data distribution to each processor is as a first touch data distribution of the operating system. The resulting distribution of data is shown in Fig. 2(d) and the references to target array A in the kernel loop are now always local.

Complicated directives such as the INDIRECT directive of HPF [5] are able to distribute data in the way shown in Fig. 2(d). It is, however, troublesome for users to insert complicated directives in their programs. In the FTC method, our compiler automatically inserts an FTC loop in the program and reduces the burden on users. Directives are not available when an appropriate data distribution must be determined during execution (e.g., for an indirect reference array). The FTC method is available in such cases (see 2.2.2).

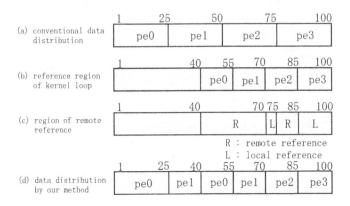

**Fig. 2** Illustration of data distribution.

Furthermore, the FTC method is effective in the following case. In real programs, arrays are passed as arguments across boundaries between procedures. When the data distribution of an array argument is statically determined by a directive, it has to be inserted into the "most ancestral procedure" that is nearest to the main procedure in the procedures where this array is referred to. However, when the shape in which the array argument is declared differs from procedure to procedure, it is not possible to create an appropriate data distribution by directive because the directive will be based on the shape of the declaration in the procedure which contains the kernel loop. In such a case, the FTC method generates both the FTC loop and the dummy procedure calls which imitate the calling relationships among related procedures, and inserts them at the head of the program. It is thus able to get an appropriate data distribution.

### 2.2.2 Extension of the FTC Method

When parameters are variables, it is necessary to change the insertion point of the FTC loop according to the points where the values of the parameters are defined. The relevant parameters are:
- the declared size of the target array;
- the upper bound, lower bound, and stride of the kernel loop; and
- any variables contained in subscripts of target arrays (except loop control variables).

When the parameters are constants, the FTC loop is inserted at the head of the execution part of the program. When, however, the parameters are variables, the FTC loop must be inserted after the points at which these parameters are defined. In the latter case, there are two possible patterns for the inserted code, and the appropriate one depends on the points at which the parameters are defined. When the parameters are defined before an initialization loop, the FTC loop is inserted just after the point at which the parameters are defined. When, on the other hand, the parameters are defined after an initialization loop, a program transformation such as is shown in Fig. 3 is necessary.

Firstly, an array (called a "clone array") is generated with a declaration in the same shape as that of the target array. Next, all references to the target array in the initialization loop are replaced by references to the clone array. The FTC loop for the target array and code to copy all elements of the clone array to the target array are inserted just after the point at which related parameters of the target array are defined. Our FTC method is applicable to a program in which the parameters are variables.

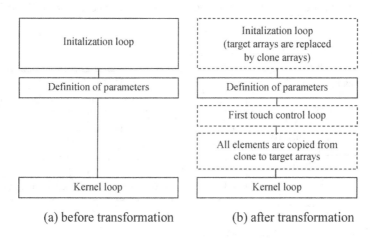

(a) before transformation          (b) after transformation

**Fig. 3**  Program transformation in the case of parameters defined after the initialization loop.

We also consider the data redistribution. When there are two or more kernel loops and each of them has a different pattern of reference to the same array, redistributing the array's data is helpful in obtaining good performance. The following program transformation is applied:

-   generate a clone array of the target array, generate the FTC loop which distributes the clone array into the redistributed shape, and insert the loop at the head of the execution part of the program;
-   copy all values of the target array to the clone array at the point for the redistribution of data; and
-   from the data redistribution point, replace all references to the target array with references to the clone array.

It is thus possible to obtain an effect that is equivalent to that of data redistribution by the operating system.

# 3. Automatic Data Distribution Method for Distributed Shared Memory

This section describes the method of automatic data distribution for DSM in which the FTC method we explained in section 2 is applied.

## 3.1 Structure of Our Compiler

The structure of the automatic parallelizing compiler for DSM that we implemented is shown in Fig. 4. We add an automatic data distribution function to the existing WPP automatic parallelizing compiler for SMP [8]. The input to the automatic parallelizing compiler for DSM is a serial Fortran77 program and the output is a Fortran90 program with OpenMP directives and data distribution code. The output program becomes the input for the SGI MIPSpro Fortran90 compiler which supports the OpenMP Fortran API and original data distribution directives for DSM. The SGI compiler outputs the parallel object program for DSM. The DSM machine is SGI Origin2000.

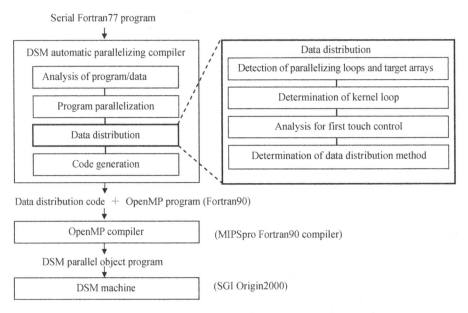

**Fig. 4**   Structure of automatic parallelizing compiler for DSM.

The data distribution part of our compiler is informed of parallelizing loops detected by the program-parallelization part [8] and detects references to target arrays from the bodies of those loops. Next, it analyzes the shape of the data distribution of each target array for each parallelizing loop. It then determines the kernel loop with the highest execution ratio of the program and the shape of the data distribution of its target arrays which fits that kernel loop. Moreover, data redistribution analysis takes place at the same time and determines whether or not a data redistribution of the target array is necessary. Finally, the analysis required for the FTC data distribution takes place, and the method of data distribution is determined.

### 3.2 Algorithm

Generally speaking, the appropriate data distribution will differ from portion to portion of a program. We designed our automatic data distribution method to operate in the following way: firstly, the data distribution is assumed to be fixed across the whole program, and an appropriate distribution is analyzed and determined statically. Next, if data redistribution analysis finds program sections where data redistribution is necessary and the cost of that redistribution is low enough, an appropriate data redistribution is determined.

Fig. 5 depicts the algorithm of the automatic data distribution method for DSM. This algorithm is divided into six parts.
(1) Detection of parallelizing loops and target arrays.
(2) Determination of the shape of data distribution for each parallelizing loop.
(3) Determination of the kernel loop.
(4) Data redistribution analysis.
(5) Analysis for first touch control.
(6) Determination of data distribution method.

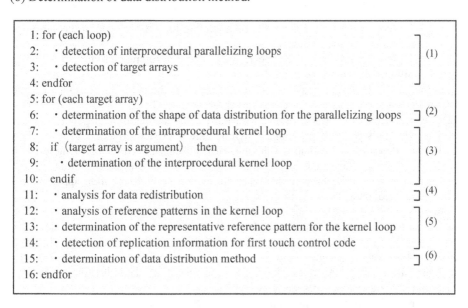

**Fig. 5**   Algorithm of the automatic data distribution method for DSM.

Each part is explained in detail below, using the example program 2 of Fig. 6. In this example, L1 and L4 assume that it is detected as parallelizing loops. Fig. 7 is the data distribution graph of the example program2. The graph consists of array nodes(rectangles), loop nodes(circles), reference pattern nodes(hexagons), and edges indicating the relation between nodes.

(1) Detection of parallelizing loops and target arrays

First, this part determines interprocedural parallelizing loops from all loops in the program according to the result of program parallelization [8]. Next, from among those arrays which are referred to from the bodies of the parallelizing loops, it detects those arrays which satisfy the following conditions. These are defined target arrays.

```
1: do i= 1, 100          ; L1
2:    do j= 1, 100        ; L2
3:       A(i,j)= · · ·
4:    enddo
5: enddo
       · · ·
11: do iter= 1, 10        ; L3
12:    do i= 2, 50        ; L4
13:       do j= 2, 99     ; L5
14:          B(j,i)= A(j+1,i+1)
15:                 + A(j+1,i-1)
16:                 + A(j-1,i-1)
17:       enddo
18:    enddo
19: enddo
```

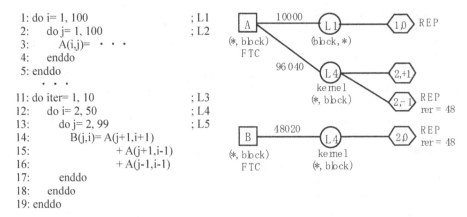

**Fig. 6**   Example program2        **Fig. 7**   Data distribution graph

- The loop-control variable of the parallelizing loop is included in the subscript expressions of the reference.
- The loop-control variable appears only once in a reference to the array and in only one dimension of that reference.

In the graph, the target arrays A and B referred to in the parallelizing loops L1 and L4 are detected, and the array nodes A and B are generated.

(2) Determination of the shape of data distribution for each parallelizing loop

This part finds parallelizing loops which include references to target arrays in their bodies and determines the shape of the data distribution of each parallelizing loop for each target array. The shape of the data distribution is a block distribution in that dimension in which the loop-control variable of the parallelizing loop appears most often in all references from the loop's body.

In the graph, the parallelizing loops L1 and L4 which have references of array A are detected, and the parallelizing loop L4 which has a reference of array B is detected. Next, (block, *) are determined as the shape of data distribution of the parallelizing loop L1 for array A because loop L1's control variable i appears most often in the indexes of the array A in the loop L1. The shape of data distribution is also determined to other loops, respectively.

(3) Determination of the kernel loop

This part determines the kernel loop for each target array. The cost of the loop is assumed to be product of the number of operations in the loop's body and the loop's length. Firstly, parallelizing loops which have the same data distribution shape are grouped, the cost of each parallelizing loop is estimated, and the group with the maximum sum of costs of the loops to be parallelized is selected. Then, let that parallelizing loop which has the maximum cost of the loops in the group be the intraprocedural kernel loop for this target array. Next, when the target array is an argument, the intraprocedural kernel loop, in each procedure to which the target array is passed, is detected. These detected intraprocedural kernel loops are grouped on the basis of the shapes of the data distributions and the group which has the maximum cost is selected. Let the intraprocedural kernel loop which has the maximum cost in this group be the interprocedural kernel loop.

In the graph, the cost of the loop, 10000, is estimated for the edge between array A and the parallelizing loop L1. Similarly, the costs of the other loops are estimated for each edge, and the parallelizing loop L4 which has the maximum cost of the loop is chosen as a kernel loop of array A. At this time, the shape of data distribution (*, block) for the kernel loop L4 becomes the shape of the data distribution of array A.

(4) Data redistribution analysis

Firstly, those target arrays which are local to the procedure are analyzed in the following way. Those parallelizing loops which satisfy the conditions below is detected and is called the data redistribution loop.

- The loop is not an intraprocedural kernel loop.
- The data distribution shape of the loop determined in (2) is not the same as that of the intraprocedural kernel loop.
- The reduction in execution time by data redistribution is greater than the threshold of data redistribution.

The equation below represents the reduction in execution time by the data redistribution.

$$N*(1-1/P)*T$$

N is the number of references to the target array in the loop. P is the number of threads. T is the difference between the access time for remote and local memory references. The threshold of data redistribution is the cost, in terms of time, of redistributing the target array's data. System-dependent parameters, the number of threads, and the size of the array determine this cost.

Secondly, the target array which is an argument is analyzed in the following way. Those intraprocedural kernel loops which satisfy the conditions below are detected and the procedure which includes the intraprocedural kernel loop is called the data redistribution procedure.

- The data distribution shape of the given intraprocedural kernel loop is not the same as that of the interprocedural kernel loop.
- The reduction in execution time gained by redistributing data is greater than the threshold of data redistribution.

In the example program2, data redistribution analysis is not made because there is no interprocedural loop.

(5) Analysis for first touch control

First, each target array is analyzed in the following way.

- Define a set of subscript expressions of all dimensions of the target array as a reference pattern, and detect all reference patterns in the kernel loop of the target array.
- Find that reference pattern which appears most often and let it be the representative reference pattern.
- Detect the upper bounds, lower bounds, and steps for those loop-control variables which are included in the subscript expressions of the representative

reference pattern, and the order of loop nesting, and hold these as information for use in generating the FTC loop.

When the target array is an argument, the calling path from the most ancestral procedure in which the target array appears to the procedure which contains the kernel loop is detected, and the following information is also held:

- the order of procedure calls,
- the order of arguments, and
- the shape of the declaration of the target array in each procedure.

When the call graph is complex, that path with the greatest number of calls is detected and the information described above, for the calls along the path, is held. This information is used to generate the FTC loop in FTC code generation. This analysis applies to constant parameters. When the parameters are variables, the extended method explained in section 2 must be applied.

In the graph, first, $(2, +1)$ and $(2, -1)$ are detected as reference patterns of the parallelizing loop L4 for array A. The first element of the reference pattern indicates the dimension containing the loop control variable of the parallelizing loop, and the second element indicates the distance from the loop control variable independent formula of the parallelizing loop (for example, in the case of I+1, distance is +1). All reference patterns are similarly detected for other loops. Next, $(2, -1)$ is chosen as a representative reference pattern REP of the parallelizing loop L4 of array A because this reference appears most often. The ratio of the number of elements of the array referred to in the kernel loop to the number of declared elements is defined as the referred-elements ratio("rer" in Fig. 7). Next, the referred-elements ratio is estimated to be 48% as the information for the FTC method of this representative reference pattern $(2, -1)$.

(6) Determination of the data distribution method

The data distribution method for each target array is determined. The FTC method is chosen when the target array satisfies the following conditions.

- The kernel loop refers to some part of the array.
- The array is an argument and the shape in which it is declared differs from procedure to procedure.

In other cases, our method chooses data distribution according to directives. When the target array is local to procedure and its referred-elements ratio is less than 50%, the FTC method is chosen for that target array. When the referred-elements ratio is greater than or equal to 50%, data distribution is by directives. When the target array is an argument with a referred-elements ratio of less than 50%, the FTC method is chosen. When the referred-elements ratio is greater than or equal to 50%, data distribution is by directives as long as all shapes in which the array is declared in procedures to which the array is passed are the same. The FTC method is chosen in all other cases [9].

In the graph, since the referred-elements ratio of the representative reference pattern of the kernel loop L4 of array A is 48% and is less than 50%, the data distribution method of array A is determined as the first touch control method FTC.

# 4. Method of Evaluation

## 4.1 Measurement Conditions

Performance was measured on Origin2000. The machine's parameters are listed in Table 1. Since each node of Origin2000 has 2 processors, the effect of improved data locality only appears with four or more processors in the performance graphs given in the next section.

**Table 1:** Machine parameters.

| Machine | SGI Origin2000 |
|---|---|
| Node | 16 nodes(2 cpu/node) |
| CPU | MIPS RISC R10000 (195 MHz) |
| Cache | L1: 32 KB, L2: 4 MB |
| Main memory | 11 GB |
| OS | IRIX 6.5.4 |
| Compier | MIPSpro Fortran90 (Version 7.3) |
| Compiler options | -mp -64 -Ofast=IP27 -OPT:IEEE_arithmetic=3 |

## 4.2 Evaluation of the Automatic Parallelizing Compiler for DSM

SPEC95fp/tomcatv and NPB2.3serial/FT, SP, and CG of NASA are used as benchmark programs. The following areas of output by the automatic data distribution function of our compiler and the resulting performance of each were analyzed:
- detected target arrays,
- determined shape of data distribution,
- determined method of data distribution, and
- performance scalability.

The results of measurement of each benchmark are given and analyzed in section 5.

# 5. Evaluation Results

Table 2 shows the results of analysis of our automatic data distribution method against each benchmark. The data size, the shape of its distribution, and the method of data distribution determined for the target arrays by our algorithm are shown. Figs. 8 to 11 represent the execution performance of each benchmark. The horizontal axes of these figures indicate the number of processors and the vertical axes indicate speedup. In these figures, "dist" and "no dist" respectively indicate whether or not our automatic data distribution method is applied. In the "no dist" case, only the operating system's first touch data distribution is applied. "class A" and "class B" indicate two data sizes of NPB2.3serial.

**Table 2:** Data distribution shapes of target arrays determined by our automatic data distribution method.

| Program | Target arrays | Data size | | Data distribution shape | Method |
|---------|---------------|-----------|---|------------------------|--------|
| | | class A | class B | | |
| FT | U1, INDEXMAP | 256x256x128 | 512x256x256 | (*,*,block) | FTC |
| | U0, U2 | 256x256x128 | 512x256x256 | (*,block,*) | |
| SP | LHS | 64x64x63x15 | 102x102x101x15 | (*,*,block,*) | DIR |
| | FORCING, RHS, U | 64x64x63x5 | 102x102x101x5 | (*,*,block,*) | |
| | SQUARE, SPEED, RHO_I AINV, QS, WS, VS, US | 64x64x63 | 102x102x101 | (*,*,block) | |
| CG | COLIDX,A | 2198000 | 15825000 | (block) | DIR |
| | ROWSTR, V, X, Z | 14001 | 75001 | (block) | |
| tomcatv | AA, DD, X, Y, RX, RY | 513x513 | | (*,block) | DIR |
| | D | 513x513 | | (block,*) | |

## (1) FT

Our algorithm detects the target arrays for automatic data distribution and determines the data distribution shapes shown in Table 2. As the data declaration shapes of those arrays differ from procedure to procedure and it is difficult to obtain an appropriate data distribution shape of the kernel loop by placing directives in the most ancestral procedure, the first touch control method (FTC) is selected. For all other benchmarks, data distribution is by directive (DIR).

The resulting speedup is shown in Fig. 8. The overhead of the FTC code is included in this figure. When the compiler doesn't use automatic data distribution, the scalability of the resulting performance is not good for classes A and B because the data locality decreases as the number of processors increases. On the other hand, when our automatic data distribution function is used, good scalability is obtained because the appropriate data distribution improves the data locality. For example, performance for class B is improved by 89% on 16 processors. In addition, as the amount of data increases, so does the difference between the speedup for "dist" and "no dist".

Data redistribution improves data locality in some parts of FT. Our method, however, doesn't use data redistribution because the cost of data redistribution by Origin2000 is estimated to be too large. If the cost of data redistribution falls, the data locality will be improved by data redistribution and the performance scalability will increase.

## (2) SP

Target arrays and the determined data distribution shapes of SP are shown in Table 2. Data distribution by directives (DIR) is chosen as the method of data distribution.

Fig. 9 represents the speedup in this case. Although the "no dist" performance of SP is comparatively good in parallel execution, SP runs, for class B on 16 processors, 12% faster than it does in the "no dist" case when our method is applied. The larger the amount of data and the greater the number of processors, the greater the performance improvement tends to be for SP.

## (3) CG

Parallel coverage of CG is very high and good scalability can be expected if data locality is good.

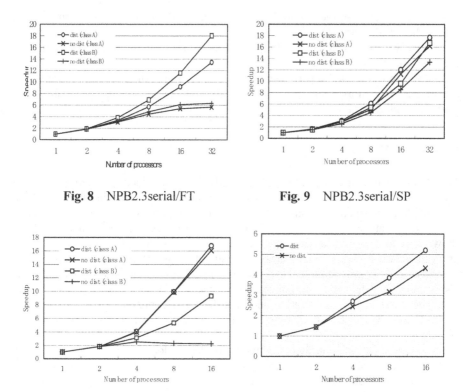

**Fig. 8**  NPB2.3serial/FT          **Fig. 9**  NPB2.3serial/SP

**Fig. 10**  NPB2.3serial/CG          **Fig. 11**  SPECfp95/tomcatv

Fig. 10 shows the speedup. In class A, good scalability is obtained for both "dist" and "no dist" since there is less data in the target arrays than the cache size. When, however, the amount of data is large, as is the case for class B, the ratio of remote references to local references increases and scalability is greatly worsened. When, on the other hand, our automatic method of data distribution is used, scalability improves sharply and performance improves by 4.1 times for class B on 16 processors.

**(4) tomcatv**

Fig.11 shows the speedup. Our automatic method of data distribution improves data locality and performance is improved by 20% on 16 processors.

**(5) Summary**

Our method distributes data on the basis of the parallelizing loops determined in the program-parallelization phase. Therefore, this method is useful in cases where an existing form of program parallelization is in use and data locality is bad. Implicit data distribution by the operating system's first touch data distribution is, in some cases, effective. This shape of data distribution, however, worsens the data locality in the following cases.

-    Where the initialization loop is not parallelizable due to dependences and/or the precision of dependence analysis.
-    When the shape in which the target array is declared is different in a procedure from the shape in the procedure that contains the kernel loop.

- The structure of the initialization loop or parallel loop nesting is different from that of the kernel loop.

FT and CG are benchmarks that represent examples of these cases. Our method is useful on these two benchmarks.

In order to obtain better performance for a wider range of practical programs, the use of analysis information from the compiler by our automatic data distribution method is indispensable.

## 6. Related Work

There has been much research into methods for automatically determining data distribution. Since the determination of an appropriate data distribution is an NP-complete problem, various heuristics for approximate solutions have been proposed by Tatsumi [6], Matsuura [7], Gupta [3], Kennedy [2], etc. Tatsumi [6] has shown how to determine a distributed dimension and its block size for a single loop, using the relative relation among arrays. Matsuura[7] has shown how to determine, on the basis of interprocedural array access information for multiple loops, the distribution of data which minimizes communication. Gupta [3] has presented an interprocedural loop parallelization and data distribution method for cc-NUMA. All methods use data distribution directives alone and do not touch on the following situations:

- where a part of an array is referred to in a kernel loop;
- where the shape in which a given array argument is declared is not the same from procedure to procedure; and
- where there is an indirect reference arrays in a kernel loop.

Our automatic data distribution method is able to distribute data appropriately even in such cases and is able to interprocedurally determine a data distribution among multiple loops.

## 7. Conclusions

In this paper, a method for interprocedural automatic data distribution in DSM systems and its implementation and evaluation have been described. We show that, in combination with the operating system's first touch data distribution and method of compiler control, our method is able to distribute data more appropriately, and evaluate its effectiveness when applied in this way. Moreover, our automatic data distribution method which uses both an FTC loop and conventional data distribution directives has been implemented in our interprocedural parallelizing compiler. This enables us to determine appropriate data distributions for indirect reference arrays, array sections in the program as a whole which conventional data distribution is unable to treat properly.

The method's performance on four benchmark programs, NPB2.3serial/FT, SP, and CG, and SPEC95fp/tomcatv, showed an improvement of 2.1 times on average on Origin2000 with 16 processors over the case where our method is not applied.

The following subjects remain for future study of this automatic data distribution method:

- the implementation of automatic data distribution for indirect reference arrays; and
- evaluation on further benchmarks and extension of our method on the basis of the results of evaluation.

For the FTC method, the following subjects remain for further study;
- the extraction of effective program patterns;
- the examination of the conditions that apply to each program pattern; and
- extension of the compiler's functions.

**Acknowledgements.** This research is partly based on the results of the Real World Computing Partnership (RWCP). We are thankful to Yuichiro Aoki and the other members of the 305 Research Unit in Hitachi Ltd.'s Systems Development Laboratory, for priceless discussions and advice.

# References

[1] Chandra, R., Chen, D., Cox, R., Maydan, D.E., Nedeljkovic, N., Anderson, J.: Data Distribution Support on Distributed Shared Memory Multiprocessors, Proc. PLDI'97, pp. 334-345 (1997).

[2] Kennedy, K., Kremer, U.: Automatic Data Layout for High Performance Fortran, Proc. Supercomputing'95, (1995).

[3] Gupta, M., Banerjee, P.: PARADIGM: A Compiler for Automatic Data Distribution on Multicomputers, Proc. ICS'93, pp. 87-96 (1993).

[4] High Performance Fortran Forum: High Performance Fortran Language Specification Version 2.0, (1997).

[5] SGI MIPSpro Fortran77 Programmer's Guide, Silicon Graphics Inc.

[6] Tatsumi, S., Kubota, A., Goshima, M., Mori, S., Nakajima, H., Tomita, S.: An Implementation of the Automatic Data Distribution Phase of the Parallelizing Compiler TINPAR, IPSJ SIG Notes, 96-PRO-8, pp. 25-30 (1996). (in Japanese).

[7] Matsuura, K., Murai, H., Suehiro, K., Seo, Y.: Fast Automatic Data Layout for Data Parallel Programs, IPSJ Journal, Vol. 41, No. 5, pp. 1420-1429 (2000). (in Japanese).

[8] Aoki, Y., Sato, M., Iitsuka, T., Sato, S., Kikuchi, S.: Prototyping of Interprocedural Parallelizing Compiler "WPP" - Performance Evaluation -, IPSJ SIG Notes, 98-ARC-130, pp. 43-48 (1998). (in Japanese).

[9] Hirooka, T., Ohta, H., Kikuchi, S.: Automatic Data Distribution Method by First  Touch Control for Distributed Shared Memory, IPSJ Journal, Vol. 41, No. 5, pp. 1430-1438 (2000). (in Japanese).

[10] The NAS Parallel Benchmarks, http://www.nas.nasa.gov/Software/NPB/

[11] SPEC Benchmarks, http://www.specbench.org/

# Balanced, Locality-Based Parallel Irregular Reductions*

Eladio Gutiérrez, Oscar Plata, and Emilio L. Zapata

Department of Computer Architecture
University of Málaga
E-29071 Málaga, Spain
{eladio,oscar,ezapata}@ac.uma.es

**Abstract.** Much effort has been devoted recently to efficiently parallelize irregular reductions. Different parallelization techniques have been proposed during the last years that can be classified into two groups: LPO (*Loop Partitioning Oriented* methods) and DPO (*Data Partitioning Oriented* methods). We have analyzed both classes in terms of a set of performance aspects: data locality, memory overhead, parallelism and workload balancing. Load balancing is not an issue sufficiently analyzed in the literature in parallel reduction methods, specially those in the DPO class. In this paper we propose two techniques to introduce load balancing into a DPO method. The first technique is generic, as it can deal with any kind of load unbalancing present in the problem domain. The second technique handles a special case of load unbalancing, appearing when there are a large number of write operations on small regions of the reduction arrays. Efficient implementations of the proposed solutions to load balancing for an example DPO method are presented. Experiments on static and dynamic kernel codes were conducted making comparisons with other parallel reduction methods.

## 1 Introduction

Many scientific/engineering applications are based on complex data structures that introduce irregular memory access patterns. In general, automatic parallelizers obtain sub–optimal parallel codes from those applications, as traditional data dependence analysis and optimization techniques are precluded. Run–time techniques have been proposed in the literature to support the parallelization of irregular codes, like those based on the inspector-executor paradigm [15], or the speculative execution of loops in parallel [16].

Run–time techniques like mentioned above are general enough to be applied to many different classes of irregular computations. However, due in part to their generality, the efficiency of the parallelized codes is usually poor. Significantly better performance may be obtained from techniques tailor-made for specific irregular operations, computational structures and/or data access patterns [1, 11].

---

* This work was supported by Ministry of Education and Culture (CICYT), Spain, through grant TIC2000-1658

H. Dietz (Ed.): LCPC 2001, LNCS 2624, pp. 162–176, 2003.

Reduction operations represent an example of such computational structures, frequently found in the core of many irregular numerical applications. The importance of these operations to the overall performance of the applications has involved much attention from compiler researchers. In fact, numerous techniques have been developed and, some of them implemented in contemporary parallelizers, to detect and transform into efficient parallel code those operations.

In this paper we classify the most important irregular reduction parallelization techniques into two main classes: *Loop Partitioning Oriented* (LPO) techniques and *Data Partitioning Oriented* (DPO) techniques. LPO methods assign blocks of reduction loop iterations to the cooperating threads, while DPO methods assign blocks of the reduction arrays to the threads (and the loop iterations that each thread execute are those that write mostly in the owned block). Further, both classes are analyzed in terms of a set of performance aspects: data locality (inter-loop and intra-loop), memory overhead, parallelism and workload balancing. These aspects have a strong influence in the overall performance and scalability of the parallel reduction code. We will discuss how the parallelization techniques usually try to optimize some of the above-mentioned aspects, missing the other(s). That is, the parallel code is usually not optimal in terms of both performance and scalability.

Load balancing is not an aspect sufficiently discussed and analyzed in the considered parallel reduction methods, specially those in the DPO class, which are very sensitive to that aspect. In this paper we propose two techniques to introduce load balancing into a DPO method. The first technique, based on the subblocking of the reduction arrays, is generic, as it can deal with any kind of load unbalancing present in the problem domain. The second technique handles a special case of load unbalancing, present when there are a large number of write operations on small regions of the reduction arrays. The proposed solution for these cases is based on the privatization of the blocks making up those regions.

In this paper we discuss efficient implementations of the proposed solutions to load balancing for the DWA–LIP DPO method, that were experimentally tested on different kernel codes and compared with other parallel reduction techniques. The main contribution from this research is that it is possible to improve the performance of a DPO method, like DWA–LIP, for unbalanced problems with no significant loss of data locality exploitation and no substantial increment in extra memory overhead and algorithmic complexity.

The remainder of the paper begins with a discussion and classification of the most important methods for irregular reduction parallelization. Using such classification, the methods are analyzed in terms of a set of relevant performance features. Next, we highlight the load balancing problem, and propose our solutions to solve it, as well as efficient implementations on a particular DPO method. Finally, experimental results that validate our analysis are presented.

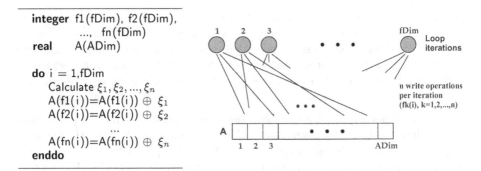

```
integer  f1(fDim), f2(fDim),
         ..., fn(fDim)
real     A(ADim)

do i = 1,fDim
   Calculate ξ₁, ξ₂, ..., ξₙ
   A(f1(i))=A(f1(i)) ⊕ ξ₁
   A(f2(i))=A(f2(i)) ⊕ ξ₂
       ...
   A(fn(i))=A(fn(i)) ⊕ ξₙ
enddo
```

**Fig. 1.** A loop with multiple reductions and a schematic representation of the irregular memory access pattern

## 2   Methods for Reduction Parallelization

Different specific solutions to parallelize irregular reductions on shared-memory multiprocessors have been proposed in the literature. We may classify them into two broad categories: *loop partitioning oriented* techniques (LPO) and *data partitioning oriented* techniques (DPO). The LPO class includes those methods based on the partitioning of the reduction loop and further execution of the resulting iteration blocks on different parallel threads. A DPO technique, on the other hand, is based on the (usually block) partitioning of the reduction array, assigning to each parallel thread preferably those loop iterations that issue write operations on a particular data block (then it is say that the thread owns that block).

To facilitate the analysis of the above classes, we consider in the rest of the paper the general case of a loop with multiple reductions, as shown in Fig. 1 (the case of multiply nested loops is not relevant for our discussion). A() represents the reduction array (that could be multidimensional), which is updated through multiple subscript arrays, f1(), f2(), ..., fn(). Due to the loop-variant nature of the subscript arrays, loop-carried dependences may be present, and can only be detected at run–time.

Taking into account this example irregular reduction loop, Fig. 2 shows a graphical representation of generic techniques in the described two classes, LPO and DPO.

The simplest solution in the LPO class is based on critical sections, where the reduction loop is executed fully parallel by just enclosing the accesses to the reduction array in a critical section. This method exhibits a very high synchronization overhead and, consequently, a very low efficiency.

The synchronization pressure can be reduced (or even eliminated) by privatizing the reduction array, as it is done by the *replicated buffer* and *array expansion* techniques. The *replicated buffer* method replicates private copies of the full reduction array on all threads. Each thread accumulates partial results on its private copy, and finally the global result is obtained by accumulating

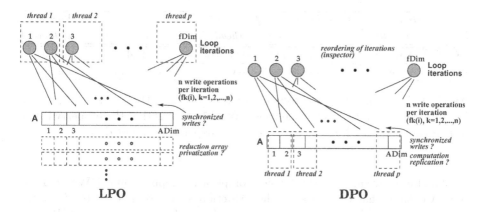

**Fig. 2.** General schematic representation of the LPO and DPO classes of reduction parallelization techniques

the partial results across threads on the global reduction array (this last step needs synchronization to ensure mutual exclusion). The other method, (*array expansion*), expands the reduction array by the number of parallel threads. Now each thread accumulates partial results on its own section of the expanded array. This approach allows to obtain the final result in a similar way than the first method, but with no need of the final synchronization.

Note that these two methods transform the reduction loop into a fully parallel one, as the possible loop-carried dependencies disappear as a result of the privatization of the reduction array. However, they have scalability problems for large data sets, as the privatization affect the whole reduction array and on all threads (the memory overhead increases in proportion to the number of parallel threads).

Methods in the DPO class avoid the privatization of the reduction array, as it is partitioned and assigned to the parallel threads. In order to determine which loop iterations each thread should execute (mostly those that write in its assigned block), an inspector is introduced at runtime whose net effect is the reordering of the reduction loop iterations (through the reordering of the subscript arrays). The selected reordering tries to minimize write conflicts, and, in addition, to exploit data (reference) locality.

Two methods has been proposed in the literature in the DPO class. One method was termed LOCALWRITE [7, 8, 10], and is based on the *owner–computes rule*. Each thread owns a portion of the reduction array (block partitioning). The inspector has reordered the subscript arrays in such a way that, in the execution phase, the set of iterations assigned to that thread only updates array elements of the owned block. Note, however, that, in order to fulfill the computes rule, those iterations that updates more than one block of the reduction array must be replicated across the owner threads. This computation replication introduces a performance penalty (parallelism loss).

| | Inter-Loop Locality | Intra-Loop Locality | Memory Overhead | Parallelism | Workload Balance |
|---|---|---|---|---|---|
| **LPO** | variable | variable | high/medium/low | high | high |
| **DPO** | high | variable | low | high/medium/low | variable |

**Table 1.** Performance characteristics for the LPO and DPO classes of parallel irregular reduction methods. The label `variable` means that the property is not intrinsically exploited by the method, but it depends on input data

An alternative method that avoids computation replication is DWA–LIP [4, 5, 6]. Consider that the blocks of the reduction array are indexed by the natural numbers. The inspector (named *loop-index prefetching* phase, or LIP) now sorts all the iterations of the reduction loop into sets characterized by the pair $(B_{min}, \Delta B)$, where $B_{min}$ ($B_{max}$) is the minimum (maximum) index of all blocks touched by the iterations in that set, and $\Delta B$ is the difference $B_{max} - B_{min}$. The execution phase (or computation phase) of the method is organized as a synchronized sequence of non-conflicting (parallel) stages. In the first stage, all sets of iterations of the form $(B_{min}, 0)$ are executed in parallel because they are all data flow independent (optimal utilization of the threads). The second stage is split into two sub-stages. In the first one, all sets $(B_{min}, 1)$ with an odd value of $B_{min}$ are executed fully parallel, followed by the second sub-stage where the rest of sets are executed in parallel. A similar scheme is followed in the subsequent stages, until all iterations are exhausted

## 2.1   Performance Characteristics

Methods in the LPO and DPO classes have, in some sense, complementary performance characteristics. Methods in the first class exhibit optimal parallelism exploitation (the reduction loop is fully parallel), but no data locality is taken into account and lack scalability (memory overhead is proportional to the number of threads). However, as the reduction loop is uniformly partitioned, these methods usually exhibit balanced workload.

Methods in the second class, however, exploit data locality and exhibit usually much lower memory overhead, and it is not dependent on the number of threads (the inspector may need some extra buffering to store subscript reorderings, independently on the number of threads). However, either the method introduces some computation replication or is organized in a number of synchronized phases. In any case, this fact represents loss of parallelism. In addition, there is the risk that the number of the loop iterations that write some specific block is much different from the same in another block (workload unbalance).

Table 1 shows typical characteristics of methods in LPO and DPO classes considering four relevant performance aspects: data locality, memory overhead, parallelism and workload balance. Data locality is in turn split into inter-loop and intra-loop localities. Inter-loop locality refers to the data locality among different reduction loop iterations. Intra-loop locality, on the other hand, corresponds to data locality inside one reduction loop iteration.

LPO methods basically exploit maximum parallelism in a very balanced way. Regarding memory overhead, they are very eager. Different solutions has been proposed recently to reduce this high memory overhead, based on the array expansion and replicated buffer basic methods. The *reduction table* method [11] assigns a private buffer to each thread of a fixed size (lower than the size of the reduction array). Then, each thread works on its private buffer indexed by using a fast hash formula. When the hash table is full, any new operation will work directly on the global reduction array within a critical section. Other method is *selective privatization* [18], where the replication include only those elements referenced by various threads. It first determine (inspector phase) which are those elements and then allocate for them private storage space. Each thread, then, works on its private buffer when updating conflicting elements, while it works on the global reduction array otherwise. This execution behavior implies a replication of each subscript array in order to store the new indexing scheme. Some sort of combination of the above both techniques has been also proposed in the literature [18].

Data locality is not exploited by a LPO method. This situation could be relieved by adding an external preprocessing stage before executing the irregular code. This stage is in charge of reordering the input data (that will fill the subscript arrays) with the aim of optimizing locality [9, 3]. However, these techniques have a high algorithmic complexity and normally they have difficulties to be used in dynamic codes.

DPO methods, on the other hand, are designed to exploit, at runtime, data locality, specially inter-loop locality, at the cost of reducing a fraction of parallelism (including computation replication). Intra-loop locality could be, additionally, exploited externally by means of a preprocessing reordering algorithm. Other interesting characteristic is that usually memory overhead is much lower than in basic LPO methods, improving significantly the scalability properties.

An important drawback of DPO methods is that they may exhibit workload unbalancing, penalizing their overall performance, depending on input data. This problem could be reduced, at least partially, by an external renumbering of input data [9, 3]. A different solution would be to introduce some load balancing support inside the DPO method. This approach is discussed in the next section.

## 3    Balancing Workload in DPO Methods

Generically, methods in the DPO class are based on an uniform block partitioning of the reduction array, as this way data locality may be exploited. However, as loop iterations are assigned to the parallel threads depending on the block they write in, this may introduce important workload unbalance. Note that this situation is not usual concerning typical numerical applications, but potentially it could appear for specific memory access patterns (that represents non uniform problem domains).

In this section we present two approaches to improve the workload balancing of DPO methods. The first approach is oriented to balance generic non uniform load distributions. It is based on the subpartitioning of the reduction array blocks into subblocks of the same size. The second approach, on the other hand, is oriented to special cases where the load unbalance is due to a high number of write operations on small regions of the reduction array (these were called regions of *high degree of contention* in [18]). The solution proposed consists of the local replication of some of these regions.

In the rest of the section we will show how we can modify in an easy and efficient way a DPO method in order to implement the above mentioned approaches. To simplify the description of these modifications the DWA-LIP technique will be taken as the working DPO method.

## 3.1   Generic Load Balancing Approach

To balance the workload among the threads while keeping exploited data locality, a good approach would be to partition the reduction array into blocks of different size, with the aim of minimizing execution time. However, the inspector cost for such solution would be presumably excessively high.

A much more lighter and simpler approach would be to partition the reduction array into small subblocks, in a number multiple of the number of parallel threads. This way, blocks of different sizes may be built by grouping, in a suitable way, certain number of contiguous subblocks.

The problem is how we can implement such an approach in a DPO method without losing its beneficial properties and keeping at most its computational structure (that is, trying to not introduce too much algorithmic complexities). We will explain next the specific case of DWA-LIP. Fig. 3 shows the parallel computational structure of the DWA-LIP method (that is, the execution phase), with no load balancing support. The inspector was in charge of assigning the reduction array to the parallel threads by blocks of the same size. As noted (and explained in the previous Section), the computation proceeds with synchronized stages, each one composed of sets of iterations (of the form $(B_{min}, \Delta B)$) that are executed in parallel.

A seamlessly modification of the DWA-LIP method to support generic load balancing is shown graphically in Fig. 4. The execution phase is practically unmodified, as the inspector is in charge of all the work. The inspector now operates as before but considering subblocks instead of blocks. It builds the synchronized iteration sets as if the number of parallel threads is equal to the number of subblocks. As the number of actual threads is much lower (a fraction) then those may be grouped into balanced supersets of different size. In Fig. 4 we have called $(i', \Delta B)$ to the $i$–th balanced group of iteration sets, that is, the $i$–th balanced superset for a certain value $\Delta B$. We observe each $(i', \Delta B)$ is an aggregation of sets of the form $(k, \Delta B)$, and so the iterations in that superset write in adjacent reduction array subblocks.

The additional complexity introduced in the inspector by the load balancer is a small fraction of the original one, as the complexity of building supersets is

$$\Delta B=0 \left[ \begin{array}{l} (1,0) \quad (2,0) \quad (3,0) \quad (4,0) \quad (5,0) \quad ..... \\ sync \end{array} \right.$$

$$\Delta B=1 \left[ \begin{array}{l} (1,1) \quad (3,1) \quad (5,1) \quad (7,1) \quad ..... \\ sync \\ (2,1) \quad (4,1) \quad (6,1) \quad (8,1) \quad ..... \\ sync \end{array} \right.$$

$$\Delta B=2 \left[ \begin{array}{l} (1,2) \quad (4,2) \quad (7,2) \quad (10,2) \quad ..... \\ sync \\ (2,2) \quad (5,2) \quad (8,2) \quad (11,2) \quad ..... \\ sync \\ (3,2) \quad (6,2) \quad (9,2) \quad (12,2) \quad ..... \end{array} \right.$$

$$\vdots \qquad (i,j): (B_{min}, \Delta B)$$

**Fig. 3.** Parallel flow computation in the original DWA-LIP method

$\mathcal{O}(nSubBlocks^2)$, being $nSubBlocks$ the total number of subblocks (and usually this number is much lower than the size of the reduction loop). The extra memory overhead becomes now $\mathcal{O}(nSubBlocks^2)$, instead of $\mathcal{O}(nThreads^2)$, being $nThreads$ the total number of threads in the system. This will not be significant while $nSubBlocks^2$ is much lower than the size of the reduction array.

The execution phase of the modified DWA-LIP handles the supersets into synchronized stages in the same way as the original DWA-LIP. In order to do that we will execute in parallel stages of supersets. In the original DWA–LIP, we have iterations sets of the form $(i + k(\Delta B + 1), \Delta B)$, $k = 0, 1, ...$, that are executed in parallel (they constitute a stage) because they issue conflict-free write operations. As a consequence, in the modified DWA–LIP, if we assure that the supersets of the form $(i', \Delta B)$ have at least $r$ sets then all supersets of the form $(i' + k\Delta^{LB}, \Delta B)$, where $\Delta^{LB} = \lfloor \frac{\Delta B - 1}{r} + 1 \rfloor$, issue also conflict-free writes, and thus may be executed fully parallel. It can be proven the best value that maximizes parallelism is $r = \min\left(\Delta B, \frac{nSubBlocks}{nThreads}\right)$. With this value, we have $\Delta^{LB} = \lceil \Delta B \frac{nThreads}{nSubBlocks} \rceil$.

The final number of supersets in each parallel stage should not be greater than the number of actual threads. The new execution phase works similarly than the original one but operating on supersets.

### 3.2   Local Expansion Load Balancing Approach

There are situations that suffer from load unbalancing that deserves to be considered as a special case. This situation arises when we find that many loop iterations write on specific and small regions of the reduction array (regions of high contention). We may deal with this case using the approach proposed in the previous section, but it is not difficult to design a more effective solution.

This contention problem can be easily detected by adding to the inspector of the DPO method a stage of histogram analysis. Indeed, in the case of the

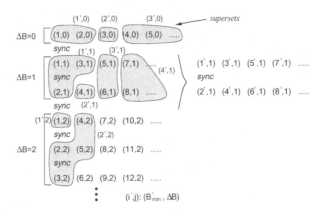

**Fig. 4.** Parallel flow computation in the DWA-LIP method after including generic load balancing support. The indices $i$ of the iteration sets $(i, j)$ correspond to subblocks. The indices $i'$ of the pairs $(i', j)$ corresponds to the balanced iteration supersets. In any case, index $j$ is $\Delta B$

DWA-LIP technique, this information is contained in the actual inspector data structure.

It can be observed that as smaller is the size of a contention region lower number of threads can execute the high number of iterations writing in such region (and thus, generating unbalancing). A easy way of relieving this problem consists of the replication on the threads of the block(s) containing the contention region. This way, write conflicts on that region disappear and thus the iterations can be redistributed on a greater number of threads.

With this approach, the data locality exploitation property of the DPO method is maintained without requiring the large amount of extra memory needed by a LPO method like array expansion or replicated buffer. Selective privatization also tries to replicate extra memory as low as possible, but no data locality is considered at all.

In the case of the DWA–LIP method, the replication of a reduction array block implies that the loop iterations in the affected sets $(B_{min}, \Delta B)$ are moved to sets with lower $\Delta B$. This fact increases the parallelism available. In addition, the iterations of sets with $\Delta B = 0$ that write in the replicated block can be assigned to any thread, allowing this way a better balancing of the workload.

The extra memory overhead that the local replication introduce is equal to the size of the reduction array multiplied by the number of replicated blocks. If the problem is very unbalanced, this last number is much lower than the total number of blocks, and thus the total extra memory cost would be much lower than in LPO methods, like array expansion or replicated buffer.

Fig. 5 depicts the access pattern histogram for the sparse matrix *av41092* [2], showing that for different numbers of threads there always exist regions of high contention. In Fig. 6 of the same figure shows the theoretical performance for

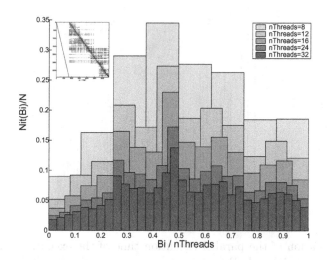

**Fig. 5.** Histogram of the reduction array access pattern for the sparse matrix *av41092* (from the Univ. of Florida Collection). $B_i$ is the reduction array block index, *nThreads* is the total number of threads, $Nit(B_i)$ is the number of iterations that write in block $B_i$, and $N$ is the total number of loop iterations

the execution phase of the locally expanded DWA–LIP on the same sparse matrix, for different values of number of expanded blocks, chosen from those that exhibit higher contention. In the figure, `Tnorm` represents the evaluated parallel reduction execution time normalized to the execution on one thread.

## 4   Experimental Evaluation

We have experimentally evaluated the proposed load balancing solutions and compared with other parallel irregular reduction methods on a SGI Origin2000 multiprocessor, with 250-MHz R10000 processors (4 MB L2 cache) and 12 GB main memory, using IRIX 6.5. All parallel codes were implemented in Fortran 77 with OpenMP [14] directives, and compiled using the SGI MIPSpro Fortran 77 compiler (with optimization level O2).

The generic load balancing approach were implemented and tested using the Spec Code [13], a kernel for Legendre transforms used in numerical weather prediction. The code includes two reduction procedures, `LTD` and `LTI`, being the former a regular one and the latter an irregular one. The experimental results corresponds only to the second routine (`LTI`). The irregular reduction is inside a nested loop, being the indices of the innermost loop also indirections. There are several reduction arrays but only one subscript array. This means that DPO methods should work efficiently because no loose of parallelism (DWA–LIP) nor computation replication (LOCALWRITE) is expected, as there is only one subscript array.

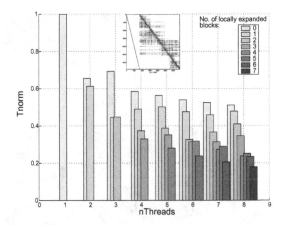

**Fig. 6.** Evaluation of the parallel execution time of the execution phase of the locally expanded DWA–LIP for the same sparse matrix than in Fig. 5

Fig. 7 shows the resulting speedup for the execution phase of several reduction methods on the LTI procedure. Pure DPO methods shows suboptimal performance, which is due mainly to the workload unbalance. When introducing the generic load balancing solution into DWA–LIP, the performance is significantly improved. The K factor represents the ration between the number of reduction array subblocks and the total number of threads. When increasing K, the speedup improves slightly. However, there is no additional improvement for values beyond 8. Note, also, that the extra memory needed for the modified DWA–LIP method is proportional to the square number of subblocks, which for the tested code is much lower than the size of the reduction array.

Array expansion performs poorly, as only the outermost loop of the irregular reduction is parallelized. In this code the innermost loop is irregular and consequently array expansion exhibits high load unbalance. In addition, this technique does not take into account data locality. A possible solution to this problem consists of fusing both loops (using, for instance, loop flattening), but that requires to add an inspector phase to the method.

For this code, the indirection array appearing in the innermost loop and the reduction subscript array are computed only once in a initialization routine. Thus the inspector phase should be executed only once also, and consequently its impact in the overall performance is negligible. For the tested code, the sequential irregular reduction time was 19 sec. while the inspector took 0.18 sec.

The local expansion load balancing approach, on the other hand, was experimented on a simple 2D short-range molecular dynamics simulation [12, 17] (MD2). This application simulates an ensemble of particles subject to a Lennard-Jones short-range potential. To integrate the equations of motion of the particles, a finite-difference leapfrog algorithm on a Nosé -Hoover thermostat dynamics is used. In the core of this code there is an irregular reduction nested loop due to

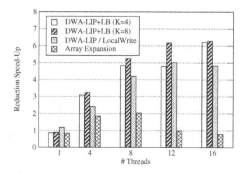

**Fig. 7.** Speedup of the generic load balancing approach implemented in the DWA–LIP method (DWA–LIP+LB) compared to the original DWA–LIP, LOCALWRITE and array expansion for the Legendre transformation (Spec Code [13])

the use of a neighbour list technique to update force contributions. Thus we have two reduction arrays and two subscript arrays. In addition, the subscript array is dynamically updated every 10 time steps. The number of particles simulated is 640K, and it has been introduced artificially a high contention region in the particle domain. To test the impact of the inter-loop locality, the iteration order of the original loop that runs over the neighbour list was randomized.

Fig. 8 the speedup for the execution phase of the local expanded load balancing technique implemented in the DWA–LIP method, compared to array expansion and selective privatization techniques. Part (a) in the figure corresponds to the original code (sorted neighbour list) while part (b) corresponds to the randomized code. As the inter-loop locality of the original code is relatively high, and the fraction of conflicting reduction array elements (elements written by more than one thread) is very low, then techniques like selective privatization performs very well. DWA–LIP works poorly due to the high unbalance of the load. When introducing local expansion, the situation improves significantly but it does not reach the level of selective privatization due to the cost of handling replicated blocks (while selective privatization works directly on the original reduction array most of the time). Array expansion performs worse due to the high overhead of operating on expanded arrays and the final collective operation.

When the neighbour list is randomized, the original inter-loop locality is lost. That produces a hard impact on the performance of selective privatization, as the number of conflicting elements increases drastically. However, DWA–LIP and its variants maintain their performance at similar levels than before, as these methods exploit at runtime inter-loop locality.

Note that beyond 8 processors, the high contention region covers more than one block. Thus, we need to locally expand two blocks in order to keep balancing the load (as shown in the above both plots).

Regarding the cost of the inspector phase, the total sequential reduction time was 10 sec. (original) and 19 sec. (randomized). The inspector execution time

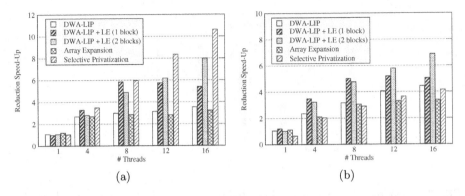

**Fig. 8.** Speedup of the local expansion load balancing approach implemented in the DWA–LIP method (DWA–LIP+LE) compared to the original method, array expansion and selective privatization for the MD2 simulation code. (a) corresponds to the original code, while in (b) the loop that runs over the neighbour list of particles was randomized

for DWA–LIP was 1.25 sec. for all cases and variants, while the same for the selective privatization was 2.4 sec.

Finally, Fig. 9 depicts the extra memory overhead that the tested reduction methods exhibit. Note that selective privatization is very sensitive to the inter-loop locality of the original code, either in performance and in extra memory, while the DPO methods succeed to exploit it at runtime. In part (b) of the figure, the memory overhead due to the inspector data structures has been included. The main overhead in DWA–LIP corresponds to the size of the subscript array (in MD2, this size is three times larger than the size of the reduction arrays). In selective privatization, a copy of each subscript array is needed to translate the indices to the selective private replicas of the reduction arrays. In MD2, this overhead is twice than in DWA–LIP.

## 5    Conclusions

There is much interest in the compiler community to parallelize efficiently ir-regular reductions, as these operations appear frequently in the core of many numerical applications. Different parallelization techniques have been proposed elsewhere, that we have classified in this paper into two classes: LPO (*Loop Partitioning Oriented* techniques) and DPO (*Data Partitioning Oriented* tech-niques). Methods in the first class assign blocks of reduction loop iterations to the cooperating threads. Methods in the second class assign blocks of the re-duction arrays to the threads, and further trying to execute most of the loop iterations that write in the owned blocks. We have analyzed both classes in terms of a set of performance aspects: data locality, memory overhead, parallelism and workload balancing.

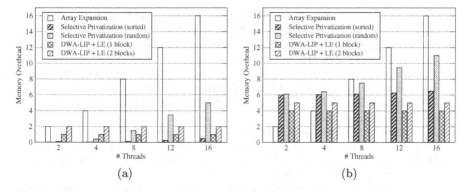

**Fig. 9.** Memory overhead for different reduction parallelization methods for the MD2 code (units are normalized to the total size of the reduction arrays): (a) concerning only replicated reduction arrays, and (b) including also the inspector data structures

The load balancing performance aspect was not sufficiently analyzed in parallel reduction methods, specially those in the DPO class, which are very sensitive to that aspect. In this paper we have proposed two new techniques to introduce load balancing into a DPO method. The first technique, based on the subblocking of the reduction arrays, is generic, as it can deal with any kind of load unbalancing present in the problem domain. The second technique handles a special case of load unbalance, appearing when there are a large number of write operations on small regions of the reduction arrays. The proposed solution is based on the privatization of the blocks making up those regions.

In this paper we show efficient implementations of the proposed solutions to load balancing for the DWA–LIP DPO method. Experimental results allow us to conclude that it is possible to improve the performance of DWA–LIP for very unbalanced problems with no significant loss of data locality and no substantial increment in extra memory overhead and algorithmic complexity.

**Acknowledgments.** The authors wish to thanks CEPBA (*European Center for Parallelism of Barcelona*, Spain) for the computing time provided on the SGI Origin2000.

# References

[1] R. Asenjo, E. Gutiérrez, Y. Lin, D. Padua, B. Pottengerg, and E. Zapata. On the Automatic Parallelization of Sparse and Irregular Fortran Codes. Technical Report 1512, University for Illinois at Urbana-Champaign, Center for Supercomputing R&D., December 1996.

[2] T. Davis, The University of Florida Sparse Matrix Collection. *NA Digest*, 97(23), June 1997.

[3] C. Ding and K. Kennedy, Improving Cache Performance of Dynamic Applications with Computation and Data Layout Transformations. In *Proceedings of the ACM International Conference on Programming Language Design and Implementation (PLDI'99)*, pages 229–241, Atlanta, GA, May 1999.

[4] E. Gutiérrez, O. Plata, and E.L. Zapata. An Automatic Parallelization of Irregular Reductions on Scalable Shared Memory Multiprocessors. In *Proceedings of the 5th International Euro-Par Conference (EuroPar'99)*, pages 422–429, Tolouse, France, August-September 1999.

[5] E. Gutiérrez, O. Plata, and E.L. Zapata. A Compiler Method for the Parallel Execution of Irregular Reductions in Scalable Shared Memory Multiprocessors. In *Proceedings of the 14th ACM International Conference on Supercomputing (ICS'2000)*, pages 78–87, Santa Fe, NM, May 2000.

[6] E. Gutiérrez, R. Asenjo, O. Plata, and E.L. Zapata. Automatic Parallelization of Irregular Applications. *J. Parallel Computing*, 26(13–14):1709–1738, December 2000.

[7] H. Han and C.-W. Tseng, Improving Compiler and Run-Time Support for Irregular Reductions Using Local Writes. In *Proceedings of the 11th Workshop on Languages and Compilers for Parallel Computing (LCPC'98)*, pages 181–196, Chapel Hill, NC, August 1998.

[8] H. Han and C.-W. Tseng, Efficient Compiler and Run–Time Support for Parallel Irregular Reductions. *J. Parallel Computing*, 26(13–14):1709-1738, December 2000.

[9] H. Han and C.-W. Tseng, Improving Locality for Adaptive Irregular Scientific Codes. In *Proceedings of the 13th Workshop on Languages and Compilers for Parallel Computing (LCPC'00)*, Yorktown Heights, NY, August 2000.

[10] H. Han and C.-W. Tseng, A Comparison of Parallelization Techniques for Irregular Reductions. In *Proceedings of the 15th IEEE International Parallel and Distributed Processing Symposium (IPDPS'2001)*, San Francisco, CA, April 2001.

[11] Y. Lin and D. Padua, On the Automatic Parallelization of Sparse and Irregular Fortran Programs. In *Proceedings of the 4th Workshop on Languages, Compilers and Runtime Systems for Scalable Computers (LCR'98)*, Pittsburgh, PA, May 1998.

[12] J. Morales and S. Toxvaerd. The Cell-Neighbour Table Method in Molecular Dynamics Simulations. *Computer Physics Communication*, 71:71–76, 1992.

[13] N. Mukherjee and J.R. Gurd, A Comparative Analysis of Four Parallelisation Schemes. In *Proceedings of the 13th ACM International Conference on Supercomputing (ICS'99)*, pages 278–285, Rhodes, Greece, June 1999.

[14] OpenMP Architecture Review Board. OpenMP: A Proposed Industry Standard API for Shared Memory Programming. http://www.openmp.org, 1997.

[15] R. Ponnusamy, J. Saltz, A. Choudhary, S. Hwang, and G. Fox. Runtime Support and Compilation Methods for User-Specified Data Distributions. *IEEE Transactions on Parallel and Distributed Systems*, 6(8):815–831, June 1995.

[16] L. Rauchwerger and D. Padua. The LRPD Test: Speculative Run-Time Parallelization of Loops with Privatization and Reduction Parallelization. In *Proceedings of the ACM SIGPLAN Conference on Programming Language Design and Implementation*, pages 218–232, La Jolla, CA, June 1995.

[17] S. Toxvaerd. Algorithms for Canonical Molecular Dynamics Simulations. *Molecular Physics*, 72(1).159–168, 1991.

[18] H. Yu and L. Rauchwerger. Adaptive Reduction Parallelization Techniques. In *Proceedings of the 14th ACM International Conference on Supercomputing (ICS'2000)*, pages 66–77, Santa Fe, NM, May 2000.

# A Comparative Evaluation of
# Parallel Garbage Collector Implementations

Clement R. Attanasio, David F. Bacon, Anthony Cocchi, and Stephen Smith

IBM T.J. Watson Research Center
P.O. Box 704, Yorktown Heights, NY  10598, U.S.A.

**Abstract.** While uniprocessor garbage collection is relatively well understood, experience with collectors for large multiprocessor servers is limited and it is unknown which techniques best scale with large memories and large numbers of processors. In order to explore these issues we designed a modular garbage collection framework in the IBM Jalapeño Java virtual machine and implemented five different parallel garbage collectors: non-generational and generational versions of mark-and-sweep and semi-space copying collectors, as well as a hybrid of the two. We describe the optimizations necessary to achieve good performance across all of the collectors, including load balancing, fast synchronization, and inter-processor sharing of free lists. We then quantitatively compare the different collectors to find their asymptotic performance both with respect to how fast they can run applications as well as how little memory they can run them in. All of our collectors scale linearly up to sixteen processors. The least memory is usually required by the hybrid mark-sweep collector that uses a copying collector for its nursery, although sometimes the non-generational mark-sweep collector requires less memory. The fastest execution is more application-dependent. Our only application with a large working set performed best using the mark-sweep collector; with one exception, the rest of the applications ran fastest with one of the generational collectors.

## 1   Introduction

This work reports the design, implementation, and performance of a family of garbage collectors that are part of the Jalapeño project, a Java Virtual Machine written in Java, targeted mainly for large symmetric multiprocessor (SMP) machines executing server applications.

These garbage collectors are type accurate both in the heap and thread stacks, stop-the-world (synchronous with respect to mutator execution), and load-balancing among all available processors. We implemented both mark-and-sweep and semi-space copying collectors, with non-generational and generational variants of each. We also implemented a hybrid collector that uses mark-and-sweep for the mature space and copying for the nursery.

In this paper we describe the novel features of our implementations and quantitatively compare their performance. We show how varying heap size affects application speed and how the collectors scale as the number of processors is varied up to 16.

H. Dietz (Ed.): LCPC 2001, LNCS 2624, pp. 177–192, 2003.

We observe a near-linear increase in throughput and decrease in delay time for garbage collection as the number of processors increases. Scalability is primarily limited by the size of the live heap; for large-scale applications like SPECjbb we observe linear scalability up to 16 processors; for others with only one or two mutators and small working sets scalability is limited to 5-8 processors.

These results were obtained by careful avoidance of delays due to load imbalance or excessive synchronization among the processors. We build work lists of objects to be scanned in buffers private to each processor, and then scan them in parallel, with the ability to exchange buffers among processors for load balancing. These techniques are similar to those described by Endo et al [7].

Jalapeño creates and manages Java threads explicitly. These threads are suspended for multiprogramming only at garbage collection safe points, so when garbage collection is triggered, all processors can begin collection as soon as the mutator thread in execution on each processor reaches a safe point. All non-executing threads are already at safe points.

In Jalapeño, everything is a Java object, including the objects that implement the JVM itself, such as thread stacks, the compiled code, and the collectors, and this requires some special considerations.

The rest of this paper is organized as follows: in Section 2 we describe the overall structure of Jalapeño and how garbage collection is integrated into the system. In Section 3 we describe the garbage collectors. In Section 4 we describe our benchmark programs and results. In Section 5 we discuss other work related to parallel garbage collection. Finally, we summarize our conclusions.

## 2     The Jalapeño Architecture and Garbage Collector Framework

In this section we describe the important features of the system in which we implemented the collectors studied in this paper, and describe the design choices that allow modular combination of different collectors and compilers.

Jalapeño [2] is a Java Virtual Machine for large symmetric multiprocessor (SMP) servers currently under development at the IBM T.J. Watson Research Center. Jalapeño is written in Java extended with unsafe primitives to allow direct manipulation of memory [1]. This simplifies some aspects of allocator and collector implementation, and complicates others.

Jalapeño uses the following well known-techniques to achieve high performance:

$M \times N$ **threading.** Java threads are multiplexed onto operating system threads, and Jalapeño schedules and migrates Java threads across operating system threads as needed. We call the operating system threads *virtual processors* (VPs).

**Processor-Local Allocation.** To avoid synchronization on every allocation, VPs allocate small objects out of larger chunks obtained from a central storage manager.

**Safe Points.** To ensure that threads are in a known state when garbage collection occurs, threads are only interrupted at safe points, for which the compiler generates maps that describe the contents of the stack. Jalapeño generates safe points at method calls and backward branches.

**Type Accuracy.** The combination of class descriptors and stack maps for safe points allows Jalapeño to perform type-accurate GC, meaning that it can locate all pointers in the system and find their correct run-time types.

**Inlined Allocation.** While many systems inline allocation code, in Jalapeño it occurs naturally because the allocation routines are also written in Java. Therefore, the general-purpose optimizer can inline allocation (system code) into the allocating methods (user code) and perform constant folding and other optimizations. When the type of an allocation is known, its size and finalization status are known, and two conditional branches can be eliminated from the allocation code.

While these are all well-known techniques, the synergy between the design choices is important. For instance, most Java Virtual Machines allocate one operating system thread per Java thread. As a result, it can take a long time to perform a barrier synchronization, since each thread must either wake up and come to some sort of safe point, or be put to sleep by the collector. Both approaches are costly, and the cost is proportional to the number of threads instead of the number of processors; therefore, these approaches do not scale. In addition, if the latter approach is taken, then the threads will be suspended at unknown points, making type-accurate collection difficult or impossible.

### 2.1  Modular System Design

Jalapeño supports multiple compilers and multiple collectors (as have other modern virtual machine designs [8, 14]). The different compilers can co-exist within a single virtual machine instance; the collector must currently be selected when the virtual machine image is generated.

There are three different compilers: *Baseline*, *Quick*, and *Opt*. The Baseline compiler performs direct translation of bytecodes into native machine instructions, simply emulating the virtual machine stack (there is no interpreter, so the Baseline compiler serves in place of an interpreter). The Quick compiler performs some simple optimizations, primarily register allocation. The Opt compiler is a full-blown multi-pass optimizing compiler. In addition, optimization levels can be dynamically controlled at run-time through feedback-directed optimization [3].

Each compiler generates `MapIterator` objects that are used to iterate over the stack frames it generates and find all of the pointers in each frame. A stack can contain a mixture of frame types generated by different compilers. The map iterator presents a common compiler independent interface used by all the collectors when scanning stacks for roots.

## 3  The Garbage Collectors

### 3.1  Storage Layout

Figure 1 illustrates how the Jalapeño address space is managed.

**Boot Image.** The boot image contains the memory image, generated by the build process, with which Jalapeño begins execution. As a minimum it contains the Java

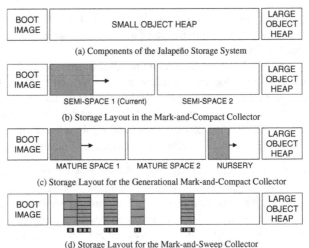

(a) Components of the Jalapeño Storage System

(b) Storage Layout in the Mark-and-Compact Collector

(c) Storage Layout for the Generational Mark-and-Compact Collector

(d) Storage Layout for the Mark-and-Sweep Collector

**Fig. 1.** Garbage Collector Storage Layout

objects necessary for bootstrapping the complete Jalapeño virtual machine. Option-ally, e.g., for faster startup, it can contain more than the minimal set. For example, the Jalapeño optimizing compiler can be produced at build time and included in the boot image.

**Small Object Heap.** All collectors divide the small object heap into "chunks," typ-ically 32KB, and allocate chunks as required to virtual processors, so that small objects can be allocated without synchronization within chunks. When needed, new chunks are obtained in a synchronized fashion from a global pool. When no more chunks are available, a garbage collection is triggered.

*Semi-space Copying Collector.* Given a chunk, the semi-space storage manager maintains a next pointer from which to satisfy a request. If the requested size does not extend beyond the chunk boundary, the next address is returned, the next pointer is updated to the end of the newly allocated space, and execution continues.

*Mark-sweep Collector.* The mark-sweep storage manager divides a chunk into fixed size slots. Currently it defines (at system build time) twelve slot sizes ranging from 12 bytes to 2KB. One chunk for each slot size is allocated to each virtual processor. A request is satisfied from the current chunk for the smallest slot size that can contain the requested size. Available slots in each chunk are maintained in a singly-linked list, and each virtual processor has a set of pointers to the next available slot for each slot size. Allocation involves updating the next pointer for the requested size for the given virtual processor. When a next pointer is zero, then a new chunk (either previously allocated or obtained from the chunk manager) becomes the current one for this virtual processor, and the list of free slots in the chunk is built.

*Allocation.* In the usual case when the allocation is satisfied in the current chunk, an optimized, inlined allocation executes ten instructions for the copying collector, and seventeen for the mark-sweep collector.

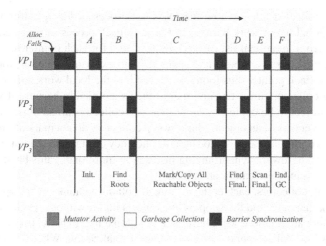

**Fig. 2.** Phases of Parallel Garbage Collection.

**Large Object Heap.** All collectors share the same large object manager. Large objects (larger than 2KB) are allocated using a first-fit strategy in contiguous 4KB pages. They are never moved during garbage collection. As large objects become garbage, their pages are automatically coalesced with adjacent free pages.

### 3.2 Parallel Collection

When an allocation request cannot be satisfied, all virtual processors are notified that a garbage collection is required. The mutator thread executing on each virtual processor, at its next garbage collection safe point, transfers execution to the Jalapeño dispatcher which suspends it and schedules the garbage collection thread. Recall that all other suspended mutator threads are already at safe points.

Coordination among executing garbage collection threads is implemented by barrier synchronization. Figure 2 illustrates the phases of garbage collection, separated by barrier synchronizations.

In phase A, initialization and collector-specific housekeeping functions are performed. The mark-sweep collector uses a side array associated with each allocated chunk for marking live objects; these must be zeroed during initialization.

The Jalapeño Table of Contents (JTOC) contains pointers to all class objects and static fields of both the Jalapeño virtual machine and applications. These, and pointers in the execution stacks of programs, comprise the roots for garbage collection. Pointers in stacks are found by the exact stack mapping mechanism implemented by all Jalapeño compilers. To accommodate relocation of code objects and execution stacks, copying collectors require the barrier after Phase B, to ensure that such objects are processed with special logic first. Mark-sweep collectors do not require barrier B because they do not move objects.

**Work Buffers.** All Jalapeño garbage collectors are carefully engineered to execute in parallel by using local work buffers that contain object pointers to process. Root pointers are collected into such buffers. When a processor fills a buffer, the buffer is added to a global list of work buffers. In Phase C, each processor repeatedly obtains a work buffer from the global list of work buffers, and for each pointer to an object not yet marked, processes the object and scans it (with exact information) for pointers to other objects. Each pointer thus found is entered into the local work buffer.

Copying collectors must test and mark objects atomically because it would be an error for an object to be copied by more than one collector thread during a collection, leading to two copies of an object. Mark-sweep collectors do not mark atomically, since the rare race condition leads only to slight inefficiency of multiple scan of an object. We feel avoiding a hardware synchronizing instruction more than gains back the time for the occasional duplicate scan of an object.

In copying collectors, each collector thread obtains a chunk of "to" space from the global chunk manager, and then copies live objects into it without synchronization.

When there are no more work buffers in the global list, Phase C is complete.

**Finalization.** All Jalapeño collectors support finalization. When an object is allocated, if its class has a finalize() method (this is checked at compile-time rather than run-time) an element identifying it is entered on a "live and finalizable object" queue. This queue, if not empty, is scanned in Phase D, and if any objects found there have become garbage, they are made live, moved to a "to be finalized" queue, and treated as roots for a mark or mark/copy phase E. Finalize methods are executed by a distinguished mutator thread after collection completes, i.e., not as part of garbage collection.

If the "to be finalized" queue is empty after phase C, phases D and E are skipped, avoiding two barrier synchronizations. Thus the mark-sweep collector usually requires four barrier synchronizations, and the copying collector usually requires five.

**Storage Reclamation.** For all Jalapeño collectors, reclaiming storage involves little additional explicit work. For semi-space copying collectors, the previous allocation space is now available for reuse. For mark-sweep collectors, unmarked entries in the side array for each chunk identify available space. The side arrays must be scanned to find chunks containing no live objects, which are returned to the global chunk manager.

### 3.3    Generational Collection

Jalapeño also contains generational variants of both the semi-space copying and mark-sweep collectors. For the copying collector, the age of the object can be determined from its address. For the mark-sweep collector, it is kept in the associated side array.

The advantage of generational collection is that old objects are not scanned unless they may contain pointers to young objects. Additionally, in copying collectors, old objects are not copied. Thus the potential advantage of generational over non-generational collection is greater for copying collectors, since these avoid the cost of copying old objects repeatedly.

Jalapeño compilers provide a write barrier for old objects: the address of the old object stored into is written into a write buffer on the first store of an address during a mutator execution cycle. During the subsequent garbage collection, the write buffer is treated as another source of root pointers.

**Hybrid Collector.** Jalapeño also contains a hybrid collector, in which new objects are allocated in a nursery using the copying manager's strategy, but when objects sur-

| Program | Description | Code Size | $T$ | Allocation | | | Smallest | | Fastest | |
|---------|-------------|-----------|-----|------|-------|-----|------|------|----------|------|
| | | | | Objs | Total | HWM | Heap | Coll. | Time (s) | Coll. |
| 213.javac | Java bytecode compiler | 561 | 1 | 8.2 M | 294 | 9.9 | 22 | MS | 14.95 | CG.2 |
| 227.mtrt | Multithreaded raytracer | 571 | 2 | 6.7 M | 165 | 7.9 | 14 | H.2 | 5.78 | CG.8 |
| 228.jack | Parser generator | 131 | 1 | 8.1 M | 331 | 2.4 | 13 | H.2 | 19.09 | CG.8 |
| SPECjbb | TPC-C for Java | 138 | 8 | 7.9 M | 280 | 148 | 180 | H.16 | [21933] | MS |
| jalapeño | Jalapeño optimizer | 1378 | 1 | 52.6 M | 1433 | 11 | 34 | H.4 | 25.8 | CP |
| gcbench | GC Benchmark | 4 | 1 | 15.4 M | 378 | 6.3 | 20 | MS | 4260 | H.8 |

**Table 1.** Benchmarks and their overall characteristics. Code size is total kilobytes of class files. $T$ is the number of simultaneous threads. Objs is the total number of objects created. All other quantities are MB of storage. Since SPECjbb is a throughput-oriented benchmark, we give its throughput score instead of the run time. HWM is the high-water-mark of allocation.

vive a garbage collection, they are copied into an old space managed by the mark-sweep collector. This collector combines the faster allocation of the copying strategy with the avoidance of copying an object more than once. Most object allocations are performed with the copying algorithm. Most live objects are assumed to be old objects, and may be repeatedly marked but are not copied after they become old.

## 4    Performance Measurements

For the performance measurements we used six programs; four are part of the SPEC benchmark suite, 213.javac, 227.mtrt, 228.jack, and SPECjbb. The remaining benchmarks are jalapeño, the Jalapeño optimizing compiler compiling a 740 class files into machine code, and the Java version of the gcbench benchmark, obtained from Hans Boehm's web site. While only mtrt and SPECjbb are parallel applications, the degree of parallelism of garbage collections was determined by the number of processors. For runs where the number of processors was not varied, eight processors were used.

All tests were run on a 24 processor IBM RS/6000 Model S80 with 50 GB of RAM. Each processor is a 64-bit PowerPC RS64 III CPU running at 450 MHz with 128 KB split first-level caches and an 8 MB unified L2 cache.

All benchmarks were run using the Jalapeño optimizing (*Opt*) compiler with the default level of optimization. All runs used the same size large object heap for each application. Since all collectors use the same large object heap code, we will not discuss large heaps in this section.

### 4.1    Benchmarks

The benchmark programs we measured are summarized in Table 1. For each benchmark, we show the code size (KB of class files), number of simultaneous threads ($T$),

| Program | Minimum Heap Size | | | | | | Std. Heap | | | Performance at Std. Heap Size | | | | | |
|---|---|---|---|---|---|---|---|---|---|---|---|---|---|---|---|
| | MS | CP | CG | | H | | Total | Minor | | MS | CP | CG | | H | |
| | | | S | L | S | L | | S | L | | | S | L | S | L |
| 213.javac | 22 | 26 | 23 | 30 | 22 | 23 | 50 | 2 | 8 | 16.0 | 20.6 | 14.9 | 15.5 | 15.6 | 15.2 |
| 227.mtrt | 17 | 18 | 19 | 24 | 14 | 18 | 50 | 2 | 8 | 6.50 | 6.21 | 5.84 | 5.78 | 6.03 | 5.91 |
| 228.jack | 16 | 13 | 14 | 20 | 13 | 17 | 50 | 2 | 8 | 20.8 | 19.5 | 19.4 | 19.1 | 19.2 | 19.1 |
| SPECjbb | 240 | 280 | 300 | 400 | 180 | 240 | 400 | 16 | 64 | 21933 | 16611 | 18927 | 17216 | 18500 | 19892 |
| jalapeño | 38 | 34 | 46 | 60 | 34 | 44 | 80 | 4 | 16 | 30728 | 25811 | 28342 | 27257 | 28374 | 27212 |
| gcbench | 20 | 28 | 20 | 28 | 24 | 28 | 36 | 2 | 8 | 5642 | 4601 | 4907 | 4385 | 4835 | 4260 |

**Table 2.** Minimum heap sizes in MB and performance for standard heap size when run with 8 CPUs. Performance is time in seconds to run the application, except for SPECjbb, for which a throughput score is calculated by the benchmark.

allocation behavior, standard heap sizes, and summarize the best performance in both time and space.

Allocation behavior is broken down into three quantities: number of objects allocated (in millions), number of megabytes allocated, and high-water-mark (HWM) of bytes allocated. The latter number shows the largest live heap size that we observed.

Throughout the measurements, different collectors are labeled **MS** for the mark-and-sweep collector, **CP** for the copying semi-space collector, **CG** for the generational copying semi-space collector, and **H** for the hybrid collector that uses copying for the minor heap and mark-and-sweep for the major heap. For the CG and H collectors, they are suffixed by the size of the heap used. Generically, CG.S refers to the copying generational collector using the small heap size. For a particular run, the size is included, for instance SPECjbb run under the copying generational semi-space collector with a 16 MB minor heap is labeled "CG.16".

Another important factor is that while we have tried to use the same benchmarks as other researchers (in particular javac, SPECjbb, and gcbench), some measurements will not be comparable due to the effects of our virtual machine being written in Java. In particular, the number of objects allocated includes objects that are allocated as part of the process of compiling and running the benchmark.

### 4.2 Absolute Performance

Table 1 provides an overview of our results on the absolute performance of the benchmarks with different collectors. We show both the minimum size in which the application ran, and the associated collector ("Smallest") as well as the best run in terms of completion time or throughput ("Fastest") when run with the standard heap size.

The results show that the hybrid collector with a small minor heap (H.S) is most likely to run the applications in the smallest heap space. There are two reasons for this: first of all, the use of the minor heap causes many short-lived objects to be collected quickly, so they never impact the space consumption of the mature space. Second, since the mature space uses the mark-sweep collector, the mature space is not divided into two semi-spaces. Put another way, the copying collector causes extremely coarse-grain

| Program | Major Collections | | | | | | Avg. Major Coll. Time | | | | | | Max. Major Coll. Time | | | | | |
|---|---|---|---|---|---|---|---|---|---|---|---|---|---|---|---|---|---|---|
| | MS | CP | CG | | H | | MS | CP | CG | | H | | MS | CP | CG | | H | |
| | | | $S$ | $L$ | $S$ | $L$ | | | $S$ | $L$ | $S$ | $L$ | | | $S$ | $L$ | $S$ | $L$ |
| 213.javac | 26 | 47 | 14 | 13 | 4 | 4 | 81 | 83 | 82 | 79 | 109 | 101 | 109 | 106 | 119 | 118 | 112 | 112 |
| 227.mtrt | 11 | 18 | 3 | 3 | 0 | 0 | 71 | 74 | 67 | 72 | — | — | 86 | 93 | 71 | 85 | — | — |
| 228.jack | 24 | 34 | 4 | 4 | 1 | 1 | 51 | 50 | 68 | 67 | 58 | 59 | 62 | 58 | 74 | 69 | 58 | 59 |
| SPECjbb | 36 | 98 | 53 | 46 | 11 | 11 | 243 | 359 | 389 | 388 | 260 | 265 | 305 | 396 | 424 | 427 | 278 | 281 |
| jalapeño | 64 | 94 | 29 | 26 | 16 | 13 | 68 | 72 | 106 | 108 | 89 | 99 | 109 | 118 | 212 | 160 | 142 | 150 |
| gcbench | 15 | 21 | 5 | 3 | 3 | 2 | 45 | 47 | 66 | 82 | 56 | 56 | 57 | 113 | 71 | 118 | 58 | 57 |

**Table 3.** Average and worst times for major collections in milliseconds when run with 8 CPUs. See Table 2 for standard heap sizes used.

fragmentation (always wasting a factor of two), while in the mark-sweep collector fragmentation is more localized and (in practice) limited.

For two benchmarks, javac and gcbench, the mark-sweep collector used less space. This is not surprising for gcbench, since it is a synthetic benchmark: there is a small number of object sizes, so fragmentation is almost zero, and the mark-sweep collector does not lose any memory to the minor heap. We are still investigating javac.

Table 1 shows that for application speed, performance varies much more. In the case of SPECjbb, the best performance is obtained with the mark-and-sweep (MS) collector, which is due to the fact that SPECjbb has a large working set — about 135 MB, which the semi-space collectors must copy on each major collection. The hybrid collector achieves almost the same speed with a large minor heap (H.64) — the gains from less object scanning seem to be offset almost exactly by the cost of the write barrier.

All but one of the other benchmarks achieved their best performance with some form of generational collector. This is due to a high allocation rate (which benefits from the cheaper allocation sequence in copying collectors) combined with a small working-set size (so that the expensive step of copying is minimized).

The SPEC benchmarks javac, mtrt, and jack all do best with the copying generational (CG) collector. For these benchmarks, the cost of the write barrier and the minor collections is gained back because fewer major collections are performed. On the other hand, gcbench does best with the hybrid (H) collector, probably due to its synthetic nature (as described above).

The jalapeño benchmark does best using the copying semi-space collector (CP), which has the lowest overhead when memory is plentiful.

In general, our results can be interpreted as strengthening the case of Fitzgerald and Tarditi [8] for profile-based selection for garbage collector selection.

Table 2 shows the minimum heap size in which each of the benchmarks ran, as well as the "standard" heap size chosen for the applications. The standard heap size is what we use for subsequent performance measurements, except those where the heap size was varied. These heap sizes were arrived at by finding a size in which each benchmark could comfortably run in all of the collectors. "Total" is the total heap size, including

| Program | No. of Minor Collections | | | | Avg. Minor Coll. Time | | | | Max. Minor Coll. Time | | | |
|---|---|---|---|---|---|---|---|---|---|---|---|---|
| | CG | | H | | CG | | H | | CG | | H | |
| | $S$ | $L$ | $S$ | $L$ | $S$ | $L$ | $S$ | $L$ | $S$ | $L$ | $S$ | $L$ |
| 213.javac | 396 | 100 | 394 | 100 | 11 | 25 | 11 | 25 | 41 | 55 | 37 | 55 |
| 227.mtrt | 184 | 45 | 184 | 45 | 6 | 11 | 6 | 11 | 33 | 41 | 32 | 41 |
| 228.jack | 385 | 96 | 384 | 96 | 5 | 9 | 5 | 9 | 56 | 72 | 56 | 66 |
| SPECjbb | 464 | 108 | 454 | 122 | 32 | 67 | 32 | 68 | 58 | 90 | 56 | 91 |
| jalapeño | 948 | 236 | 943 | 235 | 20 | 37 | 19 | 35 | 220 | 278 | 196 | 200 |
| gcbench | 181 | 45 | 181 | 45 | 4 | 6 | 4 | 6 | 15 | 52 | 16 | 56 |

**Table 4.** Average and worst times for minor collections in milliseconds when run with 8 CPUs. See Table 2 for standard heap sizes used.

space for the minor heaps, if any. "Minor" gives two minor heap sizes, a small size ($S$) and a large size ($L$) for each benchmark.

Table 2 also shows the performance for each benchmark at the standard heap size with 8 processors. From these measurements it can be seen that *application* performance can vary as much as 25% depending on the garbage collector.

### 4.3  Major and Minor Collection Times

Table 3 shows the number of major collections, and average and worst-case pause times for the different collectors running with eight processors.

Interestingly, there is not a large amount of variation in average collection time. The greatest variability is in the number of major collections. The mark-and-sweep collector (MS) performs at least a third fewer collections than the copying collector (CP), which indicates that space loss due to semi-spaces is significant.

As expected, generational collectors greatly reduce the number of major collections; in one case to zero (mtrt with the hybrid (H) collector).

Table 4 shows the number of minor collections, and the average and worst-case pause times for the different collectors running on eight processors. Since the minor heap strategies are the same for both the copying semi-space generational (CG) and hybrid (H) collectors, the total number of minor collections is always roughly the same.

The minor collection times for hybrid collector are consistently slower because the cost of allocating in the mark-and-sweep collector that the hybrid (H) uses for the mature space is longer, while the copying generational (CG) collector uses a simple bump-and-test allocator.

Note that even SPECjbb, with a live data size of about 135 MB and a 400 MB heap only experiences a 400 ms worst-case pause time for major collection and a 61 ms worst-case pause time for minor collection.

In general, the average and worst-case pause times for minor collections are very good, competitive with many times reported by "on-the-fly" collectors. Since the number of major collections is quite small, this may be acceptable for many applications.

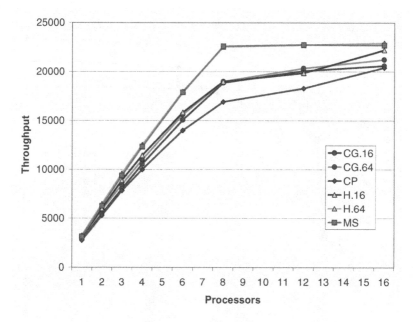

**Fig. 3.** Throughput for 8 clients as number of processors varies from 1 to 16.

### 4.4 Detailed Analysis of SPECjbb

The tables we have shown so far give a good overview of a number of different applications, and how they perform under various garbage collectors. In this section we will examine the performance of the largest and most parallel benchmark, SPECjbb, in considerably more detail.

Some previous work has only investigated collector speedups, and while this may be academically interesting, it provides no inherent benefit to the user. So the first question to answer is: what effect does varying collectors have on application performance? Figure 3 shows how the throughput of SPECjbb varies when run with 1 to 16 processors and in a 400 MB heap.

The workload consists of 8 warehouses, so after 8 processors, there is no additional parallelism in the application. The graph thus provides an interesting view of both application and collector scaling.

Two collectors, mark-sweep (MS) and the hybrid with a 64 MB minor heap (H.64), perform best across the entire range of configurations. They also scale extremely linearly, while the other collectors all show a certain amount of attenuation. In fact, the SPECjbb benchmark has better throughput with 8 processors under MS or H.64 than it does with any other collector with 16 processors.

A different view of the collectors is shown in Figure 4, in which the number of processors is fixed at 8 and the size of the heap is varied from 1GB down to the minimum in which the application can run. Once again, mark-sweep and hybrid appear to be the best collectors, but there is a distinct crossover point between them. When memory is

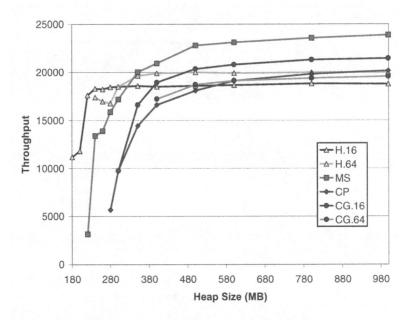

**Fig. 4.** Effect of heap size on application throughput with 8 processors (SPECjbb bench-mark).

plentiful, the mark-sweep collector considerably outperforms all others (the reason will become clear as we examine subsequent data). Below 350 MB, the mark-sweep collector begins to thrash, while the hybrid collectors defer many major collections because short-lived objects are not promoted into the mature space. In general, we observe that generational collectors degrade much more gracefully in the presence of limited memory resources.

A crucial point here is that SPECjbb achieves the same performance under the hybrid collector with an 8 MB minor heap in a 220 MB heap as the mark-sweep collector does with a 350 MB heap. Therefore, if memory resources are limited (as they often are for transaction processing systems under heavy load), the hybrid collector may be able to deliver 50% better application throughput than the next best alternative.

Some clues as to what is happening are in Figure 5, which shows the total amount of time spent in garbage collection for SPECjbb with a 400 MB heap for 1 to 16 processors. Two things are clearly visible in this graph. First, copying semi-space collectors spend much more time in garbage collection because they must, in general, perform twice as many collections as the comparable mark-sweep collector.

Generational collection significantly speeds up copying collection because the number of mature space collections drops significantly. However, in the case of mark-sweep collection, the generational hybrids (H.16 and H.64) are slower because they must perform more frequent minor collections and they also have the overhead of a write barrier, which the simple mark-sweep collector (MS) does not.

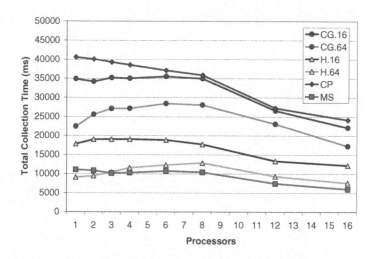

**Fig. 5.** Total garbage collection time (SPECjbb benchmark with a 400 MB Heap).

Figure 6 shows the average time for a mature-space collection as the number of processors is varied. This shows both the relative costs of collection under the different collectors, and their scaling properties. The copying collectors (CP and CG) take significantly longer per collection (as well as performing more collections due to use of semi-spaces) than the mark-sweep collectors (MS and H). In addition, the generational variants are slower because the minor heap must first be collected.

Figure 7 shows a similar trend for minor heap collection: time is dependent almost entirely on the size of the minor heap. This is not surprising since the same code is used for the minor heap in both the copying generational (CG) and hybrid (H) collectors. The hybrid collectors are slightly slower performing minor heap collection, probably due to the more expensive allocation path in the mark-sweep mature space.

For SPECjbb, which generates large amounts of data on parallel threads, garbage collection scales well, even for minor heap collection with small heaps. However, for other applications in our benchmark suite which are single-threaded and have a small working set, parallel collection of the minor heap only scales to about 5 processors.

## 5    Related Work

Research in applying parallelism to garbage collection has fundamentally focused on two issues: response time and throughput. To optimize throughput, the collector is run in *parallel* across multiple processors, usually (but not always) while the mutators are stopped. To optimize response time, the collector is run *concurrently* with the mutators, and may or may not itself be multi-threaded.

Throughput-oriented parallel collectors have generally received less attention from the research community, probably because they do not offer any solution to the fun-

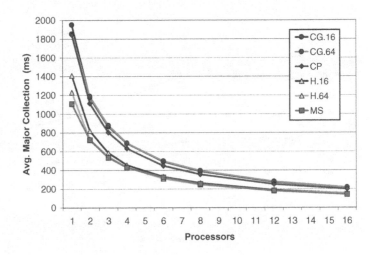

**Fig. 6.** Scalability of mature space collection (SPECjbb benchmark with a 400 MB Heap).

damental problems that garbage collection poses to time-sensitive computations. The fundamental tracing operation parallelizes fairly straightforwardly; important research questions have to do with load balancing and minimizing synchronization overhead.

Early work on parallel collection includes Halstead's implementation of a parallel copying collector for Multilisp [10] running on a 32-CPU Concert multiprocessor. His algorithm had each processor copying objects from any from-space into its local to-space.

Halstead's collector suffered from serious load-balancing problems. A similar approach was used by Crammond in the JAM Parlog collector [6]. Küchlin [13] presents a variant of Crammond's algorithm that trades time for space by using a divide-and-conquer technique that may require as many phases as there are processors but eliminates the need for tables containing inter-segment references.

Herlihy and Moss [11] describe a lock-free variant of Halstead's algorithm, but it requires multi-versioning which may significantly increase both space and time consumption.

Endo, Taura, and Yonezawa [7] implemented a parallel collector for a variant of C++ on a 64-processor Sun server. Their collector is based on the conservative Boehm collector [5]. They found that floating point numbers were often misidentified as pointers in one benchmark. Their work demonstrated that load-balancing could greatly improve scalability, and that large objects must be handled specially to maintain load balance. They also described how careful engineering of synchronization requirements improves overall performance. Unfortunately, although run on a real machine they only provide abstract speed and speedup measurements, without end-to-end performance numbers.

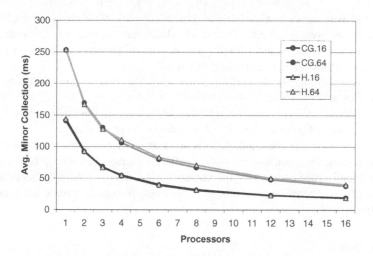

**Fig. 7.** Scalability of nursery collection (SPECjbb benchmark with 400 MB of heap space of which 16 or 64 MB is devoted to the nursery).

Recently, Boehm [4] has applied some of the techniques of Endo et al to create a version of his conservative collector that scales to small-scale (up to four CPU) multiprocessors that are becoming increasingly common, while still performing well on a single processor. He observes significant variation across benchmarks in the scalability of the collector, but also notes that due to excessive synchronization in `malloc()`, the garbage collected version often runs faster than the version that uses explicit allocation and de-allocation.

Most recently, Flood et al [9] describe parallelizing both a copying and a mark-compact collector. They compare the relative performance of the parallel versions with their serial counterparts. We have used two of the same benchmarks (`javac` and `SPEC-jbb`) for comparison. Our load balancing strategy is simpler, but seems to scale at least as well as theirs. Our scalability for `javac` is better, probably because we do not need to fragment the mature space for the compaction algorithm as they do.

## 6    Conclusions

We have shown through implementation and measurement that a variety of parallel collectors can be made scalable by careful attention to detail since all achieved near linear reduction in both major and minor collection times. The collectors can scale linearly up to 5-8 processors even when there is only a single mutator thread with a relatively small (10 MB) working set.

Performance of the collectors is very good: with eight processors we are able to collect 150 MB of live data from a 1 GB heap in 350 milliseconds.

The mark-and-sweep collector performs better when memory is tight or applications have a large working set as with the SPECjbb benchmark. Multiprocessor performance of the mark-and-sweep collector is crucially dependent on inter-processor sharing of free lists, which greatly reduces fragmentation, cuts collections by a factor of two, and allows applications to run in a considerably smaller heap.

Copying collectors clearly perform better when the creation rate of objects is high, and their lifetimes are short.

Generational collectors may be indicated when the creation rate of objects is high and at least some of them are long-lived, i.e., the working set is large.

When resources are abundant, there is no clear winner in application speed. However, when memory is limited, the hybrid collector (using mark-sweep for the mature space and semi-space copying for the nursery) can deliver at least 50% better application throughput. Therefore this collector seems best for online transaction processing applications.

# References

[1]  ALPERN, B., ET AL. Implementing Jalapeño in Java. In *Proc. of the ACM Conf. on Object-Oriented Programming, Systems, Languages, and Applications* (Oct. 1999). *SIGPLAN Notices, 34*, 10, 314–324.

[2]  ALPERN, B., ET AL. The Jalapeño virtual machine. *IBM Syst. J. 39*, 1 (2000), 211–238.

[3]  ARNOLD, M., FINK, S., GROVE, D., M.HIND, AND SWEENEY, P. Adaptive optimization in the Jalapeño JVM. In *Proc. of the ACM Conf. on Object-Oriented Programming, Systems, Languages, and Applications* (Oct. 2000). *SIGPLAN Notices, 35*, 10.

[4]  BOEHM, H.-J. Fast multiprocessor memory allocation and garbage collection. Tech. Rep. HPL-2000-165, Hewlett-Packard Laboratories, Dec. 2000.

[5]  BOEHM, H.-J., AND WEISER, M. Garbage collection in an uncooperative environment. *Software – Practice and Experience 18*, 9 (1988), 807–820.

[6]  CRAMMOND, J. A garbage collection algorithm for shared memory parallel processors. *International Journal Of Parallel Programming 17*, 6 (1988), 497–522.

[7]  ENDO, T., TAURA, K., AND YONEZAWA, A. A scalable mark-sweep garbage collector on large-scale shared-memory machines. In *Proc. of Supercomputing '97* (San Jose, California, Nov. 1997), IEEE Computer Society Press, Los Alamitos, California.

[8]  FITZGERALD, R., AND TARDITI, D. The case for profile-directed selection of garbage collectors. In ISMM [12], pp. 111–120.

[9]  FLOOD, C. H., DETLEFS, D., SHAVIT, N., AND ZHANG, X. Parallel garbage collection for shared memory multiprocessors. In *Proceedings of the Usenix Java Virtual Machine Research and Technology Symposium* (Monterey, California, Apr. 2001).

[10]  HALSTEAD, R. H. Multilisp: A language for concurrent symbolic computation. *ACM Trans. Program. Lang. Syst. 7*, 4 (Oct. 1985), 501–538.

[11]  HERLIHY, M., AND MOSS, J. E. B. Lock-free garbage collection for multiprocessors. *IEEE Transactions on Parallel and Distributed Systems 3*, 3 (May 1992).

[12]  *Proceedings of the ACM SIGPLAN International Symposium on Memory Management* (Minneapolis, MN, Oct. 2000), *SIGPLAN Notices 36*, 1.

[13]  KÜCHLIN, W. A space-efficient parallel garbage collection algorithm. In *Proceedings of Fifth ACM International Conference on Supercomputing* (June 1991), pp. 40–46.

[14]  PRINTEZIS, T., AND DETLEFS, D. A generational mostly-concurrent garbage collector. In ISMM [12], pp. 143–154.

# STAPL: An Adaptive, Generic Parallel C++ Library*

Ping An, Alin Jula, Silvius Rus, Steven Saunders, Tim Smith, Gabriel Tanase,
Nathan Thomas, Nancy Amato, and Lawrence Rauchwerger

Dept. of Computer Science, Texas A&M University,
College Station, TX 77843-3112
{pinga, alinj, silviusr, sms5644, tgs7381, gabrielt, nthomas,
amato, rwerger}@cs.tamu.edu

**Abstract.** The Standard Template Adaptive Parallel Library (STAPL) is a parallel library designed as a superset of the ANSI C++ Standard Template Library
(STL). It is sequentially consistent for functions with the same name, and executes on uni- or multi-processor systems that utilize shared or distributed memory. STAPL is implemented using simple parallel extensions of C++ that currently provide a SPMD model of parallelism, and supports nested parallelism.
The library is intended to be general purpose, but emphasizes irregular programs
to allow the exploitation of parallelism for applications which use dynamically
linked data structures such as particle transport calculations, molecular dynamics, geometric modeling, and graph algorithms. STAPL provides several different
algorithms for some library routines, and selects among them adaptively at run-
time. STAPL can replace STL automatically by invoking a preprocessing translation phase. In the applications studied, the performance of translated code was
within 5% of the results obtained using STAPL directly. STAPL also provides
functionality to allow the user to further optimize the code and achieve additional
performance gains. We present results obtained using STAPL for a molecular
dynamics code and a particle transport code.

## 1   Motivation

In sequential computing, standardized libraries have proven to be valuable tools for
simplifying the program development process by providing routines for common operations that allow programmers to concentrate on higher level problems. Similarly,
libraries of elementary, generic, parallel algorithms provide important building blocks
for parallel applications and specialized libraries [7, 6, 20]. Due to the added complexity of parallel programming, the potential impact of libraries could be even more
profound than for sequential computing. Indeed, we believe parallel libraries are crucial for moving parallel computing into the mainstream since they offer the only viable
means for achieving scalable performance across a variety of applications and architectures with programming efforts comparable to those of developing sequential codes.
In particular, properly designed parallel libraries could insulate less experienced users

* This research supported in part by NSF CAREER Awards CCR-9624315 and CCR-9734471,
  NSF Grants ACI-9872126, EIA-9975018, EIA-0103742, and by the DOE ASCI ASAP program grant B347886.

H. Dietz (Ed.): LCPC 2001, LNCS 2624, pp. 193–208, 2003.
© Springer-Verlag Berlin Heidelberg 2003

from managing parallelism by providing routines that are easily interchangeable with their sequential counterparts, while allowing more sophisticated users sufficient control to achieve higher performance gains.

Designing parallel libraries that are both portable and efficient is a challenge that has not yet been met. This is due mainly to the difficulty of managing concurrency and the wide variety of parallel and distributed architectures. For example, due to the differing costs of an algorithm's communication patterns on different memory systems, the best algorithm on one machine is not necessarily the best on another. Even on a given machine, the algorithm of choice may vary according to the data and run-time conditions (e.g., network traffic and system load).

Another important constraint on the development of any software package is its inter-operability with existing codes and standards. The public dissemination and eventual adoption of any new library depends on how well programmers can interface old programs with new software packages. Extending or building on top of existing work can greatly reduce both developing efforts and the users' learning curve.

To liberate programmers from the concerns and difficulties mentioned above we have designed STAPL (Standard Template Adaptive Parallel Library). STAPL is a parallel C++ library with functionality similar to STL, the ANSI adopted C++ Standard Template Library [17, 22, 13]. To ease the transition to parallel programming and ensure portability across machines and programs, STAPL is a superset of STL that is sequentially consistent for functions with the same name. STAPL executes on uni- or multi-processor architectures with shared or distributed memory and can co-exist in the same program with STL functions. STAPL is implemented using simple parallel extensions of C++ which provide a SPMD model of parallelism and supports nested (recursive) parallelism (as in NESL [7]). In a departure from previous parallel libraries which have almost exclusively targeted scientific or numerical applications, STAPL emphasizes irregular programs. In particular, it can exploit parallelism when dynamic linked data structures replace vectors as the fundamental data structure in application areas such as geometric modeling, particle transport, and molecular dynamics.

STAPL is designed in layers of abstraction: (i) the *interface layer* used by application programmers that is STL compatible, (ii) the *concurrency* and *communication layer* that expresses parallelism and communication/synchronization in a generic manner, (iii) the *software implementation layer* which instantiates the concurrency and communication abstractions to high level constructs, and (iv) the *machine layer* which is OS, run-time system (RTS) and architecture dependent. The *machine layer* also maintains a performance data base for STAPL on each machine and environment.

STAPL provides portability across multiple platforms by including its own (adapted from [18]) run-time system which supports high level parallel constructs (e.g., forall). Currently STAPL can interface directly to Pthreads and maintains its own scheduling. It can issue MPI and OpenMP directives and can use the native run-time system on several machines (e.g., HP V2200 and SGI Origin 2000). Thus, there is no need for user code modification when porting a program from one system to another. Only the *machine* layer needs to be modified when STAPL is ported to a new machine.

We have defined and implemented several key extensions of STL for STAPL: parallel containers and algorithms (pContainer and pAlgorithms), and an entirely new construct called pRange which allows random access to elements in a pContainer. Analogous to STL iterators, pRanges bind pContainers and pAlgorithms. Unlike STL iterators, pRanges also include a distributor for data distribution and a scheduler that can generically enforce data dependences in the parallel execution according to execution data dependence graphs (DDGs). STAPL allows for STL containers and algorithms to be used together with STAPL pContainers and pAlgorithms in the same program. STAPL provides a means of automatically transforming code that uses STL to code that uses STAPL. This parallelizes the application with very little user modification, but incurs some run-time overhead. To obtain even better performance, STAPL allows users to avoid the translation overhead by directly writing applications using pContainers, pAlgorithms, and pRanges. STAPL provides recursive data decomposition through its pRange which allows programs to be naturally mapped to hierarchical architectures.

To achieve wide adoption, STAPL must obtain reasonable performance across a wide spectrum of applications and architectures and free its users from problems related to portability and algorithm selection. This is achieved in STAPL by adaptive selection among various algorithmic options available for many STAPL library routines. Built–in performance monitors will measure actual performance, and using performance models [3, 2] that incorporate system specific information and current run-time conditions, STAPL will adaptively select an appropriate algorithm for the current situation, based on the performance monitors and performance models.

## 2  Related Work

There is a relatively large body of work that has similar goals to STAPL. Table 1 gives an overview of different projects. We will now briefly comment on some of them and attempt to compare them with STAPL. For further work in this area see [23].

| | STAPL | AVTL | CHARM++ | CHAOS++ | CILK | NESL | POOMA | PSTL | SPLIT-C |
|---|---|---|---|---|---|---|---|---|---|
| Paradigm | S/M | S | M | S | S/M | S/M | S | S | S |
| Architecture | S/D | D | S/D | D | S/D | S/D | S/D | S/D | S/D |
| Nested Par. | yes | no | no | no | yes | yes | no | no | yes |
| Adaptive | yes | no | no | no | no | no | no | no | no |
| Generic | yes | yes | yes | yes | no | yes | yes | yes | no |
| Irregular | yes | no | yes(limited) | yes | yes | yes | no | yes | yes |
| Data decomp | auto/user | auto | user | auto/user | user | user | user | auto/user | user |
| Data map | auto/user | auto | auto | auto/user | auto | auto | user | auto/user | auto |
| Scheduling | block, dyn, partial self-sched | user MPI-based | prioritized execution | based on data decomposition | work stealing | work and depth model | pthread scheduling | Tulip RTS | user |
| Overlap comm/comp | yes | no | yes | no | no | no | no | no | yes |

**Table 1.** Related Work. For the paradigm, S and M denote SPMD and MIMD, resp. For the architecture, S and D denote shared memory and distributed, resp.

The Parallel Standard Template Library (PSTL) [15, 14] has similar goals to STAPL; it uses parallel iterators in place of STL iterators and provides some parallel algorithms and containers. NESL [7], CILK [10] and SPLIT-C [9] provide the ability to exploit nested parallelism through their language support (all three are extended programming languages with NESL providing a library of algorithms). However, only STAPL is intended to automatically generate recursive parallelization without user intervention. Most of listed packages (STAPL, Amelia [21], CHAOS++ [8] and to a certain extent CHARM++ [1]) use a C++ template mechanism and assure good code reusability. STAPL emphasizes irregular data structures like trees, lists, and graphs, providing parallel operations on such structures. Charm++ and CHAOS++ also provide support for irregular application through their chare objects and inspector/executor, respectively. Both POOMA [19] and STAPL borrow from the STL philosophy, i.e., containers, iterators, and algorithms. The communication/computation overlapping mechanism is present in the STAPL executor, which also supports simultaneous use of both message passing and shared memory (MPI and OpenMP) communication models. Charm++ provides similar support through message driven execution and a dynamic object creation mechanism. The split phase assignment (:=) in Split-C also allows for overlapping communication with computation.

STAPL is further distinguished in that it emphasizes both automatic support and user specified policies for *scheduling, data decomposition and data dependence enforcement*. Furthermore, STAPL is unique in its goal to *automatically select the best performing algorithm* by analyzing data, architecture and current run-time conditions.

## 3   STAPL – Philosophy, Interface, and Implementation

STL consists of three major components: `containers`, `algorithms`, and `iterators`. Containers are data structures such as vectors, lists, sets, maps and their associated methods. Algorithms are operations such as searching, sorting, and merging. Algorithms can operate on a variety of different containers because they are defined only in terms of templated iterators. Iterators are generalized C++ pointers that abstract the type of container they traverse (e.g., linked list to bidirectional iterators, vector to random access iterators).

STAPL's interface layer consists of five major components: `pContainers`, `pAlgorithms`, `pRanges`, `schedulers/distributors` and `executors`. Figure 1 shows the overall organization of STAPL's major components. The `pContainers` and `pAlgorithms` are parallel counterparts of the STL containers and algorithms; pContainers are backwards compatible with STL containers and STAPL includes pAlgorithms for all STL algorithms and some additional algorithms supporting parallelism (e.g., parallel prefix). The `pRange` is a novel construct that presents an abstract view of a scoped data space which allows *random access* to a partition, or subrange, of the data space (e.g., to elements in a pContainer). A pRange can recursively partition the data domain to support nested parallelism. Analogous to STL iterators, pRanges bind pContainers and pAlgorithms. Unlike STL iterators, pRanges also include a `distributor` for data distribution and a `scheduler` that can generically enforce data dependences in the parallel execution according to data dependence graphs (DDGs). The STAPL `executor` is responsible for executing subranges of the pRange on processors based on the specified execution schedule. Users can write STAPL programs using pContain-

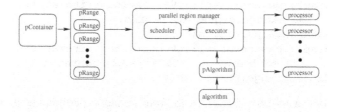

**Fig. 1.** STAPL Components

ers, pRanges and pAlgorithms, and, optionally, their own schedulers and executors if those provided by STAPL do not offer the desired functionality.

Application programmers use the interface layer and the concurrency/communication layer, which expresses parallelism and communication generically. The software and machine layers are used internally by STAPL, and only the machine layer requires modification when porting STAPL to a new system. In STAPL programmers can specify almost everything (e.g., scheduling, partitioning, algorithmic choice, containers, etc) or they can let the library decide automatically the appropriate option.

In the remainder of this section we present a more detailed discussion of the basic STAPL components and their current implementation.

## 3.1   pRanges

A pRange is an abstract view of a scoped data space providing *random access* to a partition of the data space that allows the programmer to work with different (portions of) containers in a uniform manner. Note that random access to (independent) work quanta is an essential condition for parallelism. Each subspace of the scoped data space is disjoint and can itself be described as a pRange, thus supporting nested parallelism. A pRange also has a relation determining the computation order of its subspaces and relative weights (priorities) for each subspace. If the partition, ordering relation, and relative weights (execution priorities) are not provided as input, then they can be self-computed by the pRange or imposed (by STAPL or the user) for performance gains.

**pRange Implementation** So far we have implemented the pRange for pvectors, plists and ptrees. The pRange and each of its subranges provide the same begin() and end() functions that the container provides, which allows the pRange to be used as a parallel adapter of the container. For example,

```
stapl::pRange(pContainer.begin(), pContainer.end())
```

constructs a pRange on the data in pContainer. STL has no direct sequential equivalent of pRange, but a structure to maintain a range could be implemented as a simple pair of iterators. For example, a range on a sequential STL vector of integers can be constructed as follows.

```
std::pair<std::vector<int>::iterator,std::vector<int>::iterator>
    seqRange(seqContainer.begin(),seqContainer.end());
```

```
1. stapl::pRange<stapl::pVector<int>::iterator>
      dataRange(segBegin, segEnd);
2. dataRange.partition(4);
3. stapl::pRange<stapl::pVector<int>::iterator>&
      dataSubrange = dataRange.get_subrange(3);
4. dataSubrange.partition(4);
```

**Fig. 2.** Creating a pVector `dataRange` from iterators, partitioning it into 4 subranges, selecting the 3rd subrange `dataSubrange`, and sub-partitioning it into 4 (sub)subranges.

The pRange provides random access to each of its subranges (recursively), while the elements within each subrange at the lowest level (of the recursion) must be accessed using the underlying STL iterators. For example, a pRange built on a list would provide bidirectional iterators to the begin and end of each subrange, and elements within the subranges could only be accessed in a linear fashion from either point using the bidirectional iterators. In contrast, a pRange built on a vector would provide random access iterators to the begin and end of each subrange, and internal elements of each subrange could be accessed in a random manner using them.

STAPL provides support for nested parallelism by maintaining the partition of a pRange as a set of subranges, each of which can itself be a complete pRange with its own partition of the data it represents (see Figure 2). This allows for a parallel algorithm to be executed on a subrange as part of a parallel algorithm being executed on the entire pRange. The bottom (hierarchically lowest level) subrange is the the minimum quantum of work that the executor can send to a processor.

The pRange can partition the data using a built in distributor function, by a user specified map, or it might be computed earlier in the program. A simple example of distribution tuning is static block data distribution where the chunk sizes are either precomputed, given by the user, or automatically computed by the pRange and adjusted adaptively based on a performance model and monitoring code. In the extreme case, each data element is a separate subrange, which provides fully random access at the expense of high memory usage. Usually, larger chunks of data are assigned to each subrange.

## 3.2  pContainers

A `pContainer` is the parallel equivalent of the STL container and is backward compatible with STL containers through its ability to provide STL iterators. Each pContainer provides (semi–) random access to its elements, a prerequisite for efficient parallel processing. Random access to the subranges of a pContainer's data is provided by an internal pRange maintained by the pContainer. The internal pRange is updated when the structure of the pContainer is modified (e.g., insertion or deletion of elements) so that a balanced, or user-defined, partition can be maintained.

**pContainer Implementation** The pContainers currently implemented in STAPL are `pvector`, `plist` and `ptree`. Each adheres to a common interface and maintains

```
stapl::pVector<int> pV(i,j);      std::vector<int> sV(i,j);
stapl::pSort(pV.get_pRange());    std::sort(sV.begin(),sV.end());
            (a)                                (b)
```

**Fig. 3.** (a) STAPL and (b) STL code fragments creating (line 1) and sorting (line 2) pContainers and Containers, resp.

an internal pRange. Automatic translation from STL to STAPL and vice versa requires that each pContainer provides the same data members and member functions as the equivalent STL containers along with any class members specifically for parallel processing (e.g., the internal pRange). Thus, STAPL pContainer interfaces allow them to be constructed and used as if they were STL containers (see Fig. 3).

The pContainer's internal pRange maintains (as persistent data) the iterators that mark the boundary of the subranges. The continual adjusting of subranges within the internal pRange may eventually cause the distribution to become unbalanced. When the number of updates (insertions and deletions) made to a pContainer reach a certain threshold (tracked using an update counter in the pContainer) the overall distribution is examined and the subranges and pRange are adjusted to bring the distribution back to a near balanced state, or a user-defined distribution if one is provided. The maintenance of a distributed internal pRange is critical to the performance of STAPL so that a redistribution of a pContainer's data before beginning execution of each parallel region can be avoided.

When possible, each pContainer's methods have been parallelized (e.g., the pVector copy constructor). The methods may be parallelized in two ways: (i) internal parallelization – the method's operation is parallel, and (ii) external parallelization (concurrency) – the method may be called simultaneously by different processors in a parallel region. These two approaches to parallelization coexist and are orthogonal. A pContainer method can utilize both methods of parallelism simultaneously to allow for nested parallelism.

### 3.3  pAlgorithms

A pAlgorithm is the parallel counterpart of the STL algorithm. There are three types of pAlgorithms in STAPL. First, pAlgorithms with semantics identical to their sequential counterparts (e.g., sort, merge, reverse). Second, pAlgorithms with enhanced semantics (e.g., a parallel find could return any (or all) elements found, while a sequential find generally returns only the first element). Third, pAlgorithms with no sequential equivalent in STL.

STL algorithms take iterators marking the start and end of the input as parameters. STAPL pAlgorithms take pRanges as parameters instead. STAPL provides a smooth transition from STL by providing an additional interface for each of its pAlgorithms that is equivalent to its STL counterpart and automatically constructs a pRange from the iterator arguments. The pAlgorithms express parallelism through calls to a parallel region manager, which frees the STAPL user from low level issues such as construction of parallel structures, scheduling and execution. STAPL also allows users to implement custom pAlgorithms through the same interface.

**pAlgorithm Implementation** Currently, STAPL provides parallel equivalents for all STL algorithms that may be profitably parallelized. Some algorithms perform sequentially very well and we have chosen to focus our efforts on exploiting parallelism on other algorithms (this may change as STAPL matures and more systems are studied). STAPL pAlgorithms take the pRanges to process as arguments along with any other necessary data (e.g., a binary predicate). See Fig. 3 for examples of pSort and sort.

The pAlgorithms in STAPL are implemented by expressing parallelism through the *parallel region manager* of STAPL's concurrency and communication layer. The parallel region manager (e.g., pforall) issues the necessary calls to the STAPL runtime system to generate or awaken the needed execution threads for the function, and passes the work function and data to the execution threads. Each pAlgorithm in STAPL is composed of one or more calls to the parallel region manager. Between parallel calls, the necessary post processing of the output of the last parallel region is done, along with the preprocessing for the next call. The arguments to the parallel region manager are the pRange(s) to process, and a pFunction object, which is the work to be performed on each subrange of the pRange.

The pFunction is the base class for all work functions. The only operator that a pFunction instance must provide is the () operator. This operator contains the code that works on a subrange of the provided pRanges. In addition, a pFunction can optionally provide prologue and epilogue member functions that can be used to allocate and deallocate any private variables needed by the work function and perform other maintenance tasks that do not contribute to the parallel algorithm used in the work function. The pFunction and parallel construct interfaces can be accessed by STAPL users to implement user-defined parallel algorithms. Figure 4 is an example of a simple work function that searches a subrange for a given value and returns an iterator to the first element in the subrange that matched the value. The example assumes the == operator has been defined for the data type used.

```
template<class pRange, class T>
class pSearch : public stapl::pFunction {
private:
  const T value;
public:
  pSearch(const T& v) : value(v) {}
  typename pRange::iterator operator()(pRange& pr) {
    typename pRange::iterator i;
    for (i = pr.begin(); i != p.end(); i++)
      if (*i == value) return i;
    return pr.end();
  }
};
```

**Fig. 4.** STAPL work function to search a pRange for a given value

## 3.4    Scheduler/Distributor and Executor

The scheduler/distributor is responsible for determining the execution order of the subspaces in a pRange and the processors they will be assigned to. The schedule must enforce the natural data dependences of the problem while, at the same time, minimizing execution time. These data dependences are represented by a Data Dependence Graph (DDG).

The STAPL executor is responsible for executing a set of given tasks (subranges of a pRange and work function pairs) on a set of processors. It assigns subranges to processors once they are ready for processing (i.e., all the inputs are available) based on the schedule provided by the scheduler. There is an executor that deals with the subranges at each level in the architectural hierarchy. The executor is similar to the CHARM++ message driven execution mechanism [1].

**Scheduler/Distributor and Executor Implementation** STAPL provides several schedulers, each of which use a different policy to impose an ordering on the subranges. Each scheduler requires as input the pRange(s) that are to be scheduled and the processor hierarchy on which to execute. The *static scheduling* policy allows *block scheduling* and *interleaved block scheduling* of subranges to processors. The *dynamic scheduling* policy does not assign a subrange to any given processor before beginning parallel execution, but instead allows the executor to assign the next available subspace to the processor requesting work. The *partial self scheduling* policy does not assign subspaces to a specific processor, but instead creates an order in which subspaces will be processed according to their weight (e.g., workload or other priority) and the subspace dependence graph. The executor then assigns each processor requesting work the next available subspace according to the order. Finally, the *complete self scheduling* policy enables the host code to completely control the computation by indicating an assignment of subspaces to particular processors and providing a subspace dependence graph for the pRange. If no ordering is provided, then STAPL can schedule the subspaces according to their weights (priorities), beginning with the subspaces that have the largest weights, or, if no weights are given, according to a round robin policy.

The recursive pRange contains, at every level of its hierarchy, a DAG which represents an execution order (schedule) of its subranges. In the case of a doall no ordering is needed and the DAG is degenerate. The subranges of a recursive pRange (usually) correspond to a certain data decomposition across the processor hierarchy. The distributor will, at every level of the pRange, distribute its data and associated (sub) schedule (i.e., a portion of the global schedule) across the machine hierarchy. The scheduler/distributor is formulated as an optimization problem (a schedule with minimum execution time) with constraints (data dependences to enforce, which require communication and/or synchronization). If the scheduler does not produce an actual schedule (e.g., a fully parallel loop) then the distributor will either compute an optimal distribution or use a specified one (by the user or by a previous step in the program).

Each pRange has an executor object which assigns subspaces (a set of nodes in a DDG) and work functions to processors based on the scheduling policy. The executor maintains a ready queue of tasks (subspaces and work function pairs). After the current task is completed, the executor uses point-to-point communication primitives to transmit, if necessary, the results to any dependent tasks. On shared memory systems, synchronizations (e.g., post/await) will be used to inform dependent tasks the results are ready. This process continues until all tasks have been completed. STAPL can support MIMD parallelism by, e.g., assigning each processor different DDGs, or partial DDGs, and work functions. Nested parallelism is achieved by nested pRanges, each with an associated executor.

### 3.5  STAPL Run-Time System

The STAPL run-time system provides support for parallel processing for different parallel architectures (e.g., HP V2200, SGI Origin 2000) and for different parallel paradigms (e.g., OpenMP, MPI). We have obtained the best results by directly managing the Pthread package. The STAPL run-time system supports nested parallelism if the underlying architecture allows nested parallelism via a hierarchical native run-time system. Otherwise, the run-time system serializes the nested parallelism. We are in the process of incorporating the HOOD run-time system [18].

While memory allocation can create performance problems for sequential programs, it is often a source of major bottlenecks for parallel programs [24]. For programs with very dynamic data access behavior and implicit memory allocation, the underlying memory allocation mechanisms and strategies are extremely important because the program's performance can vary substantially depending on the allocators' performance. STL provides a dynamic-behavior framework through the use of the memory heap. STAPL extends STL for parallel computation, and therefore relies heavily on efficient memory allocation/deallocation operations. The memory allocator used by STAPL is the HOARD parallel memory allocator [5]. Hoard is an efficient and portable parallel memory allocator that enhances STAPL's portability.

All algorithms and containers whose characteristics may change during execution have been instrumented to collect run-time information. For now we collect execution times of the different stages of the computation and "parallel behavior", e.g., load imbalance, subrange imbalance (suboptimal distribution). The output of the monitors is used as feedback for our development effort and, in a few instances, as adaptive feedback to improve performance.

## 4  Performance

This section examines STAPL performance and shows its flexibility and ease of use through several case studies. More details and results illustrating the performance of pContainers (a ptree) and adaptive algorithm selection can be found in [4].

All experiments were run on a 16 processor HP V2200 with 4GB of memory running in dedicated mode. All speedups reported represent the ratio between the sequential algorithm's running time and its parallel counterpart.

### 4.1  Molecular Dynamics

To illustrate the performance and the ease of coding with STAPL, we used STAPL to parallelize a molecular dynamics code which makes extensive use of STL, including algorithms and data encapsulated in containers. We have used both semi-automatic and manual parallelization modes. This code was written by Danny Rintoul at Sandia National Labs.

**Algorithm Description**  The algorithm is a discrete event simulation that computes interactions between particles. At the initialization phase, each particle is assigned an initial coordinate position and a velocity. According to their attributes (coordinates and velocity) these particles interact according to specified physics laws.

At each discrete time event, interactions between particles are computed that determine the evolution of the system at the next time step. Due to obvious flow data dependences at the event level we have parallelized the code at the event processing level. We have applied two parallelization methods with STAPL: (i) automatic translation from STL to STAPL, and (ii) manual modification to STAPL constructs.

The section of code parallelized with STAPL uses STL algorithms (e.g., for_each, transform, accumulate) and uses parallel push_back[1] operations on vectors. This section of the code represents 40% to 49% of the sequential execution time.

The rest of the program uses a set[2] for ordering the particles according to their next interaction time. Insertion and deletion operations are performed on this set.

**Automatic Translation**  STAPL provides two ways for automatically translating STL code to STAPL code: (i) *full translation* (the entire code is translated), and (ii) *partial translation* (only user defined sections of the code are translated).

There is a fundamental condition in both full and partial translation: the user must decide which sections of the STL code are safely parallelizable. It is not possible for STAPL to determine if the code is inherently sequential due to the potential existence of data dependencies. Compiler support is needed for detecting such dependencies. For full translation, the only change necessary is adding the STAPL header files. For partial translation, the sections to be parallelized are enclosed by the user inserted STAPL preprocessing directives $\#include < start\_translation >$, and $\#include < stop\_translation >$. Figure 5 and Figure 6 give an example of the manual code instrumentation needed to start automatic translation from STL to STAPL. For the molecular dynamics code we have used partial translation.

**Manual Translation**  This method takes full advantage of STAPL, by allowing the user to explicitly replace STL code with STAPL, thus reducing the run-time work STAPL needs to perform. Table 8 gives the execution times and Figure 7 plots the speedups obtained from our experiments, which show a scalable performance.

STAPL exhibits the best performance when used directly through manual modification. However, our experimental results indicate that even though automatic translation incurs some run-time overhead, it is simpler to use and the performance is very close to that obtained with manual modification (less than 5% performance deterioration).

---

[1] A push_back operation is a container method which some STL containers have. The push_back method appends an element to the end of a container.

[2] Most STL implementations implement a set with Red Black trees. We are in the process of creating a parallel set.

```
std::vector<int> v(400,000);
int sum=0;
...// Execute computation on v
std::accumulate(v.begin(),v.end(), sum);
...// Rest of the computation
```

**Fig. 5.** Original STL code

```
std::vector<int> v(400,000);
int sum=0;
...// Execute computation on v
#include <start_translation>
std::accumulate(v.begin(),v.end(), sum);
#include <stop_translation>
...Rest of the computation
```

**Fig. 6.** STL to STAPL code

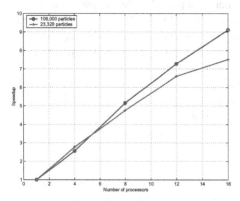

| Number of | Number of processors | | | | |
|-----------|------|------|-----|------|------|
| Particles | 1 | 4 | 8 | 12 | 16 |
| 108,000 | 2815 | 1102 | 546 | 386 | 309 |
| 23,326 | 627 | 238 | 132 | 94.2 | 86.4 |

**Fig. 8.** Molecular Dynamics Execution (*sec*)

**Fig. 7.** Molecular Dynamics Partial Speedup for manually STAPL programmed code

## 4.2 Generic Particle Transport Solver

Within the framework of the DOE ASCI project we have developed, from scratch, a particle transport code. It is a numerical intensive parallel application written entirely in C++ (so far, about 25,000 lines of code). Its purpose is the development of a general testbed for solving transport problems on regular and arbitrary grids. Its central algorithmic component is a discrete ordinate parallel sweep across a spatial grid. This involves the traversal of the spatial grid in each direction of particle travel [11, 12]. This part of the computation takes 50% to 80% of total execution time. Due to the very large data sizes and the enormous amount of computation the code has to scale up to 10,000 processors. The primary data structure is the spatial discretization grid, which is provided as input. The primary algorithm is called a solver, which usually consists mainly of grid sweeps. The solver method may also be given.

**Using STAPL** We started with a sequential version of the code written in STL and then transformed it using the pfor_each template, which applies a work function to all the elements in a domain. The application defines five entities: (1) **pContainers** to store data in a distributed fashion, (2) **pRanges** to define the domain on which to apply algorithms, (3) execution **schedules** to specify data dependencies, (4) **pFunctions** to be applied to every element of the specified domain, and (5) an **executor** to manage parallel execution. In the following we will refer to three important routines: particle scattering computation (fully parallel), sweep (partially parallel) and convergence test (reduction).

The **pContainer** that receives the input data is called the pGrid and represents a distributed spatial discretization grid. It is derived from STAPL's predefined pVector. All parallel operations use the same **pRange** because they operate on the same pGrid.

For every parallel operation we specify an execution **schedule** (by default the execution schedule is empty, i.e., no predefined order). The schedule is a directed graph whose vertices are points in the range described by the pRange built above. The scattering routines are fully parallel loops and thus have empty schedules. For the partially parallel sweep loop, the schedule is computed by the application and is given to STAPL as a Data Dependence Graph (DDG) which STAPL incorporates into the pRange.

A **pFunction** is a work function that takes as arguments elements in the pRange built above. For the scattering routines, the pFunction is a routine that computes scattering for a single spatial discretization unit (Cell Set). For the sweep, the pFunction is a routine that sweeps a Cell Set for a specific direction of particle travel. For the convergence routines, the pFunction is a routine that tests convergence for a Cell Set. *The work function (sweep) was written by the physics/numerical analysis team unaware of parallelism issues. We just needed to put a wrapper around it (the interface required by STAPL).*

The **Executor** is created by combining a set of pRanges with a set of pFunctions. Parallel execution, communication and synchronization are handled by the executor. It first maps subranges in the pRange to execution threads based on knowledge about machine, OS and underlying RTS. Nodes in the DDG stored in the pRange correspond to execution vertices and edges specify communication and synchronization. The executor ensures that the corresponding message for every incoming edge is received before it starts to execute the work function on a specific node. After the execution of the work function, the executor sends out messages for all outgoing edges. For the scattering routines (fully parallel), the executor will not initiate any communication because the DDG given as the schedule has no edges. In the convergence routines, the executor performs a reduction by using a lower-level MPI call MPI_Allreduce. It should be noted that an application can define its own executor class as long as it presents the same interface as the STAPL base executor. *In our case, creating the executor class required only 1 line of code: an instantiation of the executor constructor taking the pRanges and the pFunctions as actual parameters.*

**Experimental Results**  Experiments were run in the parallel queue (not dedicated) on a SGI Origin 2000 server with 32 R10000 processors and 8GB of physical memory. The input data was a 3D mesh with 24x24x24 nodes. The energy discretization consisted of 12 energy groups. The angular discretization had 228 angles.

The six parts of the code parallelized with STAPL, their execution profile and speedup are shown in Table 2. Speedups are for 16 processors in the experimental setup described above.

| Code Region | % Seq. | Speedup |
|---|---|---|
| Create computational grid | 10.00 | 14.50 |
| Scattering across group-sets | 0.05 | N/A |
| Scattering within a group-set | 0.40 | 15.94 |
| Sweep | 86.86 | 14.72 |
| Convergence across group sets | 0.05 | N/A |
| Convergence within group sets | 0.05 | N/A |
| Total | 97.46 | 14.70 |

**Table 2.** Profile and Speedups on 16 processor SGI Origin 2000

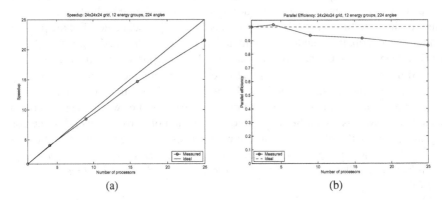

(a)                                      (b)

**Fig. 9.** (a) Speedup and (b) parallel efficiency (averaged across two runs.)

Our results are shown in Figure 9. The particular scheduling scheme used in this experiment (KBA) [16] requires that the number of processors be a perfect square, so we had to stop at 25 processors.

## 5    Conclusions and Future Work

STAPL is a parallel programming library designed as a superset of STL. STAPL provides parallel equivalents of STL containers, algorithms, and iterators, which allow parallel applications to be developed using the STAPL components as building blocks. Existing applications written using STL can be parallelized semi-automatically by STAPL during a preprocessing phase of compilation that replaces calls to STL algorithms with their STAPL equivalents. Our experiments show the performance of applications that utilize the automatic translation to be similar to the performance of applications developed manually with STAPL. The automatic translation of STL code to STAPL, the handling of the low level details of parallel execution by the parallel region manager, and the adaptive run-time system allow for portable, efficient, and scalable parallel applications to be developed without burdening the developer with the management of all the details of parallel execution.

STAPL is functional and covers almost all of the equivalent STL functionality. However much work lies ahead: Implementing several algorithmic choices for each function, full support of the recursive pRange on very large machines, a better RTS and its own, parallel memory manager are only a few of the items on our agenda.

**Acknowledgements** We would like to thank Danny Rintoul of Sandia National Laboratories for providing us with the molecular dynamics application presented in Section 4.1.

# References

[1]  *The CHARM++ Programming Language Manual.* http://charm.cs.uiuc.edu, 2000.

[2]  N. M. Amato, J. Perdue, A. Pietracaprina, G. Pucci, and M. Mathis. Predicting performance on SMPs. a case study: The SGI Power Challenge. In *Proc. International Parallel and Distributed Processing Symposium (IPDPS)*, pages 729–737, 2000.

[3]  N. M. Amato, A. Pietracaprina, G. Pucci, L. K. Dale, and J. Perdue. A cost model for communication on a symmetric multiprocessor. Technical Report 98-004, Dept. of Computer Science, Texas A&M University, 1998. A preliminary verson of this work was presented at the *SPAA'98 Revue*.

[4]  Ping An, Alin Jula, Silvius Rus, Steven Saunders, Tim Smith, Gabriel Tanase, Nathan Thomas, Nancy Amato, and Lawrence Rauchwerger. Stapl: An adaptive, generic parallel programming library for c++. Technical Report TR01-012, Dept. of Computer Science, Texas A&M University, June 2001.

[5]  Emery Berger, Kathryn McKinley, Robert Blumofe, and Paul Wilson. HOARD: A scalable memory allocator for multithreaded applications. In *International Conference on Architectural Support for Programming Languages and Operatings Systems (ASPLOS)*, 2000.

[6]  Guy Blelloch. *Vector Models for Data-Parallel Computing.* MIT Press, 1990.

[7]  Guy Blelloch. NESL: A Nested Data-Parallel Language. Technical Report CMU-CS-93-129, Carnegie Mellon University, April 1993.

[8]  C. Chang, A. Sussman, and J. Saltz. Object-oriented runtime support for complex distributed data structures, 1995.

[9]  David Culler, Andrea Dusseau, Seth Copen Goldstein, Arvind Krishnamurthy, Steven Lumetta, Thorsten von Eicken, and Katherine Yelick. Parallel programming in Split-C. In *International Conference on Supercomputing*, November 1993.

[10]  Matteo Frigo, Charles Leiserson, and Keith Randall. The implementation of the Cilk-5 multithreaded language. In *ACM SIGPLAN Conference on Programming Language Design and Implementation (PLDI)*, 1998.

[11]  Adolfy Hoisie, Olaf Lubeck, and Harvey Wasserman. Performance and scalability analysis of teraflop-scale parallel architectures using multidimensional wavefront applications. Technical Report LAUR-98-3316, Los Alamos National Laboratory, August 1998.

[12]  Adolfy Hoisie, Olaf Lubeck, and Harvey Wasserman. Scalability analysis of multidimensional wavefront algorithms on large-scale SMP clusters. In *Proceedings of Frontiers '99: The 7th Symposium on the Frontiers of Massively Parallel Computation*, pages 4–15, Annapolis, MD, February 1999. IEEE Computer Society.

[13]  International Standard ISO/IEC 14882. *Programming Languages – C++*, 1998. First Edition.

[14]  Elizabeth Johnson. *Support for Parallel Generic Programming.* PhD thesis, Indiana University, 1998.

[15]  Elizabeth Johnson and Dennis Gannon. HPC++: Experiments with the parallel standard library. In *International Conference on Supercomputing*, 1997.

[16] K. R. Koch, R. S. Baker, and R. E. Alcouffe. Solution of the first-order form of the 3D discrete ordinates equation on a massively parallel processor. *Transactions of the American Nuclear Society*, 65:198–199, 1992.

[17] David Musser, Gillmer Derge, and Atul Saini. *STL Tutorial and Reference Guide, Second Edition*. Addison-Wesley, 2001.

[18] C.G. Plaxtion N.S. Arora, R.D. Blumofe. Thread scheduling for multiprogrammed multiprocessors. In *Proceedings of the 10th ACM Symposium on Parallel Algorithms and Architectures*, June 1998.

[19] J. Reynders. Pooma: A framework for scientific simulation on parallel architectures, 1996.

[20] Robert Sedgewick. *Algorithms in C++*. Addison-Wesley, 1992.

[21] Thomas Sheffler. A portable MPI-based parallel vector template library. Technical Report RIACS-TR-95.04, Research Institute for Advanced Computer Science, March 1995.

[22] Bjarne Stroustrup. *The C++ Programming Language, Third Edition*. Addison-Wesley, 1997.

[23] Gregory Wilson and Paul Lu. *Parallel Programming using C++*. MIT Press, 1996.

[24] Paul Wilson, Mark Johnstone, Michael Neely, and David Boles. Dynamic storage allocation: A survey and critical review. In *International Workshop on Memory Management*, September 1995.

# An Interface Model for Parallel Components

Milind Bhandarkar and L. V. Kalé

Department of Computer Science
University of Illinois at Urbana-Champaign
(bhandark@csar.uiuc.edu, kale@cs.uiuc.edu)

**Abstract.** Component architectures promote cross-project code reuse by facilitating composition of large applications using off-the-shelf software components. Existing component architectures are not geared towards building efficient parallel software applications that require tighter runtime integration of largely independent parallel modules. We have developed a component architecture based on Converse, a message-driven multiparadigm runtime system that allows concurrent composition. In this paper, we describe an interface model for this component architecture, which allows reusable component modules to be developed independently of each other, and mediates, monitors, and optimizes interactions between such components.

## 1 Introduction

Developing scalable parallel applications is a difficult task. Applicability and availability of different computational techniques and programming models demands that these programs be developed as a largely independent collection of software modules based on a common framework. Several parallel languages and application frameworks have been developed to facilitate the implementation of large-scale parallel applications. These frameworks typically focus on a few techniques and applications. No single framework is suitable for all numerical, computational and software engineering techniques employed and under development in academia and research laboratories. Thus, one would need to employ different application frameworks for different modules of a complex application. However, it is currently impossible to efficiently couple together the software components built using different frameworks. This is mainly because these application frameworks have not been built with a "common component model".

One way to couple these independent software modules together is to run them as separate application processes, using mechanisms such as sockets to communicate. This tends to be extremely inefficient. While we want the individual software components to be modular and and independently developed, these components may not always have large enough grainsize to ignore the efficiency of coupling. Also, in order to be scalable to a large number of processors, especially while solving a fixed problem, it is required that the coupling efficiency be maximized. Therefore, it is imperative that the communicating software components be part of the same process in order to have efficient coupling between

H. Dietz (Ed.): LCPC 2001, LNCS 2624, pp. 209-222, 2003.

software components (known in the component terminology as "in-process components".)

In-process components eliminate the inefficiency resulting from separate application processes; do not require the data exchange to be serialized; and are close in efficiency to a procedure call. However, this efficiency must be achieved without sacrificing independence of the individual components and uniformity of data exchange.

In order to achieve this, first we make sure that the software components, which may already be parallel, coexist within a single application. Since these components often use different parallel programming paradigms and different programming languages, this is a non-trivial task. We need to keep the semantics of individual programming paradigms, while allowing these paradigms to cooperate and interact with each other. For this purpose, we need to have a *Common Language Runtime* (CLR) for all the programming paradigms we want to support. Since these programming models differ in the amount of concurrency within a process and the way control is transferred among different entities of the programming model, we have developed a runtime system called Converse, based on message-driven parallel programming paradigm. Converse employs a unified task scheduler for efficiently supporting different concurrency levels and "control regimes". Detailed description of Converse can be found in [4].

While Converse allows us to have multiple "in-process components" within an application, it does not specify how different components interact with each other. For this purpose, we need an interface model that allows components to access other components' functionality in a uniform manner. Converse being a message-driven CLR, traditional interface description languages do not perform well because they assume semantics of a blocking procedure call. Enhancing the traditional interface languages to allow asynchronous remote procedure calls results in other problems, such as proliferation of interfaces. We have developed a different interface model based on separate input and output interfaces, which enables us to overcome these problems. An orchestration language – a high level scripting language that utilizes this interface model to make it easy to construct complete applications from components – is also defined.

This paper describes the interface model for our message-driven component architecture. Our interface model encourages modular development of applications yet allows tighter integration of application components at run time.

## 1.1    Outline

The next section reviews commonly used component architectures for distributed and parallel computation, and describes their limitations. We list the desired characteristics of an ideal interface model for parallel components in section 3 and show that extensions of existing interface models do not match these characteristics. We describe our interface model, which is a crucial part of our component architecture, in section 4 with several examples, and discuss the runtime optimizations that become possible due to expressiveness of our interface model. We conclude in section 5.

## 2    Component Architectures

Software components allow composition of software programs from off-the-shelf software pieces. They aid in rapid prototyping and have been successfully used for developing GUIs, database as well as Web applications. A component model specifies rules to be obeyed by components conforming to that model. A software component is a set of objects with published interfaces, which obeys the rules specified by the underlying component model. A component model alongwith a set of "system components" defines a component architecture.

Various component architectures such as COM [9], CORBA [8], and JavaBeans [7] have been developed and have become commercially successful as distributed application integration technologies. Parallel computing community in academia and various U.S. national laboratories have recently formed a Common Component Architecture forum (CCA-Forum [1]) to address these needs for parallel computing.

Current component technologies cross language barriers, thus allowing an application written using one language to incorporate components written using another. In order to achieve this, components have to provide interface specification in a neutral language called Interface Description Language (IDL). All component architectures use some form of Interface Description Language. Though these IDLs differ in syntax, they can be used to specify almost the same concept of an interface. An interface consists of a set of "functions" or "methods" with typed parameters, and return types. Caller of a method is referred to as "Client", whereas the object whose method is called is referred to as "Server". Client and Server need not reside on the same machine if the underlying component model supports remote method invocation.

Remote method invocation involves marshaling input parameters (or serializing into a message), "stamping" the message with the component and method identifier, dispatching that message, and in case of synchronous methods, waiting for the results. On the receiving side, parameters are unmarshalled, and the specified method is called on the specified instance of the component. Similar technique is employed for creating instances of components, or locating components, by invoking methods of system component instances, which provide these services. The server machine, which contains the server component instances, employs a scheduler (or uses the system scheduler) that waits continuously for the next message indicating a method invocation, locates the specified component instance, verifies access controls, if any, and calls the specified method on that component instance.

### 2.1    Limitations of Current Component Architectures

Component architectures in the distributed programming community (such as COM, JavaBeans, CORBA) do not address issues vital for coupling parallel software components. Though all of them support in-process components, they incur overheads unacceptable for the needs of parallel application integration. Microsoft COM has limited or no cross-platform support vital for the emerging parallel computing platforms such as the Grid [3]. JavaBeans have no cross-language support, and needs components to be written only using Java, while FORTRAN dominates the parallel computing community. CORBA supports a wide variety of platforms and languages, but does not have any support for abstractions such as multi-dimensional arrays.

Common Component Architecture (CCA) [2] is one of the efforts to unify different application frameworks. The CCA approach tries to efficiently connect different applications developed using various frameworks together by providing parallel pathways for data exchange between components. They have developed a Scientific Interface Description Language (SIDL) to allow exchange of multi-dimensional arrays between components, and have proposed a coupling mechanism (CCA-ports) using *provides/uses* design pattern. For parallel communication between components, they have proposed collective ports that implement commonly used data transfer patterns such as broadcast, gather, and scatter. In-process components are connected with "direct-connect" ports, which are close in efficiency to function calls. However, these component method invocations assume blocking semantics. Also, CCA restricts itself to SPMD and threaded programming paradigms, and does not deal with coexistence of multiple non-threaded components in a single application. Hooking up components dynamically is listed among future plans, and it is not clear how the efficiency of coupling will be affected by that.

The most suitable way of combining multiple components using CCA is by developing wrappers around complete application processes to perform parallel data transfer, delegating scheduling of these components to the operating system. Heavyweight process scheduling by the operating system leads to coupling inefficiencies. If the communicating components belong to different operating system processes even on the same processor, invoking a component's services from another component requires an inefficient process context-switch. For example, on a 500 MHz Intel Pentium III processor running Linux, invocation of a "null service" (that returns the arguments passed to it) takes 330 microseconds when the service is resident in another process, while it takes 1.3 microseconds for service residing within the same process (Corresponding times on a 248 MHz Sun Ultra SPARC workstation running Solaris 5.7 are 688 and 3.2 microseconds respectively.)

Our component architecture is complimentary to the CCA effort. We support coexistence of multiple components (threaded and non-threaded; based on different programming paradigms) within an application process. Our proposed interface model uses asynchronous method invocation semantics and can be thought of as a lower-level substrate on which CCA ports could be implemented.

## 3   Interface Models

Software components in an application interact with each other by exchanging data and transferring control. An interface model defines the way these components interact with each other in an application. The ideal interface model for a parallel component architecture should have the following characteristics:

- It should allow easy assembly of complete applications from off-the-shelf components. An interface description of the component alongwith the documentation of the component's functionality should be all that is needed to use the component in an application. Thus an interface model should be able to separate the component definition from component execution.
- It should allow individual components to be built completely independently, i.e. without the knowledge of each other's implementation or execution environment or the names of entities in other components.
- Components should make little or no assumptions about the environment where it is used. For example, a component should not assume exclusive ownership of processors where it executes.
- It should be possible to construct parallel components by grouping together sequential components, and this method of construction should not be exposed to the users of the resultant parallel component.
- It should not impose bottlenecks such as sequential creation, serialization etc on parallel components. In particular, it should allow parallel data exchange and control transfer among parallel components.
- It should enable the underlying runtime system to efficiently execute the component with effective resource utilization.
- It should be language independent and cross-platform.

Traditional component architectures for distributed components use a functional representation of component interfaces. They extend the object model by presenting the component functionality as methods of an object. Thus, a component interface description is similar to declaration of a C++ object. Components interact by explicit method calls using the interface description of each other.

A straightforward extension of such interface models for parallel components would be to provide a sequential component wrapper for the parallel component, where functionality of a parallel component is presented as a sequential method invocation. This imposes serialization bottleneck on the component. For example, a parallel CSE application that interfaces with a linear system solver will have to serialize its data structures before invoking the solver. This is clearly not feasible for most large linear systems representations that need hundreds of megabytes of memory.

Another extension of the traditional interface models is to treat each parallel component as a collection of sequential components. Within this model, the interaction between two parallel components takes place by having the corresponding sequential components invoke methods on each other. While this model removes the serialization bottleneck, it imposes rigid restrictions on the structure of parallel components. For example, a parallel finite element solver will have to partition its mesh into the same number of pieces as the neighboring block-structured CFD solver, while making sure that the corresponding pieces contain adjacent nodes.

A major disadvantage of extending the interface models based on method-calls is that they make data exchange and control transfer between components explicit. Thus, they do not provide control points for flexible application composition and for effective resource management by the runtime system.

Lack of a control point at data exchange leads to reduced reusability of components. For example, suppose a physical system simulation component interacts with a sparse linear system solver component, and the data exchange between them is modelled as sending messages or as parameters to the method call. In that case, the simulation component needs to transform its matrices to the storage format accepted by the solver, prior to calling the solver methods. This transformation code is part of the simulation component. Suppose, a better solver becomes available, but it uses a different storage format for sparse matrices; the simulation component code needs to be changed in order to transform its matrices to the new format required by the solver. If the interface model provided a control-point at data-exchange, one could use the simulation component without change, while inserting a transformer component in between the simulation and the solver.

Lack of a control point for the runtime system at control transfer prevents the runtime system from effective resource utilization. For example, with blocking method invocation semantics of control transfer, the runtime system cannot schedule other useful computations belonging to a parallel component while it is waiting for results from remote method invocations.

Asynchronous remote method invocation provides a control-point for the runtime system at control-transfer. It allows the runtime system to be flexible in scheduling other computations for maximizing resource utilization. However, extending functional interface representations to use asynchronous remote method invocations pose other problems. It introduces "compositional callbacks" as a mechanism for connecting two components together.

When a component (caller) invokes services from another component (callee) using asynchronous remote method invocation, it has to supply the callee with a its own unique ID, and the callee has to know which method of the caller to call to deposit the results (see figure 1.) This is referred to as the "compositional callback" mechanism.

Compositional callback mechanism is equivalent to building an object communication graph (object network) at run-time. Such dynamic object network misses out on certain optimizations that can be performed on a static object network [10]. For example, if the runtime system were involved in establishing connections between objects, it would place the communicating objects closer together (typically on the same processor).

Another problem associated with the callback mechanism is that it leads to proliferation of interfaces, increasing programming complexity. For example, suppose a class called Compute needs to perform asynchronous reductions using a system component called ReductionManager and also participates in a gather-scatter collective operation using a system component called GatherScatter. It will act as a client of these system services. For ReductionManager and

```
Client::invokeService() {
  ServiceMessage *m = new ServiceMessage();
  // ...
  m->myID = thishandle;
  ProxyServer ps(serverID);
  ps.service(m);
}

Server::service(ServiceMessage *m) {
  // ... perform service
  ResultMessage *rm = new ResultMessage();
  // ... construct proxy to the client
  ProxyClient pc(m->myID);
  pc.deposit(rm);
}

Client::deposit(ResultMessage *m) {
  // ...
}
```

**Fig. 1.** Asynchronous remote service invocation with return results

GatherScatter to recognize Compute as their client, the Compute class will have
to implement separate interfaces that are recognized by ReductionManager and
GatherScatter. This is shown in figure 2. Thus, for each component, this would
result in two interfaces: one for the service, and another for the client of that
service. If a component avails of multiple services, it will have to implement all
the client interfaces for those services.

## 4   Our Interface Model

Our interface model requires components to specify the data they use and produce. It takes the connection specification (glue) between components out of
the component code into a scripting language that is compiled into the application. This provides the application composer and the runtime system with a
control-point to maximize reuse of components. Asynchronous remote method
invocation semantics is assumed for dispatching produced data to the component that uses them, thus supplying the runtime system with a control-point for
effective resource utilization.

We mandate that the interface of a component consist of two parts: a set
of input ports, and a set of output ports. A component publishes the data it
produces on its output ports. These data become visible (when scheduled by the
runtime system) to the connected component's input port. Connection between
an input port of an object and an output port of another object are specified

```
class ReductionClient {
  virtual void reductionResults(ReductionData *msg) = 0;
}

class GatherScatterClient {
  virtual void gsResults(GSData *msg) = 0;
}

class Compute : public ReductionClient, public GatherScatterClient
{
    // ....
    void reductionResults(ReductionData *msg) { ... }
    void gsResults(GSData *msg) { ... }
}
```

**Fig. 2.** Proliferation of interfaces

"outside" of the object's code, e.g. using a scripting language. Each object can be thought of as having its own scheduler which schedules method invocations based on the availability of data on any of its input port, and possibly emits data at the output ports. Input ports of components have methods bound to them, so that when data become available on the input port, a component method is enabled[1].

For example, a simple producer-consumer application using this interface model is shown in figure 3. Note that both the producer and the consumer know nothing about each other's methods. Yet, with very simple scripting glue, they can be combined into a single program. Thus we achieve the separation of application execution from application definition. Individual component codes can be developed independently, because they do not specify application execution. They merely specify their definitions. The scripting language specifies the actual execution.

In figure 3, the data types of the connected ports of producer and consumer match exactly. For base types, wherever transformations between data types is possible, the system will implicitly apply such transformation. For example, if the type of producer::Data is double, and the type of consumer::Data is int, the system will automatically apply the requested transformations, and will still allow them to be connected. However, if producer::Data is Rational and consumer::Data is Complex, then system will not allow the requested connection. Thus, the application composer will have to insert a transformer object (see figure 4) between the producer and the consumer. A performance improvement

---

[1] Enabling an object method is different from executing it. Execution occurs under the control of a scheduler, whereas a method is enabled upon availability of its input data. This separation of execution and enabling objects methods is crucial to our component model.

```
class producer {
  in Start(void);
  in ProduceNext(void);
  out PutData(int);
};
producer::Start(void) {
  data = 0;
  PutData.emit(0);
}
producer::ProduceNext(void) {
  data++;
  PutData.emit(data);
}
```

(a) A Producer Component

```
class consumer {
  in GetData(int);
  out NeedNext(void);
};

consumer::GetData(int d) {
  // do something with d
  NeedNext.emit();
}
```

(b) A Consumer Component

```
producer p;
consumer c;

connect p.PutData to c.GetData;
connect c.NeedNext to p.ProduceNext;
connect system.Start to p.Start;
```

(c) Application Script

**Fig. 3.** A Producer-Consumer Application

hint "inline" can be interpreted by the translator for the scripting language to execute the method associated with the input port immediately instead of putting it off for scheduling later. This hint also guides the runtime system to place the transformer object on the same processor as the object that connects to its input.

The real power of this interface model comes from being able to define collections of such objects, and with a library of system objects. For example, one could connect individual sub-image smoother components as a 2-D array (figure 5) to compose a parallel image smoother component (see figure 6).

The composite ImageSmoother component specifies connections for all the InBorder and OutBorder ports of its SubImage constituents. Note that by specifying connections for all its components' ports, and providing unconnected input and output ports with the same names and types as SubImage, ImageSmoother has become topologically similar to SubImage and can be substituted for SubImage in any application. Code for ImageSmoother methods InBorder and InSurface is not shown here for lack of space. InBorder splits the input pixels into sub-

```
class transformer {
  inline in input(Rational);
  out output(Complex);
};

transformer::input(Rational d) {
  Complex c;
  c.re = d.num/d.den; c.im = 0;
  output.emit(c);
}
```

**Fig. 4.** Transformer Component

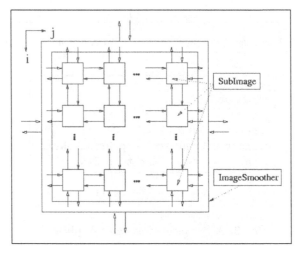

**Fig. 5.** Construction of a 2-D array component from elements

arrays and emits them on `OutSurface` ports. `InSurface` buffers the pixels until all the border pixels are handed over to it from a particular direction. It then combines all the pixels into a single array, and emits them onto corresponding `OutBorder` port.

Also, notice that the `ImageSmoother` component can configure itself with parameters N and M. N and M determine the number of rows and columns in a 2-D array of `SubImages`. They can be treated as attributes of the class `ImageSmoother`, which can be set through a script.

In this example, the interface of `SubImage` was serial. User of this component was expected to feed and receive one pixels array in each direction. The point of this example was to demonstrate the even after parallelization, the component interface can remian identical to the sequential component. If parallel interface is desired, that is also feasible, as our next example illustrates.

```
enum {EAST=0, WEST=1, NORTH=2, SOUTH=3};

class SubImage {
  in[4] InBorder(Pixels *);
  out[4] OutBorder(Pixels *);
}

class ImageSmoother <int N, int M> {
  in[4] InBorder(Pixels *);
  out[4] OutBorder(Pixels *);
  in[2*N+2*M] InSurface(Pixels *);
  out[2*N+2*M] OutSurface(Pixels *);

  SubImage si[N][M];
  // Make the east and west elements connections to surface
  for(int i=0; i<N; i++) {
    connect si[i][0].InBorder[WEST] to this.OutSurface[i];
    connect si[i][0].OutBorder[WEST] to this.InSurface[i];
    connect si[i][M-1].InBorder[EAST] to this.OutSurface[i+N];
    connect si[i][M-1].OutBorder[EAST] to this.InSurface[i+N];
  }
  // Similarly connect north and south border elements to surface
  for(int j=0; j<M; i++) {
    // ...
  }
  // Now, make internal elements connect to each other
  for(int i=1; i<=(N-1); i++) {
    for(int j=1; j<=(M-1); j++) {
      connect si[i][j].InBorder[0] to si[i-1][j].OutBorder[2];
      // ...
    }
  }
}
```

**Fig. 6.** A Parallel image smoother construction from sub-image smoother components

Consider the problem of interfacing Fluids and Solids modules in a coupled simulation. Each of the Fluids and Solids components is implemented as a parallel object. (Constituents of these modules, namely FluidsChunk and SolidsChunk, are not shown here for the sake of brevity.) A gather-scatter component FSInter specific to the application-domain can be used to connect an arbitrary number of Fluids chunks to any number of Solids chunks by carrying out the appropriate interpolations. The core interface description of this situation is shown in figure 7.

```
class Fluids<int N> {
  in[N] Input(FluidInput);
  out[N] Output(FluidOutput);
};
class Solids<int N> {
  in[N] Input(SolidInput);
  out[N] Output(SolidOutput);
};
class FSInter<int F, int S> {
  in[F] FInput(FluidOutput);
  out[F] FOutput(FluidInput);
  in[S] SInput(SolidOutput);
  out[S] SOutput(SolidInput);
};
```

(a) Component Interfaces

```
Fluids f<32>;
Solids s<64>;
FSInter fs<32,64>;

for(int i=0;i<32;i++){
  connect f.Output[i] to fs.FInput[i];
  connect fs.FOutput[i] to f.Input[i];
}
for(int i=0;i<64;i++){
  connect s.Output[i] to fs.SInput[i];
  connect fs.SOutput[i] to s.Input[i];
}
```

(b) Component Connections

**Fig. 7.** Fluids-Solids Interface in Coupled Simulation

Though most application compositions can be specified at compile (or link) time, for some applications (such as symbolic computations, branch-and-bound) it is necessary to dynamically specify connections, or to dynamically create objects. For such applications, apart from a scripting language, an API must be provided. This API will be available as an interface between the creator of the component and a "system" component. For example, creator's output port connects to the system's input port (system component is special in that it has infinite input and output ports), and emits the class type to be created, and also specifies connection information.

## 4.1 Runtime Optimizations

Several new runtime optimizations become feasible with our interface model because the composition and connectivity information is explicitly available to the runtime system. A few of them are described here.

Consider an example in a molecular dynamics application based on spatial decomposition [6], where each pair of subdomains (*patches*) has a compute object associated with it, which is responsible for computing pairwise cutoff-based interactions among atoms in those patches. If the patch neighborhood information is specified using our interface model (by constructing a 3-D grid of patches with a scripting language), these patches could be placed automatically by the runtime system on the available set of processors by taking locality of communication into account. Further, specification of connections between patches and compute object would allow the runtime system to place the compute objects closer to the patches they connect. Also, information about communication volume available from the Converse load balancing framework would enable the runtime system to place a compute object on the same processor as the patch that sends more atoms to it. We provide such runtime optimization techniques by incorporating the connectivity information in the Converse load balancing framework.

Connection specification also enables the runtime system to optimize data exchange between components that belong to the same address space. This can be achieved by allowing the components to publish their internal data buffers to the output ports. In the normal course, the published data will be sent as a message directed at the input port of the connected component. If the connected component belongs to the same address space, the runtime system may pass the same buffer to the input port of the connected component in the same process, when the corresponding input port declares itself to be readonly.

We are currently implementing the scripting language on top of the Charm++ runtime system [5], which is a C++ binding for the message-driven execution environment provided by Converse. An interface translator is being developed for translating the class definitions into C++ classes, and a small compiler is being written for the scripting language.

## 5 Conclusion

Efficient and scalable integration of independently developed parallel software components into a single application requires a component architecture that supports "in-process" components. We have developed a component architecture based on Converse, an interoperable parallel runtime system that supports message-driven execution.

We described an interface model and a scripting language to make the application composition and connectivity among components explicit. We are currently implementing this interface model and the scripting language, and carrying out optimizations enabled by them on top of the Charm++ language.

# References

1. Common          component      architecture      forum.              See
   http://www.acl.lanl.gov/cca-forum.
2. Rob Armstrong, Dennis Gannon, Al Geist, Katarzyna Keahey, Scott Kohn, Lois
   McInnes, Steve Parker, and Brent Smolinski. Toward a Common Component Architecture for High-Performance Scientific Computing. In *Proceedings of the 1999
   Conference on High Performance Distributed Computing*, pages 115–124, Redondo
   Beach, California, August 1999.
3. I. Foster and C. Kesselman (Eds). *The Grid: Blueprint for a New Computing
   Infrastructure*. Morgan Kaufmann, 1999.
4. L. V. Kalé, Milind Bhandarkar, Narain Jagathesan, Sanjeev Krishnan, and Joshua
   Yelon. Converse: An Interoperable Framework for Parallel Programming. In *Proceedings of the 10th International Parallel Processing Symposium*, pages 212–217,
   Honolulu, Hawaii, April 1996.
5. L. V. Kale and Sanjeev Krishnan. Charm++: Parallel Programming with Message-
   Driven Objects. In Gregory V. Wilson and Paul Lu, editors, *Parallel Programming
   using C++*, pages 175–213. MIT Press, 1996.
6. Laxmikant Kalé, Robert Skeel, Milind Bhandarkar, Robert Brunner, Attila Gur-
   soy, Neal Krawetz, James Phillips, Aritomo Shinozaki, Krishnan Varadarajan, and
   Klaus Schulten. NAMD2: Greater scalability for parallel molecular dynamics. *Journal of Computational Physics*, 151:283–312, 1999.
7. Richard Monson-Haefel. *Enterprise Javabeans*. O'Reilly and Associates, 2000.
8. Alan Pope. *The Corba Reference Guide : Understanding the Common Object Request Broker Architecture*. Addison-Wesley, 1998.
9. Dale Rogerson. *Inside COM*. Microsoft Press, 1997.
10. Joshua Yelon. *Static Networks Of Objects As A Tool For Parallel Programming*.
    PhD thesis, Department of Computer Science, University of Illinois, Urbana-
    Champaign, 1999.

# Tree Traversal Scheduling: A Global Instruction Scheduling Technique for VLIW/EPIC Processors

Huiyang Zhou, Matthew D. Jennings, Thomas M. Conte

Department of Electrical and Computer Engineering
North Carolina State University
{hzhou, mdjennin, conte}@eos.ncsu.edu

**Abstract.** Global scheduling in a treegion framework has been proposed to exploit instruction level parallelism (ILP) at compile time. A treegion is a single-entry / multiple-exit global scheduling scope that consists of basic blocks with control-flow forming a tree. Because a treegion scope is nonlinear (includes multiple paths) it is distinguished from linear scopes such as traces or superblocks. Treegion scheduling has the capability of speeding up all possible paths within the scheduling scope. This paper presents a new global scheduling algorithm using treegions called Tree Traversal Scheduling (TTS). Efficient, incremental data-flow analysis in support of TTS is also presented. Performance results are compared to the scheduling of the linear regions that result from the decomposition of treegions. We refer to these resultant linear regions as linear treegions (LT) and consider them analogous to superblocks with the same amount of code expansion as the base treegion. Experimental results for TTS scheduling show a 35% speedup compared to basic block (BB) scheduling and a 4% speedup compared to LT scheduling.

## 1 Introduction

Global scheduling using treegions [1,2] has been proposed to extract instruction level parallelism (ILP) at compile time. It consists of two phases: *treegion formation* and *treegion scheduling*. A treegion is a single-entry / multiple-exit nonlinear region that consists of basic blocks with control-flow forming a tree. Treegions provide more opportunities for ILP extraction as they provide a larger scheduling scope compared to linear regions such as traces [4] or superblocks [3]. Treegion schedules can utilize high issue bandwidth by speeding up more than one path of execution simultaneously.

This paper extends the previous work on treegion scheduling [1,2]. First, a new treegion scheduling algorithm, *tree traversal scheduling* (TTS) is proposed to achieve higher performance by scheduling the block-ending branches as early as possible. TTS allows high resource utilization when multiple execution paths can benefit and reduces resource contention by resolving branches early. The benefit of resolving branches early is that all of the machine's execution resources are then available for each of the possible paths that result from the branch instruction. Efficient data-flow analysis is required for TTS as it results in a lot of code motion beyond basic block scope and operand renaming in support of speculation. Therefore, liveness and reaching definition analysis changes frequently but is expensive to re-compute at a

H. Dietz (Ed.): LCPC 2001, LNCS 2624, pp. 223–238, 2003.

procedural scope. Our approach to this problem is to use incremental adjustments to the data-flow analysis during code motion and operand renaming.

For performance analysis, we compare TTS scheduling with the scheduling of the linear regions that result from the decomposition of treegions. The decomposition of treegions into linear regions favors the more frequently executed paths through the treegion. The most frequently executed path through the treegion makes up the first linear region and is removed from the treegion. The next most frequently executed path (from the remainder of the treegion) makes up another linear region, etc., until no paths remain. We refer to these resultant linear regions as Linear Treegions (LT) and consider them analogous to superblocks with the same amount of code expansion as the base treegion. Experimental results for TTS scheduling show that there is a 35% speedup compared to the basic block (BB) scheduling and a 4% speedup compared to LT scheduling.

Two architectural effects are also observed from the experiments:

(1)    In order to fully take advantage of load speculation, the in-order processor pipeline should not stall at the execution/memory stage for a D-cache miss but stall only on the first use of the missing value at the dispatch/register read stage.

(2)    Treegion scheduling has two effects on I-cache performance: fewer I-cache accesses due to fewer multi operations (mops) produced by treegion scheduling and higher I-cache and TLB miss rates due to the code expansion from treegion formation.

The remainder of the paper is organized as follows. Section 2 briefly describes the notion of the treegion and treegion formation. The TTS algorithm is discussed in Section 3 and the implementation issues for efficient data flow analysis are in Section 4. Section 5 describes the simulation environment and experimental results. Section 6 discusses related work. Finally, Section 7 concludes the paper.

## 2 Treegion and Treegion Formation

A treegion contains of a tree of basic blocks, which is a subgraph of the control flow graph (CFG) for a program. Since the treegion depends only on the topology of the CFG, it does not change when profile information varies.

Figure 1 shows an example of a CFG and the treegion formation based on it. Here we use the same treegion formation algorithm in [1] and three treegions are constructed in the CFG. Since large regions are usually better for ILP extraction in scheduling than small regions, tail duplication [3] is applied as a treegion enlarging optimization. After unconditional branches are removed, the resulting treegion is shown in Figure 2. The trade-off for exposing ILP through treegion formation is the code-expansion that results from duplicates of BB6 and BB7. Other region enlarging optimization, such as branch target expansion, loop unrolling and loop peeling [9] can be used before the treegion formation.

As each treegion contains multiple execution paths, there is more available ILP in treegions than single path regions. Treegions formation enables the scheduling of multiple paths simultaneously. The code-expansion side effect can be alleviated by compile-time transformations such as dominator parallelism [1] and the recombination of tail blocks.

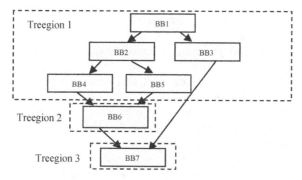

**Fig. 1.** An example CFG and the treegions constructed (each dash line box denotes a treegion)

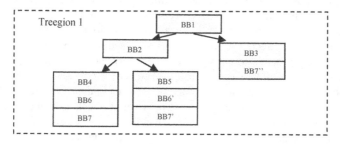

**Fig. 2.** The treegion formed with tail duplication, where BB6' is a duplicate of BB6; BB7'and BB7'' are duplicates of BB7

# 3 The Treegion Scheduling Algorithm: Tree Traversal Scheduling

The motivation of treegion scheduling is for the resultant schedule to speedup every execution path through the treegion. As treegions consist of multiple paths of execution, it will be necessary to prioritize the speculation of instructions. Speculative instructions originating from different paths will compete for the limited machine resources and execution frequency based on profile information is used to prioritize speculative instructions along the more frequently executed paths. TTS also limits the extent of speculation by prioritizing branch instructions so that branches will be resolved as early as possible. Executing branches early reduces contention for machine resources, as each path out of the branch instruction will see a full set of machine resources. TTS enables the execution of branches as early as possible by allowing branches to be scheduled even if that results in downward code motion. The TTS algorithm consists of the following two steps:

**Step1: Construct the control/data dependence graph and perform instruction ordering.**

For each treegion prioritize instructions according to:

(a)  execution frequency,

(b)  exit count heuristic to resolve ties from (a), and

(c)  data dependence height to resolve ties from (b).

In this ordering, heuristic (a) prioritizes the most frequently executed paths. The exit count heuristic (b), which is adapted from the helped count priority function of speculative hedge [6], is the number of exits that follow the instruction in the treegion. This heuristic gives priority to instructions in the basic blocks that help more exits. Instructions in the root block of the treegion have the highest priority as it is on the most often executed path and helps every exit in the treegion.

**Step2: Scheduling the instructions in the treegion.**

First we define the following terms in our discussion:

- *current_op* denotes the instruction that has just been scheduled.
- *current_block* denotes the basic block in which current_op is scheduled.
- *candidate_op* is the instruction being considered for scheduling.
- *current_cycle* is the cycle for which *candidate_op* is considered for scheduling

Tree traversal scheduling is a cycle scheduling approach. Initially, current_op is set to a default value and current_block is set as the root block of the treegion. At each cycle candidate_op is selected from instructions according to the order determined in **Step1**. Candidate_op needs to satisfy two criteria: a) candidate_op is dominated by current_block (i.e., candidate_op is either in current_block or in a child block of current_block), and b), the source operands of candidate_op are ready before current_cycle. After candidate_op is selected, we first check to make sure there are machine resources available to schedule candidate_op in current_cycle. If the scheduling of candidate_op in current_cycle is speculative, there are additional constraints to consider. First, speculative function calls and store instructions are not allowed. Next, destination operand renaming may be required to support speculation. Finally, branch candidate_ops may require downward code motion to support the *speculation* of the branch. The *speculation* of branch candidate_ops results in the formation of a multiway branch instruction in current_block. For example, in Figure 3a (instruction semantics in this paper are as follows: Operation Destination operand, Source operand 1, Source operand 2), instructions i and i+1 are not scheduled when the branch is being scheduled. These instructions are moved downwards into their child blocks (shown in Figure 3b) as a result of the branch *speculation*.

The scheduling of block-ending branches as early as possible is an important aspect of **Step2**. For the case when many instructions in the child blocks are ready to be scheduled speculatively, we need to make sure that speculation will not be over aggressive and cause a delay in executing the branch instruction. This problem is illustrated as an example shown in Figure 4.

In Figure 4a, we assume registers r6, r8, and r10 are ready at current_cycle (cycle n) and that the instructions have been ordered in **Step1** as instructions 1, 2, 3, 4, and 5. Figure 4b shows the schedule result if we apply list scheduling on a 2-way issue machine model with one alu/branch unit and one alu/load unit. Since instructions 1, 3, 4, and 5 are ready at cycle n, the list scheduler will schedule these instructions ahead of instruction 2. But, any delay in resolving this branch will delay both paths following it. Instead of scheduling the speculations right away, the TTS algorithm ensures that speculation is not too aggressive by selecting candidate_op every cycle in the instruction list based on the predetermined order. Figure 4c shows the result of the TTS scheduling algorithm. It can be seen that the TTS algorithm schedules the branch instruction at cycle n+1, prior to instructions 4 and 5. Comparing the average execution time (assuming the latency for add/branch is 1 cycle and load latency is 2 cycles for a cache hit), the schedule in Figure 4c will have 15% speed up over the scheduling in Figure 4b. Note in Figure 4c that after the branch is scheduled, TTS will move on to the next basic block, which may be basic block 1 or 2. The schedule at cycle n+2 is parenthesized to show this uncertainty.

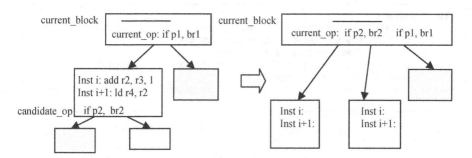

**Fig. 3.** Scheduling a branch instruction when it is in the child block of the current block. (a) the treegion before the scheduling, (b) the treegion after the scheduling

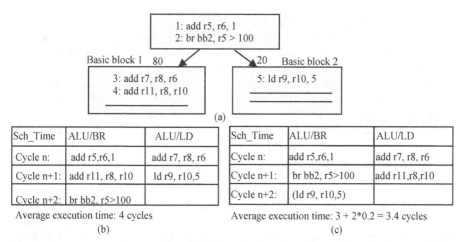

| Sch_Time | ALU/BR | ALU/LD |
|---|---|---|
| Cycle n: | add r5,r6,1 | add r7, r8, r6 |
| Cycle n+1: | add r11, r8, r10 | ld r9, r10,5 |
| Cycle n+2: | br bb2, r5>100 | |

Average execution time: 4 cycles
(b)

| Sch_Time | ALU/BR | ALU/LD |
|---|---|---|
| Cycle n: | add r5,r6,1 | add r7, r8, r6 |
| Cycle n+1: | br bb2, r5>100 | add r11,r8,r10 |
| Cycle n+2: | (ld r9, r10,5) | |

Average execution time: 3 + 2*0.2 = 3.4 cycles
(c)

**Fig. 4.** (a) An example for treegion scheduling, (b) the scheduling result using list scheduling, (c) the scheduling result using TTS.

Based on this observation of branch scheduling, conceptually we can view the TTS algorithm as applying list scheduling to a sequence of basic blocks that form a path of tree traversal, as shown in Figure 5.

There are two aspects that we can draw from the way to view TTS in Figure 5. The first is that by use of speculation on the dominated instructions the TTS algorithm achieves high resource utilization and speeds up multiple execution paths with priority given to the most often executed paths. This is an advantage over linear scheduling methods such as trace scheduling [4] and superblock scheduling [3]. Secondly, the TTS algorithm reduces resource competition since it only attempts to schedule the instructions that are dominated by the current basic block. In the example shown in Figure 4, when scheduling basic block 1 (i.e., when current_block is basic block 1), instructions from basic block 2 will not be considered. This is an advantage of TTS over the hyperblock scheduling [10].

---

**TTS algorithm**:
1. For a treegion, sort the basic blocks according to a depth-first traversal order with the child block selected with highest execution frequency.
2. Start list scheduling at the root basic block.
3. During the scheduling of a basic block, consider speculation for instructions dominated by this basic block.
4. After scheduling the block-ending branch, traverse to the next basic block and go back to step 3.

---

**Fig. 5.** A conceptually simple way to view TTS algorithm

## 4 Efficient Data Flow Analysis in the TTS Algorithm

The TTS scheduling algorithm makes extensive uses of the data flow analysis, specifically reaching definitions and live-variable analysis [18]. As this data flow analysis is computationally expensive at procedural scope, we need to be careful so that compile time does not become exceedingly long. In the TTS algorithm, there are several situations that make previous data flow analysis calculations obsolete. Those situations include: the change in liveness during speculative code motion, the change in reaching definitions when a copy operation is inserted during a renaming process, and the change in both liveness and reaching definitions in code downward motion. One obvious solution is to recalculate data flow information whenever there is a possible change during the scheduling phase. Unfortunately, this approach results in far too much compile time (analysis would be repeated thousands of times for benchmarks such as *perl*, *vortex* and *gcc*). In the TTS algorithm, speculative code motion happens frequently for wide issue processors. To alleviate the requirement of recalculating data flow analysis with each speculative code motion, we incrementally update liveness and reaching definitions in nearly all cases. The incremental updates are not always precise, but are conservative for the scheduling problem.

In the case of the speculation without renaming, as shown in Figure 6, r1 is not live along control edge 1 or edge 2. After the candidate_op (marked with *) is moved upwards, the liveness along edge 1 is not changed and r1 is included in the liveness along edge 2. Such processing is simple: liveness is extended upward for the destination operand and added to each edge that the instruction traverses during speculation. This update is conservative as r2 and r3 may no longer be live across edge 2. The conservative liveness across edge 2 may cause unnecessary renaming, when there is a definition of r2 or r3 speculated through edge 1. As we show later, most renaming cases are actually very simple to handle and take little compile time. Such additional renaming will affect compile time very slightly.

If the destination operand of the candidate_op happened to be live along edge 1, then destination operand renaming must be done before the instruction can be speculated. To investigate incremental updates to data flow analysis in speculations that require renaming, we divide renaming into three categories according to the scope of renaming: *local rename, rename with copy,* and *global rename.* Note that although the speculative code motion is used to explain the incremental data flow analysis, the same discussion holds for the renaming cases for non-speculative code motion as well.

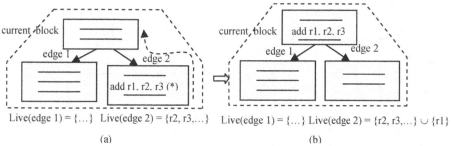

**Fig. 6.** Liveness analysis of speculation without renaming (region enclosed in dashed line is the treegion under consideration) (a) the treegion before the current speculative scheduling of candidate_op (marked with *); (b) the treegion after the current speculative scheduling of candidate_op

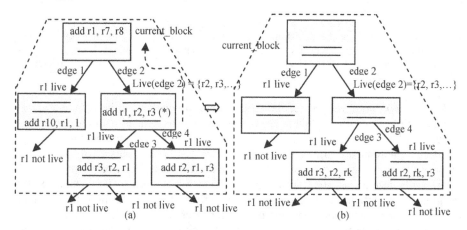

**Fig. 7.** . Liveness analysis of the speculation with local renaming (region enclosed in dashed line is the treegion under consideration) (a) the treegion before the current speculative scheduling of candidate_op (marked with *); (b) the treegion after the current speculative scheduling of candidate_op

*Local rename* represents cases where the renaming scope is contained within a treegion. The characteristics that identify a local rename case are: one definition with one or more uses in the treegion and the operand is not live out of the treegion. Since treegions have a large instruction scope and include multiple execution paths, local rename is the most common case for TTS. Figure 7 shows an example of local renaming, where the liveness of r1 along edge 1 requires the definition of r1 on the other path to be renamed before being speculated. After the definition and all the uses it reaches are renamed to rk (a new virtual register), the speculation can be performed. Since rk is a new virtual register, it has no other definitions in the program. So, we do not need to add any liveness for this operand. Also, for the same reasons as discussed before, we keep the conservative liveness of r1 along edge 3 and edge 4. In summary, in the case of local rename, all that needs to be done is renaming of the definition and all the uses it reaches (with no change to liveness information).

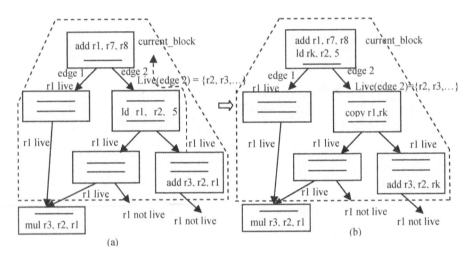

**Fig. 8.** . Liveness analysis of speculation with renaming with a copy (region enclosed in dashed line is the treegion under consideration) (a) the treegion before the current speculative scheduling of candidate_op (marked with *); (b) the treegion after the current speculative scheduling of candidate_op

*Rename with copy* is used for the cases where the operand to be renamed is live along multiple exit paths and there is a *merge problem* associated with the operand. A *merge problem* occurs when two definitions in the same treegion merge into a use and one definition dominates the other. The use in this case will be outside of the treegion scope, as treegions do not contain merge points. An example is shown in Figure 8, where both definitions of r1 inside the treegion merge into a use outside of the treegion. The definition in current_block dominates the definition in the load instruction. In rename with copy, the destination operand of candidate_op is renamed to rk and all the uses it reaches within the treegion are also renamed to rk. The instruction is speculated and a copy instruction is inserted at its original location (with the original destination operand and with rk as the source operand). Rename with copy is only applied when there are uses in the treegions that can benefit from the speculation of candidate_op. Once again, rk is a new virtual register and there are no other definitions in the program. Liveness does not change during rename with copy. However, reaching definitions need to be patched as the new copy instruction splits a previous def/use web. This update to reaching definitions is done with incremental changes and is precise.

*Global rename* is used for renaming def/use webs that span beyond the scope of a treegion and do not have the *merge problem*. Figure 9 shows one example of global renaming. Considering data flow analysis in the case of global renaming, reaching definitions do not change but liveness does. When global renaming affects another definition in the same treegion, we need to recalculate liveness immediately to ensure correctness for the current treegion scheduling scope. When global renaming only affects the definition in the candidate_op being speculated, recalculating procedural level liveness can be delayed until after scheduling of the current treegion scope is complete.

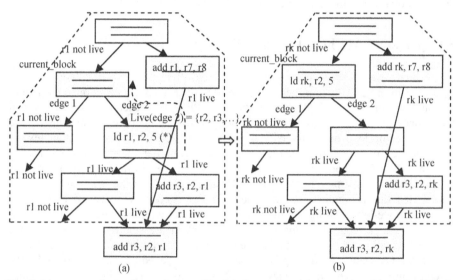

**Fig. 9.** Liveness analysis of speculation with global renaming (region enclosed in dashed line is the treegion under consideration) (a) the treegion before the current speculative scheduling of candidate_op (marked with *); (b) the treegion after the current speculative scheduling of candidate_op

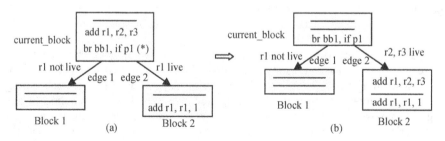

**Fig. 10.** Liveness analysis for code downward motion (a) the treegion before the scheduling of candidate_op (marked with *); (b) the treegion after the scheduling of candidate_op

Liveness information is used for the downward code motion that results from the early scheduling of block-ending branches. Downward code motion does not result in operand renaming. In downward code motion operand defining instructions are only moved down across an edge if its destination is live on that edge. Conversely, store instructions and subroutine calls are always duplicated and moved down to each successor block. An example is shown in Figure 10, where the branch instruction marked with '*' is the candidate_op and the instruction (add r1, r2, r3) is unscheduled. Since r1 is not live along edge 1, the instruction is not inserted into Block 1. Removing the destination operand from the liveness along edge 2 and adding the source operands to the liveness along edge 2 patches the liveness information. In downward code motion, the unscheduled instructions are processed in reverse program order to maintain the program semantics. Reaching definitions also need updates for downward code motion. Linking the original instruction's reaching use(s) with the downward moved instruction that dominates it does this precisely.

## 5 Experiment Methodology and Results

To evaluate the performance of the TTS algorithm, we implemented the TTS algorithm in the LEGO compiler [14], a research ILP compiler developed by Tinker Research Group at N. C. State University. The SPECint95 benchmark suite is used in the experiments. All programs are compiled with classic optimizations using the IMPACT compiler from University of Illinois [3] and converted to Rebel textual intermediate representation using the Elcor compiler from Hewlett-Packard Laboratories [20]. Then, the LEGO compiler is used to profile code, form treegion and schedule the instructions using the TTS algorithm. After the instrumentation for trace-based timing simulation, the scheduled Rebel code is converted to C code. Finally, a trace-based timing simulation is run together with the functional simulation to ensure the correctness of the program and obtain the simulation results. In our experiments, all benchmarks in SPEC95int suite run to completion.

In the experiments, the SPEC95int benchmarks are scheduled for an 8-issue VLIW machine model based on the Hewlett-Packard Laboratories HPL_PD architecture [7,8]. In this machine model, all function units are fully pipelined and all operations have a one-cycle latency except for load (two cycles for a hit), floating point add (two cycles), floating point subtract (two cycles), floating point multiply (three cycles), and floating point division (three cycles). Then in trace simulation, the same machine model is used in the execution core with the I-cache, D-cache and a branch predictor. The detailed specification of the processor model used in simulation is shown in Table 1.

In our experiments, BB scheduling and superblock scheduling are implemented in our treegion framework and results are compared to tree traversal scheduling (TTS). In BB scheduling, list scheduling with renaming support is the major scheduling technique and treegion formation is not applied. For superblock scheduling in our treegion framework, each superblock is formed by the decomposition of treegions into linear regions, which we call *linear treegions (LT)*. Figure 11 shows an example of superblock formation based on a treegion, where four superblocks (or LT) are formed from one treegion based on profile information. After superblocks have been formed, the TTS algorithm is then performed to schedule each superblock (or LT). In our experiments, LTs are used as analogous to superblocks and are compared to treegion scheduling with the same amount of initial code expansion.

**Table 1.** The specification of the machine model used in the experiment

|  | Specification |
|---|---|
| Execution | Dispatch/Issue/Retire bandwidth: 8; Universal function units: 8; Operation latency: ALU, ST, BR: 1 cycle; LD, floating-point (FP) add/subtract: 2 cycles; FP multiply/divide: 3 cycles |
| I-cache | Compressed (zero-nop) and two banks with 32KB each bank [19]. Line size: 16 operations with 4 bytes each operation. Miss latency: 12 cycles |
| D-cache | Size/Associativity/Replacement: 64KB/4-way/LRU Line size: 32 bytes. Miss Penalty: 14 cycles |
| Branch Predictor | G-share style Multi-way branch prediction [15,16]. Branch prediction table: $2^{14}$ entries. Branch target buffer: $2^{14}$ entries/8-way/LRU. Branch misprediction penalty: 10 cycles |

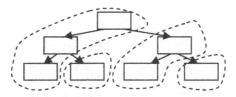

**Fig. 11.** Superblock formation in a treegion (i.e. Linear treegion formation) (each trace enclosed in dashed lines is one superblock)

One ideal machine model and one realistic machine model are used to examine the speedup effects. Ideal instruction and data caches and perfect branch prediction are assumed for the ideal machine model. Figure 12 shows speedups for TTS and LT scheduling over BB scheduling using the ideal machine model. Figure 12 shows both TTS and LT scheduling with significant speedups over BB scheduling, 35.3% and 31.3% respectively in average. Treegion scheduling also shows up to 9% speedup over linear treegion scheduling and 4% speedups in average.

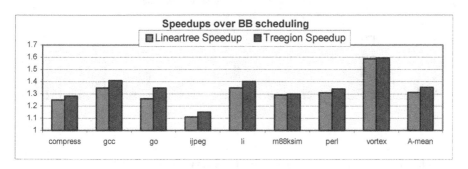

**Fig. 12.** Speedups of treegion scheduling and linear treegion scheduling over BB scheduling on an ideal processor model (ideal branch prediction and ideal caches)

If we take cache effects and branch prediction effects into consideration with cache miss latency and branch miss prediction penalty set as in Table 1, the speedups of TTS and LT scheduling over BB scheduling are as shown in Figure 13. From Figure 13, it can be seen that TTS and LT scheduling show 28.5% and 25.8% speedups over

BB scheduling. Reduced speedups for both TTS and LT scheduling are primarily the result of D-cache and I-cache performance.

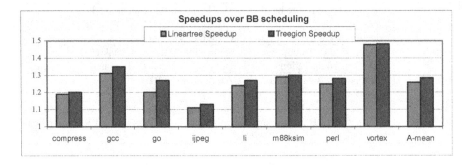

**Fig. 13.** Speedups of treegion scheduling and linear treegion scheduling over BB scheduling on a realistic processor model

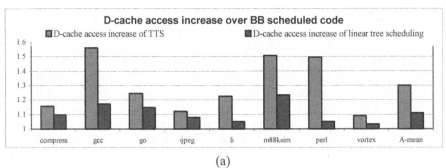

(a)

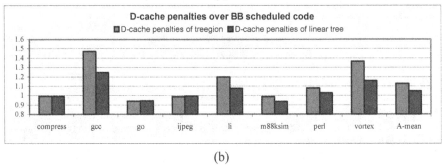

(b)

**Fig. 14.** (a) The D-cache access increase of treegion scheduled code and linear treegion scheduled code over BB scheduled code, (b) The D-cache access penalty of treegion scheduled code and linear treegion scheduled code over BB scheduled code

Speculative code motion, especially load speculation, is used extensively in both TTS and LT scheduling. The increased number of speculative loads results in an increased number of data cache (D-cache) accesses. The new D-cache accesses have a negative effect on the performance of TTS and LT scheduling, as the execution model is an in-order pipeline that stalls whenever there is a D-cache miss. As TTS enables more speculative loads (from multiple paths), the negative effect is more significant that for LT scheduling.

Figure 14a shows on average a 30% increase in D-cache read accesses for TTS over BB scheduled code. D-cache miss penalties are shown in Figure 14b. Although the D-cache miss rate is smaller for TTS (miss rate for TTS: 1.19%; miss rate for LT: 1.27%; miss rate for BB: 1.33%), TTS code still has the largest D-cache access penalties (13% more than BB scheduled code). This result shows that in order to take full advantage of load speculation, it is important for the execution pipeline not to stall at the execution/memory stage for each load miss but to stall only on the first use of the missing value at the dispatch/register read stage.

Code expansion due to treegion formation usually has negative effects on I-cache performance. In Figure 15, the code size increase for TTS is shown for each benchmark. Note that in examining the code size effect we only compare TTS with BB scheduling since the LT scheduling and TTS have similar code expansion. From Figure 15 it can be seen that TTS causes an average static code size increase of 172%. (i.e., the static code size of TTS code is 72% more than the size of BB scheduled code). Since TTS usually combines more operations into its multi-ops than BB scheduling, TTS code will have fewer multi-ops than BB scheduled code. Fewer multi-op fetches result in fewer dynamic I-cache accesses, as seen in Figure 16. On average there are 15% fewer I-cache accesses for TTS. The larger size of the multi-ops for TTS and the larger overall code size will put upward pressure on I-cache miss rate, TLB miss rate and I-cache access penalties. From our simulations, the I-cache access penalties of TTS code is 12% greater than for BB scheduled code.

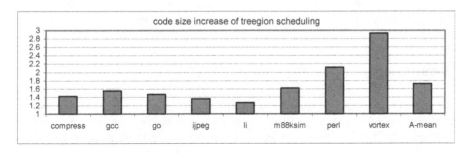

**Fig. 15.** The treegion scheduled code size over BB scheduled code size

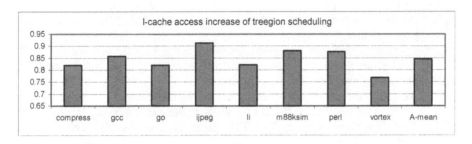

**Fig. 16.** The I-cache access of treegion-scheduled code over the BB scheduled code

# 6 Related Work

As pointed out in [1], previous work on non-linear regions has influenced our work on treegion scheduling. Among them, decision tree scheduling (DTS) [11] can be viewed as the most direct ancestor. Based on VLIW tree instructions, a finite-resource global scheduling technique [12] was developed with the help of modified percolation scheduling [13]. Tree traversal scheduling targets wider issue ILP architectures such as EPIC [21] style machines.

Tree traversal scheduling also has many similarities with other popular global scheduling techniques, such as trace scheduling [4,5], superblock scheduling [3] and hyperblock scheduling [9,10]. As mentioned previously, the heuristics used for the candidate operation selection in the TTS algorithm were motivated by the profile variation studies on superblocks [6]. In addition, superblock scheduling also uses tail duplication as an optimization step prior to scheduling. Compared with trace scheduling and superblock scheduling, TTS has the potential to speed up multiple paths simultaneously and benefits from the larger scope of instructions in treegions. Hyperblocks use predication to schedule multiple paths together but can suffer from resource contention as if-conversion linearizes the control flow. There are also works on prioritizing the blocking-ending branches in trace scheduling [22] and superblock scheduling. Comparing to them, TTS has the advantage of scheduling the branches more aggressively by allowing code downward motion and higher resource utilization by speculating instructions from more paths.

Wavefront scheduling [17] is used as a global code scheduler in Intel's reference compiler for the IA-64 architecture. It uses a path-based dependence representation to describe the data dependences and control dependences. This representation enables efficient bookkeeping for the compensation code of speculation.

# 7 Conclusion

This paper presents new developments for global scheduling in a treegion framework: the tree traversal scheduling (TTS) algorithm and efficient data flow analysis for treegions. The TTS algorithm achieves high performance by scheduling the block-ending branches as early as possible. TTS allows high resource utilization when multiple execution paths can benefit and reduces resource contention by resolving branches as early as possible. Profile information is used in the scheduling process to prioritize the most frequently executed paths. Implementation issues for efficient implementation of the data flow analysis associated with code motion and operand renaming are included.

Our experiments show that treegion scheduling using TTS has a speedup of 35% over BB scheduling and 4% over superblock scheduling. Two other important conclusions were drawn from the experiments:

1)   To fully take advantage of load speculation, the in-order processor pipeline needs to be modified so that it only stalls on the use of missing data.
2)   Fewer multi-ops as a result of TTS results in fewer I-cache accesses while code expansion due to treegion formation introduces higher miss rates.

# Acknowledgements

This research was supported by generous cash and equipment donations from Intel, IBM, Hewlett-Packard, Sun Microsystems, Texas Instruments, and an NSF CAREER award.

# References

1. W.A. Havanki, S. Banerjia, and T. M. Conte. "Treegion scheduling for wide-issue processors." *Proc. of the 4th Symp. on High-Perf. Comp. Arch. (HPCA-4)*, February 1998.
2. S. Banerjia, W. A. Havanki, and T. M. Conte. "Treegion scheduling for highly parallel processors." *Proceeding of Euro-Par'97*, August, 1997.
3. W.W. Hwu, S.A. Mahlke, W. Y. Chen, P. P. Chang, N. J. Warter, R. A. Bringmann, R. G. Ouellette, R. E. Hank, T. Kiyohara, G. E. Haab, J. G. Holm, and D. M. Lavery. "The Superblock: An effective way for VLIW and superblock compilation." *The Journal of Supercomputing*, vol. 7, pp. 229-248, January 1993.
4. J. A. Fisher. "Trace scheduling: A technique for global microcode compaction." *IEEE Trans. Computer*, vol. C-30, no.7, pp. 478-490, July 1981.
5. J. A. Fisher, "Global code generation for instruction level parallelism: Trace Scheduling-2," Tech. Rep. HPL-93-43, Hewlett-Packard Laboratories, June 1993.
6. B. L. Deitrich and W. W. Hwu. "Speculative hedge: regulating compile-tim speculation against profile variations." *Proc. 29th Int'l Symp. Microarchitecture (MICRO29)*, 1996.
7. V. Kathail, M. S. Schlansker, and B. R. Rau, "HPL PlayDoh architecture specification: version 1.0." Tech. Rep. HPL-93-80, Hewlett-Packard Laboratories, February 1994.
8. V. Kathail, M. S. Schlansker, and B. R. Rau, "HPL-PD architecture specification: version 1.1." Tech. Rep. HPL-93-80 (R.1), Hewlett--Packard Laboratories, February 2000.
9. S. A. Mahlke, "Exploiting instruction level parallelism in the presence of branches." PhD thesis, Dept. of ECE, University of Illinois at Urbana-Champaign, Urbana, IL, 1996.
10. S. A. Mahlke, D. C. Lin, W. Y. Chen, R. E. Hank, and R. A. Bringmann "Effective compiler support for predicated execution using the Hyperblock" *Proc. 25th Ann. Int'l Symp. Microarchitecture (MICRO25)*, December, 1992.
11. P. Y. T. Hsu and E. S. Davison, "Highly concurrent scalar processing", *Proc. 13th Ann. Int'l Symp. Computer Architecture (ISCA-13)*, June 1986.
12. S. M. Moon and K. Ebcioğlu. "An efficient resource-constrained global scheduling technique for superscalar and VLIW processors." *Proc. 25th Ann. Int'l Symp. Microarchitecture (MICRO25)*, December, 1992.
13. A. Nicolau. "Percolation scheduling: a parallel compilation technique." Tech. Rep. TR-85-678, Department of Computer Science, Cornell University, May 1985.
14. The LEGO Compiler. Available for download at http://www.tinker.ncsu.edu/LEGO
15. K. N. Menezes, S. W. Sathaye, and T. M. Conte. "Path Prediction for high issue-rate processors." *Conf. On Parallel Arch. and Compilation Techniques (PACT'97)*, 1997.
16. J. Hoogerbrugge. "Dynamic branch prediction for a VLIW processor." *Proc. Of the 2000 Conf. On Parallel Architectures and Compilation Techniques (PACT'00)*, October, 2000.
17. J. Bharadwaj, K. Menezes, and C. McKinsey. "Wavefront scheduling: Path based data representation and scheduling of subgraphs." *Proc. 32nd Ann. Int'l Symp. Microarchitecture (MICRO32)*, December, 1999.
18. A. V. Aho, R. Sethis, and J. D. Ullman "Compilers Principles, Techniques, and Tools." Addison-Wesley Publishing Company, March, 1988.

19. T. M. Conte, S. Banerjia, S. Y. Larin, K. N. Menezes, and S. W. Sathaye, "Instruction fetch mechanisms for VLIW architectures with compressed encodings." *Proc. 29th Ann. Int'l Symp. Microarchitecture (MICRO29)*, December, 1996.
20. S. Aditya, V. Kathail, and B. R. Rau, "Elcor's machine description system: version 3.0." Tech. Rep. HPL-98-128 (R.1), Hewlett--Packard Laboratories, October 1998.
21. M. S. Schlansker and B. R. Rau. "EPIC: Explicitly Parallel Instruction Comupting." *IEEE Computer*, Vol. 33, Issue 2, February 2000.
22. M. D. Smith. "Architectural support for compile-time speculation." In D. Lilja and P. Birds, editors. The Interaction of Compilation Technology and Computer Architecture. Kluwer Academic Publishers, Boston, 1994.

# *MIRS*: Modulo Scheduling with Integrated Register Spilling⋆

Javier Zalamea, Josep Llosa, Eduard Ayguadé, and Mateo Valero

Departament d'Arquitectura de Computadors (UPC)
Universitat Politècnica de Catalunya
{jzalamea,josepll,eduard,mateo}@ac.upc.es

**Abstract.** The overlapping of loop iterations in software pipelining techniques imposes high register requirements. The schedule for a loop is valid if it requires at most the number of registers available in the target architecture. Otherwise its register requirements have to be reduced by spilling registers to memory. Previous proposals for spilling in software pipelined loops require a two–step process. The first step performs the actual instruction scheduling without register constraints. The second step adds (if required) spill code and reschedules the modified loop. The process is repeated until a valid schedule, requiring no more registers than those available, is found.

The paper presents *MIRS* (Modulo scheduling with Integrated Register Spilling), a novel register–constrained modulo scheduler that performs modulo scheduling and register spilling simultaneously in a single step. The algorithm is iterative and uses backtracking to undo previous scheduling decisions whenever resource or dependence conflicts appear. *MIRS* is compared against a state–of–the–art two–step approach already described in the literature. For this purpose, a workbench composed of a large set of loops from the Perfect Club and a set of processor configurations are used. On the average, for the loops that require spill code a speed–up in the range 14–31% and a reduction of the memory traffic by a factor in the range 0.90–0.72 are achieved.

**Keywords:** Instruction-Level Parallelism, Software Pipelining, Register Allocation, Spill Code .

## 1  Introduction

With the improvements in the underlying technology, current processors are being designed with the aim of supporting increasing levels of instruction–level parallelism (ILP). Software pipelining [11] is an instruction scheduling technique able to exploit this ILP out of a loop by overlapping operations from various successive loop iterations. Different approaches have been proposed in the literature

⋆ This work has been supported by the Ministry of Education of Spain under contracts TIC 98/511 and TIC2001-0995-C02-01, and by CEPBA (European Center for Parallelism of Barcelona). Javier Zalamea is granted by the Agencia Española de Cooperación Internacional.

H. Dietz (Ed.): LCPC 2001, LNCS 2624, pp. 239–253, 2003.

[2] for the generation of software pipelined schedules. Some of them mainly focus on achieving high throughput [1, 13, 18, 25, 26, 28].

Register allocation consists in finding the final assignment of registers to loop variables (variants and invariants) and temporaries. It has been extensively studied in the framework of acyclic schedules [5, 7, 8, 9] based on the original graph coloring proposal [10]. However, software pipelining imposes some constraints that prevent the use of these techniques for register allocation. For instance, the lifetime of loop variables may cross the boundary of iterations and may last for more than one iteration, interfering with themselves. Several proposals have been made to handle these constraints [15, 16, 27].

The main drawback of these aggressive scheduling techniques is their high register requirements [22, 24]. This has motivated some recent modulo scheduling proposals whose main objective is the minimization of the register pressure [12, 14, 17, 20, 23]. Figure 1a (dashed lines) shows the percentage of loops in our workbench (Section 4) that require less than a specific number of registers for the set of processor configurations considered in this paper and assuming an unbounded number of registers. Figure 1a (solid lines) shows the percentage of the total execution cycles spent on them. Notice that although the percentage of loops that require a high number of registers is small, the percentage of time is important. For instance, only 8–14% of the loops require more than 32 registers but they represent 34–45% of the total execution time.

Having a schedule that uses more registers than those available in the target architecture requires some additional actions [27]. One of the options is to reschedule the loop with a reduced execution rate (i.e. with less iteration overlapping); this reduces the number of overlapped operations and variables. Unfortunately, the register reduction is at the expense of a reduction in performance. Another option is to spill some variables to memory, so that they do not occupy registers for a certain number of clock cycles. This requires the insertion of store and load instructions that free the use of these registers. The evaluation in [21]

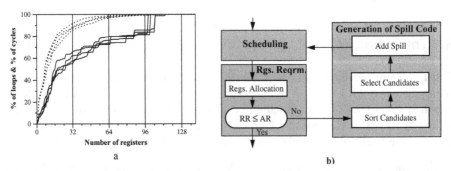

**Fig. 1.** a) Percentage of loops and percentage of execution cycles that require less than a number of registers for the processor configurations considered in this paper. b) Flow diagram for the two–step spill algorithm.

shows that reducing the execution rate tends to generate worse schedules than spilling variables.

To the best of our knowledge, all the previous approaches to register spilling for modulo scheduled loops [21, 29, 30, 31], follow a two–step process, as shown in Figure 1b. In the first step, the loop is scheduled without considering register constraints. Once the loop is scheduled, register allocation is performed over the existing schedule. If the loop requires more registers than those available, spill code is added in the original code and the loop is scheduled again. This second step is repeated until a valid schedule requiring no more registers than available is found. Unfortunately, at a given point in this process it is possible that a different set of lifetimes than those already spilled might need to be spilled.

This paper presents a novel approach for register spilling in modulo scheduled loops. In this approach, instruction scheduling, register allocation, and register spilling are simultaneously in the same step. To achieve this, it uses the ability of some previous iterative modulo scheduling techniques [12, 13, 17, 28] to backtrack, i.e. to undo previous scheduling decisions and reschedule operations. In order to have reasonable low spill code requirements, *MIRS* is based on HRMS (Hypernode Reduction Modulo Scheduling [23]), a register–sensitive modulo scheduler. Our proposal is compared with the ideal case (which is an upper bound for performance) and a representative state–of–the–art two–step approach [31].

The paper is organized as follows: Section 2 provides a brief overview of modulo scheduling, register allocation and describes some related work. Then, Section 3 presents the iterative algorithm that constitutes *MIRS*. Section 4 evaluates and compares the behavior of the proposed algorithm. Finally, Section 5 states our conclusions and outlines some future work.

# 2 Basic Concepts and Related Work

## 2.1 Modulo Scheduling

In a software pipelined loop, the schedule of an iteration is divided into stages so that the execution of consecutive iterations, which are in distinct stages, overlaps. The number of stages in one iteration is termed **Stage Count** (*SC*). The number of cycles between the initiation of successive iterations in a software pipelined loop determines its execution rate and is termed the **Initiation Interval** (*II*).

The *II* is bounded either by recurrence circuits in the dependence graph of the loop (*RecMII*) or by resource constraints of the target architecture (*ResMII*). The lower bound on the *II* is termed the **Minimum Initiation Interval** (*MII* = *max*(*RecMII*, *ResMII*)). The reader is referred to [13, 28] for an extensive dissertation on how to calculate *RecMII* and *ResMII*.

The scheduling step of a modulo scheduling technique builds the schedule progressively by adding instructions to a partial schedule. Sometimes the scheduler reaches a partial schedule in which the remaining instructions cannot be placed. In this case there are two alternative solutions: increasing the *II* [19, 20, 23], or applying backtracking [12, 17, 28]. Backtracking involves unscheduling some operations in the partial schedule in order to make room for other operations and scheduling them later. Techniques that include backtracking are also termed *iterative techniques*. In order to avoid an excessive increase in the scheduling complexity, the amount of backtracking is limited.

In this paper, a register–sensitive software pipelining technique has been used in order not to overestimate the necessity for spill code. In particular we propose an iterative version of Hypernode Reduction Modulo Scheduling (HRMS). When an unbounded number of registers is considered, the original algorithm [23] achieves the *MII* for 97.9% of the workbench considered in this paper. The iterative version proposed in this paper achieves it for 99.0% of the loops. In both implementations, schedules with very low register requirements are generated.

## 2.2    Register Allocation

Each value in a loop is alive for a certain amount of cycles termed **lifetime** (*LT*). The lifetime of a variable can be divided into several sections (called **uses**) that span from the previous consumer to the current one. The maximum number of simultaneously live values (*MaxLive*) is an accurate approximation of the number of registers required for the schedule [27]. The cycle where *MaxLive* values are alive is termed the **Critical Cycle**. In our proposal, *MaxLive* is used to estimate the registers required by a partial schedule. Notwithstanding, once the final schedule is found, registers are allocated using wands–only strategy with end–fit and adjacency ordering [27] and additional spill is added if required. This strategy usually achieves a register allocation that uses *MaxLive* registers and almost never requires more than *MaxLive* + 1 registers.

## 2.3    Adding and Scheduling Spill Operations

Previous approaches to introduce spill code [21, 29, 30, 31] are based on an algorithm similar to the one shown in Figure 1b. After instruction scheduling and register allocation, if the loop requires more registers than those available (required registers $RR$ > available registers $AR$), a set of spilling candidates is obtained and ordered. The algorithm then decides how many candidates are selected and introduces the necessary memory accesses in the original dependence graph. The loop is rescheduled again because modulo schedules tend to be very compact —the goal is to saturate the most used resource— and it is very difficult to find empty slots to allocate the new memory operations in the schedule. The process is repeated until a schedule, requiring no more registers than those available, is found. *MIRS* avoids the rescheduling of the loop by adding spill code in the partial schedule, where more empty slots are available. In addition it reschedules operations already placed in the partial schedule, when necessary, in order to make room for the spill code.

Some criteria are required in order to assign priorities to the spilling candidates. The priority is usually computed according to the *LT* (the number of cycles that the candidate is alive) [21] or to some ratio between its *LT* and the memory traffic (*trf*) that would be introduced when spilled (*LT/trf*) [21, 29, 30]. *MIRS*, like [31], uses (*LT/trf*) to select only among those uses whose lifetime spans the critical cycle.

After giving priorities to each spilling candidate, the algorithm decides how many candidates are actually spilled to memory. For instance, [21] proposes to spill one candidate at a time. This heuristic avoids overspilling at the expense of a high scheduling time. To avoid this negative aspect, the compiler described in [29] performs several tries by spilling $2^n$ candidates, where $n$ is increased by one each time. Another alternative, used in [30] consists on selecting as many candidates as necessary to saturate the memory units with the current *II*, which unfortunately produces an excessive memory traffic. In order to minimize the number of trials, [21] selects as many candidates as necessary so as to reduce, in one step, *RR* to *AR*. In order to avoid overspilling, [31] introduces a parameterizable factor, named Quantity Factor, to give more control over this process. Due to the iterative nature of the proposed algorithm, *MIRS* does not require to spill more than a lifetime per iteration; therefore, spill code is introduced in a more accurate way avoiding overspilling.

In order to guarantee that the spill effectively decreases *RR*, the spilled operations have to be scheduled as close as possible to their producer/consumer operations. This is accomplished by scheduling the spill operation and its associated producer/consumer operation as a single complex operation [21, 31]. On the contrary, *MIRS* is less restrictive and allows to schedule them some cycles apart of the producer/consumer. This feature is controlled by a parameterizable control. When set to its lowest value is equivalent as scheduling the spill operation and its associated producer/consumer as a single complex operation.

# 3   MIRS: Modulo Scheduling with Integrated Register Spilling

## 3.1   Definitions

Dependence relations between operations in a loop are usually represented using a dependence graph. This graph is used to schedule the operations so that these dependence relations are honored when the loop is executed in a specific target architecture.

**Definition 1:** The Dependence Graph $G = DG(V, E, \delta, \lambda)$ is a directed graph in which $V$ is the set of vertices and where each vertex $v \in V$ represents an operation of the loop. $E$ is the dependence edge set, where each edge $(u, v) \in E$ represents a dependence between two operations $u$ and $v$. Edges may correspond to any of the following types of dependences: register dependences, memory dependences or control dependences.

**Definition 2:** The dependence distance $\delta_{(u,v)}$ is a nonnegative integer associated with each edge $(u, v) \in E$. There is a dependence of distance $\delta_{(u,v)}$ between two nodes $u$ and $v$ if the execution of operation $v$ depends on the execution of operation $u$ , $\delta_{(u,v)}$ iterations before.

**Definition 3:** The latency $\lambda_u$ is a nonzero positive integer associated with each node $u \in V$ and is defined as the number of cycles taken by the corresponding operation to produce a result.

The iterative approach presented in this paper first pre-orders the nodes in what we call the *priority_list*. After that the actual iterative scheduling process constructs a *partial_schedule* by scheduling nodes (once at a time) following the order in the *priority_list*. During this iterative process, new nodes may be added to $G$ due to the insertion of spill code. These new store/load nodes will inherit the priority from the associated producer/consumer nodes.

The pre-ordering of nodes is done with the goal of scheduling the loop with an $II$ as close as possible to $MII$ and using the minimum number of registers. To achieve this, it gives priority to recurrences in order not to stretch any recurrence circuit. It also ensures that, when a node is scheduled, the current partial scheduling contains only *predecessors* or *successors* of the node, but never both (unless the node is the last node of a recurrence circuit to be scheduled).

During the scheduling step, each node is placed on the partial schedule as close as possible to the *neighbors* that have already been scheduled. In order to enable this, the following definitions are useful:

**Definition 4:** *Early_start* for a node $u$ in graph $G$ is the earliest cycle at which the node can be scheduled such that all its predecessors have completed their execution. It is computed as follows:

$$Early\_start_u = \max_{v \in PSP(u)} t_v + \lambda_v - \delta_{(v,u)} \times II$$

Where $t_v$ is the cycle where $v$ has been scheduled, $\lambda_v$ is the latency of $v$, $\delta_{(v,u)}$ is the dependence distance from $v$ to $u$, and $PSP(u)$ is the set of *predecessors* of $u$ that have been previously scheduled.

**Definition 5:** *Late_start* for a node $u$ in graph $G$ is the latest cycle at which the node can be scheduled such that it completes its execution before its successors start executing. It is computed as follows:

$$Late\_start_u = \min_{v \in PSS(u)} t_v - \lambda_u + \delta_{(u,v)} \times II$$

Where $PSS(u)$ is the set of *successors* of $u$ that have been previously scheduled.

In order to find a free slot where to schedule each node in $G$, the current partial schedule is scanned in a specific order. For this purpose, the following situations are possible:

- If operation $u$ has only *predecessors* in *partial_schedule*, then $u$ is scheduled as soon as possible. In this case the scheduler scans starting at cycle $Early\_start_u$ until the cycle $Early\_start_u + II - 1$ is reached.
- If operation $u$ has only *successors* in *partial_schedule*, then $u$ is scheduled as late as possible. In this case the scheduler scans starting at cycle $Late\_start_u$ until the cycle $Late\_start_u - II + 1$ is reached.
- If operation $u$ has *predecessors* and *successors*, then the scheduler scans the partial schedule starting at cycle $Early\_start_u$ until the cycle

$$\min(Late\_start_u, Early\_start_u + II - 1).$$

In order to control the iterative nature of the algorithm, the following definitions are useful.

**Definition 6:** *Budget_ratio* is the number of attempts that the iterative algorithm is allowed to perform per node in $G$.

**Definition 7:** *Budget* is the number of attempts that the iterative algorithm can still perform before giving up the current value of *II*. Initially, the *Budget* is set to the product of the number of nodes in $G$ by the *Budget_ratio*. During the iterative algorithm, every time a new node (due to spill code) is inserted in the graph, the *Budget* is increased by *Budget_ratio*. When the number of scheduled nodes exceeds *Budget*, the currently obtained partial schedule is discarded, the *II* is incremented by 1, and the scheduling process is re-started with the original graph. The *Budget_ratio* is predefined in the implementation and decides how far the algorithm can go with a fixed value of *II*, ejecting nodes of the partial schedule and trying new alternative allocations.

### 3.2   Algorithm

Figure 2 summarizes the main steps of the iterative *MIRS* algorithm. The algorithm uses the node ordering strategy defined in the HRMS modulo scheduling algorithm to assign priorities to the nodes in $G$, although other priority heuristics could be used. For each node $i$ it computes the *Early_start* and *Late_start* values, as well as the search direction between these two values.

With this information, the algorithm tries to find a cycle in the current *partial_schedule* in which the node can be placed without causing any resource conflict or dependence violation. If such a cycle is found, the *partial_schedule* is updated, including resources and registers usage. If the algorithm fails finding a scheduling cycle in the specified cycles, it applies the *Force_and_eject* heuristic which forces the node in a specific cycle and forces some nodes to be ejected due

- Step 1. Initialize *II* = *MII*.
- Step 2. Compute priorities for each node in $G$ using pre–ordering step of HRMS.
- Step 3. Set *Budget* = *Budget_ratio* * *nodes(G)*.
- Step 4. Pick node $i$ with the highest priority from priority list; Budget = Budget -1.
- Step 5. Determine *Early_start*, *Late_start* and *Direction* for node $i$.
- Step 6. Find a *cycle* in *partial_schedule* for node $i$.
- Step 7. If a valid *cycle* is not found for node $i$ Then apply the *Force_and_Eject* heuristic.
- Step 8. Schedule $i$ and apply the *Check_and_Insert_Spill* heuristic.
- Step 9. If all instructions are scheduled Then goto Step 11.
- Step 10. If (!*Restart_Schedule*) Then goto step 4; Else *II++* and goto Step 3.
- Step 11. Finalize scheduling process.

**Fig. 2.** Skeleton of the iterative integrated instruction scheduling/register spilling algorithm.

to resource constraints or dependence violations. This heuristic is defined later in this section.

Once the schedule for node $i$ is done, which includes all possible unscheduling actions, the *Check_and_Insert_Spill* heuristic is applied. This heuristic evaluates the necessity of introducing spill code and decides which lifetimes are selected for spilling. After applying spill and inserting new nodes in the dependence graph, the *Restart_Schedule* heuristic decides if the current *partial_schedule* and value of $II$ are still valid to continue with the scheduling process or it is better to restart the process with an increased value for $II$.

The scheduling process finishes in *Step 9* when the algorithm detects that the *priority_list* is empty. At this point, the algorithm performs the real register allocation[1] and generates VLIW code.

**Force_and_eject Heuristic** When the scheduler fails in finding a cycle where to schedule a node, it forces the node at a specific cycle given by:

$$forced\_cycle = max(Early\_start, (Prev\_cycle(i) + 1))$$

if the search direction is from *Early_start* to *Late_start*, or

$$forced\_cycle = min(Late\_start, (Prev\_cycle(i) - 1))$$

otherwise. In both expressions, *Prev_cycle(i)* is the cycle at which the node was scheduled in a previous partial schedule (before a possible ejection).

When forcing a node in a particular cycle, the heuristic ejects nodes that cause resource conflicts with the forced node. If for a particular resource conflict several candidate nodes are possible, the heuristic selects the one that was first placed in the *partial_schedule*. Other iterative algorithms [12, 17, 28] eject all the operations that cause each resource conflict. In our iterative algorithm, the minimum number of operations are ejected. The heuristic also ejects all previously scheduled predecessors and successors whose dependence constraints are violated due to the forced placement.

Notice that all the unscheduled operations are put back in the *priority_list* with their original priority. Therefore, they will be immediately picked up by the iterative algorithm for rescheduling.

**Check_and_Insert_Spill Heuristic** This heuristic first compares the actual number of registers used in the current *partial_schedule* ($RR$) and the total number of registers available ($AR$) and decides whether to insert spill code or proceed with the next node in *priority_list*. In our implementation, spill code is introduced whenever $RR > SG \times AR$, $SG$ being the *spill_gauge*. $SG$ may take any positive value larger or equal than one. If set to one, it means that the algorithm adds spill code as soon as the register limit is reached. When set to a very large value it causes the algorithm to perform spill after obtaining a partial schedule for all

---

[1] Since *MaxLive* is an approximation of the actual register requirements, sometimes it is needed to insert some additional spill code to ensure that the $RR$ fit in $AR$, as mentioned in Section 2.2.

the nodes in the dependence graph. The effects of intermediate values for this parameter on the quality of the schedule are discussed in an extended version of this paper [32].

In order to efficiently reduce the register requirements, the spill heuristic tries to select the use, among those that cross the *critical_cycle* in the *partial_schedule*, that has the largest ratio between its lifetime and the memory traffic its spilling would generate (number of load and store operations to be inserted). If such a use is not found or it does not spans a minimum number of cycles, one of the nodes already scheduled in the *critical_cycle* is ejected and placed back in the *priority_list*. This forces a reduction of the register requirements in the *critical_cycle* by moving the non–spillable section of the lifetime outside this cycle. The minimum number of cycles that the selected lifetime has to span (named *minimum_span_gauge MSG*) is another parameter of our algorithm that influences the quality of the schedules generated and it is experimentally evaluated in [32].

For the lifetime selected, spill load/store nodes are inserted in the dependence graph. These operations are also inserted in the *priority_list* with the priority of their associated consumer/producer nodes minus one. In addition, these nodes are forced to be placed as close as possible to their associated consumer/producer nodes. To achieve this, the *Early_start* of an spill load node is set to its *Late_start* - *DG* and the *Late_start* of an spill store node is set to its *Early_start* + *DG*, *DG* being the *distance_gauge*. The influence of this gauge is also discussedin the extended version of this paper [32].

Once spill nodes are inserted in the dependence graph, the *Budget* is increased by the number of nodes inserted times the *Budge_ratio* in order to give further chances to the iterative algorithm to complete the schedule.

**Restart_Schedule Heuristic** The iterative algorithm discards the current partial schedule in two cases: 1) if the number of trials is exhausted (*Budget* reaches 0) and 2) if the processor configuration with the current value of *II* can not support the memory traffic generated due to the newly inserted spill operations. After inserting a set of spill memory operations, it may be better to directly increase *II* instead of continuing trying with its current value. In order to forestall this situation, the heuristic estimates the memory traffic (number of load and store instructions) due to the newly introduced spill code (*NewTrf*). If the maximum traffic (*MaxTrf*) that can be supported with the current value of *II* is not enough to absorb *NewTrf*, then the algorithm directly increases the *II* and discards the current *partial_schedule*. In both situations, the algorithm is restarted with a larger value for *II*. If both tests are passed, the algorithm proceeds with the next node in the *priority_list*.

# 4    Performance Evaluation

The effectiveness of *MIRS* is statically evaluated to find out the number of loops for which it obtains better schedules than the proposal presented in [31] (from

now on named *2–STEP*). After that, a dynamic evaluation is performed in order
to show its effectiveness.

The evaluation is done using a set of statically scheduled processor configurations *PiMjLk* defined as follows: $i$ is the number of functional units used to
perform each type of computation (adders, multipliers and div/sqr units); $j$ is the
number of load/store units; and $k$ is the latency of the adders and the multipliers. In all configurations, the latencies of load and store accesses are two cycles
and one cycle, respectively. Divisions take 17 cycles and square roots take 30
cycles. All functional units are fully pipelined, except for the div/sqr functional
units. In particular, four different configurations are used: *P2M2L4*, *P2M2L6*,
*P4M2L4* and *P4M4L4*, with 32 registers.

For the evaluation we use all the innermost loops of the Perfect Club [2] benchmark suite [6] that have neither subroutine calls nor conditional exits. Loops
with conditional statements have been previously IF-converted [3] so that they
behave as a single basic block loop. The loops have been obtained with the experimental ICTINEO compiler [4]. A total of 1258 loops, that represent about
80% of the total execution time of the benchmark (measured on an HP-PA 7100)
have been scheduled.

## 4.1   Static Evaluation

The static metrics used to evaluate the performance are the following:

– $\Sigma II$, which measures the sum of the individual $II$ for the loops considered.
– $\Sigma trf$, which measures the sum of the individual number of memory operations used in the scheduling for the loops considered.

Table 1 compares *MIRS* against *2–STEP* in terms of the above mentioned
metrics. Columns on the left, under label "Loops with Spill" show the comparison
considering only the loops that require spill code. For instance, for processor
configuration *P4M2L4*, *MIRS* improves the $II$ metric in 61 loops, achieves the
same value in 74 loops and produces a worse result for 14 loops. In total, the $\Sigma II$
is reduced from 3045 to 2670. In terms of memory traffic, *MIRS* reduces $trf$ in 69
loops, achieves the same value in 42 loops and produces more $trf$ in 38 loops. In
total, the $\Sigma trf$ is reduced from 5185 to 4555. The two columns under label "All
Loops" show the comparison considering all the 1258 loops in the benchmarks.
Notice that, when only considering the loops that require spill the $\Sigma II$ is reduced
by 375 cycles and when considering all loops it is reduced by 411 cycles. This
extra benefit is caused by the iterative nature of the scheduling algorithm which
improves the $II$ in loops with complex operations. Similar results are obtained
for the other processor configurations, showing a natural tendency to produce
schedules that improve both the execution rate and reduce the memory traffic.
Only in a small number of loops, the algorithm produces schedules with both
worse $II$ and $trf$ values.

---

[2] Although the Perfect Club benchmark set is considered obsolete for the purposes of
evaluating supercomputer performance, the structure and computation performed in
the loops are still representative of current numerical codes.

**Table 1.** Static evaluation.

| Item | Loops with Spill | | | | | | | | All Loops | |
|---|---|---|---|---|---|---|---|---|---|---|
| | $II_{MIRS} < II_{2\text{-}STEP}$ | | $II_{MIRS} = II_{2\text{-}STEP}$ | | $II_{MIRS} > II_{2\text{-}STEP}$ | | Total | | Total | |
| | 2-STEP | MIRS | 2-STEP | MIRS | 2-STEP | MIRS | 2-STEP | MIRS | 2-STEP | MIRS |
| P4M2L4 | 61 | | 74 | | 14 | | 149 | | 1258 | |
| $\Sigma II$ | 1902 | 1505 | 794 | 794 | 349 | 371 | 3045 | 2670 | 8152 | 7741 |
| $\Sigma trf$ | 3272 | 2679 | 1286 | 1256 | 627 | 620 | 5185 | 4555 | 10269 | 9639 |
| $< trf$ | 21 | 31 | 9 | 33 | 8 | 5 | 38 | 69 | 38 | 69 |
| P4M4L4 | 50 | | 113 | | 19 | | 182 | | 1258 | |
| $\Sigma II$ | 1178 | 973 | 950 | 950 | 372 | 398 | 2500 | 2321 | 6838 | 6639 |
| $\Sigma trf$ | 3707 | 3208 | 2502 | 2502 | 1291 | 1198 | 7695 | 6908 | 12381 | 11594 |
| $< trf$ | 20 | 27 | 18 | 56 | 5 | 14 | 43 | 97 | 43 | 97 |
| P2M2L4 | 42 | | 58 | | 9 | | 109 | | 1258 | |
| $\Sigma II$ | 1836 | 1565 | 1089 | 1089 | 197 | 216 | 3122 | 2870 | 9398 | 9102 |
| $\Sigma trf$ | 2799 | 2552 | 1283 | 1361 | 329 | 341 | 4411 | 4254 | 9907 | 9750 |
| $< trf$ | 20 | 16 | 20 | 14 | 4 | 3 | 44 | 33 | 44 | 33 |
| P2M2L6 | 68 | | 80 | | 10 | | 158 | | 1258 | |
| $\Sigma II$ | 2581 | 2206 | 1154 | 1154 | 256 | 270 | 3991 | 3630 | 10659 | 10241 |
| $\Sigma trf$ | 4125 | 3620 | 1613 | 1572 | 465 | 473 | 6203 | 5665 | 11152 | 10614 |
| $< trf$ | 16 | 40 | 21 | 28 | 3 | 6 | 40 | 74 | 40 | 74 |

### 4.2 Dynamic Evaluation

In order to dynamically compare the two algorithms, the two following metrics are used:

- Ratio between the ideal number of execution cycles needed to execute the loops assuming an unbounded number of registers and the actual execution cycles needed to execute them once scheduled with one of the heuristics. The execution cycles are estimated as $II * (N + (SC - 1) * E)$, $N$ being the total number of iterations and $E$ the number of times the loop is executed. The values of $N$ and $E$ are obtained by profiling.
- Ratio between the memory traffic caused by the loops when scheduled with one of the heuristics and the ideal memory traffic when an unbounded number of registers is available. In both cases, the traffic is estimated as $M * N$, $M$ being the number of memory operations in the kernel code of the software pipelined loop. Although, a memory traffic reduction is not directly observable in performance, it reduces the instruction fetch bandwidth requirements for spill operations and the memory bandwidth requirements. This two factors can influence power consumption, which is a major concern in current state-of-the-art processor designs.

Figure 3a-c shows the above mentioned ratios and the speed–up for *MIRS* and *2–STEP* for the four different processor configurations considering the loops that require spill code. On the average, the reduction in execution cycles represents

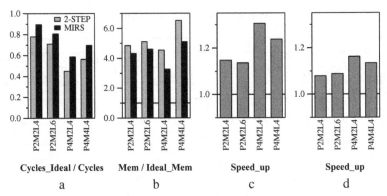

**Fig. 3.** Dynamic evaluation of relative execution cycles, memory traffic and speed–up for four processor configurations *P2M2L4*, *P2M2L6*, *P4M2L4* and *P4M4L4*.

an speed–up of 15%, 14%, 31% and 24% in those loops for for processor configurations *P2M2L4*, *P2M2L6*, *P4M2L4* and *P4M4L4*, respectively. Memory traffic is reduced by factors 0.89, 0.90 0.72 and 0.78, respectively. As shown in Figure 3d, for the whole benchmark set, the reduction in execution cycles represents a speed–up of 7.9%, 8.8%, 16.2% and 13.4% respectively.

Figure 4 shows the above mentioned ratios and the execution speed–up for each program in the Perfect Club benchmark set for processor configuration *P4M2L4*. Notice that for 5 applications *2–STEP* already reaches the optimal execution time and memory traffic, and therefore no speed-up at all can be obtained. For 5 more applications *2–STEP* is very close to the optimal and only small speed-ups (up to 3%) can be obtained with the new approach. However, there are three applications for which substantial improvements are obtained. For NASI and SMSI, whose memory traffic due to spill code is high, the proposed algorithm achieves a speed–up of 26% and 7.8% respectively. In the case of OCSI the improvement is not due to the reduction in spill code but to the iterative nature of the scheduling algorithm which favors applications with complex operations. In OCSI these kind of complex operations limit the performance of some loops and the application of an iterative algorithm produces a speed-up of 13.5%.

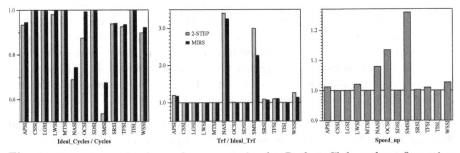

**Fig. 4.** Dynamic results for each program in the Perfect Club and configuration *P4M2L4*. Light bars correspond to the *2–STEP* algorithm and dark bars to *MIRS*.

### 4.3   Scheduling Time

*MIRS* takes between 15 and 20 minutes to schedule all 1258 loops, which is about 5 times the time required by *2–STEP*. However, this is still a very reasonable scheduling time for 13 applications. We have observed that *MIRS* spends almost 84% of this time on only three of the loops. These loops are extremely large, initially require more than 100 registers and the *II* has to be increased a large number of times (i.e. the scheduler has to be restarted 40–70 times) to reach the available number of registers. An heuristic to estimate a tight lower bound of the final *II* could dramatically reduce the scheduling time.

## 5   Conclusions

Software pipelining is a very effective technique for scheduling loops. Unfortunately software pipelined schedules have high register requirements. When the number of registers required by a schedule exceed the number of registers available in the processor, some actions are required to alleviate register pressure.

An option is to spill some registers to memory so that they became available to store other values. Unfortunately the addition of spill code degrades the performance of the schedule. On the one hand, the additional spill code (performed through store/load operations) increases the usage of the memory ports. If they became saturated, the initiation interval of the loop must be increased to accommodate the additional operations, producing a direct degradation of performance. On the other hand, even if the initiation interval of the loop is not affected by the additional memory traffic, it produces some negative side effects: 1) more instruction fetch bandwidth is required for the additional load/store operations, which may hurt performance indirectly; 2) the additional memory traffic may interfere in the cache with the regular traffic and increases miss ratio hurting also performance; and 3) the additional memory accesses and fetch bandwidth increase the overall power consumption.

Previous proposals for register spilling in software pipelined loops are based in a two–step process. First a schedule with no register constraints is generated. Then, registers are allocated and spill code is added if required. The addition of spill code requires rescheduling the loop. This process may be repeated several times since more spill might be required after the reschedule.

In this paper we have presented *MIRS*, an iterative Modulo scheduling approach with Integrated Register Spilling. *MIRS* schedules the loops, allocates registers and adds the required spill code all in a single step. It is based on the ability of iterative modulo scheduling to undo previous scheduling decisions, eject operations and leave room to schedule the spill code.

Performance figures show that *MIRS* obtains an average speed–up ranging from 14% to 31% (depending on the processor configuration) for all the loops that require spill code. This represents an average speed–up from 7.9% to 16.2% for the whole benchmark set. However for particular applications speed-ups up to 26% are obtained. In addition, noticeable traffic reductions (with all the implications mentioned above) are also obtained.

# References

[1] A. Aiken and A. Nicolau. A realistic resource-constrained software pipelining algorithm. *Advances in Languages and Compilers for Parallel Processing*, pages 274–290, 1991.

[2] V. Allan, R. Jones, R. Lee, and S. Allan. Software pipelining. *ACM Computing Surveys*, 27(3):367–432, September 1995.

[3] J. Allen, K. Kennedy, and J. Warren. Conversion of control dependence to data dependence. In *Proc. 10th annual Symposium on Principles of Programming Languages*, January 1983.

[4] E. Ayguadé, C. Barrado, A. González, J. Labarta, J. Llosa, D. López, S. Moreno, D. Padua, F.Reig, Q. Riera, and M. Valero. Ictineo: a tool for instruction level parallelism research. Technical Report UPC-DAC-96-61, Universitat Politècnica de Catalunya, December 1996.

[5] D. Bernstein, D. Goldin, M. Golumbic, H. Krawczyk, Y. Mansour, I. Nahshon, and R. Pinter. Spill code minimization techniques for optimizing compilers. In *Proc. of the ACM SIGPLAN'89 Conf. on Programming Languages Design and Implementation*, pages 258–263, July 1989.

[6] M. Berry, D. Chen, P. Koss, and D. Kuck. The Perfect Club benchmarks: Effective performance evaluation of supercomputers. Technical Report 827, Center for Supercomputing Research and Development, November 1988.

[7] P. Briggs, K. Cooper, K. Kennedy, and L. Torczon. Coloring heuristics for register allocation. In *Proc. of the ACM SIGPLAN'89 Conf. on Programming Language Design and Implementation*, pages 275–284, June 1989.

[8] P. Briggs, K. Cooper, and L. Torczon. Improvements to graph coloring register allocation. *ACM Transactions on Programming Languages and Systems*, 16(3):428–455, May 1994.

[9] D. Callahan and B. Koblenz. Register allocation via hierarchical graph coloring. In *Proc. of the ACM SIGPLAN'91 Conf. on Programming Language Design and Implementation*, pages 192–203, June 1991.

[10] G. Chaitin. Register allocation and spilling via graph coloring. In *Proc. ACM SIGPLAN Symp. on Compiler Construction*, pages 98–105, June 1982.

[11] A. Charlesworth. An approach to scientific array processing: The architectural design of the AP120B/FPS-164 family. *Computer*, 14(9):18–27, 1981.

[12] A. K. Dani, V. J. Ramanan, and R. Govindarajan. Register-sensitive software pipelining. In *Procs. of the Merged 12th International Parallel Processing and 9th International Symposium on Parallel and Distributed Systems*, april 1998.

[13] J. Dehnert and R. Towle. Compiling for the Cydra 5. *The Journal of Supercomputing*, 7(1/2):181–228, May 1993.

[14] A. Eichenberger and E. Davidson. Stage scheduling: A technique to reduce the register requirements of a modulo schedule. In *Proc. of the 28th Annual Int. Symp. on Microarchitecture (MICRO-28)*, pages 338–349, November 1995.

[15] C. Eisenbeis, S. Lelait, and B. Marmol. The meeting graph: a new model for loop cyclic register allocation. In *Proc. of the Fifth Workshop on Compilers for Parallel Computers (CPC95)*, pages 503–516, June 1995.

[16] L. Hendren, G. Gao, E. Altman, and C. Mukerji. Register allocation using cyclic interval graphs: A new approach to an old problem. ACAPS Tech. Memo 33, Advanced Computer Architecture and Program Structures Group, McGill University, 1992.

[17] R. Huff. Lifetime-sensitive modulo scheduling. In *Proc. of the 6th Conference on Programming Language, Design and Implementation*, pages 258–267, 1993.

[18] S. Jain. Circular scheduling: A new technique to perform software pipelining. In *Proc. of the ACM SIGPLAN '91 Conference on Programming Language Design and Implementation*, pages 219–228, June 1991.

[19] M. Lam. Software pipelining: An effective scheduling technique for VLIW machines. In *Proceedings of the SIGPLAN'88 Conference on Programming Language Design and Implementation*, pages 318–328, June 1988.

[20] J. Llosa, A. González, E. Ayguadé, and M. Valero. Swing modulo scheduling: A lifetime-sensitive approach. In *IFIP WG10.3 Working Conference on Parallel Architectures and Compilation Techniques (PACT'96)*, pages 80–86, October 1996.

[21] J. Llosa, M. Valero, and E. Ayguadé. Heuristics for register-constrained software pipelining. In *Proc. of the 29th Annual Int. Symp. on Microarchitecture (MICRO-29)*, pages 250–261, December 1996.

[22] J. Llosa, M. Valero, and E. Ayguadé. Quantitative evaluation of register pressure on software pipelined loops. *International Journal of Parallel Programming*, 26(2):121–142, April 1998.

[23] J. Llosa, M. Valero, E. Ayguadé, and A. González. Hypernode reduction modulo scheduling. In *Proc. of the 28th Annual Int. Symp. on Microarchitecture (MICRO-28)*, pages 350–360, November 1995.

[24] W. Mangione-Smith, S. Abraham, and E. Davidson. Register requirements of pipelined processors. In *Proc. of the Int. Conference on Supercomputing*, pages 260–246, July 1992.

[25] S. Ramakrishnan. Software pipelining in PA–RISC compilers. *Hewlett-Packard Journal*, pages 39–45, July 1992.

[26] B. Rau and C. Glaeser. Some scheduling techniques and an easily schedulable horizontal architecture for high performance scientific computing. In *Proc. of the 14th Annual Microprogramming Workshop*, pages 183–197, October 1981.

[27] B. Rau, M. Lee, P. Tirumalai, and P. Schlansker. Register allocation for software pipelined loops. In *Proc. of the ACM SIGPLAN'92 Conference on Programming Language Design and Implementation*, pages 283–299, June 1992.

[28] B. R. Rau. Iterative modulo scheduling: An algorithm for software pipelining loops. In *Proc. of the 27th Annual International Symposium on Microarchitecture*, pages 63–74, November 1994.

[29] J. Ruttenberg, G. Gao, A. Stoutchinin, and W. Lichtenstein. Software pipelining showdown: Optimal vs. heuristic methods in a production compiler. In *Proc. of the ACM SIGPLAN'96 Conf. on Programming Languages Design and Implementation*, pages 1–11, May 1996.

[30] J. Wang, A. Krall, M. A. Ertl, and C. Eisenbeis. Software pipelining with register allocation and spilling. In *Proc. of the 27th Annual Int. Symp. on Microarchitecture*, pages 95–99, November 1994.

[31] J. Zalamea, J. Llosa, E. Ayguadé, and M. Valero. Improved spill code generation for software pipelined loops. In *Procs. of the Programming Languages Design and Implementation (PLDI'00)*, pages 134–144., June 2000.

[32] J. Zalamea, J. Llosa, E. Ayguadé, and M. Valero. *MIRS*: Modulo scheduling with integrated register spilling. Technical Report UPC-DAC-2000-68, Universitat Politècnica de Catalunya, November 2000.

# Strength Reduction of Integer Division and Modulo Operations

Jeffrey Sheldon, Walter Lee, Ben Greenwald, and Saman Amarasinghe*

M.I.T. Laboratory for Computer Science

**Abstract.** Integer division, modulo, and remainder operations are expressive and useful operations. They are logical candidates to express complex data accesses such as the wrap-around behavior in queues using ring buffers. In addition, they appear frequently in address computations as a result of compiler optimizations that improve data locality, perform data distribution, or enable parallelization. Experienced application programmers, however, avoid them because they are slow. Furthermore, while advances in both hardware and software have improved the performance of many parts of a program, few are applicable to division and modulo operations. This trend makes these operations increasingly detrimental to program performance.

This paper describes a suite of optimizations for eliminating division, modulo, and remainder operations from programs. These techniques are analogous to strength reduction techniques used for multiplications. In addition to some algebraic simplifications, we present a set of optimization techniques that eliminates division and modulo operations that are functions of loop induction variables and loop constants. The optimizations rely on algebra, integer programming, and loop transformations.

## 1  Introduction

This paper describes a suite of optimizations for eliminating division, modulo, and remainder operations from programs. In addition to some algebraic simplifications, we present a set of optimization techniques that eliminates division and modulo operations that are functions of loop induction variables and loop constants. These techniques are analogous to strength reduction techniques used for multiplications.

Integer division, modulo, and remainder are expressive and useful operations. They are often the most intuitive way to represent many algorithmic concepts. For example, use of a modulo operation is the most concise way of implementing queues with ring buffers. In addition, many modern compiler optimizations heavily employ division and modulo operations when they perform array transformations to improve data locality or enable parallelization. The SUIF parallelizing compiler [2, 5], the Maps compiler-managed memory system [6], the Hot

* This research is funded in part by Darpa contract # DABT63-96-C-0036 and in part by an IBM Research Fellowship.

H. Dietz (Ed.): LCPC 2001, LNCS 2624, pp. 254–273, 2003.
© Springer-Verlag Berlin Heidelberg 2003

Pages software caching system [15], and the C-CHARM memory system [13] all introduce these operations to express the array indexes after transformations.

However, the cost of using division and modulo operations is often prohibitive. Despite their suitability for representing various concepts, experienced application programmers avoid them when they care about performance. On the MIPS R10000, for example, a divide operation takes 35 cycles, compared to six cycles for a multiply and one cycle for an add. Furthermore, unlike the multiply unit, the division unit has dismal throughput because it is not pipelined. In compiler optimizations that attempt to improve cache behavior or reduce memory traffic, the overhead from the use of modulo and division operations can potentially negate any performance gained.

Advances in both hardware and software make optimizations on modulo and remainder operations more important today than ever. While modern processors have taken advantage of increasing silicon area by replacing iterative multipliers with faster, non-iterative structures such as Wallace multipliers, similar non-iterative division/modulo functional units have not materialized technologically [16]. Thus, while the performance gap between an add and a multiply has narrowed, the gap between a divide and the other arithmetic operations has either widened or remained the same. In the MIPS family, for example, the ratio of costs of div/mul/add has gone from 35/12/1 on the R3000 to 35/6/1 on the R10000. Similarly, hardware advances such as caching and branch prediction help reduce the cost of memory accesses and branches relative to divisions. From the software side, better code generation, register allocation, and strength reduction of multiplies increase the relative execution time of portions of code that uses division and modulo operations. Thus, in accordance with Amdahl's law, the benefit of optimizing away these operations is ever increasing.

```
for(t = 0; t < T; t++)
  for(i = 0; i < NN; i++)
    A[i%N] = 0;
```

(a) Loop with an integer modulo operation

```
_invt = (NN-1)/N;
for(t = 0; t <= T-1; t++) {
  for(_Mdi = 0; _Mdi <= _invt; _Mdi++) {
    _peeli = 0;
    for(i = N*_Mdi;
        i <= min(N*_Mdi+N-1,NN-1); i++) {
      A[_peeli] = 0;
      _peeli = _peeli + 1;
    }
  }
}
```

(b) Modulo loop after strength reduction optimization

```
for(t = 0; t < T; t++)
  for(i = 0; i < NN; i++)
    A[i/N] = 0;
```

(c) Loop with an integer division operation

```
_invt = (NN-1)/N;
for(t = 0; t <= T-1; t++) {
  for(_mDi = 0; _mDi <= _invt; _mDi++) {
    for(i = N*_mDi;
        i <= min(N*_mDi+N-1,NN-1); i++) {
      A[_mDi] = 0;
    }
  }
}
```

(d) Division loop after strength reduction optimization

**Fig. 1.** Two sample loops before and after strength reduction optimizations. The run-time inputs are T=500, N=500, and NN=N*N.

This paper presents optimizations that focus on eliminating division and modulo operations from loop nests where the numerators and the denominators are linear functions of loop induction variables and loop constants. The concept is similar to strength reduction of multiplications. However, a strength reducible multiplication in a loop creates a simple linear data pattern, while modulo and division instructions create values with complex saw-tooth and step patterns. We use algebra, loop iteration space analysis, and integer programming techniques to identify and simplify these patterns. The elimination of division and modulo operations requires complex loop transformations to break the patterns at their discrete points.

We believe that if the compiler is able to eliminate the overhead of division and modulo operations, their use will become prevalent. Both user code and compiler generated code will benefit. Similar to how strength reduction of multiplications helped the acceptance of early Fortran compilers into the scientific programming community, strength reduction of modulo and division can increase the attractiveness and impact of automatic parallelization and locality optimization.

The algorithms shown in this paper have been effective in eliminating most of the division and modulo instructions introduced by the SUIF parallelizing compiler, Maps, Hot Pages, and C-CHARM. In some cases, they improve the performance of applications by more than a factor of ten.

**Related Work**    An early article by Cocke and Markstein describes one of the optimizations presented in this paper and shows how it complements locality improving array transformations [7]. Other previous work on eliminating division and modulo operations have focused on the case when the denominator is a compile-time constant [1, 12, 14]. In [12], a division with constant denominator is turned into a load-constant, a multiplication, one or two shifts, and two add/subtracts; a modulo with constant denominator is converted into those instructions plus a multiply and a subtract. In contrast, our approach focuses on loop nests, but it only requires that the denominator is loop invariant. In cases where both approaches are applicable, our approach usually leads to more efficient code, with mod cost as low as one add, and div cost as low as an add amortized over the iteration count.

The rest of the paper is organized as follows. Section 2 motivates our work. Section 3 describes the framework for our optimizations. Section 4 presents the optimizations. Section 5 presents results. Section 6 concludes.

## 2    Motivation

We illustrate by way of example the potential benefits from strength reducing integer division and modulo operations. Figure 1(a) shows a simple loop with an integer modulo operation. Figure 1(b) shows the result of applying our strength reduction techniques to the loop. Similarly, Figure 1(c) and Figure 1(d) show a loop with an integer divide operation before and after optimizations. Figure 2 shows the performance of these loops on a wide range of processors. The results show that the performance gain is universally significant, generally ranging from 4.5x to 45x.[1] The thousand-fold speedup for the division loop on the Alpha 21164 arises because, after the division has been strength reduced, the compiler is able to recognize that the inner loop is performing redundant stores. When the array is declared to be volatile, the redundant stores are not optimized away, and the speedup comes completely from the elimination of divisions. This example illustrates that, like any other optimizations, the benefit of mod/div strength reduction can be multiplicative when combined with other optimizations.

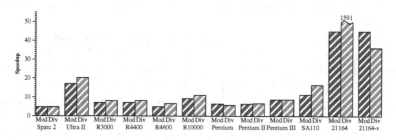

**Fig. 2.** Performance improvement obtained with the strength reduction of modulo and division operations on several machines.

## 3   Framework

**Definition 1.** *Let $x \in R$, $n, d \in Z$. We define integer operations div, rem, and mod as follows:*

$$TRUNC(x) = \begin{cases} \lfloor x \rfloor & x \geq 0 \\ \lceil x \rceil & x < 0 \end{cases}$$
$$n \ div \ d \ = TRUNC(n/d)$$
$$n \ rem \ d \ = n - d * TRUNC(n/d)$$
$$n \ mod \ d \ = n - d * \lfloor n/d \rfloor$$

*For the rest of this paper, we use the traditional symbols / and % to represent integer divide and integer modulo operations, respectively.*

To facilitate presentation, we make the following simplifications. First, we assume that both the numerator and denominator expressions are positive unless explicitly stated otherwise. The full compiler system has to check for all the cases and handle them correctly, but sometimes the compiler can deduce the sign of an expression from its context or its use, *e.g.,* an array index expression. Second,

---

[1] The speedup on the Alpha is more than twice that of the other architectures because its integer division is emulated in software.

we describe our optimizations for modulo operations, which are equivalent to remainder operations when both the numerators and the divisors are positive.

Most of the algorithms introduced in this paper strength reduce integer division and modulo operations by identifying their value patterns. For that, we need to obtain the value ranges of numerator and denominator expressions of the division and modulo operations. We concentrate our effort on loop nests by obtaining the value ranges of the induction variables, since many of the strength-reducible operations are found within loops, and optimizing modulo and division operations in loops has a much higher impact on performance. Finding the value ranges of induction variables is equivalent to finding the iteration space of the loop nests.

First, we need a representation for iteration spaces of the loop nests and the numerator and denominator expressions of the division and modulo operations. Representing arbitrary iteration spaces and expressions accurately and analyzing them is not practical in a compiler. Thus, we restrict our analysis to loop bounds and expressions that are affine functions of induction variables and loop constants. We choose to view the iteration spaces as multi-dimensional convex regions in an integer space [2, 3, 4]. We use systems of inequalities to represent these multi-dimensional convex regions and program expressions. The analysis and strength reduction optimizations are then performed by manipulating the systems of inequalities.

**Definition 2.** *Assume a p-deep (not necessarily perfectly nested) loop nest of the form:*

```
FOR i₁ = max(l_{1,1}..l_{1,m₁}) TO min(h_{1,1}..h_{1,n₁}) STEP s₁ DO
  FOR i₂ = max(l_{2,1}..l_{2,m₂}) TO min(h_{2,1}..h_{2,n₂}) STEP s₂ DO
    ....
    FOR i_p = max(l_{p,1}..l_{p,m_p}) TO min(h_{p,1}..h_{p,n_p}) STEP s_p DO
      /* the loop body */
```

*where $v_1, ..., v_q$ are loop invariant, and $l_{x,y}$ and $h_{x,y}$ are affine functions of the variables $v_1, ..., v_q, i_1, ..., i_{x-1}$. We define the context of the $k^{th}$ loop body recursively:*

$$\mathcal{F}_k = \mathcal{F}_{k-1} \wedge \left\{ i_k \left| \begin{array}{l} \bigwedge_{j=1,...,m_k} i_k \geq l_{k,j} \wedge \\ \bigwedge_{j=1,...,n_k} i_k \leq h_{k,j} \end{array} \right. \right\}$$

The loop bounds in this definition contain max and min functions because many compiler-generated loops, including those generated in Optimizations 9 and 10 in Section 4.3, produce such bounds.

Note that the symbolic constants $v_1, ..., v_q$ need not be defined within the context. If we are able to obtain information on their value ranges, we include them into the context. Even without a value range, the way the variable is used in an expression (*e.g.*, its coefficient) can provide valuable information on the value range of the expression.

We perform loop normalization and induction variable detection analysis prior to strength reduction so that all the FOR loops are in the above form. Whenever possible, any variable defined within the loop nest is written as affine expressions of the induction variables.

**Definition 3.** *Given context $\mathcal{F}$ with symbolic constants $v_1, ..., v_q$ and loop index variables $i_1, ..., i_p$, an affine integer division (or modulo) expression within it is represented by a 3-tuple $\langle N, D, \mathcal{F} \rangle$ where $N$ and $D$ are defined by the affine functions: $N = n_0 + \sum_{1 \le j \le q} n_j v_j + \sum_{1 \le j \le p} n_{j+q} i_j$, $D = d_0 + \sum_{1 \le j \le q} d_j v_j + \sum_{1 \le j \le p-1} n_{j+q} i_j$. The division expression is represented by $N/D$. The modulo expression is represented by $N\%D$.*

*We restrict the denominator to be invariant within the context (i.e., it cannot depend on $i_p$). We rely on this invariance property to perform several loop level optimizations.*

### 3.1 Expression Relation

**Definition 4.** *Given affine expressions $A$ and $B$ and a context $\mathcal{F}$ describing the value ranges of the variables in the expressions, we define the following relations:*

- *Relation$(A < B, \mathcal{F})$ is true iff the system of inequalities $\mathcal{F} \wedge \{A \ge B\}$ is empty.*
- *Relation$(A \le B, \mathcal{F})$ is true iff the system of inequalities $\mathcal{F} \wedge \{A > B\}$ is empty.*
- *Relation$(A > B, \mathcal{F})$ is true iff the system of inequalities $\mathcal{F} \wedge \{A \le B\}$ is empty.*
- *Relation$(A \ge B, \mathcal{F})$ is true iff the system of inequalities $\mathcal{F} \wedge \{A < B\}$ is empty.*

Using the integer programming technique of Fourier-Motzkin Elimination [8, 9, 10, 18, 20], we manipulate the systems of inequalities for both analysis and loop transformation purposes. In many analyses, we use this technique to identify if a system of inequalities is empty, *i.e.*, no set of values for the variables will satisfy all the inequalities. Fourier-Motzkin elimination is also used to simplify a system of inequalities by eliminating redundant inequalities. For example, a system of inequalities $\{I \ge 5, I \ge a, I \ge b, a \ge 10, b \le 4\}$ can be simplified to $\{I \ge 10, I \ge a, a \ge 10, b \le 4\}$. In many optimizations discussed in this paper, we create a new context to represent a transformed iteration space that will result in elimination of modulo and division operations. We use Fourier-Motzkin projection to convert this system of inequalities into the corresponding loop nest. This process guarantees that the loop nest created has no empty iterations and loop bounds are the simplest and tightest [2, 3, 4].

### 3.2 Iteration Count

**Definition 5.** *Given a loop* FOR $i = L$ TO $U$ DO *with context $\mathcal{F}$, where $L = max(l_1, ..., l_n)$, $U = min(u_1, ..., u_m)$, the number of iterations niter can be expressed as follows:*

$$niter(L, U, \mathcal{F}) = \min\{k | k = u_y - l_x + 1; x \in [1, n]; y \in [1, m]\}$$

*The context is included in the expression to allow us to apply the max/min optimizations described in Section 4.4.*

# 4    Optimization Suite

This section describes our suite of optimizations to eliminate integer modulo and division instructions.

## 4.1    Algebraic Simplifications

First, we describe simple optimizations that do not require any knowledge about the value ranges of the source expressions.

**Algebraic Axioms** Many algebraic axioms can be used to simplify division and modulo operations [11]. Even if the simplification does not immediately eliminate operations, it is important because it can lead to further optimizations.

**Optimization 1** *Simplify the modulo and division expressions using the following algebraic simplification rules.* $f_1$ *and* $f_2$ *are expressions,* $x$ *is a variable or a constant, and* $c$, $c_1$, $c_2$ *and* $d$ *are constants.*

$$(f_1 x + f_2)\% x \implies f_2 \% x$$
$$(f_1 x + f_2)/x \implies f_1 + f_2/x$$
$$(c_1 f_1 + c_2 f_2)\% d \implies ((c_1 \% d) f_1 + (c_2 \% d) f_2)\% d$$
$$(c_1 f_1 + c_2 f_2)/d \implies ((c_1 \% d) f_1 + (c_2 \% d) f_2)/d$$
$$+ (c_1/d) f_1 + (c_2/d) f_2$$
$$(c f_1 x + f_2)\% (dx) \implies ((c \% d) f_1 x + f_2)\% (dx)$$
$$(c f_1 x + f_2)/(dx) \implies ((c \% d) f_1 x + f_2)/(dx) + (c/d) f_1$$

**Reduction to Conditionals** A broad range of modulo and division expressions can be strength reduced into a conditional statement. Since we prefer not to segment basic blocks because it inhibits other optimizations, we attempt this optimization as a last resort.

**Optimization 2** *Let* $\langle N, D, \mathcal{F} \rangle$ *be a modulo or division expression in a loop of the following form:*

```
FOR i = 0 TO U DO
    x = N%D
    y = N/D
ENDFOR
```

Let n be the coefficient of i in N, and let $N^- = N - n * i$. Then if $n < D$, the loop can be transformed to the following:

```
_Mdx = N^-%D
_mDy = N^-/D
FOR i = 0 TO U DO
    x = _Mdx
    y = _mDy
    _Mdx = _Mdx + n
    IF _Mdx ≥ D THEN
        _Mdx = _Mdx - D
        _mDy = _mDy + 1
    ENDIF
ENDFOR
```

The code shown is for $N > 0$ and $n > 0$. Other cases can be handled by changing signs appropriately.

## 4.2  Optimizations Using Value Ranges

The following optimizations not only use algebraic axioms, they also take advantage of compiler knowledge about the value ranges of the variables associated with the modulo and division operations.

**Elimination via Simple Continuous Range**  Suppose the context allows us to prove that the range of the numerator expression does not cross a multiple of the denominator expression. Then for a modulo expression, we know that there is no wrap-around. For a division expression, the result has to be a constant. In either case, the operation can be eliminated.

**Optimization 3** *Given a modulo or division expression* $\langle N, D, \mathcal{F} \rangle$*, if Relation* $(N \geq 0 \wedge D \geq 0, \mathcal{F})$ *and Relation* $(kD \leq N < (k+1)D, \mathcal{F})$ *for some* $k \in Z$*, then the expressions reduce to* $k$ *and* $N - kD$ *respectively.*

**Optimization 4** *Given a modulo or division expression* $\langle N, D, \mathcal{F} \rangle$*, if Relation* $(N < 0 \wedge D \geq 0, \mathcal{F})$ *and Relation* $((k+1)D < N \leq kD, \mathcal{F})$ *for some* $k \in Z$*, then the expressions reduce to* $k$ *and* $N + kD$*, respectively.*

**Elimination via Integral Stride and Continuous Range**  This optimization is predicated on identifying two conditions. First, the numerator must contain an index variable whose coefficient is a multiple of the denominator. Second, the numerator less this index variable term does not cross a multiple of the denominator expression. These conditions are common in the modulo and division expressions that are part of the address computations of compiler-transformed linearized multidimensional arrays.

**Optimization 5** *Given a modulo or division expression* $\langle N, D, \mathcal{F} \rangle$*, let* $i$ *be an index variable in* $\mathcal{F}$*,* $n$ *be the coefficient of* $i$ *in* $N$*, and* $N^- = N - n * i$*. If* $n \% D = 0$ *and there exists an integer* $k$ *such that* $kD \leq N^- < (k+1)D$*, then the modulo and division expressions can be simplified to* $N^- - kD$ *and* $(n/D)i + k$*, respectively for* $k > 0$ *and to* $N^- - (k+1)D$ *and* $(n/D)i + k + 1$ *for* $k < 0$*.*

If alignment of the loop, $k$, is not constant, or cannot be determined one can instead perform a slightly more general transformation.

**Optimization 6** *Let* $\langle N, D, \mathcal{F} \rangle$ *be a modulo or division expression in a loop of the following form:*

```
FOR i = 0 TO U DO
    x = N%D
    y = N/D
ENDFOR
```

Let n be the coefficient of i in N and $N^- = N - n * i$. Then if $n \% D = 0$, the loop can be transformed to the following:

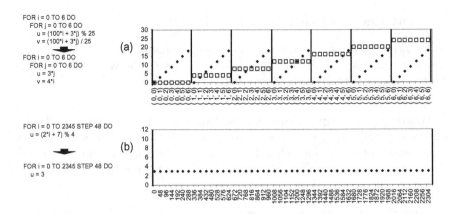

**Fig. 3.** Original and optimized code segments for several modulo and division expressions. The x-axes are the iteration spaces. The y-axes are numeric values. The solid diamonds are values of the modulo expression. The open squares are the values of the division expression. The solid lines represent the original iteration space boundaries. The dash lines represent the boundaries of the transformed loops.

```
_Mdx = N⁻%D
_mDy = N⁻/D
FOR i = 0 TO U DO
    x = _Mdx
    y = _mDy
    _mDy = _mDy + (n/D)
ENDFOR
```

**Elimination through Absence of Discontinuity**  Many modulo and division expressions do not create discontinuities within the iteration space. If this can be guaranteed, then the expressions can be simplified. Figure 3(a) shows an example of such an expression with no discontinuity in the iteration space.

**Optimization 7**  *Let $\langle N, D, \mathcal{F} \rangle$ be a modulo or division expression in a loop of the following form:*

```
FOR i = 0 TO U DO
    x = N%D
    y = N/D
ENDFOR
```

Let n be the coefficient of i in N, $N^- = N - n * i$, and $k = N^-\%D$. For $n > 0$ the loop can be transformed into the following if $Relation(n * niter(0, U, \mathcal{F}) \leq D - k + n - 1, \mathcal{F})$ while for $n < 0$ the loop can be transformed into the following if $Relation(n * niter(0, U, \mathcal{F}) \geq n - k$, the loop can be transformed to the following:

```
_mDy = N⁻/D
_Mdx = k
FOR i = 0 TO U DO
    x = _Mdx
    y = _mDy
    _Mdx = _Mdx + n
ENDFOR
```

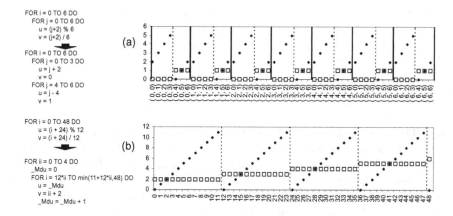

**Fig. 4.** Original and optimized code segments for several modulo and division expressions. See caption for Figure 3.

### 4.3 Optimizations Using Loop Transformations

The next set of optimizations perform loop transformations to create new iteration spaces that have no discontinuity. For each loop, we first analyze all its expressions to collect a list of necessary transformations. We then eliminate any redundant transformations.

**Loop Partitioning to Remove One Discontinuity** For some modulo and division expressions, the number of iterations in the loop will be less than the distance between discontinuities. But a discontinuity may still occur in the iteration space if it is not aligned to the iteration boundaries. When this occurs, we can either split the loop or peel the iterations. We prefer peeling iterations if the discontinuity is close to the iteration boundaries. This optimization is also paramount when a loop contains multiple modulo and division expressions, each with the same denominator and whose numerators are in the same uniformly generated set [22]. In this case, one of the expressions can have an aligned discontinuity while others may not. Thus, it is necessary to split the loop to optimize all the modulo and division expressions. Figure 4(a) shows an example where loop partitioning eliminates a single discontinuity.

**Optimization 8** Let $\langle N, D, \mathcal{F} \rangle$ be a modulo or division expression in a loop of the following form:

```
FOR i = 0 TO U DO
    x = N%D
    y = N/D
ENDFOR
```

Let n be the coefficient of i in N and $N^- = N - n * i$. Then if $D\%n = 0$ and $Relation(niter(0, U, \mathcal{F}) \leq D/n, \mathcal{F})$, the loop can be transformed to the following:

```
k = N⁻%D                                    IF _Mdx ≥ D THEN
_Mdx = k                                       _Mdx = _Mdx − D
_mDy = N⁻/D                                    _mDy = _mDy + 1
_cut = min((D − _kx + n − 1)/n + L − 1, U)  ENDIF
FOR i = 0 TO _cut DO                         FOR i = _cut + 1 TO U DO
   x = _Mdx                                     x = _Mdx
   y = _mDy                                     y = _mDy
   _Mdx = _Mdx + n                              _Mdx = _Mdx + n
ENDFOR                                       ENDFOR
```

**Loop Tiling to Eliminate Discontinuities** In many cases, the value range identified contains discontinuities in the division and modulo expressions. This section explains how to perform loop transformations to move discontinuities to the boundaries of the iteration space. The result is that modulo and division operations can be eliminated or propagated out of the inner loops. Figure 4(b) shows an example requiring this optimization.

When the iteration space has a pattern with a large number of discontinuities repeating themselves, breaking a loop into two loops such that the discontinuities occur at the boundaries of the second loop will let us optimize the modulo and division operations. Optimization 9 adds an additional restriction to the lower bound so that no preamble is needed. Optimization 10 eliminates that restriction.

**Optimization 9** *Let* $\langle N, D, \mathcal{F} \rangle$ *be a modulo or division expression in a loop of the following form:*

```
FOR i = 0 TO U DO
   x = N%D
   y = N/D
ENDFOR
```

Let n be the coefficient of i in N and $N^- = N − n * i$. Then if $D\%n = 0$ and $N^- = 0$, the loop can be transformed to the following:

```
_mDy = N⁻/D
FOR ii = 0 TO U/(D/n) DO
   _Mdx = 0
   FOR i = ii * (D/n) TO
           min((ii + 1) * (D/n) − 1, U) DO
      x = _Mdx
      y = _mDy
      _Mdx = _Mdx + n
   ENDFOR
   _mDy = _mDy + 1
ENDFOR
```

**Optimization 10** *For the loop nest and the modulo and division statements described in optimization 9, if* $D\%n = 0$ *then the above loop nest is transformed to the following:*

```
_Mdx = N⁻%D                    _Mdi = (n * _brklb + N⁻)%D
_mDy = N⁻/D                    FOR ii = 0 TO U/(D/n) DO
FOR i = 0 TO _brklb − 1 DO        _Mdx = _Mdi
   x = _Mdx                       FOR i = ii * (D/n) + _brklb
   y = _mDy                               TO min((ii + 1) * D/n − 1 + _brklb, U) DO
   _Mdx = _Mdx + n                   x = _Mdx
ENDFOR                               y = _mDy
IF _brklb ≥ 0 THEN                   _Mdx = _Mdx + n
   _mDy = _mDy + 1                ENDFOR
ENDIF                             _mDy = _mDy + 1
                               ENDFOR
```

*The expression to determine _brklb depends on the sign of both $N$ and $n$. If $N > 0$ and $n > 0$, _brklb $= (N^-/D + 1)(D/n) - N^-/n$. If $N < 0$ and $n > 0$, _brklb $= (-N^-\%D)/n + 1$. If $N > 0$ and $n < 0$, _brklb $= (-N^-/D + 1) * (D/|n|) * (D/|n|) - (-N^-)/|n|$. If $N < 0$ and $n < 0$, _brklb $= (N^-\%D)/|n| + 1$.*

**General Loop Transformation: Single Access Class** It is possible to transform a loop to eliminate discontinuities with very little knowledge about the iteration space and value ranges. The following transformation can be applied to any loop containing a single arbitrary instance of affine modulo/division expressions.

**Optimization 11** *Let $\langle N, D, \mathcal{F} \rangle$ be a modulo or division expression in a loop of the following form:*

```
FOR i = L TO U DO
    x = N%D
    y = N/D
ENDFOR
```

Let n be the coefficient of i in N and $N^- = N - n * i$. Then the loop can be transformed to the following:

```
SUB FindNiceL(L, D, n, N^-)
    IF n = 0 THEN
        RETURN L
    ELSE
        VLden = ((L * n + N^- - 1)/D) * D
        VLbase = L * n + N^- - VLden
        NiceL = L + (D - VLbase + n - 1)/n
        RETURN NiceL
    ENDIF
ENDSUB

k = n/D
r = n - k * D

IF r ≠ 0 THEN
    perIter = D/r
    niceL = FindNiceL(L, D, r, N^-)
    niceNden = (U - niceL + 1)/D
    niceU = niceL + niceNden * D
ELSE
    perIter = U - L
    niceL = L
    niceU = U + 1
ENDIF

modval = (n * L + N^-)%D
divval = (n * L + N^-)/D
i = L
FOR i2 = L TO niceL - 1 DO
    x = modval
    y = divval
    modval = modval + r
    divval = divval + k
    i = i + 1
    IF modval ≥ D THEN
        modval = modval - D
        divval = divval + 1
    ENDIF
ENDFOR
```

```
WHILE i < niceU DO
    FOR i2 = 1 TO perIter DO
        x = modval
        y = divval
        modval = modval + r
        divval = divval + k
        i = i + 1
    ENDFOR
    IF modval < D THEN
        x = modval
        y = divval
        modval = modval + r
        divval = divval + k
        i = i + 1
    ENDIF
    IF modval ≠ 0 THEN
        modval = modval - D
        divval = divval + 1
    ENDIF
ENDWHILE

FOR i2 = niceU TO U DO
    x = modval
    y = divval
    modval = modval + r
    divval = divval + k
    i = i + 1
    IF modval ≥ D THEN
        modval = modval - D
        divval = divval + 1
    ENDIF
ENDFOR
```

The loop works as follows. First, note that within the loop, $N$ is a function of i only and D is a constant.

For simplicity, consider the case when $n < D$. We observe that if $N(i) \% D \in [0, n)$, then there is no discontinuity in the functions $N(i)/D$, $N(i)\%D$ in the range $[i, i + \lfloor D/n \rfloor)$. Furthermore, the discontinuity must occur either after $i + \lfloor D/n \rfloor$ or $i + \lfloor D/n \rfloor + 1$.

Thus, the transformation uses a startup loop that executes iterations of i until $N(i)$ falls in the range $[0, n)$. It then enters a nested loop whose inner loop executes $\lfloor D/n \rfloor$ iterations continuously, then conditionally executes another iteration if the execution has not reached the next discontinuity. This main loop continues for as long as possible, and a cleanup loop finishes up whatever iterations the main loop is unable to execute.

The loop handles the case when $n \geq D$ by using $n\%D$ as the basis for calculating discontinuities.

Note that the FindNiceL subroutine can be shared across optimized loops.

**General Loop Transformation: Arbitrary Accesses** Finally, the following transformation can be used for loops with arbitrarily many affine accesses.

**Optimization 12** *Given a loop with affine modulo or division expressions:*

```
FOR i = L TO U DO
    x₁ = (a₁ * i + b₁) op₁ d₁
    x₂ = (a₂ * i + b₂) op₂ d₂
    ...
    xₙ = (aₙ * i + bₙ) opₙ dₙ
ENDFOR
```

where $op_j$ is either mod or div, the loop can be transformed into:

```
SUB FindBreak(L, U, den, n, k)
    IF n = 0 THEN
        RETURN U + 1
    ELSE
        VLden = ((L * n + k)/den) * den
        VLbase = L * n + k - VLden
        Break = L + (den - VLbase + n - 1)/n

        RETURN Break
    ENDIF
ENDSUB

FOR j = 1 TO n DO
    kⱼ = aⱼ/dⱼ
    rⱼ = aⱼ - kⱼ - dⱼ

    valⱼ[mod] = (aⱼ * L + bⱼ)%dⱼ
    valⱼ[div] = (aⱼ * L + bⱼ)/dⱼ

    breakⱼ = FindBreak(L, U, dⱼ, rⱼ, bⱼ)
ENDFOR
```

```
i = L
WHILE i ≤ U DO
    Break =
        min(U + 1, {breakⱼ|j ∈ [1, n]})
    FOR i = i TO Break DO
        x₁ = val₁[opⱼ]
        val₁[mod] = val₁[mod] + r₁
        val₁[div] = val₁[div] + k₁
        x₂ = val₂[opⱼ]
        val₂[mod] = val₂[mod] + r₂
        val₂[div] = val₂[div] + k₂
        ...
    ENDFOR

    FOR j = 1 TO n DO
        IF Break = breakⱼ THEN
            valⱼ[mod] = valⱼ[mod] - dⱼ
            valⱼ[div] = valⱼ[div] + 1
            breakⱼ =
                FindBreak(i + 1, U, dⱼ, rⱼ, bⱼ)
        ENDIF
    ENDFOR
ENDWHILE
```

Note that the *val*[] associative arrays are used only for the purpose of simplifying the presentation. In the actual implementation, all the $op_j$'s are known at compile time, so that for each expression only one of the array values needs to be computed. Also, note that the FindBreak subroutine can be shared across optimized loops.

The loop operates by keeping track of the next discontinuity of each expression. Within an iteration of the WHILE loop, the code finds the closest discontinuity and executes all iterations until that point in the inner FOR loop. Note, however, that because one needs to perform at least one division within the outer loop to update the set of discontinuities, the more complex control flow in the transformed loop may lead to slowdown if the iteration count of the inner loop is small (possibly due to a small $D$ or a large $n$).

## 4.4   Min/Max Optimizations

Some loop transformations, such as those in Section 4.3, produce minimum and maximum operations. This section describes methods for eliminating them. For brevity, we only present the Min optimizations when the Max optimizations can be defined analagously (Optimizations 13, 14, and 17).

**Min/Max Elimination by Evaluation**   If we have sufficient information in the context to prove that one of the operand expressions is always greater (smaller) than the rest of the operands, we can use that fact to get rid of the max (min) operation from the expression.

**Optimization 13** *Given a min expression $min(N_1, ..., N_m)$ with a context $\mathcal{F}$, if there exists $k$ such that for all $0 \leq i \leq m$, $Relation(N_k \leq N_i, \mathcal{F})$, then $min(N_1, ..., N_m)$ can be reduced to $N_k$.*

**Min/Max Simplification by Evaluation**   Even if we are able to prove few relationships between pairs of operands, it can result in a min/max operation with fewer number of operands.

**Optimization 14** *Given a min expression $min(N_1, ..., N_m)$ with a context $\mathcal{F}$, if there exists $i, k$ such that $0 \leq i, k \leq m$, $i \neq k$, $Relation(N_i \leq N_k, \mathcal{F})$ is valid, then $min(N_1, ..., N_m)$ can be reduced to $min(N_1, ..., N_{k-1}, N_{k+1}, ..., N_m)$.*

**Division Folding**   The arithmetic properties of division allow us to fold a division instruction into a min/max operation. This folding can create simpler division expressions that can be further optimized. If further optimizations do not eliminate these division operations, however, the division folding should be un-done to remove potential negative impact on performance.

**Optimization 15** *Given an integer division expression with a min/max operation $\langle min(N_1, ..., N_m), D, \mathcal{F} \rangle$ or $\langle max(N_1, ..., N_m), D, \mathcal{F} \rangle$, if $Relation(D > 0, \mathcal{F})$ holds, rewrite min and max as $min(\langle N_1, D, \mathcal{F} \rangle, ..., \langle N_m, D, \mathcal{F} \rangle)$ and $max(\langle N_1, D, \mathcal{F} \rangle, ..., \langle N_m, D, \mathcal{F} \rangle)$ respectively.*

For brevity, we omit the dual optimization when $D < 0$.

**Min/Max Elimination in Modulo Equivalence** Since $a \leq b$ does not lead to $a\%c \leq b\%c$, there is no general method for folding modulo operations. If we can prove that the results of taking the modulo of each of the min/max operands are the same, however, we can eliminate the min/max operation.

**Optimization 16** *Given an integer modulo expression with a min /max oper-ation* $\langle min(N_1, ..., N_m), D, \mathcal{F} \rangle$ *or* $\langle max(N_1, ..., N_m), D, \mathcal{F} \rangle$ *if* $\langle N_1, D, \mathcal{F} \rangle \equiv ... \equiv \langle N_m, D, \mathcal{F} \rangle$, *then we can rewrite the modulo expression as* $\langle N_1, D, \mathcal{F} \rangle$.

Note that all $\langle N_k, D, \mathcal{F} \rangle$ $(1 \leq k \leq m)$ are equivalent, thus we can choose any one of them as the resulting expression.

**Min/Max Expansion** Normally min/max operations are converted into con-ditionals late in the compiler during code generation. However, if any of the previous optimizations are unable to eliminate the mod/div instructions, low-ering the min/max will simplify the modulo and division expressions, possibly leading to further optimizations. To simplify the explanation, we describe Opti-mizations 17 with only two operands in the respective min and max expressions.

**Optimization 17** *A mod/div statement with a min operation,* $res = \langle min(N_1, N_2), D, \mathcal{F} \rangle$, *gets lowered to*

```
IF N₁ < N₂ THEN
    res = ⟨N₁, D, F ∧ {N₁ < N₂}⟩
ELSE
    res = ⟨N₂, D, F ∧ {N₁ ≥ N₂}⟩
ENDIF
```

## 5    Results

We have implemented the optimizations described in this paper as a compiler pass in SUIF [21] called Mdopt. We are also in the process of implementing the optimizations in SUIF2 using the Omega integer programming solver pack-age [17]. Mdopt has been used as part of several compiler systems: the SUIF par-allelizing compiler [2], the Maps compiler-managed memory system in the Raw parallelizing compiler (Rawcc) [6], the Hot Pages software caching system [15], and the C-CHARM memory system [13]. All those systems introduce modulo and division operations when they manipulate array address computations dur-ing array transformations. This section presents some of the performance gain when applying Mdopt to code generated by those systems.

### 5.1    SUIF Parallelizing Computer

The SUIF parallelizing compiler uses techniques based on linear inequalities to parallelize dense matrix programs [2, 5]. This section uses a hand coded example to illustrate how such a system benefits from Mdopt.

We begin with a five-point stencil code. The stencil code involves iterating over the contents of a two dimensional matrix with a 5-point stencil writing

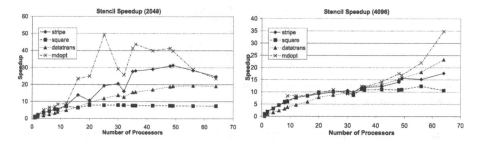

**Fig. 5.** Performance of stencil code using varying parallelization techniques.

resulting values into another matrix, swapping the matrixes, and repeating. In a traditional parallelizing compiler, the matrix is divided into as many stripes as there are processors, with each stripe assigned to a single processor. Each processor portion of the matrix is a contiguous block of memory, thus ensuring good cache locality. In Figure 5, the *stripe* lines show the performance of this parallelization technique for two matrix sizes on an SGI Origin with MIPS R10000 processors, each with a 4MB L2 cache.

This parallelization technique suffers the drawback that it has a large edge-to-area ratio. Edges are undesirable because the processors need to communicate edge values to their neighbors in each iteration. This interprocessor communication can be reduced by dividing the original matrix into roughly square sections rather than stripes. The *square* lines in Figure 5 show the performance of these square partitions. In this approach, however, each processor's data is no longer a contiguous block of memory. This property increases the likelihood of conflict misses. As a result, *square* actually performs uniformly worse than *stripe*.

Square partitions can be made contiguous through array transformations. This transformation restores cache locality, but it introduces division and modulo operations into address computations. The *datatrans* and *mdopt* lines in Figure 5 show the performance of this approach without and with Mdopt optimizations, respectively. Using a 4096x4096 matrix, little speedup is gained by performing the data transformation and modulo/division optimizations on small processor configurations. This is because each processor's working set is sufficiently large that the computation is memory bound. As the number of processors increase past 32, the working set of each processor begins to fit in the L2 caches. The application becomes CPU bound, so that the benefits of div/mod optimizations becomes visible. For a smaller 2048x2048 matrix, the application is CPU bound for correspondingly smaller configurations, and we see an overall performance gain for up to 48 processors. For larger configurations, however, synchronization costs at the end of each iteration overshadows any performance gains from Mdopt.

| Benchmarks | Speedup |
|---|---|
| convolution | 15.6 |
| jacobi | 17.0 |
| median-filter | 2.8 |
| sor | 8.0 |

**Table 1.** Speedup from applying Mdopt to C-CHARM generated code run on an Ultra 5 Workstation.

| Number of Tiles | 1 | | 2 | | 4 | | 8 | | 16 | | 32 | |
|---|---|---|---|---|---|---|---|---|---|---|---|---|
| Benchmarks | Slow down | Speed up | Slow down | Speed up | Slow down | Speed up | Slow down | Speed up | Slow down | Speed up | Slow down | Speed up |
| life | 1.02 | 1.00 | 3.23 | 2.20 | 2.86 | 2.17 | 3.85 | 6.03 | 2.86 | 19.42 | 3.57 | 17.64 |
| jacobi | 1.00 | 1.00 | 4.76 | 4.22 | 8.33 | 6.51 | 10.00 | 3.33 | 10.00 | 2.52 | 33.33 | 6.44 |
| cholesky | 1.00 | 1.00 | 3.57 | 3.62 | 4.35 | 4.12 | 5.00 | 3.41 | 5.55 | 2.54 | 11.11 | 1.85 |
| vpenta | 1.00 | 1.00 | 1.39 | 1.18 | 1.92 | 1.48 | 2.50 | 1.98 | * | * | * | * |
| btrix | 1.00 | 1.00 | 2.94 | 3.19 | 3.45 | 2.26 | 1.35 | 1.00 | 1.25 | 1.00 | 1.28 | 0.96 |
| tomcatv | 0.88 | 1.00 | 3.13 | 2.81 | 4.17 | 3.19 | 5.89 | 7.49 | 7.14 | 6.86 | * | * |
| ocean | 1.00 | 1.00 | 1.37 | 1.60 | 1.69 | 1.70 | 1.41 | 2.00 | 2.44 | 2.33 | 2.94 | 3.82 |
| swim | 1.00 | 1.00 | 1.00 | 1.00 | 1.06 | 1.00 | 1.00 | 1.00 | 1.00 | 1.00 | 1.00 | 0.95 |
| adpcm | 1.10 | 1.00 | 1.10 | 1.00 | 1.23 | 1.00 | 1.10 | 1.00 | 1.10 | 1.00 | 1.10 | 1.00 |
| moldyn | 1.00 | 1.03 | 0.99 | 1.00 | 0.99 | 1.03 | 1.00 | 1.00 | 1.06 | 1.00 | 1.14 | 0.97 |

**Table 2.** Performance of Maps code during transformation targeting a varying number of Raw tiles. For each configuration, the left column shows the slowdown from low-order interleaving array transformation. The right column shows the performance recovered when Mdopt optimization is applied. * indicates missing entries because gcc runs out of memory.

## 5.2 C-CHARM Memory Localization System

The C-CHARM memory localization compiler system [13] attempts to do much of the work traditionally done by hardware caches. The goal of the system is to generate code for an exposed memory hierarchy. Data is moved explicitly from global or off-chip memory to local memory before it is needed and vice versa when the compiler determines it can no longer hold the value locally.

C-CHARM analyses the reuse behavior of programs to determine how long a value should be held in local memory. Once a value is evicted, its local memory location can be reused. This local storage equivalence for global memory values is implemented with a circular buffer. References are mapped into the same circular buffer, and their address calculations are rewritten with modulo operations. It is these modulo operations that map two different global addresses to the same local address. It is these operations that Mdopt removes.

Table 1 shows the speedup from applying modulo/division optimizations on C-CHARM generated code running on a single processor machine.

## 5.3 Maps Compiler Managed Memory

Maps is the memory management front end of the Rawcc parallelizing compiler [6], which targets the MIT Raw architecture [19]. It distributes the data in a sequential input program across the individual memories of the Raw tiles. The system low-order-interleaves arrays whose accesses are affine functions of enclosing loop induction variables. That is, for an N-tile Raw machine, the $k^{th}$ element of an "affine" array $A$ becomes the $(k/N)^{th}$ element of partial array $A$ on tile $k\%N$. Mdopt is used to simplify the tile number into a constant, as well as to eliminate the division operations in the resultant address computations.

Table 2 shows the impact of the transformations. It contains results for code targeting a varying number of tiles, from 1 to 32. The effects of the transformations depend on the number of affine-accessed arrays and the computation to data ratio. Because Mdopt plays an essential correctness role in the Rawcc compiler (Rawcc relies on Mdopt to reduce the tile number expressions to constants), it is not possible to directly compare performance on the Raw machine with and without the optimization. Instead, we compile the C sources before and after the optimization on an Ultrasparc workstation, and we use that as the basis for comparison.

The left column of each configuration shows the performance measured in slowdown after the initial low-order interleaving data transformation. This transformation introduces division and modulo operations and leads to dramatically slower code, as much as 33 times slowdown for 32-way interleaved jacobi. The right column of each configuration shows the speedup attained when we apply Mdopt on the low-order interleaved code. These speedups are as dramatic as the previous slowdown, as much as an 18x speedup for 32-way interleaved life. In many cases the Mdopt is able to recover most of the performance lost due to the interleaving transformation. This recovery, in turn, helps make it possible for the compiler to attain overall speedup by parallelizing the application [6].

# 6   Conclusion

This paper introduces a suite of techniques for eliminating division, modulo, and remainder operations. The techniques are based on number theory, integer programming, and strength-reduction loop transformation techniques. To our knowledge this is the first extensive work that provides modulo and division optimizations for expressions whose denominators are non-constants.

We have implemented our suite of optimizations as a SUIF compiler pass. The compiler pass has proven to be useful across a wide variety compiler optimizations which does data transformations and manipulate address computations. For some benchmarks with high data to computation ratio, an order of magnitude speedup can be achieved.

We believe that the availability of these techniques will make divisions and modulo operations more useful to programmers. Programmers will no longer need to make the painful tradeoff between expressiveness and performance when deciding whether to use these operators. The optimizations will also increase the impact of compiler optimizations that improve data locality or enable parallelization at the expense of introducing modulo and division operations.

**Acknowledgments**   The idea of a general mod/div optimizer was inspired from joint work with Monica Lam and Jennifer Anderson on data transformations for caches. Chris Wilson suggested the reduction of conditionals optimization. Rajeev Barua integrated Mdopt into Rawcc; Andras Moritz integrated the pass into Hot Pages. We thank Jennifer Anderson, Matthew Frank, and Andras Moritz for providing valuable comments on earlier versions of this paper.

# References

[1] R. Alverson. Integer Division Using Reciprocals. In *Proceedings of the Tenth Symposium on Computer Arithmetic*, Grenoble, France, June 1991.

[2] S. Amarasinghe. Parallelizing Compiler Techniques Based on Linear Inequalities. In *Ph.D Thesis, Stanford University. Also appears as Techical Report CSL-TR-97-714*, Jan 1997.

[3] C. Ancourt and F. Irigoin. Scanning Polyhedra with Do Loops. In *Proceedings of the Third ACM SIGPLAN Symposium on Principles and Practice of Parallel Programming*, pages 39–50, Williamsburg, VA, Apr. 1991.

[4] M. Ancourt. *Génération Automatique de Codes de Transfert pour Multiprocesseurs à Mémoires Locales*. PhD thesis, Université Paris VI, Mar. 1991.

[5] J. M. Anderson, S. P. Amarasinghe, and M. S. Lam. Data and Computation Transformations for Multiprocessors. In *Proceedings of the Fifth ACM SIGPLAN Symposium on Principles and Practice of Parallel Programming*, pages 166–178, Santa Barbara, CA, July 1995.

[6] R. Barua, W. Lee, S. Amarasinghe, and A. Agarwal. Maps: A Compiler-Managed Memory System for Raw Machines. In *Proceedings of the 26th International Symposium on Computer Architecture*, Atlanta, GA, May 1999.

[7] J. Cocke and P. Markstein. Strength Reduction for Division and Modulo with Application to Accessing a Multilevel Store. *IBM Journal of Research and Development*, 24(6):692–694, November 1980.

[8] G. Dantzig. *Linear Programming and Extensions*. Princeton University Press, Princeton, NJ, 1963.

[9] G. Dantzig and B. Eaves. Fourier-Motzkin Elimination and its Dual. *Journal of Combinatorial Theory (A)*, 14:288–297, 1973.

[10] R. Duffin. On Fourier's Analysis of Linear Inequality Systems. In *Mathematical Programming Study 1*, pages 71–95. North-Holland, 1974.

[11] R. L. Graham, D. E. Knuth, and O. Patashnik. *Concrete Mathematics*. Addison-Wesley, Reading, MA, 1989.

[12] T. Granlund and P. Montgomery. Division by Invariant Integers using Multiplication. In *Proceedings of the SIGPLAN '94 Conference on Programming Language Design and Implementation*, Orlando, FL, June 1994.

[13] B. Greenwald. A Technique for Compilation to Exposed Memory Hierarchy. Master's thesis, Massachusetts Institute of Technology, Department of Electrical Engineering and Computer Science, September 1999.

[14] D. Magenheimer, L. Peters, K. Peters, and D. Zuras. Integer Multiplication and Division On the HP Precision Architecture. *IEEE Transactions on Computers*, 37:980–990, Aug. 1988.

[15] C. A. Moritz, M. Frank, W. Lee, and S. Amarasinghe. Hot Pages: Software Caching for Raw Microprocessors. Technical Memo LCS-TM-599, Laboratory for Computer Science, Massachusetts Institute of Technology, Sept 1999.

[16] S. Oberman. *Design Issues in High Performance Floating Point Arithmetic Units.* PhD thesis, Stanford University, December 1996.

[17] W. Pugh. The Omega test: A fast and practical integer programming algorithm for dependence analysis. In *Proceedings of Supercomputing '91*, Albuquerque, NM, Nov. 1991.

[18] A. Schrijver. *Theory of Linear and Integer Programming.* John Wiley and Sons, Chichester, Great Britain, 1986.

[19] M. B. Taylor. Design Decisions in the Implementation of a Raw Architecture Workstation. Master's thesis, Massachusetts Institute of Technology, Department of Electrical Engineering and Computer Science, September 1999.

[20] H. Williams. Fourier-Motzkin Elimination Extension to Integer Programming Problems. *Journal of Combinatorial Theory*, 21:118–123, 1976.

[21] R. Wilson, R. French, C. Wilson, S. Amarasinghe, J. Anderson, S. Tjiang, S.-W. Liao, C.-W. Tseng, M. Hall, M. Lam, and J. Hennessy. SUIF: An Infrastructure for Research on Parallelizing and Optimizing Compilers. *ACM SIGPLAN Notices*, 29(12), Dec. 1996.

[22] M. E. Wolf. *Improving Locality and Parallelism in Nested Loops.* PhD thesis, Dept. of Computer Science, Stanford University, Aug. 1992.

# An Adaptive Scheme for Dynamic Parallelization*

Yonghua Ding and Zhiyuan Li

Department of Computer Sciences
Purdue University
West Lafayette, IN 47907, USA
{ding,li}@cs.purdue.edu

**Abstract.** In this paper, we present an adaptive dynamic parallelization scheme which integrates the inspector/executor scheme and the speculation scheme to enhance the capability of a parallelizing compiler and reduce the overhead of dynamic parallelization. Under our scheme, a parallelizing compiler can adaptively apply the inspector/executor scheme or the speculation scheme to a candidate loop that cannot be parallelized statically. We also introduce several techniques which enable dynamic parallelization of certain programs, including SPICE,TRACK and DYFESM in the Perfect Benchmark suite. The experimental results show that our adaptive scheme and techniques are quite effective.

## 1 Introduction

Over the last two decades compiler techniques for automatic parallelization have been studied extensively, however, a significant fraction of parallelizable loops still cannot be identified statically by a state-of-the-art parallelizing compiler due to irregular or input-dependent access patterns. Recently, researchers introduced dynamic parallelization schemes which detect and exploit loop parallelism at run-time. Under such schemes, the parallelizing compiler performs dependence analysis and parallelization of a candidate loop at run-time [8,10]. One can categorize the candidate loops as follows.

- Statically parallelizable loops.
- Loops which are statically determined as sequential.
- Dynamically parallelizable loops which can be
  - Fully parallelizable.
  - Partially parallelizable.
- Loops that cannot be parallelized dynamically.

Dynamic parallelization schemes apply to the candidate loops that cannot be statically determined as sequential or parallel loops, and they complement the

---

* This work is supported in part by the National Science Foundation through grants ACI/ITR-0082834 and CCR-9975309

parallelizing compiler to extract parallelism automatically at run-time. Nevertheless, dynamic parallelization schemes cannot always improve performance because they have overhead for dynamic dependence analysis and a candidate loop may turn out to have little parallelism.

Currently there exist two general schemes for dynamic parallelization, namely inspector/executor and speculation. In the inspector/executor scheme, the compiler generates the inspector which dynamically analyzes the dependences in the original loop, and the executor that schedules and executes the loop using the dependence information extracted by the inspector [3,10,15]. In the speculation scheme, the compiler uses shadow structures in the candidate loop to mark the reference information of the modified variables whose dependences cannot be determined at compile-time. After the execution of the speculative parallel loop, a dynamic dependence analysis is performed to check if any cross-iteration dependences exist. If they do, the execution backtracks to a previous checkpoint and the original loop is executed sequentially [4,9].

In previous work, there has been little discussion on how the compiler decides whether to apply dynamic parallelization and which scheme to choose. In this paper, we present an adaptive scheme that integrates the inspector/executor scheme and the speculation scheme, under which the compiler can select the proper scheme. We organize the paper as follows. We first analyze the overhead of the inspector/executor scheme vs. the speculation scheme. After that, in section 3, we introduce our adaptive scheme for dynamic parallelization. We present several overhead reduction techniques which can improve the capability of our adaptive scheme in section 4. The experimental results are given in section 5. Related work and conclusions are discussed in section 6 and section 7.

## 2   Overhead Analysis of Inspector/Executor Vs. Speculation

Although much work has been done to reduce the overhead of dynamic parallelization [3,4,12,13], such overhead still be significant due to the extra computation for dependence analysis at run-time. However, a specific dynamic parallelization scheme applied to different loops may have different overhead, and different schemes applied to a specific loop may also have different overhead.

In the inspector/executor scheme, the overhead is due to the execution of the inspector. The ratio of the workload of the inspector to that of the original loop, $R_{ie}$, is critical to the overhead of the inspector/executor scheme. If $R_{ie}$ approachs 1, the inspector would be the entire original loop and most likely cannot be parallelized, so it will have as high an overhead as the workload of the original loop. Yet in most cases, $R_{ie} \ll 1$ and the inspector, extracted from the original loop, is a fully parallelizable loop that analyzes the dependence dynamically. Thus the overhead of the inspector/executor scheme will inversely scale the number of processors as follows.

- $W$ = workload of the original loop,    $W'$ = workload of the inspector.

- Overhead of the inspector/executor scheme = $\frac{W'}{p} = \frac{W*R_{ie}}{p}$    $R_{ie} = \frac{W'}{W}$,
  $p$ = number of processors

No matter whether the candidate loop is a dynamically parallelizable loop or a dynamically undeterminable loop, the overhead of the inspector/executor scheme will conform to the above formula if we assume the inspector can be successfully parallelized. However, in some cases, it is difficult to extract the inspector from the original loop, and the inspector may be the entire original loop in the worst case. Then the inspector/executor scheme will gain nothing, and may even degrade the performance.

In the speculation scheme, the overhead comes from checkpointing the program state before entering speculation, initialization of shadow structures, and analysis of the shadow structures after the speculation if the speculation succeeds. However, if the speculation fails, the overhead includes those above and the speculative execution of the parallelized original loop augmented with marking shadow structures and the restoration of checkpointing for sequential re-execution [9]. So the overhead of the speculation scheme applied to a dynamically undeterminable loop or partially parallelizable loop is different from that applied to a dynamically fully parallelizable loop. For a dynamically undeterminable loop or partially parallelizable loop, the speculative execution of the parallelized original loop will fail, and the speculation scheme need restore the program state at the checkpoint and re-execute the original loop sequentially. In this case, the overhead of speculation will be greater than $\frac{W}{p}$ even if we ignore the overhead of checkpointing and initialization. If a candidate loop is a dynamically fully parallelizable loop and we suppose speculation will not fail, the overhead only comes from the checkpointing, initialization, marking shadow structures in the speculative execution of the parallelized loop and the analysis of shadow structures for the dependence test. These overheads are correlative with the features of the candidate loop. For example, a sparse code and a dense code will have extremely different overheads on the checkpointing and initialization. And different speculation techniques will have different overheads for marking shadow structures and dependence analysis. So it is difficult to have a general formula for the overhead of a speculation scheme on dynamically fully parallelizable loops. But in most cases if the speculation does not fail, the overhead of speculation scheme will be less than $\frac{W*r}{p}$ for some r. Previous empirical studies indicate that $r < R_{ie}$ is often the case [9].

From the above discussion, one can see that it is quite complicated, and likely quite time-consuming, to measure speculation overhead and to compare it against inspector/executor overhead at run-time. Thus, it is desirable to devise a run-time scheme to choose between the two parallelization techniques without explicit estimation of their overhead. On the other hand, based on the above discussions, a basic adaptive scheme can be based on the following assumptions.

- A speculation scheme has a lower overhead than an inspector/executor scheme if the candidate loop is a dynamically fully parallelizable loop.
- An inspector/executor scheme has a lower overhead than a speculation scheme if the candidate loop is a dynamically undeterminable loop or partially parallelizable loop.

In the next section, we discuss an implementation of such an adaptive scheme. We also discuss certain circumstances in which the basic assumptions may not hold and how we can extend the scheme to a more sophisticated one.

## 3   The Paradigm of Adaptive Dynamic Parallelization

Though there are many dynamic parallelization techniques, like Zhu-Yew's scheme [15], LRPD test [9] and Softspec [2] etc, the inspector/executor and speculation are two general schemes. Lots of work show they can enhance a parallelizing compiler to gain good performance for some specific applications which cannot be parallelized statically due to dynamic features. However, a parallelizing compiler cannot statically determine whether or not to apply these schemes and which scheme is better for the dynamic parallelization, and currently there is no published work solving this problem. It is a critical decision for parallelizing compiler using an inspector/executor scheme or speculation scheme(whether or not to parallelize a specific loop dynamically), because the overhead of the two schemes are different for a specific loop and the features of candidate loops are also different. From the discussion of the previous section, in most cases, if a loop is fully parallelizable, it will have lower overhead using the speculation scheme than the inspector/executor scheme. However, if a loop cannot be fully parallelized, speculation will fail, and it need restore the modified shared variables and re-execute the loop sequentially. Thus the inspector/executor scheme will have lower overhead than speculation. In dynamic applications, most of the crucial candidate loops have more than one invocation, and the loop behavior is similar in different invocations or in some neighbor invocations. Thus we can predict the loop behavior and determine the exploitation of inspector/executor or speculation scheme dynamically. Table 1 illustrates the number of invocations of parallelizable loops in some dynamic applications.

| Loops | number of invocations |
|---|---|
| Loop 10 in mosfet of SPICE | 631 |
| Loop 10 in mxmult of DYFESM | 11011 |
| Loop 300 in nlfilt of TRACK | 55 |
| Loop 400 in extend of TRACK | 55 |
| Loop 17 in preseq of RELAP5 | 3433 |

**Table 1.** The number of invocations of some dynamically parallelizable loops

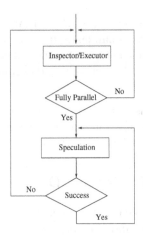

**Fig. 1.** Basic adaptive scheme for dynamic parallelization

Figure 1 illustrates our basic organization of an adaptive scheme for dynamic parallelization. In the first invocation of a candidate loop that cannot be parallelized statically, we apply the inspector/executor scheme to the candidate loop to attempt dynamic parallelization. If we know it is a dynamically fully parallelizable loop after applying the inspector/executor scheme, we apply the speculation scheme to it for the next invocation because the loop more likely has similar behavior in the neighbor invocations. Otherwise, it's a partially parallelizable or dynamically undeterminable loop, and we still apply the inspector/executor scheme to it in the next invocation because the speculation will more possibly fail and may have higher overhead. After the switch from inspector/executor scheme to speculation scheme, the speculation scheme will continue as long as it succeeds. When it fails the speculation scheme switches back to inspector/executor scheme in the next invocation. There will definitely be sequential loops, so after we try several invocations of the loop without gaining any parallelism, we should terminate the attempts to dynamically parallelize the loop. For example, after we try 3 consecutive invocations of inspector/executor scheme without parallelism, we'll execute the loop sequentially in the remain invocations.

Based on our preliminary results, we are optimistic that our basic adaptive scheme which integrates the inspector/executor scheme and speculation scheme can be both general and efficient for dynamic parallelization. In common cases, the speculation scheme should achieve better performance than the inspector/executor scheme if the candidate loop is a fully parallelizable loop, otherwise, the inspector/executor scheme should have lower overhead than the speculation scheme. However, in some cases, this criterion is incorrect as we discussed in section 2. For example, the overhead of conventional speculation techniques applied to sparse applications will be extremely high even if the loop is fully parallelizable, because the speculation wastes much time on the checkpointing, initialization and computation of shadow structures for dependence analysis, while the useful computation refers only a small fraction of the original array. In this case, the inspector/executor scheme will have better performance compared with the speculation scheme. Another example is from loop 17 in subroutine PRESEQ of RELAP5, the granularity of computation on the modified array elements is not big enough, so the overhead of checkpointing in the speculation scheme will outweigh the benefits of speculation, making the inspector/executor scheme the better choice. A sophisticated adaptive scheme should consider these cases. We extend our basic adaptive scheme by adding dynamic performance analysis in the sequential execution,inspector/executor execution and speculation execution and choose the proper scheme with best performance adaptively as figure 2 shows.

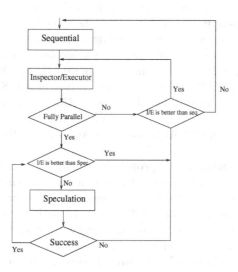

**Fig. 2.** Extended adaptive scheme

The performance analysis dynamically collects the computation quantity of the original codes(excluding the overhead of dynamic parallelization) and consumed CPU time in each invocation of the loop. The computation quantity can be achieved by dynamic granularity analysis which is a compiler aided interprocedural analysis augmented with summation insertion in the branch statements, i.e., the compiler computes the granularity for each basic block and inserts statement to collect the granularity in each branch statement. We define the performance as the ratio of computation quantity to CPU time and average the performance of each scheme by the formula $P_i = \lambda P_{i-1} + (1 - \lambda)Performance$ in which $\lambda$ is an averaging factor chosen between 0 and 1. Currently we choose $\lambda$ as 0.5 in our experiment. However, how to choose $\lambda$ for the best prediction is still under way for our future work. After we have tried all the sequential execution, inspector/executor scheme and speculation scheme, we can decide which scheme is the best for the next invocation of the candidate loop according to the comparison of their averaged performance, not just according to the success or failure of the speculation.

# 4    Some Techniques to Enhance the Capability of Speculation and Inspector/Executor

## 4.1    Dynamic Range Test

Some features of dynamic programs can greatly reduce the overhead of dynamic parallelization. We introduce an overhead reducing technique using the monotonous references information, i.e., the addresses of read or write references increase or decrease monotonously in a loop [5]. According to our empirical study, we found that many dynamic applications have this kind feature. For example, the Perfect Benchmark program SPICE has the monotonous references in most of its loops, and in the most time consuming loop (loop 10 in subroutine MOS-FET) all the read and write references are monotonous except the reduction references. In another Perfect Benchmark program DYFESM, the write region MX(PPTR(ISS)+1:PPTR(ISS)+IBLEN(ISS)), in which ISS is the loop index, is critical to parallelize loop 10 in subroutine MXMULT which is the most time consuming loop, and PPTR(ISS) increases monotonously with constant stride. The nuclear application RELAP5 also has many loops with monotonous references.

Under the observation in real programs: in parallel loops different iterations usually access adjacent array ranges, static range test can handle array subscripts with symbolic expression [1]. Based on the monotony feature, our dynamic range test can efficiently determine the parallelization of the loops with all monotonous references, and it has lower overhead compared with other dynamic dependence tests because it need less temporary memory(shadow structures) and computation for the analysis of shadow structures. Figure 3 shows the algorithm of our dynamic range test. In the algorithm description, we focus on the references of a shared array A which cannot be analyzed at compile time.

In the inspector phase, the computation of MAX_r,MIN_r,MAX_w and MIN_w references can be executed concurrently, but the comparing should be sequential. The executor runs the original loop sequentially or concurrently according to the dependence test result in the inspector. Though we illustrate our dynamic range test in the inspector/executor scheme, we can implement the method with the speculation scheme, i.e., we add the computation of MAX_r,MIN_r,MAX_w and MIN_w references in the speculative execution of the doall loop then do the comparing after the speculative execution. If the comparison fails we need restore the modified variables and re-execute the loop sequentially. Although our algorithm is based on loop iterations, we can compute the MAX_r,MIN_r, MAX_w and MIN_w references and do comparing based on processors, i.e., we partition the iteration space into processor number blocks and compute the MAX_r,MIN_r,MAX_w and MIN_w references for each block, then do comparing for blocks.

```
Inspector phase:
isdoall = true
read_is_OK = true
read_is_increase = true
read_is_decrease = true
In each iteration, compute the minimum and maximum address of read references MI
N_r and
MAX_r, also compute the minimum and maximum address of write references MIN_w an
d MAX_w.
/* Check the first two iterations' MIN_w or MAX_w and determine the increase or
decrease
of write references */
if ( MIN_w(1) < MIN_w(2) )
    write_is_increase = true
else
    write_is_increase = false
/* Compare the i'th iteration with i−1'th iteration for references overlap */
for ( i=2, n ) {
  If (write_is_increase) {
    if ( MIN_w(i) <= MAX_w(i−1) )
        isdoall = false
    if ( MIN_r(i) <= MAX_r(i−1) )
        read_is_increase = false
    if ( read_is_increase )
        if ( not(MAX_r(i−1) < MIN_w(i) and MAX_w(i−1) < MIN_r(i)) )
            read_is_OK = false
    else
        read_is_OK = false
  }
  else {
    if ( MAX_w(i) >= MIN_w(i−1) )
        isdoall = false
    if ( MAX_r(i) >= MIN_r(i−1) )
        read_is_decrease = false
    if ( read_is_decrease )
        if ( not(MIN_r(i−1) > MAX_w(i) and MIN_w(i−1) > MAX_r(i)) )
            read_is_OK = false
    else
        read_is_OK = false
  }
}
if ( isdoall and ( not read_is_OK ) ) {
    MIN_w = min( MIN_w(i) ) i=1...n
    MAX_w = max( MAX_w(i) ) i=1...n
    MIN_r = min( MIN_r(i) ) i=1...n
    MAX_r = max( MAX_r(i) ) i=1...n
    if ( not(MAX_r < MIN_w or MIN_r > MAX_w) ) isdoall = false
}

Executor phase:
if ( isdoall )
    run parallel version
else
    run sequential version
```

**Fig. 3.** The algorithm of dynamic range test

## 4.2   Partial Reduction

Reduction operation is common in scientific applications and critical for parallelization in some applications. Much work has been done in this field, and the LRPD test is the representative in dynamic parallelization [6,12]. However, in the case of sparse programs the normal reduction parallelization may not gain any enhancement because the loop updates only a small fraction of the reduction array and the parallelization consumes lots of memory and traversal time to privatize the reduction array and perform the reduction operation across processors. Though hashing reduction is a solution to the reduction operations in some sparse codes, the overhead of constructing a hash table may be too high to profit the parallelization [12]. Especially in some scientific applications like SPICE and RELAP5, a large common array is defined and many other arrays are equivalent to this array. Although the number of references in a loop is sparse compared with the entire array space, it may not be sparse in the references region of the loop. For example, in loop 10 of subroutine MOSFET in SPICE, the reduction operations refer about 500 elements of array VALUE defined with 200000 elements. However, the minimum address of reduction references is lvn which is a loop invariant and the maximum address of reduction references is lvn+590. This reduction array is certainly not sparse in a local sense since 500 references fall in a space of 590 elements.

We extend our dynamic range test by separating the computation of maximum and minimum address of reduction references, MAX_reduction and MIN_reduction, from other read and write references. In the comparing phase, we need make sure there is no overlap between the reduction references and other read write references, then perform the reduction operation on the array elements from MIN_reduction to MAX_reduction of the array subscripts. We can use the span of references region and the number of references in the loop to compute the local sparseness of the loop, and according to the local sparseness we can decide which method is beneficial from the partial reduction and hashing reduction.

## 4.3   Extended Reduction Recognition

In the normal reduction operations, the initializations of the reduction array elements are prior to the loop of the reduction. However, in the Perfect Benchmark program DYFESM, some initializations are in the same loop with the reduction operations. So the conventional reduction recognition methods couldn't be applied to this program. Our method can combine with the LRPD test to speculatively execute the loop as a doall loop, i.e., execute all its iterations concurrently and apply a run-time test to check if there were any cross-iteration dependences. If the run-time test fails, we will pay a penalty in that we need to backtrack and re-execute the loop sequentially. Next we'll focus our analysis on reduction recognition. We extend the reduction pattern as figure 4 shows. In the loop body, EXP is an expression without the reference of array A. To parallelize the loop, we need guarantee that S1 has no cross-iteration output dependence with itself, and there's no overlap between the reference sets in S1 and S2 for conventional reduction recognition. However, if the reference sets in S1 and S2 do overlap like loop 10 in MXMULT of DYFESM, we need extend the reduction recognition to make sure that the reference of each element of array A in S1 must occur before that in S2 for the parallelization. We present the extended reduction recognition below.

1. Marking Phase. This phase is performed during the speculative parallel execution of the loop. For array A[1:m], we declare write and reduction shadow arrays WA[1:m,1:p] and RDA[1:m,1:p] respectively(p is the number of processors). They both initialize to 0. RDA records the first iteration in which the relative reference occurred, and WA records the last iteration in which the relative reference occurred.

2. Analysis Phase. This phase is performed after the speculative parallel execution. For each element A(i), the LRPD test guarantees that the write of A(i) in S1 is referred at most once if the loop can be parallelized. However, the reduction reference of A(i) may be referred many times, so we need to get its minimum iteration number $RDA'(i) = min(RDA(i,j))$  $j = 1...p$. For each nonzero element of $RDA'$, we compare the value in $RDA'$ with that in $WA$. If there exist such a pair $WA[i]$ and $RDA'[i]$, $RDA'[i] \neq 0$ and $RDA'[i] < WA[i]$, then the reduction parallelization is invalid and we need to re-execute the loop sequentially, otherwise, the speculative parallel execution is correct.

```
        DO I = 1, N
   S1     A(K(I)) = ...
   S2     A(L(I)) = A(L(I)) + EXP
        ENDDO
```

**Fig. 4.** Extended reduction pattern

## 4.4   Inspector/Executor Scheme for Crucial Loop Variables

This method deals with the crucial loop variables which will restrict the parallelization if we cannot know their values in the beginning of each iteration concurrently, and it can only be implemented with the inspector/executor scheme. In the inspector phase, we compute the value of these kind of variables for each iteration and record them in a newly declared array, then do the data dependence test and determine whether the loop can be parallelized. In the executor phase, we execute the original loop sequentially or concurrently according to the inspector result. Because the inspector need execute the loop sequentially for the computation of the crucial variables' value, to reduce overhead we should try to exclude the statements which do not relate to the computation of those crucial loop variables in the loop body. Figure 5 shows an example loop with a crucial loop variable IND. If we cannot know its value in each iteration concurrently, we cannot parallelize the loop. We apply loop fission to split the loop into two loops.

In the first loop, we compute the value of the crucial loop variable IND in each iteration. It is a sequential loop and it only contains the necessary statements relating to the computation of the crucial loop variable IND. After we compute the value of the loop variable IND in each iteration, we can execute the original loop sequentially or concurrently according to the dependence test result in the inspector.

```
DO I = 1, N
    IF ( A(I) .GT. 0 ) THEN
        IND = IND + 1
    ELSE IF ( A(I) .LT. 0 ) THEN
        IND = IND + 2
    ENDIF
    B(IND) = ....
    C(IND) = ....
ENDDO
```

**Fig. 5.** A loop with crucial loop variable IND

To implement our method in a parallelizing compiler, we assume the compiler can identify the crucial loop variables in static analysis. Because we need to execute the inspector sequentially, the overhead of the inspector may outweigh the benefits of parallelism. If so, our method will gain nothing, or it may even degrade the performance. So the compiler needs to compare the computation of these variables and that of the entire loop to decide whether it should exploit this method.

## 5    Experimental Results

We apply our adaptive dynamic parallelization scheme and these techniques to four applications. Though we parallelize these applications manually, we believe our adaptive scheme and techniques can be implemented in a parallelizing compiler to obtain the same performance automatically. Table 2 shows which techniques are used to parallelize the critical loops in these applications dynamically. We obtain the experimental results on an SGI origin 2000 with 32 R10K CPUs, and we use the SGI MIPSpro f77 compiler with automatic parallelization switch -pfa for comparison. When we test our manual parallel version, we only use the switch -mp without any optimization options. Because RELAP5 is a large application, it is difficult to get precise result if we test loop 17 of subroutine PRESEQ in the original program, so we extract the loop as a test program and expand the iteration space.

Table 3 shows the speedups of the two schemes, inspector/executor and speculation, applied to the loops in which most of them are critical loops in the test program except loop 17 in PRESEQ of RELAP5. Most of the loops have apparent speedup except loop 400 in EXTEND of TRACK. That is because of

| Program | Dynamic Range Test | Partial Reduction | Extended Reduction | Crucial Loop Variable |
|---------|:---:|:---:|:---:|:---:|
| SPICE | √ | √ | | |
| DYFESM | √ | | √ | |
| TRACK | √ | | | √ |
| RELAP5 | √ | | | |

**Table 2.** The techniques used to parallelize 4 dynamic programs.

| Loops | Speculation | Inspector/Executor |
|-------|:---:|:---:|
| Loop 10 in mosfet of SPICE | 1.52 | 1.75 |
| Loop 10 in mxmult of DYFESM | 2.83 | 2.76 |
| Loop 300 in nlfilt of TRACK | 2.76 | 0.71 |
| Loop 400 in extend of TRACK | N/A | 0.75 |
| Loop 17 in preseq of RELAP5 | 2.53 | 3.50 |

**Table 3.** The speedups of two schemes applied to some critical loops on 4 processors

the overhead of the inspector and the small granularity of parallelism. In fact, when we parallelize loop 400 in subroutine EXTEND of TRACK, we need to execute more than half of the statements in the loop body for computation of the crucial loop variables, and we also need to backup and restore some arrays modified in the inspector. However, under our extended adaptive dynamic parallelization scheme, the performance degradation will not occur because it will terminate the dynamic parallelization after several trials without parallelism. And the speedups of these loops are near the higher speedups of the speculation execution and the inspector/executor execution because the adaptive scheme always selects the scheme with better performance to execute the next invocation of the candidate loop.

| Program | Basic Adapt. | Extended Adapt. | Speculation | Inspector/Executor | PFA | SUIF |
|---------|:---:|:---:|:---:|:---:|:---:|:---:|
| SPICE | 1.21 | 1.26 | 1.21 | 1.28 | N/A | N/A |
| DYFESM | 1.59 | 1.59 | 1.61 | 1.60 | 0.9 | 0.9 |
| TRACK | 1.33 | 1.31 | 1.33 | 0.74 | 1.0 | 0.9 |
| Average | 1.38 | 1.39 | 1.38 | 1.21 | 0.95 | 0.9 |

**Table 4.** The speedup of entire program on 4 processors

Table 4 shows the speedup of the three Perfect Benchmark programs parallelized by the PFA,SUIF and different dynamic parallelization schemes. In our manual parallelization, we apply the dynamic parallelization schemes only to the critical loops as table 3 shows excluding loop 400 in extend of TRACK. Our extended adaptive scheme has the best average performance compared with other schemes and parallelizing compilers. The SUIF speedup is from [14], and was tested on a DEC8400 with 4 alpha 21164 350MHz CPUs. We get the PFA speedup on the same platform as our manual speedup. Our speedup of SPICE is not good on the SGI origin 2000, however on a SUN SPARC machine with 4 processors, our speedup can reach 1.5 for the entire program. Figure 6 illustrates our dynamic range test achieved speedups scaling fairly well with the number of processors, and the performance of speculation without checkpointing is better than that of the inspector/executor scheme, however speculation with checkpointing is worse than the inspector/executor scheme. That is because the overhead of checkpointing outweighs the benefits of speculation, i.e., the granularity of the computation on the modified variables is not big enough to apply the speculation scheme. Our extended adaptive scheme will identify this situation according to the dynamic performance analysis and will switch back from the speculation scheme to the inspector/executor scheme even the speculation succeeds. We extracted loop 17 in PRESEQ of RELAP5, which has quite a few loops like this, and simplified some data references without losing the essence of the original loop. Figure 7 compares the performance of our dynamic range test with that of the LRPD test on loop 300 of subroutine NLFILT in TRACK, both implemented with the speculation scheme.

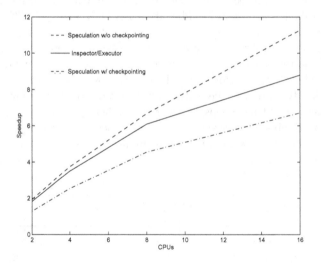

**Fig. 6.** Inspector/Executor and speculation speedup of Loop Relap_Preseq_17

## 6   Related Work

Since the advent of research interest in dynamic parallelization in the early 1990's, several schemes have been proposed. In general, the inspector/executor scheme and the speculation scheme are the most popular. J. Saltz [10] proposed

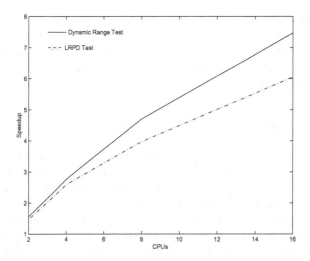

**Fig. 7.** Dynamic Range test and LRPD test speedup of Loop TRACK_NLFILT_300

an effective iteration-level inspector/executor scheme for loops without output dependences. The inspector partitions the iteration space into subsets which maintain the cross-iteration flow dependences, then the executor runs the iterations in the same subset concurrently and runs the different subsets in order. Zhu and Yew's scheme [15] integrates the dependence test and scheduling into the executor and has a fully parallel executor, but the memory requirement is very high. Midkiff and Padua [7] improved Zhu-Yew's scheme by allowing concurrent reads to the same array element in several iterations, however, the requirement of high communication is same as Zhu-Yew's scheme. Chen [3] advanced the scheme by decoupling the dependence test and the executor. The separation of the inspector and executor not only reduces the overhead of synchronization in the executor, but also provides the possibility of reusing the dependence information developed in the inspector across multiple invocations of the same loop. Rauchwerger and Padua's LRPD test [9] is a speculation scheme. Instead of distributing the loop into inspector and executor loops, it speculatively executes the loop as doall and applies a run-time test to check the cross-iteration dependences. It also does privatization and reduction recognition dynamically. However, it needs much extra memory for shadow arrays and the computation on these shadow arrays, and it cannot deal with the reduction with prior write references. Yu and Rauchwerger's adaptive reduction parallelization [12] characterizes the reference pattern and chooses the appropriate method for reduction parallelization dynamically. Currently, Bruening et.[2] presented software-based speculative parallelization which can dynamically parallelize loops with stride-predictable memory references. In their method the overhead of dependence test at run-time is lower, but the capability of parallelization is restricted because it only work with the constant stride memory references. Actually, it cannot be applied to any application we mentioned in our experimental results section because none of them always has constant stride memory references. In [11],Voss presents a compiler-supported high-level adaptive optimization system which applies the optimizations dynamically at run-time, but he does not address the dynamic parallelization.

## 7   Conclusions

In this paper, we present an adaptive dynamic parallelization scheme which integrates an inspector/executor scheme and a speculation scheme. Our adaptive scheme dynamically switches between the inspector/executor scheme and speculation scheme to enhance the capability of parallelizing compilers while reducing the overhead of dynamic parallelization. We have also proposed some dynamic parallelization techniques which can efficiently parallelize some applications and be implemented with our adaptive scheme to enhance a parallelizing compiler. Experimental results show our techniques can efficiently parallelize some Perfect Benchmark programs SPICE, DYFESM and TRACK, and some loops in nuclear application RELAP5.

## References

1. William Blume and Rudolf Eigenmann. *Non-Linear and Symbolic Data Dependence Testing*. IEEE Trans. on Parallel and Distributed Systems, Vol.9,No.12,pages 1180-1194, December 1998.
2. Derek Bruening, Srikrishna Devabhaktuni, and Saman Amarasinghe. *Softspec: Software-based Speculative Parallelism*. 3rd ACM Workshop on Feedback-Directed and Dynamic Optimization (FDDO-3), December 10, 2000, Monterey, California.
3. D. K. Chen, J. Torrellas, and P. C. Yew. *An Efficient Algorithm for the Run-Time Parallelization of Do-Across Loops*. In Supercomputing' 94, pp518-527, November 1994.
4. Manish Gupta and Rahul Nim. *Techniques for Speculative Run-Time Parallelization of Loops*. Proceedings of SC'98: High Performance Networking and Computing Conference, November 1998.
5. M. Gupta,S. Mukhopadhyay, N. Sinha. *Automatic Parallelization of Recursive Procedures*. Proceedings of International Conference on Parallel Architectures and Compilation Techniques (PACT), October 1999.
6. Hwansoo Han and Chau-Wen Tseng. *A Comparison of Parallelization Techniques for Irregular Reductions*. 15th International Conference on Parallel and Distributed Computing(IPDPS'01), San Francisco, CA, April 2001.
7. S. Midkiff and D. Padua. *Compiler algorithms for synchronization*. IEEE Trans. on Computers, C-36(12), December 1987.
8. L. Rauchwerger. *Run-Time Parallelization: It's Time Has Come*. Journal of Parallel Computing, Special Issue on Languages and Compilers for Parallel Computers, 24(3-4), 1998, pp527-556.
9. L. Rauchwerger and D. Padua. The *LRPD Test: Speculative run-time parallelization of loops with privatization and reduction parallelization*. IEEE Trans. on Parallel and Distributed Systems, 10(2) pp160-1 80, February 1999.

10. J. Saltz, R. Mirchandaney, and K. Crowley. *Run-time parallelization and scheduling of loops*. IEEE Trans. Comput., 40(5), May 1991.
11. Michael J. Voss and Rudolf Eigenmann. *High-Level Adaptive Program Optimization with ADAPT*. In Proc. of PPOPP'01, Symposium on Principles and Practice of Parallel Programming, 2001.
12. Hao Yu and L. Rauchwerger. *Adaptive Reduction Parallelization*. Proceedings of the ACM 14th International Conference on Supercomputing, Santa Fe, NM, May 2000.
13. Hao Yu and L. Rauchwerger. *Techniques for Reducing the Overhead of Run-time Parallelization*. Proc. of the 9th Int. Conference on Compiler Construction, Berlin, Germany, March 2000.
14. Binyu Zang. *Constructing the Parallelizing Compiler AFT*. PhD thesis, Fudan University, P.R. China, April 1999.
15. C.-Q. Zhu and P.-C. Yew. *A synchronization scheme and its application for large multiprocessor systems*. In 4th Int. Conf. on Distributed Computing Systems, pp486-493, May 1984.

# Probabilistic Points-to Analysis*

Yuan-Shin Hwang[1], Peng-Sheng Chen[2], Jenq Kuen Lee[2], and Roy Dz-Ching Ju[3]

[1] Department of Computer Science
National Taiwan Ocean University
Keelung 202 Taiwan
[2] Department of Computer Science
National Tsing Hua University
Hsinchu 300 Taiwan
[3] Microprocessor Research Lab.
Intel Corporation
Santa Clara, CA 95052 U.S.A

**Abstract.** Information gathered by the existing pointer analysis techniques can be classified as *must* aliases or *definitely*-points-to relationships, which hold for all executions, and *may* aliases or *possibly*-points-to relationships, which might hold for some executions. Such information does not provide quantitative descriptions to tell how likely the conditions will hold for the executions, which are needed for modern compiler optimizations, and thus has hindered compilers from more aggressive optimizations. This paper addresses this issue by proposing a probabilistic points-to analysis technique to compute the probability of each points-to relationship. Initial experiments are done by incorporating the probabilistic data flow analysis algorithm into SUIF and MachSUIF, and preliminary experimental results show the probability distributions of points-to relationships in several benchmark programs. This work presents a major enhancement for pointer analysis to keep up with modern compiler optimizations.

## 1 Introduction

There have been considerable efforts on pointer analysis by researchers [1, 4, 6, 7, 8, 12, 17, 18, 20, 22, 24, 25]. They have proposed various algorithms to compute either aliases or points-to relationships at program points. They categorize aliases or points-to relationships into two classes: *must* aliases or *definitely*-points-to relationships, which hold for all executions, and *may* aliases or *possibly*-points-to relationships, which might hold for some executions. However, the information gathered by these algorithms based on this classification does not provide the quantitative descriptions needed for modern compiler optimizations, e.g. data speculation, data prefetching, etc., and thus has hindered compilers from more aggressive optimizations. Neither *may* aliases nor *possibly*-points-to relationships can tell how likely the conditions will hold for the executions,

* The work was supported in part by NSC of Taiwan under grant no. NSC-89-2213-E-019-019, NSC-90-2213-E-019-016, NSC-89-2218-E-007-023, NSC-89-2219-E-007-012, and MOE research excellent project under grant no. 89-E-FA04-1-4.

H. Dietz (Ed.): LCPC 2001, LNCS 2624, pp. 290–305, 2003.

and consequently compilers have to make a conservative guess and assume the conditions hold for all executions. This paper addresses this issue by proposing a *probabilistic points-to analysis* approach to give a quantitative description for each points-to relationship to represent the probability that it holds.

Useful optimizations and transformations can be performed if it is known that certain alias or points-to relationships hold with high or low probabilities. One application is to guide data speculation on advanced architectures. For example, IA-64 [5], which relies on static scheduling, may provide hardware support for speculative motion of loads across possibly aliasing stores. This allows the loads to be executed early but with potentially incorrect values. The hardware in conjunction with software provides a recovery mechanism to recover from any mis-speculation. This feature allows a compiler to generate optimal code by breaking memory dependences, which are often on performance critical paths. However, a mis-speculation on such architecture typically incurs a large recovery penalty. Therefore, to properly guide data speculation, it is important for a compiler to derive the aliasing probability for a pair of data speculation candidates (i.e. a load and a store) and compare an amortized recovery cost with the benefit of a 'good' speculation. A probabilistic memory disambiguation approach was proposed for numeric applications [11]. However, the problem remains open for pointer-induced memory references.

```
foo(int a, int b, int c) {
    int *p; ...
    p = ..
    if( a < b ) { p = &c; }
    st  c = ..;
    ld  = *p
}
```

Above is an example of using aliasing probability to guide data speculation. Before the if-clause, p does not point to c, but it does so in the clause. After the if-clause, a store to c is followed by a load from *p. Assume that the load is on a critical path, and hence a compiler wants to schedule the load before the store. However, since *p may alias with c, a compiler would not be able to do so without a support like data speculation (or alternatively some code duplication). The compiler must be able to estimate the aliasing probability between the load and the store and hence how often p points to c. If the amortized recovery cost outweighs the benefit of the shortened critical path after moving the load across the store, this data speculation is unprofitable and should not be performed.

Another application will be optimizations for pointer-based objects on distributed shared memory parallel machines. With affinity analysis [3] and data distribution analysis [13], the advanced analyzer will be able to know or estimate which processor an object is resided in. For task allocations, the optimizer will attempt to assign the processor that owns most of the objects for that task for executions. For programs employing pointer usages, a pointer will be pointing to a set of objects with may-aliases. Therefore, the ability for the analyzer to be able to tell the probability of the aliasing objects for a pointer reference will help the analyzer calculate the amortized amount of objects a processor owns for a task execution.

Probabilistic points-to analysis can be applied to compiler optimizations with memory hierarchies as well. Suppose a pointer, $p$, points to a set of may-aliasing objects.

With the limited amount of the fast memory and working set, only the objects among the aliased objects with high probabilities should be brought into the faster memory of the memory hierarchies. In that case, we should use the information gathered during the probabilistic points-to analysis to have the one with higher probability. In general, the probabilistic points-to information help the compilers to estimate an amortized cost for object placements among memory hierarchies.

This paper proposes a probabilistic points-to analysis approach to address these open issues by giving quantitative descriptions which represent the probabilities that points-to relationships might hold. A probabilistic data flow analysis framework is presented for the probabilistic points-to analysis. In this framework, transfer functions are first computed to identify the probabilities each points-to relationship will be generated and preserved respectively, and then the probabilities of each points-to relationship that might hold at program points will be computed from the transfer functions. This work, to the authors' best knowledge, is the first algorithm for probabilistic points-to analysis. Initial experiments are done by incorporating the intraprocedural probabilistic points-to analysis algorithm into SUIF [9] and MachSUIF [21]. Preliminary experimental results reporting the probability distributions of probabilistic points-to relationships will be given as well.

## 2    Probabilistic Points-to Analysis

### 2.1    Problem Specifications

The goal of probabilistic points-to analysis is to compute at every program point the probability of each points-to relationship that might hold. For each points-to relationship, say that $p$ points to $v$, denoted as a tuple $(p, v)$, it computes the probability that pointer $p$ points to $v$ at every program point during the program execution. In other words, a *probabilistic points-to relationship* $(p, v, P)$ is computed for each points-to relationship $(p, v)$ at every program point, where $P$ is the probability that $(p, v)$ holds. When $P$ is equal to 1, the points-to relationship $(p, v)$ always holds every time the program point is visited. On the other hand, if $P$ is equal to 0, then $p$ will never points to $v$ at this program point. Consequently, if $P$ is between 0 and 1, $p$ will point to $v$ at some instances when the program control reaches the program point, while $p$ will not point to $v$ at other instances.

**The Domain**  The probability $P$ of each probabilistic points-to relationship $(p, v, P)$ at a program point $s$ can be defined as follows:

$$P = \frac{E(s, (p, v))}{E(s)}$$

where $E(s)$ is the number of times $s$ is expected to be visited during program execution and $E(s, (p, v))$ denotes the number of times the points-to relationship $(p, v)$ holds at $s$ [15]. Consequently, all the possible values of $P$ for each probabilistic points-to relationship will be the real numbers ranging from 0 to 1. In addition, before the probability $P$ is computed, it is set as $\perp$, and hence the domain of $P$ will be

$$Domain(P) = \{p \mid p \in [0, 1] \vee p = \perp\}$$

**Program Representations**    Programs will be represented by control flow graphs (CFGs) whose edges are labeled with a static assigned execution frequency [15, 23] or an actual frequency from profiling. An empty node will be added at the entry of every loop as the *header* node, while an empty node will be augmented as the header node and an empty node as the *join* node.

**Meet Operator** ⊓    Although the domain of the probabilistic points-to analysis is not a semilattice, the notion of *meet* operations is used to represent the actions of merging values at join nodes. Suppose the probabilities that the points-to relationship $(p, v)$ holds at the program point right after $B_1$ and $B_2$ in the control flow graph shown in Figure 1 are $P_1$ and $P_2$, respectively. In other words, $(p, v, P_1) \in OUT_{B_1}$ and $(p, v, P_2) \in OUT_{B_2}$, where $OUT_{B_1}$ and $OUT_{B_2}$ are the sets of probabilistic points-to relationships at the program points right after $B_1$ and $B_2$. Then the possibility $P$ that the points-to relationship $(p, v)$ holds at the join node will be

$$P = \frac{P_1 \cdot E(B_1) + P_2 \cdot E(B_2)}{E(B_1) + E(B_2)}$$

where $E(B_1)$ and $E(B_2)$ are the numbers of times $B_1$ and $B_2$ are expected to be visited during program execution. Consequently, the probabilistic points-to relationship $(p, v, P)$ at the join node can be computed by the following the meet operation:

$$(p, v, P) = E(B_1) \cdot (p, v, P_1) \sqcap E(B_2) \cdot (p, v, P_2) = (p, v, \frac{P_1 \cdot E(B_1) + P_2 \cdot E(B_2)}{E(B_1) + E(B_2)})$$

where the scalar multiplication operator '·' over probabilistic points-to relationships is defined as

$$E(B_1) \cdot (p, v, P_1) \stackrel{def}{=} (p, v, E(B_1) \cdot P_1)$$

Furthermore, the meet operation on $OUT_{B_1}$ and $OUT_{B_2}$ can be defined:

$$OUT_{B_1} \sqcap OUT_{B_2} = \{E(B_1) \cdot (p, v, P_1) \sqcap E(B_2) \cdot (p, v, P_2) \,|$$
$$(p, v, P_1) \in OUT_{B_1} \wedge (p, v, P_2) \in OUT_{B_2}\}$$

$$\bot \sqcap \bot = \bot$$
$$P_1 \sqcap \bot = \bot$$
$$\bot \sqcap P_2 = \bot$$
$$P_1 \sqcap P_2 = P \equiv \frac{P_1 \cdot E(B_1) + P_2 \cdot E(B_2)}{E(B_1) + E(B_2)}$$

**Fig. 1.** Meet Operation              **Fig. 2.** Rules for ⊓

The meet operator ⊓ merges the possibilities of each probabilistic points-to relationship of different inedges at a join node. If the possibilities of any incoming probabilistic points-to relationships are unknown, i.e. ⊥, the possibility $P$ at the join node will be computed following the rules for ⊓ operator shown in Figure 2.

### 2.2   Approach

The probabilistic points-to analysis can be formulated as a data flow framework [4, 10, 14]. The data flow framework for the probabilistic points-to analysis includes *transfer functions*, which formulate the effect of statements on probabilistic points-to relationships. Suppose the sets of probabilistic points-to relationships at the program points right before and after $S$ are $IN_S$ and $OUT_S$, respectively. Then the effect of $S$ on probabilistic points-to relationships can be represented by the transfer function $F_S$:

$$OUT_S = F_S\,(IN_S)$$

**Transfer Functions**    For every statement $S$, a transfer function will be computed for each points-to relationship. Therefore, a transfer function $\langle p,\ v,\ P_{gen}(S),\ P_{prv}(S)\rangle$ will be computed at $S$ for the points-to relationship $(p,\ v)$, where $P_{gen}(S)$ and $P_{prv}(S)$ are defined as follows:

- $P_{gen}(S) \equiv$ probability that $(p,\ v)$ will be generated at $S$.
- $P_{prv}(S) \equiv$ probability that $(p,\ v)$ will be preserved at $S$.

where $P_{gen}(S) + P_{prv}(S) \leq 1$. Consequently, the transfer function $F_S$ of statement $S$ consists of the transfer functions for all probabilistic points-to relationships, i.e.

$$F_S = \{\langle p,\ v,\ P_{gen}(S),\ P_{prv}(S)\rangle \mid (p,\ v,\ P_{in}(S)) \in IN_S\}$$

Suppose the probability that the points-to relationship $(p,\ v)$ holds at the program point before $S$ is $P_{in}(S)$, i.e. $(p,\ v,\ P_{in}(S)) \in IN_S$. Then the probabilistic points-to relationship $(p,\ v,\ P_{out}(S))$ holds at the program point after $S$ will be

$$(p,\ v,\ P_{out}(S)) = F_S\,((p,\ v,\ P_{in}(S))) = (p,\ v,\ P_{gen}(S) + P_{in}(S) \cdot P_{prv}(S))$$

where $\langle p,\ v,\ P_{gen}(S),\ P_{prv}(S)\rangle \in F_S$.

**Default Transfer Functions**    The transfer functions that are computed in this paper model how the probabilistic points-to relationships are modified by statements. When a probabilistic points-to relationship, say $(p,\ v,\ P)$, will not be modified by a statement $S$, the transfer function $F_S$ of the statement $S$ will not include the transfer function $\langle p,\ v,\ 0,\ 1\rangle$ for $(p,\ v,\ P)$. Instead, $\langle p,\ v,\ 0,\ 1\rangle$ will be considered as a *default transfer function* of $S$, and hence will not be explicitly listed. For the rest of the paper, when the transfer functions for any probabilistic points-to relationships are not specified, the default transfer functions will be applied.

**Composition of Transfer Functions**    The composition of transfer functions $F_{S_1}$ and $F_{S_2}$ of two contiguous statements $S_1;\ S_2$ can be denoted as $F_{S_1} \circ F_{S_2}$ and is defined as

$$F_{S_1} \circ F_{S_2}\,(x) \overset{def}{=} F_{S_2}(\,F_{S_1}\,(x))$$

Suppose $\langle p,\ v,\ P_{gen}(S_1),\ P_{prv}(S_1)\rangle$ and $\langle p,\ v,\ P_{gen}(S_2),\ P_{prv}(S_2)\rangle$ are the transfer functions of two contiguous statement $S_1;\ S_2$ for the points-to relationship $(p,\ v)$, respectively. That is, $\langle p,\ v,\ P_{gen}(S_1),\ P_{prv}(S_1)\rangle \in F_{S_1}$ and $\langle p,\ v,\ P_{gen}(S_2),$ $P_{prv}(S_2)\rangle \in F_{S_2}$. Then the transfer function of $S_1;\ S_2$ for the points-to relationship $(p,\ v)$ can be computed by the following formula

$$P_{gen}(S_1;\ S_2) = P_{gen}(S_1) \cdot P_{prv}(S_2) + P_{gen}(S_2)$$
$$P_{prv}(S_1;\ S_2) = P_{prv}(S_1) \cdot P_{prv}(S_2)$$

and consequently $\langle p,\ v,\ P_{gen}(S_1;\ S_2),\ P_{prv}(S_1;\ S_2)\rangle \in F_{S_1;\ S_2}$.

**Meet Operator $\sqcap$ of Transfer Functions**   Given transfer functions $F_{B_1}$ and $F_{B_2}$, the merge of $F_{B_1}$ and $F_{B_2}$ is the transfer function $E(B_1) \cdot F_{B_1} \sqcap E(B_2) \cdot F_{B_2}$ which is defined by

$$(E(B_1) \cdot F_{B_1} \sqcap E(B_2) \cdot F_{B_2})(x) \stackrel{def}{=} E(B_1) \cdot F_{B_1}(x) \sqcap E(B_2) \cdot F_{B_2}(x)$$

Therefore, the corresponding transfer functions for each probabilistic points-to relationship in $F_{B_1}$ and $F_{B_2}$ will be merged. Suppose the transfer functions of $F_{B_1}$ and $F_{B_2}$ for the probabilistic points-to relationship $(p, v, P)$ are $\langle p, v, P_{gen}(B_1), P_{prv}(B_1)\rangle$ and $\langle p, v, P_{gen}(B_2), P_{prv}(B_2)\rangle$, respectively. Then the merge of the transfer functions $F_{B_1}$ and $F_{B_2}$ for the probabilistic points-to relationship $(p, v, P)$ will be defined as follows:

$$P_{gen}(E(B_1) \cdot F_{B_1} \sqcap E(B_2) \cdot F_{B_2}) = \frac{P_{gen}(B_1) \cdot E(B_1) + P_{gen}(B_2) \cdot E(B_2)}{E(B_1) + E(B_2)}$$

$$P_{prv}(E(B_1) \cdot F_{B_1} \sqcap E(B_2) \cdot F_{B_2}) = \frac{P_{prv}(B_1) \cdot E(B_1) + P_{prv}(B_2) \cdot E(B_2)}{E(B_1) + E(B_2)}$$

and hence $\langle p, v, P_{gen}(E(B_1) \cdot F_{B_1} \sqcap E(B_2) \cdot F_{B_2}), P_{prv}(E(B_1) \cdot F_{B_1} \sqcap E(B_2) \cdot F_{B_2})\rangle \in E(B_1) \cdot F_{B_1} \sqcap E(B_2) \cdot F_{B_2}$.

**Comparison with Bitvector Data Flow Framework**   The data flow analysis framework proposed in this paper can be called as the *probabilistic data flow analysis framework*, which is adapted from the bitvector data flow analysis framework [14]. As a bitwise transfer function $f$ is computed for every bit of bitvectors with the bitvectors $GEN_f$ and $THRU_f$ in the bitvector data flow analysis framework, where $f$ is defined by bitwise logical operations:

$$f(x) = GEN_f \vee (x \wedge THRU_f)$$

a probabilistic transfer function is computed for every points-to relationship in probabilistic data flow analysis framework. Therefore, the relationships between the transfer functions of these two data flow analysis frameworks are listed in the following table:

|          | $P_{gen}$ | $P_{prv}$ |
|----------|-----------|-----------|
| $GEN_f$  | 1         | 0         |
| $THRU_f$ | 0         | 1         |

The main difference is for every condition the probabilistic data flow analysis framework computes a real number ranging from 0 to 1 as the possibility that the condition might hold, whereas the bitvector data flow analysis framework computes a boolean number either true or false to indicate whether the condition might hold or not.

Similar to the composition of probabilistic transfer functions defined in Section 2.2, the composition $f \circ g$ of bitvector transfer functions $f$ and $g$ is defined by

$$f \circ g(x) \stackrel{def}{=} g(f(x))$$

while the computation of $f \circ g$ can be computed by

$$GEN_{f \circ g} = (GEN_f \wedge THRU_g) \vee GEN_g$$

$$THRU_{f \circ g} = THRU_f \wedge THRU_g$$

## 2.3  Algorithm

The algorithm is adapted from the elimination methods [14, 19]. It performs probabilistic points-to analysis in two phases:

1. Regions are reduced to *abstract CFG nodes* repeatedly to obtain a sequence of *abstract CFGs (ACFGs)* [14]. Their transfer function will be computed during the transformation process and then annotated to the corresponding ACFG nodes.
2. Traverse the sequence of ACFGs to compute the probabilistic points-to relationships at every region using the transfer functions computed in the first phase.

**Basic Pointer Assignment Statements**   Basic pointer assignment statements can be classified into four types: *address-of assignment, copy assignment, load assignment,* and *store assignment* [18]. For every basic pointer assignment of the first three types, i.e. $p = \cdots$, it first kills all the points-to relationships of the pointer $p$, before generating any new points-to relationships. Therefore, it will be semantically equivalent if it is preceded immediately by the statement $p = nil$. Similarly, it will be semantically equivalent if any store assignment $\star p = q$ is preceded immediately by the statement $\star p = nil$. Therefore, programs will be normalized such that each basic pointer assignment of the first three types $p = \cdots$ will be preceded by a $p = nil$ while each store assignment $\star p = q$ will be preceded by a $\star p = nil$. Consequently, in addition to the transfer functions of the four basic types of pointer assignment statements, transfer functions of statement types $p = nil$ and $\star p = q$ will be computed as well.

- $S: p = nil$   Statement $S: p = nil$ kills all the points-to relationships of $p$. Therefore, the transfer function $F_S$ of $S$ is

$$F_S = \{\langle p, \star, 0, 0 \rangle\}$$

where $\star$ is a wildcard character that means that $p$ points to every variable.

- **Address-of Assignment** $S: p = \&q$   Statement $S: p = \&q$ generates a points-to relationship $(p, q)$. Therefore, the transfer function $F_S$ of $S$ for $(p, q)$ will be

$$F_S = \{\langle p, q, 1, 0 \rangle\}$$

while the transfer functions for other points-to relationships are default transfer functions $\langle \neg p, \star, 0, 1 \rangle$, where $\neg p$ represents the pointers other than $p$, and consequently are not listed explicitly.

- **Copy Assignment** $S: p = q$   The copy assignment $S: p = q$ will generate new points-to relationships of $p$ by copying all the points-to relationships of $q$. Consequently, the transfer function $F_S$ of $S$ will be

$$F_S = \{\langle p, v, P, 0 \rangle \mid (q, v, P) \in IN_S\}$$

- **Load Assignment** $S: p = \star q$

$$F_S = \{\langle p, v, \sum_x P_1^x \cdot P_2^x, 0 \rangle \mid \forall_x (q, x, P_1^x) \in IN_S \wedge (x, v, P_2^x) \in IN_S\}$$

- $S$: $\star p = nil$

$$F_S = \{\langle x, \star, 0, 1 - P\rangle \mid (p, x, P) \in IN_S\}$$

- **Store Assignment** $S$: $\star p = q$

$$F_S = \{\langle x, v, P_1 \cdot P_2, 0\rangle \mid (p, x, P_1) \in IN_S \wedge (q, v, P_2) \in IN_S\}$$

Sequence of ACFG Nodes $S_1; S_2; \cdots; S_n$

$$F_{S_1; S_2; \cdots; S_n} = F_{S_1} \circ F_{S_2} \circ \cdots \circ F_{S_n}$$

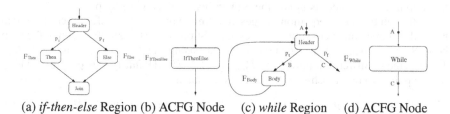

(a) *if-then-else* Region  (b) ACFG Node    (c) *while* Region    (d) ACFG Node

**Fig. 3.** Computing Transfer Functions of *if-then-else* and *while* Regions

*if-then-else* **Construct**    The merge of the $Then$ and $Else$ branches summarizes all paths through the *if-then-else* construct shown in Figure 3(a) and (b).

$$F_{IfThenElse} = p_t \cdot F_{Then} \sqcap p_f \cdot F_{Else}$$

where $F_{Then}$ and $F_{Else}$ are the transfer functions of Then and Else branches respectively while $p_t$ and $p_f$ are the branching probabilities of Then and Else branches respectively and $p_t + p_f = 1$.

Suppose $\langle p, v, P_{gen}(Then), P_{prv}(Then)\rangle$ and $\langle p, v, P_{gen}(Else), P_{prv}(Else)\rangle$ are the transfer functions for the points-to relationship $(p, v)$ at $Then$ and $Else$ branches, respectively. Then the transfer function for $(p, v)$ of the *if-then-else* construct will be $\langle p, v, P_{gen}(IfThenElse), P_{prv}(IfThenElse)\rangle$, where $P_{gen}(IfThenElse)$ and $P_{prv}(IfThenElse)$ can be computed by the follow equations:

$$P_{gen}(IfThenElse) = p_t \cdot P_{gen}(Then) + p_f \cdot P_{gen}(Else)$$
$$P_{prv}(IfThenElse) = p_t \cdot P_{prv}(Then) + p_f \cdot P_{prv}(Else)$$

Once the transfer function of an *if-then-else* construct is computed at the first phase, the sets of probabilistic points-to relationships at program points within the *if-then-else* region can be computed:

$$OUT_{IfThenElse} = F_{IfThenElse}(IN_{IfThenElse})$$
$$IN_{Then} = IN_{IfThenElse}$$
$$IN_{Else} = IN_{IfThenElse}$$

***while* Loops**  Figure 3(c) and (d) depicts the process of summarizing the region of a *while* loop at the first phase. Since a loop can iterate an arbitrary number of times, its transfer function can be defined by the following equation:

$$F_{While} = \prod_{i=0}^{\infty} (p_f \cdot p_t^i) \cdot (F_{Body})^i$$

where $F_{Body}$ is the transfer function of the loop body, while the probability of entering the loop from the header is $p_t$ and the probability of leaving the loop is $p_f$.

Although the above equation merges an infinite number of transfer functions, it can be easily reduced into very simple expressions. Suppose the transfer function of the loop body *Body* for each probabilistic points-to relationship, say $(p, v, P)$, is $\langle p, v, P_g(B), P_p(B) \rangle$, then transfer function $\langle p, v, P_{gen}(While), P_{prv}(While) \rangle \in F_{While}$ of the loop for the points-to relationship $(p, v)$ can be computed:

$$
\begin{aligned}
P_{prv}(While) &= p_f + p_t \cdot P_p(B) \cdot p_f + (p_t \cdot P_p(B))^2 \cdot p_f + \cdots + (p_t \cdot P_p(B))^n \cdot p_f + \cdots \\
&= p_f(1 + p_t \cdot P_p(B) + (p_t \cdot P_p(B))^2 + \cdots + (p_t \cdot P_p(B))^n + \cdots) \\
&= p_f / (1 - p_t \cdot P_p(B)) \\
P_{gen}(While) &= p_t \cdot P_g(B) \cdot (p_f + p_t \cdot P_p(B) \cdot p_f + (p_t \cdot P_p(B))^2 \cdot p_f + \cdots) + \\
&\quad\; p_t^2 \cdot P_g(B) \cdot (p_f + p_t \cdot P_p(B) \cdot p_f + (p_t \cdot P_p(B))^2 \cdot p_f + \cdots) + \cdots + \\
&\quad\; p_t^n \cdot P_g(B) \cdot (p_f + p_t \cdot P_p(B) \cdot p_f + (p_t \cdot P_p(B))^2 \cdot p_f + \cdots) + \cdots \\
&= P_g(B) \cdot P_{prv}(While) \cdot (p_t + p_t^2 + \cdots + p_t^n + \cdots) \\
&= p_t \cdot P_g(B) \cdot P_{prv}(While) / (1 - p_t) \\
&= p_t \cdot P_g(B) \cdot p_f / (1 - p_t \cdot P_p(B)) \cdot (1 - p_t) \\
&= p_t \cdot P_g(B) / (1 - p_t \cdot P_p(B))
\end{aligned}
$$

The first equation computes $P_{prv}(While)$ as the summation of the probabilities that $(p, v)$ is preserved at the loop exit after zero, one, two, $\cdots$ iterations. The second equation specifies that $(p, v)$ will be generated by the loop when it is generated at the first iteration and preserved hereafter or it is generated at the second iteration and preserved hereafter, and so on. It also can be proved that the ranges of $P_{prv}(While)$ and $P_{gen}(While)$ fall between 0 and 1.

Once the transfer function of a *while* loop is computed at the first phase, the sets of probabilistic points-to relationships at program points within the *while* region can be computed

$$OUT_{While} = F_{While}(IN_{While})$$
$$IN_{Body} = F_{Header}(IN_{While})$$

where the function $F_{Header}$ (which summarizes the effects from the program point $A$ to $B$ in Figure 3(c)) is defined as follows:

$$F_{Header} = \prod_{i=0}^{\infty} (p_t \cdot p_t^i) \cdot (F_{Body})^i$$

Suppose the probabilistic points-to relationship $(p, v, P_{in})$ is in $IN_{While}$, then the probabilistic points-to relationship $(p, v, P_{out}) \in OUT_{While}$ can be calculated:

$$(p, v, P_{out}) = F_{While}((p, v, P_{in}))$$
$$= (p, v, \frac{p_f \cdot P_{in} + p_t \cdot P_g(B)}{1 - p_t \cdot P_p(B)})$$

Similarly, $(p, v, P_i) \in IN_{Body}$ can be calculated:

$$(p, v, P_i) = F_{Header}((p, v, P_{in})) = (p, v, \frac{p_f \cdot P_{in} + p_t \cdot P_g(B)}{1 - p_t \cdot P_p(B)})$$

***do-while* or *repeat-until* Loops**    The transfer function of a *do-while* or *repeat-until* loop can be defined by the following equation:

$$F_{DoWhile} = \prod_{i=1}^{\infty} (p_f \cdot p_t^{i-1}) \cdot (F_{Body})^i$$

***for* Loops**    The transfer function of a *for* $(E_{init\_stmt}; E_{cond.}; E_{iteration\_stmt})$ $Body$ loop can be defined by the following equation:

$$F_{For} = F_{E_{init\_stmt}} \circ \prod_{i=0}^{\infty} (p_f \cdot p_t^i) \cdot (F_{Body} \circ F_{E_{iteration\_stmt}})^i$$

**Computing Transitive Transfer Functions**    The transfer functions that are generated by copy, load, and store statements can be called as *transitive transfer functions* since they depends on the sets of probabilistic points-to relationships right before the statements. These transfer functions complicate the process of the probabilistic points-to analysis especially for loops since the sets of probabilistic points-to relationships, which will be computed at the second phase, must be known before transfer functions are generated at the first phase. This problem can be solved by assigning a symbolic probability for each probabilistic points-to relationship at the entry of a loop body. Consider the program shown in Figure 4. The symbolic probabilities $P_1$, $P_2$, $P_3$, and $P_4$ are assigned as the probabilities of the probabilistic points-to relationships for $(p, v, P_1)$, $(p, u, P_2)$, $(q, v, P_3)$, and $(q, u, P_4)$ respectively at the loop entry, i.e. $OUT_{S_3}$. The statement $S_5 : p = q$; generates a set of transitive transfer functions $F_{S_5} = \{\langle p, v, P_3, 0\rangle \langle p, u, P_4, 0\rangle\}$, while $S_7$ generates a set of transitive transfer functions $F_{S_7} = \{\langle q, v, P_1, 0\rangle \langle q, u, P_2, 0\rangle\}$. Consequently, $F_{S_4} = \{\langle p, v, 0.5P_3, 0.5\rangle\langle p, u, 0.5P_4, 0.5\rangle\langle q, v, 0.5P_1, 0.5\rangle\langle q, u, 0.5P_2, 0.5\rangle\}$ will be the transfer function of the loop body. Furthermore, $F_{S_3}$ will be the transfer function of the loop with elements $\langle p, v, 9P_3/11, 2/11\rangle$, $\langle p, u, 9P_4/11, 2/11\rangle$, $\langle q, v, 9P_1/11, 2/11\rangle$, and $\langle q, u, 9P_2/11, 2/11\rangle$.

| Program | $INS_{i}$ | $OUTS_{i}$ | $F_{S_i}$ |
|---|---|---|---|
| $S_1$: p = &v; | | $(p, v, 1)$ | $\langle p, v, 1, 0 \rangle$ |
| $S_2$: q = &u; | $(p, v, 1)$ | $(p, v, 1)\ (q, u, 1)$ | $\langle q, u, 1, 0 \rangle$ |
| $S_3$: while (...) { | $(p, v, 1)\ (q, u, 1)$ | $(p, v, P_1)\ (p, u, P_2)\ (q, v, P_3)\ (q, u, P_4)$ | $\langle p, v, 9P_3/11, 2/11\rangle\ \langle p, u, 9P_4/11, 2/11\rangle$ |
| | | | $\langle q, v, 9P_1/11, 2/11\rangle\ \langle q, u, 9P_2/11, 2/11\rangle$ |
| $S_4$:  if (...) | $(p, v, P_1)\ (p, u, P_2)\ (q, v, P_3)\ (q, u, P_4)$ | $(p, v, P_1)\ (p, u, P_2)\ (q, v, P_3)\ (q, u, P_4)$ | $\langle p, v, 0.5P_3, 0.5\rangle\ \langle p, u, 0.5P_4, 0.5\rangle$ |
| | | | $\langle q, v, 0.5P_1, 0.5\rangle\ \langle q, u, 0.5P_2, 0.5\rangle$ |
| $S_5$:   p = q; | $(p, v, P_1)\ (p, u, P_2)\ (q, v, P_3)\ (q, u, P_4)$ | $(p, v, P_3)\ (p, u, P_4)\ (q, v, P_3)\ (q, u, P_4)$ | $\langle p, v, P_3, 0\rangle\ \langle p, u, P_4, 0\rangle$ |
| $S_6$:  else | | | |
| $S_7$:   q = p; | $(p, v, P_1)\ (p, u, P_2)\ (q, v, P_3)\ (q, u, P_4)$ | $(p, v, P_1)\ (p, u, P_2)\ (q, v, P_1)\ (q, u, P_2)$ | $\langle q, v, P_1, 0\rangle\ \langle q, u, P_2, 0\rangle$ |
| $S_8$: } | | | |

**Fig. 4.** Solving Transitive Transfer Functions

The symbolic probabilities $P_1$, $P_2$, $P_3$, and $P_4$ can be solved by the linear system $OUT_{S_3} = F_{Header}(INS_{S_3})$, where $F_{Header} = \prod_{i=0}^{\infty}(p_t \cdot p_t^i) \cdot (F_{S_4})^i$. The set of probabilistic points-to relationships at the loop entry will be $OUT_{S_3} = \{(p, v, 0.55)\ (p, u, 0.45)\ (q, v, 0.45)\ (q, u, 0.55)\}$ if the branching probabilities are $p_t = 0.9$ and $p_f = 0.1$.

# 3    Experimental Results

## 3.1    Platform and Benchmarks

A prototype compiler has been implemented upon the SUIF system [9] and CFG library of MachSUIF [21] to perform the intraprocedural probabilistic points-to analysis (PPA). Programs are first transformed from the high-SUIF format to the low-SUIF format by SUIF and then represented by CFGs using the CFG library of MachSUIF. The compiler will then traverse the CFGs to compute the probability of each probabilistic points-to relationship at every program point. This section will present the preliminary experimental results of this implementation.

| Program | Procedure | Description |
|---|---|---|
| *reverse* | *InsertElement* | A small program that builds a binary tree and then recursively swaps the left and right children of each node. (McGill [8]) |
| *hash* | *AddToTable* | A program builds a hash table (McGill) |
| *misr* | *create_link_list* | A program creates and uses linked list. (McGill) |
| *queens* | *find* | A program that finds solutions to the eight-queens chess problem. |
| *cq* | *s81* | A test program from lcc-4.0 testsuite. |
| *20000801-2.c* | *test* | Test programs from gcc-3.0 snapshot testsuite |
| *990127-1.c* | *main* | (from directory: c-torture/execute/) |

**Table 1.** Benchmark Programs and Selected Procedures

Several applications have been chosen as the benchmarks and a procedure of each benchmark program has been instrumented, as listed in Table 1. These benchmark programs will then be executed to gather the detailed points-to information of these procedures at runtime. The runtime results will be compared with the following three variations of points-to analysis:

- Probabilistic points-to analysis based on static probabilities (PPA-S)
  A probability will be assigned to each outgoing edge of CFG, say $p_t = p_f = 0.5$ for *if* statements and $p_t = 0.9$ and $p_f = 0.1$ for loops, and the probabilistic points-to analysis algorithm described in Section 2 will be executed based on these edge probabilities.
- Probabilistic points-to analysis based on profiling information (PPA-P)
  The TCOVSUIF profiling tool [2] is used to gather loop counts and branch frequencies, and probabilistic points-to analysis will be performed based on the profiling information to compute the probabilities of points-to relationships in these selected procedures.
- Traditional points-to analysis (TPA)
  The probability of each points-to relationship is assumed to be 1.

The preciseness of these points-to analysis methods respective to the runtime results will be compared by the statistics *average error* $\xi = \sum_{i=1}^{n} |P_{estimated}(i) - P_{runtime}(i)|/n$ and *standard deviation* $\sigma = \sqrt{\sum_{i=1}^{n} (P_{estimated}(i) - P_{runtime}(i))^2/(n-1)}$.

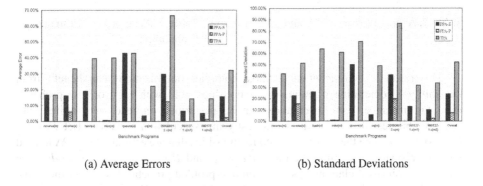

(a) Average Errors                    (b) Standard Deviations

**Fig. 5.** Experimental Results

## 3.2   Results

Figure 5(a) shows the average errors of estimated probabilities of points-to relationships by these methods respective to the profiled frequencies at runtime. At each chosen program point, the estimated probabilities of all points-to relationships will be compared with the profiled probabilities. For example, *reverse(m)* in Figure 5(a) is computed at the middle point (randomly selected) of the instrumented procedure in the program *reverse*, while *reverse(e)* compares the errors at the end of the procedure in *reverse*. Similarly, Figure 5(b) depicts the standard deviations of these points-to analysis techniques respective to the profiled frequencies at runtime. Table 2 summarizes the average errors and standard deviations depicted in Figure 5(a) and Figure 5(b) in a tabular format.

The above figures and table show that probabilistic points-to analysis approach can estimate how likely each points-to relationship would hold with relatively small errors.

Even with statically assigned edge probabilities, the average error of estimated probabilities by PPA-S compared to the runtime frequencies is about 15.58%. With the aid of edge profiling information, PPA-P reduces the average error down to 2.27%. Furthermore, the 7.38% standard deviation of PPA-P demonstates that almost all of estimated probabilities are quite accurate, with errors less than 7.38%.

| Programs | Average Errors | | | Standard Deviations | | |
|---|---|---|---|---|---|---|
| | PPA-S | PPA-P | TPA | PPA-S | PPA-P | TPA |
| *reverse(m)* | 16.67% | 0% | 16.67% | 29.70% | 0% | 42.01% |
| *reverse(e)* | 16.16% | 5.99% | 33.19% | 22.60% | 15.55% | 51.46% |
| *hash(e)* | 19.10% | 0% | 39.58% | 26.11% | 0% | 63.96% |
| *misr(m)* | 0.72% | 0.61% | 40% | 0.86% | 0.71% | 60.91% |
| *queens(e)* | 42.86% | 0.0002% | 42.86% | 50% | 0.0004% | 70.71% |
| *cq(m)* | 3.56% | 0.0174% | 22.22% | 5.66% | 0.0277% | 49.01% |
| *20000801-2.c(m)* | 29.7% | 12.50% | 66.67% | 40.91% | 19.76% | 86.60% |
| *990127-1.c(m1)* | 6.49% | 0% | 14.29% | 13.12% | 0% | 31.71% |
| *990127-1.c(m2)* | 5% | 1.30% | 14.29% | 10.10% | 2.62% | 33.67% |
| Overall | 15.58% | 2.27% | 32.19% | 24.11% | 7.38% | 52.20% |

**Table 2.** Average Errors and Standard Deviations

| Probability Range | PPA-S | PPA-P | PPA-S | PPA-P |
|---|---|---|---|---|
| 0%~10% | 83.33% | 100% | 80% | 100% |
| 10%~20% | 0% | 0% | | |
| 20%~30% | 0% | 33.33% | 0% | 33.33% |
| 30%~40% | 0% | 0% | | |
| 40%~50% | 0% | 66.67% | 0% | 100% |
| 50%~60% | 0% | 50% | | |
| 60%~70% | 0% | 100% | 10% | 100% |
| 70%~80% | 0% | 100% | | |
| 80%~90% | 0% | 100% | 94.64% | 97.10% |
| 90%~100% | 95.74% | 97.10% | | |

**Table 3.** Accuracy of Estimated Probabilities

This result is significant since most compiler optimizations can benefit from the ability to determine if points-to relationships hold with high or low probabilities. For instance, data speculation can be performed on reads and writes with low possibilities of conflicts to avoid costly mis-speculation penalties. Let $Points\text{-}to_{PPA}(l\%{\sim}h\%)$ be the set of points-to relationships that are estimated by PPA to hold with the probabilities within the range $l\%{\sim}h\%$, and $Points\text{-}to_{Runtime}(l\%{\sim}h\%)$ be the set of points-to relationships with runtime-profiled probabilities within the range $l\%{\sim}h\%$ and are also in the set $Points\text{-}to_{PPA}(l\%{\sim}h\%)$. Then the *accuracy within the probability range* $l\%{\sim}h\%$ of PPA is defined as the ratio of the size of the sets $Points\text{-}to_{Runtime}(l\%{\sim}h\%)$ over the size of $Points\text{-}to_{PPA}(l\%{\sim}h\%)$, i.e. $|Points\text{-}to_{Runtime}(l\%{\sim}h\%)| / |Points\text{-}to_{PPA}(l\%{\sim}h\%)|$. Table 3 presents the accuracy of PPA-S and PPA-P within different probability ranges based on the above definition. The first section of Table 3 shows the accuracy of PPA-S and PPA-P in the probability range 0%~10% are 83.33 and 100% respectively, while the accuracy of both PPA-S and PPA-P in the range 90%~100% are 95.74% and 97.10%. If the interval of the probability ranges is extended to 20%, the accuracy of PPA-S and PPA-P in the probability range 0%~20% is 80% and 100% respectively, and while the accuracy of both PPA-S and PPA-P in the range 80%~100% is 94.64% and 97.10%, respectively, as shown in the second section of Table 3. This result demonstrates that the probabilistic points-to analysis can identify the points-to relationships with high or low probabilities with very high accuracy.

Table 4 lists the distributions of probabilities of all points-to relationships estimated by points-to analysis techniques and profiled at runtime. For most of the benchmarks, the probability distributions of PPA-P are the same as the profiled probability distributions. It shows that the probabilities estimated by the probabilistic points-to analysis are very accurate.

| program | analysis method | 0% ℓ 10% | 10% ℓ 20% | 20% ℓ 30% | 30% ℓ 40% | 40% ℓ 50% | 50% ℓ 60% | 60% ℓ 70% | 70% ℓ 80% | 80% ℓ 90% | 90% ℓ 100% |
|---|---|---|---|---|---|---|---|---|---|---|---|
| reverse(m) | Runtime | 16.7% | 0 | 0 | 0 | 0 | 0 | 0 | 0 | 0 | 83.3% |
| | PPA-P | 16.7% | 0 | 0 | 0 | 0 | 0 | 0 | 0 | 0 | 83.3% |
| | PPA-S | 0 | 0 | 0 | 0 | 33.3% | 0 | 0 | 0 | 0 | 66.7% |
| | TPA | 0 | 0 | 0 | 0 | 0 | 0 | 0 | 0 | 0 | 100% |
| reverse(e) | Runtime | 19% | 0 | 0 | 0 | 9.5% | 19% | 0 | 0 | 0 | 52.5% |
| | PPA-P | 19% | 0 | 0 | 0 | 9.5% | 9.5% | 0 | 0 | 0 | 62% |
| | PPA-S | 0 | 14.3% | 14.3% | 0 | 0 | 0 | 0 | 14.3% | 14.3% | 42.8% |
| | TPA | 0 | 0 | 0 | 0 | 0 | 0 | 0 | 0 | 0 | 100% |
| hash(m) | Runtime | 39.1% | 0 | 0 | 0 | 0 | 0 | 0 | 0 | 0 | 60.9% |
| | PPA-P | 39.1% | 0 | 0 | 0 | 0 | 0 | 0 | 0 | 0 | 60.9% |
| | PPA-S | 13% | 0 | 0 | 26.1% | 0 | 0 | 26.1% | 0 | 0 | 34.8% |
| | TPA | 0 | 0 | 0 | 0 | 0 | 0 | 0 | 0 | 0 | 100% |
| misr(m) | Runtime | 40% | 0 | 0 | 0 | 0 | 0 | 0 | 0 | 0 | 60% |
| | PPA-P | 40% | 0 | 0 | 0 | 0 | 0 | 0 | 0 | 0 | 60% |
| | PPA-S | 40% | 0 | 0 | 0 | 0 | 0 | 0 | 0 | 40% | 20% |
| | TPA | 0 | 0 | 0 | 0 | 0 | 0 | 0 | 0 | 0 | 100% |
| queens(e) | Runtime | 42.9% | 0 | 0 | 0 | 0 | 0 | 0 | 0 | 0 | 57.1% |
| | PPA-P | 42.9% | 0 | 0 | 0 | 0 | 0 | 0 | 0 | 0 | 57.1% |
| | PPA-S | 0 | 0 | 0 | 85.7% | 0 | 0 | 0 | 0 | 0 | 14.3% |
| | TPA | 0 | 0 | 0 | 0 | 0 | 0 | 0 | 0 | 0 | 100% |
| cq(m) | Runtime | 22.2% | 0 | 0 | 0 | 0 | 0 | 0 | 0 | 0 | 77.8% |
| | PPA-P | 22.2% | 0 | 0 | 0 | 0 | 0 | 0 | 0 | 0 | 77.8% |
| | PPA-S | 22.2% | 0 | 0 | 0 | 0 | 0 | 0 | 0 | 22.2% | 55.6% |
| | TPA | 0 | 0 | 0 | 0 | 0 | 0 | 0 | 0 | 0 | 100% |
| 20000801-2.c(m) | Runtime | 33.3% | 0 | 0 | 0 | 66.7% | 0 | 0 | 0 | 0 | 0 |
| | PPA-P | 0 | 33.3% | 33.3% | 0 | 33.4% | 0 | 0 | 0 | 0 | 0 |
| | PPA-S | 100% | 0 | 0 | 0 | 0 | 0 | 0 | 0 | 0 | 0 |
| | TPA | 0 | 0 | 0 | 0 | 0 | 0 | 0 | 0 | 0 | 100% |
| 990127-1.c(m1) | Runtime | 0 | 14.3% | 0 | 0 | 0 | 0 | 0 | 14.3% | 0 | 71.4% |
| | PPA-P | 0 | 0 | 14.3% | 0 | 0 | 0 | 0 | 14.3% | 0 | 71.4% |
| | PPA-S | 0 | 0 | 0 | 14.3% | 0 | 0 | 14.3% | 0 | 0 | 71.4% |
| | TPA | 0 | 0 | 0 | 0 | 0 | 0 | 0 | 0 | 0 | 100% |
| 990127-1.c(m2) | Runtime | 0 | 0 | 14.3% | 0 | 0 | 0 | 0 | 14.3% | 0 | 71.4% |
| | PPA-P | 0 | 0 | 14.3% | 0 | 0 | 0 | 0 | 14.3% | 0 | 71.4% |
| | PPA-S | 0 | 0 | 0 | 28.6% | 0 | 0 | 0 | 0 | 0 | 71.4% |
| | TPA | 0 | 0 | 0 | 0 | 0 | 0 | 0 | 0 | 0 | 100% |
| overall | Runtime | 24.8% | 0.9% | 1.0% | 0 | 3.8% | 3.8% | 0 | 1.9% | 0 | 63.8% |
| | PPA-P | 23.8% | 0.9% | 2.9% | 0 | 2.9% | 1.9% | 0 | 1.9% | 0 | 65.7% |
| | PPA-S | 11.4% | 2.9% | 2.9% | 6.6% | 13.3% | 0 | 6.6% | 2.9% | 8.6% | 44.8% |
| | TPA | 0 | 0 | 0 | 0 | 0 | 0 | 0 | 0 | 0 | 100% |

**Table 4.** Distributions of probabilities of Points-to Relationships

### 3.3  Discussion

PPA-P can accurately estimate probabilities of points-to relations of most selected procedures in the benchmark programs with errors less than 1%. However, the errors of the programs *reverse* and *20000801-2.c* are quite significant compared to the errors of the other programs. The reason is that the current implementation can not handle heap and recursive data structures properly. Heap locations are named after the program points where they are allocated. This naming scheme can not provide enough information for probabilistic points-to analysis to make accurate estimations. It will be improved in the future implementation.

## 4  Related Work

There have been considerable efforts on pointer analysis by researchers [1, 4, 6, 7, 8, 12, 17, 18, 20, 22, 24, 25]. The proposed techniques compute at program points either aliases or points-to relationships. They categorize aliases or points-to relationships into two classes: *must* aliases or *definitely*-points-to relationships, which hold for executions, and *may*-aliases or *possibly*-points-to relationships, which hold for at least one execution. However, they can not tell which *may*-aliases or possibly-points-to relationships hold for the most of executions and which for only few executions. Such information is crucial for compilers to determine if certain optimizations and transformations will be beneficial. The probabilistic points-to analysis approach proposed in this paper is the first algorithm to compute such information.

The most closely related work is the *data flow frequency analysis* proposed by Ramalingam [15]. It provides a theoretical foundation for data flow frequency analysis, which computes at program points the expected number of times that certain conditions might hold. The probabilistic points-to analysis approach proposed in this paper is built upon the probabilistic data flow analysis framework, which is adapted from Ramalingam's data flow frequency analysis. However, this paper focuses on points-to analysis, which is a complicated issue because of the dynamic associations property of pointers. Extra cares are needed for probabilistic points-to analysis with the recent establishments for foundations of probabilistic data flow equations. Furthermore, this technique solves the probabilistic data flow analysis problem on CFGs, eliminating the overhead of generating the *exploded graphs* [16].

In the work related to data speculations for modern computer architectures, such as IA-64 [5], Ju et al. [11] gives a probabilistic memory disambiguation approach for array analysis and optimizations. However, the problem remains open for pointer-induced memory references. This work tries to provide a solution to fill-in the open areas. In the work related to compiler optimizations for pointer-based programs on distributed shared-memory parallel machines, affinity analysis [3] and data distribution analysis [13] are currently able to estimate which processor an object is resided in. For programs with pointer usages, a pointer will be pointing to a set of objects with may-aliases. In this case, our analyzer can be integrated with the conventional affinity analyzer, and the integrated scheme can calculate the amortized amount of objects a processor owns for a task execution. Thus it will help program optimizations.

# References

[1] Michael Burke, Paul Carini, Jong-Deok Choi, and Michael Hind. Flow-insensitive interprocedural alias analysis in the presence of pointers. In *Proceedings of the 8th International Workshop on Languages and Compilers for Parallel Computing*, Columbus, Ohio, August 1995.

[2] Tim Callahan and John Wawrzynek. Simple profiling system for suif. In *Proceedings of the First SUIF Compiler Workshop*, January 1996.

[3] M. C. Carlisle and A. Rogers. Software caching and computation migration in olden. In *Proceedings of ACM SIGPLAN Conference on Principles and Practice of Parallel Programming*, pages 29–39, July 1995.

[4] Jong-Deok Choi, Michael Burke, and Paul Carini. Efficient flow-sensitive interprocedural computation of pointer-induced aliases and side effects. In *Conference Record of the Twentieth Annual ACM SIGPLAN-SIGACT Symposium on Principles of Programming Languages*, pages 232–245, Charleston, South Carolina, January 1993.

[5] Intel Corporation. *IA-64 Application Developer's Architecture Guide*. 1999.

[6] Manuvir Das. Unification-based pointer analysis with directional assignments. *SIGPLAN Notices*, 35(5):35–46, May 2000. *Proceedings of the ACM SIGPLAN '00 Conference on Programming Language Design and Implementation*.

[7] Alain Deutsch. Interprocedural May-Alias analysis for pointers: Beyond $k$-limiting. *SIGPLAN Notices*, 29(6):230–241, June 1994. *Proceedings of the ACM SIGPLAN '94 Conference on Programming Language Design and Implementation*.

[8] Maryam Emami, Rakesh Ghiya, and Laurie J. Hendren. Context-sensitive interprocedural Points-to analysis in the presence of function pointers. *SIGPLAN Notices*, 29(6):242–256,

June 1994. *Proceedings of the ACM SIGPLAN '94 Conference on Programming Language Design and Implementation*.

[9]  The Stanford SUIF Compiler Group. The suif library. Technical report, Stanford University, 1995.

[10] M.S. Hecht. *Flow Analysis of Computer Programs*. Elsevier North-Holland, 1977.

[11] R. D.C. Ju, J.-F. Collard, and K. Oukbir. Probabilistic memory disambiguation and its application to data speculation. In *Proceedings of the 3rd Workshop on Interaction between Compilers and Computer Architecture*, Oct 1998.

[12] William Landi and Barbara G. Ryder. A safe approximate algorithm for interprocedural pointer aliasing. *SIGPLAN Notices*, 27(7):235–248, July 1992. *Proceedings of the ACM SIGPLAN '92 Conference on Programming Language Design and Implementation*.

[13] Jenq Kuen Lee, Dan Ho, and Yue-Chee Chuang. Data distribution analysis and optimization for pointer-based distrib uted programs. In *Proceedings of the 26th International Conference on Parallel Proces sing (ICPP)*, Bloomingdale, IL, August 1997.

[14] Steven S. Muchnick. *Advanced Compiler Design & Implementation*. Morgen Kaufmann, 1997.

[15] G. Ramalingam. Data flow frequency analysis. *SIGPLAN Notices*, 31(5):267–277, May 1996. *Proceedings of the ACM SIGPLAN '96 Conference on Programming Language Design and Implementation*.

[16] Thomas Reps, Susan Horwitz, and Mooly Sagiv. Precise interprocedural dataflow analysis via graph reachability. In *Conference Record of POPL '95: 22nd ACM SIGPLAN-SIGACT Symposium on Principles of Programming Languages*, pages 49–61, San Francisco, California, January 1995.

[17] Erik Ruf. Context-insensitive alias analysis reconsidered. *SIGPLAN Notices*, 30(6):13–22, June 1995. *Proceedings of the ACM SIGPLAN '95 Conference on Programming Language Design and Implementation*.

[18] Radu Rugina and Martin Rinard. Pointer analysis for multithreaded programs. *SIGPLAN Notices*, 34(5):77–90, May 1999. *Proceedings of the ACM SIGPLAN '99 Conference on Programming Language Design and Implementation*.

[19] B. G. Ryder and M. C. Paull. Elimination algorithms for data flow analysis. *ACM Computing Surveys*, 18(3):277–316, September 1986.

[20] Marc Shapiro and Susan Horwitz. Fast and accurate flow-insensitive points-to analysis. In *Conference Record of POPL '97: 24nd ACM SIGPLAN-SIGACT Symposium on Principles of Programming Languages*, pages 1–14, Paris, France, January 1997.

[21] Michael D. Smith. The suif machine library. Technical report, Division of of Engineering and Applied Science, Harvard University, March 1998.

[22] Bjarne Steensgaard. Points-to analysis in almost linear time. In *Conference Record of POPL '96: 23nd ACM SIGPLAN-SIGACT Symposium on Principles of Programming Languages*, pages 32–41, St. Petersburg Beach, Florida, January 1996.

[23] Tim A. Wagner, Vance Maverick, Susan L. Graham, and Michael A. Harrison. Accurate static estimators for program optimization. *SIGPLAN Notices*, 29(6):85–96, June 1994. *Proceedings of the ACM SIGPLAN '94 Conference on Programming Language Design and Implementation*.

[24] Robert P. Wilson and Monica S. Lam. Efficient context-sensitive pointer analysis for C programs. *SIGPLAN Notices*, 30(6):1–12, June 1995. *Proceedings of the ACM SIGPLAN '95 Conference on Programming Language Design and Implementation*.

[25] Suan Hsi Yong, Susan Horwitz, and Thomas Reps. Pointer analysis for programs with structures and casting. *SIGPLAN Notices*, 34(5):91–103, May 1999. *Proceedings of the ACM SIGPLAN '99 Conference on Programming Language Design and Implementation*.

# A Compiler Framework to Detect Parallelism in Irregular Codes

Manuel Arenaz, Juan Touriño, and Ramón Doallo

Computer Architecture Group
Department of Electronics and Systems
University of A Coruña, Spain
{arenaz,juan,doallo}@udc.es

**Abstract.** This paper describes a compiler framework that enhances the detection of parallelism in loops with complex irregular computations. The framework is based on the static analysis of the Gated Single Assignment (GSA) program representation. A taxonomy of the strongly connected components (SCCs) that appear in GSA dependence graphs is presented as the basis of our framework. Furthermore, an algorithm for classifying the set of SCCs associated with loops is described. We have implemented a prototype of the SCC classification algorithm using the infrastructure provided by the Polaris parallelizing compiler. Experimental results for a suite of real irregular programs are shown.

## 1 Introduction

The development of efficient applications for parallel computers is a difficult task. The problem can be significantly simplified if the compiler is able to translate automatically a sequential program into a parallel counterpart. Current parallelizing compilers are able to efficiently detect and parallelize loop patterns that appear in regular codes, but irregular codes are still a challenge due to the presence of subscripted subscripts that complicate the compiler analysis. In this work, we present a compiler framework to enhance the detection of loop-level parallelism in codes with irregular computations. The technique is based on the classification of the strongly connected components (SCCs) that are found in the dependence graphs that arise in the Gated Single Assignment program representation.

Static Single Assignment (SSA) [2] is a standard program representation used in modern optimizing compilers. SSA captures data-flow information for scalar variables by inserting *pseudo-functions* at the confluence nodes of the control flow graph where multiple reaching definitions of a scalar variable exist. Parallelizing compilers are faced with the analysis of programs with subscripted subscripts, so the information provided by SSA is insufficient. Two extensions of SSA that capture data-flow information for arrays at the element level have been proposed in the literature: *Partial Array SSA* (PA-SSA) [8, 9] and Gated Single Assignment (GSA) [14]. Both program representations support static program analysis. Nevertheless, for our purposes, GSA presents several advantages over PA-SSA.

H. Dietz (Ed.): LCPC 2001, LNCS 2624, pp. 306–320, 2003.

Array assignment statements are represented in GSA using only one statement (while two statements are used in PA-SSA) that captures the data-flow information for the array being defined. This fact has important implications in our technique. On the one hand, the statements associated with array definitions in GSA belong to a unique SCC, which simplifies the SCC classification algorithm. On the other hand, the conversion of real codes into PA-SSA form could lead to code explosion. Another advantage of GSA form is that the pseudo-functions located at the confluence nodes associated with branches capture the condition for each definition to reach the confluence node. Such information, which is not represented in PA-SSA, contributes to improve the efficiency of the implementation of the classification algorithm described further on.

Demand-driven implementations of SSA-based program representations have been used in solving data-flow analysis problems efficiently [3, 14]. From the point of view of the work we present here, special mention deserves the paper of Gerlek et al. [3]. They describe an algorithm for classifying the strongly connected components that appear in SSA graphs. This algorithm enables the detection of sequences of values (such as induction or wrap-around variables) in loops with complex control flow. Nevertheless, only sequences defined in terms of integer-valued scalar operators are considered.

In this work, a method for classifying the strongly connected components that appear in GSA dependence graphs is presented; SCCs defined in terms of expressions that contain subscripted subscripts are considered. Several approaches have been proposed to detect loop-level parallelism in irregular codes. Pottenger and Eigenmann [11] describe a pattern-matching-based method to recognize induction variables and reduction operations (regular constructs are also treated in that work). Techniques that recognize patterns directly from the source code have two major drawbacks: dependence on the code quality and difficulty in analyzing complex control structures. Keßler [7] describes a pattern-driven automatic parallelization technique based on the recognition of syntactical variations of sparse matrix computation kernels, which limits its scope of application. Unlike pattern-matching techniques, our method is independent of the source code and rests on a normalized program representation provided by the GSA form.

The method presented in this paper is based on a demand-driven implementation of the GSA form. Very interesting implications in the context of parallelizing compilers can be derived from our approach, as it enables the recognition of recurrence forms defined on arrays with irregular access patterns, even in the presence of complex control structures. Several recurrence forms, defined both on scalar and array variables, are considered. Detection of recurrence forms that are hidden in the source code behind conditional constructions is enabled too. A representative, yet simple, example is the computation of the minimum/maximum value of an array. This recurrence form is associated with computational kernels that appear very often in real codes. A previous work of Suganuma et al. [13] has addressed the detection of these constructions, though it uses a non-standard program representation, and limits its scope of application to scalar variables.

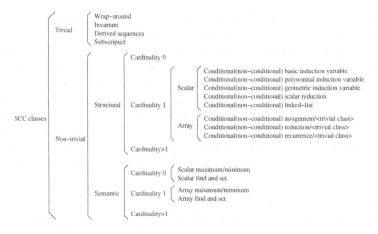

**Figure1.** Taxonomy of strongly connected components in GSA graphs.

Our framework also extends the algorithm proposed in [3] to detect scalar reduction operations within complex control structures.

This paper is organized as follows. In Section 2 a taxonomy of the SCCs that appear in GSA dependence graphs is presented. In Section 3 a demand-driven method to classify the SCCs is described. Section 4 is devoted to experimental results for the SparsKit-II library [12], which was chosen because it covers a wide range of irregular patterns; the example codes presented in this work have been abstracted from this library. We close with the conclusions of the paper in Section 5.

## 2    Taxonomy of GSA Strongly Connected Components

Our framework is based on the classification of the strongly connected components that appear in GSA dependence graphs. Four types of pseudo-functions are defined in GSA: the $\mu$-function, which appears at loop headers, selects the initial and loop-carried values of a variable; the $\gamma$-function, which is located at the confluence node associated with a branch, captures the condition for each definition to reach the confluence node; the $\alpha$-function replaces an array assignment statement; and the $\eta$-function determines the last value of a variable at the end of the loop.

In this section we present a taxonomy in which the properties of different classes of SCCs are defined. Components defined both in terms of scalar and array variables are considered. Furthermore, components associated with recurrence forms that set the value of scalar and array variables are classified. A scheme of the taxonomy is depicted in Figure 1.

First, we introduce notations used in the rest of the paper. Let $SCC(X_1, ..., X_n)$ denote a strongly connected component composed of $n$ nodes of a GSA dependence graph. The nodes are associated with the GSA assignment statements where the variables $X_k$ $(k = 1, ..., n)$ are defined. Let $OCCURS_e(v)$ represent the number of occurrences of variable $v$ that appear in expression $e$. In general,

$$OCCURS_{e_1,...,e_r}(v_1, ..., v_s) = \sum_i \sum_j OCCURS_{e_i}(v_j)$$

denotes the number of occurrences of $v_1, ..., v_s$ in $e_1, ..., e_r$. Let $CLASS_X(e)$ denote the class of expression $e$ with regard to variable $X$. We extend this notation to cope with assignment statements as $CLASS_X(v = e)$, where $v = e$ is a statement that sets the scalar/array variable $v$ to the value of expression $e$.

Next, we define some of the basic concepts that will appear in different parts of this work.

**Definition 1.** Let $v = e$, with $e = \oplus(e_1, ..., e_r)$, be an assignment statement. Expressions $v, e, e_1, ..., e_r$ and operator $\oplus$ are defined to have *level* zero. If $v, e_1, ..., e_r$ contain occurrences of array variables, say $a(s)$, then expression $s$ and all its subexpressions (and operators) are defined to have level one.

**Definition 2.** Let $X_1, ..., X_n$ be a set of variables defined in the GSA form. Let $Y_1, ..., Y_m$ $(m \le n)$ be the set of variables corresponding to $X_1, ..., X_n$ in the source code. The *cardinality* of a strongly connected component, $|SCC(X_1, ..., X_n)|$, is defined as the number of different variables contained in $Y_1, ..., Y_m$.

**Definition 3.** A *direct dependence* $SCC(X_1, ..., X_n) \to SCC(Y_1, ..., Y_m)$ exists if the assignment statements associated with the strongly connected component $SCC(Y_1, ..., Y_m)$ contain at least one occurrence of the variables $X_1, ..., X_n$. This relation can be easily generalized to *indirect dependences* between SCCs, which is denoted as $SCC(X_1, ..., X_n) \xrightarrow{+} SCC(Y_1, ..., Y_m)$.

**Definition 4.** Two components $SCC(X_1, ..., X_n)$ and $SCC(Y_1, ..., Y_m)$ are classified as *mutually dependent* if and only if $SCC(X_1, ..., X_n) \xrightarrow{+} SCC(Y_1, ..., Y_m)$ and $SCC(Y_1, ..., Y_m) \xrightarrow{+} SCC(X_1, ..., X_n)$.

Finally, the difference between what we have called trivial and non-trivial SCCs, which will be used in the taxonomy proposed below, is defined.

**Definition 5.** Let $SCC(X_1, ..., X_n)$ be a strongly connected component. The component is *trivial* if it consists of exactly one node of the GSA dependence graph $(n = 1)$. Otherwise, the component is *non-trivial* $(n > 1)$.

## 2.1   Trivial SCCs

Trivial components, $SCC(X_1)$, consist of only one node that is associated with a scalar assignment statement [1] $v = e$, where $v$ is a scalar variable that is

---

[1] Note that array assignment statements are always included in non-trivial components due to the fact that the definition of an array element is represented using, at least, two pseudo-functions in the GSA form.

set to the value of expression $e$. Variable $v$ is not defined in terms of itself $(OCCURS_e(v) = 0)$, otherwise the component would be composed of at least two nodes. The properties of expression $e$ allow to distinguish different classes of trivial components. Several trivial SCCs are associated with some sequences defined in [3]: *wrap-around*, *invariant* and the different forms of *derived sequences*, such as *derived linear/polynomial/geometric induction variables*; however, forms involving subscripted subscripts are not considered. In order to cope with such forms we define a new class of trivial components called *subscripted*. In this class, expression $e$ contains at least one array reference whose subscript expression is loop-variant, i.e., its value changes in each loop iteration. The definition of the class subscripted enables the classification of those SCCs that contain expressions defined in terms of array references with irregular access patterns. The cardinality of a trivial SCC is always one except for the members of the wrap-around class whose cardinality is zero. Figure **2** shows an example code that computes a gather operation on a sparse matrix. The loop body contains two trivial components, $SCC(j_1)$ and $SCC(j_2)$, that belong to the classes wrap-around and subscripted, respectively.

## 2.2   Non-trivial SCCs

Non-trivial components consist of at least two nodes of the GSA graph. The nodes may contain pseudo-function or scalar assignment statements. Besides, non-trivial SCCs always contain at least one $\mu$-function, and can be classified as structural and semantic according to the following definition.

**Definition 6.** Let $SCC(X_1, ..., X_n)$ be a non-trivial strongly connected component of a loop. Let $C_1, ..., C_m$ be the set of conditional expressions associated with the $\gamma$-functions of the loop body. Then, $SCC(X_1, ..., X_n)$ is called *structural* if $OCCURS_{C_1,...,C_m}(X_1, ..., X_n) = 0$. Otherwise, $SCC(X_1, ..., X_n)$ is *semantic*.

**i. Structural SCCs.** Two criteria will be used for further classification of structural SCCs (see Figure 1). The first criterium, explained in the following definition, is based on the concept of conditionality of an SCC.

**Definition 7.** A structural component $SCC(X_1, ..., X_n)$ is *conditional* if it contains at least one node associated with a $\gamma$-function. Otherwise, the component is *non-conditional*.

The second criterium rests on the concept of cardinality of a strongly connected component.

**Cardinality zero.** This class of structural SCC arises only when a scalar variable is defined inside an if–endif construction. In this situation, two SCCs appear in the GSA graph associated with the scalar variable: a trivial SCC that contains the scalar assignment statement and a non-trivial SCC with cardinality zero. This class of non-trivial SCC always consists of one $\mu$-function and one or more $\gamma$-functions. Figure **3** shows a code for computing the minimum value $m$ of a set of rows of a sparse matrix. The location $l$ of the minimum value is also computed. In the GSA graph of the innermost loop a component $SCC(l_3, l_5)$ that belongs to this class appears.

**Cardinality one.** This class of SCCs defines the value of only one variable of the original source code. The variable is defined in terms of itself. Exactly one $\mu$-function is included in the SCC. Structural SCCs with cardinality one can be classified as well.

**Definition 8.** Let $SCC(X_1, ..., X_n)$ be a structural component with cardinality one. $SCC(X_1, ..., X_n)$ is *scalar* if a scalar variable is defined in the original source code. Otherwise, $SCC(X_1, ..., X_n)$ is *array*.

Some scalar sequences associated with scalar structural SCCs are presented in [3]: *basic, polynomial, geometric induction variables*, and a set of *monotonic sequences*. Monotonic sequences correspond to conditional scalar structural components in our taxonomy. In order to cope with subscripted subscripts, we define two additional classes:

- *Scalar reduction*: The operations within the component contain at least one loop-variant subscripted subscript. An example code is the computation of the sum/product of some elements of an array.
- *Linked list*: No arithmetic operator is allowed within the component. Only array references whose subscript expressions consist of one occurrence of the variable defined in the SCC are allowed. An example code is the traversal of a linked list implemented by means of an array, i.e., $i = next(i)$ within the loop body.

With respect to array structural SCCs, several subclasses are also distinguished. Let $A(s) = e$ be an array assignment statement where the $s-th$ element of the array $A$ is assigned the value of expression $e$. The set of occurrences of $A$ in $e$ is $OCCURS_e(A) = \{A(s_1), ..., A(s_r)\}$. Depending on the structure of the array assignment statements within the array structural SCC, we have obtained the following classes:

- *Assignment/CLASS$_A(s)$*, where $|OCCURS_e(A)| = 0$.
- *Reduction/CLASS$_A(s)$*, where $|OCCURS_e(A)| > 0$ and $s = s_j$ $(j = 1, ..., r)$.
- *Recurrence/CLASS$_A(s)$* otherwise.

Possible values for $CLASS_A(s)$ are the classes of trivial SCCs defined previously in this section. Some examples can be introduced to illustrate this last subclassification: the component $SCC(a_1, a_2, a_3)$ that appears in Figure **2** belongs to the class conditional/assignment/linear; the component $SCC(a_3, a_4, a_5)$ contained in the loop *do_h* of Figure **4**, which computes an irregular reduction, is classified as conditional/reduction/subscripted.

```
                                    k₁ = 1
                                    DO h₁ = 1, n
         k = 1                        k₂ = μ(k₁, k₄)
         DO h = 1, n                  j₁ = μ(j₀, j₂)
           j = f(h)                   a₁ = μ(a₀, a₃)
           IF (j ≠ 0) THEN            j₂ = f(h₁)
             a(k) = b(j)              IF (j₂ ≠ 0) THEN
             k = k + 1                  a₂(k₂) = α(a₁, b(j₂))
           END IF                       k₃ = k₂ + 1
         END DO                       END IF
                                      k₄ = γ(j₂ ≠ 0, k₃, k₂)
                                      a₃ = γ(j₂ ≠ 0, a₂, a₁)
         (a) Source code.          END DO


                                          (b) GSA form.
```

$$k_1 = 1$$
$$\text{DO } h_1 = 1, n$$
$$k_2 = \mu(k_1, k_4)$$
$$j_1 = \mu(j_0, j_2)$$
$$a_1 = \mu(a_0, a_3)$$
$$j_2 = f(h_1)$$
$$\text{IF } (j_2 \neq 0) \text{ THEN}$$
$$a_2(k_2) = \alpha(a_1, b(j_2))$$
$$k_3 = k_2 + 1$$
$$\text{END IF}$$
$$k_4 = \gamma(j_2 \neq 0, k_3, k_2)$$
$$a_3 = \gamma(j_2 \neq 0, a_2, a_1)$$
$$\text{END DO}$$

**Figure2.** Gather operation of an array with irregular access pattern.

```
                                    m₁ = a(f(1))
                                    l₁ = f(1)
                                    DO row₁ = n1, n2
   m = a(f(1))                        l₂ = μ(l₁, l₃)
   l = f(1)                           m₂ = μ(m₁, m₃)
   DO row = n1, n2                    h₁ = μ(h₀, h₂)
     DO h = begin(row), end(row)      DO h₂ = begin(row₁), end(row₁)
       IF (a(f(h)) < m) THEN            l₃ = μ(l₂, l₅)
         m = a(f(h))                    m₃ = μ(m₂, m₅)
         l = f(h)                       IF (a(f(h₂)) < m₃) THEN
       END IF                             m₄ = a(f(h₂))
     END DO                               l₄ = f(h₂)
   END DO                               END IF
                                        l₅ = γ(a(f(h₂)) < m₃, l₄, l₃)
                                        m₅ = γ(a(f(h₂)) < m₃, m₄, m₃)
     (a) Source code.                 END DO
                                    END DO


                                          (b) GSA form.
```

**Figure3.** Computation of the minimum value of the rows of a sparse matrix.

```
                                    DO h₁ = 1, n
     DO h = 1, n                      a₃ = μ(a₁, a₅)
       IF (f(h) ≠ 0) THEN             IF (f₁(h₁) ≠ 0) THEN
         a(f(h)) = a(f(h)) + 2          a₄(f₁(h₁)) = α(a₃, a₃(f₁(h₁)) + 2)
       END IF                         END IF
     END DO                           a₅ = γ(f₁(h₁) ≠ 0, a₄, a₃)
                                    END DO

       (a) Source code.
                                          (b) GSA form.
```

**Figure4.** Source code for computing an irregular reduction.

**ii. Semantic SCCs.** Semantic SCCs are associated with recurrence forms that are hidden behind conditional structures in the source code of a loop. These hidden recurrences are widely used in real applications. An important contribution of this work is to propose a framework that enables the detection of structural and semantic SCCs in a unified manner. Semantic SCCs always contain at least one $\gamma$-function. As structural SCCs, semantic SCCs are classified according to their cardinality. In this work, only semantic components with one $\gamma$-function, and with cardinality zero or one are considered. In fact, all the semantic components that appear in our test code fulfill these conditions.

**Cardinality zero.** These components, $SCC(X_1, ..., X_{j-1}, X_{j+1}, ..., X_n)$, appear in loop bodies where a scalar variable is defined inside an if–endif construction. Consequently, there is always a trivial component $SCC(X_j)$ whose assignment statement matches $X_j = e$, which defines the variable $X$ in the original source code. This SCC class is divided according to the structure of the conditional expression $C$ of the $\gamma$-function (see Figure **1**).

- *Scalar maximum/minimum*: Expression $C$ matches $e \odot X_k$, where $\odot$ represents a relational operator ($<$, $\leq$, $>$ or $\geq$), and $k \in \{1, ..., j-1, j+1, ..., n\}$. Note that $e$ is the right-hand side expression of the assignment statement associated with $SCC(X_j)$. A representative source code pattern is the computation of the maximum/minimum value of an n-dimensional array (see $SCC(m_3, m_5)$ in the innermost loop of Figure **3**).
- *Scalar find and set*: Expression $C$ matches $(X_k == v).AND.e'$, with $k \in \{1, ..., j-1, j+1, ..., n\}$, $v$ and $e'$ being expressions that do not contain occurrences of $X_k$. Besides, the assignment statement associated with the trivial component $SCC(X_j)$ matches $X_j = v'$, $v' \neq v$. On the other hand, variable $X$ must be set to the value $v$ before starting the execution of the loop, and it can be only modified in $SCC(X_j)$ inside the loop body. Figure **5** shows a loop that contains a component of this class, $SCC(flag_2, flag_4)$. The recognition of this class of semantic SCCs can enable the parallelization of a wider set of loops, as this construction may prevent the parallelization of other irregular patterns.

**Cardinality one.** These semantic components appear in loop bodies where an array variable is defined inside an if–endif construction. Consequently, they contain at least one $\alpha$-function. Two classes are distinguished: *Array maximum/minimum* and *Array find and set*. These classes verify the same conditions as scalar maximum/minimum and scalar find and set, respectively, the difference being that an array element is involved, not a scalar variable. Figure **6** shows a source code example where the maximum of each row of a two-dimensional array is computed. Besides, an irregular access pattern is used within each row. The component $SCC(m3, m4, m5)$ of the innermost loop belongs to subclass array maximum/minimum. Figure **7** presents a loop where non-zero array elements are set to zero. The loop body contains a component $SCC(a_1, a_2, a_3)$ of class array find and set.

```
flag = .TRUE.
DO h = 1, n
    IF (flag.AND.(...)) THEN
        flag = .FALSE.
        /* Other irregular pattern */
        ...
    END IF
    ...
END DO
```

(a) Source code.

```
flag₁ = .TRUE.
DO h₁ = 1, n
    flag₂ = μ(flag₁, flag₄)
    IF (flag₂.AND.(...)) THEN
        flag₃ = .FALSE.
        /* Other irregular pattern */
        ...
    END IF
    flag₄ = γ(flag₂.AND.(...), flag₃, flag₂)
    ...
END DO
```

(b) GSA form.

**Figure5.** Semantic SCC with cardinality zero: Scalar find and set.

```
DO h = 1, n
    m(h) = b(h, f(1))
    DO k = 2, n
        IF (b(h, f(k)).gt.m(h)) THEN
            m(h) = b(h, f(k))
        END IF
    END DO
END DO
```

(a) Source code.

```
DO h₂ = 1, n
    m₁ = μ(m₀, m₃)
    k₁ = μ(k₀, k₂)
    m₂(h₂) = α(m₁, b(h₂, f(1)))
    DO k₂ = 2, n
        m₃ = μ(m₂, m₅)
        IF (b(h₂, f(k₂)).gt.m₃(h₂)) THEN
            m₄(h₂) = α(m₃, b(h₂, f(k₂)))
        END IF
        m₅ = γ(b(h₂, f(k₂)).gt.m₃(h₂), m₄, m₃)
    END DO
END DO
```

(b) GSA form.

**Figure6.** Semantic SCC with cardinality one: Array maximum/minimum.

```
DO h = 1, n
    IF (a(f(h)) ≠ 0) THEN
        a(f(h)) = 0
    END IF
END DO
```

(a) Source code.

```
DO h₁ = 1, n
    a₁ = μ(a₀, a₃)
    IF (a₁(f(h₁)) ≠ 0) THEN
        a₂(f(h₁)) = α(a₁, 0)
    END IF
    a₃ = γ(a₁(f(h₁)) ≠ 0, a₂, a₁)
END DO
```

(b) GSA form.

**Figure7.** Semantic SCCs with cardinality one: Array find and set.

Structural and semantic SCCs are divided in subclasses on the basis of the concept of cardinality. In this paper, only components with cardinality zero or one are considered because the percentage of loops that contain SCCs with cardinality greater than one is very low in the SparsKit-II library (see Section 4).

# 3   Classification Algorithm

The core of our compiler framework consists of a non-deadlocking demand-driven algorithm to classify the SCCs that appear in the GSA representation of a loop body.

## 3.1   Classification of Strongly Connected Components

Our demand-driven algorithm proceeds as follows. For each non-classified component $SCC(X_1, ..., X_n)$, the component is pushed onto a stack of SCCs and its classification procedure is started. If the SCC is independent, $SCC(X_1, ..., X_n)$ is successfully classified, then it is popped from the stack, and the classification process of the SCC located on top of the stack continues at the same point where it had been deferred. The classification process of a component $SCC(X_1, ..., X_n)$ is deferred only when a dependence $SCC(Y_1, ..., Y_m) \rightarrow SCC(X_1, ..., X_n)$ is found. In that situation, the classification of $SCC(Y_1, ..., Y_m)$ starts.

The algorithm described so far reaches a deadlock state when mutually dependent SCCs exist in the loop body. Such situations are detected by using the stack of SCCs as follows. If a dependence $SCC(Y_1, ..., Y_m) \rightarrow SCC(X_1, ..., X_n)$ is found, the contents of the stack are checked before starting the classification of $SCC(Y_1, ..., Y_m)$. If $SCC(Y_1, ..., Y_m)$ is already in the stack, then a dependence $SCC(X_1, ..., X_n) \overset{+}{\rightarrow} SCC(Y_1, ..., Y_m)$ exists. Consequently, $SCC(X_1, ..., X_n)$ and $SCC(Y_1, ..., Y_m)$ are mutually dependent.

The taxonomy of SCCs presented in Section 2 defines the properties of each SCC class. Trivial components $SCC(X_1)$ inherit $CLASS_{X_1}(e)$, $e$ being the right-hand side expression of the assignment statement $X_1 = e$. Non-trivial components $SCC(X_1, ..., X_n)$ are classified as follows. The class $CLASS_{X_k}(X_k(s_k) = e_k)$ of each assignment statement $X_k(s_k) = e_k$, $k \in \{1, ..., n\}$, contained in the component, is determined. If all the assignment statements belong to the same class, then the component inherits $CLASS_{X_k}(X_k(s_k) = e_k)$. Otherwise, the SCC remains unclassified. Finally, if the SCC is semantic, the algorithm determines the appropriate subclass by checking the properties of the corresponding conditional expressions.

## 3.2   Classification of Assignment Statements

A demand-driven propagation mechanism is used for classifying assignment statements. This subsection begins with the description of an algorithm to classify arbitrary complex expressions. As we will see, this algorithm enables the classification of scalar and array assignment statements.

The class $CLASS_{X_k}(v = e)$ of an assignment statement $v = e$ within a component $SCC(X_1, ..., X_n)$, $X_k$ ($k \in \{1, ..., n\}$) being the identifier of variable $v$, is determined on the basis of the types of operators and operands (scalar/array variables) that appear in the right-hand side expression $e$. A post-order traversal of $e$ is performed. Whenever an operator $\oplus$ is found, the class of the operands

**Table1.** Transfer functions for addition $(T_+)$ and array references $(T_{X(s)})$.

| | $T_+$ | | | | $T_{X(s)}$ | |
| | *inv* | *lin* | *red* | *subs* | *inv* | *subs* |
| --- | --- | --- | --- | --- | --- | --- |
| *inv* | *inv* | *lin* | *red* | *subs* | *inv* | *subs* |
| *lin* | *lin* | *lin* | *red* | *red/subs* | *subs* | *subs* |
| *red* | *red* | *red* | *red* | *red* | *subs* | *subs* |
| *subs* | *subs* | *red/subs* | *subs* | *red* | *subs* | *subs* |

$e'_1, e'_2, ..., e'_r$ is determined. Next, the class of the operator is inferred by means of a *transfer function* $T_\oplus$ that combines $CLASS_{X_k}(e'_1), ..., CLASS_{X_k}(e'_r)$. Table **1** presents a tabular representation of the transfer function for the binary addition $(T_+)$. The transfer function for the $r$-ary addition can be easily built from the binary case. Possible operand classes are the trivial classes of the taxonomy presented in Section 2. The table only shows the classes that appear most frequently in our test code: invariant $(inv)$, linear induction variable $(lin)$, scalar reduction $(red)$ and subscripted $(subs)$. In the first column and the first row of the table, classes are ordered by set containment. Note that the result of combining two classes is always the wider class. The only exception consists of the combination of *lin* and *subs* classes. In such case, two different results are possible: *red* if the addition appears in the right-hand side expression of the assignment statement (addition operator with level zero), and *subs* if it appears in the subscript expression of an array reference (level one). A special transfer function to derive the class of array references $(T_{X(s)})$ is presented in Table **1**, too. Rows and columns correspond to the classes of the subscript expression $s$ and the array identifier $X$, respectively. If the classes of $X$ and $s$ are both invariant, then the array reference is classified as invariant. Otherwise, it is set to subscripted. All transfer functions verify that if at least one operand cannot be classified, then the class of the operator cannot be inferred.

Next, the application of this algorithm in order to classify an assignment statement is explained. On the one hand, scalar statements $X_k = e_k$ inherit the class of the right-hand side expression $CLASS_{X_k}(X_k = e_k) = CLASS_{X_k}(e_k)$. On the other hand, array statements $X_k(s_k) = e_k$ are classified as follows. The class $CLASS_{X_k}(s_k)$ is first determined. Next, $CLASS_{X_k}(X_k(s_k) = e_k)$ is set to the structural array SCC class $Assignment/CLASS_{X_k}(s_k)$. Finally, $CLASS_{X_k}(e_k)$ is inferred. Whenever an array reference $X_j(s_j)$, $j \in \{1, ..., n\}$, $j \neq k$ is found during the traversal of expression $e$, $CLASS_{X_k}(X_k(s_k) = e_k)$ is set to $Reduction/CLASS_{X_k}(s_k)$ if the following conditions fulfill: $s_j = s_k$ and $CLASS_{X_k}(X_k(s_k) = e_k) \neq Recurrence/CLASS_{X_k}(s_k)$. Otherwise, the class of the array statement is $Recurrence/CLASS_{X_k}(s_k)$. The procedure described above is applied to each assignment statement within a SCC, and then the class of the SCC is inferred.

# 4   Experimental Results

We have developed a prototype of our SCC classification algorithm using the
infrastructure provided by the Polaris parallelizing compiler [1]. Table **2** presents
statistics about the number ($\#SCCs$) and percentage (%) of each SCC class in
the SparsKit-II library [12]. A set of costly subroutines that perform operations
on sparse matrices was analyzed, in particular: basic linear algebra operations
(e.g. matrix-matrix product and sum), non-algebraic operations (e.g. extracting
a submatrix from a sparse matrix, filter out elements of a matrix according
to their magnitude, or performing a mask operation with matrices), and some
sparse storage conversion procedures. In the first column of the table, the SCC
taxonomy is depicted as a tree that reveals the subclasses of each SCC class.
The last two rows show the total number of trivial and non-trivial SCCs. The
rest of rows present the details of non-trivial structural/semantic SCCs.

Cardinality-one structural SCC is the most frequent class of component in
SparsKit-II. The frequency of non-conditional classes is high. Nevertheless, we
will focus on conditional ones because non-conditional constructions are particular, simpler cases. A negligible percentage of SCCs remain unclassified due
to limitations of the current version of our prototype. Next, two examples that
illustrate how the properties of relevant irregular loop patterns are captured by
cardinality-one structural SCCs, are presented. The parallelization of *irregular
reductions* (see Figure **4**) has been an active research area in recent years [5, 6]
due to their importance in many scientific applications. In the context of our
framework, irregular reductions are associated with the class of *conditional(non-
conditional)/reduction/subscripted* components. Another interesting case is an
array whose elements $a(k)$ are written one after another in consecutive locations using an induction variable $k$ (see Figure **2**). Note that there is no
closed form expression of the array subscript because the value of the subscript is changed conditionally. In the GSA dependence graph, this pattern is
represented by two non-trivial cardinality-one structural SCCs: $SCC(a_1, a_2, a_3)$
and $SCC(k_2, k_3, k_4)$, which belong to the classes *conditional/linear* and *condi-
tional/assignment/linear*, respectively. The remaining SCCs are trivial and do
not characterize this loop pattern. The loop pattern can be recognized by checking the existence of an SCC dependence $SCC(k_2, k_3, k_4) \rightarrow SCC(a_1, a_2, a_3)$
that arises as a result of using induction variable $k$ for indexing array $a$. This
irregular pattern was reported as *consecutively written array* in [10]. In our suite
of real codes, we have found other patterns that share this SCC dependence,
the difference being the location of the occurrence of variable $k$. In SparsKit-II
this occurrence also appears in the right-hand side expression of the assignment
statement either as an operand or as the subscript expression of an array reference. In our framework, these patterns are detected in the same manner. The
statistics shown in Table **2** were obtained by processing 238 loops of SparsKit-II
using our prototype. We have found that 96 loops (approx. 40%) carry out irregular computations, of which only 4 loops correspond to irregular reductions and
15 loops compute different forms of the consecutively written array pattern.

**Table2.** Classification of the SCCs of SparsKit-II.

| | | #SCCs | % |
|---|---|---|---|
| **Non-trivial Structural** | | 351 | 68 |
| Cardinality=0 ............................................................. | | 19 | 4 |
| Cardinality=1 ............................................................. | | 307 | 59 |
| Scalar ............................................................. | | 59 | 11 |
| conditional/ | invariant | 0 | 0 |
| | linear | 25 | 5 |
| | reduction | 0 | 0 |
| non-conditional/ | invariant | 15 | 3 |
| | linear | 6 | 1 |
| | reduction | 13 | 2 |
| Array ............................................................. | | 248 | 48 |
| conditional/ | assignment/invariant | 6 | 1 |
| | assignment/linear | 32 | 6 |
| | assignment/subscripted | 7 | 1 |
| | assignment/unknown | 7 | 1 |
| | reduction/invariant | 1 | 0 |
| | reduction/linear | 0 | 0 |
| | reduction/subscripted | 4 | 1 |
| | reduction/unknown | 0 | 0 |
| | recurrence/invariant | 0 | 0 |
| | recurrence/linear | 5 | 1 |
| | recurrence/subscripted | 1 | 0 |
| | recurrence/unknown | 6 | 1 |
| non-conditional/ | assignment/invariant | 0 | 0 |
| | assignment/linear | 91 | 18 |
| | assignment/subscripted | 22 | 4 |
| | assignment/unknown | 13 | 3 |
| | reduction/invariant | 0 | 0 |
| | reduction/linear | 3 | 1 |
| | reduction/subscripted | 13 | 3 |
| | reduction/unknown | 0 | 0 |
| | recurrence/invariant | 0 | 0 |
| | recurrence/linear | 33 | 6 |
| | recurrence/subscripted | 3 | 1 |
| | recurrence/unknown | 1 | 0 |
| Cardinality>1 ............................................................. | | 25 | 5 |
| **Non-trivial Semantic** | | 11 | 2 |
| Cardinality=0 ............................................................. | | 7 | 1 |
| Cardinality=1 ............................................................. | | 4 | 1 |
| Cardinality>1 ............................................................. | | 0 | 0 |
| Trivial SCCs | | 155 | 30 |
| Non-trivial SCCs | | 362 | 70 |

Semantic SCCs represent a low percentage of the total number of components. Nevertheless, we consider that the detection of this SCC class is a significant advance for two reasons. On the one hand, the corresponding source code patterns appear very often in scientific applications that work with very large matrices. The computational cost associated with these patterns usually depends on matrix size. On the other hand, loop bodies can contain a combination of semantic and structural SCCs. Thus, the detection of semantic SCCs can enable the parallelization of a wider class of loops. The 11 semantic components that appear in SparsKit-II are divided as follows: 7 cardinality-zero SCCs (5 and 2 of classes scalar maximum/minimum and scalar find and set, respectively) and 4 cardinality-one SCCs (in particular, array find and set).

## 5   Conclusions

Previous works in the area of detection of parallelism address the problem of recognizing specific and isolated irregular patterns within loop bodies (usually using pattern-matching to analyze the source code). Nevertheless, these techniques do not describe a general framework to enable the detection of any sort of irregular pattern.

In this paper a GSA-based compiler framework that enhances the detection of loop-level parallelism in irregular codes has been proposed. Strongly connected components are associated with recurrence forms that set the value of either scalar or array variables. Consequently, our framework enables the detection of all recurrence forms in a unified manner. The properties of the different SCC classes are established in the taxonomy that we present in this work. As far as we know, researchers have mainly concentrated their efforts on recognizing the recurrence forms associated with structural components. The detection of recurrence forms corresponding to semantic components is addressed here using a standard program representation.

Our SCC classification algorithm can be used for analyzing real irregular codes statically. We have presented experimental results for SparsKit-II, a library for manipulating sparse matrices that contains a wide range of irregular patterns. A high percentage of the loops processed in SparsKit-II contain irregular computations (approx. 40%), fact that demonstrates the applicability of our algorithm in practice. Furthermore, we have checked that the SCC classes defined in our taxonomy appear, among others, in finite element applications (e.g. Featflow [15]), computer graphics (e.g. generic convex polygon scan conversion [4]), and well-known benchmark suites. As future work we intend to refine our SCC taxonomy and to extend our prototype so that a wider set of real codes can be analyzed.

## References

1. Blume, W., Doallo, R., Eigenmann, R., Grout, J., Hoeflinger, J., Lawrence, T., Lee, J., Padua, D.A., Paek, Y., Pottenger, W.M., Rauchwerger, L., Tu, P.: Parallel Programming with Polaris. IEEE Computer **29**(12) (1996) 78–82

2. Cytron, R., Ferrante, J., Rosen, B.K., Wegman, M.N., Zadeck, F.K.: Efficiently Computing Static Single Assignment Form and the Control Dependence Graph. ACM Transactions on Programming Languages and Systems **13**(4) (1991) 451–490

3. Gerlek, M.P., Stoltz, E., Wolfe, M.: Beyond Induction Variables: Detecting and Classifying Sequences Using a Demand-Driven SSA Form. ACM Transactions on Programming Languages and Systems **17**(1) (1995) 85–122

4. Glassner, A.S.: Graphics Gems. Academic Press (1993)

5. Gutiérrez, E., Plata, O., Zapata, E.L.: A Compiler Method for the Parallel Execution of Irregular Reductions in Scalable Shared Memory Multiprocessors. Proceedings of the 14th ACM International Conference on Supercomputing (2000) 78–87

6. Han, H., Tseng, C.-W.: Efficient Compiler and Run-Time Support for Parallel Irregular Reductions. Parallel Computing **26**(13-14) (2000) 1861–1887

7. Keßler, C.W.: Applicability of Automatic Program Comprehension to Sparse Matrix Computations. Proceedings of the 7th International Workshop on Compilers for Parallel Computers (1998) 218–230

8. Knobe, K., Sarkar, V.: Array SSA Form and Its Use in Parallelization. Proceedings of the 25th ACM SIGACT-SIGPLAN Symposium on the Principles of Programming Languages (1998) 107–120

9. Knobe, K., Sarkar, V.: Enhanced Parallelization via Analyses and Transformations on Array SSA Form. Proceedings of the 8th International Workshop on Compilers for Parallel Computers (2000) 199–212

10. Lin, Y., Padua, D.A.: On the Automatic Parallelization of Sparse and Irregular Fortran Programs. In: David R. O'Hallaron (Ed.): Languages, Compilers, and Run-Time Systems for Scalable Computers. Lecture Notes in Computer Science, Vol. 1511, Springer-Verlag (1998) 41–56

11. Pottenger, W.M., Eigenmann, R.: Idiom Recognition in the Polaris Parallelizing Compiler. Proceedings of the 9th ACM International Conference on Supercomputing (1995) 444–448

12. Saad, Y.: SPARSKIT: A Basic Tool Kit for Sparse Matrix Computations. http://www.cs.umn.edu/Research/darpa/SPARSKIT/sparskit.html (1994)

13. Suganuma, T., Komatsu, H., Nakatani, T.: Detection and Global Optimization of Reduction Operations for Distributed Parallel Machines. Proceedings of the 1996 ACM International Conference on Supercomputing, Philadelphia, PA, USA (1996) 18–25

14. Tu, P., Padua, D.: Gated SSA-Based Demand-Driven Symbolic Analysis for Parallelizing Compilers. Proceedings of the 9th ACM International Conference on Supercomputing, Barcelona, Spain (1995) 414–423

15. Turek, S., Becker, Chr.: Featflow: Finite Element Software for the Incompressible Navier-Stokes Equations. User Manual. http://www.featflow.de (1998)

# Compiling for a Hybrid Programming Model Using the LMAD Representation

Jiajing Zhu[1], Jay Hoeflinger[2], and David Padua[1]

[1] University of Illinois at Urbana-Champaign, Urbana, IL 61801
{zhu,padua}@cs.uiuc.edu
[2] Intel Corporation Champaign, IL 61820
jay.p.hoeflinger@intel.com

**Abstract.** There are two typical ways for a compiler to generate parallel code for distributed memory multiprocessors. One is to generate explicit message passing code and the other is to generate code for a distributed shared memory software layer. In this paper, we propose a new compiler design that combines message passing and distributed shared memory for a single program, depending on how data is accessed. The Linear Memory Access Descriptor (LMAD) is used to represent data distribution and data accesses in our compiler. The LMAD can represent complex distribution and access patterns accurately. We show how LMADs may be used to generate message passing operations. Experimental results indicate that our technique is useful for programs with both regular and irregular access patterns.

## 1 Introduction

Distributed memory multiprocessors are a popular choice for scientific computation. In many cases, these computers are more appealing than shared memory computers due to their relatively low cost and potentially high performance.

The main drawback comes from the complication of programming for distributed systems. Since the memory system of these machines is distributed, the most natural and efficient way to program them is via explicit message passing, which is well known to be a programming model that is difficult to use and may lead to errors.

Many distributed systems also provide programmers with a shared memory abstraction via additional hardware or software. Such systems are referred to as distributed shared memory (DSM) systems. Although the shared memory view alleviates the difficulty in programming, naive use of it often degrades performance at the same time.

Compilers designed for distributed memory systems could play an important role in easing the programming burden caused by distributed machines. Currently, there are two typical ways for a compiler to generate parallel code for distributed memory multiprocessors. One is to generate explicit message passing code and the other is to generate code for a DSM software layer.

H. Dietz (Ed.): LCPC 2001, LNCS 2624, pp. 321–335, 2003.

Both kinds of compilers have difficulty in generating efficient code for a wide range of applications. Many compilers designed for distributed systems can only produce good performance on a particular group of applications, while failing on others.

One factor that limits the success of distributed-system compilers is the rigid programming model applied by the compilers. Therefore, in this paper, we propose a flexible combination of these two programming models, and integrate them into a new compiler framework.

The mechanism discussed in this paper is based on partitioning the program memory space into data to be handled by the DSM system and data to be handled explicitly via message passing. A compiler will partition the data into these two components and will generate all message passing and DSM operations needed to maintain the integrity of the data. Data that is accessed in a regular way, with the regularity made explicit in the source program, will usually be handled by a message-passing mechanism, while irregularly accessed data, or data with a statically unknown access pattern, will tend to remain under the aegis of the DSM system.

In this paper, a new internal representation, the Linear Memory Access Descriptor (LMAD) [11, 6], is applied to represent data distribution and memory accesses in our compiler. An LMAD can represent complex distribution and access patterns accurately. It may be translated precisely across procedure boundaries. Simplification [12] and intersection [7] operations have been defined for the LMAD. In this work, we will show how to use the LMAD to represent data distributions and for generating message passing calls.

The remainder of this paper is organized as follows. Section 2 describes our hybrid programming model and compares it to the pure message passing and DSM models. Section 3 introduces the LMAD internal representation. Section 4 gives the detailed algorithm that targets the compiler to hybrid code. Section 5 provides some experimental results. Section 6 discusses related work and Section 7 is a conclusion.

## 2   Programming Models

### 2.1   Existing Models: Private Memory and Shared Memory

Currently, the target programming models for distributed memory machines may be divided into two categories: the private memory model (communicating by explicit message passing) and the shared memory model (communicating by an underlying DSM platform). Current strategies to improve the performance of compiler-generated code are developed within the limitations of the chosen programming model.

One of the key differences between these programming models is their view of user data. In the private memory model, the address space seen by each processor is separate, so there is no way for one processor to address the data of another. Remote data may only be accessed via explicit message passing. In the shared memory model, on the other hand, although the architecture remains distributed, a single address space is shared by all processors via the support of the additional DSM system, which makes it possible for two processors to refer to the same variable by simply issuing its address.

In recent years, researchers have designed compilers targeted at software DSM systems [8, 2, 5, 14]. These compilers translate sequential or explicitly parallel codes for execution on distributed computers, using the DSM layer to provide the shared memory view of data.

In the private memory model, all data is private to each processor. Data may be exchanged between processors only by explicit message passing. A paralleliz-ing compiler targeting the private memory model must take responsibility for collecting and analyzing the access pattern information from a sequential code, determining the distribution of data, and then inserting message passing calls in the proper places to exchange data between processors.

When the access patterns are very complicated, or determined by input data, the compiler may not have enough information to generate the precise message passing code necessary to move data to where it is needed. Since the compiler must generate correct code, it can compensate for the lack of information by either transfering more data than is necessary, or by generating a large number of very small messages. Either case causes extra overhead, which can hinder program performance.

In the shared memory model, the compiler is relieved of the task of determin-ing where each data value is stored, and which data value is referred to by each memory reference. Resources that it might have used for ensuring correctness with the private memory model, it can use for optimizing the program with the shared memory model. The compiler typically must periodically generate sim-ple code to trigger automatic DSM consistency-maintenance mechanisms (such as barriers). The DSM system itself then maintains data consistency through a run-time mechanism. Due to this run-time support, the shared memory model out-performs the private memory model in compiler-generated codes for some programs with irregular access patterns [3].

The drawbacks of the DSM model are also significant. The overhead for maintaining a virtual shared memory can be large. Although various efforts have been made to reduce this overhead [8], the communication caused by exchanging control information among processes still occupies a significant percentage of the total amount of communication. In addition, a DSM system may transfer more data than is needed if it maintains consistency on a unit that is bigger than the size of the data accessed.

From the point of view of a compiler, both the message passing and the shared memory model have limitations as the target programming model for automatic code generation. Each model works efficiently on only a limited application set.

Furthermore, the patterns for which the two models are successful are com-plementary. Research [3], mostly done on small benchmark codes or application kernels, indicates that the compiler targeting message passing code is more ef-fective on programs with regular access patterns, while the compiler targeting to DSM code shows an obvious advantage in programs with irregular access patterns. In real applications, however, the problem could be more serious, because many real programs exhibit both regular and irregular accesses.

Thus, we find that neither the private memory nor the shared memory model is a good output model in all cases. A single, fixed model (either private or shared) will prevent the compiler from handling both regular and irregular access patterns efficiently.

## 2.2   Hybrid Programming Model

We propose a new programming model for distributed systems. It is a synthesis of the private memory and shared memory models. The new model inherits the strong points from both existing models. By targeting this model, we believe that the compiler can generate efficient parallel code easily and automatically, on regular, irregular and mixed access pattern programs. We assume an environment that supports both message passing and a (hardware or software) DSM mechanism.

In our hybrid programming model, we include both the private memory and the shared memory model. Since the most efficient mechanism for communicating data differs, depending on how the data is used within the code, we apply two different communication mechanisms to handle data with different communication features. The user data is classified by its usage patterns. We divide data into three classes: **private data**, **distributed data**, and **shared data**.

**Private data** consists of variables that are only accessed by a single processor. No communication is needed for this data.

**Distributed data** consists of variables, with simple usage patterns, which might need to be communicated between processors. Communication of these variables is handled by the message passing mechanism. Since they have a simple usage pattern, the precise message passing code can be easily generated by the compiler automatically.

**Shared data** consists of variables with statically unknown or irregular access patterns. The consistency of shared variables across processors is handled by a DSM mechanism. Shared data is data for which precise message passing code cannot be generated, due to lack of precise access information.

In this hybrid model, explicit message passing and the DSM system are independent and equal-level mechanisms. They work separately on different data classes. Distributed data can be located outside the shared memory space of the software DSM system, eliminating the overhead that would be otherwise necessary to manage it within the DSM system.

In the following sections, we will discuss a compiler framework that supports this hybrid model.

# 3    Internal Representation

## 3.1   Introducing Linear Memory Access Descriptors

Before discussing the details about the compiler framework, we must introduce the Linear Memory Access Descriptor (LMAD), which is applied in this framework. We use the LMAD to describe both array distribution and access patterns. By unifying the internal representation of distribution and access, we can facilitate the message passing path in an efficient and precise way.

An LMAD has several components to describe a access pattern. The **base offset** is the offset, from the first element of the array, for the first location accessed. A **dimension** is a movement through memory with a consistent stride and a computable number of steps. **Stride** gives the distance between two consecutive array accesses in one dimension. **Span** is the distance (in memory units) between the offsets of the first and last elements that are accessed in one dimension.

The LMAD of a reference to array A is represented as $\mathcal{A}^{\text{stride}_1,\text{stride}_2,\cdots}_{\text{span}_1,\text{span}_2,\cdots} +$ base_offset. The stride$_k$ is the stride for the k-th dimension of array A and the span$_k$ is the span for the k-th dimension. An example of an array access, its access pattern and its LMAD representation are shown in Figure 1. The memory locations touched by a memory reference, driven by an enclosing loop nest, may be accurately represented by an LMAD [6].

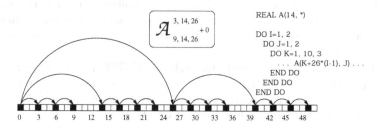

**Fig. 1.** LMAD

## 3.2   Using an LMAD to Represent Data Distribution

The LMAD was designed to represent data accesses [12, 6]. In this paper, we will discuss how to use an LMAD to represent data distributions and to generate message passing code.

When an array is distributed, each processor owns a different part of the overall array space. The data owned by a processor is physically stored on that processor. Since the LMAD can represent memory references inside loops, one way to represent the data owned by a processor is to construct a virtual *distributing loop* that touches each owned location within the overall array space.

When several dimensions are distributed, the distributing loops would be nested. The dimension whose elements are stride-one (left-most in Fortran, right-most in C) would have its distributing loop nested inner-most. The LMAD representing the memory accesses within the distributing loop nest then also represents the distribution of the data to processors.

| Distribution | Distributing loop on $P_i$ | LMAD distribution |
|---|---|---|
| A(N): A(BLOCK) | block= N/p_num $(A(i), i = block*P_i+1, block*(P_i+1))$ | $\mathcal{A}^1_{block-1} + block * P_i$ |
| A(N): A(CYCLIC) | $(A(i), i = P_i+1, N, p\_num)$ | $\mathcal{A}^{p\_num}_{N-p\_num} + P_i$ |
| A(N): A(BLOCK-CYCLIC(k)) | $((A(i,j), i = 1,k),$ $j = k*p\_num*P_i+1, N, k*p\_num)$ | $\mathcal{A}^{1,k*p\_num}_{k-1,N-k*p\_num} + k * p\_num * P_i$ |
| Align A(i+k) with template T(M) distribute T(BLOCK) | block= M/p_num $(A(i+k), i=block*P_i+1, block*(P_i+1))$ | $\mathcal{A}^1_{block-1} + k + block * P_i$ |

**Table 1.** Distributions based on LMADs ($P_i$ is the processor number, with values: $0 : p\_num - 1$).

An LMAD can represent standard data distribution patterns, like BLOCK, CYCLIC, BLOCK-CYCLIC, distribution with an offset, etc, by summarizing the data accesses in a virtual distributing loop. The formulas in Table 1 show the LMAD representations of these distributions for a one dimensional array A (boundary conditions are eliminated here for simplicity). We use the implicit loop notation of Fortran in the table. In Table 1, p_num is the total number of the processors, and $P_i$ is the ID of a processor which is an integer in the range $[0 : p\_num - 1]$.

In Table 1 (c) that represents the A(BLOCK-CYCLIC) distribution. The block length of the distribution is k. The inner loop accesses each element in a single block while the outer loop accesses the array in a cyclic way. Table 1 (d) represents the distribution with a constant offset.

Figure 2 gives some examples to show how the array distributions are represented by LMADs. In these examples, array A(30) is distributed between 2 processors.

The formulas in Figure 1 can be extended to represent distributions in multi-dimensions, by simply nesting the virtual distributing loops. Using a set of LMADs, we can represent even more complex distribution patterns.

## 4    Targeting a Compiler to the Hybrid Model

### 4.1    Overview of the Code Generating Framework

The framework of the compiler algorithm to implement the hybrid model consists of four phases. We give a brief outline of the algorithm framework here, followed by a more detailed description in the next subsections.

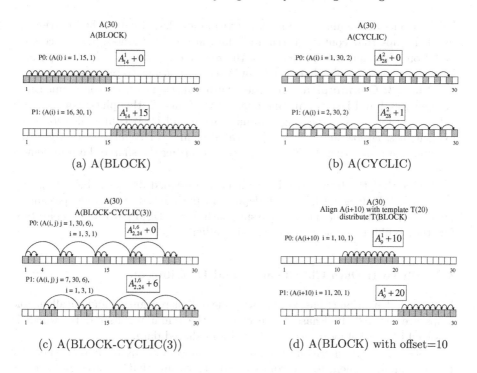

**Fig. 2.** Use LMAD to represent distributions

**Phase 0: Parallelization** The parallelization phase produces a preliminary parallelized shared memory program. Parallelization can be done by a compiler or by hand. The result of this phase is a parallel program for shared memory, with variables privatized as necessary, reductions indicated, and parallel regions marked. In this step, we assume that data will be privatized within single parallel loop nests, and that it will be replicated in all processors.

**Phase 1: Data classification and distribution** In this phase, we classify unprivatizable user data as either *distributed data* or *shared data*. Distributed data is divided among the processors, while shared data is apportioned according to the rules for the DSM being used (TreadMarks replicates its shared data on each processor). The communication of distributed data will be handled by the explicit message passing mechanism, while the shared data will be handled via the DSM mechanism.

Data access patterns are analyzed in this phase. Data having *simple-enough* access patterns is considered as distributed data. All the other data in the program is considered as shared data, except the privatizable data, which was identified in the original parallelization of the code (Phase 0).

**Phase 2: Computation Division** In this phase, the compiler divides the iteration space and assigns iterations to each processor. The code is organized in the SPMD model. This phase includes two subphases: computation division for distributed data and computation division for shared data. The iterations of parallel loops that contain distributed data are divided among the processors, based on, although not restricted to, the *owner-computes* rule. For the parallel loops that contain only shared data, we assign iterations to processors evenly.

**Phase 3: Communication generation** Function calls for communications are generated and inserted in this phase. Like Phase 2, this phase consists of 2 subphases: for message passing communication and DSM communication. The explicit message passing calls are generated at first for communicating the distributed data, and then DSM calls for synchronizing the shared data are generated.

Notice that the framework is particularly designed for the hybrid programming model. It does not have an independent path for either message passing or DSM code. Neither the message passing path or the DSM path work separately, but they build a complete algorithm altogether.

### 4.2    Phase 1: Data Classification and Distribution

In the parallelization (Phase 0), privatizable data is recognized and parallelizable loops are marked. In Phase 1, we classify the remaining user data, which is involved in parallel loops, as distributed and shared data.

Notice that the algorithms used in our framework are quite simple, especially when comparing them to the complicated algorithms that researchers have developed to distribute and access data in distributed system. This is one of the important advantages of our system. By applying an appropriate communication mechanism to each type of data, we hope to generate efficient code, even by very simple algorithms.

The algorithm is designed to operate in an incremental way. In the basic algorithm, only the data with very simple access patterns will be considered as distributed data, but the algorithm can be made more sophisticated and open to further optimization. New techniques can be added incrementally to push more data into the distributed data set, to achieve better performance.

The outline of the data distribution algorithm is given in Figure 3. The input to the algorithm is RefSet(A), the set of references to a given array A, found in a program, and the loop information for loops surrounding each reference. The output of the algorithm is the distribution decision vector D for array A.

The distribution vector D has the same number of elements as the number of dimensions for array A. Each element of vector D represents the distribution decision of the corresponding dimension of array A. Each element of vector D can have one of the following three values: "*" representing an *undecided* dimension, "**D**" representing a *distributable* dimension, and "**N**" representing a *non-distributable* dimension.

In the main loop of the algorithm, we first analyze the access pattern for every dimension of each reference with respect to the loop index. The access pattern could be *separated*, *simply overlapped*, or *irregular*. This is the basic step for the following analysis.

```
Input:
    Array A, RefSet(A), and involved loop information.
Output:
    the distribution decision vector D for Array A,
Algorithm:
main function:
    dims = number of dimensions in array A
    Initialize D[1:dims] = ''*'' (Undecided)
    For(each ref ∈ RefSet(A))
        For(dim = 1 : dims) analyze the access pattern EndFor
        if( loop_index(dim) refer to a parallelizable loop)
            if(access pattern is separated or simply overlapped)
                set_distribution(dim, ''D'') (distributable)
            else set_distribution(dim, ''N'') (non-distributable)
        if( loop_index(dim) refer to a sequetial loop)
            set_distribution(dim, ''N'')
        if(subscript(dim) loop-invariant)
            // leave the corresponding dimension untouched
            continue;
        else set_distribution(dim, ''N'')
    EndFor

set_distribution(dim, distribution)
        if(D[dim] < distribution) D[dim] = distribution
        // ''N''>''D''>''*''
```

**Fig. 3.** Data distribution algorithm

In the next step, consider the corresponding loop for a given dimension. Three cases are considered here. First, if there is loop index involved in the dimension, and the loop is parallelizable, then, for separated or simply overlapped access, set the dimension as distributable ("**D**"), if not, set the dimension as non-distributable ("**N**"). Second, we consider if the loop involved in this dimension is sequential. If the loop is sequential, we set the dimension as "**N**", because in a parallel program, a sequential loop implies the iteration space is not distributed among processors. Therefore, that data is not suitable for distributing. Third, if there is no loop index involved in this dimension (the subscript is loop-invariant), then we will keep its current distribution unchanged. For all the other cases, the dimension will be set as *non-distributable*.

The same array may be referred to in different ways at different places in the program. The conflict is resolved by the precedence of the types of distributions. Distribution **N** has higher precedence than **D**, which has higher precedence than *.

As the final step of the Phase 1, we take the output of the data distribution algorithm and classify the arrays as distributed data or shared data. The arrays

```
do i = 3,N              do i = 2,N-1              do i = max(2, dist_init),
   A(i-1) = ...            A(i) = ...                      min(N-1, dist_limit)
   E(i) = ...             E(i+1) = ...                A(i) = ...
   C(i-1) = ...            C(i) = ...                 E(i+1) = ...
enddo                   enddo                         C(i) = ...
                                                   enddo
```

(a) Choose i-1 as       (b) shift the loop        (c) Divide the loop
the owner               if necessary

**Fig. 4.** Computation division.

with at least one distributable dimension are distributed data. The others are shared data.

### 4.3  Phase 2: Computation Division

Parallel loops that contain distributed data are divided according to the layout of the distributed data, decided in Phase 1, and iterations are assigned to each processor by the owner-computes rule.

In the cases that there are different access patterns in the same loop, we use an evaluation strategy to pick up the most frequently visited pattern as the owner pattern of the loop.

For example, the loop in Figure 4 (a) has both i and i-1 access on the left hand side. We assume that each array has the same access cost. So we try to make the most frequently accessed pattern to be computed on its owner. In the case of Figure 4 (a), the most frequent pattern is i-1. The loop is then shifted, as in Figure 4 (b).

In Figure 4 (c) the loop is divided and the iteration space is assigned to each processor. dist_init is the beginning of the distribution on the local processor, dist_limit is the end of the distribution.

For parallel loops that only contain references to shared data, we divide the iteration space evenly for each processor.

### 4.4  Phase 3: Communication Generation

In this phase, function calls for communications are generated and inserted. There are two kinds of communication function calls: the functions for message passing communication and the functions for DSM communication. The explicit message passing calls are generated first, for communicating the distributed data, and then the DSM calls are generated to synchronize the shared data.

**Message Passing Communication** In the first step of this phase, we compute the region of distributed data that needs to be transferred. Message passing

```
For(each reference ref(A) of distributed array)
   access(P_my_id) = computeLMAD(ref(A))
   for(each distribution on P_i, i != my_id)
      if(ref(A) is read) mode = superset
      else mode = precise
      overlap = intersect(distribute(P_i), access(P_my_id), mode)
      if(overlap != NULL)
         success = generate_message(overlap, i, my_id)
      if(!success) push_back(A)
   endfor
endfor
```

**Fig. 5.** Message Passing Communication

calls are inserted to perform the communication for distributed data, in a copy-in/copy-out manner. Data that is read within a parallel loop nest is fetched from its owner before the loop. Data that is written within the loop must be written back to its owner afterward.

Figure 5 gives the algorithm for message passing call generation. For each reference to array A, we must determine a **send/receive** pair for a given processor and a remote processor by intersecting the LMAD representing its accesses in the given processor with the distribution LMAD of array A in the remote processor.

The LMAD intersection algorithm can be found in [7]. Before calling the intersect function, we specify a value for the "mode" parameter to indicate what to do if the function cannot calculate the precise intersection. If the access is a read reference, it would not affect the correctness of the code if we fetch more data than needed from the remote processor, so "superset" is specified for "mode". If the access is a write reference, the precise write-back is required. In that case, "precise" is specified. Then, if the intersection operation cannot be done precisely, the intersection function will report a failure.

For example, consider a complicated reference like A(B(i), j-1), distributed as A(**N, Block**). If the access is a read, then we can conservatively fetch the whole column of A, so, the "superset" mode can be used. But if the access is a write, then the write-back must be precise. If the intersection procedure fails, due to being in "precise" mode, the array must be pushed back to the shared data set.

A non-empty overlap result from the intersect operation indicates that communication is necessary. In the routine **generate_message**, we try to convert the overlap LMAD to the proper message passing calls by the transformations in Figure 6. The LMADs in Figure 6 are the non-empty results from intersecting the distribution LMAD on processor $P_i$ with the access LMAD on processor $P_j$.

Figure 6 gives three kinds of transformations from LMAD to the equivalent MPI message passing calls. Figure 6 (a) shows the transformation from a dense LMAD, which has the stride of 1, to the equivalent MPI calls. The processor of

LMAD $L_{ij}$: $\mathcal{TT}^1_{span}$ + **offset**
if(my_id == i)
   Send(TT(offset), span+1, data_type, j)
if(my_id == j)
   Receive(TT(offset), span+1, data_type, i)

(a) Transformation 1

LMAD $L_{ij}$: $\mathcal{TT}^{stride}_{span}$ + **offset**
MPI_type_vector(span+1, 1, stride,
    data_type, NewT)
if(my_id == i)
   Send(TT(offset), 1, NewT, j)
if(my_id == j)
   Receive(TT(offset), 1, NewT, i)

(b) Transformation 2

LMAD $L_{ij}$: $\mathcal{TT}^{1,stride2}_{span1span2}$ + **offset**
MPI_type_vector(span2/stride2+1, span1+stride1, stride2, data_type, NewT)
if(my_id == i)
   Send(TT(offset), 1, NewT, j)
if(my_id == j)
   Receive(TT(offset), 1, NewT, i)

(c) Transformation 3

**Fig. 6.** Transfer LMADs to Message Passing Code.

the distribution LMAD sent the overlap data to the processor with the access LMAD. The beginning address of the message buffer is the offset of the overlap LMAD. The length of the message buffer is **span+1**.

For the LMADs with *stride* > 1, as shown in Figure 6 (b), we build an MPI user data type to transfer the data. The MPI type vector can be used to build the user data type with the stride. It has the following interface [10]:

$$MPI\_type\_vector(count, blocklength, stride, oldtype, newtype)$$

The transformation is shown in Figure 6 (b).

The transformation in Figure 6 (b) can be extended to two dimensional LMADs, as shown in Figure 6 (c), as long as *the stride of the first dimension = 1.*

For read references, the message passing calls are generated before the loop, to get the data before it is needed. For write references, the message passing calls are generated after the loop, to write the data back to its owner. The message passing codes in Figure 6 are for read references. The communication codes for write references can be generated by simply switching the sender and the receiver.

If some LMADs are too complicated to be converted into proper message passing calls, the **generate_message** function will return a failure status. If a failure happens, the **push_back** function will push the array back to the shared data set, letting the DSM mechanism handle its communication.

**DSM Communication** The DSM communication calls are generated as the last step of the whole framework. DSM calls are inserted to maintain the synchronization of shared data. At the time of this writing, we use a conservative strategy to handle shared data. Shared data is synchronized after it is updated and at the end of each parallel loop in which the shared data is involved.

## 5   Experimental Results

We applied the algorithm of Section 4 by hand to several benchmarks. We are using MPICH, an implementation of MPI, as our explicit message passing platform. We chose TreadMarks [1], a page-based, lazy-release consistency DSM system as our DSM platform.

Our test-bed consisted of a cluster of Sun workstations connected by Ethernet and a Linux PC cluster connected by Myrinet. Programs were executed on 1, 2, 4, and 8 processors on each cluster. The benchmark set includes Jacobi, Swim, Tomcatv, and SpMatMul.

Jacobi is a partial differential equation solver, using an iterative method. Swim is a benchmark for weather prediction from SPEC, solving difference equations on a two dimensional grid. Tomcatv is a SPEC benchmark. We used the modified version of tomcatv from Applied Parallel Research, Inc., containing better data locality than the SPEC version. Most of the access patterns in these codes are regular.

SpMatMul is a code for multiplying a sparse matrix by a vector. The sparse matrix is stored in the compressed row storage (CRS) format. This program has both regular and irregular access patterns.

The results of the experiments are shown in Figure 7 (a-e). With the first three benchmarks, Jacobi, Swim and Tomcatv, in which regular accesses dominate the access patterns, the pure DSM codes show heavy overhead due to excessive overhead and synchronization. By introducing explicit message passing, the code with our hybrid model reduced overhead and improved performance.

SpMatMul has both regular and irregular accesses. We compare it here with both pure DSM code and pure message passing code. The DSM mechanism is inefficient for the regular part, while the pure message passing code is inefficient for the irregular part. But the code using our hybrid model works efficiently on both parts and achieves the highest speedup.

## 6   Related Work

Dwarkadas, Cox and Zwaenepoel [4] designed an integrated compile-time and run-time software DSM system. The run-time system was augmented with two additional functions: Validate and Push. Using the program access pattern information provided by the compiler, Validate and Push are applied in a program to improve performance.

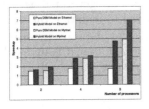

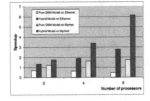

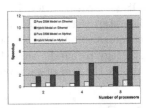

(a) Speedup of Jacobi     (b) Speedup of Swim     (c) Speedup of Tom-catv

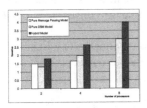

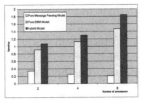

(d) Speedup of Spmat-Mul on Myrinet     (e) Speedup of Spmat-Mul on Ethernet

**Fig. 7.** Experimental Results

Chandra and Larus [2] worked on techniques similar to those used by Dwarkadas et al. They combined the PGI HPF compiler and the Tempest software DSM system [13] in the context of fine-grained software shared memory.

Tseng [14] presented compiler optimizations for reducing synchronization overhead. The SUIF parallelizing compiler was used to produce hybrid fork-join/SPMD parallel codes, targeting the CVM system [9]. Barriers were eliminated or replaced by low-overhead synchronization functions.

Our research differs from all these works by proposing a new programming model rather than an augmented interface for the DSM system. In fact, we know of no other work that combines DSM and message passing as equal partners, as we have done.

Another difference is that we use a new internal representation LMAD rather than the traditional triplet representation. LMAD can represent complex distribution and access patterns accurately. It may also be translated accurately across procedure boundaries, thereby facilitating interprocedural analysis.

## 7   Conclusion

We have proposed a new programming model that merges the private and shared memory models. To support the hybrid programming model, we presented a compiler algorithm. The compiler generates message passing code where the access patterns are simple, and relies on the shared memory mechanism where the access patterns are too complex.

# References

[1] C. Amza, A. Cox, S. Dwarkadas, P. Keleher, H. Lu, R. Rajamony, W. Yu, and W. Zwaenepoel. TreadMarks: Shared Memory Computing on Networks of Workstations. *IEEE Computer*, 29(2):18–28, February 1996.

[2] Satish Chandra and James R. Larus. Optimizing communication in HPF programs on fine-grain distributed shared memory . *ACM. Sigplan Notices (Acm Special Interest Group on Programming Languages)*, 32(7):100–11, July 1997.

[3] Alan L. Cox, Sandhya Dwarkadas, Honghui Lu, and Willy Zwaenepoel. Evaluating the performance of software distributed shared memory as a target for parallelizing compilers . *11th International Parallel Processing Symposium(Cat. No.97TB100107). IEEE Comput. Soc. Press.*, pages 474–82, 1977.

[4] Sandhya Dwarkadas, Alan L. Cox, and Willy Zwaenepoel. An integrated compile-time/run-time software distributed shared memory system . *ACM. Sigplan Notices (Acm Special Interest Group on Programming Languages)*, 31(9):186–97, Sept. 1996.

[5] Sandhya Dwarkadas, Honghui Lu, and Alan L. Cox. Combining compile-time and run-time support for efficient software distributed shared memory . *Proceedings of the IEEE*, 87(3):476–86, March 1999.

[6] J. Hoeflinger. *Interprocedural Parallelization Using Memory Classification Analysis*. PhD thesis, University of Illinois at Urbana-Champaign, July 1998.

[7] J. Hoeflinger and Y. Paek. A Comparative Analysis of Dependence Testing Mechanisms. In *Thirteenth Workshop on Languages and Compilers for Parallel Computing*, August 2000.

[8] Liviu Iftode and Jaswinder Pal Singh. Shared virtual memory: progress and challenges . *Proceedings of the IEEE*, 87(3):498–507, March 1999.

[9] P. Keleher. The relative importance of concurrent writers and weak consistency models . *16th International Conference on Distributed Computing Systems*, May 1996.

[10] Message Passing Interface Forum. *MPI: A Message-Passing Interface Standard* , 1995.

[11] Y. Paek. *Automatic Parallelization for Distributed Memory Machines Based on Access Region Analysis*. PhD thesis, University of Illinois at Urbana-Champaign, April 1997.

[12] Y. Paek, J. Hoeflinger, and D. Padua. Simplication of Array Access Patterns for Compiler Optimizations. *Proceedings of the SIGPLAN Conference on Programming Language Design and Implementation*, June 1998.

[13] Steven K. Reinhardt, James R. Larus, and David A. Wood. Tempest and Typhoon: User-level shared memory . *Proceedings the 21st Annual International Symposium on Computer Architecture (Cat. No.94CH3397-7). IEEE Comput. Soc. Press.*, pages 325–36, 1994.

[14] Chau-Wen Tseng. Compiler optimizations for eliminating barrier synchronization . *Sigplan Notices (Acm Special Interest Group on Programming Languages)*, 30(8):144–55, Aug. 1995.

# The Structure of a Compiler for
# Explicit *and* Implicit Parallelism[*]

Seon Wook Kim and Rudolf Eigenmann

School of Electrical and Computer Engineering
Purdue University, West Lafayette, IN
eigenman@purdue.edu

**Abstract.** We describe the structure of a compilation system that generates code for processor architectures supporting both explicit and implicit parallel threads. Such architectures are small extensions of recently proposed speculative processors. They can extract parallelism speculatively from a sequential instruction stream (implicit threading) *and* they can execute explicit parallel code sections as a multiprocessor (explicit threading). Although the feasibility of such mixed execution modes is often tacitly assumed in the discussion of speculative execution schemes, little experience exists about their performance and compilation issues. In prior work we have proposed the Multiplex architecture [1], supporting such a scheme. The present paper describes the compilation system of Multiplex.

Our compilation system integrates the Polaris preprocessor with the Gnu C code generating compiler. We describe the major components that are involved in generating explicit and implicit threads. We describe in more detail two components that represent significant open issues. The first issue is the integration of the parallelizing preprocessor with the code generator. The second issue is the decision when to generate explicit and when to generate implicit threads. Our compilation process is fully automated.

## 1 Introduction

Automatic program parallelization for shared-memory multiprocessor systems has made significant progress over the past ten years, and it has been most successful in Fortran code, as demonstrated by the Polaris and the SUIF compilers [2, 3]. However, substantial challenges still exist when detecting parallelism in irregular and non-numeric applications. One serious limitation of the current generation of compilers is that they have to provide absolute guarantees about program data dependences between sections of code believed to be parallel. Both software and hardware techniques have been proposed to overcome this limitation. Multi-version codes and run-time dependence test [4, 5] are examples of

---

[*] This work was supported in part by NSF grants #9703180-CCR and #9974976-EIA. Seon Wook Kim is now with KAI Software Lab, A Division of Intel Americas, Inc., Champaign, IL, seon.w.kim@intel.com.

software techniques, while speculative multiprocessors are proposals for hardware solutions [6, 7, 8, 9, 10]. The software's run-time dependence test instruments codes to track data dependences during speculative parallel execution. Speculative multiprocessors provide such speculative support in hardware.

Combining explicit parallelization and speculative execution may appear straightforward. In fact, some recent proposals for speculative architectures make this tacit assumption. However, little experience exists with combined schemes. In [1] we have presented an architecture that supports such an execution mechanism. The present paper describes the issues and the structure of a compiler generating code for such an architecture.

A compiler that supports both explicit and implicit parallelism must perform the following tasks.

**Recognition of parallelism:** The basis for explicit threading is the automatic or manual recognition of code sections that can execute in parallel. In this paper we consider automatic parallelization.

**Selecting explicit and implicit threads:** Explicit threads can be selected from the code sections identified as parallel. The remaining code may be split into implicit threads, that is, into code sections that the hardware can then execute speculatively in parallel.

**Thread preprocessing:** High-level transformations of the selected threads may be necessary. For example, our compiler transforms all explicitly parallel code sections such that the absence of cross-thread dependences is guaranteed.

**Thread code generation:** The actual code generation may include steps such as inserting calls to thread management libraries, identifying threads (e.g., adding thread header code), and setting up thread environments (e.g., defining thread-private stacks).

A number of issues arise when realizing such a compilation system. For this paper we rely on state-of-the-art technology for recognizing parallelism. Although there are many open issues in the detection of parallel code, they are the same as for automatic parallelization on today's multiprocessor systems. In our work we make use of the capabilities of the Polaris parallelizer [2].

Selecting explicit and implicit threads is an important new issue. A straightforward scheme would select all recognized outermost parallel loop iterations as explicit threads, which is the scheme chosen in today's parallelizing compilers. For the rest of the program it would select one or a group of basic blocks as implicit threads, which is the scheme used in the Wisconsin Multiscalar compiler [11]. In [12], preliminary studies showed that such a simplistic scheme would lead to suboptimal performance. Both execution schemes incur intrinsic overheads. For fully independent threads, the choice between implicit and explicit execution is important for best performance. An improved scheme must estimate overheads incurred by the two threading schemes and find the best tradeoff. We will discuss these issues and present a thread selection algorithm in Section 4.

Thread preprocessing is important in our compiler to insert code that makes runtime decisions if static thread selection was judged insufficient. Preprocessing is also necessary to guarantee the absence of data dependences among explicit threads. In Section 2.3 will will describe why code sections that are recognized as fully parallel may still incur dependences in the generated code. We use state-of-the-art compiler techniques to resolve this problem.

The actual code generation must properly identify and coordinate code sections that are to be executed as explicit or implicit threads. The start of each thread must be marked in the binary code, the thread mode (explicit or implicit) must be specified, and thread management code must be inserted.

One of the biggest implementation issues arises because the first three steps above are typically done in the preprocessor, whereas the last step is performed by the code generating compiler. Integrating the two different compilers involves expressing the results of the preprocessor's analysis in a way that can be communicated to the code generator. One also must extend the code generator to understand and use this information. We describe the interface between preprocessor and code generator in our compilation system in Section 3.

The specific contributions of this paper are as follows:

– We describe the structure and the tasks of a compiler for an architecture that supports both explicit and implicit parallelism.
– We describe techniques for integrating a parallelizing preprocessor and a code generating compiler to accomplish these tasks.
– We describe an algorithm for selecting explicit and implicit threads.

The remainder of the paper is organized as follows. Section 2 gives an overview of our compilation system in terms of the tasks identified above. The modules for which we used state-of-the-art compiler components will be briefly explained. The next two sections describe in more details the two most difficult issues we encountered. These are (1) the integration of the preprocessor and the code generating compiler (Section 3) and (2) the implicit/explicit thread selection algorithm (Section 4). We present performance results in Section 5, followed by conclusions in Section 6.

## 2    Overview of the Compilation System

Figure 1 gives an overview of the compilation system for our experimental architecture, Multiplex [1]. It consists of an extended version of the Polaris preprocessor [2], a modified f2c translator [13], an extended version of the Gnu C compiler [14], and Multiplex-specific thread libraries.

### 2.1    Recognition of Parallelism

Fortran applications are analyzed by the preprocessor to identify parallel loops. We use the existing Polaris infrastructure for this purpose. Polaris is a parallelizing preprocessor that contains advanced techniques, such for data-dependence

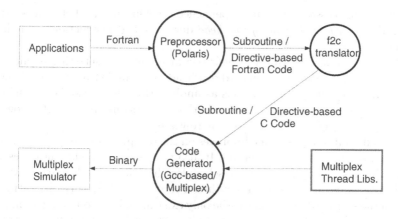

| Compiler / Tool | Multiplex Extension | Purpose |
|---|---|---|
| Polaris | Thread selector pass | Select either explicit or implicit threading at compile time and runtime (multi-versioning) to minimize explicit threading overhead. |
| | Subroutine-based postpass | Guarantee absence of dependences among explicit threads. Enable thread-private stacks for allocating private variables |
| | Directive-based postpass | Implicit threads: Control thread selection of the code generator. |
| f2c | Parser | Parse Fortran Multiplex directives. |
| Gnu C | Parser | Parse C Multiplex directives. |
| Code generator | Multiplex backend | Insert special instructions to mark thread execution attributes. |
| Library | Thread management | Fork and join explicit/implicit threads. Pass arguments from parent to child threads. |
| | Utilities | Provide thread identification numbers and the number of threads. |

**Fig. 1.** Overview of the compilation system for the Multiplex architecture

analysis, array privatization, idiom recognition, and symbolic analysis [2]. Although the present paper uses automatic parallelization techniques for identifying explicit threads, this is not a prerequisite. For example, explicitly parallel programs (e.g., OpenMP source code) could be used. In such programs, parallel regions would provide candidate explicit threads, while implicit threads would be derived from the "serial" program section.

## 2.2   Thread Selection

All iterations of parallel loops are candidates for explicit threads. The rest of the program is considered for creating implicit threads. While explicit threading eliminates unnecessary runtime dependence tracking in parallel code sections, it introduces *explicit threading overhead* due to added instructions and thread management costs.

In Section 4 we describe the heuristic algorithm for selecting explicit and implicit threads. Based on estimated overheads at compile time it may choose to execute fully parallel loop iterations as implicit threads. If insufficient information is available at compile time, then both code versions are generated together with code choosing between the two at runtime.

Our fully-automatic scheme improves on the one presented in [1], in which we have used a semi-automatic method. It also relates to the techniques presented in [15]. In this work, the compiler schedules the outermost loop that will not overflow the speculative storage for thread-level execution, only estimating the usage of the storage. Our scheme is the only existing fully automated technique to consider various characteristics of the applications and to deliver the performance as good as a profiling scheme. The algorithm is a novel part of our compilation system.

## 2.3   Thread Preprocessing

Thread preprocessing performs two tasks. First, it generates code that makes runtime decisions about whether to execute a thread as implicit or explicit. Second, it transforms explicit loops that are selected for explicit threading into subroutine form.

**Two-Version Code for Explicit/Implicit Threading** If the thread selection algorithm decides that there is insufficient information at compile time, it generates conditional expressions that determine the best threading mode. The preprocessing step inserts an IF statement containing this conditional, with the THEN and ELSE part being the explicit and implicit threading version of the loop, respectively. The explicit threading version selects each iteration of this loop as an explicit thread. The implicit version selects each innermost loop iteration as an implicit thread. Creating this code was straightforward, given the available Polaris infrastructure.

**Subroutine Conversion of Explicit Threads** Our compiler transforms explicit threads into subroutine form. This transformation is the same as routinely applied by compilers for generating thread-based code from parallel loop-oriented languages. Polaris already contains such a pass, which we have used with small modifications [16]. Figure 2 shows examples of the code transformation in thread preprocessing.

This transformation accomplishes two tasks. First, it provides the explicit thread with a proper stack frame so that a private stack can be used during its execution. Section 2.5 describes the process of setting up stacks for each thread. Second, it guarantees explicit threads to be dependence-free. We have found two causes of false dependences introduced in otherwise fully-independent threads.

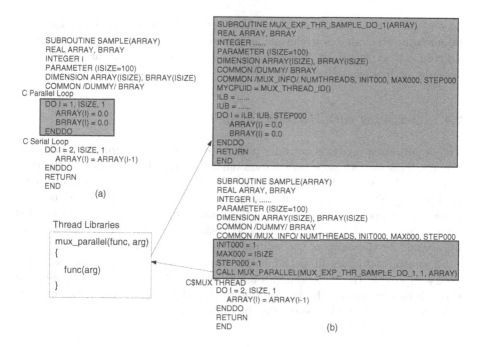

```
          SUBROUTINE SAMPLE(ARRAY)
          REAL ARRAY, BRRAY
          INTEGER I
          PARAMETER (ISIZE=100)
          DIMENSION ARRAY(ISIZE), BRRAY(ISIZE)
          COMMON /DUMMY/ BRRAY
C Parallel Loop
          DO I = 1, ISIZE, 1
             ARRAY(I) = 0.0
             BRRAY(I) = 0.0
          ENDDO
C Serial Loop
          DO I = 2, ISIZE, 1
             ARRAY(I) = ARRAY(I-1)
          ENDDO
          RETURN
          END
                         (a)


          Thread Libraries

          mux_parallel(func, arg)
          {

             func(arg)

          }
```

```
SUBROUTINE MUX_EXP_THR_SAMPLE_DO_1(ARRAY)
REAL ARRAY, BRRAY
INTEGER ......
PARAMETER (ISIZE=100)
DIMENSION ARRAY(ISIZE), BRRAY(ISIZE)
COMMON /DUMMY/ BRRAY
COMMON /MUX_INFO/ NUMTHREADS, INIT000, MAX000, STEP000
MYCPUID = MUX_THREAD_ID()
ILB = ......
IUB = ......
DO I = ILB, IUB, STEP000
   ARRAY(I) = 0.0
   BRRAY(I) = 0.0
ENDDO
RETURN
END

SUBROUTINE SAMPLE(ARRAY)
REAL ARRAY, BRRAY
INTEGER I, ......
PARAMETER (ISIZE=100)
DIMENSION ARRAY(ISIZE), BRRAY(ISIZE)
COMMON /DUMMY/ BRRAY
COMMON /MUX_INFO/ NUMTHREADS, INIT000, MAX000, STEP000
INIT000 = 1
MAX000 = ISIZE
STEP000 = 1
CALL MUX_PARALLEL(MUX_EXP_THR_SAMPLE_DO_1, 1, ARRAY)
C$MUX THREAD
DO I = 2, ISIZE, 1
   ARRAY(I) = ARRAY(I-1)
ENDDO
RETURN
END                              (b)
```

**Fig. 2.** Code transformation by the preprocessor. (a) Original code. (b) Transformed code. The subroutine MUX_EXP_THR_SAMPLE_DO_1 is created from a parallel loop, and it is called by the thread manager mux_parallel (Section 2.5). The function mux_parallel copies shared variables (ARRAY) into child threads and control the explicit threads. The newly created subroutines are executed explicitly, while the serial loop is executed implicitly. The serial loop is annotated whith the directive c$mux thread.

Although their explanation needs some implementation details, both issues are intrinsic to the architecture and compilation system.

The first type of dependence is introduced as a result of using a state-of-the-art, sequential compiler for low-level code generation. Standard register allocation techniques performed by such compilers attempt to place values in registers. If the lifetime of such a value spans two threads, the two processors executing the threads need to perform *register communication* with proper synchronization. This mechanism is well understood in speculative architectures and is part of our execution scheme for implicit threads. However, for explicit threads such dependences are not allowed. In our compiler we found that the *strength reduction* technique is a major cause of such dependences. The transformation into subroutine form prevents this optimization across explicit threads.

The second type of dependence is only an apparent dependence, in which the processor falsely assumes that register communication is necessary. It is caused by the typical register-save instructions at the beginning and end of a subroutine, which look to the architecture as if the register value were written to memory. In actuality, the value is irrelevant for the subroutine. This problem was identified in [17] as "artificial dependences" and can cause significant performance degradation in speculative architectures.

## 2.4   Interfacing with Backend Compiler

The preprocessor analyzes not only parallel loops, but also explicit and implicit threads. This preprocessor information must be correctly passed on to the code generator. The information includes the thread boundaries and attributes (implicit or explicit). It is communicated to the backend code generator in two different forms: Loops that are selected to become implicit threads are annotated with a directive. Explicit threads are identified by a call to a special runtime library and by the name of the subroutine passed as an argument.

A substantial effort in implementing our code generation scheme was necessary to enable the code generator to understand the information obtained through this interface. The issue of interfacing the preprocessor with the code generator is described in more detail in Section 3.

## 2.5   Code Generation for Implicit and Explicit Threads

The goal of the code generator is to mark implicit and explicit threads in the binary code and insert data necessary for proper threads operation. We use the compiler techniques already provided by the Wisconsin Multiscalar compiler [11]. It inserts thread header information that marks the start of a new thread and expresses cross-thread register dependences. We extended the thread header to mark the thread attributes. We describe the library implementation next.

**Thread Libraries** The thread libraries provide three functions: a stack manager to initialize the stack space, a thread manager to fork explicit threads, and thread utilities to support the threads' intrinsic functions.

The stack manager initializes a private stack pointer and allocates a private stack space to each processor at the beginning of the program. Private stacks eliminate dependences in thread-private variables of explicit threads.

Figure 3 shows the implementation of the thread manager. It consists of two parts: copying arguments into the private stacks and forking/executing/joining explicit threads.

Two additional thread utility functions are provided: mux_thread_id and mux_num_threads. The function mux_thread_id returns the processor identification number, and mux_num_threads returns the number of processors. These functions are used for thread scheduling.

```
void mux_parallel(void (*pdo_func)(),       /* newly created subroutine from a parallel loop */
                  int        *num_argc, /* number of shared variables in arguments */
                  unsigned int *reg_argv2, /* the first argument through a register */
                  unsigned int *reg_argv3, /* second argument through a register */
                  void        *stk_argv)   /* the first argument through a global stack */
{
    int i;
    unsigned int stack_argv = (unsigned int)&stk_argv;

    /* stack argument copy */
    if(*num_argc >= 5){
        for(i=0;i<numThreads;i++)
            memcpy((unsigned int *)MUX_StkBase[i]+16),
                   (unsigned int *)(stack_argv+8),
                   (*num_argc - 4) * sizeof(unsigned int));

    /* store a global stack pointer into a temporary space */
    asm("sw   $29,glb_stk_addr");

$mux parallel
    for(i=0;i<numThreads;i++){
        /* get a private stack pointer */
        pri_stk_addr = MUX_StkBase[i];
        /* assign the private stack pointer to a stack register */
        asm("lw    $29,pri_stk_addr");
        /* execute loop body */
        pdofunc(reg_argv2, reg_argv3,
            *(unsigned int)stack_argv, *(unsigned int*)(stack_argv+4));
        /* restore a global stack pointer */
        asm("lw    $29,glb_stk_addr");
    }

    return;
}
```

Copy shared variables into thread workspace.

Fork/execute/join explicit threads

**Fig. 3.** The explicit thread manager `mux_parallel`. It copies the shared variables into the child thread workspace and controls the explicit threads. The real implementation is done at the assembly level. The program gives an overview of the implementation.

## 3   Integrating Preprocessor and Code Generator

A substantial effort in implementing our code generation scheme was necessary to build an interface such that the analysis information generated by the preprocessor can be passed on to the code generator. The preprocessor identifies threads and passes their attributes to the code generator. For this purpose, the preprocessor uses a naming scheme for explicit threads. It creates a name prefix of the newly created subroutine for explicit threads, as illustrated in Section 2.3, as `mux_exp_thr_`. The actual code invoking the explicit thread is the call to the `mux_parallel` library routine.

For implicit threads, the preprocessor uses two Multiplex directives: c$mux thread to select an iteration of the annotated loop, c$mux serial_thread to assign the whole loop to one implicit thread. By default, an iteration of the innermost loop is selected as an implicit thread.

We extended the code generator so that it understands this information. We implemented parsing capabilities for the input directives. We also extended the code generator's internal data structure (RTL, Register Transfer Language) [14] to represent the directive information in the form of *RTL notes*. These notes are used by the code generating pass that selects implicit threads. For the subroutines of explicit threads the code generator simply produces one-thread code.

Figure 4 shows examples of the implicit thread generation scheme in the original Multiscalar and the new Multiplex compiler. The scheme combines several basic blocks into a thread and marks it as such. The Multiscalar scheme always picks iterations of innermost loops as threads (Figure 4 (b)), whereas the Multiplex compiler picks threads according to the provided mux$ thread directives (Figure 4 (c)). Our code generator uses directives from the preprocessor, in the form of extended RTL notes. They describe the boundaries of threads, which can be at any loop level. The basic blocks belonging to the inner loop are copied because the outer loop has two basic blocks 0 and 1 forming the loop entry. The details are described in [12].

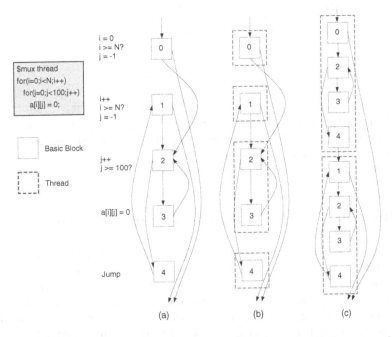

**Fig. 4.** Thread selection using the Multiplex directive set. (a) Source code and control flow graph (CFG). (b) The Multiscalar compiler. (c) The Multiplex compiler. The thread selection in Multiplex is controlled by the preprocessor, whereas that of Multiscalar is done by the code generator itself, walking through the CFG.

# 4   Implicit/Explicit Thread Selection

Careful thread selection is important for good performance. A naive scheme may select all iterations of fully parallel loops as explicit threads and all innermost iterations of the remaining loop nests as implicit threads. Such a scheme would incur overheads that can be reduced with a better selection algorithm. The following factors must be considered.

For our consideration, the most important overhead of implicit threads is *speculative storage overflow*. It occurs when the speculative state (all speculatively written values) built up in the course of the thread execution exceeds the capacity of the speculative storage [18]. Explicit threads do not incur this overhead because they do not use speculative storage. However, they incur overheads due to the added instructions generated by the preprocessing step (subroutine conversion). This overhead is significant in small threads.

Fully parallel code sections can be executed as either implicit or explicit threads. The thread selection algorithm makes this decision by considering the above overheads. Although there are more choices, the algorithm will only consider the outermost parallel loops for explicit execution and the innermost loops for implicit executions. In our experiments we have found that alternative choices can rarely improve performance further. Thus, for each outermost parallel loop $\mathcal{L}$ the algorithm considers the following factors:

*Speculative storage overflow:* The compiler determines whether the implicit execution of any innermost loop would incur speculative storage overflow. In our architecture, the speculative storage is organized as a direct-mapped L1 cache. Speculative storage overflow occurs on a cache conflict. That is, if the conflicting cache line is currently speculative then it cannot be replaced, hence execution stalls. Our algorithm inspects *read–read* and *write–read* reference pairs in innermost loops of $\mathcal{L}$. If it is able to calculate the address distance of the two references and this distance is a multiple of the number of cache blocks, then a cache conflict is caused by the second reference. The resulting speculative storage overflow can stall the processor execution for several hundred cycles. Therefore, if the compiler detects any such overflow, it chooses explicit thread execution for $\mathcal{L}$. If insufficient information is available at compile time, the compiler marks the loop as needing a dynamic decision and generates the expression that needs to be evaluated at runtime. Note that the algorithm ignores cache conflicts if the second reference is a write. We have found that the store queue, to which write references go, provides sufficient buffering so that the processor does not incur significant stalls.

*Loop workload:* To estimate $\mathcal{L}$'s workload, the algorithm multiplies the ranges of all indices of enclosing loops. If the result is less than a threshold and there is no speculative storage overflow, then the loop is selected for implicit execution. If the workload is not a constant, then the compiler again marks the loop as needing a runtime decision.

*Loop attributes:* A candidate loop $\mathcal{L}$ is also executed in explicit mode if any of the following attributes hold. (1) $\mathcal{L}$ is more than doubly-nested (the workload is assumed to be large enough). (2) There is any inner, serial loop, i.e., the loop has compiler-detected cross-iteration dependences (executing inner loop iterations as implicit threads would result in high dependence overhead). (3) $\mathcal{L}$ contains function calls (the algorithm assumes that an implicit execution would incur stalls due to artificial dependences, see Section 2.3).

**Algorithm 1 (Selecting Explicit/Implicit Thread Execution Mode)**
*For each outermost parallel loop $\mathcal{L}$ in the program,*

1. *Estimate the workload of $\mathcal{L}$ and the speculative storage overflow of all innermost loops as described above.*
2. *Select thread execution mode:*
   (a) *Mark $\mathcal{L}$ as explicit if at least one of the following conditions is true:*
      i. *$\mathcal{L}$ is more than doubly nested.*
      ii. *$\mathcal{L}$ encloses any serial loop.*
      iii. *$\mathcal{L}$ contains any function call.*
      iv. *The compiler detects any speculative storage overflow.*
      v. *The workload is greater than the threshold.*
   (b) *Else if both overflow and workload are compile-time decidable, mark all innermost loops of $\mathcal{L}$ as implicit.*
   (c) *Else mark $\mathcal{L}$ as needing runtime decision.*

Figure 5 shows an example of the thread selection decision made in SWIM INITAL_do70. The speculative storage is a 4K direct-mapped cache. The algorithm considers only two pairs of accesses: $(u(1, j), v(1, 1+j))$, and $(u(1+m, j), v(1, 1+j))$. At compile time the value of the variable $m$ is not known, so a function call is inserted, mux_test_overflow, to test for speculative storage overflow of the two accesses $(u(1+m, j), v(1, 1+j))$ at runtime. The compiler can estimate the overflow of the two variables, $u(1, j)$ and $v(1, 1+j)$, because they are in the same common block and the sizes of all variables belonging to the common block are known at compile time. The algorithm also estimates the workload for the loop using the loop index range.

```
        IF (.NOT.mux_test_overflow(u(1+m, 1), v(1, 2)).AND.(-419)+n.LE.0)
      *THEN
C$MUX LOOPLABEL 'INITAL_do70'
C$MUX THREAD
        DO j = 1, n, 1
          u(1, j) = u(1+m, j)
          v(1+m, 1+j) = v(1, 1+j)
  70    CONTINUE
        ENDDO
        ELSE
          init000 = 1
          max000 = n
          step000 = 1
          CALL mux_parallel(mux_exp_thr_inital_do70, 0)
        ENDIF
```

**Fig. 5.** Code generation for runtime thread selection in SWIM INITAL_do70.

The presented scheme is the only existing fully automated technique that considers various characteristics of the application and the hardware to select the best thread execution mode. In the next section we will show that it performs as well as a scheme that uses profile information.

# 5   Performance Analysis

## Overall Evaluation of the Compiler Infrastructure

Figure 6 shows the speedups of our benchmarks, consisting of the SPECfp95 and three Perfect Benchmarks applications. The bars show (1) the original Multiscalar codes (implicit-only execution, not using our new compiler techniques), (2) our Multiplex execution with a naive thread selection algorithm, (3) the Multiplex execution with our new thread selection algorithm, and (4) the Multiplex execution with a thread-selection scheme based on profile information. The speedups measure the four-CPU execution relative to a one-CPU execution. These results correspond closely to the ones presented in [1], which described the Multiplex hardware system. However, in [1] we used a semi-automatic thread selection scheme, while the measurements in Figure 6 show the performance using our new algorithm. The hardware system has four dual-issue, out-of-order superscalar CPU cores. Each processor has its own private 16K DM L1 data cache as a speculative storage, and the cache coherence protocol is extended to maintain the speculative states. We profiled the performance on a loop-by-loop basis, and manually selected the better execution mode. The Multiplex-naive code executes *all* parallel loops as explicit threads.

For presentation, we classify the measured applications into two: Class 1 (FPPPP, APSI, TURB3D, APPLU and WAVE5) applications have many small-grain parallel loops inside a serial loop, and Class 2 (the rest of applications) codes have large-grain parallel loops. In the Class 1 applications, the implicit-only execution is better than the naive Multiplex scheme by 6.2% due to the explicit threading overhead. In the other applications (Class 2 applications), the performance in the naive Multiplex codes is better than implicit-only by 43.7%. This improvement is due to the elimination of speculative execution overheads in compiler-identified parallel code sections. Using our compiler infrastructure, the hardware can turn off speculation in compiler-identified parallel code sections. It allows us to exploit large-grain thread-level parallelism, and eliminate the speculative overheads. The results also show that our thread selection algorithm is most effective in the applications of Class 1. We discuss this effect in more detail in the next subsection.

## Evaluation of the Thread Selection Algorithm

Figure 6 shows that our heuristic thread selection algorithm improves the naive Multiplex performance in the Class 1 applications by a significant 13.1% on average. The performance of the compiler heuristics does not match that of the

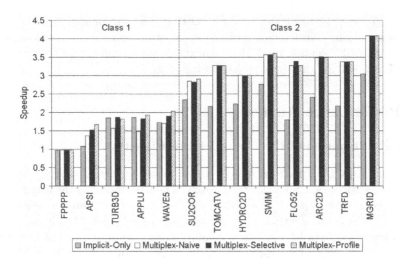

**Fig. 6.** Overall speedup with respect to the superscalar execution. The "Multiplex-Naive" executes all parallel loops in explicit mode. "Multiplex-Selective" uses our new heuristic algorithm, which executes some of the parallel loops in explicit mode. For comparison, in "Multiplex-Profile" the execution mode is selected manually based on profiling.

profiling scheme in all applications. The main reason is that the compiler does not make a correct choice between implicit and explicit execution because the array subscripts are not analyzable (not affine). For example, this is the case in the loop BESPOL_do10 in SU2COR.

Figure 7 shows the instruction overhead, which is the ratio of the committed instructions of the four-processor execution schemes to those of a superscalar execution. In the Class 1 applications, the instruction overhead of the naive thread selection algorithm is much higher, resulting in the implicit-only execution performing better. The reason is again the many small explicit loops in those applications, which incur significant explicit threading overhead. The compiler heuristic reduces the instruction overhead in the Class 1 naive Multiplex codes significantly.

## 6    Conclusions

Speculative architectures have been proposed in order to relieve the compiler from the burden of providing absolute guarantees about program data dependences between sections of code believed to be parallel. However, internally speculative architectures make use of sophisticated techniques that incur intrinsic overheads. Compiler techniques are important to reduce these overheads.

In this paper, we presented the structure of a compilation system that exploits both implicit and explicit thread-level parallelism. The system integrates

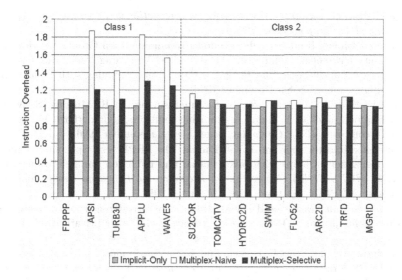

**Fig. 7.** Instruction overhead of implicit-only, the naive Multiplex and Multiplex using our thread selection algorithm with respect to the superscalar execution. Our algorithm reduces explicit threading overhead significantly in the Class 1 applications.

a parallelizing preprocessor with a code generator for the Multiplex architecture. A preprocessor identifies parallel code sections, and selects the execution mode for each section. It also transforms the parallel loops into subroutine-based forms in order to guarantee that there is no dependence for explicit threading. The preprocessor's analysis information (thread boundaries and attributes) is passed to the code generator through an appropriate interface, integrating the two compilers tightly. We also presented a compiler algorithm that decides between implicit and explicit thread execution mode. Where the algorithm cannot make static decisions, it generates runtime decision code. We showed that all of our compiler techniques improve the performance significantly.

There are many related projects in speculative CMPs [6, 7, 8, 9, 10]. However, there has not been an emphasis of compilation issues. Our system is the first that can exploit both explicit and implicit thread-level parallelism. Furthermore, our compiler infrastructure is the only existing fully automated translator system for speculative architectures that integrates the preprocessor's analysis capabilities with the code generator.

# References

[1] Chong-Liang Ooi, Seon Wook Kim, Il Park, Rudolf Eigenmann, Babak Falsafi, and T. N. Vijaykumar. Multiplex: Unifying conventional and speculative thread-level

parallelism on a chip multiprocessor. In *International Conference on Supercomputing (ICS'01)*, pages 368–380, June 2001.

[2] William Blume, Ramon Doallo, Rudolf Eigenmann, John Grout, Jay Hoeflinger, Thomas Lawrence, Jaejin Lee, David Padua, Yunheung Paek, Bill Pottenger, Lawrence Rauchwerger, and Peng Tu. Parallel programming with Polaris. *IEEE Computer*, pages 78–82, December 1996.

[3] M. W. Hall, J. M. Anderson, S. P. Amarasinghe, B. R. Murphy, S.-W. Liao, E. Bugnion, and M. S. Lam. Maximizing multiprocessor performance with the SUIF compiler. *IEEE Computer*, pages 84–89, December 1996.

[4] Lawrence Rauchwerger and David Padua. The LRPD test: Speculative run-time parallelization of loops with privatization and reduction parallelization. In *The ACM SIGPLAN '95 Conference on Programming Language Design and Implementation (PLDI'95)*, pages 218–232, June 1995.

[5] Lawrence Rauchwerger and David Padua. The privatizing DOALL test: A runtime technique for DOALL loop identification and array privatization. In *International Conference on Supercomputing (ICS'94)*, pages 33–43, 1994.

[6] Gurindar S. Sohi, Scott E. Breach, and T. N. Vijaykumar. Multiscalar processors. In *The 22th International Symposium on Computer Architecture (ISCA-22)*, pages 414–425, June 1995.

[7] Kunle Olukotun, Lance Hammond, and Mark Willey. Improving the performance of speculatively parallel applications on the Hydra CMP. In *International Conference on Supercomputing (ICS'99)*, pages 21–30, 1999.

[8] J. Gregory Steffan and Todd C. Mowry. The potential for thread-level data speculation in tightly-coupled multiprocessors. Technical Report CSRI-TR-350, University of Toronto, Department of Electrical and Computer Engineering, Feb. 1997.

[9] J.-Y. Tsai, Z. Jiang, Z. Li, D.J. Lilja, X. Wang, P.-C. Yew, B. Zheng, and S. Schwinn. Superthreading: Integrating compilation technology and processor architecture for cost-effective concurrent multithreading. *Journal of Information Science and Engineering*, March 1998.

[10] Ye Zhang, Lawrence Rauchwerger, and Josep Torrellas. Hardware for speculative run-time parallelization in distributed shared-memory multiprocessors. In *The Fourth International Symposium on High-Performance Computer Architecture (HPCA-4)*, pages 162–173, February 1998.

[11] T. N. Vijaykumar and Gurindar S. Sohi. Task selection for a multiscalar processor. In *The 31st International Symposium on Microarchitecture (MICRO-31)*, pages 81–92, December 1998.

[12] Seon Wook Kim. *Compiler Techniques for Speculative Execution*. PhD thesis, Electrical and Computer Engineering, Purdue University, April 2001.

[13] S. I. Feldman, David M. Gay, Mark W. Maimone, and N. L. Schryer. A Fortran-to-C converter. Technical Report Computing Science No. 149, AT&T Bell Laboratories, Murray Hill, NJ, 1995.

[14] Richard M. Stallman. *Using and Porting GNU Gcc version 2.7.2*, November 1995.

[15] J.-Y. Tsai, Z. Jiang, and P.-C. Yew. Compiler techniques for the superthreaded architectures. *International Journal of Parallel Programming*, 27(1):1–19, February 1999.

[16] Seon Wook Kim, Michael Voss, and Rudolf Eigenmann. Performance analysis of parallel compiler backends on shared-memory multiprocessors. In *Compilers for Parallel Computers (CPC2000)*, pages 305–320, January 2000.

[17] J. Oplinger, D. Heine, and M. S. Lam. In search of speculative thread-level parallelism. In *The 1999 International Conference on Parallel Architectures and Compilation Techniques (PACT'99), Newport Beach, CA*, pages 303–313, October 1999.

[18] Seon Wook Kim, Chong-Liang Ooi, Rudolf Eigenmann, Babak Falsafi, and T. N. Vijaykumar. Reference idempotency analysis: A framework for optimizing speculative execution. In *ACM SIGPLAN Symposium on Principles and Practice of Parallel Programming (PPOPP01)*, pages 2–11, June 2001.

# Coarse Grain Task Parallel Processing with Cache Optimization on Shared Memory Multiprocessor

Kazuhisa Ishizaka, Motoki Obata, and Hironori Kasahara

Dept.EECE, Waseda University
3-4-1 Ohkubo, Shinjuku-ku, Tokyo, 169-8555, Japan
Advanced Parallelizing Compiler Project
{ishizaka,obata,kasahara}@oscar.elec.waseda.ac.jp
http://www.apc.waseda.ac.jp/

**Abstract.** In multiprocessor systems, the gap between peak and effective performance has getting larger. To cope with this performance gap, it is important to use multigrain parallelism in addition to ordinary loop level parallelism. Also, effective use of memory hierarchy is important for the performance improvement of multiprocessor systems because the speed gap between processors and memories is getting larger.

This paper describes coarse grain task parallel processing that uses parallelism among macro-tasks like loops and subroutines considering cache optimization using data localization scheme. The proposed scheme is implemented on OSCAR automatic multigrain parallelizing compiler. OSCAR compiler generates OpenMP FORTRAN program realizing the proposed scheme from a sequential FORTRAN77 program. Its performance is evaluated on IBM RS6000 SP 604e High Node 8 processors SMP machine using SPEC95fp tomcatv, swim, mgrid. In the evaluation, the proposed coarse grain task parallel processing scheme with cache optimization gives us up to 1.3 times speedup on 1PE, 4.7 times speedup on 4PE and 8.8 times speedup on 8PE compared with a sequential processing time.

## 1 Introduction

Shared memory multiprocessor architecture is widely used from a single chip multiprocessor to a high performance computer. The difference between peak performance and effective performance has been getting larger with the increase of the number of processors. Moreover, the speed gap between processors and memories is getting significant. Therefore, optimal use of hierarchical memories and task parallelism are very important for the improvement of effective performance of multiprocessor systems. However, the optimization requires high expertise for the parallel processing and the data distribution to the hierarchical memories, scheduling and so on. Considering the above facts, to improve effective performance and ease of use, an automatic parallelizing compiler realizing coarse grain parallel processing in addition to loop parallel processing with memory hierarchy optimization is required.

H. Dietz (Ed.): LCPC 2001, LNCS 2624, pp. 352–365, 2003.

As automatic parallelizing compilers, loop parallelizing compilers are very popular for SMPs currently available on the market.

Also, advanced research compilers, such as Polaris[1] exploiting loop parallelism by using inline expansion of subroutine, symbolic propagation, array privatization, range test and run-time data dependence analysis [2, 3] and SUIF[4] which parallelizes loop by using inter-procedure analysis unimodular transformation and data locality optimization have been developed. [5, 6, 7].

The data locality optimization is essential to cope with increasing speed gap between processors and memories. Many researches for data locality optimization using program restructuring techniques such as blocking, tiling, padding and data localization have been performed for high performance computers and multiprocessor systems [8, 9, 10].

In spite of those efforts, the gap between peak and effective performance has been getting larger with increase of the number of processors. Therefore, the exploitation of multigrain parallelism in addition to the loop parallelism is required. Multigrain parallel processing, which has been realized in OSCAR compiler, uses not only loop level parallelism but also coarse grain task parallelism among basic blocks, loops and subroutines and near fine grain task parallelism among statements. Based on the OSCAR multigrain parallelizing techniques, "Advanced Parallelizing Compiler(APC)" project[11] has been started since the autumn in 2000 as a part of Japanese Government Millennium project IT21. A target of this project is to develop a practical multigrain parallelizing compiler in cooperation with Government, Industry and Academia.

Also, PROMIS compiler[12] aims at integration of loop and instruction level parallelism using a common intermediate representation. NANOS compiler[13] exploits the multi level parallelism using extended OpenMP API.

This paper describes coarse grain task parallel processing considering cache optimization using data localization[10] in order to enhance the performance of coarse grain task parallel processing. The proposed scheme is implemented on OSCAR automatic multigrain parallelizing compiler. OSCAR compiler generates a parallelized FORTRAN program using OpenMP API[14, 15], which is a standard API for shared memory multiprocessor. OSCAR compiler realizes hierarchical coarse grain task parallel processing with cache optimization without special extension of OpenMP [16].

The rest of this paper is organized as follows. In section 2, coarse grain task parallel processing is described. Section 3 proposes cache optimization scheme for coarse grain task parallel processing. Section 4 describes the overview of OSCAR compiler. The effectiveness of the proposed schemes is evaluated on IBM RS6000 604e High Node using several benchmarks in SPEC95fp in section 5. Finally, concluding remarks are described in section 6.

## 2   Coarse Grain Task Parallel Processing

This section describes coarse grain task parallel processing, which is a part of multigrain parallel processing. Coarse grain task parallel processing uses parallelism among three kinds of macro-tasks or coarse grain tasks, namely block of pseudo assignment statements(BPA) repetition block(RB), subroutine block(SB). The compiler decomposes a source program into the macro-tasks. Also, it hierarchically generates macro-tasks inside inside of a sequential repetition block and a subroutine block.

Coarse grain task parallel processing in OSCAR compiler is performed in the following steps.

1. Decomposition of a source program into macro-tasks.
2. Analysis of data dependencies and control flows among macro-tasks and generation of Macro Flow Graph (MFG) that represents them.
3. Analysis of Earliest Execution Condition(EEC) that represents the condition on which macro-task may start its execution earliest and generation of Macro Task Graph (MTG).
4. Scheduling macro-tasks to processors or processor groups. When a macro-task graph has no conditional dependencies, macro-tasks are scheduled to processors or processor clusters at a compiler time and parallelized code is generated for each processor according to the scheduling results. When macro-task graph contains control dependencies, compiler generates dynamic scheduling routine to assign macro-tasks to processors or processor clusters at a run time and embeds the dynamic scheduling routine to the generated parallelized code with macro-task code in order to cope with runtime uncertainties.

## 2.1   Generation of Macro-Tasks

The compiler first generates macro-tasks namely block of pseudo assignment statements(similar to basic blocks), repetition blocks and subroutine blocks from a source program. Furthermore, compiler hierarchically decomposes the body of sequential repetition block and a subroutine block.

If a repetition block(RB) is a parallelizable loop, it is divided into partial loops by loop iteration direction taking into consideration the number of processors, cache size and so on. These partial loops are defined as different macro-tasks that are executed in parallel.

## 2.2   Generation of Macro Flow Graph

After generation of macro-tasks, the data dependency and control flow among a macro-tasks for each layer are analyzed hierarchically, and represented by macro flow graph(MFG) as shown in Fig.1(a).

In the Fig. 1(a), nodes represent macro-tasks, solid edges represent data dependencies among macro-tasks and dotted edges represent control flow. A small circle inside a node represents a conditional branch inside a macro-task. Though arrows of edges are omitted in the macro flow graph, it is assumed that the directions are downward.

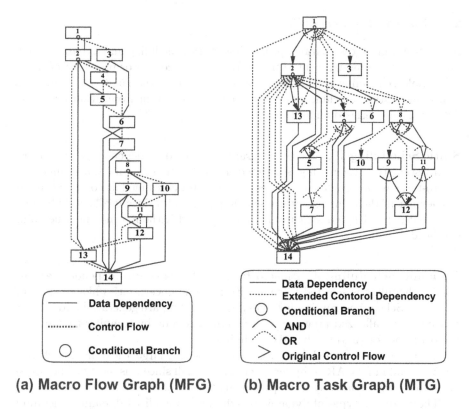

**(a) Macro Flow Graph (MFG)     (b) Macro Task Graph (MTG)**

**Fig. 1.** Macro Flow Graph and Macro Task Graph

## 2.3  Generation of Macro Task Graph

To extract parallelism among macro-tasks from macro flow graph, compiler analyses Earliest Executable Condition of each macro-task. Earliest Executable Condition represents the conditions on which macro-task may begin its execution earliest.

Earliest execution condition of macro-task is represented in macro task Graph (MTG) as shown in Fig. 1(b).

In macro task graph, nodes represent macro-tasks. A small circle inside nodes represents conditional branches. Solid edges represent data dependencies. Dotted edges represent extended control dependencies. Extended control dependency means ordinary normal control dependency and the condition on which a data dependence predecessor macro-task is not executed. Solid and dotted arcs connecting solid and dotted edges have two different meanings. A solid arc represents that edges connected by the arc are in AND relationship. A dotted arc represents that edges connected by the arc are in OR relation ship. In macro task graph, though arrows of edges are omitted assuming downward, an edge having arrow represents original control flow edges, or branch direction in macro flow graph.

## 2.4   Macro-Task Scheduling

In the coarse grain task parallel processing, static scheduling and dynamic scheduling are used for assignment of macro-tasks to processors or processor clusters. A suitable scheduling scheme is selected considering the shape of macro task graph and target machine parameters such as the synchronization overhead, data transfer overhead and so on.

**Static Scheduling** If a macro task graph has only data dependencies and is deterministic, static scheduling is selected. In the static scheduling, assignment of macro-tasks to processors or processor clusters is determined at compile time by a scheduler in the compiler. Static scheduling is useful since it allows us to minimize data transfer and synchronization overhead without run-time scheduling overhead.

**Dynamic Scheduling** If a macro task graph has control dependencies, dynamic scheduling is selected to cope with runtime uncertainties like conditional branches. Scheduling routine for dynamic scheduling are generated and embedded into a parallelized program with macro-task code by compiler to eliminate the overhead for runtime thread scheduling.

Though dynamic scheduling overhead is generally large, the dynamic scheduling overhead in OSCAR compiler is relatively small since it is used for the coarse grain tasks with relatively large processing time.

There are two types of dynamic scheduling; Centralized dynamic scheduling and Distributed dynamic scheduling. The centralized dynamic scheduling routine is executed by one processor specified as the scheduler and other processors execute only macro-task code according to scheduling result. In the distributed dynamic scheduling, scheduling routines are distributed to the all processors with exclusive accesses to scheduling information such as ready task queues, earliest exclusive conditions and so on.

## 3   Cache Optimization for Coarse Grain Task Parallel Processing

This section describes the scheme to use cache effectively in order to enhance the performance of coarse grain task parallel processing.

If macro-tasks that access the same data are executed on the same processor as consecutively as possible, data can be transfered among these macro-tasks using fast memory near a processor such as cache, distributed shared memory or local memory.

To realize such task assignments, the data localization scheme[10] has been proposed.

In this paper, this data localization scheme is extended to use cache effectively on the shared memory machine. A task scheduler for coarse grain task parallel processing is extended to assign macro-tasks that access the same data to be executed as consecutively as possible on the same processor considering task parallelism.

A simple example of the proposed scheme is shown in Fig. 2. In the macro task graph in Fig. 2(b), macro-task 1 and 6 access the same data. However, execution order in the original program is the increasing order of the task number as shown in Macro Flow Graph in Fig.2(a). Therefore, macro-task 2, 3, 4 and 5 are executed after macro-task 1 prior to the macro-task 6.In this case, shared data accessed by macro-task 1 may be forced out of cache by macro-task 2 through 5 before macro-task 6 is executed. However, because macro-task 6 depends on only macro-task 1 and 5, macro-task 6 can be executed immediately after macro-task 1 and macro-task 6 can access data in the cache.

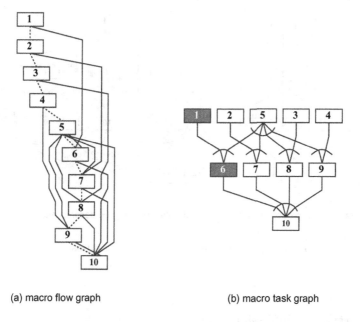

(a) macro flow graph                    (b) macro task graph

**Fig. 2.** An example of cache optimization for a macro task graph

The proposed cache optimization scheme using data localization mainly consists of two techniques; loop aligned decomposition and partial static task assignment.

## 3.1 Loop Aligned Decomposition

To avoid cache misses, Loop Aligned Decomposition(LAD)[17] is applied to loops that use large size of data. LAD divides a loop into partial loops with the smaller number of iterations so that data size used in the divided loops is smaller than cache size.

The partial loops are treated as coarse grain tasks. Next, the partial loops connected by data dependence edge on the macro task graph are grouped into "Data Localization Group(DLG)" [10]. The partial loops, or tasks, inside a DLG are assigned to the same processor by static or dynamic scheduler.

In macro-task graph in Fig. 3(a), it is assumed that macro-tasks 2, 3 and 7 are parallel loops and they access the same data and its size exceeds cache size. In this example, these loops are divided into four partial loops by LAD. For example, macro-task 2 in Fig. 3(a) is divided into macro-task 2 through 5 in Fig. 3(b). In this case, the Data Localization Groups of macro-tasks with large share data are respectively (2, 6, 13), (3, 7, 14), (4, 8, 15), (5, 9, 16) in Fig. 3(b). In Fig. 3(b), the light gray band shows DLG. For example, DLG0 contains macro-tasks 2, 6 and 13 and DLG1 contains macro-tasks 3, 7 and 14 and so on.

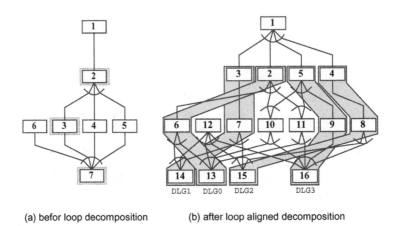

(a) befor loop decomposition          (b) after loop aligned decomposition

**Fig. 3.** Example of Loop Align Decomposition

## 3.2   Partial Static Assignment

As mentioned above, in the proposed cache optimization scheme, a task scheduler for coarse grain task parallel processing is extended to assign macro-tasks inside DLG to be executed on same processor consecutively.

This extension is called as partial static assignment[17] and it can be applied to both centralized and distributed dynamic scheduling. It is implemented in distributed dynamic scheduling routine at present in OSCAR compiler. This extended distributed dynamic scheduling routine with partial static assignment for cache is summarized as follows.

1 Execute its distributed scheduling routine to determine the macro-task to be executed next. This scheduler assigns, or acquires, macro-tasks outside DLG to own processor from the ready macro-task queue. At this time, if there is

**Fig. 4.** An example of schedule for a single processor

no macro-task outside DLG in the ready macro-task queue, scheduler assigns macro-tasks inside DLG.
**2** Execute the assigned macro-task. If an executed macro-task is the special macro-task which represents the end of the macro task graph, the execution of this hierarchy of the macro task graph is finished. Otherwise goto step3.
**3** If the last executed macro-task is inside the DLG, goto 3.1, otherwise goto 3.2.
 **3.1** Assign macro-task in the same DLG from ready queue. If there is no macro-task inside the same DLG, assign macro-task outside DLG. If there is no ready macro-task outside DLG, assign macro-task in another DLG.
 **3.2** Assign macro-task outside DLG. If there is no such macro-task, assign macro-task inside the DLG.
**4** Goto 2.

Fig. 4 shows a schedule when the proposed partial static task assignment for cache optimization is applied to macro task graph in Fig. 3(b) for a single processor. As described above, macro-tasks are executed in the increasing order of the node number on the macro task graph in original program. Fig. 4 shows that macro-tasks in the same DLG are executed consecutively to use cache effectively by using partial static assignment. As shown in Fig. 4, macro-task 3, 7 and 14 in DLG1 and macro-task 4, 8 and 15 in DLG2 are executed consecutively.

## 4   OSCAR Multigrain Parallelizing Compiler

Fig. 5 shows the overview of OSCAR compiler. It consists of frontend, middle path and backends. OSCAR compiler has various backends for different target multiprocessor systems like OSCAR type distributed/shared memory single chip multiprocessor system[18], UltraSparc, MPI-2 and OpenMP. OpenMP backend used in this paper generates the parallelized FORTRAN source code with OpenMP directives.

In OpenMP backend, OSCAR compiler is used as a preprocessor that transforms an ordinary sequential FORTRAN program to OpenMP FORTRAN program for shared memory multiprocessor system.

### 4.1   Realization of the Proposed Scheme Using OpenMP

This section describes the program generated by OSCAR compiler which realizes the proposed scheme using OpenMP API. A code image for eight threads

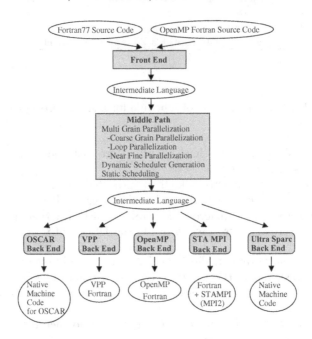

**Fig. 5.** Configuration of OSCAR compiler

generated by OpenMP backend for a macro task graph in Fig. 6(a) is shown in Fig. 6(b).

In this figure, eight threads are generated by OpenMP PARALLEL SECTIONS directive and these generated threads join only once at the end of program based on "one time single level thread generation"[16].

In this example, static scheduling is applied to the first layer. In this case, the eight threads are grouped into two thread groups, each of which has four threads. Macro-task 1_1 and 1_3 are statically assigned to thread group0 and macro-task 1_2 is assigned to thread group1. When static scheduling is applied, compiler generates different codes into each OpenMP SECTION for each thread according to the static scheduling result. The assigned macro-tasks to thread groups are processed in parallel by threads inside the thread group by using static scheduling or dynamic scheduling hierarchically.

Macro-task 1_2 in Fig. 6 assigned onto thread group1 is processed by four threads in parallel using the centralized dynamic scheduling. In this example, thread 4 works as the centralized scheduler and thread 5 to 7 execute sub macro-tasks 1_2_1, 1_2_2 and so on, which generated by decomposition of the inside of macro-task 1_2, according to the dynamic scheduling result of the centralized scheduler.

Macro-task 1_3 shows an example of distributed dynamic scheduling. In this case, macro-task 1_3 is decomposed into sub macro-tasks and assigned thread

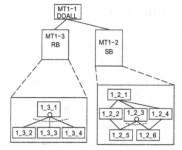

(a) An example of macro task graph

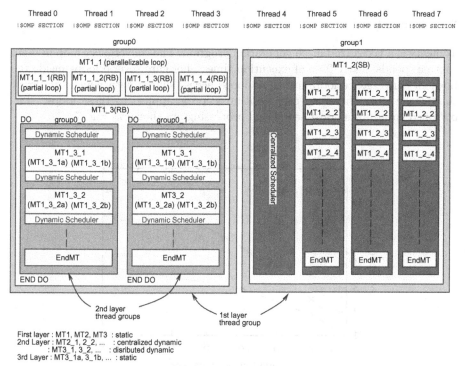

(b) An image of generated parallel code

**Fig. 6.** Generated code image using OpenMP (eight threads)

group0_0 and 0_1 defined inside thread group0. In this example, the thread group0_0 and 0_1 has two threads. The distributed dynamic scheduling routines that perform partial static task assignment for cache optimization are embedded into before each macro-task code as shown in Fig. 6. Furthermore, Fig. 6 shows macro-task 1_3_1, 1_3_2 and so on are processed by two threads inside thread group0_0, or 0_1.

## 5    Performance Evaluation

This section describes the result of the performance evaluation of the proposed scheme on a commercial SMP machine, IBM RS6000 SP 604e High Node. The generated OpenMP FORTRAN programs by OSCAR compiler are compiled by IBM XL FORTRAN compiler version 6.1 for RS6000. RS6000 used in this evaluation has eight 200MHz PowerPCs each of which has 32KB L1 instruction and data cache respectively, 2MB unified L2 cache per two processors and 512MB main memory. Programs used for this evaluation are tomcatv, swim and mgrid in SPEC95fp benchmarks.

### 5.1    Tomcatv

Tomcatv is a vectorized mesh generation program. The convergence loop in main routine spends nearly 99% of execution time. There are several loops inside the body of convergence loop and these loops access shared data which are larger than cache size. Therefore, cache optimization is applied to these loops. The obtained speedups against sequential processing are shown in Fig. 7.

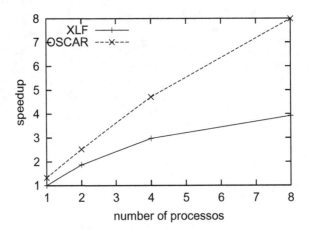

**Fig. 7.** Speedup of tomcatv

The sequential execution time of tomcatv was measured with XL FOR-TRAN compiler option "-O3 -qhot -qmaxmem=-1 -qarch=auto -qtune=auto -qcach=auto" and it was 693 seconds. The execution times of automatic loop parallelization by XL FORTRAN compiler were 370 seconds for 2PEs (1.9 times speedup), 233 seconds for 4PEs (3.0 times speedup) and 177 seconds for 8PEs (3.9 times speedup). When OSCAR compiler was used as a preprocessor of XL FORTRAN compiler, the execution times were reduced to 523 seconds for 1PE

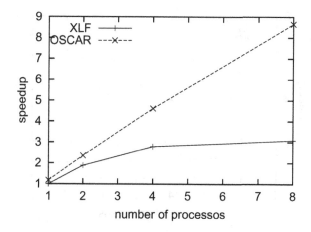

**Fig. 8.** Speedup of swim

(1.3 times speedup), 275 seconds for 2PEs (2.5 times speedup), 147 seconds for 4PEs (4.7 times speedup) and 86.8 seconds for 8PEs (8.0 times speedup).

## 5.2  Swim

Swim solves the system of shallow water equation using difference approxima-tions and has large loop level parallelism. The most execution time is spent in three subroutines, namely "calc1", "calc2", "calc3" called from main loop. These subroutines contain several loops which access larger data than cache size. There-fore, coarse grain task parallel processing with cache optimization is applied to these loops inside subroutines. The evaluation results are shown in Fig. 8

When swim was compiled by only XL FORTRAN compiler for single pro-cessor, the sequential execution time was 521 seconds. The execution times were reduced to 277 seconds for 2PE (1.9 times speedup), 183 seconds for 4PE (2.8 times speedup), and 169 seconds for 8PE (3.1 times speedup) by using XLF FORTRAN compiler automatic parallelization. The execution times of OSCAR compiler were 443 seconds for 1PE (1.2 times speedup), 221 seconds for 2PEs (2.4 times speedup), 113 seconds for 4PEs (4.6 times speedup) and 60.2 seconds for 8PEs (8.7 times speedup).

## 5.3  Mgrid

Mgrid is the 3 dimensional multi-grid solver. About 70% of execution time is spent in subroutine "resid" and "psinv". These subroutines contain loops which access larger data than the cache size. The proposed coarse grain task parallel processing with cache optimization is applied inside these subroutines. Fig. 9 shows the speedups against sequential processing by XL FORTRAN compiler.

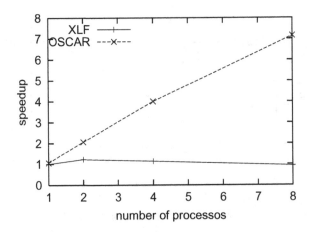

**Fig. 9.** Speedup of mgrid

Mgrid by XL FORTRAN compiler needed 676 seconds for a single processor. The execution times of OSCAR compiler were 637 seconds for 1PE (2.1 times speedup), 352 seconds for 2PEs (4.0 times speedup), 174 seconds for 4PE and 94.5 seconds for 8PEs (7.2 times speedup) in Mgrid. Scalable speedups was obtained and it was shown that OSCAR compiler gave us lager speedup than XL FORTRAN compiler which spent 552 seconds for 2PEs (1.2 times speedup), 594 seconds for 4PEs (1.1 times speedup) and 722 seconds for 8PEs (0.9 times speedup).

## 6   Conclusions

This paper has proposed coarse grain task parallel processing with cache optimization to enhance the effective performance of shared memory multiprocessor systems. The proposed schemes are implemented on OSCAR automatic multigrain parallelizing compiler. OSCAR compiler generates parallelizing code using ordinary OpenMP API for portability.

In the performance evaluation, tomcatv, swim, mgrid in SPEC95fp were parallelized by OSCAR compiler and were run on the commercial shared memory multiprocessor IBM RS 6000 SP 604e High Node. Evaluation results show that coarse grain task parallel processing with cache optimization gave us speedups for tomcatv, swim and mgrid on 8 processors such as 8.0, 8.6 and 7.2 respectively complared with single processor. Furthermore, the proposed scheme show 2.0, 2,8 and 7.6 times speedup compared with XL FORTRAN loop parallelizing compiler on 8 processors.

A part of this research has been supported by METI/NEDO Millennium project IT21 "Advanced Parallelizing Compiler".

# References

[1] R. Eigenmann, J. Hoeflinger, and D. Padua. On the automatic parallelization of the perfect benchmarks. *IEEE Trans. on parallel and distributed systems*, 9(1), Jan. 1998.

[2] P. Tu and D. Padua. Automatic array privatization. *Proc. 6th Annual Workshop on Languages and Compilers for Parallel Computing*, 1993.

[3] L. Rauchwerger, N. M. Amato, and D. A. Padua. Run-time methods for parallelizing partially parallel loops. *Proceedings of the 9th ACM International Conference on Supercomputing, Barcelona, Spain*, pages 137–146, Jul. 1995.

[4] M. W. Hall, J. M. Anderson, S. P. Amarasinghe, B. R. Murphy, S. Liao, E. Bugnion, and M. S. Lam. Maximizing multiprocessor performance with the suif compiler. *IEEE Computer*, 1996.

[5] M. W. Hall, B. R. Murphy, S. P. Amarasinghe, S. Liao, , and M. S. Lam. Interprocedural parallelization analysis: A case study. *Proceedings of the 8th International Workshop on Languages and Compilers for Parallel Computing*, Aug. 1995.

[6] A. W. Lim, G. I. Cheong, and M. S. Lam. An affine partitoning algorithm to maximize parallelism and minimize communication. *Proc. of the 13th ACM SIGARCH International Conference on Supercomputing*, Jun. 1999.

[7] J. M. Anderson, S. P. Amarasinghe, and M. S. Lam. Data and computation transformations for multiprocessors. *Proc. of the Fifth ACM SIGPLAN Symposium on Principles and Practice of Parallel Processing*, Jul. 1995.

[8] H. Han, G. Rivera, and C-W. Tseng. Software support for improving locality in scientific codes. *8th Workshop on Compilers for Parallel Computers*, Jan. 2000.

[9] G. Rivera and C-W. Tseng. Locality optimizations for multi-level caches. *Super Computing '99*, Nov. 1999.

[10] A. Yoshida, Y. Ujigawa, M. Obata, K. Kimura, and H. Kasahara. Data-localization among doall and sequential loops in coarse grain parallel processing. *Seventh Workshop on Compilers for Parallel Computers*, Jul. 1998.

[11] Advanced Parallelizing Compiler Project. http://www.apc.waseda.ac.jp/.

[12] C. J. Brownhill, A. Nicolau, S Novack, and C. D. Polychronopoulos. Achieving multi-level parallelization. *Proc. of the International Symposium on High Performance Computing*, 1997.

[13] X. Martorell, E. Ayguade, N. Navarro, J. Corbalan, M. Gonzalez, and J. Labarta. Thread fork/join techniques for multi-level parallelism exploitatio in numa multiprocessors. *Proc. of the 1999 International Conference on Supercomputing*, June 1999.

[14] Portable Scalable SMP Programing OpenMP: Simple. http://www.openmp.org/.

[15] L. Dagum and R. Menon. Openmp: An industry standard api for shared memory programming. *IEEE Computational Science & Engineering*, 1998.

[16] H. Kasahara, M. Obata, and K. Ishizaka. Automatic coarse grain task parallel processing on smp using openmp. *Proc. of 13 th International Workshop on Languages and Compilers for Parallel Computing 2000*, Aug. 2000.

[17] H. Kasahara A. Yhoshida, K. Koshizuka. Data-localization using loop aligned decomposition for macro-dataflow processing. *Proc. of 9th Workshop on Languages and Compilers for Parallel Computing*, Aug. 1996.

[18] K. Kimura and H. Kasahara. Near fine grain parallel processing using static scheduling on single chip multiprocessors. *Proc. of International Workshop on Innovative Architecture for Future Generation High-Performance Processors and Systems*, Nov. 1999.

# A Language for Role Specifications*

Viktor Kuncak, Patrick Lam, and Martin Rinard

Laboratory for Computer Science
Massachusetts Institute of Technology
Cambridge, MA 02139
{vkuncak, plam, rinard}@lcs.mit.edu

**Abstract.** This paper presents a new language for identifying the changing roles that objects play over the course of the computation. Each object's points-to relationships with other objects determine the role that it currently plays. Roles therefore reflect the object's membership in specific data structures, with the object's role changing as it moves between data structures. We provide a programming model which allows the developer to specify the roles of objects at different points in the computation. The model also allows the developer to specify the effect of each operation at the granularity of role changes that occur in identified regions of the heap.

## 1 Introduction

In standard type systems for object-oriented languages, each object is created as an instance of a specific class, with the object's type determined by that class. Because the object's class does not change, the object has the same type for its entire existence in the computation. This property limits the ability of the type system to capture dynamically changing object properties. Specifically, a given object may play many different roles during its lifetime in the computation, with the distinctions between these roles crucial to the computation's safety and correctness. The inability of the type system to model these changing roles prevents it from capturing these important distinctions.

This paper presents a new kind of type system, called a *role system*, which enables a developer to express the different roles that each object plays during its lifetime in the computation. The role of each object is determined by its points-to relationships with other objects. As these relationships change, the object's type changes to reflect its changing role in the computation. Our system can therefore capture important distinctions between objects of the same class as they play different roles in the computation.

Because roles are determined by the linking relationships, role changes often correspond to movements between data structures. Our role system is therefore designed to capture the linking relationships at a level of precision that makes it

---

* This research was supported in part by DARPA Contract F33615-00-C-1692, NSF Grant CCR00-86154, NSF Grant CCR00-63513, and an NSERC graduate scholarship.

possible to track the removals and insertions that implement movements between data structures. We realize this goal by providing three mechanisms:

1. **Role Definitions:** The role definitions specify the referencing relationships for each role. For all references to an object *o* playing a given role, the role definition specifies the field where the reference to *o* is stored and the role of the object containing this reference. On the other hand, for each reference originating at the object playing the role, the role definitions specify the roles of the objects to which it refers. The role definitions therefore provide complete heap aliasing information for each object at the granularity of roles.
2. **Role Declarations:** The programmer can declare the role of the object to which each local variable or parameter refers. In effect, these role declarations express additional application-specific safety properties not captured by standard type systems.
3. **Operation Effects:** The programmer can declare how operations change the roles of the objects that they access, providing useful information about the effect of each operation at the granularity of roles.

## 2   Examples

We next present several examples that illustrate the role specification language. The first example illustrates how roles capture distinctions that arise from the semantics of the underlying application domain. The second example illustrates how roles capture shape invariants of linked data structures at sufficient precision to capture removals (and corresponding insertions) from the data structure.

### 2.1   Aircraft Example

Our first example illustrates how roles can capture the distinction between aircraft that are parked at a gate, aircraft that are taxiing on the ground, and flying aircraft. Each parked or taxiing aircraft is associated with an airport, with the ground controllers at the airport responsible for its movements. Flying aircraft are not associated with a specific airport; instead, the controllers at a control center are responsible for its flight path.

Aircraft are represented in the system by instances of the `Aircraft` class from Figure 1. Each `Aircraft` object has two instance variables: `cc` is its control center when it is flying, and `ap` is its airport when it is parked or taxiing. Figure 1 also presents the definitions of the roles that `Aircraft` objects can play. The `Parked` and `Taxiing` role definitions specify that the `ap` field of each `Parked` and `Taxiing` aircraft refers to a specific, non-null `Airport` object where the aircraft is located. The `cc` field is null for objects playing these roles, as an airport is controlling these aircraft.

Conceptually, each role has a set of slots filled by incoming references from other objects; the role definitions specify the number of slots and the roles and fields of the references that may fill each slot. In our example, each `Parked` aircraft has an incoming slot filled by a reference from the `Gate` object where the aircraft is parked; this reference is the only heap reference to a `Parked` aircraft. `Taxiing` aircraft have a slot filled by a reference from the runway that the aircraft is on; this reference is the only heap reference to a `Taxiing` aircraft. The `cc` field of `Flying` aircraft refers to a non-null `ControlCenter` object that represents the control center responsible for the aircraft's flight plan; the `ap` field is null. `Flying` aircraft have a single slot, filled by a reference from the controlling center's list of aircraft.

In addition to the textual representation, Figure 1 presents a graphical representation of the roles and their referencing relationships. Each box in the picture represents either a role or a class. Arrows with closed heads represent references between objects, while arrows with open heads represent the partition of a class into the roles that objects from that class can play.

```
class Aircraft {
    ControlCenter cc;
    Airport ap;
}
role Parked of Aircraft {
    fields ap: Airport, cc: null;
    slots Gate.p;
}
role Taxiing of Aircraft {
    fields ap: Airport, cc: null;
    slots Runway.p;
}
role Flying of Aircraft {
    fields cc: ControlCenter, ap: null;
    slots ControlCenterListNode.aircraft;
}
```

**Fig. 1.** Aircraft Example Role Definitions

The developer can use roles to improve the precision of operation interfaces. Figure 2 presents a sample operation on an aircraft. The `land` operation executes when an aircraft lands at an airport. The parameter declarations state that landing aircraft must be playing the `Flying` role. The effects declarations specify that control of the landing aircraft passes from the control center to the airport, with the aircraft's role changing from `Flying` to `Taxiing`. Other operations (`takeoff`, `pushback`, etc.) place similar requirements on the roles that their parameters play and have similar effects on these roles. From these operations, it is possible to automatically extract the role transition diagram for `Aircraft` objects, which is presented in Figure 3.

```
void land(Flying p, Runway r, Airport a)
effects { p.ap = a; p.cc = null; r.p = p;
          roleChange(p : Taxiing); }
{
    p.ap = a; p.cc = null; r.p = p;
    roleChange(p : Taxiing);
}
```

**Fig. 2.** The land Operation

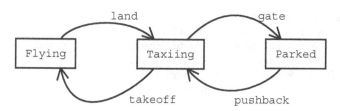

**Fig. 3.** Role Transition Diagram for Aircraft Objects

## 2.2  Doubly Linked List Example

This example illustrates the use of roles with a simple doubly-linked list data structure. The data structure has a dummy header node followed by some inner nodes which refer to the elements stored in the list. Figure 4 presents the role definitions for the list data structures. The nodes in the linked list are all objects of the doubleNode class, which has three roles. The dummy header plays the doubleHeader role, which requires the header to have a null content field. Inner nodes play the doubleInner role, which require the inner nodes to have a non-null content field. An object playing the doubleNode role can play either the doubleHeader or doubleInner role. Finally, the soloNode is a node that has been deleted from the list.

The role definitions for the doubleHeader and doubleInner roles require the next and prev fields of objects playing these roles to point to non-null objects playing either the doubleHeader or doubleInner role, and that prev.next and next.prev paths terminate at the object where they started, i.e., the two links are inverses. The next and prev fields of objects playing the soloNode role are null, and there are no heap references to soloNode roles.

We next discuss the removal of a node from a doubleNode list. The procedure navigates the list until it reaches the node to remove or returns back to the header node. If it finds the node to remove, it removes it, changing the node's role from doubleInner to soloNode. The effects statement of the remove operation states that the operation may set the content field of one of the nodes in the list to null and change the role of a list node to soloNode. The operation may also read and write some of the fields of the nodes in the list.

```
class doubleNode {
    doubleNode next, prev;
    Element content;
}
role doubleHeader of doubleNode {
    fields next: doubleHeader | doubleInner,
           prev: doubleHeader | doubleInner, content: null;
    slots (doubleHeader | doubleInner).prev,
          (doubleHeader | doubleInner).next;
    identities prev.next, next.prev;
}
role doubleInner of doubleNode {
    fields next: doubleHeader | doubleInner,
           prev: doubleHeader | doubleInner, content: stored;
    slots (doubleHeader | doubleInner).prev,
          (doubleHeader | doubleInner).next;
    identities prev.next, next.prev;
}
role soloNode of doubleNode {
    fields next: null, prev: null;
    slots ;
}
role stored of Element {
    slots doubleInter.content;
}
role soloElem of Element {
    slots ;
}
```

**Fig. 4.** Roles for the Circular Linked List

## 3   The Role Definition Language

We next present the full role definition language.

### 3.1   Basic Constraints

The heart of the role definition language is a set of basic constraints that the programmer can use to identify the relationships that define a role. There are several kinds of constraints:

**Field constraints:** Each field constraint is of the form

$$\text{field} : \text{role}_1 | \cdots | \text{role}_k$$

```
void remove(doubleHeader d, stored c)
effects {
    read(d.next);
    (([x, y : d.next*] x.* = y;
     [x : d.next*] x.content = null; changeRole(x : soloNode);
     [x : d.next*] read(x.*);
     changeRole(c : soloElem)
    ) | skip) }
{
    doubleNode n = d.next;
    do {
        if (n.content == c) {
            assert(n : doubleInner);
            doubleNode nn = n.next, np = n.prev;
            nn.prev = n.prev; np.next = n.next;
            n.next = null; n.prev = null;
            n.content = null;
            changeRole(n : soloNode);
            changeRole(c : soloElem);
            return;
        }
        n = n.next;
    } while (n != d);
}
```

**Fig. 5.** Code for Removing a Node from a Doubly Linked List

where field is the name of a field in the object and $role_1$ through $role_k$ are the names of roles. If this constraint appears in the definition of a given role, all objects playing the role have a field named field that refers to an object playing one of the roles $role_1$ through $role_k$.

**Slot constraints:** Each role has a number of *slots*, or incoming references. There is a slot constraint associated with each slot that defines the kinds of references that can fill the slot. Each slot constraint has the form

$$role_1.field_1 \mid \cdots \mid role_k.field_k$$

where $role_1$ through $role_k$ are role names and $field_1$ through $field_k$ are field names. If a given object is playing a role whose definition contains this constraint, there must exist an $i$ such that the field $field_i$ in some object playing role $role_i$ contains a reference to the given object.

**Identity constraints:** Each identity constraint is of the form $field_1.field_2$, where $field_1$ and $field_2$ are two field names. If this constraint appears in the definition of a given role and an object $o$ is playing the role, $o.field_1.field_2$ refers back to $o$. The standard example is a doubly linked list node l, where l.next.prev = l.

**Property constraints:** Each property constraint consists of a predicate over the primitive fields (integers, booleans, doubles, etc.) of the object. When an object satisfies a role which contains some property constraint $p$, then $p$ must evaluate to true on this object. In this way, properties allow the specification of user-defined abstractions of object state.

**Acyclicity constraints:** Each acyclicity constraint is a specification of the form regExp, where regExp is a regular expression over the field names. Given an object playing the role, this constraint states that there are no cycles in the subgraph obtained by following paths that 1) start from the given object and 2) conform to the regular expression.

Figure 6 summarizes the syntax for basic role definitions.

```
role r{
     fields      f₁ :r₁₁ | r₁₂ | ··· | r₁ₚ₁,
                 ...
                 fₙ :rₙ₁ | rₙ₂ | ··· | rₙₚₙ;

     slots       r′₁₁.f′₁₁ | ··· | r′₁q₁.f′₁q₁,
                 ...
                 r′ₘ₁.f′ₘ₁ | ··· | r′ₘqₘ.f′ₘqₘ

     identities f₁.g₁,...,fₖ.gₖ;
     properties p₁,...,pₗ;
     acyclic     regExp₁,...,regExpₜ
}
```

**Fig. 6.** General Form of Basic Role Specification

## 3.2   Multislots

An object of basic role with $k$ slots requires exactly $k$ references from other objects. In some cases an object may be referred to by a statically undetermined number of other objects. This possibility can be specified using *multislots.*

$$\texttt{multislots } \text{role}_1.\text{field}_1,\ldots,\text{role}_k.\text{field}_k;$$

A multislot allows arbitrary number of references of types $\text{role}_1.\text{field}_1$ through $\text{role}_k.\text{field}_k$. All references must be distinct and they must also to be distinct from all references mentioned in the **slots** declaration.

## 3.3   Compound Roles

As described so far, each object plays a single role at any given time, with its role changing over time as it moves between data structures and its relationships with other objects change. It is also sometimes useful for an object to play multiple roles at the same time. For example, an object may participate in both a linked list and a tree, playing the linked list and tree roles at the same time. We support this concept by allowing the programmer to define compound roles, which combine multiple roles into a single new role. Syntactically, the programmer declares a compound role as follows.

$$\texttt{role}\, r = r_1 + \ldots + r_n\,;$$

The fields and slots of the role r are the disjoint union of the fields and slots of roles $r_1$ through $r_n$. A object of role r satisfies all identity, property, and acyclicity constraints of roles $r_1$ through $r_n$.

## 3.4 Parameterized Roles

It is useful to parameterize roles with respect to other roles or with respect to individual references.

**Role Parameters** allow the definition of a role to be parametrized by names of other roles. This is a form of parametric polymorphism for role definitions. For example, a list can be parametrized by the role of its elements. Role parameters are introduced by < > brackets in the role definition. Once introduced, role parameters can be used inside the role definition in all places where a fixed role name is expected. In order to be used as an ordinary role, a parametrized role needs to be supplied with actual role arguments, written in < > brackets.

```
role List<T> {
  fields  first : ListNode<T>;
}
role ListNode<T> {
  fields next : ListNode<T> | null,
         elem : T;
  slots  ListNode<T>.next | List<T>.first;
}
role Airport {
  fields landed : List<Aircraft>;
}
```

**Fig. 7.** Parametrization by Roles

**Reference Parameters** allow role definitions to be parametrized by individual references from some object, where the identity of the object may not be known until run-time. This allows very fine-grained role definitions, suitable even for descriptions of nested data structures. Reference parameters are introduced into role definitions using [ ] brackets after the role name. Reference parameters can be used in slots or to instantiate other reference-parametrized roles. Every reference-parametrized role must be instantiated with an appropriate number of reference arguments supplied in [ ] brackets. Arguments can be field names or other role parameters.

The example in figure 8 illustrates the use of reference parameters. The GraphList role represents a list of disjoint graphs: there are no edges between nodes of graphs reachable from different nodes of the GraphListNode role. Nodes of the list are represented by objects with GraphListNode role. Each graph is made up of GraphNodes. The disjointness of the graphs is ensured by parametrizing the GraphNode role.

```
role GraphList {
  fields first : GraphListNode;
}
role GraphListNode {
  fields next  : GraphListNode | null,
         graph : GraphNode[graph];
  slots  GraphListNode.next | GraphList.first;
}
role GraphNode[f] {
  fields succ : List<GraphNode[f]>
  slots f | ListNode<GraphNode[f]>.elem;
}
```

**Fig. 8.** Parametrization by References: List of Disjoint Graphs

Reference parameters for roles, unlike role parameters, cannot in general be eliminated by source-to-source transformation at the role definition time. Note, however, that parametrization by individual references does not prevent the static analysis of data structures. If, for references $o_1.f_1$ and $o_2.f_2$, either $f_1 \neq f_2$ or the alias analysis implies $o_1 \neq o_2$, then two data structures parametrized by roles $o_1.f_1$ and $o_2.f_2$ are known to be disjoint.

### 3.5   Roles and Classes

Our role system can be realized as a refinement of a static class system where each role is a refinement of some class, with one class being refined into multiple roles. To indicate that a role rl refines a class cl, we write the name of c after the definition of role r.

$$\text{role rl of cl } \{\ldots\}$$

We note that it is also possible to use roles as a stand-alone type system.

```
      roleDef ::= "role" roleName
                  ("<" roleParams ">")? ("[" refParams "]")?  "of" ClassName "{"
                  ("fields" fieldDecls ";")?
                  ("slots" slotDecls ";")?
                  ("multislots" multislotDecl ";")?
                  ("identities" identDecls ";")?
                  ("acyclic" acyclicDecls ";")?  "}"
                | "role" roleName "=" disjRole ";"
                | "role" roleName "=" roleSum ";"
   fieldDecls ::= fieldDecl | fieldDecls "," fieldDecl
    fieldDecl ::= field ":" disjRole
     disjRole ::= role | disjRole "|" role
    slotDecls ::= slotDecl | slotDecls "," slotDecl
     slotDecl ::= reference | slotDecl "|" reference
multislotDecl ::= reference | multislotDecl "," reference
   identDecls ::= identDecl | identDecls "," identDecl
    identDecl ::= field "." field
 acyclicDecls ::= acyclicDecl | acyclicDecls "," acyclicDecl
  acyclicDecl ::= regExp
    reference ::= role "." field
      roleSum ::= role | roleSum "+" role
         role ::= roleName("<" roleArg ">")? ("[" refArg "]")?
      roleArg ::= role | roleArg "," role
       refArg ::= field | refParam
   roleParams ::= ID | roleParams "," ID
    refParams ::= ID | refParams "," ID
```

**Fig. 9.** Syntax of Role Specifications

# 4    The Role Programming Model

Due to the fine-grained nature of load statements `x.f=y` and store statements `x=y.f`, role constraints tend to be temporarily violated at certain program points. In this section we provide a programming model that gives the minimal requirements for a program to be role correct. A static program analysis can enforce a stronger role checking policy; it may not accept a weaker role checking policy. We assume a type safe programming language with a clean memory model, such as Java [5]. In the absence of acyclicity constraints, at any given program point, the set of all objects on the heap can be partitioned into:

1. **onstage objects** which are referenced by at least one local variable of the currently executing procedure;
2. **offstage objects** which are not referenced by any of the local variables of the currently executing procedure.

Only onstage objects can have their role constraints temporarily violated. More precisely, we have the following invariant.

**Local Role Consistency Invariant:** At *every program point*, there exists an assignment of roles to all objects of the heap such that the constraints for all *offstage* objects are satisfied.

Next, we introduce the notion of program checkpoints. The checkpoints include at least procedure entry, procedure exit, and procedure call points. They may also include additional program points specified by the programmer using the `roleCheck()` command.

**Global Role Consistency Invariant:** At *every program checkpoint*, there exists an assignment of roles to all objects of the heap such that the constraints for *all* objects are satisfied.

Note that it is not neccessary to have a checkpoint in every loop of the control-flow graph. This allows the verification of nonlocal changes to the heap without complex global loop invariants.

Role changes to onstage objects are specified using the `changeRole` construct. The statement `changeRole(x : r)` changes the current role of the onstage object *o*, referenced by local variable x, to role r. Local role consistency implies that the constraints of all offstage objects adjacent to *o* must be consistent with the new role of *o*. (The consistency of the object *o* with its own role is not checked until *o* goes offstage, or until a checkpoint is reached.)

In some cases it is useful to change roles of multiple offstage objects, without bringing them onstage first. The `changeRoles` statement is used for this purpose. It specifies a regular expression denoting a region of the heap, and a set of role transitions to be performed on this region. Every role transition specifies an initial role and a final role. As in Section 5, a regular expression denotes all objects reachable from the given variable without passing though other variables in the current scope.

```
statement ::= ...
            | "changeRole" "(" var ":" role ")"              onstage role change
            | "changeRoles" "(" regExp "," "{"roleTrans"}" ")"  offstage role changes
            | "roleCheck()"                                   global role check
 roleTrans ::= roleTrans "," roleTran                        role transition list
  roleTran ::= role₁ "->" role₂                              role transition
```

**Fig. 10.** Role Changing Statements

**Acyclicity Constraints:** Acyclicity constraints introduce the need to take into account the reachability of one onstage object from another to ensure that the program does not introduce a cycle into a region of the heap that the roles require to be free of cycles.

# 5  The Invariant Specification Language

Invariants allow the programmer to specify properties that hold at a given program point. The **assert** statement is used to enforce invariants. An invariant is a propositional formula over atomic properties. Atomic properties allow stating 1) roles of objects at a given program point; 2) aliasing between two given references; and 3) an upper bound on the set of paths between two objects in the current heap.

| | | |
|---|---|---|
| statement ::= ... | | |
| | "assert" "(" prop ")" | assertion |
| prop ::= atomic | | atomic proposition |
| | "!" prop | negation |
| | $prop_1$ "\|\|" $prop_2$ | disjunction |
| | $prop_1$ "&&" $prop_2$ | conjunction |
| atomic ::= $obj_1$ ":" role | | role assertion |
| | $obj_1$ "==" $obj_2$ | aliasing |
| | $obj_1$ "*>" $obj_2$ ":" regExp | reachability |
| obj ::= var \| obj "." field | | object reference |
| regExp ::= "empty" \| "none" | | empty path, empty set |
| | field | single field |
| | $regExp_1$ "." $regExp_2$ | concatenation |
| | $regExp_1$ "\|" $regExp_2$ | union |
| | regExp "*" | Kleene star |
| | regExp "&" | Infinite paths |

**Fig. 11.** Invariant Specifications

Roles at a given program point are asserted by the proposition obj : role. This allows the developer to verify the statically computable role of an object at a given program point.

To specify that objects $obj_1$ and $obj_2$ must be aliased, the assertion $obj_1 == obj_2$ is used. Objects are referred to using a sequence of fields starting from program variables. To specify that $obj_1$ and $obj_2$ must not be aliased, the assertion $!(obj_1 == obj_2)$ is used. Omitting the aliasing relation between these two objects allows for both cases. Note that both must and may aliasing information can be specified.

The expression $obj_1$ *> $obj_2$ denotes the set of all finite and infinite directed paths in the heap that lead from $obj_1$ to $obj_2$ without going through any onstage objects. (Paths that may pass through onstage objects can be split into segments that pass only through offstage objects.) Concrete sets of paths are specified using regular expressions, extended with the & operator, which allows the specification of infinite paths. This allows the precise specification of cyclicity. The symbol ":" denotes path subset, so $obj_1$ *> $obj_2$ : regExp gives may-reachability information in the form of an upper bound on the set of paths between two objects. For example, in the context of variables $x$ and $y$, the constraint x *> y : none implies that any sequence of operations that has access only to $x$ cannot perform structural modifications on the object pointed to by $y$. Using negation, it is possible to express must reachability information, which is a poweful tool when combined with aliasing constraints in role definitions, allowing the analysis of nonlocal operations on tree-like data structures.

## 6    Procedure Specifications

In this section we present the sublanguage for specifying procedure effects. It is designed to convey detailed yet concise procedure summaries which can be used as a basis for a compositional flow-sensitive interprocedural analysis with strong updates. The use of procedure summaries allows the use of precise analysis techniques inside procedures while retaining an overall linear analysis complexity in the total size of the program. Among our design goals for procedure specifications were:

1. the ability to approximate incremental changes to the regions of the heap;
2. easy instantiation of procedure specification in the context of the caller;
3. the ability to precisely specify the effects of simple procedures that perform local transformations on the heap;
4. the ability to specify aliasing contexts among procedure parameters as well as regions of heap reachable from parameters.

The first goal led us to a language whose primitives are local effects similar to loads and stores. These effects can be combined using nondeterministic choice, and their location specified using regular expressions. The second goal implied the decision to interpret all regular expressions in a procedure specification with respect to the state of the heap at procedure invocation time. The effects of simple procedures can be easily specified as a combination of elementary effects. The procedure contexts can be specified in a flexible way using the conditional effect construction. The syntax of procedure effects is given in figure 12.

Formally, an effect with no free variables is a binary relation between the initial heap and the final heap. We define the following hierarchy of effects: 1) primitive effects 2) simple effects 3) effects. Each class includes the previous ones.

**Primitive effects** are the building blocks of all effects. A *write* effect corresponds to a store statement or modification of a primitive field. A *read* effect specifies a load statement or read of a primitive field of a given object, without specifying which local variable receives the value. The *role change* effects specify a change of roles for one or more objects and correspond to the changeRole and changeRoles statements in the procedure. The skip statement denotes an

$$
\begin{array}{rll}
\text{effect} ::= & \text{simpleEffect} & \text{simple effect} \\
| & \text{effect}_1 \ "\,|\," \ \text{effect}_2 & \text{nondeterministic choice} \\
| & \text{effect}_1 \ "\,;\," \ \text{effect}_2 & \text{sequence} \\
| & \text{prop} \ "\text{->}" \ \text{effect} & \text{conditional effect} \\
| & "\,[\,"\ \text{bindings} \ "\,]\,"\ \text{simpleEffect} & \text{variable bindings} \\
| & \text{simpleEffect} \ "*" & \text{iteration} \\
\text{simpleEffect} ::= & \text{primitive} & \text{primitive effect} \\
| & \text{simpleEffect}_1 \ "\,|\," \ \text{simpleEffect}_2 & \text{nondeterministic choice} \\
| & \text{simpleEffect}_1 \ "\,;\," \ \text{simpleEffect}_2 & \text{sequence} \\
| & \text{prop} \ "\text{->}" \ \text{simpleEffect} & \text{conditional simple effect} \\
\text{primitive} ::= & \text{obj} \ "\,.\," \ \text{fieldSpec} \ "=" \ \text{valSpec} & \text{write} \\
| & "\text{read}" \ "\,(\," \ \text{obj} \ "\,.\," \ \text{fieldSpec} \ "\,)\," & \text{read} \\
| & "\text{changeRole}" \ "\,(\," \ \text{var} \ "\,:\," \ \text{role} \ "\,)\," & \text{onstage role change} \\
| & "\text{changeRoles}" \ "\,(\," \ \text{regExp} \ "\,,\," \ \{\ \text{roleTrans}\} \ "\,)\," & \text{offstage role changes} \\
| & "\text{skip}" & \text{empty effect} \\
| & "\text{fail}" & \text{failure} \\
\text{bindings} ::= & \text{binding} \ | \ \text{bindings} \ "\,,\," \ \text{binding} & \text{binding sequence} \\
\text{binding} ::= & \text{var} \ "\,:\," \ "\text{regExp}" & \text{existing object binding} \\
| & \text{var} \ "\,:\," \ "\text{new}" \ \text{role} & \text{new object binding} \\
\text{valSpec} ::= & \text{obj} \ | \ "\text{null}" \ | \ "\text{any}" & \text{value specification} \\
\text{fieldSpec} ::= & \text{field} \ | \ "\text{any}" & \text{field specification} \\
\text{obj} ::= & \text{var} \ | \ \text{paramRef} & \text{object} \\
\text{paramRef} ::= & \text{param} \ | \ \text{global} \ | \ \text{paramRef} \ "\,.\," \ \text{field} & \text{object at fixed path} \\
\end{array}
$$

**Fig. 12.** Procedure Effects

empty effect; it does nothing. The expression `fail` denotes the effect which always fails. It is allowed to call the procedure only from contexts for which the procedure effect does not fail.

Objects can be referred to via a fixed sequence of field names starting from parameters (and global variables), or via a variable bound to a region of the heap or a new object identifier. In both write and read effects it is possible to abstract away from the value written or the field name by using the **any** keyword.

**Simple effects** are built out of primitive effects using nondeterministic choice, sequence, and conditional. The *nondeterministic choice* operator " $|$ " specifies the union of the effect relations. In the expression $\text{effect}_1 \mid \text{effect}_2$, both $\text{effect}_1$ and $\text{effect}_2$ can occur; the called precedure is free to choose either one of them. The *sequence* of the effects $\text{effect}_1$; $\text{effect}_2$ denotes execution of $\text{effect}_1$ followed by the execution of $\text{effect}_2$. This corresponds to the composition of the effect relations. The *conditional* effect prop $\rightarrow$ effect is the restriction of effect to the states which satisfy the proposition prop. The effect relation acts as the identity on all states for which prop predicate is not satisfied. The syntax for propositions is the same as in Section 5.

**Effects** are built out of simple effects using variable binding and iteration in addition to nondeterministic choice, sequence, and conditional. A *variable binding* specifies a list of bindings for the free variables of an effect expression. A variable can be bound either to a nondeterministically chosen object in the region of the initial heap specified by a given regular expression (notation var : regExp), or to a newly allocated object of a given role (notation var : new role). The first form summarizes structural changes of a given region of the heap. The second form allows naming of objects created inside the procedure. This is important since new objects are often incorporated into existing data structures, so that effects that involve them determine the reachability properties of the heap after the procedure execution. The *iteration* operator ∗ denotes repetition of the effect an unspecified number of times. It can be used to summarize the effect of loops in the procedure.

## 7   Parallelization with Roles

It is possible to use the role definitions and operation effect statements as a basis for the automatic parallelization of programs that manipulate linked data structures. Because the role definitions characterize the aliasing relationships in which objects engage, the compiler can use the role definitions to discover computations that access disjoint regions of recursive data structures. The role definitions of the objects in a tree data structure, for example, enable the compiler to determine that different subtrees rooted at the same node are disjoint. The combination of this information with the operation effects information enables the compiler to, for example, parallelize standard recursively-defined computations that update tree nodes but do not change the structure of the tree. Similar transformations are possible for other computations that access linked data structures.

## 8   Related Work

The concept of role models as a generalization of the static class system has been present in the object modelling community for some time [13], but usually with no formal relationship with program code. The idea of static analysis of types which change at run-time was explored in [17], but without any treatment of relationships between objects in the heap. A system for object reclassification is presented in [3], but the class changes are designed to be transparent to aliasing; in our approach, the roles change when the aliases change, which is a requirement for reasoning about the role changes that take place when objects move between data structures. Our system also associates a set of invariants with the current role of every object, allowing stronger structural properties to be expressed. Another difference is that implementation of the language in [3] is based on performing additional run-time checks whereas our language is primarily an interface to a static program analysis system.

The sublanguage we use for specifying context-specific invariants is similar to the logic described in [1] which also explains the relationship with [8]. A more general system used for dependence testing is described in [9].

There appears to be surprisingly little work on languages for describing precise effects procedures with respect to the heap. The importance of procedure specifications for pointer analysis was indicated in [14]. A language for annotating software libraries is described in [6]. Effects systems in general were used in functional languages with side effects [10]. Our specification language bears some similarities to propositional dynamic logic [7]. Similarly to [4], our effect language specifies operations on heap. Unlike graph rewrite rules, our effect specifications are based on primitive effects which correspond to statements in imperative programs. The effects of complex procedures also tend to be more nondeterministic than graph rewrite rules due to their approximate nature.

Although the focus in this paper is on the specification language, the analyzability of the language was our major concern. The techniques useful for role analysis are discussed in [15], [12], [4]. More restrictive approaches rely on the extensions of linear type systems or on ownership types [16], [11], [2].

## 9    Conclusion

We have proposed a language for specifying invariants of objects which move between dynamically changing data structures. We have given the syntax and semantics of the language and illustrated its use on several examples.

The role definition sublanguage enables the classification of objects according to their membership in different data structures as well as the specification of some essential data structure heap invariants. The invariant specification sublanguage allows the communication of additional context-specific reachability and aliasing properties. Finally, the procedure effect sublanguage is designed to capture precise effects of short procedures and to summarize complex modifications performed in regions of the heap reachable from procedure parameters.

We have constructed this language to serve as a foundation for a compositional flow-sensitive interprocedural program analysis. Such an analysis can increase a programmer's confidence in program correctness. Moreover, it can enable a variety of program transformations.

## References

[1] Michael Benedikt, Thomas Reps, and Mooly Sagiv. A decidable logic for linked data structures. In *Proc. 8th European Symposium on Programming*, 1999.

[2] David G. Clarke, John M. Potter, and James Noble. Ownership types for flexible alias protection. In *Proc. 13th Annual Conference on Object-Oriented Programming, Systems, Languages, and Applications*, 1998.

[3] S. Drossopoulou, F. Damiani, M. Dezani-Ciancaglini, and P. Giannini. Fickle: Dynamic object re-classification. In *Proc. 15th European Conference on Object-Oriented Programming*, LNCS 2072, pages 130–149. Springer, 2001.

[4] Pascal Fradet and Daniel Le Metayer. Shape types. In *Proc. 24th ACM POPL*, 1997.

[5] James Gosling, Bill Joy, Guy Steele, and Gilad Bracha. *The Java Language Specification*. Sun Microsystems, Inc., 2001.

[6] Samuel Z. Guyer and Calvin Lin. An annotation language for optimizing software libraries. In *Second Conference on Domain Specific Languages*, 1999.

[7] David Harel, Dexter Kozen, and Jerzy Tiuryn. *Dynamic Logic*. The MIT Press, Cambridge, Mass., 2000.

[8] Joseph Hummel, Laurie J. Hendren, and Alexandru Nicolau. Abstract description of pointer data structures: An approach for improving the analysis and optimization of imperative programs. *ACM Letters on Programming Languages and Systems*, 1(3), September 1993.

[9] Joseph Hummel, Laurie J. Hendren, and Alexandru Nicolau. A language for conveying the aliasing properties of dynamic, pointer-based data structures. In *Proc. 8th International Parallel Processing Symposium*, Cancun, Mexico, April 26–29 1994.

[10] Pierre Jouvelot and David K. Gifford. Algebraic reconstruction of types and effects. In *Proc. 18th ACM POPL*, 1991.

[11] Naoki Kobayashi. Quasi-linear types. In *Proc. 26th ACM POPL*, 1999.

[12] Anders Møller and Michael I. Schwartzbach. The Pointer Assertion Logic Engine. In *Proc. ACM PLDI*, 2001.

[13] Trygve Reenskaug. *Working With Objects*. Prentice Hall, 1996.

[14] Radu Rugina and Martin Rinard. Design-driven compilation. In *Proc. 10th International Conference on Compiler Construction*, 2001.

[15] Mooly Sagiv, Thomas Reps, and Reinhard Wilhelm. Solving shape-analysis problems in languages with destructive updating. In *Proc. 23rd ACM POPL*, 1996.

[16] F. Smith, D. Walker, and G. Morrisett. Alias types. In *Proc. 9th European Symposium on Programming*, Berlin, Germany, March 2000.

[17] Robert E. Strom and Shaula Yemini. Typestate: A programming language concept for enhancing software reliability. *IEEE Transactions on Software Engineering*, January 1986.

# The Specification of Source-to-Source Transformations for the Compile-Time Optimization of Parallel Object-Oriented Scientific Applications

Daniel J. Quinlan[1], Markus Schordan[1], Bobby Philip[1], and Markus Kowarschik[2]

[1] Center for Applied Scientific Computing
Lawrence Livermore National Laboratory, Livermore, CA, USA
[2] System Simulation Group, Department of Computer Science
University of Erlangen-Nuremberg, Germany

**Abstract.** The performance of object-oriented applications in scientific computing often suffers from the inefficient use of high-level abstractions provided by underlying libraries. Since these library abstractions are user-defined and not part of the programming language itself there is no compiler mechanism to respect their semantics and thus to perform appropriate optimizations.

In this paper we outline the design of ROSE and focus on the discussion of two approaches for specifying and processing complex source code transformations. These techniques are intended to be as easy and intuitive as possible for potential ROSE users; i.e., for designers of object-oriented scientific libraries, people most often with no compiler expertise.

## 1 Introduction

The future of scientific computing depends upon the development of more sophisticated application codes. The original use of Fortran represented higher-level abstractions than the assembly instructions that preceded it, but exhibited performance problems that took years to overcome. However, the abstractions represented in Fortran were *standardized* within the language; today's much higher-level object-oriented abstractions are more difficult to optimize because they are *user-defined*.

The introduction of parallelism greatly exacerbates the compile-time optimization problem. While serial languages serve well for parallel programming, they know only the semantics of the serial language. As a result a serial compiler cannot introduce scalable parallel optimizations. Significant potential for optimization of parallel applications is lost as a result. There is a significant opportunity to capitalize upon the parallel semantics of the object-oriented framework and drive significant optimizations specific to both shared memory and distributed memory applications.

H. Dietz (Ed.): LCPC 2001, LNCS 2624, pp. 383–394, 2003.
© Springer-Verlag Berlin Heidelberg 2003

384 Daniel J. Quinlan et al.

We present a preprocessor based mechanism, called *ROSE*, that optimizes parallel object-oriented scientific application codes that use high-level abstractions provided by object-oriented libraries. In contrast to compile-time optimization of basic language abstractions (loops, operators, etc.), the optimization of the *use* of library abstractions within applications has received far less attention. With ROSE, library developers define customized optimizations and build specialized preprocessors. Source-to-source transformations are then used to provide an efficient mechanism for introducing such custom optimizations into user applications. A significant advantage of our approach is that preprocessors can be built which are tailored to user-defined high-level abstractions, while vendor supplied C++ compilers know only the lower-level abstractions of the C++ language they support. So far, our research has focused on applications and libraries written in C++.

This approach permits us to leverage existing vendor C++ compilers for architecture specific back-end optimizations. Significant improvements in performance associated with source-to-source transformations have already been demonstrated in recent work, underscoring the need for further research in this direction.

| Statement/GridSize | 5x5 | 25x25 | 100x100 |
|---|---|---|---|
| w=1 | 3.0 | 1.8 | 1.3 |
| w=u | 3.0 | 1.9 | 1.3 |
| w=u*2+v*3+u | 13.0 | 5.0 | 2.4 |
| indirect addressing | 44.0 | 41.0 | 32.5 |
| where statements | 23.0 | 5.0 | 3.0 |
| 9pt stencil | 77.0 | 14.0 | 5.6 |

**Table 1.** Speedups associated with optimizing source-to-source transformations of abstractions within Overture applications. Results are presented for 2D array objects u,v,w.

Table 1 shows some of these improvements for the use of optimizing source-to-source transformations within the *OVERTURE* framework [3]. Speedups are listed for several common types of statements, the values are the ratios of execution times without and with the optimizing source-to-source transformations. In each case the optimizing transformation results in better performance. The degree of improvement depends upon the abstraction being optimized within the application code and the problem size. For example, in the case of indirect addressing the performance improvement for 100×100 size problems is 3250%, showing the rich potential for indirect addressing optimizations. We can expect that ROSE will duplicate these results through the fully automated introduction of such optimizing transformations into application codes.

Other work exists which is related to our own research. Internally within ROSE a substantially modified version of the *SAGE II* [6] AST restructuring tool is used. *Nestor* [8] is a similar AST restructuring tool for Fortran 77, Fortran 90, and HPF2.0, which, however, does not attempt to recognize and optimize high-level user-defined abstractions. Work on *MPC++* [9,10] has led to the development of a C++ tool similar to SAGE, but with some additional capabilities for optimization. However, it does not attempt to address the sophisticated scale of abstractions that we target or the transformations we are attempting to introduce.

Related work on *telescoping languages* [7] shares some of the same goals as our research work and we look forward to tracking its progress in the coming years. Other approaches we know of are based on the definition of library-specific *annotation languages* to guide optimizing source code transformations [11] and on the specification of both high-level languages and corresponding sets of axioms defining code optimizations [12].

Work at University of Tennessee has lead to the development of *Automatically Tuned Linear Algebra Software* (ATLAS) [4]. Within this approach numerous transformations are written to define a search space and the performance of a given architecture is evaluated. The parameters associated with the best performing transformation are thus identified. Our work is related to this in the sense that this is one possible mechanism for the identification of optimizing transformations that could be used within preprocessors built using ROSE to optimize application codes. Our approach to the specification of transformations in this paper is consistent with the source code generation techniques used to generate transformations within ATLAS.

The remainder of this paper is organized as follows. In section 2 we give a survey on the ROSE infrastructure; we describe the process of automatically generating library-specific preprocessors and explain their source-to-source transformation mechanisms. The main focus of this paper is on the specification of these source-to-source transformations by the developer of the library. We will thus discuss two alternative specification approaches and an AST query mechanism in section 3. In section 4 we finally summarize our work.

## 2    ROSE Overview

We have developed ROSE as a preprocessor mechanism because our focus is on optimizing the use of user-defined high-level abstractions and not on lower-level optimizations associated with back-end code generation for specific platforms. Our approach permits ROSE to work as a preprocessor independent of any specific C++ compiler.

In the following we will briefly describe the internal structure of a preprocessor which has been automatically generated using ROSE; particularly the recognition of high-level abstractions (section 2.1), the overall preprocessor design (section 2.2), and finally the specification of the transformations (section 3), which is the main focus of this paper.

## 2.1  Recognition of Abstractions

We recognize abstractions within a user's application much the same way a compiler recognizes the syntax of its base language. To recognize high-level abstractions we build a hierarchy of *high-level abstract grammars* and the corresponding *high-level ASTs* using ROSE. This hierarchy is what provides for a relationship to telescoping languages [7].

These high-level abstract grammars are very similar to the base language abstract grammar — in our case an abstract C++ grammar. They are modified forms of the base language abstract grammar with added terminals and non-terminals associated with the abstractions we want to recognize. They cannot be modified in any way to introduce new keywords or new syntax, so clearly there are some restrictions. However, we can still leverage the lower-level compiler infrastructure; the parser that builds the base language AST. New terminals and nonterminals added to the base language abstract grammar might represent specific user-defined functions, data-structures, user-defined types, etc. More detail about the recognition of high-level abstractions can be found in [2]

## 2.2  Preprocessor Design

Figure 1 shows how the individual ASTs are connected in a sequence of steps; automatically generated translators generate higher level ASTs from lower level ASTs. The following describes these steps:

1. The first step generates the Edison Design Group (EDG) AST. This AST has a proprietary interface and is translated in the second step to form the abstract C++ grammar's AST.
2. The C++ AST restructuring tool is generated by ROSETTA [1] and is essentially comformant with the SAGE II implementation. This second step is representative of what SAGE II provides and presents the AST in a form where it can be modified with a non-proprietary public interface. At this second step the original EDG AST is deleted and afterwards is unavailable.
3. The third step is the most interesting since at this step the abstract C++ Grammar's AST is translated into higher level ASTs. Each parent AST (associated with a lower level abstract grammar) is translated into all of its child ASTs so that the hierarchy of abstract grammars is represented by a corresponding hierarchy of ASTs (one for each abstract grammar). Transformations can be applied at any stage of this third step and modify the parent AST recursively until the AST associated with the original abstract C++ grammar is modified. At the end of this third step all transformations have been applied.
4. The fourth step is to traverse the C++ AST and generate optimized C++ source code (unparsing). This completes the source-to-source preprocessing.

An obvious next and final step is to compile the resulting optimized C++ source code using a vendor's C++ compiler.

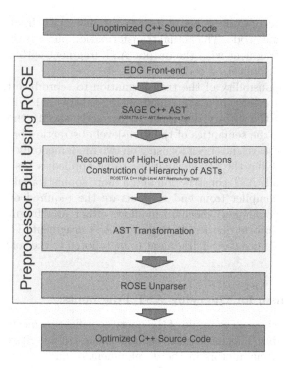

**Fig. 1.** Source-to-source C++ transformation with preprocessors using the ROSE infrastructure.

## 3   Specification of Transformations

This paper is primarily about the specification of transformations for use within preprocessors built using ROSE. The purpose of any transformation is to locally rewrite a statement or collection of statements — the *target* — using the semantics of the high-level abstractions being optimized and the context of their use within the application.

All transformations share a common set of requirements. Internally, the application has been parsed to build the corresponding AST within the AST hierarchy, using either the abstract C++ grammar or a higher-level abstract grammar. This forms the starting point for the internal processing. The ending point is the AST which has been modified according to the specification of the transformation. Since at this point all fragments of the AST where transformations will be applied have been identified in the recognition phase, we can associate transformations with specific terminals of the high-level abstract grammar. This approach permits the transformations to be performed within a single traversal of the AST at each node corresponding to a specific terminal of the abstract grammar.

The definition of the interface for the specification of transformations is straightforward. Inputs are fragments of the application's AST representing

C++ code to be optimized. Outputs are the new AST fragments representing the transformed code. The actual transformation phase is the substitution of the input AST fragment with the output AST fragment within the larger AST representing the application code.

It is the responsibility of the transformation to reproduce the semantics of the statement or collection of statements being substituted. Ultimately, it is the responsibility of the library developer to correctly specify the transformation which represents the semantics of the high-level abstraction being optimized.

Our recent research has been focusing on two fundamentally different methodologies for specifying the transformations to be applied; a first approach based on direct (manual) AST construction and a more sophisticated second approach leveraging the compiler front-end to generate the required output AST fragment. An orthogonal query mechanism allows either AST fragment construction mechanism to perform queries on the input AST fragment. This query mechanism permits the output AST fragment to be tailored to the context of the input AST fragment.

## 3.1  Mechanism for Querying AST Fragments

Figures 2 and 3 show an example of the query specification mechanism using synthesized attributes. This mechanism permits the use of inherited and synthesized attributes and accumulators in the development of queries upon any fragment of the AST. The mechanism is backed up by an automatically generated tree traversal mechanism generated by ROSETTA as part of the AST restructuring tool associated with each level of an abstract grammar in the hierarchy.

## 3.2  Direct Construction of AST Fragments

From the perspective of the compiler, at the start of the optimization phase the user's application is already parsed and represented by an AST. Any optimization must modify this representation. Evidently, the simplest approach is to modify the AST directly. Numerous specialized tools are based around techniques that directly manipulate the internal forms used within compilers. The AST and the source code are semantically equivalent in the sense that they represent the same code. However, the AST is more complex for users to manipulate as a tree, at least partly because programmers are used to manipulating source code as text.

Figure 5 shows an example of code required to construct a `for` loop within Sage++ [6] (predecessor to Sage II and our *modified* version of Sage II). Debugging the code generated from this AST fragment, requires a level of indirection which makes the specification of larger transformations particularly difficult.

figure 4 shows the code generated from the specification of the AST fragment in figure 5. Within this approach, and specifically in this example, there is a dramatic difference in the amount of code required to specify the AST fragment (figure 5) and the source code unparsed from the AST fragment (figure 4). Specific to this example there is a factor of 12 expansion in complexity as

```
class Query : public AstBottomUpProcessing< list<SgName> > {
    list<SgName> evaluateSynthesizedAttribute(SgNode*,SubtreeSynthesizedAttributes);
    ...
};

// This function returns a list of variable names as synthesized attribute
list<SgName>
Query::evaluateSynthesizedAttribute(SgNode* astNode,
                                    SubTreeSynthesizedAttributes childList)
{
    list<SgName> variableNameList;
    SgVarRefExp* varRefExp = isSgVarRefExp(astNode);
    if (varRefExp != NULL)
    {
        SgVariableSymbol* variableSymbol = varRefExp->get_symbol();
        SgInitializedName* initializedName = variableSymbol->get_declaration();
        SgName variableName = initializedName->get_name();
        variableNameList.push_back (variableName);
    }
    return mergeLists(variableNameList, childList);
}
```

**Fig. 2.** Example of evaluateSynthesizedAttribute function used in the templated query interface for a query of variable names in AST fragments. The Query class inherits from AstBottomUpProcessing with list<SgName> as template parameter.

```
Query localQueryOperator;  // build query operator
list<SgName> operandNameList = localQueryOperator.traverse( astNode );
```

**Fig. 3.** Example source code fragment specifying the query of variable names using synthesized attributes.

measured in the number of lines of code. It is also immediately obvious that the final code representation (figure 4) is easier to understand. The source code building the AST fragment (figure 5) additionally assumes a working knowledge of a particular AST restructuring tool (in this case Sage++).

However, conventional methods for the specification of transformations — which we have found in the literature — are characterized by the direct construction or alteration of AST fragments (e.g., declaration statement objects, for loop statement objects, etc.). Alternative compiler tools (Nestor [8], Sage [6], etc.) are similarly limited to such direct transformation approaches and, as a result, are most appropriate for simple transformations. These direct approaches also assume a high degree of compiler expertise which additionally limit their applicability within scientific computing.

### 3.3   Source-String Based Construction of AST Fragments

Since scientific library writers represent our target audience, we cannot assume any compiler expertise or familiarity with ASTs. Additionally, it is our experience that transformations for cache-based optimizations, which we are particularly

```
A.redim(size);
for (i_loopxx = 0; i_loopxx < 100; i_loopxx++)
{
  xxx_dA_T[i_loopxx] = xxx_dB[i_loopxx];
}
```

**Fig. 4.** Unparsed source code from the AST formed in figure 5.

interested in, are complex [13,14]. Implementing these kinds of transformations using the approach of direct AST construction is rather tedious, if not impractical. We therefore require a more compact representation of the transformation. Clearly, from the user's perspective, the transformation would be best represented as source code in the application's programming language, even if this representation cannot immediately be substituted into the AST.

Our more sophisticated second approach is therefore based on the source code representation of the transformations and leveraging the compiler front-end in order to generate the equivalent AST fragment to be substituted into the application's AST. There are several advantages of this transformation mechanism:

- The source code represents the most compact representation of the equivalent AST and is familiar to the programmer.
- The source code representing the transformation can be most easily examined for correctness by the user.
- Since the source code can be extracted from files, transformations can be built from working versions of the code representing the transformations. This approach thus allows test codes representing the transformations to be built separately and introduced as optimizing transformations into applications. We expect this approach will permit an interface to optimization tools such as ATLAS.
- The transformation source code can be parsed directly by the internal compiler infrastructure to generate the AST fragment required. Thus the process of generating the AST fragment for insertion into the AST at compile-time can be automated.

With sufficient exercise of the query mechanism the source-string can be tailored (programmed) to build most source code transformations. Figure 6 shows the source code and function call required to generate the identical AST fragment as in figure 5.

We consider the manipulation of strings, as an alternative way to specify the AST transformation at compile time, to be an added approach especially useful for larger transformations. This approach is direct from the user's point of view, since the source-to-source transformation is specified using source code. But our approach should be considered indirect from the compiler's point of view, since the AST fragment is subsequently generated from source-strings and *it* (the AST fragment) is what is needed at compile-time.

The optimization of object-oriented array class libraries can form an interesting example problem. The array statements elegantly represent mathematical

```
SgExpression *Expression = CExpressionStatement->expr()->lhs();
SgSymbol *Argument = (Expression->lhs()->symbol() == NULL) ?
    Expression->lhs()->lhs()->symbol() : Expression->lhs()->symbol();
SgExpression dimen_call(RECORD_REF);
dimen_call.setLhs(SgVarRefExp(*TemporaryArrayPtr));
SgSymbol *FieldSymbol = FindFieldWName("redim", TemporaryArrayPtr );
SgFunctionCallExp dimen_func (*FieldSymbol);
dimen_func.addArg(SgVarRefExp(*Argument));
dimen_call.setRhs(dimen_func);
SgCExpStmt RedimMemberFunction (dimen_call);
SgExpression *Expression = getRootExpression ( Statement );
SgVariableSymb *TemporaryArrayPtr = new SgVariableSymb ("xxx_dA_T");
TemporaryArrayPtr->declareTheSymbol( *( StatementPtr->controlParent() ) );
SgExpression *le = Expression->lhs();
SgDerivedType *dtp = NULL;
SgSymbol *vsb = le->symbol();
TemporaryArrayPtr->setType(vsb->type());
SgExpression *Expression = getRootExpression ( Statement );
SgVariableSymb *TemporaryArrayPtr = new SgVariableSymb ("xxx_dB");
TemporaryArrayPtr->declareTheSymbol( *( StatementPtr->controlParent() ) );
SgExpression *le = Expression->lhs();
SgDerivedType *dtp = NULL;
SgSymbol *vsb = le->symbol();
TemporaryArrayPtr->setType(vsb->type());
SgVariableSymb *LoopInductionVariable = new SgVariableSymb ("i_loopxx");
LoopInductionVariable->setType( SgTypeInt() );
LoopInductionVariable->declareTheSymbol( *( StatementPtr->controlParent() ) );
SgCExpStmt *AssignmentExpression =
  new SgCExpStmt( SgAssignOp(*LhsExpression, SgVarRefExp(*TemporaryArrayPtr) ) );
SgBasicBlock* LoopBody = new SgBasicBlock ();
LoopBody.insert(AssignmentExpression);
int upperBound = 100;
SgForStmt *ForStatementPtr =
  new SgForStmt( SgAssignOp(SgVarRefExp(*LoopInductionVariable),SgValueExp(0)),
                 SgVarRefExp(*LoopInductionVariable) < SgValueExp(upperBound),
                 SgUnaryExp(PLUSPLUS_OP,1,SgVarRefExp(*LoopInductionVariable)),
                 SgCExpStmt(*LoopBody));
```

**Fig. 5.** Code to build manually an AST fragment for the `for` loop shown in fig. 4

expressions because of the operator overloading made possible within the C++ language. In figure 7 we show a sample array statement from the A++/P++ array class library [15,16]. This library permits the specification of serial and parallel array objects and their manipulation using overloaded operators. The library permits the evaluation of expressions using pair-wise operator or expression template mechanisms. Both of these approaches have performance problems. The pair-wise evaluation of expressions within a statement is not cache friendly and results in a loss of performance (factor of 1-6) [16,13]. While the expression templates have long compile times and limits on their application [13].

Figure 8 shows the semantically equivalent transformation generated from the above A++/P++ target (figure 7). In this case the optimizing transformation removes all array class overhead and provides the same performance as C or Fortran 77, since the data is accessed through **restrict** pointers. More sophisticated transformations could provide fusion between statements to provide improved temporal locality of array statement expressions (providing larger internal loops).

```
buildAST_Fragment (
  "A.redim(size); \n for (i_loopxx = 0; i_loopxx < 100; i_loopxx++) \n \
  { \n xxx_dA_T[i_loopxx] = xxx_dB[i_loopxx]; }" );
```

**Fig. 6.** Function call using a source-string to create an AST representing the
source code in figure 4.

```
// A and B are declared as array objects (not shown)
// and used in an array statement
A(I) = ( B(I-1) + B(I+1) ) * 0.5;
```

**Fig. 7.** Target of optimizing transformation (transformation shown in figure 8).

## 4    Conclusions

ROSE is a library to simplify the construction of optimizing preprocessors. The
specification of the transformation is done within the program that is compiled
to be the preprocessor. This program leverages both the ROSE library for internal infrastructure and the source code generated by ROSETTA (part of ROSE).
Source code generated by ROSETTA implements AST restructuring tools corresponding to abstract grammars and higher-level abstractions, this source code
is compiled to build the preprocessor. Infrastructure within ROSE permits the
specification of transformations, either directly modifying the AST or indirectly
through the specification of source-strings which are processed to form AST
fragments which are used to modify the AST.

We have presented the ROSE infrastructure to automatically generate library-
specific source-to-source compilers (preprocessors). These preprocessors can be
used to optimize the use of high-level abstractions in parallel object-oriented
applications.

We have presented two basic approaches for specifying transformations. While
our first approach of direct AST construction turned out to be tedious (especially
for complex cache-based transformations), our second approach, which leverages
the compiler front-end instead, provides an elegant and comfortable alternative.

## References

1. Quinlan, D., Philip, B., "ROSETTA: The Compile-Time Recognition Of Object-
   Oriented Library Abstractions And Their Use Within Applications", Proceedings
   of the PDPTA'2001 Conference, Las Vegas, Nevada, June 24-27 2001
2. Quinlan, D. Schordan, M. Philip, B. Kowarschik, M. "Parallel Object-Oriented
   Framework Optimization", (submitted to) Special Issue of Concurrency: Practice and Experience, also in Proceedings of Conference on Parallel Compilers
   (CPC2001), Edinburgh, Scotland, June 2001.

```
// Transformation Target: A(I) = ( B(I-1) + B(I+1) ) * 0.5;
int rose_index [8];
int rose_stride[8];
int rose_base  [8];
int rose_bound [8];
double restrict* B_rose_pointer = B.getDataPointer();
double restrict* A_rose_pointer = A.getDataPointer();
rose_base[0]   = (B.getBase)(0);
rose_bound[0]  = (B.getBound)(0);
rose_stride[0] = (B.getStride)(0);
for (int i = rose_base[0]; i <= rose_bound[0]; i += rose_stride[0])
{
   A_rose_pointer[i] = (B_rose_pointer[i-1] + B_rose_pointer[i+1] ) * 0.5;
}
```

**Fig. 8.** Unparsed source code represented by an AST of the transformed target code (figure 7). The specification uses the internal ROSE infrastructure (not shown). A source-string is processed to generate an AST fragment and then unparsed to form the text.

3. Brown, D., Henshaw, W., Quinlan, D., "OVERTURE: A Framework for Complex Geometries", Proceedings of the ISCOPE'99 Conference, San Francisco, CA, Dec 7-10 1999.

4. ATLAS homepage, http://www.netlib.org/atlas.

5. Edison Design Group, http://www.edg.com.

6. Bodin, F. et. al., "Sage++: An object-oriented toolkit and class library for building fortran and C++ restructuring tools", Proceedings of the Second Annual Object-Oriented Numerics Conference, 1994.

7. Broom, B., Cooper, K., Dongarra, J., Fowler, R., Gannon, D., Johnsson, L., Kennedy, K., Mellor-Crummey, J., Torczon, L., "Telescoping Languages: A Strategy for Automatic Generation of Scientific Problem-Solving Systems from Annotated Libraries", Journal of Parallel and Distributed Computing, 2000.

8. Silber, G.-A., http://www.ens-lyon.fr/~gsilber/nestor.

9. Ishikawa, Y., et. al., "Design and Implementation of Metalevel Architecture in C++ — MPC++ Approach —", Proceedings of Reflection'96 Conference, April 1996.

10. Chiba, S., "Macro Processing in Object-Oriented Languages", Proc. of Technology of Object-Oriented Languages and Systems (TOOLS Pacific '98), Australia, November, IEEE Press, 1998.

11. Guyer, S.Z., Lin, C., "An Annotation Language for Optimizing Software Libraries", Proceedings of the Second Conference on Domain-Specific Languages, October 1999.

12. Menon, V., Pingali, K., "High-Level Semantic Optimization of Numerical Codes", Proceedings of the ACM/IEEE Supercomputing 1999 Conference (SC99), Portland, OR, 1999.

13. Bassetti, F., Davis, K., Quinlan, D., "Optimizing Transformations of Stencil Operations for Parallel Object-Oriented Scientific Frameworks on Cache-Based Architectures" Proceedings of the ISCOPE'98 Conference, Santa Fe, NM, 1998.

14. Weiß, C., Karl, W., Kowarschik, M., Rüde, U., "Memory Characteristics of Iterative Methods", Proceedings of the ACM/IEEE Supercomputing 1999 Conference (SC99), Portland, OR, 1999.

15. Lemke, M., Quinlan, D., "P++, a C++ Virtual Shared Grids Based Programming Environment for Architecture-Independent Development of Structured Grid Applications", published as part of CONPAR/VAPP V, September 1992, Lyon, France; also published in Lecture Notes in Computer Science, Springer Verlag, September 1992.
16. Parsons, R., Quinlan, D., "A++/P++ Array Classes for Architecture Independent Finite Difference Computations", Proceedings of the Second Annual Object-Oriented Numerics Conference, pages 408-418, Sunriver, OR, April 1994.

# Computing Array Shapes in MATLAB[*]

Pramod G. Joisha, U. Nagaraj Shenoy, and Prithviraj Banerjee

Department of Electrical and Computer Engineering, Northwestern University, USA.
[pjoisha, nagaraj, banerjee]@ece.nwu.edu

**Abstract.** This paper deals with the problem of statically inferring the shape of an array in languages such as MATLAB. Inferring an array's shape is desirable because it empowers better compilation and interpretation; specifically, knowing an array's shape could permit reductions in the number of run-time array conformability checks, enable memory preallocation optimizations, and facilitate the in-lining of "scalarized" code. This paper describes how the shape of a MATLAB expression can be determined statically, based on a methodology of systematic matrix formulations. The approach capitalizes on the algebraic properties that underlie MATLAB's shape semantics and exactly captures the shape that the MATLAB expression assumes at run time. Some of the highlights of the approach are its applicability to a large class of MATLAB functions and its uniformity. Our methods are compared with the previous shadow variable scheme, and we show how the algebraic view allows inferences not deduced by the traditional approach.

## 1   Introduction

In languages such as MATLAB[1] and APL that lack type declarations, static knowledge of an array's intrinsic type and shape could improve the translated code's execution efficiency. For instance, it could enable the system to avoid conformability checks on a function's operands at run time, if certain guarantees can be made on the nature of those operands at compile time. Besides, knowing how an array's shape will evolve during the course of a loop's execution may permit the system to arrive at some estimate of its size, thereby allowing the preallocation of the array outside the loop. This greatly enhances performance, since the overhead of incremental array growth is avoided.

In this work, we examine the problem of statically inferring an array's shape in the MATLAB programming language. The language is representative of numerous other interactive array languages such as APL and SETL, and was primarily chosen on account of the immense popularity that it enjoys in the programming community. In fact, the language's extensive array support, coupled with its simplicity and interactive nature, is the chief reason behind its emergence as the tool of choice for fast prototyping and analysis.

---

[*] This research was supported by DARPA under Contract F30602–98–2–0144.
[1] MATLAB is a registered trademark of The MathWorks, Inc.

H. Dietz (Ed.): LCPC 2001, LNCS 2624, pp. 395–410, 2003.
© Springer-Verlag Berlin Heidelberg 2003

## 1.1   Motivation

Consider the synthetic MATLAB code fragment shown in Figure 1.[2] Here, the invocations rand(m, n) and rand(x, y) return a pair of two-dimensional arrays (i.e., matrices) having the extents m, x and n, y along the first and second dimensions respectively. Thus, even though there is no way of establishing the values of m, n, x and y at compile time, we can still safely conclude at compile time that a and b have $\langle m, n \rangle$ and $\langle x, y \rangle$ as their respective shape tuples. However, what should the shape tuple of c be? Note that c is the outcome of a*b where * is the MATLAB matrix multiply operation [10]. According to the semantics of this operation, the answer "$\langle m, y \rangle$, if n = x" is only partly correct. This is because, if either a or b evaluate to scalars at run time (i.e., $m = 1 \wedge n = 1$ or $x = 1 \wedge y = 1$), the shape of c will be $\langle x, y \rangle$ or $\langle m, n \rangle$ respectively. In fact, can we even determine the dimensionality of c at compile time? This is because, if either a or b are scalars at run time, c will have as many dimensions as the other operand. Since there is no "unique" shape tuple that can be statically ascribed to c, should we maintain a list of candidate shapes against c, each of which could potentially be the final shape of c? How then do we infer the shape of d in the given code excerpt so as to take into consideration all possible "reaching" shapes of c?

```
m ← round(4*rand+1);
n ← round(5*rand+1);
x ← round(5*rand+1);
y ← round(6*rand+1);

a ← rand(m, n);
b ← rand(x, y);

c ← a*b;
d ← c+a;
e ← d-a;
f ← e./d;
```

**Fig. 1.** A Motivating Code Fragment

## 1.2   Related Work

In the recent past, the compiler community has witnessed much activity in the area of compilation for the MATLAB language [4, 5, 13, 2, 9, 11]. The work due to Kaplan et al. [8], based on the theory of lattices, was among the first that dealt with the problem of automatically determining the type attributes in a programming language requiring no declarations. In the work due to Budd [1], a partial ordering of intrinsic type and shape was used in the type determination process. Data-flow techniques were then applied to propagate type information

---

[2] The symbol ← will be used to denote the assignment operation in MATLAB.

across expressions, statements and procedures. However, the notion of shape as used in [1] corresponded to the broad attributes of scalar, vector, "fixed-size" array and "arbitrary" array, and it is not clear how the actual array extents were automatically computed. The FALCON project [5] was among the early works to examine the type determination problem in MATLAB. The FALCON system relies on a static shape inference mechanism that essentially propagates an array's "rank" and shape when possible, and resorts to a dynamic strategy based on shadow variables otherwise. Similar techniques have been adopted in the "Otter" MATLAB compiler [13] and in Menhir [2]. Investigations into shape, using alternate approaches such as category theory, have also been done [6]. These efforts have attempted to consider shape in a broad context—that is, as structures not just limited to matrices and arrays, but encompassing lists, trees and unlabeled graphs as well. The type of operations considered were confined to those that permitted a complete static analysis of shape—that is, operations in which the shape of the output was completely determined by the shapes of the inputs.

## 1.3  Contributions

This paper presents a framework that makes it possible to statically describe the shape of a MATLAB expression. The main contribution is that, unlike previous approaches, the framework empowers useful inferences even in situations wherein the actual array extents may not be statically determinable. This difference is important because current techniques do not attempt further inferences from a statically unknown shape. The following are the specific contributions of this work.

- A framework that, in addition to enabling a compact and exact static representation of shape for a large class of MATLAB functions, reveals useful properties borne by the language's shape semantics.
- We show how a compiler or interpreter could use the framework to reduce two overheads: that due to array conformability checks, and that due to the incremental growth of arrays in loops.

## 1.4  Outline

The rest of this paper is organized as follows. We begin with the underpinnings of the framework in § 2. In § 3, we describe the framework by showing its application to an important operator in MATLAB. Continuing with the same operator, we show in § 4 how the framework uncovers some of the important properties associated with its shape semantics. In § 5, we discuss the applicability of the framework. Comparisons with the current state of the art in shape determination are done in § 6. In § 7, we explain how the framework can handle arbitrary control flow. Two important optimizations that the framework allows, namely reduction in the array conformability check overhead and array preallocation, are presented and discussed in § 8 and § 9. Finally, we conclude the paper in § 10.

## 2   Preliminaries

All data in MATLAB is ultimately an array. For example, a scalar is an array of size $1 \times 1$. We use the shape-tuple notation $\langle p_1, p_2, \ldots, p_m \rangle$ to represent the shape of an $m$-dimensional array whose respective extents from the first to the $m$th dimension are $p_1$, $p_2$ and so on until $p_m$.

In MATLAB, any $m$-dimensional array can be considered to have $n$ dimensions, where $n > m$, simply by regarding the higher dimensions to have unit extents. Since higher dimensions are indicated to the right of lower dimensions in the shape-tuple notation, *trailing extents* of unity are effectively of no significance to an array's shape in MATLAB. In other words, the shape tuples $\langle 2, 3, 4 \rangle$, $\langle 2, 3, 4, 1 \rangle$, $\langle 2, 3, 4, 1, 1 \rangle$ and so on represent the same shape. We therefore say that these shape tuples are *MATLAB-equivalent*.

For the sake of convenience, we impose the restriction that the shape tuple of an array must have at least two components in its representation. With this proviso, a column vector with three elements could have any of the shape tuples $\langle 3, 1 \rangle$, $\langle 3, 1, 1 \rangle$ and so on, but not $\langle 3 \rangle$.

The notion of equivalent shape tuples leads to the idea of an array's *canonical shape tuple*. An array's canonical shape tuple is obtained from any of its equivalent shape tuples by discarding all trailing extents of unity from the third component onwards. For the column vector discussed above, the canonical shape tuple would be $\langle 3, 1 \rangle$ while the canonical shape tuple for a scalar would be $\langle 1, 1 \rangle$.

We next define an array's *rank* as the number of its dimensions. Because an array will have an infinite set of shape tuples, it will also have an infinite set of ranks. For example, an array having $\langle 5, 1, 2 \rangle$ as its canonical shape tuple will have a rank of 3 or more. We therefore call the smallest rank that can be ascribed to an array its *canonical rank*; this equals the number of components in its canonical shape tuple.

### 2.1   Terminology

In the context of MATLAB expressions, we shall use the terms illegal arrays, scalars, row vectors, column vectors and matrices to mean the following:

**illegal array**: An array that is the "outcome" of an ill-formed MATLAB expression.

**scalar**: A legal array whose canonical rank is 2, and whose extents along the first and second dimensions are 1 each.

**row vector**: A legal array whose canonical rank is 2, and whose extent along the first dimension is 1.

**column vector**: A legal array whose canonical rank is 2, and whose extent along the second dimension is 1.

**matrix**: A legal array whose canonical rank is 2.

Illegal arrays are an artificial construct introduced only for completeness. They are meant to represent the result of an illegal MATLAB expression. For example, when a $2 \times 3$ matrix is multiplied with a $4 \times 5$ matrix in MATLAB, the run-time system will complain of an error. The concept of an illegal array is meant to abstract such error situations.

Notice the overlap in the above definitions. For instance, that which is a scalar could also be regarded as a row vector, a column vector or a matrix. And a row vector or a column vector is also a matrix. We shall use the phrase "higher dimensional array" to describe legal arrays whose canonical ranks are at least 3. The term "array" by itself (without any qualification) could mean an illegal array, a scalar, a row vector, a column vector, a matrix or a higher dimensional array. MATLAB also supports *empty arrays* [10]; these are legal arrays that contain no data but yet have a shape. To encompass the empty array construct, we allow the shape-tuple components to also be zero.

## 2.2   Shape Algebra Basics

Consider the set $\mathbb{L}_\mathbb{S}$ of all square diagonal matrices of order 2 or more, in which the principal diagonal elements belong to the set of nonnegative integers $\mathbb{W}$. We shall follow the convention of denoting an $n \times n$ square diagonal matrix having $p_1$, $p_2$ and so on until $p_n$ as its principal diagonal elements by $\langle p_1, p_2, \ldots, p_n \rangle$. Thus,

$$\langle p_1, p_2, \ldots, p_n \rangle = \begin{pmatrix} p_1 & 0 & \ldots & 0 \\ 0 & p_2 & \ldots & 0 \\ \vdots & \vdots & \ddots & \vdots \\ 0 & 0 & \ldots & p_n \end{pmatrix}.$$

By using $\langle p_1, p_2, \ldots, p_n \rangle$ to also represent the shape tuple of a MATLAB array, we in effect infuse the notation the power of matrix arithmetic. The choice of square diagonal matrices to capture the essence of an array's shape was motivated by the fact that under the usual matrix arithmetic operations of addition, subtraction, division (i.e., inverse), and multiplication by a scalar, the result is also square diagonal.

We additionally include the concept of "illegal shape tuples" so as to represent the shape of an illegal MATLAB array. We do this by considering a set $\mathbb{I}_\mathbb{S}$ of integer square diagonal matrices whose members do not belong to $\mathbb{L}_\mathbb{S}$. A suitable choice for $\mathbb{I}_\mathbb{S}$ would be:

$$\mathbb{I}_\mathbb{S} = \{\langle \pi_1, \pi_2 \rangle, \langle \pi_1, \pi_2, 1 \rangle, \langle \pi_1, \pi_2, 1, 1 \rangle, \ldots\} \tag{1}$$

where $\pi_1$ and $\pi_2$ are integers such that either $\pi_1 < 0$ or $\pi_2 < 0$ or both. Consider the augmented set $\mathbb{S} = \mathbb{L}_\mathbb{S} \cup \mathbb{I}_\mathbb{S}$. We can easily define an equivalence relation $\wp$ on $\mathbb{S}$ such that two elements in this set are related by $\wp$ if they are MATLAB-equivalent. That is, for any $s, t \in \mathbb{S}$, $s \wp t$ if and only if either $s$ and $t$ are identical or differ by trailing extents of unity from the third component on. Hence, if $s = \langle p_1, p_2, \ldots, p_k \rangle$ and $t = \langle q_1, q_2, \ldots, q_l \rangle$ where $k, l \geq 2$, then

$$s \wp t \implies \begin{cases} s = t & \text{if } k = l, \\ s = \langle q_1, q_2, \ldots, q_l, 1, \ldots, 1 \rangle & \text{if } k > l, \\ t = \langle p_1, p_2, \ldots, p_k, 1, \ldots, 1 \rangle & \text{if } k < l. \end{cases} \tag{2}$$

Notice that the set of illegal shape tuples $\mathbb{I}_\mathbb{S}$ forms an equivalence class by this relation. Furthermore, observe that the shape tuple of a MATLAB expression can be any element in some equivalence class under $\wp$. Each equivalence class in the set of equivalence classes under $\wp$—called the *quotient set* of $\mathbb{S}$ by $\wp$ (see [14])—corresponds to a canonical shape tuple and vice versa.

# 3   Shape Inferring Framework

The shape inferring framework determines the shape tuple of a MATLAB expression, given the shape tuples of its operands. Every MATLAB function can have its shape semantics modelled algebraically by a *shape-tuple operator*. The shape-tuple operator (also called the *shape-tuple function*) gives us the shape of a MATLAB function's result, given the shapes of its operands.

To illustrate the actual mechanics of the shape inferring process, we shall consider the problem of determining the shape of a MATLAB matrix multiply expression. That is, given the MATLAB statement c ← a*b where the shape tuples of a and b are $s = \langle p_1, p_2, \ldots, p_k \rangle$ and $t = \langle q_1, q_2, \ldots, q_l \rangle$ respectively and where $k, l \geq 2$, we shall see how the shape tuple $u = \langle r_1, r_2, \ldots, r_m \rangle$ of the outcome c can be computed. We begin by reprising the shape semantics of the matrix multiply operation in MATLAB [10]:

> The function * is defined when one of the operands is a legal array and the other is a scalar. If both operands are nonscalars, then they must be matrices such that the extents along the second dimension of a and the first dimension of b match. Any other combination of shapes produces a run-time error.

The first question that needs to be addressed is what should the rank of the result c be. By answering this question, we would know the number of array extent components $m$ in the shape tuple $u$ of c. However, we cannot "accurately" answer this question at compile time in the sense that the canonical rank will, in the most general setting, be determinable only at run time. For instance, in the case of c ← a*b, the canonical rank of c could be anywhere between 2 to $\max(k, l)$ depending on the run-time values of $p_1, p_2, \ldots, p_k$ and $q_1, q_2, \ldots, q_l$. Whatever may be the canonical shape tuple of the result, by virtue of the equivalence relation $\wp$ introduced in § 2.2, it will be equivalent to a shape tuple having $\max(k, l)$ components. Therefore, we can conservatively determine the rank of c at compile time as being

$$\mathcal{R}(c) = \max(k, l). \tag{3}$$

## 3.1   Shape Predicates

The next issue that needs to be addressed is detecting when a MATLAB matrix multiply operation is well defined. For this, we enlist the services of three "shape-predicate" functions—$\theta$, $\beta$ and $\alpha$—that map a shape tuple $s$ to the 0/1 set $\mathbb{B}$. These functions predicate three conditions that could be associated with a given shape tuple. The function $\theta : \mathbb{S} \mapsto \mathbb{B}$ is called the *correctness shape predicate* and maps all legal shape tuples to 1 and all illegal shape tuples to 0. If the shape tuple $s$ indicates a MATLAB matrix, the *matrix shape predicate* $\beta : \mathbb{S} \mapsto \mathbb{B}$ is defined to be 1; otherwise it is 0. If $s$ indicates a MATLAB scalar, the *scalar shape predicate* $\alpha : \mathbb{S} \mapsto \mathbb{B}$ is defined to be 1, and 0 otherwise. Note that the terminology of § 2.1 is used here.

From their definitions, each of the shape-predicate functions can be expressed mathematically in terms of the shape-tuple components. If $u = \langle r_1, r_2, \ldots, r_m \rangle$, we have the following:

$$\beta(u) = \theta(u)\delta(r_3 - 1)\delta(r_4 - 1)\ldots\delta(r_m - 1), \tag{4}$$

$$\alpha(u) = \delta(r_1 - 1)\delta(r_2 - 1)\delta(r_3 - 1)\ldots\delta(r_m - 1). \tag{5}$$

In Equations (4) and (5), $\delta$ denotes the *discrete Delta function* defined on the integer domain:

$$\delta(i) = \begin{cases} 0 & \text{if } i \neq 0, \\ 1 & \text{if } i = 0. \end{cases} \tag{6}$$

The way the $\theta$ function is connected to the shape-tuple components is dependent on the actual choice for the two-component illegal shape tuple $\pi = \langle \pi_1, \pi_2 \rangle$ in Equation (1), and does not affect the formulation of our framework. Observe that by Equations (4) and (5), whenever $\beta(u)$ or $\alpha(u)$ is 1, $\theta(u)$ must also be 1.

Getting back to the MATLAB statement c ← a*b, the correctness shape predicate $\theta(u)$ should be 1 if the MATLAB expression a*b is well formed, and 0 otherwise. When is a MATLAB matrix multiply well defined? According to the earlier stated semantics, the outcome of a*b is a legal array so long as a and b are both legal, and either a is a scalar, or b is a scalar, or a and b are matrices such that the extent of a along its second dimension equals the extent of b along its first dimension. Couching these semantics in mathematical language, we get

$$\theta(u) = \theta(s)\theta(t)\big(1 - (1 - \alpha(s))(1 - \alpha(t))(1 - \beta(s)\beta(t)\delta(p_2 - q_1))\big). \tag{7}$$

It is easy to verify that Equation (7) evaluates to 1 for a well-defined MATLAB matrix multiply operation, and to 0 otherwise. For instance, if a were a scalar and b a legal array, $\theta(s)$, $\theta(t)$ and $\alpha(s)$ would all become 1, so that $\theta(u)$ would simplify to 1, irrespective of what $\beta(t)$, $p_2$ and $q_1$ actually are. We therefore say that a scalar shape tuple and any legal shape tuple *always* form a "legal shape-tuple combo" for the * built-in function.

## 3.2   Shape Tuple

To formulate the shape tuple of the result, we take advantage of the fact that the shape-tuple representation synonymously denotes a square diagonal matrix. This allows us to algebraically calculate the shape tuple of the result using elementary matrix arithmetic on the shape tuples of the operands. In the case of c ← a*b, we get

$$u = (1 - \theta(u))\pi^* + \theta(u)\big(s^*\alpha(t) + t^*\alpha(s)(1 - \alpha(t)) + (s^*\Gamma_1 + t^*\Gamma_2 \\ + \iota^* - \Gamma_1 - \Gamma_2)(1 - \alpha(s))(1 - \alpha(t))\big). \tag{8}$$

In the above equation, each of the quantities $\boldsymbol{\pi}^*$, $\boldsymbol{s}^*$, $\boldsymbol{t}^*$, $\boldsymbol{\iota}^*$, $\boldsymbol{\Gamma}_1$ and $\boldsymbol{\Gamma}_2$ designate $\mathcal{R}(\mathsf{c}) \times \mathcal{R}(\mathsf{c}) = \max(k, l) \times \max(k, l)$ integer square diagonal matrices. In $\boldsymbol{\Gamma}_1$, only the first principal diagonal element is 1 and the rest are 0. In $\boldsymbol{\Gamma}_2$, only the second principal diagonal element is 1 and the remaining are 0. The symbols $\boldsymbol{\pi}^*$ and $\boldsymbol{\iota}^*$ respectively represent the two-component illegal shape tuple $\boldsymbol{\pi} = \langle \pi_1, \pi_2 \rangle$ and the two-component scalar shape tuple $\boldsymbol{\iota} = \langle 1, 1 \rangle$, appropriately "promoted" to $\mathcal{R}(\mathsf{c})$ components by appending unit extents. The quantities $\boldsymbol{s}^*$ and $\boldsymbol{t}^*$ are also obtained by promoting $\boldsymbol{s}$ and $\boldsymbol{t}$ to $\mathcal{R}(\mathsf{c})$ components. By having all the matrices in Equation (8) to be of the same size (i.e., $\mathcal{R}(\mathsf{c}) \times \mathcal{R}(\mathsf{c})$), the computation in the equation is well defined.

EXAMPLE 1: *Matrix Multiplication*
Let us reconsider the previous MATLAB statement c ← a*b, and suppose that the shape tuples for a and b are $\boldsymbol{s} = \langle p_1, p_2 \rangle$ and $\boldsymbol{t} = \langle q_1, q_2, q_3 \rangle$ respectively. From Equation (3), $\mathcal{R}(\mathsf{c}) = 3$; after promoting the shape tuples $\boldsymbol{s}$ and $\boldsymbol{t}$ to $\mathcal{R}(\mathsf{c})$ components, we get

$$\boldsymbol{s}^* = \begin{pmatrix} p_1 & 0 & 0 \\ 0 & p_2 & 0 \\ 0 & 0 & 1 \end{pmatrix}, \qquad \boldsymbol{t}^* = \begin{pmatrix} q_1 & 0 & 0 \\ 0 & q_2 & 0 \\ 0 & 0 & q_3 \end{pmatrix}.$$

From Equation (4), we have $\beta(\boldsymbol{s}) = \theta(\boldsymbol{s})$ and $\beta(\boldsymbol{t}) = \theta(\boldsymbol{t})\delta(q_3 - 1)$. From Equation (5), we also have $\alpha(\boldsymbol{s}) = \delta(p_1 - 1)\delta(p_2 - 1)$ and $\alpha(\boldsymbol{t}) = \delta(q_1 - 1)\delta(q_2 - 1)\delta(q_3 - 1)$. These values can be plugged into Equation (7) to obtain $\theta(\boldsymbol{u}) = \theta(\boldsymbol{s})\theta(\boldsymbol{t})\big(1 - \big(1 - \delta(p_1 - 1)\delta(p_2 - 1)\big)\big(1 - \delta(q_1 - 1)\delta(q_2 - 1)\delta(q_3 - 1)\big)\big(1 - \theta(\boldsymbol{s})\theta(\boldsymbol{t})\delta(q_3 - 1)\delta(p_2 - q_1)\big)\big)$. Hence, from Equation (8), we get the shape tuple $\boldsymbol{u}$ of c to be

$$\boldsymbol{u} = \begin{pmatrix} C\big(p_1 B + q_1 A (1 - B) \\ + p_1 (1 - A)(1 - B)\big) \\ + (1 - C)\pi_1 & 0 & 0 \\[2ex] 0 & \begin{matrix} C\big(p_2 B + q_2 A(1 - B) \\ + q_2(1 - A)(1 - B)\big) \\ + (1 - C)\pi_2 \end{matrix} & 0 \\[2ex] 0 & 0 & \begin{matrix} C\big(B + q_3 A(1 - B) \\ + (1 - A)(1 - B)\big) \\ + (1 - C) \end{matrix} \end{pmatrix},$$

where $A = \alpha(\boldsymbol{s})$, $B = \alpha(\boldsymbol{t})$, $C = \theta(\boldsymbol{u})$ and $\boldsymbol{\pi}^* = \langle \pi_1, \pi_2, 1 \rangle$. Thus, if the respective values for $\langle p_1, p_2 \rangle$ and $\langle q_1, q_2, q_3 \rangle$ are, say $\langle 3, 2 \rangle$ and $\langle 4, 4, 1 \rangle$ at run time, $\theta(\boldsymbol{u})$ will become 0, giving $\boldsymbol{\pi}^*$ for $\boldsymbol{u}$. The key point is that we now have a compact static representation for the shape tuple of c that takes into account all possibilities. ∎

## 4   Exposing an Algebra

The right-hand side of Equation (8) is essentially a linear sum of four terms:

$(1 - \theta(\boldsymbol{u}))\boldsymbol{\pi}^*, \qquad \theta(\boldsymbol{u})\boldsymbol{s}^*\alpha(\boldsymbol{t}),$

$\theta(\boldsymbol{u})\boldsymbol{t}^*\alpha(\boldsymbol{s})(1 - \alpha(\boldsymbol{t})), \qquad \theta(\boldsymbol{u})(\boldsymbol{s}^*\boldsymbol{\Gamma}_1 + \boldsymbol{t}^*\boldsymbol{\Gamma}_2 + \boldsymbol{\iota}^* - \boldsymbol{\Gamma}_1 - \boldsymbol{\Gamma}_2)(1 - \alpha(\boldsymbol{s}))(1 - \alpha(\boldsymbol{t})).$

It is easy to see that at any one time, only one of these four terms contributes to the sum. For example, for an illegal shape-tuple combo, $\theta(\boldsymbol{u})$ will be 0 so that only $(1 - \theta(\boldsymbol{u}))\boldsymbol{\pi}^*$ contributes to the sum. Thus, the expression computed in Equation (8) will always equal one of the following: $\boldsymbol{\pi}^*$, $\boldsymbol{s}^*$, $\boldsymbol{t}^*$ or $\boldsymbol{s}^*\boldsymbol{\Gamma}_1 + \boldsymbol{t}^*\boldsymbol{\Gamma}_2 + \boldsymbol{\iota}^* - \boldsymbol{\Gamma}_1 - \boldsymbol{\Gamma}_2$. Since these are all clearly members of $\mathbb{S}$, Equation (8) defines a mapping $\ddot{\circledast}$ from $\mathbb{S} \times \mathbb{S}$ to $\mathbb{S}$. In other words, $[\mathbb{S}, \ddot{\circledast}]$ forms an *algebraic system* [14].

## 4.1   The Substitution Property

Let $[X, \bullet]$ be an algebraic system in which $\bullet$ is a binary operation. An equivalence relation $E$ on $X$ is said to have the *substitution property* with respect to the operation $\bullet$ if for any $x_1, x_2, x_1', x_2' \in X$, $(x_1 \, E \, x_1') \wedge (x_2 \, E \, x_2')$ implies that $(x_1 \bullet x_2) \, E(x_1' \bullet x_2')$ [14]. It can be shown that with respect to the algebraic system $[\mathbb{S}, \ddot{\circledast}]$, the equivalence relation $\wp$ has the substitution property [7]. The substitution property implies that it does not matter which among the equivalent shape tuples is chosen while computing Equation (8); we are guaranteed to always arrive at shape tuples that will at worst differ only by trailing extents of unity.

## 4.2   A Simpler Algebra

Equivalence relations such as $\wp$ that satisfy the substitution property with respect to some algebraic system are usually called *congruence relations* [14]. Such relations enable the construction of new and simpler algebraic systems from a given algebraic system. For example, in the case of $[\mathbb{S}, \ddot{\circledast}]$, the $\ddot{\circledast}$ operation suggests the simpler operation $\dot{\circledast} : \mathbb{S}_\wp \times \mathbb{S}_\wp \mapsto \mathbb{S}_\wp$ that works directly on the quotient set $\mathbb{S}_\wp$ of $\mathbb{S}$ by $\wp$. Algebraic systems such as $[\mathbb{S}_\wp, \dot{\circledast}]$, called *quotient algebras* [14], preserve many of the properties of the parent algebras from which they are derived. Because these algebras operate on equivalence classes, "relationship properties" seen in the parent algebra become "equality properties" in the quotient algebra. For instance, if $\overline{\boldsymbol{s}}$ were to denote the equivalence class of the shape tuple $\boldsymbol{s}$ under $\wp$, then, for $[\mathbb{S}_\wp, \dot{\circledast}]$, the following two properties can be shown to hold [7]:

$$\overline{\boldsymbol{\pi}} \, \dot{\circledast} \, \overline{\boldsymbol{s}} = \overline{\boldsymbol{s}} \, \dot{\circledast} \, \overline{\boldsymbol{\pi}} = \overline{\boldsymbol{\pi}}, \qquad \text{(Annihilation)} \qquad (9)$$

$$\overline{\boldsymbol{\iota}} \, \dot{\circledast} \, \overline{\boldsymbol{s}} = \overline{\boldsymbol{s}} \, \dot{\circledast} \, \overline{\boldsymbol{\iota}} = \overline{\boldsymbol{s}}. \qquad \text{(Identity)} \qquad (10)$$

# 5   Shape Inferring for MATLAB's Built-In Functions

From the perspective of shape determination, it suffices to focus attention on only those language operators that are built directly into the MATLAB system. These operators, known as *built-in functions*, are similar to the primitives in APL, and ultimately comprise all MATLAB programs. Once we know how shape inferring works for each of these functions, the hope is to determine the shapes of arbitrary MATLAB expressions by composing the shape-tuple functions across the program.

The shape inferring framework presented here is aimed at a particular class of MATLAB functions that we call Type I. (A detailed discussion of a novel shape-based taxonomy of MATLAB's built-in functions is available in [7].) Members of the Type I class, which appear to be a significant majority in the language, produce results whose shapes are completely determined by the shapes of the inputs. Common MATLAB operators, such as matrix multiply and array addition, are Type I; in fact, we have have been able to so far uncover nine quotient algebras to which are isomorphic the shape semantics of over 50 Type I built-in functions [7]. These quotient algebras, called *shape-tuple class algebras*, are summarized in Table 1. The table displays the various shape-tuple class operators (such as the ⊛ operator discussed in § 4), along with specimen MATLAB expressions whose shape semantics they capture, as well as certain common properties that they can be shown to possess (or not possess) [7]. As we shall in § 6, these simple properties can often be leveraged to make useful inferences even when the shapes are not statically known.

**Table 1.** Shape-Tuple Class Algebras

| Shape-Tuple Class Operator | Identity | Associativity | Commutativity | Idempotent Law |
|---|---|---|---|---|
| $\dot{\circledast}$ (e.g., a*b) | $\bar{\iota}$ | ✗ | ✗ | ✗ |
| $\dot{\oplus}$ (e.g., a+b, a-b, a.*b) | $\bar{\iota}$ | ✓ | ✓ | ✓ |
| $\dot{\nabla}$ (e.g., fft(a)) | - | - | - | - |
| $\dot{\odot}$ (e.g., a^b) | $\bar{\iota}$ | ✓ | ✓ | ✗ |
| $\dot{\neg}$ (e.g., a') | - | - | - | - |
| $\dot{\oslash}$ (e.g., a/b) | ✗ | ✗ | ✗ | ✗ |
| $\dot{\circ}$ (e.g., a.\b) | ✗ | ✗ | ✗ | ✗ |
| $\dot{\odot}$ (e.g., [a; b]) | ✗ | ✓ | ✓ | ✗ |
| $\dot{\ominus}$ (e.g., [a, b]) | ✗ | ✓ | ✓ | ✗ |

## 6 Comparisons

The following two examples demonstrate the power of the framework. In both of these examples, the algebraic properties of the shape-tuple operators involved are exploited to perform a static inference.

EXAMPLE 2: *Comparisons with Rose's Approach*
For the code fragment shown in Figure 1, the static inference mechanism due to Rose will fail because the extents of the matrices a and b will not be known exactly at compile time. For both a and b, shadow variables will be generated at compile time to resolve

the shape information at run time. The approach will not be capable of important static inferences such as (1) if the assignment to d succeeds, then the subsequent assignment to e will also succeed and (2) that e and d will then have the same shape. In our framework, we obtain the following two equations corresponding to those two statements after consulting Table 1:

$$\overline{s_d} = \overline{s_c} \,\dot\oplus\, \overline{s_a}, \tag{Eg-2.1}$$

$$\overline{s_e} = \overline{s_d} \,\dot\oplus\, \overline{s_a}, \tag{Eg-2.2}$$

where $s_c$, $s_a$, $s_d$ and $s_e$ are the shape tuples of c, a, d and e respectively. By substituting Equation (Eg-2.1) into Equation (Eg-2.2), we obtain

$$\overline{s_e} = (\overline{s_c} \,\dot\oplus\, \overline{s_a}) \,\dot\oplus\, \overline{s_a},$$

which by associativity becomes $\overline{s_e} = \overline{s_c} \,\dot\oplus\, (\overline{s_a} \,\dot\oplus\, \overline{s_a})$. By the idempotent law, this simplifies to

$$\overline{s_e} = \overline{s_c} \,\dot\oplus\, \overline{s_a}. \tag{Eg-2.3}$$

Comparing Equations (Eg-2.1) and (Eg-2.3), we can conclude that $\overline{s_e} = \overline{s_d}$. Thus, if the assignment to d succeeds (in which case, $\overline{s_d}$ won't be $\overline{\pi}$), the subsequent assignment to e will also succeed and e and d will then have the same shape. Therefore at run time, we need to perform conformability checking only for the first statement. Furthermore, since e and d will always have the same shape, a simpler version of the ./ operator could be used to compute f, which incidentally, can be inferred to have the same shape as e and d.

Observe that this result is deducible by our framework even when a and b are *arbitrary* arrays, not necessarily just matrices. For example, if the last four statements in Figure 1 were part of a function definition in which a and b were the formal parameters, the framework would still arrive at the above result. Such a generalized inference is not possible in Rose's scheme. ∎

EXAMPLE 3: *Inferring in the Presence of Loops*
Consider the following code fragment that involves a while loop:

```
S₁:  a ← ...;
S₂:  b ← ...;
S₃:  while (...),
S₄:        c ← a.*b;
S₅:        a ← c;
S₆:  end;
```

From statement $S_4$ and Table 1, we get

$$\overline{u_i} = \overline{s_{i-1}} \,\dot\oplus\, \overline{t}, \tag{Eg-3.1}$$

where $s_i$, $t$ and $u_i$ denote the respective shape tuples of a, b and c in the $i$th iteration ($i \geq 1$) of the loop. From statement $S_5$, we also have

$$\overline{s_i} = \overline{u_i}. \tag{Eg-3.2}$$

Hence, by substituting Equation (Eg-3.1) into Equation (Eg-3.2), we arrive at

$$\overline{s_i} = \overline{s_{i-1}} \,\dot\oplus\, \overline{t}.$$

Reusing the above, we get

$$\overline{s_i} = (\overline{s_{i-2}} \oplus \overline{t}) \dot\oplus \overline{t} = \overline{s_{i-2}} \oplus (\overline{t} \oplus \overline{t}) = \overline{s_{i-2}} \oplus \overline{t}.$$

Proceeding thus, we can arrive at the following:

$$\overline{s_i} = \overline{s_0} \dot\oplus \overline{t} \text{ for all } i \geq 1. \tag{Eg-3.3}$$

The result in Equation (Eg-3.3) is important because it leads to the following useful inferences and optimizations: (1) the code fragment is *shape correct* if the assignments to a and b in $S_1$ and $S_2$ are shape correct, and if a and b are initially shape conforming with respect to the .* built-in function (both of these requirements are expressible by the single condition $\overline{s_0} \dot\oplus \overline{t} \neq \overline{\pi}$); (2) the shape of c will remain the same throughout the loop's execution; (3) the shape of a can potentially change only at the first iteration of the loop; and (4) c can therefore be preallocated and a resized before executing the loop.

It should be emphasized that these deductions are possible even when full knowledge of the initial shapes of a and b is lacking; such inferences cannot be drawn if Rose's approach is used. ■

## 7   Handling Control Flow

To handle arbitrary control flow, we consider the SSA representation [3] of a MATLAB program. By introducing an ancillary variable $P$, called the *shadow-path variable*, the framework could be extended to support the $\phi$ construct that is central to the SSA representation.

Consider a join node c ← $\phi$(a, b) in the SSA form of a MATLAB program. The shape of c could be inferred as follows:

$$\mathcal{R}(c) = \max(\mathcal{R}(a), \mathcal{R}(b)), \tag{11}$$
$$\theta(u) = \delta(P - h)\theta(s) + (1 - \delta(P - h))\theta(t), \tag{12}$$
$$u = (1 - \theta(u))\pi^* + \theta(u)\big(s^*\delta(P - h) + t^*(1 - \delta(P - h))\big). \tag{13}$$

In Equations (12) and (13), $P$ takes on an integer value at run time depending on how execution flows. Each of the edges in the program's control-flow graph that merge at a join node are labeled with integers. At run time, the shadow-path variables assume these values whenever control flows along those edges. The particular value $h$ in Equations (12) and (13) is the integer label of the edge between the definition node for a and the join node in question. Thus, though it may not be possible to exactly determine $u$ at compile time in such situations, we will still have an exact and compact symbolic representation for it.

## 8   Reducing Array Conformability Checks

By enabling the computation of a shape-tuple expression prior to invoking the associated built-in function, the framework effectively permits an implementation to in-line a built-in function's conformability checking code at the call site. This in turn may facilitate a reduction in the overall conformability checking overhead through the application of traditional compiler techniques such as copy propagation, common-subexpression elimination (CSE) and dead-code elimination.

Figure 2 shows a translation of the code excerpt in Figure 1, with code due to the framework indicated by a ▶ prefix. The inferences that were made in Example 2 are responsible for the invocation rdivide= (a version of ./ that expects identically shaped arguments), and for the assignments $s_e \leftarrow s_d$ and $s_f \leftarrow s_d$. The actual conformability checks occur through the *assert* calls—*assert*(B) tests whether the Boolean expression $B$ is true at run time and exits if false. Note that for the first four shape tuples in Figure 2, no run-time assertions need to be made since the correctness shape predicates for them are statically determinable. The same applies to the correctness shape predicates $\theta(s_a)$ and $\theta(s_b)$ since they can be statically ascertained to be 1 each [7]. After applying copy propagation to $s_e$ and $s_f$, two redundant calls to $assert(\theta(s_d) = 1)$ are generated. By applying CSE, these two redundant calls can be identified and eliminated. Dead-code elimination could then be used on the shape-tuple computations to produce the final result shown in Figure 3.

```
▶ sₘ ← ⟨1, 1⟩
m ← round(4*rand+1);
▶ sₙ ← ⟨1, 1⟩
n ← round(5*rand+1);
▶ sₓ ← ⟨1, 1⟩
x ← round(5*rand+1);
▶ s_y ← ⟨1, 1⟩
y ← round(6*rand+1);

▶ sₐ ← ⟨m, n⟩
a ← rand(m, n);
▶ s_b ← ⟨x, y⟩
b ← rand(x, y);

▶ s_c ← sₐ ⊛̈ s_b; assert(θ(s_c) = 1)
c ← mtimes(a, b);
▶ s_d ← s_c ⊕̈ sₐ; assert(θ(s_d) = 1)
d ← plus(c, a);
▶ s_e ← s_d; assert(θ(s_e) = 1)
e ← minus(d, a);
▶ s_f ← s_d; assert(θ(s_f) = 1)
f ← rdivide=(e, d);
```

**Fig. 2.** Checking Code In-lined

```
m ← round(4*rand+1);
n ← round(5*rand+1);
x ← round(5*rand+1);
y ← round(6*rand+1);

▶ sₐ ← ⟨m, n⟩
a ← rand(m, n);
▶ s_b ← ⟨x, y⟩
b ← rand(x, y);

▶ s_c ← sₐ ⊛̈ s_b; assert(θ(s_c) = 1)
c ← mtimes(a, b);
▶ s_d ← s_c ⊕̈ sₐ; assert(θ(s_d) = 1)
d ← plus(c, a);
e ← minus(d, a);
f ← rdivide=(e, d);
```

**Fig. 3.** After CSE and Dead-code Elimination

Note that all of the shape-tuple component arithmetic in the embedded code of Figure 3 can be efficiently mapped by an interpreter or a compiler to a machine's instruction set since they only involve scalar, floating-point calculations.

# 9    Preallocation

Preallocation is an optimization that can often improve the performance of MATLAB and APL codes. In [12], an improvement by a factor of 4 was observed for the Euler-Cromer program in the FALCON benchmark suite, when this optimization was manually applied. The basic idea behind using the framework to realize this optimization is to move all shape-tuple computations associated with the body of the loop, outside the loop. This can be done if all the shape-tuple computations are of the Type I kind, since in that case, each shape-tuple expression would be dependent only on earlier shape-tuple expressions. For example, consider the for loop construct shown in Figure 4. Given for i = $expr$, ...; end, MATLAB executes the loop $n$ times, where $n$ is the number of columns in the MATLAB expression $expr$ [10]. With every iteration of the loop, i will be assigned the successive column vectors in $expr$. Modifications to either $expr$ or i within the body of the loop do not change the initially determined iteration count $n$. (In that way, these loops resemble the do loops in FORTRAN 77.)

```
a ← ...; b ← ...;
c ← ...; e ← ...;
for i = e,
    a ← [a; b];
    c ← a.*c;
end;
```

**Fig. 4.** A MATLAB for Loop

```
▶ s_a ← ...; s_b ← ...; s_c ← ...
▶ s_e ← ⟨p_1, p_2, ..., p_k⟩
  a ← ...; b ← ...; c ← ...; e ← ...;
▶ A ← 0; C ← 0
▶ for j from 1 to p_2 × ⋯ × p_k
      s_a ← s_a ⊚ s_b; s_c ← s_a ⊕̈ s_c
      A ← max(A, |s_a|); C ← max(C, |s_c|)
  endfor
▶ resize a to A elements
▶ resize c to C elements
  for i = e,
      a ← [a; b];
      c ← a.*c;
  end;
```

**Fig. 5.** After Preallocation

The first statement in the loop body of Figure 4 will cause the array a to grow; the construction [a; b] concatenates a and b along the first dimension. If an interpreter were to directly execute the loop, the array a would be incrementally increased in size with every iteration of the loop, thereby impacting performance. Instead, we move the shape-tuple computations associated with these two MATLAB statements—which are $s_a \leftarrow s_a \circledcirc s_b$ and $s_c \leftarrow s_a \ddot{\oplus} s_c$ from Table 1—outside the loop. This is shown in Figure 5, where for brevity, the conformability checking code has been omitted. The code hoisting is valid because these shape-tuple computations are only dependent on the initial values of $s_a$, $s_b$ and $s_c$. In addition, we execute the hoisted shape-tuple computations $p_2 \times \cdots \times p_k$ times where $s_e = \langle p_1, p_2, \ldots, p_k \rangle$, since this is the number of times that the original loop would actually be executed. In the hoisted code, we also track the maximum sizes of a and c through the variables $A$ and $C$; these are updated in every iteration to the maximum of their current value and the determinant of the corresponding shape tuple. Thus, once the hoisted code finishes execution, we would know exactly the sizes to which a and c must be finally grown.

The shape tuples themselves do not arbitrarily grow in size. This is because most Type I built-in functions exhibit an important characteristic known as the *bounded property* [7]: Whenever the ranks of their arguments are bounded by a suitable constant, the ranks of their results will also be bounded by the same constant. Thus, if we were to consider the MATLAB statement c $\leftarrow$ $\varphi$(a, b) where $\varphi$ is a Type I built-in function that exhibits the bounded property, it will be possible to find a constant $\mathfrak{R}_\varphi$ such that for all $\mathcal{R}(\mathsf{a})$ and $\mathcal{R}(\mathsf{b})$,

$$\mathcal{R}(\mathsf{a}) \leq \mathfrak{R}_\varphi \wedge \mathcal{R}(\mathsf{b}) \leq \mathfrak{R}_\varphi \implies \mathcal{R}(\mathsf{c}) \leq \mathfrak{R}_\varphi. \tag{14}$$

The bounded property is crucial because it enables us to conservatively estimate at compile time the ranks of *all* expressions in programs that comprise solely of these operators. Such an estimate would be possible even in the presence of general loops since the arrays produced by these built-in functions will not arbitrarily grow in rank. Thus, in the case of Figure 4, if $k$, $l$, $m$ are the initial ranks of a, b and c respectively, then during the loop's execution, the canonical ranks of a and c will not be larger than $\max(k, l)$ and $\max(k, l, m)$ respectively [7]. Hence, because the substitution property is honored by the corresponding shape-tuple functions, we can perform all the shape-tuple computations in Figure 5 assuming $\max(k, l, m)$ components. In this way, none of the shape tuples have to be grown at all.

Note that in the case of many Type I built-in functions, Rose's approach could be adapted to implement preallocation as described above. This is because for this class of built-in functions, the generated shadow variables will be dependent on only previously generated shadow variables; thus, the shadow variable code will also be eligible for code hoisting. However, unlike Rose's approach, the framework may permit tighter inferences in specific cases, such as that shown in Example 3.

## 10   Summary

In this paper, we have described a framework using which the shape of a MATLAB expression can be expressed exactly and succinctly at compile time. The framework covers a large class of built-in functions and reveals and exploits the algebras that underlie each of them. The unique advantage of our framework over other approaches is that it enables useful static inferences even in the absence of statically determinable array extents. The framework's utility is not restricted to MATLAB alone—it could be applied to infer shapes in other array-based languages such as APL that share many of MATLAB's features.

# References

[1] T. Budd. **An APL Compiler**. Springer-Verlag New York, Inc., New York City, NY 10010, USA, 1988. ISBN 0–387–96643–9.

[2] S. Chauveau and F. Bodin. "Menhir: An Environment for High Performance MATLAB". *Lecture Notes in Computer Science*, 1511:27–40, 1998. Proceedings of the 4th International Workshop on Languages, Compilers and Run-Time Systems, Pittsburgh, PA, USA, May 1998.

[3] R. Cytron, J. Ferrante, B. K. Rosen, and M. N. Wegman. "Efficiently Computing Static Single Assignment Form and the Control Dependence Graph". *ACM Transactions on Programming Languages and Systems*, 13 (4):451–490, October 1991.

[4] P. Drakenberg, P. Jacobson, and B. Kågström. "A CONLAB Compiler for a Distributed-Memory Multicomputer". In the *Proceedings of the 6th SIAM Conference on Parallel Processing for Scientific Computing*, pages 814–821, Norfolk, VA, USA, March 1993.

[5] L. A. De Rose. "Compiler Techniques for MATLAB Programs". Ph.D. dissertation, University of Illinois at Urbana-Champaign, Department of Computer Science, May 1996.

[6] B. C. Jay. "A Semantics for Shape". *Science of Computer Programming*, 25:251–283, 1995.

[7] P. G. Joisha, U. N. Shenoy, and P. Banerjee. "An Approach to Array Shape Determination in MATLAB". Technical Report CPDC–TR–2000–10–010, Center for Parallel and Distributed Computing, Department of Electrical and Computer Engineering, Northwestern University, Evanston, IL 60208–3118, USA, October 2000.

[8] M. A. Kaplan and J. D. Ullman. "A Scheme for the Automatic Inference of Variable Types". *Journal of the ACM*, 27(1):128–145, January 1980.

[9] The MAJIC Project, at `http://polaris.cs.uiuc.edu/majic/majic.html`.

[10] The MathWorks, Inc., 24 Prime Park Way, Natick, MA 01760–1500, USA. *MATLAB—The Language of Technical Computing*, January 1997. Using MATLAB (Version 5).

[11] MATLAB Compiler and C/C++ Math Library 2.0.2, at `http://www.mathworks.com/products/compilerlibrary/`.

[12] V. Menon and K. Pingali. "A Case for Source-Level Transformations in MATLAB". In the *Proceedings of the 2nd Conference on Domain-Specific Languages*, pages 53–65, Austin, TX, USA, October 1999.

[13] M. J. Quinn, A. Malishevsky, N. Seelam, and Y. Zhao. "Preliminary Results from a Parallel MATLAB Compiler". In the *Proceedings of the 12th International Parallel Processing Symposium*, pages 81–87, Orlando, FL, USA, April 1998.

[14] J. P. Tremblay and R. Manohar. **Discrete Mathematical Structures with Applications to Computer Science**. Computer Science Series. McGraw-Hill, Inc., New York City, NY 10121, USA, 1975. ISBN 0–07–065142–6.

# Polynomial Time Array Dataflow Analysis

Robert Seater and David Wonnacott

Haverford College, Haverford, PA 19041
davew@cs.haverford.edu
http://www.cs.haverford.edu/people/davew/index.html

**Abstract.** Array dataflow analysis is a valuable tool for supercomputer compilers. However, the worst-case asymptotic time complexities for modern array dataflow analysis techniques are either not well understood or alarmingly high. For example, the Omega Test uses a subset of the $2^{2^{2^{O(n)}}}$ language of Presburger Arithmetic for analysis of affine dependences; its use of uninterpreted function symbols for non-affine terms introduces additional sources of complexity. Even traditional data dependence analysis of affine dependences is equivalent to integer programming, and is thus NP-complete. These worst-case complexities have raised questions about the wisdom of using array dataflow analysis in a production compiler, despite empirical data that show that various tests run quickly in practice.

In this paper, we demonstrate that a polynomial-time algorithm can produce accurate information about the presence of loop-carried array dataflow. We first identify a subdomain of Presburger Arithmetic that can be manipulated (by the Omega Library) in polynomial time; we then describe a modification to prevent exponential blowup of the Omega Library's algorithm for manipulating function symbols.

Restricting the Omega Test to these polynomial cases can, in principle, reduce the accuracy of the dataflow information produced. We therefore present the results of our investigation of the effects of these restrictions on the detection of loop-carried array dataflow dependences (which prevent parallelization). These restrictions block parallelization of only a few unimportant loop nests in the approximately 18000 lines of benchmark code we studied. The use of our subdomain of Presburger Arithmetic also gives a modest reduction in analysis time, even with our current unoptimized implementation, as long as we do not employ our modified algorithms for function symbols. The data collected in our empirical studies also suggest directions for improving both accuracy and efficiency.

## 1 Introduction

Array dataflow analysis is an important tool for supercomputer compilers. This analysis provides information that can be used to determine the legality of array privatization, a critical technique for automatic parallelization [1]. It can also serve as the basis for optimization of communication [2] or memory locality [3]. Unfortunately, the worst-case asymptotic time complexities for array dataflow analysis techniques are either not well understood or alarmingly high.

H. Dietz (Ed.): LCPC 2001, LNCS 2624, pp. 411–426, 2003.
© Springer-Verlag Berlin Heidelberg 2003

Array dataflow analysis can be seen as an extension of traditional array dependence analysis to produce information about the flow of values rather than simple memory aliasing. We thus refer to it as a *value-based* analysis, in contrast to the traditional *memory-based* analysis. The Omega Test implements both memory-based [4] and value-based [5, 6] analyses by generating and simplifying sets of constraints that describe dependences. The complexity of these constraints depends on the subscripts and control flow expressions (hereafter referred to as *dependence expressions*) and the kind of analysis being performed. Memory-based dependence analysis in the presence of arbitrary affine (i.e. linear plus a constant) dependence expressions is equivalent to integer programming, and thus is NP-complete [7]. Value-based analysis includes negated constraints, and thus requires a richer constraint language; the Omega Test uses Presburger Arithmetic [8], which appears to have time complexity $2^{2^{2^{O(n)}}}$ [9, 10].

Empirical studies of benchmark programs have found that affine dependence expressions are generally very simple. As we shall see, this lets the Omega Test run quickly. It also lets simple memory-based tests provide fairly accurate information. Compiler writers thus choose between the risk of missing an optimization and the risk of a non-terminating compilation due to an exponential case in a more general test. However, the simple memory-based tests carry a hidden cost, in that they do not provide the Omega Test's exact description of each dependence. More accurate information is needed for value-based and conditional analyses, which can be much more important than exact affine memory-based testing [11, 1]. Empirical studies have shown that these analyses can be efficient practice (see Section 6), but the lack of a polynomial bound still raises questions about the use of such techniques in production compilers.

In addition to leaving open the possibility that some unusual program may require years of dependence analysis, empirical studies provide very little information about *why* an exponential algorithm works well in practice. An $O(2^n)$ algorithm may run well because the test data do not exercise the exponential behavior of the algorithm, or because n is small: a compiler can afford to perform some tasks with $2^{10}$ operations (taking about a microsecond), or even a few with $2^{20}$. In contrast, $2^{2^{2^n}}$ is disastrous, even for small n: A petaflop computer would have to run for about $10^{45}$ times the age of the universe to do $2^{2^{2^3}}$ operations. Clearly there is some other factor working in our favor here.

In this paper, we identify a subdomain of Presburger Arithmetic for which we can perform polynomial-time satisfiability testing; this lets us define a polynomial-time array dataflow algorithm by simply introducing an approximation for any term outside of this subdomain. We begin, in Section 2, with a brief restatement of the constraint-based approach to dependence analysis. Section 3 then describes our polynomial subdomain of Presburger Arithmetic and our technique for preventing exponential blowup of the Omega Library's algorithm for manipulating function symbols. Section 4 discusses the kinds of programs that produce constraints in our polynomial subdomain. Section 5 presents our investigation of the impact of our restrictions on the speed and accuracy of our analysis. Section 6 covers related work, and Section 7 presents our conclusions.

## 2  Constraint-Based Dependence Analysis

In this section, we review the Omega Test's constraint-based approach to dependence analysis. Space limitations prevent a full review; readers who are not familiar with this work may wish to consult [12, 6].

In its most general form, a dependence is a relation between tuples of integers that correspond to the values of the loop index variables at the source and sink of the dependence. Since we may not have a bound on the number of loop iterations, we cannot hope to enumerate them, and thus we represent dependence relations with constraints on integer variables. For example, in Figure 1, the memory-based flow dependence from iteration $[\,n1, k1\,]$ to iteration $[\,n1', k1'\,]$ is

$$\{\,[\,n1, k1\,] \rightarrow [\,n1', k1'\,] \mid n1' = n1 \wedge k1' = k1 + 1 \wedge 2 \leq k1 < n1 \leq n\,\}$$

The constraints under which memory aliasing occurs can be obtained from the loop bounds and array subscripts, as well as the fact that the source of any dependence must precede its sink. In some cases, other program analyses are also useful: For the relation above, we substituted the closed form n1-k1+1 for the induction variable nn.

```
do n1 = 2, n {
    nn = n1-1
    c(1,n1) = 1.0
    do k1 = 2, n1 {
        c(k1,nn) = c(k1-1,nn+1) * ...
        nn = nn-1
    }
}
```

**Fig. 1.** Excerpt from CNSTNT in MDG [13]

When a dependence relation can be expressed as a conjunction of affine constraints on the symbolic constants and loop indices, memory-based dependence testing is equivalent to integer programming [7], which is NP-Complete [14].

The Omega Test performs value-based analysis by subtracting, from the set of memory-based dependences, the dependences in which the array element is overwritten between the original write and the read. This can be done by eliminating iterations in which the dependence is *killed* or, in some cases, by eliminating iterations in which the sink of the dependence is *covered*. In either case, we must negate a conjunction of constraints that may involve existentially quantified variables. For example, we can find the set of iterations that are exposed above the aforementioned dependence as:

$$\underbrace{\{[n1, 2] \mid 2 \leq n1 \leq n\}}_{\text{iterations exposed}} = \underbrace{\{[n1, k1] \mid 2 \leq k1 \leq n1 \leq n\}}_{\text{iterations executed}} - \underbrace{\{[n1, k1{+}1] \mid 2 \leq k1 < n1 \leq n\}}_{\text{iterations reached by dependence}}$$

The need to negate constraints increases the complexity of our constraint system beyond the level of integer programming (NP-complete) to a larger subclass of Presburger Arithmetic [8]. Presburger Arithmetic appears to have time complexity $2^{2^{2^{O(n)}}}$ [9, 10].

Since our simplified dependence relations contain constraints on the symbolic constants, we could use variable elimination (selectively) to detect conditions on these constants that are necessary for any dependence to exist. For example, if we existentially quantify all variables *except* $n$ in the dependence constraints for the flow dependence discussed above, we find it exists iff $n \geq 3$. We could therefore parallelize this loop when there is no dependence, i.e. when $n < 3$.

To avoid wasting time trying to parallelize such single-trip loops and other useless cases, we search for conditions that are not redundant with a set of constraints that define the non-useless cases (such as $n \geq 3$). We perform this test with the *gist* operation [15, 16]. Intuitively, given two conjunctions of equality and inequality constraints $p$ and $q$, *gist p given q* yields constraints in $p$ which are not implied by $q$. That is, $(gist\ p\ given\ q) \wedge q$ is equivalent to $p \wedge q$. In the worst case, finding a gist forces us to perform one satisfiability test of $p \wedge \neg e$ for each equation $e$ in $q$, and thus has exponential time complexity.

The Omega Test provides two approaches to dealing with a term that cannot be expressed as an affine function of the symbolic constants and loop indices. First, such terms (or, indeed, any term) can safely be replaced with *unknown*, a special term that holds the place of any fact that cannot be represented any other way. In some cases, it is still possible to disprove a dependence; in others, the *unknown* remains in the simplified dependence relation, indicating an approximate answer. Second, each non-affine term can be replaced with an application of an *uninterpreted function symbol* [17, 18, 6]: Any program expression produces a value each time it is executed, and can thus be viewed as a function of the loop indices (or, in some cases, a smaller set of parameters).

Presburger Arithmetic with arbitrary uses of uninterpreted function symbols is undecidable [19]. The algorithms in [16] allow each argument to a function to be any affine combination of loop indices and symbolic constants; the current implementation requires that the list of arguments be a prefix of the set of loop indices (i.e. in a loop nest $i$, $j$, $k$, a binary function could be only be applied to the argument list $i, j$). If the Omega Library is forced to apply a function to some other argument, it simply replaces it with *unknown*.

The Omega Library simplifies a formula containing a function symbol by splitting it into cases in which the arguments are provably equal or distinct. That is, if the formula $F$ contains $f(i, j)$ and $f(i', j')$, then $F$ is replaced with

$$(F \wedge i = i' \wedge j = j') \vee (F \wedge \neg(i = i' \wedge j = j')).$$

When the arguments are equal, the function applications can be treated as a single scalar variable; otherwise, they can be treated as independent scalars [17].

This simple technique greatly increases the accuracy of the Omega Test (see [6] or Section 5.4). Unfortunately, this makes the size of a formula with $u$ uses of a function grow by a factor equal to the number of ways to partition a set of size $u$, or *Bell number* [20], which is exponential (note that every subset defines a partition). All but one of the terms in the resulting disjunction will have at least one negated set of $a$ equalities (for a function of arity $a$), and the Omega Library treats these as as a $2^a$-way disjunction, multiplying the size of the formula $O(2^a)$. (For example, $F$ above is split into five formulas, with $(i = i' \wedge j = j')$, $(i < i')$, $(i > i')$, $(i = i' \wedge j < j')$, and $(i = i' \wedge j > j')$, respectively). Even with the limitations of the current implementation, which allow at most two distinct sets of arguments for each function, a formula with any number of functions of arity up to $a$ can increase in size by this factor of $O(2^a)$.

## 3   An Efficient Subdomain

Many of the Presburger Formulas that arise during dependence analysis fall into the following subdomain of Presburger Arithmetic, and can be tested for satisfiability in polynomial time:

a. The individual "atomic" constraints are drawn from the *LI(2)-unit* subdomain (i.e. constraints with up to two variables and unit coefficients).

b. These constraints are only combined in the form $\exists\, v_1, v_2, ...v_n$ s.t. $C_0 \wedge \neg C_1 \wedge \neg C_2 ... \wedge \neg C_m$, where each $C_i$ term is a conjunction of atomic constraints involving $v_{0..n}$ and possibly additional existentially quantified variables local to $C_i$.

c. $C_1..C_m$ can be ordered such that $C_1$ contains at most one constraint that is not *obviously redundant* (see Section 3.3) with respect to $C_0$, and which must be an inequality or simple stride constraint (e.g. $x$ is a multiple of 3); $C_2$ contains at most one such constraint that is not obviously redundant with respect to $C_0 \wedge \neg C_1$; $C_3$ contains at most one such constraint that is not obviously redundant with respect to $C_0 \wedge \neg C_1 \wedge \neg C_2$; etc.

Property (b) holds for all formulas for memory-based analysis (when $m = 0$) and value-based analysis (whether using the kill or cover test). Property (a) ensures that the Omega Library will perform satisfiability tests on individual conjuncts in polynomial time, and Property (c) defines the cases in which the Omega Library can handle negation in polynomial time. It is possible to produce programs with affine loops bounds and subscripts that still violate Property (a) or (c), though these appear to be very rare in practice, as we show in Section 5.

### 3.1   Conjunctions of LI(2)-unit Equations

An equation is said to be *LI(2)* if it has the form $ax + by + c = 0$ or $ax + by + c \geq 0$. It is *LI(2)-unit* if $a, b \in \{+1, -1, 0\}$. The satisfiability testing algorithm of the Omega Library can process any conjunction of LI(2)-unit equations on existentially quantified integer variables in polynomial time.

The Omega Library uses repeated variable elimination to test satisfiability (a formula with no variables is either *true* or *false*). Substitution is used for a variable that is involved in an equality constraint, and Pugh's extension of Fourier's method of variable elimination is used for the remaining variables [4]. Fourier's method produces all combinations of an upper bound and a lower bound on the given variable. This can cause the number of inequalities to grow exponentially with the number of variables eliminated.

Within the LI(2)-unit domain, all constraints on a pair of variables $(x, y)$ must be parallel to either $x + y = 0$ or $x - y = 0$. Furthermore, the LI(2)-unit domain is, like LI(2), closed under variable elimination. These facts ensure that Pugh's techniques for parallel redundant constraint detection will succeed in limiting the number of inequalities produced during each variable elimination, allowing the removal of $v$ variables in $O(v^3)$ time[1] [4]. Thus, satisfiability testing of an LI(2)-unit formula of size $n$ is done in $O(n^3)$ time.

Note that constraints like $j1 + j2 - i = j2$ and $2x \leq 7$ can easily be made LI(2)-unit, since they can be rewritten as $j1 - i = 0$ and $x \leq 3$ (respectively). These conversions are performed during the normal processing by the Omega Library. We have investigated techniques for converting other classes non-LI(2)-unit constraints into this domain, but we have not found this to be important in practice. The details of these conversions are covered in [12].

## 3.2   Gist Operations and Conditional Analysis

In the worst case, the gist operation discussed in Section 2 may need to perform $O(|q|)$ satisfiability tests to produce *gist p given q* (where $|q|$ is the number of equations in $q$). When $p$ and $q$ are both in LI(2)-unit, these each take $O(v^3)$ time, for a total of $O(v^3 |q|)$ steps.

## 3.3   Negation

Our value-based analysis produces queries of the form

$$\exists v_1, v_2, ...v_n \text{ s.t. } C_0 \wedge \neg C_1 \wedge \neg C_2 ... \wedge \neg C_m$$

as described above. The Omega Library tests such a system for satisfiability by converting it into disjunctive normal form (hereafter, we refer to a formula in this form as "a DNF") and applying Pugh's extension of Fourier's method to test the satisfiability of each term of the disjunction.

Consider first the case of $m = 1$, in which $C_1$ is a conjunction of $g$ inequalities. Simply negating $C_1$ and distributing it over $C_0$ would produce a DNF of size $g |C_0|$. However, any inequality of $C_1$ that is redundant with respect to $C_0$ (that is, $x \wedge C_0 \equiv C_0$) would produce an unsatisfiable conjunction, which would then be eliminated by the subsequent satisfiability tests. The Omega Library uses the gist operation to improve the efficiency of this process by eliminating such redundant terms before converting to DNF, replacing $C_1$ with *gist $C_1$ given $C_0$*.

---

[1] If a formula includes large numbers of redundant constraints, satisfiability testing may take $O(v^3 + c)$ for $v$ variables and $c$ LI(2)-unit constraints.

For this step, it uses a less complex variant of the gist operation [15, 16] that may leave some redundant constraints in $C_i$. This test will detect any constraint that is redundant with respect to a single constraint or pair of constraints in $C_0$ (we term such constraints *obviously redundant* with respect to $C_0$), and runs in time $O(|C_0|^2|C_1|)$.

A simple stride constraint, such as $\exists\ \alpha$ s.t. $i = 3\alpha$, can be negated without introducing disjunction. However, other equality constraints are treated as a pair of inequalities. Property (c) ensures that, after our simple gist test, $\neg C_1$ will not include disjunction, so checking any $C_0 \wedge \neg C_1$ in our domain requires a single simple gist operation and a single satisfiability test.

When $m > 1$, it may be the case that, for each $C_i$, $\neg(gist\ C_i\ given\ C_0)$ does not introduce disjunction. In this case, the Omega Library simply processes the $C_i$ as above, using $m$ simple gist operations and $m$ simplifications (a single simplification at the end would suffice for this case). In other cases, the Omega Library makes up to $m$ passes over these terms to find cases in which a constraint in some $C_i$ is made redundant by the negation of a constraint in some other $C_j$. For any formula in our domain, this will produce a single conjunction after at most $\frac{m(m+1)}{2}$ gists and $m$ satisfiability tests. Thus, the total time is $O(m^2((|C_0| + m)^2 max_i(|C_i|)))$ for gists plus $O(mv^3)$ for simplifications, which is $O(n^5)$ for a formula of size $n$.

For queries outside of our domain, the Omega Library will eventually perform a pass in which no new $C_i$ can be negated without introducing disjunction. At this point, it introduces disjunction: negating a $C_i$ with $g$ inequalities, $s$ strides, and $e$ equalities produces a $(g + s + 2e)$-way disjunction. Doing this for $m$ such negated conjuncts produces a DNF with $(g + s + 2e)^m$ terms, each of which must be tested for satisfiability.

Note that this restriction does not take into account the possibility of doing analysis with a different set of constraints that could fit within our domain. For example, it is always legal to replace the cover test with a collection of kill tests, which sometimes produce simpler negations.

## 3.4   Non-affine Terms

Property (a) allows only affine terms, so no dependence problem within this domain will involve function symbols. Unfortunately, a significant number of dependences involve non-affine terms. As with the full Omega Test, we have the option of treating each non-affine term as an *unknown* or an uninterpreted function; the former introduces a large number of false dependences [6, Table I].

To retain our polynomial time bound while allowing the use of function symbols, we modify the algorithm for manipulating uninterpreted function symbols to replace the constraints describing the conditions under which the arguments are distinct (e.g. $\neg(i = i' \wedge j = j')$) with *unknown*. Furthermore, if there are functions of different arities, we use a single formula with *unknown* to represent all cases in which arguments differ. Under this restriction and the restriction that any given function may only be applied to two distinct lists of arguments (as in the current implementation), the presence of any number of applications of any number of functions can only increase the size of a formula by a factor of the largest arity of any function. This modification does not restrict the domain of our test, but it could force our test to produce an approximate answer.

## 4    Programs Fitting This Domain

To ensure that all memory-based dependence tests involve conjunctions of LI(2)-unit constraints, we restrict programs as follows: Control flow statements must be only `for` loops with bounds that are LI(1)-unit expressions (i.e. variable + constant or just a constant) of the symbolic constants and outer loop indices, `if`'s that perform LI(2)-unit inequality tests, or `else`-less `if`'s with LI(2)-unit equality tests. Furthermore, all pairs of corresponding subscript expressions for a given array must have a difference that is LI(2)-unit.

It is tempting to restrict each individual subscript to the LI(1)-unit domain, but this would be overly severe: Subscript expressions that are not LI(1)-unit can still produce LI(2)-unit constraints. For example, the `trip` routine of the ARC2D benchmark contains references with the subscripts `j1+j2-i` and `j2`, which produce the LI(2)-unit constraint $j1 + j2 - i = j2$.

We can still perform dependence analysis in the presence of expressions outside of our domain by handling them as if they were not affine (i.e. by introducing an *unknown* or a function symbol).

As stated in Section 2, all of the constraint sets for our analysis have Property (b). Thus there is no need to restrict programs to produce this property.

Describing the set of programs that do not violate Property (c) is somewhat tricky. We believe that this property will hold in any procedure in which each array use is covered by a single write statement, or when an array is defined as a collection of chunks, organized along in a single dimension of the array. This domain should include many programs, but it also omits some interesting cases. Instead of attempting to avoid building constraints that violate Property (c), we simply build the constraints and introduce *unknowns* when we would otherwise have to introduce disjunction (this can still be done in polynomial time).

Our current implementation does not include any system to determine that an alternate set of equations might have Property (c).

## 5    Empirical Results

Identifying a domain in which our analysis is both fast and exact is only valuable if real programs produce analysis problems from this domain. We have developed a restricted version of the Omega Test, and applied it to a set of benchmarks, to measure the impacts of the restrictions given in Section 3.

### 5.1    Experimental System

We based our restricted Omega Test on a modified version of Release 1.2 of Petit and the Omega Library (our modifications will be included in the next bug fix release). We use the "-X" flag (no eXponential cases) of this release to cause Petit to introduce an *unknown* for any non-LI(2)-unit constraint, any conditional statement that introduces disjunction, or any negation that would introduce disjunction. This flag also enables our modifications of algorithm for uninterpreted function symbols given in Section 3.4.

We have not implemented a system for using the dependence killing test selectively when the cover test loses accuracy due our limitations on negation. To factor out this effect, we disabled the cover analysis during our experiments (this has no impact on the accuracy of the full Omega Test). We also made several minor enhancements and bug fixes to Release 1.2, and increased the variable `maxVars` to 56 to handle all dependences from the benchmark set we used. Our timing results were produced on a 400 MHz Intel Linux system.

## 5.2   Programs to Be Tested

We applied our modified version of the Omega Test to the five programs from the Perfect Club Benchmarks [13] that were studied by Maydan [11] and in our previous work [16, 6]. To allow comparison with earlier results, we reinstated the old definition of reduction dependence (via a new compile-time option in Petit 1.2). We also collected data only for dependences due to arrays of type real, and only dependences that fundamentally inhibit loop-level parallelism: loop-carried value-based flow dependences that are part of a dependence cycle (via the Petit flags "-g -r -j -Fvcf"). In this study, as in the past, we only consider only intra-procedural dependences. With these flags set, the full Omega Test prints 271 dependences.

## 5.3   Results

Table 1 shows the number of intra-procedural loop-carried value-based flow dependences that arise from arrays of type real and are part of a dependence cycle, given various restrictions on the Omega Test.

The "Exp" column gives a baseline of information about the full (exponential) test. The "Exp Cond" and "Exp UFS" columns give data for runs in which we applied several, but not all, of our restrictions. In "Exp Cond", we prevented all forms of exponential growth except those created by a disjunction in a program term (such as the conditions describing the else clause of the conditional if (i==1)); In "Exp UFS", we restricted our test to the polynomial subdomain of Presburger Arithmetic, but did not restrict disjunction from uninterpreted function symbols beyond the limitations of the current implementation. The "Poly" column gives the results for the fully polynomial algorithm. For this column, we have also given the number of loops and loop nests for which parallelization is blocked by a dependence in the restricted test, but not in the original test. Finally, the "LI(1)" column gives the results if we restrict our test to LI(1)-unit dependence expressions rather than LI(2)-unit dependence  constraints.

The new dependences introduced by our restriction to the polynomial-time test have the following effects on parallelization of the benchmarks:

**Table 1.** Number of Parallelism-Blocking Dependences (and Newly Blocked Loops)

| Benchmark | Dependence Test | | | | |
|---|---|---|---|---|---|
| | Exp | Exp Cond | Exp UFS | Poly | LI(1) |
| QCD2 | 65 | 65 | 151 | 151 (3/1) | 151 |
| MDG | 64 | 78 | 78 | 78 (3/2) | 78 |
| DYFESM | 53 | 72 | 112* | 111 (11/5) | 223 |
| ARC2D | 89 | 89 | 89 | 89 (0/0) | 114 |
| TRFD | 0 | 0 | 0 | 0 (0/0) | 0 |
| Total | 271 | 304 | 430* | 429 (17/8) | 566 |

* Numbers marked * are 1 higher than they should be due to an Omega Library bug.

QCD2 (**86 new dependences**) 10 new dependences block the parallelization of a loop nest in the main routine of qcd2 (this nest contains I/O statements). 74 of the remaining 76 are due to statements in the else branches of two conditionals of the form if (i==1) in choos (this loop already carries a conditional dependence).

MDG (**14 new dependences**) Two of these block the parallelization of the loop from cnstnt shown in Figure 1, and twelve block parallelization of a pair of nested loops from initia (these all include the single non-LI(2)-unit constraint $3i + j - 3 = 3i' + j' - 3$).

DYFESM (**58 new dependences**) 15 of these dependences arise from a single pattern of dependences that occur in hop, hop0, and solxdd. This pattern, shown in Figure 2, is responsible for dependences carried by 8 loops in 3 nests in this benchmark. These dependences involve the expression $iloc + i - 1 = iloc' + i' - 1$, which is not LI(2)-unit. However, for the loop-independent dependence, $i = i'$ and $iloc = iloc'$, and the expression is simply *true*. We are investigating techniques for encorporating this type of information.

```
do iblock = 1, nblock {
  iloc = pptr(iblock)
  do i = 1, iblen(iblock) {
    xdplus(iloc+i-1) = xd(iloc+i-1) +
        deltat * .5 * xdd(iloc+i-1)
    xplus(iloc+i-1)  = x(iloc+i-1) +
        deltat * xdplus(iloc+i-1)
  } }
```

**Fig. 2.** Excerpt from HOP0 in DYFESM [13]

The remaining dependences include 4 that block outer loop parallelism in compl, 3 that block a pair of loops in matinv, and 36 that block the outer loop of matinv, which already carries conditional dependences.

This program also contained a dependence that brought to light a subtle bug in the Omega Library, causing the system to produce an approximate answer when it should have been able to disprove a dependence.

In total, the 158 new dependences introduced by the fully polynomial test block the parallelization of nine loop nests, two of which were already blocked by conditional dependences. According to [1, Table 3], none of the newly blocked loops contains important parallelism.

## 5.4 Discussion

Most of the dependences introduced by our restriction to polynomial-time analysis come from our refusal to incorporate information from conditions that could introduce disjunction (i.e. the restriction from "Exp Cond" to "Poly"). However, most of the newly blocked loops were a consequence of our restriction to LI(2)-unit constraints. The restriction to LI(1)-unit subscripts, rather than LI(2)-unit differences between pairs of subscripts, would almost double the number of false dependences introduced. Our techniques for controlling disjunction created by uninterpreted function symbols had no impact whatsoever on dependence detection or parallelism (except by uncovering a bug in the library).

As a point of comparison, restricting the Omega Test to use only affine constraints (i.e. treat all functions as *unknown*) introduces 944 false dependences. For these benchmarks, information about non-affine terms is far more important than information about affine terms outside of our polynomial subdomain.

## 5.5 Analysis Time

To determine the practical value of our polynomial-time algorithm, we measured the speed of our implementation. Table 2 gives the results of our timing measurements (in seconds). Our restriction to a polynomial time subdomain of Presburger Arithmetic gives a clear speed advantage: The "Exp UFS" column has the fastest analysis time of all. However, the inclusion of our restrictions on function symbols increases the analysis time (in the "Poly" column) beyond the time needed for full analysis.

We believe there are three significant factors slowing down our analysis: First, our technique for preventing exponential blowup during the processing of function symbols is not a practical benefit. Recall that we replace a potentially large disjunction with one *unknown*; when each element of the disjunction contains an easily discovered contradiction, eliminating it appears to be faster than testing the single conjunction containing the *unknown*. Second, our test for LI(2)-unit constraints appears to be too expensive: when we run the simpler LI(1)-unit test on the dependence expressions, we once again find a significant speedup in analysis time (though at a cost of significantly more dependences). Finally, the

**Table 2.** Analysis Times (in Seconds) for Various Tests

| Benchmark | Dependence Test | | | | |
| --- | --- | --- | --- | --- | --- |
| | | Exp | Exp | | |
| | Exp | Cond | UFS | Poly | LI(1) |
| QCD2 | 11.8 | 29.6 | 6.6 | 17.5 | 9.1 |
| MDG | 10.5 | 16.4 | 10.4 | 16.1 | 2.8 |
| DYFESM | 14.1 | 16.1 | 6.1 | 6.8 | 12.8 |
| ARC2D | 6.8 | 6.8 | 6.8 | 6.7 | 6.7 |
| TRFD | 1.6 | 3.0 | 1.5 | 2.9 | 1.0 |
| Total | 44.8 | 71.9 | 31.4 | 50.0 | 32.4 |

failure to accurately describe a loop-independent dependence that covers a read can force us to spend a lot of time analyzing loop-carried dependences that it would have killed. For example, our refusal to introduce terms like $i \neq 1$ in the analysis of `choos` in the `QCD2` benchmark more than doubles both the number of loop-carried dependences and the analysis time for this benchmark.

At the moment, the most practical result of our work is the combination of the polynomial subset of Presburger Arithmetic and the current Omega Library implementation of function symbols ("Exp UFS"). This guarantees polynomial-time analysis of affine dependences and consistently speeds up our analysis.

## 6  Related Work

Most traditional dependence tests, such as Banerjee's inequalities or the GCD test [21], run in polynomial time, but do not produce dataflow information.

Early work on array dataflow analysis was not exact over our entire polynomial domain. Brandes [22] and Ribas [23] each developed extensions of array dependence analysis that eliminate killed dependences. Brandes's analysis requires rectangular loop nests, and Ribas's techniques require perfectly nested loops. Rosene [24, Chapter 3] and Gross and Steenkiste [25] extended scalar dataflow analysis to describe regions of arrays. Gross and Steenkiste restrict their analysis to represent only rectangular regions in arrays, allow only LI(1) subscripts for which each loop counter appears in only one subscript expression (which must be the same subscript in all references to each array in a given loop). Rosene described a system with a somewhat more general representation, but his system was never implemented.

More recent work, including our previous work on array dataflow [5, 6], has focused on producing more general results, without provably polynomial time bounds. Feautrier's array dataflow analysis [26] also involves extending an integer programming system to allow the removal of iterations from which dependences are killed. His techniques appear to be more expensive than our general system, primarily due to differences in our techniques for negated constraints [5].

Maydan and Lam [11] developed algorithms to produce Feautrier's results more efficiently in certain common cases. However, they note that, in general, "the complexity of our algorithm grows exponentially with the number of write statements" [11, Section 4.5].

More recently, Hall, Murphy, Amarasinghe, Liao, and Lam [27, 28] developed an array dataflow algorithm based on the use of affine constraints to represent exposed regions of an array. They produce efficient results by introducing approximations in some cases where negation is required, but use Fourier's (exponential) algorithm to test for satisfiability [28, Section 5.4.1]. Moon, Hall, and Murphy [29, 30] have modified this system to produce information about conditional dependences, but did not limit the asymptotic complexity.

Li's techniques [31, 32, 33], like those of Rosene and Gross and Steenkiste, produce information about exposed regions of arrays. Li gives extensive empirical evidence that his techniques are efficient [33], but does not give a polynomial time bound. Tu and Padua [34, 35] convert code into gated single assignment form and then perform a demand-driven backward substitution to detect inter-iteration flow of values. They do not provide any polynomial bound on the amount of backward substitution that must be performed.

Another possible approach to polynomial-time analysis is to use an interrupt timer or a limit on the size or number of terms in a dependence, recording any dependence that exceeds the limit as *unknown*. This would allow us to produce exact results for many dependences that are slightly outside of the domain given in this paper, such as the dependences from CNSTNT shown in Section 2. However, this solution lacks the elegance of a true polynomial bound, the results might vary significantly for different limits, and a system based on a timer could even produce unpredictable results from run to run.

# 7    Conclusions

Most of the affine loop bounds and subscripts that occur in real programs are quite simple. This property allows polynomial-time analysis that is generally accurate in practice, or exact analysis that is generally efficient in practice, for programs with affine dependence expressions. We have produced a modified version of the Omega Test that allows the user of a compiler to switch between these two options with a command-line argument. Our restricted algorithm improves on recent (post-1990) work in that it has a polynomial-time upper bound; it improves on earlier (pre-1991) systems with exact analysis for cases that had been handled approximately (i.e. imperfectly nested or triangular loops, certain kinds of coupled subscripts, or LI(2)-unit equations that stem from non-LI(1) subscripts).

Our algorithm is based on a subdomain of Presburger Arithmetic for which satisfiability testing can be performed in polynomial time. The existing algorithms in the Omega Library are polynomial in this subdomain. Thus, we can select either "approximate but provably fast" or "exact but potentially slow" options for all our existing array analysis algorithms (memory-based, value-based (dataflow), and conditional analyses) and process the results with a single set of algorithms.

We can maintain our polynomial time bound when manipulating function symbols by making a slight modification to the Omega Library's original algorithm, though this does not appear to be useful in practice.

In the benchmarks we studied, most dependences that fell outside of our subdomain of Presburger Arithmetic did so because of non-affine terms rather than complex yet still affine terms. Dependences with "complex yet still affine" terms often include only a single deviant constraint, such as the subscript equality in the `initia` routine, or the conditional in `choos`. By restricting ourselves to our polynomial subdomain of Presburger arithmetic, we can reduce total analysis time for the benchmarks we studied from 44.8 to 31.4 seconds (as long as we do *not* use our modified function symbol algorithm). Most of the loop-carried dataflow dependences that were introduced were carried by loops that already carried conditional dataflow. None of the previously dependence-free loops that were blocked by false dependences contained significant parallelism.

This work is essentially a formalization and experimental validation of some of the intuitions that have developed in the constraint-based array analysis community over the past decade. It is our hope that this formalization can serve as a guide to help identify other cases in which constraint-based techniques can be used effectively.

# 8    Acknowledgments

This work is supported by NSF grant CCR-9808694.

# References

[1] R. Eigenmann, J. Hoeflinger, Z. Li, and D. Padua. Experience in the automatic parallelization of 4 Perfect benchmark programs. In *Proceedings of the 4th Workshop on Programming Languages and Compilers for Parallel Computing*, August 1991. Also Technical Report 1193, CSRD, Univ. of Illinois.

[2] Paul Feautrier. Toward automatic distribution. *Parallel Processing Letters*, 4(3):233–244, September 1994.

[3] David Wonnacott. Using Time Skewing to eliminate idle time due to memory bandwidth and network limitations. In *Proceedings of the 2000 International Parallel and Distributed Processing Symposium*, May 2000. An earlier version is available as Rutgers University DCS TR 388.

[4] William Pugh. The Omega test: a fast and practical integer programming algorithm for dependence analysis. *Communications of the ACM*, 35(8):102–114, August 1992.

[5] William Pugh and David Wonnacott. An exact method for analysis of value-based array data dependences. In *Proceedings of the 6th International Workshop on Languages and Compilers for Parallel Computing*, volume 768 of *Lecture Notes in Computer Science*. Springer-Verlag, Berlin, August 1993. Also available as Tech. Report CS-TR-3196, Dept. of Computer Science, University of Maryland, College Park.

[6] William Pugh and David Wonnacott. Constraint-based array dependence analysis. *ACM Trans. on Programming Languages and Systems*, 20(3):635–678, May 1998.

[7] D. E. Maydan, J. L. Hennessy, and M. S. Lam. Efficient and exact data dependence analysis. In *ACM SIGPLAN '91 Conference on Programming Language Design and Implementation*, pages 1–14, June 1991.

[8] G. Kreisel and J. L. Krevine. *Elements of Mathematical Logic*. North-Holland Pub. Co., 1967.

[9] Michael J. Fischer and Michael O. Rabin. Super-exponential complexity of Presburger arithmetic. In Richard M. Karp, editor, *Proceedings of the SIAM-AMS Symposium in Applied Mathematics*, volume 7, pages 27–41, Providence, RI, 1974. AMS.

[10] D. Oppen. A $2^{2^{2^{pn}}}$ upper bound on the complexity of presburger arithmetic. *Journal of Computer and System Sciences*, 16(3):323–332, July 1978.

[11] Dror Eliezer Maydan. *Accurate Analysis of Array References*. PhD thesis, Computer Systems Laboratory, Stanford U., September 1992.

[12] Robert Seater and David Wonnacott. Polynomial time array dataflow analysis. Technical Report 2000-38, Center for Discrete Mathematics and Theoretical Computer Science, November 2000.

[13] M. Berry et al. The PERFECT Club benchmarks: Effective performance evaluation of supercomputers. *International Journal of Supercomputing Applications*, 3(3):5–40, March 1989.

[14] Michael R. Garey and David S. Johnson. *Computers and Intractability: A Guide to the Theory of NP-Completeness*. W.H. Freeman and Company, 1979.

[15] William Pugh and David Wonnacott. Eliminating false data dependences using the Omega test. In *SIGPLAN Conference on Programming Language Design and Implementation*, pages 140–151, San Francisco, California, June 1992.

[16] David G. Wonnacott. *Constraint-Based Array Dependence Analysis*. PhD thesis, Dept. of Computer Science, The University of Maryland, August 1995. Available as ftp://ftp.cs.umd.edu/pub/omega/davewThesis/davewThesis.ps.

[17] Robert E. Shostak. A practical decision procedure for arithmetic with function symbols. *Journal of the ACM*, 26(2):351–360, April 1979.

[18] William Pugh and David Wonnacott. Nonlinear array dependence analysis. In *Third Workshop on Languages, Compilers, and Run-Time Systems for Scalable Computers*, Troy, New York, May 1995.

[19] P. Downey. Undecidability of presburger arithmetic with a single monadic predicate letter. Technical Report 18-72, Center for Research in Computing Technology, Havard Univ., 1972.

[20] Louis Comtet. *Advanced Combinatorics*. D. Reidel Publishing Company, Dordrecht, Holland, 1974.

[21] M. J. Wolfe. *Optimizing Supercompilers for Supercomputers*. The MIT Press, Cambridge, Mass., 1989.

[22] Thomas Brandes. The importance of direct dependences for automatic parallelism. In *Proceedings of the 2nd International Conference on Supercomputing*, pages 407–417, July 1988.

[23] Hudson Ribas. Obtaining dependence vectors for nested-loop computations. In *Proceedings of 1990 International Conference on Parallel Processing*, pages II–212 – II–219, August 1990.

[24] Carl Rosene. *Incremental Dependence Analysis*. PhD thesis, Dept. of Computer Science, Rice University, March 1990.

[25] Thomas Gross and Peter Steenkiste. Structured dataflow analysis for arrays and its use in an optimizing compiler. *Software—Practice and Experience*, 20:133–155, February 1990.

[26] Paul Feautrier. Dataflow analysis of scalar and array references. *International Journal of Parallel Programming*, 20(1):23–53, February 1991.

[27] M. W. Hall, B. R. Murphy, S. P. Amarasinghe, S. Liao, and M. S. Lam. Interprocedural analysis for parallelization. In *Proceedings of the 8th International Workshop on Languages and Compilers for Parallel Computing*, August 1995.

[28] Saman P. Amarasinghe. *Parallelizing Compiler Techniques Based on Linear Inequalities*. PhD thesis, Computer Systems Laboratory, Stanford U., January 1997.

[29] Sungdo Moon, Mary W. Hall, and Brian R. Murphy. Predicated array data-flow analysis for run-time parallelization. In *Proceedings of the 1998 International Conference on Supercomputing*, July 1998.

[30] Sungdo Moon and Mary W. Hall. Evaluation of predicated array data-flow analysis for automatic parallelization. In *Proceedings of the 7th ACM SIGPLAN Symposium on Principles and Practice of Parallel Programming*, pages 84–95, May 1999.

[31] Zhiyuan Li. Array privatization for parallel execution of loops. In *Proceedings of the 1992 International Conference on Supercomputing*, pages 313–322, July 1992.

[32] Junjie Gu, Zhiyuan Li, and Gyungho Lee. Symbolic array dataflow analysis for array privatization and program parallelization. In *Supercomputing '95*, San Diego, Ca, December 1995.

[33] Junjie Gu, Zhiyuan Li, and Gyungho Lee. Experience with efficient array data flow analysis for array privatization. In *Proceedings of the 6th ACM SIGPLAN Symposium on Principles and Practice of Parallel Programming*, pages 157–167, Las Vegas, Nevada, June 1997.

[34] Peng Tu and David Padua. Array privatization for shared and distributed memory machines. In *Workshop on Languages, Compilers, and Run-Time Environments for Distributed Memory Multiprocessors*, September 1992.

[35] Peng Tu. *Automatic Array Privatization and Demand-Driven Symbolic Analysis*. PhD thesis, Dept. of Computer Science, University of Illinois at Urbana-Champaign, 1995.

# Induction Variable Analysis without Idiom Recognition: Beyond Monotonicity

Peng Wu[1], Albert Cohen[2], and David Padua[3]

[1] IBM T.J. Watson Research Center
Yorktown Heights, NY 10598
pengwu@us.ibm.com

[2] A3 Project, INRIA Rocquencourt
78153 Le Chesnay, France
Albert.Cohen@inria.fr

[3] Dept. of Computer Science, U. of Illinois
Urbana, IL 61801
padua@cs.uiuc.edu

**Abstract.** Traditional induction variable (IV) analyses focus on computing the closed form expressions of variables. This paper presents a new IV analysis based on a property called *distance interval*. This property captures the value changes of a variable along a given control-flow path of a program. Based on distance intervals, an efficient algorithm detects dependences for array accesses that involve induction variables. This paper describes how to compute distance intervals and how to compute closed form expressions and test dependences based on distance intervals.

This work is an extension of the previous induction variable analyses based on *monotonic evolution* [11]. With the same computational complexity, the new algorithm improves the monotonic evolution-based analysis in two aspects: more accurate dependence testing and the ability to compute closed form expressions.

The experimental results demonstrate that when dealing with induction variables, dependence tests based on distance intervals are both efficient and effective compared to closed-form based dependence tests.

## 1 Introduction

Dependence analysis is useful to many parallelization and optimization algorithms. To extract dependence information, array subscripts must be compared across statements and loop iterations. However, array subscripts often include variables whose value at each loop iteration is not easily available. An important class of such variables are *induction variables*.

In classical dependence analyses, occurrences of induction variable are often replaced by their closed form expressions. Since most dependence tests handle affine expressions only, this approach only applies to induction variables with affine closed form expressions. To handle more general induction variables, in our previous work, we proposed a dependence test based on a light-weight IV

H. Dietz (Ed.): LCPC 2001, LNCS 2624, pp. 427–441, 2003.

```
1      do i = 0,n
2        do j = 0,m
3          k = k+1
4            a(k) = ⋯
5        end do
6      end do
```

```
1    do i = 1,10
2      ⋯
3      a(k) = ⋯
4      ⋯ = a(k+1)
5      k = k+2
6    end do
```

**Fig. 1.** Non-affine closed form expression

**Fig. 2.** IV incremented by step of 2

property called *monotonic evolution* [11]. In essence, monotonic evolution captures whether the value of a variable is increasing or decreasing along a given execution path. For example, consider the loop nest in Fig. 1 where $m$ is not a compile time constant. The closed form expression of k is not affine. However, knowing that the value of k at statement 4 is strictly increasing, one can prove that statement 4 is free of output-dependences.

Nevertheless, there are cases where monotonic evolution is not sufficient for accurate dependence testing. Consider the loop in Fig. 2. Knowing that the value of k is strictly increasing is not enough. A dependence test needs to know that the value of k increases by a minimum of 2 to determine statement 3 and 4 as dependence-free. To obtain such additional information, this paper extends the concept of monotonic evolution to *distance interval*, which captures the minimal and maximal value changes of a variable along any given execution path. We also extend the algorithms in [11] to compute distance intervals and to perform dependence tests based on distance intervals. In addition, we present a method to compute closed form expressions from distance intervals.

Experimental results show that when dealing with induction variables, dependence tests based on distance intervals are both efficient and effective compared to closed-form based dependence tests (implemented in Polaris). In particular, our technique misses three loops that can be parallelized by Polaris, but finds 74 more parallel loops than can Polaris.

The rest of the paper is organized as follows. Section 2 gives an overview of monotonic evolution. Section 3 defines distance interval. Section 4 and 5 describe how to use distance intervals in dependence testing and closed form computation. Section 6 proposes a technique to handle IVs defined by arbitrary assignments. Section 7 presents the experimental results. Section 8 compares our technique with others, and Section 9 concludes.

## 2    Overview of Monotonic Evolution

Monotonic evolution of a variable describes the *direction* in which the value of the variable changes along a given execution sequence. Possible values of an evolution are described by the lattice of *evolution states* as shown in Fig. 3. We define two types of evolutions:

- The notation $p \dashv_i^N q$ represents the *join* ($\sqcup$) of the evolution of i over all paths that starts from $p$ and ends at $q$ *excluding* those that traverse any edge in the set $N$. Intuitively, $p \dashv_i^N q$ captures how the value of i changes when the program executes from an instance of p to an instance of q. When $q$ can not be reached from $p$, $p \dashv_i^N q$ is $\bot$.
- The notation $p \dashv_i^N r \dashv_i^N q$ represents an evolution that must traverse an intermediate node, i.e., the evolution of $i$ along all paths from $p$ *via* $r$ to $q$, excluding those that traverse any edge in $N$.

Lattice elements:

$\top$  unknown evolution;

$\trianglelefteq$  monotonically increasing;

$\triangleleft$  strictly monotonically increasing;

$\trianglerighteq$  monotonically decreasing;

$\triangleright$  strictly monotonically decreasing;

$\diamond$  constant evolution;

$\bot$  no evolution.

Ordering:

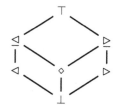

**Fig. 3.** The lattice of evolution states

To compute the value of an evolution, each statement in the program is interpreted as a transfer function of evolution values. Given a variable i, a statement is classified as: *identity statement* if it does not change the value of i, such as j = n; *forward induction* if it always increases the value of i, such as i = i+1; *backward induction* if it always decreases the value of i, such as i = i-3; *arbitrary assignment* if it assigns any value to i, such as i = n. The corresponding transfer functions are given in Table 1.

|  | $\bot$ | $\triangleleft$ | $\trianglelefteq$ | $\diamond$ | $\trianglerighteq$ | $\triangleright$ | $\top$ |
|---|---|---|---|---|---|---|---|
| Identity | $\bot$ | $\triangleleft$ | $\trianglelefteq$ | $\diamond$ | $\trianglerighteq$ | $\triangleright$ | $\top$ |
| Forward | $\bot$ | $\triangleleft$ | $\triangleleft$ | $\triangleleft$ | $\top$ | $\top$ | $\top$ |
| Backward | $\bot$ | $\top$ | $\top$ | $\triangleright$ | $\triangleright$ | $\triangleright$ | $\top$ |
| Arbitrary | $\bot$ | $\top$ | $\top$ | $\top$ | $\top$ | $\top$ | $\top$ |

**Table 1.** Transfer functions of evolution values

## 3   Distance-Extended Evolution

This section defines distance interval and its operations, and describes the algorithm to compute distance interval.

## 3.1  Distance Interval

A distance interval captures the minimal and maximal value changes of a variable along a given execution sequence. More precisely, for any $a$ and $b$ such that $-\infty \le a \le b \le +\infty$, $[a, b]$ describes any evolution where the value difference of the variable at the starting and ending nodes of the evolution is *no less* than $a$ and *no greater* than $b$. When $a = b$, $[a, b]$ is *exact*. In this case, we may use the shorter $a$ for $[a, a]$. The lattice of distance intervals is formally defined in Table 2. $\perp$ describe unreachable evolutions. For example, consider the loop in Figure 2, we have $5 \dashv_k 5 = [2, 18]$.

| $\sqcup$ | $\perp$ | $[a, b]$ |
|---|---|---|
| $\perp$ | $\perp$ | $[a, b]$ |
| $[c, d]$ | $[c, d]$ | $[\min(a, c), \max(b, d)]$ |

**Table 2.** Distance-extended lattice

A distance interval can always be mapped to an evolution state according to the signs of the interval's bounds. For instance, $[0, 0]$ corresponds to $\diamond$; $[a, b]$ corresponds to $\trianglelefteq$ when $a \ge 0$, to $\trianglerighteq$ when $b \le 0$, and to $\top$ when $a$ and $b$ are of opposite signs.

## 3.2  Distance Intervals of Expressions

Distance intervals can be computed for expressions, i.e., $p \dashv_e^N q$ where $e$ is an arithmetic expression. We define two operations, "$\times$" and "$+$", on distance intervals in Table 3 and Table 4, respectively.

| $\times$ | $a\ (> 0)$ | $0$ | $a\ (< 0)$ |
|---|---|---|---|
| $\perp$ | $\perp$ | $[0, 0]$ | $\perp$ |
| $[c, d]$ | $[ac, ad]$ | $[0, 0]$ | $[ad, ac]$ |

**Table 3.** The $\times$ operator

| $+$ | $\perp$ | $[a, b]$ |
|---|---|---|
| $\perp$ | $\perp$ | $\perp$ |
| $[c, d]$ | $\perp$ | $[a + c, b + d]$ |

**Table 4.** The $+$ operator

The rules to compute evolution of expressions are as follows. When $e$ is a constant expression, $p \dashv_e^N q = [0, 0]$ if $q$ is reachable from $p$; otherwise, $p \dashv_e^N q = \perp$. When $e$ is of the form $ae_1$ where $a$ is a constant, $p \dashv_{ae_1}^N q = p \dashv_{e_1}^N q \times a$. Lastly, when $e$ is of the form $e_1 + e_2$, $p \dashv_{e_1 + e_2}^N q = p \dashv_{e_1}^N q + p \dashv_{e_2}^N q$.

For example, suppose that $e$ is 2i-3j+6,

$$p \dashv_{2i - 3j + 6}^N q = p \dashv_i^N q \times 2 + p \dashv_j^N q \times (-3) + [0, 0].$$

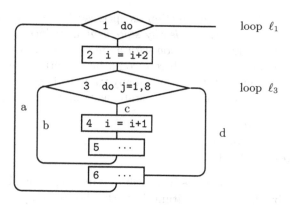

**Fig. 4.** Stride information

## 3.3  Stride Information

We define a special evolution, called *stride*, that traverses *at most* one iteration of a loop. Consider a loop $\ell$ with a header $h$ and a statement $p$ enclosed in $\ell$. We define three strides between $p$ and $h$:

$\mathbf{Up}_{i,N}(p, h)$ denotes an evolution from $p$ *up* to the first $h$ reached excluding edges in $N$. It is called an **up-stride** of $p$.

$\mathbf{Down}_{i,N}(h, p)$ denotes an evolution from $h$ *down* to $p$ *without* traversing $h$ twice, excluding edges in $N$. It is called a **down-stride** of $p$.

$\mathbf{Stride}_{i,N}(\ell)$ denotes an evolution from $h$ to the next $h$, excluding edges in $N$ and the exit edge of $\ell$. It is called a **stride** of loop $\ell$. In fact, $\mathrm{Stride}_{i,N}(\ell)$ is a special case of $\mathrm{Down}_{i,N}(h, p)$ and $\mathrm{Up}_{i,N}(p, h)$ when $p = h$.

Let us illustrate these definitions on the example shown in Fig. 4 where nodes are named by statement labels.

- $\mathrm{Stride}_i(\ell_3) = [1, 1]$ since it traverses exactly one iteration of the inner loop;
- $\mathrm{Stride}_i(\ell_1) = [10, 10]$ since it traverses statement 2 and the entire inner loop exactly once (knowing $\ell_3$ has 8 iterations);
- $\mathrm{Down}_i(3, 5) = [1, 1]$ since it traverses the single path from statement 3 to the first statement 5 reached;
- $\mathrm{Up}_i(5, 1) = [0, 7]$ since statement 4 is traversed at most 7 times.

## 3.4  Computing Distance Interval

The non-iterative algorithm described in [11] can be extended to compute distance intervals of evolutions. Due to space constraints, we only briefly describe the algorithm here. The full algorithm can be found in [12].

The core of the non-iterative algorithm is the basic algorithm, which is based on a depth-first traversal of a non-cyclic control-flow graph. For each statement traversed, it applies the transfer function as specified below. Given a variable i, a statement is classified as: an *identity statement* if it does not change the value of i, such as j = n; an *induction with a step* $c$ if it always changes the value of i by $c$, such as i = i+c, where $c$ could be a runtime constant of any sign; an *arbitrary assignment* if it may assign any value to i, such as i = n. The corresponding transfer functions for these statements are:

- Identity$(state) = state$
- Induction$_c(state) = state + [c, c]$
- Arbitrary$(state) = [-\infty, +\infty]$

Then, the algorithm decomposes any evolution into segments, each of which can be computed by the basic algorithm. In particular, to compute $p \dashv_i^N q$, the evolution is decomposed into an up-stride of $p$, a down-stride of $q$, and some strides of the surrounding loops of $p$ and $q$. Since evolutions are decomposed into the same segments over and over again, we can reuse values of intermediate segments to compute different evolutions. This leads to a very efficient algorithm to compute multiple evolutions.

## 4    Dependence Test Using Distance Information

Distance intervals can be used for dependence testing. Such a dependence test shares some similarities with the range test [2].

### 4.1    Dependence Test

Consider two array accesses, a(i) at $p$ and a(i+d) at $q$, where d is a constant.[1] The dependence test computes the value difference between i at $p$ and i+d at $q$, and use this information to decide whether the two accesses are independent. It is obvious that, at any given run-time program point, the value of i will differ from that of i+d by $d$. Therefore, the value difference between i at $p$ and i+d at $q$ can be computed as the evolution of i from $p$ to $q$ summed with $[d, d]$.

Consider a loop $\ell$, two accesses, a[e] at $p$ and a[e+d] at $q$. Let $B$ and $E$ denote the sets of back-edges and exit edges of $\ell$, respectively.

1. There is *no* intra-loop dependence between $p$ and $q$ for loop $\ell$ when

$$p \dashv_e^B q + [d, d] \in \{[a, b] \mid ab > 0\}$$
$$\wedge \quad q \dashv_e^B p + [-d, -d] \in \{[a, b] \mid ab > 0\}. \quad (1)$$

2. There is *no* loop-carried dependence between $p$ and $q$ for loop $\ell$ with a header $h$ when

$$p \dashv_e^E h \dashv_e^E q + [d, d] \in \{[a, b] \mid ab > 0\}$$
$$\wedge \quad q \dashv_e^E h \dashv_e^E p + [-d, -d] \in \{[a, b] \mid ab > 0\}. \quad (2)$$

```
1    do i = 1,100
2       k = k+2
3       t = a(k)
4       a(k) = a(k+1)
5       a(k+1) = t
6    end do
```

**Fig. 5.** Example of dependence test

Consider the loop in Fig. 5 that swaps every pair of consecutive elements of array a. Since k is incremented by 2 per iteration, we have,

$$3 \dashv_k 1 \dashv_k 5 + [1,1] = [2,2] + [1,1] = [3,3]$$
$$5 \dashv_k 1 \dashv_k 3 + [-1,-1] = [2,2] + [-1,-1] = [1,1].$$

According to (2), this proves that there is no loop-carried dependence between 3 and 5.

## 4.2 Practical Computation

The dependence test computes two evolutions for any pair of accesses and for each surrounding loop to be tested (e.g., from $p$ to $q$, and from $q$ to $p$). Obviously, computation will not be efficient without optimizing computations across different evolutions. We propose to cache and reuse intermediate evolutions. We can compute and tabulate the results for each statement and loop to be tested. To further optimize the algorithm, for each basic block, we compute local evolutions that traverse an entire block, and store the results. During later computation, the algorithm may "short-cut" the basic block by summing its cached local state with the input state. The full algorithm is described in [12].

## 4.3 Complexity Analysis

Since dependence tests are local to individual loop nests, we consider an arbitrary loop nest $L$ and an induction variable i. Let $e$ be the number of edges in $L$, and $m$ be the maximal nesting of $L$. Suppose that $k$ statements in $L$ are involved in the dependence test. The dependence test computes $p \dashv_i^N h \dashv_i^N q$ and $p \dashv_i^N q$, for all possible $p$, $q$ and $h$, where $N$ may only contain back-edges and exit edges. In fact, when computing intermediate evolutions, we can drop $N$ and explicitly compute those evolutions for each loop. We showed that the dependence test complexity is

$$O(ek + m^2 k^2). \tag{3}$$

---

[1] Accesses of the form a[i+$d_1$] and a[i+$d_2$] can be handled as a[j] and a[j+($d_2-d_1$)].

Any flow-sensitive, statement-wise dependence test for $k$ statements in a loop nest of depth $m$ must take at least $mk^2$ steps, our test is no exception. In our scheme, dependency is tested individually for each loop of a nest (as reflected by the occurrence of $m$ in (3)). Therefore, compared to classical dependence tests *without induction variable recognition*, our scheme requires more steps.[2] However, (3) estimates the number of operations (i.e., $\times$, $+$, and $\sqcup$) involved in the dependence test: the formula gives a fairly accurate account of the cost of the test. On the other hand, for classical dependence tests, the cost of individual operations is difficult to estimate. Depending on the mathematical tools employed, some operations may be as expensive as solving a system of linear equations.

## 5    Closed Form Computation

Although our dependence test requires no closed form computation, closed form expressions are still needed by subsequent loop transformations to break the dependence inherent to inductions. Distance intervals can be used to compute closed form expressions.

Given a variable $v$ and a statement $p$, the closed form expression of $v$ at $p$ explicitly computes the value of $v$ at any instance of $p$. Suppose that $p$ is enclosed in a loop nest, $\ell_n, \ldots, \ell_1, \ell_0$, where $\ell_0$ immediately encloses $p$. Assume that all loop indices have an initial value of 1 and a step of 1. Let $i_k$ denote the loop index of any loop $\ell_k$, and $v_k$ denote the value of $v$ before entering $\ell_k$. The closed form computation is conducted in the following steps:

– First, we compute the closed form expression of $v$ at $p$ for loop $\ell_0$. If $\mathrm{Stride_v}(\ell_0)$ and $\mathrm{Down_v}(\ell_0, p)$ are exact,[3] the value of $v$ at $p$ at iteration $i_0$ of loop $\ell_0$ can be expressed as

$$v = v_0 + \mathrm{Stride_v}(\ell_0) \times (i_0 - 1) + \mathrm{Down_v}(\ell_0, p). \qquad (4)$$

– Then, consider $\ell_1$ that immediately enclose $\ell_0$. Applying (4) again, $v_0$ can be computed as

$$v_0 = v_1 + \mathrm{Stride_v}(\ell_1) \times (i_1 - 1) + \mathrm{Down}_{v, O_0}(h_1, h_0)$$

where $O_0$ is the set of outgoing edges of $h_0$. Basically, $\mathrm{Down}_{v, O_0}(h_1, h_0)$ computes the evolution from $h_1$ down to the first $h_0$. Replacing $v_0$ in (4) by the above equation, the closed form expression of $v$ for $\ell_1$ and $\ell_0$ is

$$v = v_1 + \mathrm{Stride_v}(\ell_1) \times (i_1 - 1) + \mathrm{Down}_{v, O_0}(h_1, h_0)$$
$$+ \mathrm{Stride_v}(\ell_0) \times (i_0 - 1) + \mathrm{Down_v}(h_0, p). \qquad (5)$$

---

[2] $m$ times, when testing a large number of array accesses, i.e., when $k$ is close to $e$.
[3] This ensures that (4) indeed computes a singleton interval.

```
1    k = 1
2    do i = 1, 10
3       do j = 1, 10
4          k = k+2
5          a[k] = ...
6       end do
7    end do
```

**Fig. 6.** Closed form computation

- Finally, generalizing (4) and (5), the closed form expression of $v$ at $p$ for any loop nest $\ell_n, \ldots, \ell_0$ is

$$v = v_n + \text{Stride}_v(\ell_1) \times (i_1 - 1) + \text{Down}_{v,O_0}(h_1, h_0)$$
$$+ \text{Stride}_v(\ell_2) \times (i_2 - 1) + \text{Down}_{v,O_1}(h_2, h_1)$$
$$+ \cdots + \text{Stride}_v(\ell_n) \times (i_n - 1) + \text{Down}_{v,O_{n-1}}(h_n, h_{n-1})$$
$$+ \text{Stride}_v(\ell_0) \times (i_0 - 1) + \text{Down}_v(h_0, p) \quad (6)$$

where $O_k$ is the set of outgoing edges of loop $\ell_k$ and provided that $\text{Stride}_v(\ell_k)$, $\text{Down}_{v,O_0}(h_k, h_{k-1})$, and $\text{Down}_v(h_0, p)$ are exact.

For example, consider the loop nest in Fig. 6. Let $O$ denote the exit-edge of loop 3. Applying (6), the closed form expression of $k$ at 5 is

$$k = 1 + \text{Stride}_k(\ell_2) \times (i - 1) + \text{Down}_{k,O}(2, 3)$$
$$+ \text{Stride}_k(\ell_3) \times (j - 1) + \text{Down}_k(3, 5).$$

Hence, $k = 1 + 20(i - 1) + 2(j - 1) + 2 = 20(i - 1) + 2(j - 1) + 3$.

## 6   Handling Arbitrary Assignments

The transfer function of arbitrary assignment given in Section 3.4 conservatively maps any input state to $[-\infty, +\infty]$. We would like to provide a more precise transfer function for arbitrary statements.

Consider an assignment $s$ of the form i = j. Suppose that $i < j$ holds at any statement instance of $s$, then the value of $i$ always increases after an execution of $s$. This means that the effect of $s$ on $i$ is equivalent to that of an induction statement (with a positive step). Therefore, we define the transfer function of $s$, denoted as $f_s$, according to the inequality between $i$ and $j$ at $s$: if $c \le i - j \le d$ at $s$, then

$$f_s(in) = in + [c, d]. \quad (7)$$

In order to obtain $[c, d]$, we need to estimate the bounds of $i - j$ at $s$. Obviously, $i$ and $j$ have the same value immediately after $s$, hence after denoted as

```
1   do i = 1,100
2      k = n
3      ...
4      do j = 1,10
5         a[k] = ...
6         k = k+1
7      end do
8      n = n + 11
9   end do
```

**Fig. 7.** Example of arbitrary assignment

$s^+$. Therefore, $s^+$ can be used as a reference point to compare the values of $i$ and $j$ at $s$.

Let $[a, b]$ (resp. $[a', b']$) denote the evolution of $i$ (resp. $j$) from an instance of $s^+$ to the instance of $s$ from the very next iteration of $\ell_s$. We assume that $s$ is executed at every iteration of $\ell_s$. This condition can be checked as whether $h_s$ can reach itself without traversing incoming edges of $s$ and exit edges of $\ell_s$. Then, $[a, b]$ and $[a', b']$ can be computed as follows:

$$[a, b] = \mathrm{Up}_i(s^+, h_s) + \mathrm{Down}_i(s, h_s) \qquad [a', b'] = \mathrm{Up}_j(s^+, h_s) + \mathrm{Down}_j(s, h_s).$$

Knowing $i = j$ at $s^+$, the difference between values of $i$ and $j$, at any instance of $s$ executed after an instance of $s^+$, is bounded by the "difference" between $[a, b]$ and $[a', b']$:

$$c \leq i - j \leq d \text{ where } [c, d] = [a - b', b - a']. \tag{8}$$

Since $s$ is executed at every iteration of $\ell_s$, any instance of $s$ executed after the first iteration of $\ell_s$ follows some instance of $s^+$. When computing evolutions, (8) holds at node $s$ only after a back-edge has been traversed along the path.

We now apply the method to compute $5 \dashv_k 5$ in Fig. 7, where statement 2 is an arbitrary assignment. Corresponding distance intervals are computed as

$$[a, b] = \mathrm{Up}_k(3, 1) + \mathrm{Down}_k(1, 2) = [10, 10]$$
$$[a', b'] = \mathrm{Up}_n(3, 1) + \mathrm{Down}_n(1, 2) = [11, 11].$$

Since any path from statement 5 to 2 always traverses the back-edge of loop 1 first, $1 \leq k - n \leq 1$ holds at each traversal of 2 along paths of $5 \dashv_k 5$. Hence, applying (7), the transfer function of statement 2 is $f_2(in) = in + [1, 1]$.

## 7   Experimental Results

For our experimental studies, we used Polaris [3], a Fortran source-to-source parallelizing compiler, as the basis for comparison. In Polaris, induction variables are substituted by their closed form expressions before the dependence test is performed. In the context of dependence testing for array accesses, we focus on *integer induction variables* (IIVs) which are used in *array subscripts*, and we do not deal with IIVs unrelated to any dependences, e.g., IIVs used in subscripts for arrays that only appear in right-hand side.

In the experiment, we used Polaris to find candidate IIVs from the Perfect Club benchmark suite. Applying our dependence test by hand (for dependences involving IIVs) and using the dependence information reported by Polaris (for other dependences), we detected parallel loops involving IIVs. Table 5 presents the experimental results.[4] The first three columns classify loops with IIVs into three sets: loops containing IIVs (Total); loops where IIVs appear as subscripts (Subscript); and loops where the analysis of IIVs is required for parallelization (Targeted), that is, loops that are the target of our technique. The next five columns give the number of loops with IIVs parallelized by different techniques: by Polaris (Polaris), by our dependence analysis with either the original (Monotonic) or the distance-extended (w/ Distance) lattice, combined with the method to handle arbitrary assignments (w/ Assign), combined with a run-time test for stride and loop bounds (w/ Test). Note that, in columns Monotonic and w/Distance, a loop counted as parallel simply means that when disabling IV substitution in Polaris and "plugging in" our analysis, Polaris reports no loop-carried dependence for the loop except for those due to assignments to IVs themselves. Such dependences can be handled either by finding closed form expressions and performing the substitution, or by the techniques described in the next paragraph.

| | Loops with IIVs | | | Parallel Loops with IIVs | | | | |
|---|---|---|---|---|---|---|---|---|
| | Total | Subscript | Targeted | Polaris | Monotonic | w/ Distance | w/ Assign | w/ Test |
| adm | 17 | 17 | 5 | 3 | 2 | 3 | 3 | 4 |
| bdna | 63 | 62 | 60 | 22 | 34 | 34 | 34 | 34 |
| dyfesm | 15 | 11 | 8 | 7 | 8 | 8 | 8 | 8 |
| flo52 | 15 | 15 | 15 | 12 | 12 | 12 | 12 | 12 |
| mdg | 29 | 29 | 24 | 14 | 12 | 13 | 13 | 16 |
| mg3d | 97 | 97 | 89 | 5 | 5 | 5 | 39 | 58 |
| ocean | 11 | 6 | 4 | 4 | 4 | 4 | 4 | 4 |
| qcd | 69 | 69 | 69 | 58 | 64 | 64 | 64 | 64 |
| spec77 | 99 | 59 | 54 | 44 | 1 | 44 | 44 | 44 |
| trfd | 13 | 13 | 9 | 7 | 6 | 6 | 7 | 7 |

**Table 5.** Experiments with the Perfect Club benchmark suite

Let us comment on the results. Our dependence test matches or outperforms Polaris on all loops with IIVs but one (in mdg). We discovered 74 new loops whose only dependences came from operations on induction variables themselves. Among them, 56 (1 in adm, 1 in mdg, 53 in mg3d and 1 in qcd) do have

---

[4] Three programs have been omitted: arc2d and track because they contain no loop with IIVs, and spice because it could not be handled by Polaris.

closed form expression (but the dependence test in Polaris failed to handle these closed form expressions). Twelve (11 in **bdna** and 1 in **dyfesm**) have no closed form expressions because the loop bounds involve array references; but they can be parallelized without much overhead, using a parallel reduction scheme. The other six (1 in **bdna** and 5 in **qcd**) involve conditional induction variable updates; one may resort to a more general **doacross** technique to parallelize such loops: the loop body is split into a "head" sequential part for induction variable computation and a "tail" part which can be run in parallel with the next iteration.

Notice that unknown symbolic constants (for loop bounds and induction variable strides) are sometimes a reason for unsuccessful parallelization by Polaris. Using our technique, a run-time test is inserted to check for inequalities assumed during monotonic evolution and dependence testing.

## 7.1   Additional Patterns That Can Be Handled

This section describes the patterns that can be handled by our method, in addition to the four patterns already described in [11].

**Pattern 5: monotonic small- and big-step.**   In this case, variable **mrsij** is incremented by a "small" step (1) in every iteration of the inner loop, and is re-assigned to the value of **mrsij0** in every iteration of the outer loop. Variable **mrsij0** itself is an induction variable incremented by a "big" step **nrs** by the outer loop. As opposed to the stride and offset pattern, proving there is no dependence requires comparing the accumulative effect of the "small" step of the *inner* loop—which usually depends on the bounds of the inner loop and the step—with the big step of the *outer* loop.

```
—— trfd olda do100 —— line 331 ——
do mrs = 1,nrs
   ...

   mrsij = mrsij0
   do mi = 1,morb
      ...

      do mj = 1,mi
         mrsij = mrsij+1
         xrsij(mrsij) = xij(mj)
      end do
   end do
   mrsij0 = mrsij0+nrs
end do
```

big steps

small steps

Polaris detects no dependences carried by any of the loops because the closed form expression of **mrsij** yielded disjoint intervals [2]. This is illustrated on the right-hand side figure: there are no dependences carried by the outer loop because the dotted lines—the last value of **mrsij**—always precede the dashed ones—the next value of **mrsij0**. Our technique may parallelize the two inner loops based on the strict monotonicity of **mrsij**. Using the dedicated technique to handle arbitrary assignments (`mrsij = mrsij0`) and the distance-extended lattice, the outer loop may also be parallelized. We found 35 loops (1 in `trfd` and 34 in `mg3d`) share this pattern.

## 7.2   Patterns That Could Not Be Handled

The following nests illustrate the two most common cases where our technique could not successfully detect parallel loops.

**Pattern $a$: complex small- and big-step** The following nest is similar to pattern 5, but induction variables appear in loop bounds instead of array accesses. Neither Polaris nor our technique can parallelize the outer loop. Nevertheless, it should not be difficult to extend the arbitrary assignment method to loop counter assignments, and detect that array accesses span disjoint regions across iterations of the outer loop.

```
— mdg nrmlkt do300 — line 494 —
do j = 1,3
    . . .
    kmin = kmax+1
    kmax = kmax+natmo
    do k = kmin,kmax
      var(k) = var(k) * · · ·
    end do
end do
```

**Pattern $b$: interleaved big- and small-step** Our distance-extended lattice handles complex combinations of offsets and strides spanning multiple loops, as long as offsets are explicit in every reference. In many benchmarks, a comparison is required between the stride of an *inner* loop and an *outer* loop bound (the opposite of the previous pattern).

```
— mdg correc do1000 — line 989 —
do i = 1,nt
    . . .
    jj = i
    do j = 1,nor1
      var(jj) = var(jj) + · · ·
      jj = jj+nt
    end do
end do
```

big steps

small steps

To parallelize the outer loop, one has to show that i—hence the initial value of `jj`—is always greater than 0 and less than or equal to `nt`. This is illustrated on the right-hand side figure: there are no dependences carried by the outer loop because the dotted line—the greatest possible value of i—precedes the dashed one—the stride of `jj`. On this example, our improvement to handle arbitrary assignments is not very helpful: values of `jj` are interleaved across iterations of the outer loop. We found 20 loops sharing this pattern in the perfect benchmarks (1 in `bdna` and 19 in `mg3d`). Polaris cannot handle this pattern either.

## 8    Related Work

Most induction variable analyses focus on idiom recognition and closed form computation. Using patterns proposed by Pottenger and Eigenmann [10], the Polaris compiler recognizes polynomial sequences that are not limited to scalar and integer induction variables. Abstract interpretation is used by Ammarguellat and Harrison [1] to compute symbolic expressions. Two general classification techniques have been designed. The first one [6] by Gerlek, Stoltz and Wolfe is based on a SSA representation [5] optimized for efficient demand-driven traversals. The second one [8] is designed by Haghighat and Polychronopoulos for the Parafrase 2 compiler. It combines symbolic execution and recurrence interpolation. Both techniques handle a broad scope of closed form expressions, such as linear, arithmetic (polynomial), geometric (with exponential terms), periodic, and wrap-around.

IV properties other than closed form expressions have also been studied. Gupta and Spezialetti [7] extended the linear IV detection framework with arithmetic and geometric sums as well as *monotonic* sequences, but for non-nested loops only. Their technique is applied to efficient run-time array bounds checking. Lin and Padua [9] studied monotonicity for values of index arrays in the context of parallelizing irregular codes. This property is used later to detect dependences between accesses to sparse matrices through index arrays. However, their technique does not target general induction variables. Gerlek, Stoltz and Wolfe [6] also detect *monotonic* sequences as a special class of induction variables. But details were not provided as how to use such information in dependence testing.

## 9    Conclusion and Future Work

We presented an extension of our previous work [11] on using monotonic evolution to test dependence for array subscripts that involve induction variables. It is a natural step to extend monotonic evolution states with the minimal and maximal distance information. Distance interval enables precise dependence testing in presence of interleaved variable assignments, symbolic constants, evolutions between different variables, non-monotonic evolutions, and closed form computation. In the experiment carried out with the Perfect benchmarks, we showed that our technique matches the precision of Polaris when closed forms are available, and when there are no closed form expressions, we can still detect additional parallel loops.

The immediate future work is to implement this technique in Polaris and validate its use for fast dependence testing. Since arbitrary assignments link the values of two variables, they may be used as reference points to relate (compare) values of different variables. We would also like to apply monotonic evolution on other forms of induction operations, such as pointer chasing in recursive data structures and *container* traversals through *iterators* [4], either for pointer analysis or for paralllization. Monotonic evolution is well-suited for dynamic structures since traversals of such structures are likely to be monotonic, and closed form abstractions are impractical for such accesses.

# References

[1] Z. Ammarguellat and W.L. Harrison. Automatic recognition of induction & recurrence relations by abstract interpretation. In *ACM Symp. on Programming Language Design and Implementation (PLDI'90)*, pages 283–295, Yorkton Heights, NY, June 1990.

[2] W. Blume and R. Eigenmann. The range test: A dependence test for symbolic, non-linear expressions. In *Supercomputing'94*, pages 528–537, Washington D.C., November 1994. IEEE Computer Society Press.

[3] W. Blume, R. Eigenmann, K. Faigin, J. Grout, J. Hoeflinger, D. Padua, P. Petersen, W. Pottenger, L. Rauchwerger, P. Tu, and S. Weatherford. Parallel programming with Polaris. *IEEE Computer*, 29(12):78–82, December 1996.

[4] A. Cohen, P. Wu, and D. Padua. Pointer analysis for monotonic container traversals. Technical Report CSRD 1586, University of Illinois at Urbana-Champaign, January 2001.

[5] R. Cytron, J. Ferrante, B.K. Rosen, M.N. Wegman, and F.K. Zadeck. Efficiently computing static single assignment form and the control dependence graph. *ACM Trans. on Programming Languages and Systems*, 13(4):451–490, October 1991.

[6] M.P. Gerlek, E. Stoltz, and M. Wolfe. Beyond induction variables: Detecting and classifying sequences using a demand-driven ssa form. *ACM Trans. on Programming Languages and Systems*, 17(1):85–122, January 1995.

[7] R. Gupta and M. Spezialetti. Loop monotonic computations: An approach for the efficient run-time detection of races. In *ACM Symp. on Testing Analysis and Verification*, pages 98–111, 1991.

[8] M. Haghighat and C. Polychronopoulos. Symbolic analysis for parallelizing compilers. *ACM Trans. on Programming Languages and Systems*, 18(4):477–518, July 1996.

[9] Y. Lin and D. Padua. Compiler analysis of irregular memory accesses. In *ACM Symp. on Programming Language Design and Implementation (PLDI'00)*, Vancouver, British Columbia, Canada, June 2000.

[10] B. Pottenger and R. Eigenmann. Parallelization in the presence of generalized induction and reduction variables. In *ACM Int. Conf. on Supercomputing (ICS'95)*, June 1995.

[11] P. Wu, A. Cohen, D. Padua, and J. Hoeflinger. Monotonic evolution: An alternative to induction variable substitution for dependence analysis. In *ACM Int. Conf. on Supercomputing*, Sorrento, Italy, June 2001.

[12] Peng Wu. Analyses of pointers, induction variables, and container objects for dependence testing. Technical Report UIUCDCS-R-2001-2209, University of Illinois at Urbana-Champaign, May 2001. Ph.D Thesis.

# Author Index

# Lecture Notes in Computer Science

For information about Vols. 1–2589

please contact your bookseller or Springer-Verlag

Vol. 2627: B. O'Sullivan (Ed.), Recent Advances in Constraints. Proceedings, 2002. X, 201 pages. 2003. (Subseries LNAI).

Vol. 2628: T. Fahringer, B. Scholz, Advanced Symbolic Analysis for Compilers. XII, 129 pages. 2003.

Vol. 2631: R. Falcone, S. Barber, L. Korba, M. Singh (Eds.), Trust, Reputation, and Security: Theories and Practice. Proceedings, 2002. X, 235 pages. 2003. (Subseries LNAI).

Vol. 2632: C.M. Fonseca, P.J. Fleming, E. Zitzler, K. Deb, L. Thiele (Eds.), Evolutionary Multi-Criterion Optimization. Proceedings. XV, 812 pages. 2003.

Vol. 2633: F. Sebastiani (Ed.), Advances in Information Retrieval. Proceedings, 2003. XIII, 546 pages. 2003.

Vol. 2634: F. Zhao, L. Guibas (Eds.), Information Processing in Sensor Networks. Proceedings, 2003. XII, 692 pages. 2003.

Vol. 2636: E. Alonso, D, Kudenko, D. Kazakov (Eds.), Adaptive Agents and Multi-Agent Systems. XIV, 323 pages. 2003. (Subseries LNAI).

Vol. 2637: K.-Y. Whang, J. Jeon, K. Shim, J. Srivastava (Eds.), Advances in Knowledge Discovery and Data Mining. Proceedings, 2003. XVIII, 610 pages. 2003. (Subseries LNAI).

Vol. 2638: J. Jeuring, S. Peyton Jones (Eds.), Advanced Functional Programming. Proceedings, 2002. VII, 213 pages. 2003.

Vol. 2639: G. Wang, Q. Liu, Y. Yao, A. Skowron (Eds.), Rough Sets, Fuzzy Sets, Data Mining, and Granular Computing. Proceedings, 2003. XVII, 741 pages. 2003. (Subseries LNAI).

Vol. 2641: P.J. Nürnberg (Ed.), Metainformatics. Proceedings, 2002. VIII, 187 pages. 2003.

Vol. 2642: X. Zhou, Y. Zhang, M.E. Orlowska (Eds.), Web Technologies and Applications. Proceedings, 2003. XIII, 608 pages. 2003.

Vol. 2643: M. Fossorier, T. Høholdt, A. Poli (Eds.), Applied Algebra, Algebraic Algorithms and Error-Correcting Codes. Proceedings, 2003. X, 256 pages. 2003.

Vol. 2644: D. Hogrefe, A. Wiles (Eds.), Testing of Communicating Systems. Proceedings, 2003. XII, 311 pages. 2003.

Vol. 2645: M.A. Wimmer (Ed.), Knowledge Management in Electronic Government. Proceedings, 2003. XI, 320 pages. 2003. (Subseries LNAI).

Vol. 2646: H. Geuvers, F, Wiedijk (Eds.), Types for Proofs and Programs. Proceedings, 2002. VIII, 331 pages. 2003.

Vol. 2647: K.Jansen, M. Margraf, M. Mastrolli, J.D.P. Rolim (Eds.), Experimental and Efficient Algorithms. Proceedings, 2003. VIII, 267 pages. 2003.

Vol. 2648: T. Ball, S.K. Rajamani (Eds.), Model Checking Software. Proceedings, 2003. VIII, 241 pages. 2003.

Vol. 2649: B. Westfechtel, A. van der Hoek (Eds.), Software Configuration Management. Proceedings, 2003. VIII, 241 pages. 2003.

Vol. 2651: D. Bert, J.P. Bowen, S. King, M, Waldén (Eds.), ZB 2003: Formal Specification and Development in Z and B. Proceedings, 2003. XIII, 547 pages. 2003.

Vol. 2653: R. Petreschi, Giuseppe Persiano, R. Silvestri (Eds.), Algorithms and Complexity. Proceedings, 2003. XI, 289 pages. 2003.

Vol. 2656: E. Biham (Ed.), Advances in Cryptology – EUROCRPYT 2003. Proceedings, 2003. XIV, 649 pages. 2003.

Vol. 2657: P.M.A. Sloot, D. Abramson, A.V. Bogdanov, J.J. Dongarra, A.Y. Zomaya, Y.E. Gorbachev (Eds.), Computational Science – ICCS 2003. Proceedings, Part I. 2003. LV, 1095 pages. 2003.

Vol. 2658: P.M.A. Sloot, D. Abramson, A.V. Bogdanov, J.J. Dongarra, A.Y. Zomaya, Y.E. Gorbachev (Eds.), Computational Science – ICCS 2003. Proceedings, Part II. 2003. LV, 1129 pages. 2003.

Vol. 2659: P.M.A. Sloot, D. Abramson, A.V. Bogdanov, J.J. Dongarra, A.Y. Zomaya, Y.E. Gorbachev (Eds.), Computational Science – ICCS 2003. Proceedings, Part III. 2003. LV, 1165 pages. 2003.

Vol. 2660: P.M.A. Sloot, D. Abramson, A.V. Bogdanov, J.J. Dongarra, A.Y. Zomaya, Y.E. Gorbachev (Eds.), Computational Science – ICCS 2003. Proceedings, Part IV. 2003. LVI, 1161 pages. 2003.

Vol. 2663: E. Menasalvas, J. Segovia, P.S. Szczepaniak (Eds.), Advances in Web Intelligence. Proceedings, 2003. XII, 350 pages. 2003. (Subseries LNAI).

Vol. 2665: H. Chen, R. Miranda, D.D. Zeng, C. Demchak, J. Schroeder, T. Madhusudan (Eds.), Intelligence and Security Informatics. Proceedings, 2003. XIV, 392 pages. 2003.

Vol. 2667: V. Kumar, M.L. Gavrilova, C.J.K. Tan, P. L'Ecuyer (Eds.), Computational Science and Its Applications – ICCSA 2003. Proceedings, Part I. 2003. XXXIV, 1060 pages. 2003.

Vol. 2668: V. Kumar, M.L. Gavrilova, C.J.K. Tan, P. L'Ecuyer (Eds.), Computational Science and Its Applications – ICCSA 2003. Proceedings, Part II. 2003. XXXIV, 942 pages. 2003.

Vol. 2669: V. Kumar, M.L. Gavrilova, C.J.K. Tan, P. L'Ecuyer (Eds.), Computational Science and Its Applications – ICCSA 2003. Proceedings, Part III. 2003. XXXIV, 948 pages. 2003.

Vol. 2670: R. Peña, T. Arts (Eds.), Implementation of Functional Languages. Proceedings, 2002. X, 249 pages. 2003.

Vol. 2674: I.E. Magnin, J. Montagnat, P. Clarysse, J. Nenonen, T. Katila (Eds.), Functional Imaging and Modeling of the Heart. Proceedings, 2003. XI, 308 pages. 2003.

Vol. 2675: M. Marchesi, G. Succi (Eds.), Extreme Programming and Agile Processes in Software Engineering. Proceedings, 2003. XV, 464 pages. 2003.

Vol. 2676: R. Baeza-Yates, E. Chávez, M. Crochemore (Eds.), Combinatorial Pattern Matching. Proceedings, 2003. XI, 403 pages. 2003.

Vol. 2686: J. Mira, J.R. Álvarez (Eds.), Computational Methods in Neural Modeling. Proceedings, Part I. 2003. XXVII, 764 pages. 2003.

Vol. 2687: J. Mira, J.R. Álvarez (Eds.), Artificial Neural Nets Problem Solving Methods. Proceedings, Part II. 2003. XXVII, 820 pages. 2003.

Vol. 2692: P. Nixon, S. Terzis (Eds.), Trust Management. Proceedings, 2003. X, 349 pages. 2003.

Vol. 2707: K. Jeffay, I. Stoica, K. Wehrle (Eds.), Quality of Service – IWQoS 2003. Proceedings, 2003. XI, 517 pages. 2003.